THE INVENTION OF ALTRUISM
Making Moral Meanings in Victorian Britain

THE INVENTION
OF ALTRUISM
Making Moral Meanings
in Victorian Britain

by
Thomas Dixon

A British Academy
Postdoctoral Fellowship Monograph

Published for THE BRITISH ACADEMY
by OXFORD UNIVERSITY PRESS

Oxford University Press, Great Clarendon Street, Oxford OX2 6DP

Oxford New York

Auckland Cape Town Dar es Salaam Hong Kong Karachi
Kuala Lumpur Madrid Melbourne Mexico City Nairobi
New Delhi Shanghai Taipei Toronto

With offices in
Argentina Austria Brazil Chile Czech Republic France Greece
Guatemala Hungary Italy Japan Poland Portugal Singapore
South Korea Switzerland Thailand Turkey Ukraine Vietnam

Published in the United States
by Oxford University Press Inc., New York

British Library Cataloguing in Publication Data
Data available

Library of Congress Cataloging in Publication Data
Data available

Typeset by
J&L Composition Ltd, Filey, North Yorkshire
Printed in Great Britain
on acid-free paper by
Antony Rowe Limited
Chippenham, Wiltshire

ISBN 978-0-19-726426-3

For Emily

Contents

Illustrations

Acknowledgements

This book would not have been possible without the support of the British Academy in the form of a three-year Postdoctoral Fellowship and subsequently a publishing contract for the resulting monograph. I am grateful to Ken Emond, Ivana Markova, and Janet English at the British Academy for their efficiency, support, and encouragement. The first stages of the research for this book were undertaken in Cambridge and supported by a Junior Research Fellowship at Churchill College, and by the Faculty of Divinity. I also benefited immensely from my association in Cambridge with the Department of History and Philosophy of Science, whose seminars and reading groups provided a particularly stimulating environment within which to develop research ideas. I completed the later stages of this project as a member of the Department of History at the University of Lancaster, where I have been extremely grateful for the supportive research environment the department has provided. The final stages of my research were facilitated by travel grants both from my Department and from the Scouloudi Foundation in association with the Institute of Historical Research. The final writing, production, illustration, and indexing of the book were supported by a generous writer's award from the John Templeton Foundation, in connection with which I am very grateful indeed to Charles Harper and Stephen G. Post. Jane Robson ensured the text was copy-edited to the highest standard.

The staff of several libraries and archives provided essential assistance. I benefited particularly from help received from the following: La Maison d'Auguste Comte, Paris; the British Library Manuscripts Department; the British Library Newspaper Library; Martin Maw at the Oxford University Press archives and Beverley Hunt, the *OED* archivist; George Turnbull and the staff of the Archives and Local Studies Unit of the Central Library, Manchester; Stephen Bird at the Labour History Archive and Study Centre, Manchester; Kenneth Dunn of the Manuscripts Department of the National Library of Scotland, Edinburgh; Cressida Annesley at the Canterbury Cathedral Archives; Godfrey Waller and the staff of the Cambridge University Library Manuscripts Department; the Darwin Correspondence Project at the University of Cambridge; Sue Donnelly, archivist at the LSE library; Jeff Abbott at the Bishopsgate Reference

Library, London; Matt Skidmore and the staff of the Senate House Library Special Collections, London; Lorna Hyland at the Maritime Archives and Library, Liverpool; the staff of the Special Collections, Glasgow University Library; and Roger Bristow, Information Services Librarian at Hastings Library. Jonathan Smith, Archivist at Trinity College, Cambridge, provided invaluable assistance on several occasions in connection with questions about Henry Sidgwick, W. F. Trotter, and G. E. Moore. In Lancaster, I have benefited from the help of the staff of the University Library, especially Jenny Brine, who arranged for many items to be made available through inter-library loan.

I am grateful for the opportunities I have had to discuss my research at seminars and conferences over the past several years, including papers given at: Heythrop College, London; Canterbury Christ Church University College; the British Academy Postdoctoral Fellowship Symposium organized by Ken Emond; two annual conferences of the British Society for the History of Science; the Martineau Society Annual Conference in Oxford; the Galton Institute symposium marking the centenary of the death of Herbert Spencer, organized by Greta Jones and Betty Nixon; a panel organized by Ilana Blumberg on altruism and egoism in Victorian literature at the Annual Convention of the Modern Language Association in Philadelphia; a panel on the evolution of sex with Chris Renwick and Greg Radick at the 'Electrifying Experimentation' conference at the University of Sheffield; and a departmental research seminar in Lancaster. I am grateful for the questions and suggestions that I received on all these occasions, which substantially altered the trajectory of my research.

Many friends and colleagues have contributed advice and assistance, directing me towards sources, answering queries by email, or suggesting new lines of inquiry. I am very grateful to all of them. In Lancaster, Gordon Phillips advised on James Hinton and Victorian philanthropy, Thomas Rohkrämer helped me with German translations on more than one occasion, Mike Winstanley directed me towards the publications of the Manchester Literary Club, and Marcus Morris offered assistance on aspects of Victorian socialism. Tim Hickman, Paolo Palladino, Stephen Pumfrey, and Thomas Rohkrämer all encouraged me to articulate more clearly the distinction between word history and conceptual history. On this question I particularly benefited from my attendance at the conference on 'Slippery Words' organized by Gavin Edwards at the University of Glamorgan in 2004. Charlotte Brewer gave me invaluable advice about the history of the *OED* and the use of its archives. I benefited from the guidance of several colleagues with expertise in linguistics. I am grateful to Mick Short and

Jonathan Culpeper at Lancaster University, and to Merja Kytö of Uppsala University who kindly searched various linguistic corpora on my behalf and put me in touch with Hendrik de Smet of the University of Leuven. I am grateful to Neil Kenny for very rewarding discussions about word histories, and to Stefan Collini who responded encouragingly to my questions about the scope and feasibility of this project. Jim Moore has been generous with his time and his expertise on questions of evolution, politics, and Victorian religion, especially in connection with Herbert Spencer. John van Wyhe directed me towards the anti-altruistic *Eagle and the Serpent*. Charlotte Sleigh kindly helped me improve the section on 'Insect Ethics'. Greg Radick, Jon Hodge, Jean Gayon, and Jim Endersby offered expert help on Darwin. Others to whom I am very grateful for advice and encouragement at various stages of this project are: Naomi Beck, Charles Cashdollar, Emma Dixon, Gordon Dixon, Kay Dixon, Matthew Eddy, Kevin Foster, James Harris, James Humphreys, Chris Insole, Greta Jones, David Knight, Abigail Lustig, Lewis Owens, Heath Pearson, Jane Platt, Chris Renwick, Rebecca Stott, Léon Turner, Paul White, Angus Winchester, and two anonymous assessors and an anonymous reader appointed by the British Academy. Finally, I am indebted to John Hedley Brooke, Janet Browne, Robert Richards, and Fraser Watts, all of whom have offered advice and support over several years.

When it came to the final writing of this book, I relied disproportionately on the help of two people in particular, to whom I am enormously grateful for countless substantive and stylistic improvements to the text. Emily Butterworth read the entire manuscript and gave up a large amount of her time to discuss each chapter with me in detail, offering greatly appreciated criticism and encouragement. Jim Secord, who very generously agreed to take on the role of academic editor, also read the entire manuscript and provided strategic advice, invaluable expert guidance on the literature of the period, and pertinent methodological criticism at every stage.

A small amount of the material in this book has been published in different forms previously. I am grateful to the Galton Institute for permission to reuse material from 'Herbert Spencer and Altruism: The Sternness and Kindness of a Victorian Moralist', in G. Jones and R. A. Peel (eds), *Herbert Spencer: The Intellectual Legacy* (Galton Institute, 2004), pp. 85–124; and to Ashgate for permission to reuse material from 'The Invention of Altruism: Auguste Comte's *Positive Polity* and Respectable Unbelief in Victorian Britain', in D. Knight and M. Eddy (eds), *Science and Beliefs: From Natural Philosophy to Natural Science* (Ashgate, 2005), pp. 195–211.

The support of the John Templeton Foundation meant that I was able to engage the expert assistance of a picture researcher. Sandra Assersohn's resourcefulness and diligence have made the process of selecting, sourcing, and crediting the illustrations for this book efficient and painless. I am grateful to the following for permission to reproduce images in their possession: the Syndics of Cambridge University Library; the Secretary to the Delegates of Oxford University Press; the Astor, Lenox, and Tilden Foundation, New York; the Library of the London School of Economics and Political Science; the British Library; the Mary Ward Settlement; La Maison d'Auguste Comte, Paris. Although every effort has been made, in a few instances we have been unable to trace the copyright holder of an image prior to publication. If notified, the publishers will be pleased to amend the acknowledgements in any future edition.

For their permission to quote from unpublished material in their possession, I am very grateful to the following: the Senate House Library; the Master and Fellows of Trinity College, Cambridge; the Syndics of Cambridge University Library; the Secretary to the Delegates of Oxford University Press; the British Library; the Maritime Archives, Liverpool; the Library of the London School of Economics and Political Science; Glasgow University Library, Department of Special Collections.

Abbreviations

CUL	Cambridge University Library
LSE	London School of Economics and Political Science
NLS	National Library of Scotland
ODNB	*Oxford Dictionary of National Biography*
OED	*Oxford English Dictionary*
OUP	Oxford University Press

Introduction

There was no 'altruism' before 1852.[1] There was love, beneficence, Christianity. There was sympathy, philanthropy, utilitarianism. But prior to 1852 nobody used the word 'altruism' to refer to moral sentiments, actions, or ideologies. In that year the philosopher and critic G. H. Lewes approvingly introduced the term to a British readership in an article in the *Westminster Review* about the latest work by the atheistic French thinker who was credited with its coining—Auguste Comte.[2] The creation and acceptance of this new word made it possible to experience oneself and the world in new ways, to communicate new ethical concepts, and to create new moral and religious identities. Its introduction was resisted by many, and mocked by others, for a mixture of philosophical, theological, and political reasons.

In 1901, the year of Queen Victoria's death, a clergyman in George Gissing's novel *Our Friend the Charlatan* was depicted sitting at his breakfast table reading a newspaper article that condemned 'altruism' as a 'silly word' often associated with nauseating moral self-deceit.[3] This, however, is the latest complaint about 'altruism' as an unwelcome new word that I have found. For the most part, by the 1890s, although some still regretted this neologism, they accepted it with resignation as a term that had been almost

---

[1] I will, as here, use quotation marks to indicate when I am discussing the word 'altruism' rather than the feelings, behaviours or concepts the word has been used to signify. At some points I refer to 'the language of altruism' as shorthand for the set of words 'altruism', 'altruistic', 'altruist', and others directly derived from them.

[2] Full details of periodical and newspaper articles published before 1914, and of all archival material, will be given in footnotes and are not included in the list of references in the bibliography below. Where anonymous authors are identified within square brackets, the source of the identification is Houghton 1966–89, unless otherwise stated. [G. H. Lewes], 'Contemporary Literature of France', *Westminster Review* 58 (1852), 614–30, at 618. The first published use of the French *altruisme*, from which the English 'altruism' derives came one year earlier in 1851. For more on Lewes as the importer of 'altruism', and on the exact origins of the French term, see Ch. 2 below.

[3] Gissing 1901: 1–6; see also Ch. 3 below.

universally accepted. By 1910, one writer was referring to 'the two traditional terms, *egoism* and *altruism*, which may be roughly but clearly defined
as denoting the self-regarding and the other-regarding impulses, respectively'.[4] Stefan Collini, in a chapter of his *Public Moralists* (1991) on 'The
Culture of Altruism', having noted the speed with which Comte's neologism was adopted, writes that the intellectual historian should 'pause and
reflect upon what is revealed by this linguistic success story'.[5] The present
book is the result of a fairly lengthy reflective pause of exactly this kind. It
explains how and why the language of altruism was imported, adopted,
resisted, and finally accepted between its first introduction as a strange and
unwelcome neologism and its successful naturalization as a 'traditional
term' in ethical discourse around the turn of the twentieth century.

Setting out to write the history of a particular word, rather than of a
generally conceived idea or concept, has allowed me to produce a more
focused narrative than might otherwise have been possible. My decisions
about what material to include have been driven primarily by the desire to
establish how this key term in modern moral thought came into general
use. This has involved paying attention to stodgy theoretical tracts by
Auguste Comte and his English followers, which were almost as little read
in the nineteenth century as they are now, as well as to relatively well-
known philosophical works by John Stuart Mill and Herbert Spencer, and
to popular publications by best-selling novelists, religious writers, and political propagandists who picked up on the language of altruism towards the
end of the nineteenth century. My focus has been more on writers and the
texts they produced than on their readers or on more everyday uses of
'altruism', but by no means exclusively so. And, as with all controversial new
words and the ideas they stand for, in the case of 'altruism' it was conservative opponents, many of them Christians, who did as much as anyone to
spread the word. That linguistic resistance movement accordingly features
prominently in this account alongside those who enthusiastically adopted
the language of altruism as a welcome new idiom with which to articulate
their most cherished ideals.

Although this book is primarily a study in Victorian intellectual and
cultural history, I hope that it will also have something to say to those who
are interested in recent debates about altruism. My own interest in the history of the language of altruism initially arose from thinking about such
debates. Two provocative and influential works of the 1970s—E. O. Wilson's

---

[4] Sisson 1910: 158.
[5] Collini 1991: 60–90, at 60.

Sociobiology (1975) and Richard Dawkins's *The Selfish Gene* (1976)—have both cast long shadows over these controversies. One of the key questions these two books raised was whether human altruism could be explained as a product of Darwinian evolution. Some mistakenly believed, as some still do, that Darwinian evolution had always been thought of as a process favouring ruthless selfishness. In fact, as will become clear below, it was recognized by Darwin himself, and by virtually all other scientific writers throughout the Victorian period too, that instincts of sympathy, cooperation, and love were just as much a product of nature, and in certain circumstances just as necessary for survival, as were instincts of aggression, competition, and self-preservation.[6]

Different scientists have produced different answers in recent decades to questions about the origins and functions of altruism. Some, such as Dawkins, following W. D. Hamilton's work on the theory of 'kin selection', have focused on the genetic level and thought about how genes that pre-disposed people to help their close family might successfully spread through a population. Dawkins's conclusion in 1976 was that we should 'try to *teach* generosity and altruism' as an act of rebellion against our essentially selfish genes.[7] Other writers on the subject, such as Elliott Sober and David Sloan Wilson, have preferred to follow Darwin's own approach by concentrating on explanations in terms of the relative evolutionary advantage that a coop-erative community or group might have over one composed of more self-ish individuals.[8] Social psychologists have contributed to the debate by trying to design experiments that establish whether we humans are ever motivated by pure altruism when we help others or if there is always a hid-den selfish motive—such as the desire to relieve our own discomfort at the sight of another's suffering.

Philosophers have asked whether or not we can ever draw moral imperatives from facts about our evolutionary past or our psychological make-up. Even if our genes do predispose us to be altruistic, does it follow that we should be? After all, our genes might also dispose us to be aggres-sive, violent, and selfish. This has raised the question of whether any attempt to identify ethical statements about what is good with factual ones about the evolution of human morality will always commit what G. E. Moore, in 1903, called the 'naturalistic fallacy'.[9] Finally, religious and theological writers

---

[6] See Chs 4, 5, and 7 below.
[7] Dawkins 1989: 201.
[8] Sober and Wilson 1998.
[9] I return to G. E. Moore in Ch. 8 below.

have often accepted the hidden premise of most of these debates that altruism is indeed the highest, or even the only, moral virtue, and one required and celebrated by the great faith traditions. They have, however, tended to resist both the Dawkinsian idea that our behaviour is determined by 'selfish genes' and also sceptical social-scientific and philosophical arguments suggesting that self-interest lies behind most or all human altruism.[10]

Looking back at how the language of altruism became an accepted part of scientific, religious, and moral vocabularies throws fresh light on these recent debates. Most fundamentally, it encourages us to ask whether 'altruism' is a useful scientific, ethical, or religious category at all.[11] A specific problem that has hampered discussions about science and ethics in recent decades is the very ambiguity of the word 'altruism'. Some writers suggest that there are two totally different meanings of 'altruism'—the everyday moral meaning and a quite different technical evolutionary-biological meaning.[12] Confusion has also been caused by lack of clarity over whether 'altruism' refers to behaviours or intentions.[13] In other words, although 'altruism' is a single word, it is not associated with any single concept. Instead there are three different clusters of concepts that have been associated with the term. Some have used 'altruism' to refer to selfless or other-regarding instincts, emotions, or motives. This was the meaning initially given to the term by Comte. Others have preferred to use the word to refer to actions that benefit another and not the agent. This second sort of meaning first emerged through the influence of Herbert Spencer's writings about evolution, sociology, and ethics from the 1870s onwards. Thirdly, 'altruism' is sometimes used to signify a doctrine, ideology or ethical principle based on the belief that 'morally good' generally means for the good of others. From the 1850s onwards, 'altruism' was sometimes used in this third sense, initially to refer to Comte's proposed 'Religion of Humanity', and later to stand for other humanistic and socialistic ideologies quite different from Comte's positivism. These three different sets of 'altruism' con-

---

[10] An excellent introduction to these scientific, philosophical and theological debates is Post *et al.* 2002. See also Dixon 2005a. On the debate about scientific explanations of altruism see Sober and Wilson 1998. For a recent theological study, see Grant 2001.

[11] I come back to this question in the Conclusion below.

[12] See, for example, Dawkins 1989: 4; Sober and Wilson 1998: 6–8; Sober 2002; Dawkins 2006: 214–22.

[13] This confusion was at the heart of much debate about the implications of Dawkins's argument in *The Selfish Gene*. Dawkins did not deny that humans and other animals performed actions that helped others. But he did deny that these were brought about by altruistic intentions. He interpreted them instead, rather tortuously, as being self-interested actions performed by genes seeking to replicate themselves.

cepts could be described as psychological altruism, behavioural altruism, and ethical or ideological altruism.[14] And within each of these general clusters of concepts there have of course been many different nuances. Tracing the emergence of these multiple meanings of 'altruism' will hopefully help to draw attention to the ambiguities still present in contemporary debates.

There are certainly continuities between Victorian and more recent debates about 'altruism'. Both involve comparable concerns and conceptual confusions. 'Altruism' still has connotations both of social science and of a certain humanistic religiosity, as it did from the outset. Theories of altruism today, as in the nineteenth century, often have clear political implications about the ideal human society, about the boundaries of moral communities, and about mechanisms of social improvement. However, I want to emphasize the strangeness as well as the familiarity of the Victorian discussions that this book is about. Even words in our own language coined in the relatively recent past have not always meant what they mean to us now. 'Altruism', for most of the period under discussion in this book, would have been either an unknown or else a novel and strange-sounding term to virtually all users of the English language. Many of the uses and discussions of the term that I investigate below revolved around that very strangeness.

There are other important differences too. Both the scientific and the religious contexts have changed. Instead of genetics, evolutionary biology, and game theory, which tend to inform contemporary discussions, the contested sciences of phrenology and, especially, sociology were at the centre of Auguste Comte's original theory of altruism. Only in the later nineteenth century did evolutionary biological accounts start to take a more central role. In recent debates, it has often been the scientists who have denied the existence of 'genuine' altruism, and the theologians who have contradicted them. In the nineteenth century, positions on this question were often reversed. Comte trumpeted it as one his great scientific discoveries that humans were innately altruistic. He contrasted this with the traditional theological teaching that humans were innately selfish and sinful. Several Christian critics of Comte felt he had illegitimately overlooked the innate strength of individual self-regard. On the other hand other Christian writers, such as the Scottish evangelical Henry Drummond, would later, like the atheistic Comte, put a lot of emphasis on the naturalness of altruism.[15] The Victorian debates with which I am concerned, unlike recent discussions, took place in an intensely religious culture, and one in which

---

[14] See Sober and Wilson 1998: 6–8; Dixon 2005a: 4.
[15] See Ch. 7, below.

Christianity still played a very prominent, albeit a contested role. As we shall see, different situations produced different meanings.

Chapter 1 explains how 'altruism' made its way into the first published part of the greatest record of the English language, the *Oxford English Dictionary*. I use this story of lexicographers, readers, definitions, and illustrative quotations as an initial vignette of the world of Victorian moral thought, and to lead into some further reflections on processes of moral meaning-making in Victorian Britain. I also discuss a methodological question that is central to this study: what is the relationship between words and concepts, and what different assumptions and methods are appropriate to writing the histories of each? In his *History in English Words*, Owen Barfield noted that the nineteenth century saw a proliferation of English words formed in combination with 'self-'. Mentioning especially 'self-help' and a newly positive sense of 'self-respect', he saw this development as an aspect of the rise of Victorian 'individualism' and 'humanism'. How different these words all sounded, Barfield wrote, 'from the Christian vocabulary of the human and social virtues— *charity, lovingkindness, mercy, pity*, and the like!' Barfield regretted that the new vocabulary lacked 'the suppressed poetic energy' of the former Christian terms, and noted with disapproval that the later semantic development of 'humanity' and 'humanitarian' had come to signify a kind of moral obligation that extended even 'to the brutes'.[16] Although Barfield did not include Auguste Comte's 'altruism' in his list of the de-Christianized moral terms bequeathed to the English language by the nineteenth century, his comments could very well be applied to it.

As I argue in Chapters 2 and 3, one of the main appeals of the language of altruism, especially in the first twenty or thirty years of its existence, was its association with a scientific and humanistic religiosity. It was a word which was used by respectable unbelievers and denounced by clergymen precisely because it was seen to embody a scientific and humanistic vision of the world. Its growing acceptance by users of the English language both enabled and reflected intellectual and institutional shifts away from Christianity and towards some form of humanism. Complaints about the new ideal of 'altruism' focused on the alleged impotence of any worldview that lacked the promise of heaven and the threat of hell to provide moral motivation. In sermons, books, and articles in periodicals, defenders of Christianity found this and other reasons to resist the humanistic ideology which they believed the advocacy of 'altruism' entailed, and which they

---

[16] He quantifies the number of new hyphenated 'self-' words as 'upwards of forty'. Barfield 1954: 192–4.

associated with positivists and high-minded unbelievers such as Frederic Harrison and George Eliot.

It was against the backdrop of these existing debates about scientific and religious authority in the world of ethics that readers would have viewed theories of the evolution of morality in the 1870s. In other words, famous Victorian anxieties about science and religion existed before either Charles Darwin or Herbert Spencer made evolution a popular and controversial topic. Science and religion were debated in connection with sociology, positivism, and ethics as much as with biology, Darwinism, and evolution, both before and after 1859. In Chapters 4 and 5, I elaborate on these ideas by looking at the relative places of Darwin and Spencer in the history of the science of altruism. Their shared belief in the heritability of acquired characteristics was central to their mid-Victorian optimism about the prospects for moral progress in future generations. Spencer taught that, in the future, human society would be increasingly altruistic. Darwin, using different language, believed that in coming generations, 'the struggle between our higher and lower impulses will be less severe, and virtue will be triumphant'.[17]

Although Darwin himself neither used nor explicitly resisted the language of altruism, many others, from the 1870s to the present, have made claims about Darwin as a theorist of altruism and selfishness. There is a popular impression that the Victorian age was dominated by a competitive and individualistic ethos that was essentially 'selfish'. This is often connected with the further idea that Darwin saw the natural world as an arena of ruthless and violent competition which could be used to legitimate such an ethos. As I will explain much more fully in Chapter 4, Darwin in fact saw sympathy and love, alongside selfishness and violence, throughout the natural world. In insect societies as well as human ones, cooperation and benevolence had evolved for good reasons. The theory of the evolution of the moral sense that Darwin developed in *The Descent of Man* (1871) was complicated and—to modern readers familiar with neo-Darwinism—not entirely 'Darwinian'. It combined ideas taken from eighteenth- and nineteenth-century moral philosophy with observations of the instincts of insects, all within a theoretical framework that included a belief in the heritability of acquired characteristics and the ability of nature to select at the level of communities as well as individuals.

---

[17] C. Darwin 1871: i. 104; C. Darwin 1882: 125.

Darwin's speculations about the evolutionary origins of feelings of sympathy and benevolence need to be put firmly back where they belong, in the context of mid-Victorian evolutionary, entomological, and ethical debates. Journalists and popularizers found the parallels between human and insect ethics suggested by Darwin's work just as stimulating and concerning as the more famous comparisons it made between men and monkeys. And although he was perceived by some as a prophet of competition and selfishness, there were others, including the popular science writer Arabella Buckley, who from the outset promoted the Darwinian vision of natural history as an evolutionary training ground for those moral qualities of self-sacrifice and altruism that were so valued in modern human societies.

Aside from Darwin, the writer most commonly associated with evolution in Victorian Britain, and the country's most famous living philosopher, was the cantankerous and individualistic Herbert Spencer. Spencer certainly seems an unlikely altruist, but it was the influence of his writings, including his *Data of Ethics* (1879), that did most to guarantee the wider dissemination of the language of altruism from the 1870s onwards. Chapter 5 explains what 'altruism' meant to Spencer; how he used it in his attacks on the brutality and hypocrisy of British imperialism; how it led many readers, to his great frustration, to identify him as a disciple of Comte; and how he finally dropped the term as it came to be associated with socialism. Spencer's combination of altruism abroad and egoism at home made sense as two sides of his resistance to political and ideological movements identified by some as a 'New Liberalism' but which he thought represented instead the 'New Toryism'. Authoritarian and interventionist social policies and expansionist and jingoistic attitudes to empire were both signs, for the old radical Spencer, of a Tory approach to government. His view was that an altruistic Tory was still a Tory.

The popularity and influence of Herbert Spencer's work guaranteed a much wider dissemination of the language of altruism into a range of literary, religious, and political contexts from the late 1870s onwards. The 1880s was the pivotal decade in Victorian moral thought, and is the main focus of Chapter 6. A new wave of awareness of the plight of the urban poor was expressed in a range of both practical and intellectual activities. Some, such as Charles Booth, committed themselves to a vast project of social-scientific surveying and classifying of the urban poor. Others undertook missionary work amongst them, seeking to bring the same religious and moral enlightenment to English cities as had been exported for decades to the further reaches of the empire. At the same time that religious philanthropists were setting up university 'settlements' that would bring culture to the London poor, others were founding socialist organizations advocating more fundamental structural reform of society. The 1880s was also the decade that saw the flourishing of respectable unbelief. The atheist Charles Bradlaugh took his seat in Parliament, and the agnostic Thomas Huxley became president of the Royal Society. The best-selling novel of the decade, Mrs Humphry Ward's *Robert Elsmere* (1888), told the story of an Anglican clergyman losing his faith and founding a new religious brotherhood in the East End of London based on a humanistic reinterpretation of Christianity. Elsmere's new faith drew on the philosophical idealism of his Oxford tutor 'Mr Grey' (widely recognized to be a representation of T. H. Green). He was the sort of idealistic altruist who found his true self through self-renunciation.

All of these developments provided new meanings and contexts for discussions of altruism. This was also the time when the most dramatic single shift in the meaning of 'altruism' occurred. During the last two decades of the century, the dominant association of 'altruism'—now the fashionable watchword of the day, on the lips of many a campaigner and social reformer—was with various forms of socialist and collectivist political and economic thought. This new collectivist altruism, championed by such widely read socialist writers as Robert Blatchford, was perceived by individualists as a most unwelcome new fad, became the object of novelistic satire in Ouida's *An Altruist* (1897) and W. H. Mallock's *The Individualist* (1899), and was the target of a sustained campaign of resistance in the pages of the weekly *Spectator* in the 1890s. This flurry of writing on the subject late in the century saw the creation of a new type—the 'altruist'—generally portrayed as a sentimental, idealistic, overly intellectual, and ultimately muddle-headed young reformer.

Although the language of altruism had been widely disseminated and accepted by the end of the nineteenth century, the various rationalistic, humanistic, and optimistic ideologies with which it had been associated, especially in the mid-Victorian years, were no longer in the ascendancy. Chapters 7 and 8 are about the meanings of 'altruism' at the *fin de siècle*, as the mid-Victorian consensus disintegrated. Chapter 7 looks at three different ways that evolutionary science developed from the 1880s onwards to give rise to some quite different visions of altruism—including those which featured in two of the best-selling non-fiction works of the 1890s. Henry Drummond's *The Ascent of Man* (1894) provided a theistic version of human evolution dominated by motherhood and altruism. Benjamin Kidd's *Social Evolution* (1894) endorsed August Weismann's rejection of the inheritance of acquired characteristics and consequently argued that increased altruism could only be guaranteed by the cultural impact of religion rather than by heritable moral improvements in the race. Nonetheless, advocates of eugenics continued to put forward proposals for how to achieve moral progress through selective human breeding. Despite their scientific and political differences, these writers all agreed about the desirability of altruism and shared the hope that it might somehow be increased.

The final naturalization of 'altruism', around the time of Queen Victoria's death, coincided with the emergence of the most radical critiques of the collectivist, progressivist, and humanistic ideologies with which the term had become associated. Chapter 8 surveys varieties of post-Victorian moral thought at the turn of the century, as exemplified in the individual-istic, egoistic, and aesthetic philosophies of Oscar Wilde, Friedrich Nietzsche and his British followers, and G. E. Moore. All of these new philosophies involved radical redefinitions and revaluations of 'altruism' and marked the beginnings of a post-Victorian 'egomania', which looked for ways to escape from the dull and cloying cult of sentimental selflessness that characterized high Victorian moralism. Wilde mocked the idea of living for others and instead celebrated Jesus Christ as the first and greatest of all indi-vidualists. Nietzsche and his British admirers waged war on Christian pity and Spencerian altruism as different varieties of a single decadent value-system. G. E. Moore used analytic philosophy to articulate and justify a neo-pagan ethics of art and emotion.

The story that I tell below, which could perhaps have been subtitled 'British Moral Thought from Comte to Nietzsche', looks at examples of Victorian moralizing in some of their less well-known contexts, as well as offering reappraisals of canonical texts of nineteenth-century intellectual history. It confirms that ideas about selfishness and altruism were of wide concern in Victorian Britain, but shows that any picture in which the Victorians generally endorsed an individualistic, competitive, or even self-ish ethos is certainly a misleading caricature. Debates about 'altruism' (or 'Other-ism' as Henry Drummond sometimes called it) offered an oppor-tunity for Victorians to think, discuss, and agonize over the moral relation-ship between themselves and a variety of others: those of other classes, other nationalities, other races, and even other species. They also invited discussion of the roots of altruistic feelings and the justification of altruistic actions. Were other-regarding motives derived from God's love, from ani-mal ancestry, or from rational calculation? Which others should we help, and why? And political questions were never far away either. Proposals about altruism were very often also proposals about political authority, economic inequality, and the future of society.

In the Conclusion I use this historical account of Victorian science, religion, and ethics as the basis for some brief reflections on philosophical problems and political pitfalls that are in some cases still associated with concepts of altruism. It is easy to become trapped and confined by the intellectual categories we inherit. It was a sense of intellectual confinement that led nineteenth-century theorists such as Auguste Comte and Herbert Spencer to invent new words with which to construct new scientific visions of humanity and society. Terms such as 'sociology' and 'altruism' made those new visions possible. We have now inherited the categories that they created, and those categories can themselves be confining rather than liberating. By providing accounts of the contingent circumstances in which they were created, the intellectual historian can draw attention to the provisional nature of our categories and can thus help to undermine the sense that they are inevitable, or even natural. As Quentin Skinner has put it, 'it is easy to become bewitched into believing that the ways of thinking about them bequeathed to us by the mainstream of our intellectual traditions must be *the* ways of thinking about them'. One of the contributions of the historian, he suggests, is to 'offer us a kind of exorcism' from the bewitching power of the categories we inherit.[18] I aim to perform such an exorcism in relation to 'altruism'.

In writing this book I have of course drawn on the research of many other historians. I have already mentioned Stefan Collini's excellent study of the cluster of values which helped to create a Victorian culture of altruism. Like Collini, I have taken James Murray's definition of 'altruism' as one of my starting points, and I look at several of the same key figures.[19] Given the greater length and different concerns of my own study, however, I hope that it adds to Collini's findings by delving further into the various scientific, religious, social, and political meanings of the language of altruism, and by reflecting on reasons for resistance to 'altruism' as well as its adoption. Where the material I cover is associated with individuals and subjects that have been extensively written about by other historians I have tried to avoid replication of too much that has been said elsewhere and, instead, to

---

[18] Skinner 2002: 6.

[19] In addition to Collini's chapter, two other studies have also taken the spread of the language of altruism as one of their starting points. L. J. Budd 1956 is a study of the arrival of 'altruism' in North America and its association with varieties of communism there in the 1890s. Pearson 2004 looks at 'altruism' in late nineteenth-century economic thought.

provide sufficient information to provide meaningful context for my own account, while using footnotes to direct readers to the existing studies for fuller analyses. This applies especially to four areas: the impact of Comte's 'Religion of Humanity' on Victorian Britain,[20] the history of Victorian Christianity in its encounters with secular and scientific challenges,[21] the writings and impact of canonical figures of Victorian moral thought such as John Stuart Mill, Charles Darwin, Herbert Spencer, Henry Sidgwick, and T. H. Green,[22] and Victorian encounters with urban poverty.[23]

[20] The key works on positivism and the Religion of Humanity are Wright 1986; Cashdollar 1989.
[21] Works that have particularly informed my own understanding of these issues include Chadwick 1966–70; Royle 1974; F. M. Turner 1974; J. R. Moore 1979; Royle 1980; Lightman 1987; Helmstadter and Lightman 1990; J. R. Moore 1989a; Brooke 1991; F. M. Turner 1993; Brooke and Cantor 1998; Secord 2000.
[22] Three of the most important existing intellectual histories of Victorian moral thought are Schneewind 1977; Collini 1991; Himmelfarb 1991. Among studies of the particular impact of Darwin, Spencer, and other evolutionary theorists on moral thought, I have particularly drawn on R. J. Richards 1987; P. Crook 1994; R. J. Richards 2003. Intellectual and cultural histories dealing with some of the same moral philosophers and moral questions covered in the present book are F. M. Turner 1974; Cowling 1985; Weiner 1990; Himmelfarb 1995; Searle 1998; Levine 2002; Richardson 2003; Offer 2006.
[23] The classic study is Stedman Jones 1971. On many other aspects of moral and scientific approaches to poverty in late-Victorian Britain, such as Charles Booth's social surveys, the world of Victorian philanthropy, the university settlements, and the rise of socialism, I have drawn especially on Himmelfarb 1991 and Koven 2004. The latter analyses the voyeuristic as well as the philanthropic, the erotic as well as the altruistic aspects of Victorian 'slumming' in the 1880s.

Chapter One

Making Moral Meanings

> Words are something more than the clothes of thought; they are its incarnation. We inherit words; we use them in our service, ennobling them or, more frequently, debasing them; they lived before us, and they will long outlive our very memory. We are the fleeting shadows; they are the substances.
>
> Robert Mackintosh, *From Comte to Benjamin Kidd* (1899), 249

In the scriptorium

Although the words 'altruism' and 'altruistic' entered the English language in the early 1850s, some people were still wondering exactly what they meant in 1880. One individual, signing their letter just with the initial 'C', wrote to *Notes and Queries*, a weekly publication describing itself as *A Medium of Intercommunication for Literary Men, General Readers, Etc*. The query was published in the number for 7 February 1880: '"Altruism."—What are the etymology and meaning of this word as used by a certain school of philosophers and sociologists?'[1]

Eight weeks later, three replies were published.[2] The briefest, but most informative of the three responses to the original inquiry came from one E. H. Marshall, who quoted from Émile Littré's *Dictionnaire de la Langue Française*. Littré, a follower of Comte's philosophy of positivism, as well as France's leading lexicographer, provided the following definition of 'altruisme': 'Terme de philosophie. Ensemble des penchants bienveillants. L'altruisme est opposé à l'egoisme. Mot dû à A. Comte. Etym. *autrui*.'[3]

Edward Marshall was the book-loving son of a landowning Oxfordshire clergyman. He had graduated from Oxford in 1874, and was subsequently called to the bar. But instead of pursuing a legal career,

---

[1] *Notes and Queries* (7 Feb. 1880), 117.
[2] *Notes and Queries* (2 Apr. 1880), 286.
[3] Quoted by Marshall, ibid. See Littré 1863: i. 120.

Marshall, in 1880, at the age of 29, moved to the south-coast English town of Hastings and took up the post of librarian at the Reference Library that had been founded there by Lord Brassey (see Fig. 1).[4] Marshall held this post until his death nearly thirty years later. During that time, as one of his obituarists noted, 'he was a well-known and frequent contributor to *Notes and Queries*, a periodical dealing with knotty points in literature'.[5] His response on the subject of 'altruism' was just one of over twenty contributions he made to the periodical in 1880 alone. Other subjects on which he offered information and opinions that year included the spelling of 'awful', Grimm's memoirs, Lincolnshire expressions, literary forgeries, the earliest uses of the French word *prestidigitateur*, and the meaning of the word 'prudent'. This last subject, along with the meaning of 'altruism', held particular interest for Marshall who was a man of 'deep religious instincts', and for many years the honorary secretary of the Hastings and St Leonard's Mendicity Society, which sought to ensure that charitable donations were directed to the deserving rather than the undeserving poor.[6] On the meaning of 'prudent', Marshall wrote that this term should not be construed in a narrow way to mean 'cunning' or 'worldly-wise' but should be taken to refer to 'man in the whole economy of his nature', that is to say to 'his spiritual and future, no less than to his social and temporal life'. True prudence, he wrote, was to choose good over evil with a view for the whole of man's destiny, in this world and the next. This, he thought, was the meaning of the 'prudent man' frequently referred to in the book of Proverbs.[7]

Another reader of *Notes and Queries* was the Scottish schoolteacher, philologist and lexicographer James Murray who, since March 1879, had been the editor of the Philological Society's new English dictionary.[8] This huge project had been started in response to criticisms of existing dictionaries made in a speech by the dean of Westminster, Richard Chenevix

---

[4] Obituaries of E. H. Marshall: *The Times* (13 Sept. 1909); *Hastings Observer* (11 Sept. 1909); *Hastings Weekly Mail and Times* (11 Sept. 1909). I am grateful to Roger Bristow at the Hastings Reference Library for copies of these obituaries and other information regarding E. H. Marshall.
[5] Obituary of E. H. Marshall, *Hastings Weekly Mail and Times* (11 Sept. 1909), 8.
[6] Ibid. Henry Sidgwick was also involved in a similar society in Cambridge (brief notes relating to his work with the society can be found in the Sidgwick Papers, Trinity College Library, Add.ms.c.96/3); and Herbert Spencer expressed his approval of benevolent societies and mendicity societies as, in some cases, 'less objectionable' ways for private individuals to give to the poor; Spencer 1892–3: ii. 381.
[7] *Notes and Queries* (12 June 1880), 480.
[8] Winchester 2003: 93. On the history of the dictionary, see also Sutcliffe 1978: 53–65, 92–7; McKusick 1992.

Figure 1. The Hastings Reference Library, from *The Builder*, 26 May 1877.
Reproduced by permission of the Syndics of Cambridge University Library.

Trench, in 1857.[9] It would eventually come to fruition with the publication of the completed *Oxford English Dictionary* in 1928.[10] This was an international, collaborative attempt to provide a single, comprehensive, scientific,
and historical work of reference charting the uses of all English words since
the earliest developments of the language up until the present. The two
most important parts of this project were the hundreds of thousands of
illustrative quotations sent in on slips of paper by a huge army of volunteer
readers, and the ordering and analysis of these quotation slips by the editor
and his assistants. At the time of his appointment as editor, James Murray
was working as a schoolteacher in Mill Hill, North London. He undertook
his work in a corrugated-iron shed in his back garden, a structure which he
called 'the Scriptorium' (see Fig. 2).[11] In the years immediately following
his appointment, Murray received about a thousand quotation slips from
readers each day.[12] Murray used *Notes and Queries* as a medium through
which to request illustrative quotations, from '*Literary Men, General Readers,
Etc.*' for particular words. On Saturday, 28 January 1882, a request appeared:
'The New English Dictionary of the Philological Society.—Quotations
wanted: send direct to the editor, Dr Murray, Mill Hill, London, N. W.'[13]
This notice divided words into three lists: those for which any quotations
should be sent; those for which quotations were wanted earlier than a given
date; and those where a quotation was wanted that was later than a given
date. The first list included the word 'altruist'. The second included: 'altruism,
1865; altruistic, 1874; altruistically, 1879'.[14]

   In the Hastings Library two days later, Edward Marshall, having read
Murray's appeal in *Notes and Queries*, copied onto a postcard two illustra-
tive quotations (see Fig. 3): one each for 'altruism' and 'altruistic', both from
G. H. Lewes's 1853 book, *Comte's Philosophy of the Sciences*; and sent it to Dr
Murray's Mill Hill home.[15] These quotations both significantly predated the

---

[9] Winchester 2003: esp. 36–45.

[10] From here onwards, *OED*. The dictionary was initially known as the Philological Society's
Dictionary, and then the New English Dictionary. It only later became known as the *Oxford
English Dictionary*.

[11] Winchester 2003: 103–4. Murray would later move to Oxford and install a similar second
'Scriptorium' in his garden there.

[12] Ibid. 112.

[13] *Notes and Queries* (28 Jan. 1882), 66.

[14] Ibid.

[15] This card from Marshall to Murray, dated 30 Jan. 1882, is held in the OUP archive in Oxford,
in the correspondence relating to the dictionary, at BL/297/33. The first published use of
'altruism' in fact came, as we have seen, a year earlier than the book cited by Marshall, in a review
of 'Contemporary Literature of France', also by G. H. Lewes, in the *Westminster Review*, 58 (1852),
614–30, at 618. For more on Lewes as the importer of 'altruism', see Ch. 2 below.

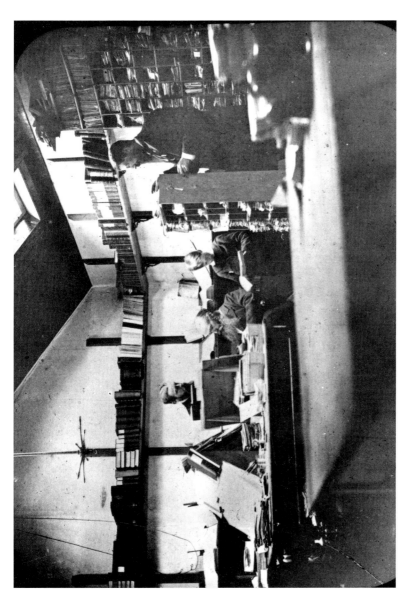

Figure 2. The means of semantic production: James Murray in his Mill Hill 'Scriptorium' in the 1880s. Reproduced by permission of the Secretary to the Delegates of Oxford University Press.

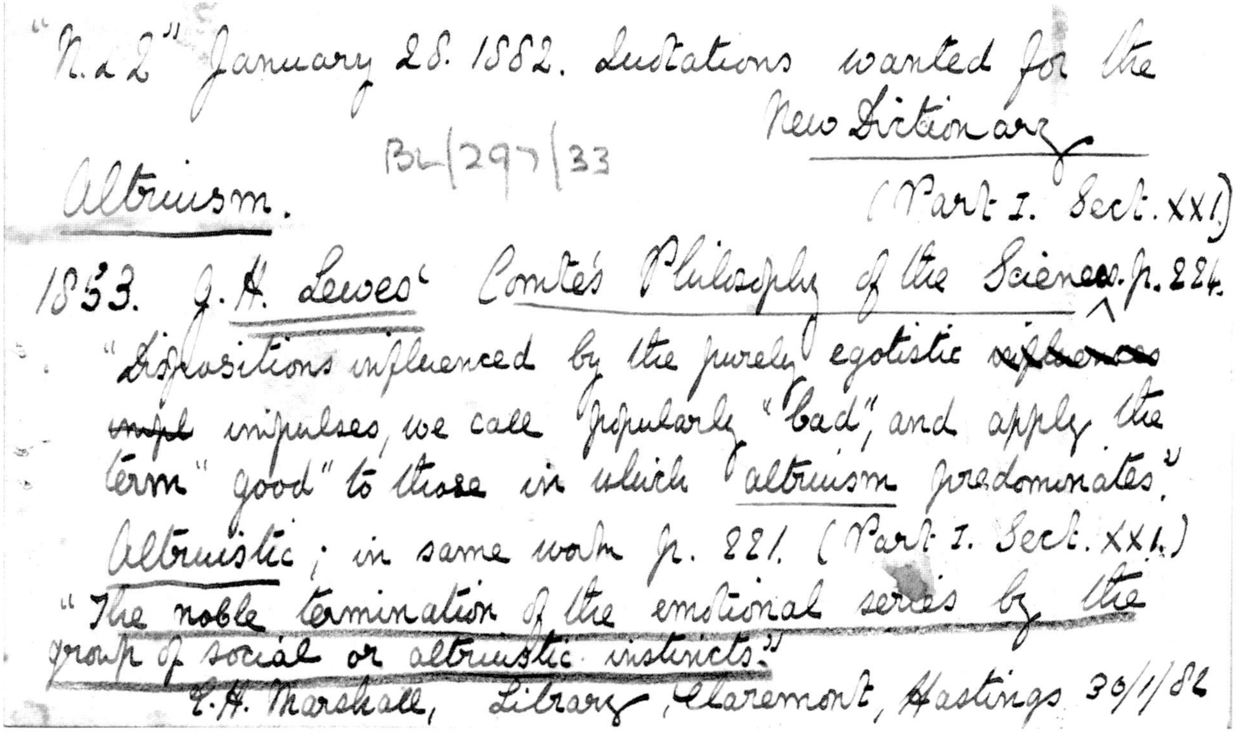
"N. & Q." January 28. 1882. Quotations wanted for the New Dictionary

Bl/297/33

Altruism. (Part I. Sect. XXI.)

1853. G. H. Lewes' Comte's Philosophy of the Science^ p. 224.

"Dispositions influenced by the purely egotistic impulses, we call popularly "bad," and apply the term "good" to those in which altruism predominates."

Altruistic; in same work p. 221. (Part I. Sect. XXI.)

"The noble termination of the emotional series by the group of social or altruistic instincts."

E. H. Marshall, Library, Claremont, Hastings 30/1/82

Figure 3. Illustrative quotations sent by Edward Marshall to James Murray in response to the latter's advertisement in *Notes and Queries* in January 1882. Reproduced by permission of the Secretary to the Delegates of Oxford University Press.

earliest quotations that Murray already had for those words (from John Stuart Mill and Herbert Spencer, respectively). Two years later, almost to the day, the first part of the dictionary was published (see Fig. 4). An advertisement in the *Times* on 29 January 1884 announced: 'This Day, Part I. A–Ant (pp. xvi, 352), price 12s. 6d., A NEW ENGLISH DICTIONARY, on Historical Principles, founded mainly on the materials collected by the Philological Society, Edited by JAMES A. H. MURRAY, LL.D., President of the Philological Society, with the assistance of many scholars and men of science.' The advertisement went on to explain that this was a publication produced on 'the principle of co-operation', and based on over three million distinct quotations, sent to the editor by over thirteen hundred readers. The resulting publication would 'represent in a condensed form the accumulated knowledge of very many of the first scholars of our time' and would be found 'in all respects abreast of the actual state of science'. The work was addressed 'not only to the advanced student of English literature' but also to 'the general reader, who will here find, ready to his hand, the derivation and accepted pronunciation, the past history and present use, of every word which may occur in his reading, and concerning which he may desire to be further informed'. The advertisement included two sample entries. One was for 'alternately', the other for 'agnosticism', including the journalist R. H. Hutton's assertion that the term was coined by the religiously sceptical evolutionist, Professor Thomas Huxley, at a party held prior to the formation of the Metaphysical Society in 1869.[16]

From now on, any reader who wondered, as 'C' had in 1880, what 'altruism' meant, could turn to the appropriate page of the *New English Dictionary* (see Fig. 5).[17] There they would find, among other illustrative quotations, the two from G. H. Lewes's book on Comte sent to Murray by Edward Marshall in 1882. Murray's definition informed readers who may not have benefited from the discussion in *Notes and Queries* that the word 'altruism' had been coined, in French, by Comte, who had derived the term from the Italian *altrui* meaning 'of or to others, what is another's, somebody else'. This, in turn, was based on the Latin *alteri huic*, meaning 'to this other'. Murray noted that '*Altruisme* was apparently suggested by the Fr. law-phrase *l'autrui*, standing according to Littré for *le bien, le droit d'autrui*', and that it had been introduced into English by 'the translators and expounders of Comte'. Its meaning was given as 'Devotion to the welfare of others, regard

---

[16] On the history of 'agnosticism' and its meanings and dissemination see Lightman 1987, 2002. For more on Hutton and the Metaphysical Society, see Chs 2 and 3 below.
[17] The dictionary was known as the *Oxford English Dictionary* from 1894 onwards.

A NEW

ENGLISH DICTIONARY

ON HISTORICAL PRINCIPLES;

FOUNDED MAINLY ON THE MATERIALS COLLECTED BY

The Philological Society.

EDITED BY

JAMES A. H. MURRAY, LL.D.,

PRESIDENT OF THE PHILOLOGICAL SOCIETY,

WITH THE ASSISTANCE OF MANY SCHOLARS AND MEN OF SCIENCE.

PART I.   A — ANT.

OXFORD:

AT THE CLARENDON PRESS.

1884.

Price Twelve Shillings and Sixpence.

Figure 4. The title page of the first published fascicle of the *New English Dictionary* (1884). Reproduced by permission of the Secretary to the Delegates of Oxford University Press.

ALTOGETHER. 259 ALUM.

Altogether (ǭltŭge·ðəɹ), *a.*, *adv.*, and *sb.* [comb. of ALL and TOGETHER. Orig. a mere strengthening of *all*, but, like *all* itself, gradually becoming adverbial, in which sense alone it is now used when written in combination.]

A. *adj.* A strengthened form of ALL *a.*

†**1.** The whole together, the entire; everything, the whole, the total. (Often *absol.*; cf. ALL A II.) *Obs.*

1154 *O. E. Chron.* (Laud MS.) an. 1137 § 4 & brenden sythen þe cyrce & al te gædere. *c* 1200 ORMIN 9581 Issraæle þeod.. all togeddre att Drihhtin Godd. 1526 TINDALE 1 *Cor.* vii. 19 Circumcision is nothynge.. but the keppynge of the commaundmentes of god is altogether. 1528 MORE *Heresyes* IV. Wks. 1557, 285/1 Ananias & Saphyra.. made semblance as though they brought to the apostles altogether. 1611 BIBLE *Ex.* xix. 18 And mount Sinai was altogether on a smoke. — *Ps.* cxxxix. 4 There is not a worde in my tongue: but lo, O Lord, thou knowest it altogether.

†**2.** *pl.* All united, all in a company; all inclusively; all without exception. Now written separately *all together*.

1330 R. BRUNNE *Chron.* 264 Bot alle þei were forholn, & failed þam alle togider. *c* 1400 *Ywaine & Gaw.* 2955 Cumes forth, he said, ye altogeder. 1535 COVERDALE *Ezek.* xxxiv. 13 Proude wordes agaynst me, which I haue herde altogether. 1590 SHAKS. *Com. Err.* V. i. 245 Then altogether They fell vpon me. 1663 GERBIER *Counsel* 102 Solidity, Conveniency, and Ornament, altogether to be observed in true Building. [*Mod.* They came separately, but went away all together.]

B. *adv.* [by gradual transference from the sb. to the predicate; cf. ALL C 1.]

1. Everything being included; in all respects, in every particular; entirely, wholly, totally, quite.

c 1200 *Trin. Coll. Hom.* 19 Here fifealde mihte was altegeder attred. *c* 1330 *Kyng of Tars* 601 Whon he hedde altogedere ipreyd, And al that evere he couthe iseyd. 1534 MORE *On the Passion* Wks. 1557, 1373/1 Were he as bad as Judas altogiter. 1611 BIBLE *John* ix. 34 Thou wast altogether born in sins. 1712 ADDISON *Spect.* No. 441 ¶ 9 Scenes and Objects, and Companions that are altogether new. 1782 PRIESTLEY *Nat. & Rev. Relig.* I. 30 The idea of chance is altogether excluded. 1857 BUCKLE *Civiliz.* I. ii. 125 In Greece, we see a country altogether the reverse of India. 1881 TROLLOPE *Ayala's Angel* III. lvi. 163 That kept me from being altogether wretched.

2. Uninterruptedly, without deviation or admixture. (Cf. ALL C 4.)

1700 *Lond. Gaz.* mmmdcix/4 A dark Iron-grey Horse.. Paces altogether. 1709 *Ibid.* mmmmdcviii/4 A Bay Mare, .. Trots altogether.

3. For altogether: for all time to come, as a permanent arrangement, finally, definitely, permanently, 'for good.' (*For* is sometimes omitted.)

1548 UDALL etc. *Erasm. Paraphr. Luke* xxiv. 44 Did he not once for altogether.. take awaie all autoritie from the priestes? 1580 NORTH *Plutarch* (1676) 311 Perswading themselves he was fled for altogether. 1674 SCHEFFER *Lapland* xxvi. 121 Most of them then were baptized very late.. some deferred it for altogether. 1825 *Bro. Jonathan* II. 40 Walter and Edith were not in a humour.. for separating.. altogether.

C. *sb.* A whole, a *tout ensemble*.

1667 WATERHOUSE *Fire of Lond.* 141 Her Congregations, Her Citizens, Her altogether has been as orderly, etc. 1674 N. FAIRFAX *Bulk & Selv.* 33 We only call.. Gods All-fillingness an altogether, to loosen it from any thing of sundership. 1865 *Pall Mall G.* 26 June 9 American fingers.. impart a finish and an altogether (this is much better than to steal *tout-ensemble* from the wicked Emperor).

Altogetherness (ǭltŭge·ðəɹnės). *rare.* [f. prec. + -NESS.] Wholeness, unity of being.

1674 N. FAIRFAX *Bulk & Selv.* 60 So Gods All-fillingness is in the world.. in an indivisible altogetherness. 1824 J. GALT *Rothelan* II. III. vii. 67 His courteous mildness, his altogetherness of fraud and smiles.

†**Altoge·thers,** *adv. Obs.* [f. ALL + TOGETHERS a variant of TOGETHER, with genitival ending: cf. *afterward, -s, elsewhere, -s.*] = ALTOGETHER.

c 1175 *Lamb. Hom.* 81 Þe an is aquenched al to geðeres. *c* 1450 LONELICH *Grail* xxxvii. 842 Now Altogederis we ben present. 1569 J. ROGERS *Glasse of Godly Love* 180 Christe only is her comfort all togethers. 1586 J. HOOKER *Giraldus's Hist. Irel.* in *Holinshed* II. 114/1 The present state of all Ireland, altogethers deuoured with robberies, murders, riots.

Alto-relievo (ɑ·lto rǐlī·vo). Pl. -os. [It. *alto-rilievo* high relief; this spelling is sometimes used in Eng.] High relief; sculpture or carved work in which the figures project more than one half of their true proportions from the wall or surface on which they are carved. Hence *concr.* A sculpture or carving in high relief.

1717 BERKELEY in Fraser *Life* (1871) 550 The infinite profusion of alto-relievo. 1762 H. WALPOLE *Vertue's Anecd. Paint.* (1786) I. 276 A fine bust of queen Elizabeth on onyx, alto relievo in profile. 1773 BRYDONE *Sicily* xix. (1809) 199 The representation of a boar-hunting in alto relievo, on white marble. 1878 LADY HERBERT tr. *Hübner's Round the World* II. v. 342 There are no alto-relievos.

Altricate, -tion, obs. ff. ALTERCATE, -TION.

Altruism (æ·ltru͡iz'm). [a. Fr. *altruisme* formed by Comte on It. *altrui* (Fr. *autrui*) of or to others, what is another's, somebody else, f. L. *alteri huic* 'to this other,' the dative afterwards passing into a general oblique case. See -ISM. *Altruisme* was apparently suggested by the Fr. law-phrase *l'autrui*, standing according to Littré for *le bien, le droit d'autrui*. Introd. into Eng. by the translators and expounders of Comte.] Devotion to the welfare of others, regard for others, as a principle of action; opposed to egoism or selfishness.

1853 LEWES *Comte's Philos. Sc.* I. xxi. 224 Dispositions influenced by the purely egotistic impulses we call popularly 'bad,' and apply the term 'good' to those in which altruism predominates. 1865 MILL in *Westm. Rev.* July, To make altruism (a word of his [Comte's] own coining) predominate over egoism. 1871 FARRAR *Witn. Hist.* iv. 144 Is altruism a sweeter, or better word than charity? 1876 — *Marlb. Serm.* xvi. 157 A good and wise modern philosopher summed up the law and duty of life in Altruism—*Vive pour autrui*—'Live for others.' 1877 C. ROW *Bampt. Lect.* (1881) 106 The religion of humanity, whose great moral principle is altruism. 1879 GEO. ELIOT *Theophr. Such* viii. 147 The bear was surprised at the badger's want of altruism.

Altruist (æ·ltru͡ist). [f. ALTRUISM: see -IST. Cf. Fr. *altruiste* adj.] One who professes the principles of altruism.

1868 NETTLESHIP *Browning's Poetry* vi. 167 His development as a great altruist. 1881 *Daily News* 27 Aug. 5/1 If they were thorough altruists, a sweet reasonableness would induce them to avoid inflicting.. distress.

Altruistic (æltru͡i·stik), *a.* [f. Fr. *altruiste* (adj. f. *altruisme*) + -IC. Earlier than ALTRUIST.] Of or pertaining to altruism; actuated by regard for the well-being of others; benevolent.

1853 LEWES *Comte's Philos. Sc.* I. xxi. 221 The noble termination of the emotional series by the group of social or altruistic instincts. 1862 HINTON *Let.* in *Life* (1878) 194 The word altruistic I borrow from Comte. Is it not a capital word? I am resolved to naturalise it. 1873 H. SPENCER in *Contemp. Rev.* Feb., Up to a certain point altruistic action blesses giver and receiver, beyond that point it curses giver and receiver.

Altruistically (æltru͡i·stikăli), *adv.* [f. prec. + -AL + -LY.] In an altruistic manner; benevolently.

1874 H. SPENCER *Sociol.* viii. 186 A means to furthering the general happiness altruistically. 1879 — *Data of Eth.* xi. 197 The most altruistically-natured leave no like-natured posterity.

Altruize (æ·ltru͡əiz), *v. nonce-wd.* [f. It. *altrui* some one else + -IZE; suggested by ALTRUISM.] To change into some one else.

1878 T. SINCLAIR *Mount* 300 Etherealised or converted, altruised, or.. artisticised into a third world of thought.

†**A·ltry.** *Obs. rare*$^{-1}$. [f. ALTER + -Y; purely imitative: cf. *enter, entry.*] Alteration, change.

1527 *Acct. of Gibson, Master of Revels*, Payd to John Skut, yᵉ quenys tayler for makynge of yᵉ ladies aparell by altry.

‖**A·ltus.** *Mus. Obs.* [L. *altus* high (sc. *cantus* singing).] = ALTO *sb.*2

1609 DOULAND *Ornithop. Microl.* 86 The Base requires a third below, and the Altus the same aboue. *a* 1659 CLEVELAND *Comm. Place* (1677) 163 A Deep Base that must reach as low as Hell to describe the Passion, and thence rebound to a joyful *Altus*, the high-strain of the Resurrection.

†**A·ltumal,** *a. Obs.* ? *slang.* [f. L. *altum* the deep, *i.e.* the sea + -AL.] (See quot.)

1711 *Medleys* 29 Jan. (1712) 186 His Altumal Cant, a Mark of his poor Traffick and Tar-Education. 1753 CHAMBERS *Cycl. Supp.*, *Altumal*, a term used to denote the mercantile style, or dialect. In this sense, we meet with altumal cant, to denote the language of petty traders and tars.

†**A·lture.** *Obs.* [ad. It. *altura* height; f. *alto*:—L. *altum* height: see -URE.] Height, altitude.

a 1547 EARL SURREY *Ps.* lv. 29 From that the sun descends, Till he his alture win. 1598 BARRET *Theor. Warres* V. i. 127 Casamats.. so low that they arriued not vnto the alture of the ditch.

†**Alu·co.** *Obs. rare.* [f. L. *alūcus* an owl.] A book-name given by some to the White, by others to the Tawny, Owl.

1753 CHAMBERS *Cycl. Supp.*, *Aluco*, the name by which authors have called the common white owl. 1785 LATHAM *Synopsis* 134 Tawny Owl, *Syrnium Stridula*, Aluco Owl.

Aludel (æ·liudel). *Chem.* [a. Fr. *aludel*, in 13th c. *alutel*, ad. Arab. *al-uthāl* (quoted by Dozy with this sense in 9th c.), i.e. *al* the + *uthāl*, prob. variant of *ithāl* pl. of *athla* utensil, apparatus.] A pear-shaped pot of earthenware or glass, open at both ends, so that a series could be fitted one above another; used by the alchemists in sublimation.

1559 MORWYNG *Evonym.* 6 Putting wull of wode, or bombice into the upper hoole of the aludel. 1610 B. JONSON *Alchem.* II. iii. (1616) 624 Let your heat, still, lessen by degrees, To the Aludels. 1677 HARRIS tr. *Lemery's Chem.* (1686) Introd. 44 Aludels.. are Pots without a bottom, joyned together and are placed over another Pot with a hole in the middle to serve for Sublimations. 1731 HALES *Stat. Ess.* I. 201 We luted a German retort to two or three large alodals. 1881 RAYMOND *Gloss. Mining Terms*, *Aludel*, an earthen condenser for mercury.

A-luff, obs. form of ALOOF.

Alum (æ·ləm). Forms: 4 **alem**, 4–5 **alym**, 4–8 **alom**, 5–7 **alume**, **alome**, 6 **alme**, 6–7 **allume**, 6–8 **allom(e**, **allum**, 4– **alum**. [a. OFr. *alum*:—L. *alūmen*, the same substance: cf. *alūta* tawed skin.]

1. A whitish transparent mineral salt, crystallizing in octahedrons, very astringent, used in dyeing, tawing skins, and medicine, also for sizing paper, and making materials fire-proof; chemically a double sulphate of aluminium and potassium ($AlK(SO_4)_2 + 12H_2O$ water of crystallization).

Burnt Alum, A. deprived of its water of crystallization so as to become a white powder; *Rock* or *Roman Alum*, that prepared from the Alum-stone in Italy; *Saccharine Alum*, an artificial composition of alum, rosewater, and egg albumen, boiled to a paste, which hardens when cold.

c 1325 *E. E. Allit. P.* B. 1035 As alum & alka[t]ran, that angré arn boþe. 1366 MAUNDEV. ix. 99 About that see growethe moche Alom. *c* 1386 CHAUCER *Chan. Yem. Prol.* 260 Tartre, alym, glas [*v.r.* alum, alumglas(se, alem]. 1436 *Pol. Poems* II. 172 Coton, roche-alum, and gode golde of Jene. 1453 in Heath *Grocers' Comp.* (1869) 422 Alum, foyle or rooch, yᵉ bale.. iiij*d.* 1551 TURNER *Herbal* II. (1568) 123 Layed to with honey and allome. 1585 JAMES I *Ess. Poesie* 16 Cleare and smothe lyke glas or alme. 1587 HOLINSHED *Chron.* III. 1199/1 A mightie great hulke, laden with wood & allume. 1601 HOLLAND *Pliny* (1634) II. 559 Alume brought from Melos, is the best. 1622 HEYLYN *Cosmogr.* I. (1682) 75 Well furnished with Allom, Sulphur, and Bitumen. 1660 R. COKE *Power & Subj.* 208 The Pope had excommunicated all persons whatsoever, who had bought alume of the Florentines. 1671 SALMON *Syn. Med.* III. xxii. 437 A lotion with Honey, Alome, and White wine. 1703 MOXON *Mech. Exerc.* 238 A fat Earth full of Allom. 1718 MRS. EALES *Receipt* 38 Put in a good piece of Roach-Allum. 1718 QUINCY *Compl. Disp.* 106 Alum is dug out of the earth as we find it in the Shops. 1768 BOSWELL *Corsica* i. (ed. 2) 52 There are also mines of allum. 1815 BAKEWELL *Introd. Geol.* 201 The sulphuric acid uniting with the alumine, forms the well-known salt called alum. 1855 TENNYSON *Maud* I. i. x, While chalk and alum and plaster are sold to the poor for bread. 1875 URE *Dict. Arts* I. 105 [Alum] seems to have come to Europe in later times as *alum of Rocca*, the name of Edessa; but it is not impossible that this name was an Italian prefix, which has remained to this day under the name of *Rock Alum, Allume di Rocca*.

2. *Mod. Chem.* (with *pl.*) A series of isomorphous double salts, including the foregoing, consisting of aluminium sulphate in combination with the sulphate of a monatomic metal, as potassium, sodium, ammonium, silver, etc., with general formula $Al'''M(SO_4)_2 + 12H_2O$; all of which crystallize in octahedrons: distinguished as *Common* or *Potash alum*, *Soda alum*, *Ammonia alum*, *Silver alum*, etc.

1868 WATTS *Dict. Chem.* V. 580 Argento-aluminic sulphate or Silver alum. Potassio-aluminic sulphate or Potash-alum: this is the salt to which the name alum is most generally applied. 1873 WILLIAMSON *Chem.* § 185 These alums cannot be separated by crystallization; and a crystal of one of them grows regularly in a solution of another alum. 1873 FOWNES *Chem.* 373 Sodium alum is much more soluble. 1875 URE *Dict. Arts* I. 107 The composition of potash-, soda-, and ammonia-alums found ready formed in nature.

3. *Mod. Chem.* (with *pl.*) Extended to a family of compounds analogous to and including the preceding series, in which the Alumina itself is absent, and replaced by the isomorphous sesquioxide of iron, chrome, or manganese; whence *Iron alum* (Potassio-ferric sulphate), *Manganese alum* (Potassio-manganic sulphate), *Chrome alum* (Potassio-chromic sulphate), *Chrome-ammonia alum* (Ammonio-chromic sulphate), etc.

1868 WATTS *Dict. Chem.* V. 578 The dodecahydrated double sulphates of the alkali-metals and triatomic metals constitute the true alums. The sulphates of ammonium, potassium, and sodium are capable of forming alums with the aluminic, ferric, chromic, and manganic sulphates. 1874 ROSCOE *Elem. Chem.* 247 Chromium sulphate forms a series of alums with potassium and ammonium sulphates, which have a deep purple tint, and are isomorphous with common alum.

4. *Min.* Applied to various native minerals, which are chemically alums proper, as *Native alum* or Kalinite; also to others (pseudo-alums), which are compounds of aluminium sulphate with the sulphate of some other base, as *Magnesia alum* (Magnesio-aluminic sulphate) or Pickeringite; or with the protoxides of iron, manganese, etc., as *Feather* or *Plume alum* (Ferroso-aluminic sulphate) or Halotrichite, *Manganese alum* or Apjohnite, *Manganoso-magnesian alum* or Bosjemanite.

The name *Feather alum* has been applied also to *magnesia alum* and *alunogen*.

a 1661 HOLYDAY *Juvenal* (1673) 122 Plume-alume burns the skin.. rock-alume dissolves metals, shrivels the skin, loosens the teeth. 1868 DANA *Min.* 655 Hallotrichine is a silky alum from the Solfatara near Naples. 1868 WATTS *Dict. Chem.* V. 583 Manganoso-aluminic sulphate, or *manganese alum*.. occurs in snow-white silky fibres at Lagoa Bay.

5. *Comb.*, in which *alum* stands in obj. relation to pr. pple. or vbl. sb., as *alum-bearing, -maker, -making, -manufacture*; in instrumental relation to pa. pple., as *alum-steeped*; in simple attrib. relation, as *alum-crystal, -liquor, -water*; or attrib. relation of material, as *alum-styptic*.

1869 ROSCOE *Elem. Chem.* 215 Ammonium Sulphate is largely employed for alum making. 1870 YEATS *Nat. Hist. Comm.* 381 The chief localities of alum manufacture in this country. 1837 SYD. SMITH *Let.* Wks. 1859 II. 277/1 Let him drive his alum-steeped loaves a little further. 1587 HARRISON *Engl.* I. II. xxiii. 348 A tast much like to allume liquor. 1875 URE *Dict. Arts* I. 117 *Alum Liquors*,—In the alum works on the Yorkshire coast, eight different liquors are met with. 1578 LYTE *Dodoens* VI. xxx. 697 Soked, or delayed in allom water. 1656 DU GARD *Lat. Unlocked* § 443 Hee wetteth with allom-water every sheet of thinner paper. 1711 POPE *Rape Lock* II. 131 Alom-stypticks with contracting pow'r Shrink his thin essence like a rivelled flow'r.

Also **alum cake**, a massive and porous sulphate of alumina, mixed with silica, manufactured from fine clay; **alum earth**, applied to various earthy or loose substances yielding alum; †**alum-farmer**, one who farmed the royal alum-works; †**alum-flower**, alum calcined and powdered; †**alum-glass**, crystallized alum; **alum-rock**, **-schist**, **-shale**, **-slate**, thin-bedded rocks found

33 – 2

Figure 5. Entries for 'altruism' and related terms in the first published fascicle of the *New English Dictionary* (1884). Reproduced by permission of the Secretary to the Delegates of Oxford University Press.

for others, as a principle of action; opposed to egoism or selfishness.'[18] There
followed illustrative quotations from G. H. Lewes, John Stuart Mill, the
Anglican clergyman and philologist Frederic Farrar, another churchman,
C. A. Row, and George Eliot who, in *Theophrastus Such* (1879), had included
the sentence: 'The bear was surprised at the badger's want of altruism.'[19] An
'altruist' was defined as 'One who professes the principles of altruism';
and 'altruistic' as 'Of or pertaining to altruism; actuated by regard for the
well-being of others; benevolent.'[20]

One review of the first part of the *New English Dictionary*, published in
the *British Quarterly Review* in April 1884, was written by Richard Lovett,
a biblical scholar and the book editor of the Religious Tract Society in
London.[21] Lovett placed the work in a religious and moral context,
describing it as a labour of love, which had been produced by the selfless
efforts of men and women 'deeply interested in the welfare of English'. He
also thought it was a 'worthy monument of the noble language which God
has entrusted to the English-speaking peoples'.[22] Looking in more detail at
some of the entries included in this first part, Lovett wrote that 'The ful-
ness of treatment received by modern words is well exemplified in *altruism*
and its derivatives.' Having summarized the origins of these words, and
noted the range of quotations used to illustrate them, Lovett emphasized
how recently this set of terms had entered the language, and noted that 'the
names of those who use it most freely, Herbert Spencer, Lewes, and Hinton,
show to what school of thought it belongs'. 'An interesting chapter of
modern philosophical controversy', Lovett concluded, 'is condensed in the
definitions and illustrations of the use of these words.'[23] He ended his
review by urging readers to buy their own copies of the successive parts of
the dictionary in order to make sure that the project would be a financial
success, since 'English governments will give little or nothing to help on
literary enterprises', even ones of such national importance.[24] Rather, it
would fall on well intentioned individuals to finance the project by digging
into their own pockets to buy each new part of the dictionary.

---

[18] Murray 1888: 259.
[19] Quoted ibid.
[20] Ibid.
[21] *ODNB*.
[22] Richard Lovett, 'Dictionary Making, Past and Present', *British Quarterly Review*, 79 (1884),
336–54. Repr. in *Littell's Living Age*, 47 (1884), 145–55, at 155.
[23] Ibid. 153.
[24] Ibid. 155.

Three kinds of meaning:
definition, connotation, significance

I have recounted the process by which 'altruism' made its way into the first of the 125 fascicles of the first edition of the *OED* in some detail since it provides a very useful preliminary vignette of the processes of moral meaning-making which this book is about. The earnest young Hastings librarian Edward Marshall combined his love of books and words with a religious and moral concern about prudence and the appropriate forms of philanthropy. The Calvinistic and meticulous Dr Murray exemplified in his career two classically Victorian moral passions—scientific classification and obsessively hard work. The enormous lexicographical project over which he presided illustrated how the goods that could be produced by cooperative labour hugely exceeded anything that the effort of a single individual might achieve. The relationship between intentions and actions in moral life, tacitly raised by Murray's definitions, was one that would be debated throughout the Victorian period. The use of another Victorian key word, 'agnosticism', as one of the examples with which to sell the first part of the new dictionary is a helpful indicator of some of the intellectual and religious preoccupations of the world in which the meanings of 'altruism' were being debated. Finally, Lovett's suggestion that worthy and selfless endeavours such as those behind the production of the new dictionary would and should be financed by private individuals rather than out of the public purse gestures towards debates about socialism, with which the language of altruism was increasingly associated from the 1880s onwards.

However, consulting a dictionary, even such an informative dictionary as Murray's, is of course by no means the only way that one might go about trying to establish the meaning of a key term in a particular period. Having consulted dictionaries and other works of reference, one might next look at the uses of the term in a much broader range of published works, from theoretical and academic works through to literary, popular, and journalistic publications. Finally, one could focus on particular individuals, perhaps looking at unpublished papers and correspondence as well as their published writings, to try to establish what the term meant to them, and why they used it in the ways that they did. Pursuing these different research strategies will result in the recovery of different kinds of meaning. The first approach will give us definitions of a term, or its formal denotation. The second approach will provide further definitions and more detailed discussions. It will also tell us more about the way the term was actually used in particular conversations and controversies, how its use changed from one

context to another, how its use developed over time, and how various connotations of the term thus accumulated and evolved. The various uses and
connotations might or might not conform to formal definitions of the
term. Finally, a more detailed consideration of the motivations of the users
of a term and of the impact their uses of it had on others, will produce a
sense of what the term meant in the context of particular individuals'
projects and identities: a sense of its significance in their lives.[25] Having pursued the strategies just outlined, what I hope to show in what follows,
amongst other things, is how the definitions, connotations, and significance
of a key term can be closely intertwined. Adopting or resisting a particular
use or definition of a key term might often be a way of inaugurating, welcoming, or struggling against the intellectual, cultural or political changes it
connotes — changes which might be central to the projects and identities
either of individuals or of whole groups, movements, classes, or nations.
Changes in the lexicon need not be merely lexical.

The dictionary definitions produced by Littré and Murray are certainly
of value to the historian, as they also were to curious readers in the nineteenth century. They reveal some early tensions between psychological,
behavioural, and ideological definitions of 'altruism'. Looking beyond the
formal definitions of terms, however, Murray's use of volunteer readers and
illustrative quotations provides the historian with a still more valuable
resource for discovering a wider range of uses and the significance attached
to them. As Lovett recognized in his 1884 review, the quotations used to
illustrate the definitions of 'altruism' and related terms provide something
approaching a condensed history of a philosophical controversy. The fact
that the term was initially adopted by those who sympathized with Auguste
Comte's atheistic and sociological visions of nature and history was a particularly problematic fact for Christian commentators on the new word,
some of whose sceptical remarks were quoted by Murray. George Eliot's
use of the term, alluding to the idea that animals shared some human moral
instincts, hinted at another particularly important element of Victorian
concerns about the meaning of altruism.

One invaluable resource in making the transition from the entries for
words in the new dictionary in 1884 to the historical contexts in which the

---

[25] Skinner 2002: 90–3 distinguishes three different kinds of meaning in relation to a text or statement: the formal meaning of the words, what the text means to a reader, and what an author
means by it. Bevir 2001 distinguishes between semantic, conventional and hermeneutic meanings.
My adoption of the less technical terms, 'definition', 'connotation', and 'significance' in relation
to the meaning of a particular term is not identical to either of these other tripartite schemes.

terms were used is the collection of slips still held in the *OED* archives. These are divided into the 'copy slips' (see Fig. 6), which include the definitions and quotations actually used in the final published dictionary, and the 'superfluous slips'. The latter include both illustrative quotations sent in by readers but which were not ultimately selected by Murray or his colleagues for inclusion in the relevant entries, and also discarded definition slips.[26] From the point of view of the historian, these slips are anything but superfluous. The discarded definition slip for 'altruist', for example, written in Murray's hand, reveals that he could not decide whether an altruist was someone who 'professes' altruism or 'practises' it. This hints again at the ambiguity between ideological and behavioural meanings of the term. Still more valuable, however, are the discarded quotation slips: nineteen illustrating 'altruism', two for 'altruist', and seventeen for 'altruistic'. These reveal that Murray decided to omit quotations from Herbert Spencer's *Data of Ethics* (1879) in which altruism was defined behaviourally, even though they were sent in by several readers. He preferred to stick to his psychological and ideological definition of altruism as a 'principle of action' rather than a kind of action, and so discarded these quotations from Spencer. Other discarded slips were equally illuminating. They revealed an array of fascinating theological, literary and journalistic uses of the language of altruism—uses which, even with the wealth of electronically searchable catalogues, databases, and online texts now available, I might not otherwise have found. This was the route through which I was first directed, for instance, to novels by 'Ouida' and W. H. Mallock; to the sermons of Canon James B. Mozley; to a discussion of egoism and altruism by Ernst Haeckel in *Nature* in 1882; and to several other newspaper and periodical articles.

It is through immersion in this wide range of writings about altruism from the 1850s to around 1900 that I have tried to reconstruct, in addition to the technical definitions of 'altruism' and its cognate terms, a second, contextual kind of meaning—the uses and connotations of those terms. This network of writings by sociologists, philosophers, natural historians, theologians, novelists, and journalists constitutes the arena in which the meanings of altruism were contested and transformed. To disagree about the proper meaning of 'altruism' (or, frequently, about the validity or propriety of adopting the language of altruism at all) was to contest the validity of a wide range of intellectual schemes, including Comtean positivism,

---

[26] Held in the OUP archive in Oxford. The copy slips relating to altruism and related words are numbered from 895 to 911. The superfluous slips are not numbered.

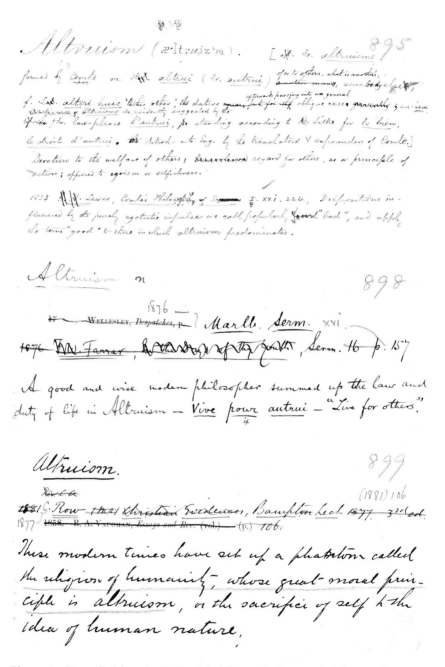

Figure 6. 'Copy slips' from the *OED* archive. The top slip is Murray's definition of 'altruism'. The lower slips are illustrative quotations taken from works by Frederic W. Farrar and Charles A. Row respectively. Reproduced by permission of the Secretary to the Delegates of Oxford University Press.

Mill's utilitarianism, Darwinian and Spencerian theories of evolution, Anglicanism, agnosticism, neo-Christianity, idealism, socialism, individualism, pessimism, or even nihilism.

These debates took place both in private and in public. Individuals, such as the young Henry Sidgwick in Cambridge in the 1860s, the social surveyors and reformers Charles Booth and Beatrice Potter (later Beatrice Webb) in the 1880s, and less well-known figures, including a Liverpool businessman and amateur philosopher called John Towne Danson, all recorded in diaries or personal notes their thoughts about the meaning of 'altruism'. Under Sidgwick's supervision, G. E. Moore wrote an undergraduate essay about egoism and altruism in the 1890s, which he discussed with his tutor. Intellectual, political, and religious groups provided opportunities for public discussions of altruism amongst like-minded individuals. Positivist meetings in London, Manchester, and elsewhere; meetings of intellectual coteries including the Metaphysical Society and the Cambridge Apostles; public lectures at Mechanics Institutes and secularist societies; sermons, church congresses, meetings of co-operative societies or dinners in the Conservative Club: all of these provided occasions to discuss the importance and significance of altruism. And the results of many of these musings, private or public, often reached a still wider audience through publication in newspapers, periodicals, volumes of lectures, textbooks, philosophical and religious tracts, political pamphlets, stories, novels, and verse.

The sentimentally selfless 'altruist' started to appear in works of fiction, including a story about 'The Altruist in Corduroy' in 1892, and a short novel by 'Ouida' entitled simply *An Altruist* in 1897. The same year saw the publication of a book of purportedly true confessions by a reformed convict named Archie, amongst them a farcical tale entitled 'Altruism' about Archie's bungled attempts to put the world to rights by stealing from a wealthy and unpopular landowner. 'Altruism', 'altruistic', and 'altruist' were words that appealed to novelists as well as sociologists, Christians as well as positivists, socialists as well as individualists, working men as well as bishops and statesmen. These terms were parts of the projects of Victorian social and religious reformers of many different kinds. Two nice examples of the broad appeal of the language of altruism are to be found in the adoption of 'Altruism' as a pen-name by a Manchester writer called Robert Melsom, author of a successful *Gas Consumers' Manual* in 1882 (see Fig. 16 below); and in the choice of 'Altruistic' as an identity for the receipt of telegrams by William Kirby, the manager of Queen's Gate Mansions in London, in his

advertisements offering rooms and suites for rent in *The Times* in the 1890s
(see Fig. 21 below).[27]

Thinking about why the language of altruism might have resonated
with individuals, from Beatrice Potter and Henry Sidgwick to Robert
Melsom and William Kirby, brings us on to a third and final semantic category—significance. When reading the definitional and intellectual debates
about moral meanings briefly described in the preceding paragraphs, and
which are documented and interpreted in detail below, I have frequently
asked myself what was really at stake for the protagonists. Various explanations suggest themselves. Some of the more minute disagreements about
definitions of terms resulted from nothing more than the pursuit of philosophical rigour and analytic precision. And, undoubtedly, some of the arguments were constructed with an eye to what might satisfy the editor of a
journal or entertain the reading public. However, the explanations that I
have emphasized more often below relate to the significance that these disputes had for the individuals engaged in them (and for those Victorians
who participated in such disputes through their reading). The details of
what I mean by this will become clear in the course of the book. However,
there are three preliminary considerations concerning personal identities
and projects that will indicate the essence of my approach.

First, the reason that people care about the meanings of particular words
is that those words either constitute or threaten cherished intellectual categories. People experience the world through their mental categories, which
are, consequently, integral to their sense of self and to their identity. For the
meaning or applicability of those categories to be questioned, therefore, can
constitute a threat to an important part of an individual's identity. Secondly,
to have the authority to define which parts of reality are picked out by a
particular term, and what that term says about those realities, is to have a
powerful influence on how others perceive and think about the world.
Finally, turning to the particular case of the language of altruism, to disagree
about whether human beings were naturally altruistic, about whether they
should aspire to be more completely altruistic, about whether God required
them to be altruistic, about whether society could and should develop to
become more completely altruistic, and about what, in any case, assenting to
any of those propositions would really mean, was to disagree about questions
the answers to which were central to a range of political and religious visions
of the world, and related schemes for transforming it. In short, debates about

---

[27] For specific references see fuller discussions of these individuals and contexts in later chapters.

'altruism' were connected to the creation and redefinition of a range of social roles, religious identities, and political projects, the details and meanings of which are central to this book.

I should perhaps acknowledge at the outset that to say that I am endeavouring to recover what disputes about 'altruism' meant to the individuals engaged in them, by immersing myself in the texts that those individuals wrote and read, is to admit that I am engaged in the enterprise of seeking to recover the motives and beliefs of people who read and wrote, thought and spoke, live and died in the past. This kind of historical undertaking is one that seems to have the ability to cause anxiety even amongst its ablest practitioners. Quentin Skinner, for instance, writes with a certain defensiveness that his aspiration 'is not of course to perform the impossible task of getting inside the heads of long-dead thinkers' (elsewhere he phrases this more soberly as a denial of the aspiration to 'enter into the thought-processes of long-dead thinkers').[28] Rather, Skinner continues, he aims 'simply to use the ordinary techniques of historical enquiry to grasp their concepts, to follow their distinctions, to recover their beliefs and, so far as possible, to see things their way'. But if grasping the concepts, following the distinctions, recovering the beliefs, and seeing again the visions of long-dead thinkers is not the same thing as getting inside their heads, nor as following their thought-processes, then it is hard to imagine what is. I suspect that the reason for this apparent equivocation is Skinner's acute awareness of the criticisms that many historians and literary critics have made of the aspiration to recover authors' intentions (as well as the intentions of readers, speakers, and listeners).[29] However, his own work is ample testimony to the value and plausibility of historical work based upon this sort of aspiration.

Although it is certainly true that we can never ascribe beliefs and intentions to historical actors in a certain or infallible way, the impossibility of certainty or infallibility need not deter us from the attempt.[30] We cannot ascribe beliefs and intentions infallibly and certainly to the living people with whom we interact daily, nor even to ourselves. To attempt to recover the thought-processes of the dead is, then, a task of the same order as the attempt to recover the thought-processes of the living. Of course these comments barely scratch the surface of this issue, but hopefully they at least

---

[28] Skinner 2002: pp. vii, 3.

[29] See Skinner 2002: esp. chs 4 and 5.

[30] This line of argument is similar to that pursued by Skinner in defending his own approach against the sceptical critiques of Derrida and others; see Skinner 2002: esp. ch. 6.

serve as an acknowledgement and partial defence of the historical approach
I have taken in this book.

Witnesses, maps, mirrors, keys, tools, motors

Historians have long recognized the value of words and their changing uses
as sources of information about the past. The lexicographical project headed
by Murray which gave rise to the *OED* was founded on the recognition that
the current meanings of a word could not be fully appreciated without some
knowledge of the history of its uses. Studying past uses of a word can throw
light on more than simply the processes by which it took on its present
meanings, however. Richard Chenevix Trench, the scholarly clergyman
whose speech was one of the driving forces behind the Philological Society's
plans for a new dictionary, was someone who recognized the potential of
words as historical sources, arguing that past uses of a word could also illuminate the cultures and societies within which they had occurred. His book
The Study of Words (1851), which was made up of lectures delivered to an
audience of trainee teachers, used the history of words to explore the
history of humanity. Trench endorsed Samuel Taylor Coleridge's view,
expressed in the latter's *Aids to Reflection* (1825), that there were cases when
'more knowledge of more value may be conveyed by the history of a word
than by the history of a campaign'.[31] In his second lecture, 'On the Morality
in Words', Trench told his audience that the philologist could deduce from
the existence of elevated moral and religious language that humanity was 'of
divine birth and stock', but from the words that existed to stand for dark and
wicked realities, that man had 'deeply fallen' from 'the heights of his original creation'. The existence of a word, he argued, 'bears testimony' to the
existence of a corresponding reality. Hence his sense of fear and shame at the
existence of words such as 'assassin', 'atheist', and 'avarice'.[32]

In the twentieth century, other writers adopted Trench's idea that words
could bear testimony to past realities; that they could act as witnesses. Two
members of the Oxford group of writers known as the Inklings, C. S. Lewis
and Owen Barfield, both wrote historical studies based on the same central
idea. Barfield, in his *History in English Words*, first published in 1926, compared the English language, along with the other languages of the world,

[31] Quoted in McKusick 1992: 17.
[32] Trench n.d.: 25–6. On Trench's philological works and his admiration for Coleridge's conception
of words as 'living powers', see McKusick 1992, esp. 12–17.

with 'an imperishable map' which 'has preserved for us the inner, living history of man's soul'.[33] His friend C. S. Lewis's *Studies in Words*, first published in 1960, and based on lectures given to Cambridge students in the 1950s, consisted of a series of essays on words chosen for 'the light they throw on ideas and sentiments' that prevailed in past societies and as an 'aid to more accurate reading' of the literature within which they were used.[34] The words chosen included 'nature', 'wit', 'simple', and 'conscience', and were illustrated with a wealth of examples from philosophical, literary, and religious works in classical, medieval, and modern languages. Although Lewis claimed that his studies were 'merely lexical', they in fact shed considerable light on historical matters; and Lewis took a particular interest in the social and moral status associated with certain uses of key words. His essay on the interrelated connotations of 'free', 'frank', 'villain', and 'liberal' is a particularly good illustration of this approach.[35]

Historians of modern Britain and its language have noted that the eighteenth and nineteenth centuries, with their dramatic industrial and scientific transformations, saw the English vocabulary expanded and enriched by a wide range of new terms. Eric Hobsbawm opened his study of the *Age of Revolution* with the observation that 'Words are witnesses which often speak louder than documents', and went on to mention 'factory', 'railway', 'scientist', 'proletariat', 'Utilitarian', 'sociology', and 'ideology' as examples of key English words which 'were invented, or gained their modern meanings' in the period between 1789 and 1848. Their importance for Hobsbawm was as pointers to the arrival or transformation of 'the things and concepts for which they provide names'.[36] The French linguist Georges Matoré, writing in the 1950s, made a distinction between *mots témoins* and *mots clés*—witness words and key words. The former category consisted of neologisms arising from material, technological, social, or intellectual changes or turning-points.[37] The terms on Hobsbawm's list would fit into this category. Key words, on the other hand, for Matoré, were words that captured the leading idea or sentiment of a whole society or period. He suggested *prud'homme* and *philosophe* as early modern French key words.[38]

---

[33] Barfield 1954: 14; quoted in G. Hughes 1988: 1.
[34] C. S. Lewis 1967: p. vii.
[35] Ibid. 111–32.
[36] Hobsbawm 1973: 13–14.
[37] Matoré 1953: 65–7.
[38] Ibid. 67–70; see also G. Hughes 1988: 24–5; G. Hughes 2000: 30–2. I have found Geoffrey Hughes's books on the history of the English language extremely helpful in thinking about historical approaches to words and semantics.

The most influential study of witness words and key words in the
English language has undoubtedly been Raymond Williams's 1976 book,
Keywords: A Vocabulary of Culture and Society. Williams explained that, on
returning to Cambridge after the war in 1945, it seemed to him that the
whole vocabulary of the place had changed—that people were speaking a
different language. He heard the word 'culture' much more often, for
example, to signify a cluster of values or a way of life.[39] The resulting study,
eventually completed thirty years later, was an alphabetically arranged dictionary of key words in modern English, such as 'art', 'bourgeois', 'charity',
'democracy', 'elite', 'family', and so on. Each entry offered etymological,
historical, and semantic reflections on the developing definitions, connotations, and significance of the chosen words. Williams himself struggled to
classify his book but suggested it might be considered a contribution to
cultural history, historical semantics, literary history, sociology, and the
history of ideas.[40] When I refer to 'altruism' as a 'key word' in this book, I
intend something closer to Williams's quite broad sense of that term than
to Matoré's more ambitious idea of a *mot-clé*.

Many of the suggestions surveyed in the previous paragraphs inform *The
Invention of Altruism* in quite obvious ways. 'Altruism' could be described both
as a witness to significant shifts in the sources of moral authority, and also as
a key word that captured some of the most characteristic sentiments and ideas
of the Victorian period. The pattern of its dissemination from its Comtean
origins, via the writings of a small group of intellectuals, into a wide and various range of other texts, in which it took on multiple meanings, could be
thought of as constituting a map of intellectual and social connections. I hope
to go somewhat beyond these characterizations, however. While it is useful to
think of words as witnesses to historical transformations, and of linguistic
change as a map or mirror of social change, metaphors such as these are very
passive. They rely on the idea that real historical change is material, social,
political, technological, or even emotional and intellectual, and that we can
map or track such fundamental change by looking at linguistic change, which
is then little more than a marker or by-product.[41] These passive metaphors

---

[39] R. Williams 1976: 9.

[40] Ibid. 11. A recent, multi-authored volume, directly inspired by Williams's 1976 book, is *New
Keywords: A Revised Vocabulary of Culture and Society*. It includes 'alternative', 'biology', 'celebrity',
'deconstruction', 'ethnicity', 'fundamentalism', and so on; Bennett *et al.* 2005. This new volume
seems generally to put rather less emphasis than Williams on historical semantics and more on
cultural and social theory.

[41] This is the model that I tended to favour myself in my study of the transition from theories of
'passions' to theories of 'emotions' in the 19th century. Dixon 2003: 249–51.

can be supplemented by more active ones. The image of a word as a key with which to unlock and open up the texts and values of a previous culture is certainly less passive than the idea of language as a map or mirror. However, it depicts the word as something in the hands of the historian rather than of its past users. If we want to think about linguistic change as more than merely epiphenomenal, then we could look at the history of words as a branch of the history of technology. Doing so would be to recognize the obvious fact that words are tools that allow people to do things such as creating identities for themselves, arguing with each other, and articulating new visions of the natural and social worlds.[42] Linguistic change can be seen as a kind of social, technological, ethical, and intellectual change itself, rather than as a map or mirror of such change. One could go even further and think of linguistic change as the motor of other kinds of change. Many new identities, new ideas, and new ideologies rely for their existence on the creation of new words or on the transformation of the meanings of old ones. As Skinner puts it, by tracing the genealogy of our evaluative vocabularies, we 'find ourselves looking not merely at the reflections but at one of the engines of social change'.[43]

Words or concepts?

Intellectual historians are used to the idea that we must pay close attention to the exact terms and categories employed by historical actors, and not try to make them speak in our own modern language, if we want to 'see things their way'.[44] Jacques Le Goff, commenting on the new twelfth-century use of the word *purgatorium* as the name for a particular place, suggests that paying attention to even apparently minor linguistic changes is a key task for 'historians of ideas and of *mentalités*, historians of the *longue durée*, historians of the deeply rooted and slowly changing'.

Writing about twenty-five years ago, Le Goff thought that, although new words and new meanings clearly provided 'valuable chronological evidence' of shifting mentalities, generally speaking, 'historians doubtless do

---

[42] My approach here is similar to Neil Kenny's. He has written that his approach to the history of the language of 'curiosity' is 'designed to replace any approach that would see language as a mere epiphenomenon of underlying social, cultural, or intellectual contexts, as a mere "effect" that is "caused" by them'. Kenny 2004: 24.

[43] Skinner 2002: 178.

[44] Ibid., p. vii.

not yet attach sufficient importance to words'.[45] For the most part, even intellectual and conceptual historians have continued to resist the idea that they are engaged in writing the histories of words rather than of concepts. This book is about the uses and meanings of a key Victorian word (and its derivatives), but it is also a contribution to intellectual and conceptual history. So, is it the history of a word or of a concept? And what difference does it make? My own starting point is the assumption that a word is a lexical item and a concept is an intellectual one. The former is a signifier, the latter a thought that is signified.[46] The history of a single signifier will be the history of many signified concepts and ideas.

In an essay discussing Raymond Williams's *Keywords*, Quentin Skinner considers the idea that possessing a concept is the same as knowing the meaning of a corresponding word. Although he admits that possessing a concept normally involves understanding the meaning of a corresponding term, Skinner denies that such an understanding is either a necessary or a sufficient condition for the possession of the concept. His two reasons for this denial are, first, that someone can possess a concept without understanding the correct application of a corresponding term and, secondly that an individual or a whole community of language users may have an agreed use of a term without there being a concept that corresponds to that agreed use.[47] Let us look at these two arguments in turn. The example Skinner gives of someone having a concept but lacking the corresponding word is Milton, who he claims possessed the concept of originality even though the word 'originality' did not enter the language until long after his death. Skinner illustrates the importance of originality to Milton by quoting a comment by that author about the need to deal with 'things unattempted yet in prose or rhyme'. This certainly sounds like an appreciation of what we would call 'originality'. But is that thematic resemblance an adequate basis for the anachronistic claim that Milton possessed the concept of originality, which surely depends in large part on the definition, significance, and connotations of the modern term 'originality'? While I would not argue that historians should never think or write in any way that employs words and concepts anachronistically, it is certainly strange for a historian such as Skinner, whose approach to his actors is normally to try to 'see

[45] Le Goff 1984: 3, 227.
[46] For a discussion of the application of Saussurian linguistics to conceptual history, see Freeden 1996: esp. 48–54.
[47] Skinner 2002: 158–60.

things their way', to advocate doing so.[48] I prefer to stick to the belief that possession of a concept does involve understanding the meaning of a corresponding word. However, that does not mean that there must be a unitary conceptual meaning for that word, shared by all its users.

Skinner's second argument is that an individual, or whole community, might be capable of regularly using a key word, such as 'being' or 'infinity', but not possess a clear concept 'that answers to any of their agreed usages'.[49] It is certainly possible for an individual to use a key word while neither understanding the concept that most users of the language consider it to signify nor having a coherent alternative concept of their own. But can a whole community of language users have 'agreed usages' of a term in the absence of a concept that answers to those usages? Presumably articulate and reflective users of the word, in such cases, would be able to give it a definition of some kind. It might be, however, that others might think, as twentieth-century logical positivists did about certain religious and ethical terms, that the definitions offered were incoherent and the words, in effect, meaningless. That is certainly possible. However, there is a much more obvious reason why competent use of a word is not the same thing as possession of a single corresponding concept—a reason that does not need to invoke incompetence or incoherence on the part of language-users— namely that the meaning of any interesting word will be contested, and different users of the term will, with good reasons, think it means different things. I have already indicated the three different clusters of concepts that 'altruism' has been used to signify, and I will develop the general point a little further below. While I disagree with Skinner's suggestion that one can possess a concept without having at least some idea of the meaning of a corresponding word, I do not doubt that most key words will be associated with more than one concept, by virtue of being believed to have different meanings by different users of the term. Indeed, it is a feature of any key word in intellectual, cultural, and political history that its proper meaning and the right to define it are hotly contested by interested parties.

A kind of intellectual history that has paid close attention to the histories of particular key words, mainly in the German and French languages, is the discipline of *Begriffsgeschichte*. Although *Begriffsgeschichte* is usually translated as 'conceptual history' or 'the history of concepts', it is an approach to history strongly grounded in linguistics, etymology, and historical semantics. In the

---

[48] For an interesting discussion of the virtues and limits of avoiding anachronism in historical writing, which takes Skinner's own anti-anachronistic approach as a starting point, see Jardine 2000.
[49] Skinner 2002: 160.

writings of one of its leading exponents, Reinhart Koselleck, the objects of
analysis are often key words or phrases whose meanings have changed over
time. As Koselleck himself puts it, in his *Futures Past*, the methods of
Begriffsgeschichte include the 'philosophical history of terminology' and 'historical philology', and one of its leading methodological principles is that
social and political conflicts of the past should 'be interpreted and opened
up via the medium of the contemporary conceptual limits and in terms of
the mutually understood past linguistic usage of the participating agents'.[50]
Koselleck argues that changing linguistic uses should be understood in relation to material and institutional change on the one hand and intellectual
or conceptual change on the other, but he avoids treating linguistic change
as a mere epiphenomenon.[51] On the particular question of the relationship
between words and concepts, Koselleck states that, within the sort of socio-
political terminology with which he is concerned, 'Each concept is associated with a word, but not every word is a social and political concept.' For
him, a word becomes a concept when 'the plenitude of a politicosocial
context of meaning and experience in and for which a word is used can be
condensed into one word'.[52]

In the writings of Koselleck, and of his most influential English-
language interpreter, Melvin Richter, the word 'concept' is sometimes used
in contexts where 'word' or 'term' would serve better. For instance,
Koselleck has written that users of the English phrase 'civil society' 'cannot
dispense with the traditional meanings of this concept'; elsewhere he refers
to the many shifts in meaning 'of the concept "revolution"', which signified, at different times, cyclical recurrence, political action, or structural
change. Similarly, he writes about one whole class of 'concepts whose content has changed so radically that, despite the existence of the same word
as a shell, the meanings are barely comparable'.[53] In cases such as these, it
might be better to translate *Begriff* as 'term' rather than 'concept', since multiplicity of meanings is something more normally associated with words
than with concepts.[54] Indeed, a concept, unlike a word, must surely have a
definite and specified meaning even to qualify as a concept. There is a sim-

---

[50] Koselleck 1985: 74, 79.
[51] Ibid. 86.
[52] Ibid. 83, 84.
[53] Ibid. 69, 82; Koselleck 2002: 209. My understanding of Koselleck's approach relies primarily on
his chapter on '*Begriffsgeschichte* and Social History' in *Futures Past*, and on Melvin Richter's very
helpful book on *Begriffsgeschichte* and its relationship with other approaches to intellectual and
conceptual history, *The History of Political and Social Concepts*. Koselleck 1985: 73–91; Richter 1995.
[54] I am grateful to Thomas Rohkrämer for alerting me to this question of the translation of *Begriff*.

ilar problem in Melvin Richter's statement that the major works of *Begriffsgeschichte* have provided valuable information about 'the past and present meanings of concepts' and have shown how 'changes in the meaning of concepts proceeded at an extremely rapid pace' in modern Europe.[55] The way in which I would resolve some of these ambiguities is to say that it is 'words' or 'terms' that have multiple and changing meanings (often by virtue of the fact that they invoke different concepts for different users at different times). A 'concept', then, is more like a definition or denotation, and is an intellectual thing clearly distinguished from the lexical thing— the word—with which it is associated.

To put the argument another way, it seems to me that what is particularly valuable about *Begriffsgeschichte* is that it traces the changing meanings of words and shows that they have sometimes been used to pick out quite different concepts over time. The three different concepts that Koselleck identifies as having been associated with the word 'revolution' are nice examples of this. It is therefore unhelpful to use 'concept' to refer to the word which, as Koselleck himself puts it, is sometimes little more than a 'shell' for a range of conceptual meanings. The word is the signifier, the concept is the signified intellectual content. On this point, I am in sympathy with the way that Skinner puts things in a recent 'Retrospect', where he writes that the various shifts we try to chart in intellectual histories are best described not as changes in concepts, but as 'transformations in the applications of the terms by which our concepts are expressed'.[56] To acknowledge the active role of language in the construction and communication of concepts, however, I would want to add 'created' to Skinner's 'expressed' in the foregoing quotation.

An intellectual history that traces the changing uses of a key word will differ in several ways from one that is designed to communicate the history of a concept. We can illustrate some of these differences by imagining how a history of the concept of altruism might differ from the history of the language of altruism that I have actually written. A history of the concept (as opposed to the language) of altruism would have to start by stipulating what 'altruism' meant. This would be necessary in order to know when one had found a discussion of the concept in writings from past eras. Even if, as I did above, the author of this imagined conceptual history acknowledged that 'altruism' could signify at least three different concepts, there would still need to be an initial stipulation as to the content of each concept, expressed

---

[55] Richter 1995: 5, 13, 17.
[56] Skinner 2002: 179.

in general terms that did not include the term 'altruism' itself.[57] Such a history might, then, take as its source material texts written in any language and in any period so long as they were judged to deal with the basic concepts and themes that 'altruism' had been stipulated to connote. A key aspect of selecting material for this conceptual history would be identifying other terms such as, for instance, self-sacrifice, charity, benevolence, sympathy, or philanthropy which were supposed to be synonyms or near-synonyms of 'altruism', discussions of which would then qualify for inclusion. Such a history would be more obviously shaped by the concerns and categories of the historian, and would have a much wider scope than the present study.

The approach that I have in fact taken, which could be labelled 'historical semantics' or simply 'word history', is more historically grounded and less presentist. Instead of starting with contemporary concepts of 'altruism' and working backwards towards their origins, this study starts with the coining of the term and traces its development forwards and outwards from there, along various branches, only some of which could be extended all the way up to the present. Paying attention to the words that nineteenth-century people themselves used to create and communicate their concepts, rather than translating them into a preconceived conceptual scheme, should make it easier to try to see things their way. Although the present study surveys and analyses a range of ethical concepts and moral ideas, its overall historical coherence is primarily linguistic rather than conceptual. By tracing the shifting uses and meanings of the language of altruism, I have been led to read a wide range of sources that would not have suggested themselves on thematic or conceptual grounds alone, but which provide rich illustrations of what 'altruism' meant to those who used it.[58] Tracing the various uses of a single word or family of words allows an account to emerge which encompasses material from several different genres, theories, and disciplines without losing overall coherence and thus, hopefully, broadening the canon and the contexts of intellectual history. By paying attention to the connotations acquired by 'altruism' as a result of its associations with other words, practices, beliefs, and institutions, the present study also draws attention to the lack of synonymy between 'altruism' and conceptu-

---

[57] Collini 2006 is an interesting example of how to deal with this problem, since it takes both a lexical and a conceptual approach. The first chapter traces the history of various uses of term 'intellectual' as a noun; the second stipulates one particular concept of the intellectual which will inform the rest of the book.

[58] The increasing availability of searchable electronic versions of texts makes this approach much more feasible. I have included a list of some of the most useful online and electronic resources that I have used in the Bibliography.

ally related terms with different connotations, such as benevolence, charity, and so on. Instead of collecting together a range of broadly semantically related terms into a single conceptual history, I try to explain how one key word—'altruism'—derived its meanings by differentiation from as well as association with other important words and concepts within the world of Victorian moralism.[59] Finally, focusing on discussions about the propriety and meaning of key words draws attention to the phenomenon of what could be called 'linguistic resistance'. Looking at the reasons why some people objected to the use of the new language of altruism reveals how resistance to linguistic change can be a key part of resistance to intellectual and social change.

Several other intellectual historians have approached their subjects through the history of a key word or set of words. There have been book-length studies of 'enthusiasm', 'purgatory', 'inhibition', 'emotions', 'curiosity', 'serendipity', and 'democracy', all of which have been at least partly conceived as histories of words rather than as histories of unitary concepts or ideas.[60] Of these, Neil Kenny's *The Uses of Curiosity in Early Modern France and Germany* (2004) is particularly notable. Unlike the present work, which is almost entirely confined to the English language, Kenny's study analyses and compares early-modern uses of 'curiosity', *curiositas, curiosité*, and *Curiosität*, with a particular emphasis on the French and German terms. What the resulting historical account particularly successfully illustrates is the way that approaching the past through the uses of words can reveal connections between many different aspects of a culture—connections which would probably not be so apparent to someone setting out to write

[59] In this respect, I agree with David Wootton, who in a review of John Dunn's book on the history of 'democracy' emphasizes that words exist 'within a network or framework of other words', especially those considered to be antonyms or synonyms. I do not agree with Wootton's argument, however, that the need to pay attention to the place of a key word in a network of other related terms means that one can never successfully or coherently tell the story of a single word, or that 'words don't have a story'. See Dunn 2005; Wootton 2005: 7.

[60] Tucker 1972; Le Goff 1984; R. Smith 1992; Kenny 2004; Merton and Barber 2004; Dunn 2005. My own previous work on the meanings of 'passions' and 'emotions' also falls into this category; see Dixon 2003, 2006. Cheung 2006 investigates the occurrences and meanings of the word 'organism' in the history of science from the 17th to the 19th centuries. On the history of 'scientist', which was coined in the 1830s, but was still being resisted in the 1890s, see Ross 1962, and Ch. 7 below. Gertrude Himmelfarb has discussed the uses of the term 'unemployment' in the 1880s; Himmelfarb 1991: 40–53. Stefan Collini's recent book on the question of intellectuals in 20th-century Britain pays close attention to the history of the word 'intellectual' and its plural; Collini writes that 'the spell cast by the actual word "intellectuals" is extraordinary, an indication that the term must be serving as a kind of place-holder for a whole collection of cultural attitudes'. Collini 2006: esp. 1–65, quotation at 4.

the history of a determinate concept. In writing the history of the uses of 'curiosity', Kenny discovers new connections between the worlds of science, religion, philosophy, and morals in early modern Europe. My hope is that the present study of 'altruism' will do something similar for Victorian Britain.

Chapter Two

Encounters with Positivism

Thus the expression, *Live for Others*, is the simplest summary of the whole moral code of Positivism. And Biology should indicate the germ of this principle, presenting it in a form uncomplicated by disturbing influences.

Auguste Comte, *System of Positive Polity* (1851–4)[1]

10 Rue Monsieur-le-Prince, Paris

To employ the language of altruism was, for much of the Victorian period, to associate oneself directly with Auguste Comte and his philosophy of 'positivism'. Even in 1897, almost half a century after its first introduction, the dean of Rochester, addressing the working men's section of the Church Congress, spoke not just about 'altruism' but about 'Comte's "Altruism"'.[2] 'Sociology', 'positivism', and 'altruism' were all Comtean terms which could be used as philosophical watchwords or as political banners, and whose fortunes were tied to a greater or lesser extent to the reputation of Auguste Comte. But who exactly was the inventor of 'altruism' and how did he come to have an impact on the English language?

Comte's major work, on the basis of which his reputation as a historian and philosopher of the sciences was established, was the six-volume *Cours de Philosophie Positive* (1830–42). In the *Cours* Comte introduced the idea of a 'Hierarchy of the Sciences', rising from mathematics, through astronomy, physics, and chemistry, to biology and finally 'social physics' or, to give it the new name he proposed, 'sociology'. Two other distinctive teachings of the *Cours* were its epistemology and its theory of evolutionary progress. To be a positivist was to be an empiricist: knowledge was of

---

[1] Quotations from Comte's *Système de Politique Positive*, published in French 1851–4, are taken from the English translation published 1875–7; Comte 1875–7: i. 566.

[2] This address is discussed further in Ch. 8, below.

observable phenomena and science produced only empirical laws connecting those phenomena. Comte's 'Law of the Three States' declared that the development of the human mind, and of the various sciences, always passed through three states: the theological, the metaphysical, and the 'positive' or scientific. The commitment to attaining the positive state in all areas of study—the state in which all supernatural and metaphysical agencies and abstractions would be abandoned in favour of purely empirical laws—was to be the central commitment of the 'positivist' philosopher. Comte's empiricist, progressivist, scientific vision of nature and society was attractive to a certain kind of radical intellectual in Britain in the 1840s. John Stuart Mill's *System of Logic* (1843) was substantially indebted to Comte and contained enthusiastic praise for him. The sensational scientific epic, *The Vestiges of the Natural History of Creation* (1844), also made use of Comte (although misspelling his name).[3] G. H. Lewes's *Biographical History of Philosophy* (1846) told the story of the history of philosophy as one of ascent towards its single crowning achievement—Comte's *Cours de Philosophie Positive*. Lewes's book rapidly sold 10,000 copies, and established both Lewes and Comte as recognized authorities on philosophy and science.[4]

From the later 1840s onwards, however, Auguste Comte's writings took a new turn—one which would introduce *altruisme* to the world, and which would alienate many of his British followers. Having established himself as the father of sociology and the founder of the philosophical school of positivism, Comte now started to reshape his philosophical thought under the influence of an intense romantic and spiritual devotion to Madame Clotilde de Vaux, a friend whose husband was a criminal sentenced for life to the galleys. Inspired by his ardent, chaste, and ultimately mystical attachment to Madame de Vaux, Comte set himself the task of developing a whole new social and religious system for the West, which would facilitate the ascendancy of the heart over the intellect, and of altruism over egoism. Comte's four-volume *Système de Politique Positive* (1851–4) was dedicated to the memory of his 'Saint Clotilde', who had died in 1846.[5] He conceived of this whole work, which was subtitled 'A Treatise of Sociology, instituting

---

[3] On the early British reception of Comte see Wright 1986: 40–72; Cashdollar 1989: 21–56. Comte was spelled 'Compte' in the *Vestiges*, but this was corrected in the *Explanations* which was published as a sequel the following year. Comte was invoked by the anonymous author, Robert Chambers, as an authority on the 'nebular hypothesis' of the origins of the solar system. See Chambers 1994: pp. xxxvi–xxxvii, V16–17, E8, E180. On the authorship and reception of the *Vestiges*, see Secord 2000. On Mill and Comte see n. 112 below.

[4] *ODNB*.

[5] See 'Dedication' to Comte 1875–7: i, pp. xxxi–xlv.

the Religion of Humanity', as an attempt to solve the 'great problem of human life', namely how to subordinate egoism to altruism.[6]

Comte's briefer *Catéchisme Positiviste* (1852) announced that the new positivist religion would soon eliminate the Catholicism on which it was modelled, and all other forms of theology. The *Catéchisme* was cast in the form an imagined dialogue between a male positivist priest and a female initiate. The routine of religious devotions prescribed by the priest included daily readings of Thomas à Kempis's *Imitation of Christ*, during which the positivist worshipper was mentally to replace 'God' with 'Humanity'.[7] Another central idea of the new religion was that the desired altruistic social synthesis would be achieved by 'man thinking under the inspiration of woman'.[8] All of this was to be achieved through humanistic prayers, social sacraments, and public festivals of humanity. Comte drew up a new calendar of thirteen months named after religious leaders of the past, as well as men of science, literature, and philosophy; months included Moses, St Paul, Aristotle, Descartes, Shakespeare, and Gutenberg.[9] The apparatus of the positivist religion was thus a cross between medieval Roman Catholicism and Robespierre's Cult of Reason.

As he sat in his small apartment at 10 Rue Monsieur-le-Prince in Paris, churning out volume after volume of these doctrinaire scientific, philosophical, and religious writings, reclassifying the functions of the human brain, inventing his new humanistic religion, appointing himself its high priest, and complaining about its lack of adherents, Comte was an increasingly isolated figure. It soon became common for writers in the British periodical press to ridicule Comte as an egotistical, eccentric, tedious, humourless, and artless writer. Since it was in the writings of this monomaniacal, slightly ridiculous, atheistical Frenchman that British readers in the 1850s and 1860s first came across the terms *altruisme* and *altruiste*, one might wonder how those terms ever succeeded in becoming naturalized English words. Comte's reputation as the author of the *Cours*, and as a scientific and philosophical thinker admired by British authorities including Mill and Lewes, guaranteed some initial interest in his later speculations.

---

[6] Comte 1875–7: i. 558–9.

[7] Quotations from the *Catéchisme Positiviste*, published in French in 1852, are taken from the revised 3rd edn of Richard Congreve's English translation, first published in 1858; Comte 1891: 218.

[8] Comte 1891: 18.

[9] The positivist calendar is included in Comte 1875–7: iv, facing 348; Comte 1891: table D, facing 300. It is also reproduced in C. M. Davies 1874: ii. 260–3; Wright 1986: 34; Brooke and Cantor 1998: 53–4.

But that alone was not enough. Comte's later works needed to be read, reviewed, interpreted, translated, admired, and talked about if his language was really to have an impact.

This chapter explains how that impact was achieved by tracing the uses and meanings of the language of altruism, from its Parisian origins, via the agency of writers who formed a coterie centred around the London publisher John Chapman and his *Westminster Review*, through to its role in the lives of three specific individuals who were amongst the first to encounter this language. All three of these individuals were sons of clergymen who, in the era of the Victorian crisis of faith, were questioning Christian ideas about divine moral authority and its supernatural basis. They sought more scientific and philosophical sources of ethical enlightenment.[10] One was an Oxford-educated physician and translator of Comte, the positivist John Henry Bridges. The second was a young Cambridge philosopher, Henry Sidgwick. Finally, James Hinton was a leading ear surgeon and eclectic philosophical writer who was a founding member of the famous Metaphysical Society and an inspiration to a later generation of freethinking social reformers and sexologists. Tracing the role of the language of altruism in the reading, thinking, writing, and conversation of these three figures will illustrate some of the impacts that Comte's later writings had on Victorian language and society. The language of altruism was physically spread from one place to another, carried and transmitted through direct human contact as well as through the mediation of the printed word. Each section of this chapter is consequently focused around a particular geographical place, starting with Comte's Paris apartment.[11]

Alexander Bain visited 10 Rue Monsieur-le-Prince at the time that Comte was composing the works that introduced *altruisme* to the world.[12] Bain had been one of Comte's earliest and most enthusiastic British readers. With a group of like-minded friends in Aberdeen, he had worked his

[10] Comte's scientific philosophy, as this and subsequent chapters suggest, was an important resource for many struggling with their Christian faith and looking for alternatives from the 1840s onwards. On other scientific ideas that contributed to intellectual and political debates about Christian belief between the 1820s and 1850s, most notably transmutationist biology and materialistic physiology, see Desmond 1989; Hilton 2000; Secord 2000: esp. ch. 9; Clifford 2003: esp. ch. 1. See also the discussion of Darwinism and Positivism in Ch. 4 below.

[11] Geographical methods have been applied very successfully to the history of science. In adopting a geographical approach in this chapter, I have been influenced by the approaches taken by Livingstone 1992, 1994, 2003; Numbers and Stenhouse 1999; and especially Secord 2000: part 2.

[12] At this time Bain was a lecturer at Bedford Ladies College in London. During the 1850s he produced several important psychological works, and in 1860 was appointed Professor of Logic at Aberdeen. On Bain, see Rylance 2000: 147–202; Dixon 2003: 150–9.

way through the *Cours de Philosophie Positive*, which had been recommended by his mentor John Stuart Mill as 'very nearly the grandest work of this age'.[13] Reading it confirmed Bain in his decision to abandon his Christian faith.[14] His meeting with Comte in Paris took place in the summer of 1851, around the time that the first volume of the *Politique Positive* was published, and a year before the publication of the *Catéchisme Positiviste*. Bain remembered Comte's home as 'modest enough, being only a half-floor of some three or four rooms altogether, and looked after by a single female servant'. Comte himself 'received us in a bright-coloured dressing-gown,—which only meant that, in regard to dress, he was a Frenchman'. In the midst of developing the political and religious part of his system, Comte held forth to his visitor on 'the advancement of his own scheme of political reconstruction, of which he had, as we know from his writings, a most extravagant anticipation'. The Frenchman's whole attitude, Bain found, was one of 'severe denunciation or self-aggrandisement' devoid of any sense of humour. 'Of such men as Aristotle, Milton, Bishop Butler, and Wordsworth, it may be safely said that they wanted the sense of humour', Bain wrote, 'but, in sheer negation, probably, they never approached to Auguste Comte.'[15]

When another British well-wisher called at 10 Rue Monsieur-le-Prince in 1853, he was surprised to find Comte living in such a well-to-do part of the city. The apartment was not large, but it was well kept, and was located in the sixième arrondissement, in the Latin quarter, near the Luxembourg Gardens and the Sorbonne. Sir Erskine Perry, recently returned from ten years as president of the colonial board of education in India, was visiting Comte to offer him financial assistance. Having heard that the founder of positivism was in financial difficulty, he had not expected to find him living in this relative style and comfort. Comte explained that he stayed in the apartment because it had been the setting for his meetings with his beloved Clotilde. Perry noticed that there were very few books in the room which doubled as Comte's library, where he wrote, and the salon where he received his guests. One of a handful of books on the mantelpiece in the salon was Corneille's translation of *The Imitation of Christ*. His host explained that he pursued a regime of 'cerebral hygiene' which involved reading virtually nothing apart from a small amount of poetry and a couple of other favourite

[13] Bain 1904: 112.
[14] Ibid. 153–9.
[15] Ibid. 223–5.

works, such as the *Imitation*. By 1853, when Perry visited, most of the *Politique* had been completed. Comte outlined some of the leading religious and political doctrines of the work to Perry, explaining his view that Christianity was an 'egotistical' religion and that some modern substitute for Catholicism was needed in order to promote 'altruism'. Paris by this time was under the rule of Louis Napoléon, who had come to power in a coup at the end of 1851. This was an encouraging sign to Comte, since he envisaged that the positivist religion and polity would be brought about within a republican dictatorship rather than either a monarchy or a democracy.[16]

In England, despite Mill, Bain, and Perry all being unimpressed by Comte's proposed religion, it started to receive more attention thanks to Richard Congreve. A product of Thomas Arnold's regime at Rugby school, and subsequently a schoolmaster there, Congreve had taken Anglican orders and become a tutor at Wadham College, Oxford. But in June 1854 he decided to resign his college fellowship in order to devote himself to a deeper and freer study of positivism. Three years later Congreve formally renounced his Anglican orders, and Comte appointed him the official head of his British disciples. In 1858 Congreve's English translation of the *Catéchisme Positiviste* was published by John Chapman.[17] Through the activities of Congreve, and a group of his former Oxford pupils including Frederic Harrison, Edward Spencer Beesly, and John Henry Bridges, positivism as an organized religious movement with its own chapels and temples of humanity managed to attract a few hundred adherents over the following decades. There were centres in London, Manchester, Newcastle-upon-Tyne, and Liverpool.[18] For some English positivists, the room in which Comte had composed the *Système de Politique Positive* took on special religious significance. In the 1890s, the artist Thomas Sulman and his wife sent new year cards to their fellow positivists, offering 'Fraternal Greetings from Finchley', which bore an image of the library in Comte's

---

[16] Erskine Perry, 'A Morning with Auguste Comte', *The Nineteenth Century*, 2 (1877), 621–31. R. H. Hutton, the editor of *The Spectator*, wrote a commentary on Perry's 1877 recollection: R. H. Hutton, 'Auguste Comte's Aspiration' (1877) repr. in Hutton 1894: i. 303–9. Some of Comte's views on the political situation in France in the 1840s and 1850s are contained in his preface to the *Catéchisme Positiviste* and in his preface to vol. iii of the *Politique Positive*; see Comte 1875–7: iii, pp. ix–xliv; Comte 1891: 1–26, esp. 8–9.

[17] On Congreve's career, see *ODNB*, the obituary in *The Times* (8 July 1899), 9, and a leader in the same newspaper two days later; *The Times* (10 July 1899), 11.

[18] On the spread of organized positivism in England, see McGee 1931; Wright 1986. On Liverpool in particular, where Charles Booth, amongst others, came into contact with positivist circles, see Wright 1986: 255–60.

apartment, with the caption 'Room in which *La Politique Positive* was written' (see Fig. 7). During a visit to Paris in 1865, George Eliot and G. H. Lewes had thought Comte's former home the most interesting thing they saw. Eliot wrote to Maria Congreve: 'We thought the apartment very *freundlich*, and I flattered myself that I could have written better in the little study there than in my own.'[19]

It was towards the end of the first volume of the *Politique Positive*, in the section laying the biological groundwork of his social system, that Comte introduced the term *altruisme*. In earlier sections of the work, dealing with social and political subjects, he had used a different terminology, writing

THE LIBRARY,
10, RUE MONSIEUR-LE-PRINCE,
PARIS.
Room in which La Politique Positive was written.

I. MOSES, $\frac{44}{110}$—*With Fraternal Greetings from Finchley.*

Figure 7. Card sent by Thomas and M. A. Sulman to their fellow positivists to celebrate the new year in 1890. London Positivist Society Papers, LSE, LPS 5/3/A, f. 10.

[19] To Mrs Richard Congreve, 27 Jan. 1865; Haight 1954–78: iv. 176–7.

that 'the object of Morals is to make our sympathetic instincts preponder-
ate as far as possible over the selfish instincts; social feelings over personal
feelings'.[20] When Comte came to write the section on biology, perhaps
seeking a more technical, scientific vocabulary, he rephrased this contrast in
terms of *egoisme* and *altruisme*. *Egoisme* was not, of course, a word of Comte's
own coining. And, in fact, *altruisme* might not have been either. Although it
became standard, following Lewes and Mill, to describe *altruisme* as a
Comtean coinage, several French sources suggested that it was in fact the
creation of François Andrieux, who had taught Comte grammar and literature at the École Polytechnique in Paris in 1817. One of Comte's French
disciples claimed that Comte himself had said that the word was coined by
Andrieux.[21] Certainly Comte never made any direct claim to the parentage of *altruisme*. Nonetheless, he made the term his own, and it was only an
inner circle of French positivists who knew, or thought they knew, its true
origins.

Comte had never been averse to linguistic innovation. He complained
in the preface to the fourth volume of the *Politique Positive* of the difficulty
innovative thinkers such as himself must encounter in trying to work out
their 'new conceptions in the old language'.[22] The obvious solution to this
problem was to create a new language. A more particular etymological reason for Comte's approval of *altruisme* was that it was based on an Italian
word (*altrui*, meaning 'of others' or 'to others'). Comte believed that Italian
was the greatest of the European languages. He hoped it would eventually
be adopted universally, since it was 'the language spoken by the noblest pre-
cursors of the definitive social order' and had been shaped 'by the most
peaceful and most artistic of European nations'. 'When the language of
Dante and Ariosto shall have become the universal language', Comte predicted, it would be used by all worshippers of the 'Great Being', humanity,
in the 'daily expressions of their emotion, both in private and in public'.[23]
It was this association of positivism in general, and of 'altruism' in particular, with the Italian language which led the author of an article in *Fraser's*

---

[20] Comte 1875–7: i. 73.
[21] Deroisin wrote that another positivist, Blignières, had asserted that the word was coined by
Andrieux; Deroisin claimed that the possible sources for Blignières's claim were either Deroisin
himself or Comte, from whom he had heard it directly. See Deroisin 1909: 139; Gouhier 1933: i.
167–8; M. Leroy 1946–54: iii. 102–3. On Comte's early years, and his contact with Andrieux, see
Pickering 1993: esp. 45–6.
[22] Comte 1875–7: iv, p. xii. Thomas Hardy copied out this passage in his extensive notes on the
Politique Positive; Björk 1985: i. 133; Wright 1986: 203.
[23] Comte 1875–7: iv. 67, 85.

Magazine in 1879 to mock 'the Italian sweet sound of Altruism' which had lately been heard in certain religious and literary quarters.[24]

The ultimate Latin root of the Italian *altrui* was *alter*, meaning 'other'. To combine this Latin root with a Greek suffix, *-ism* (signifying a doctrine or theory), was to break one of the cardinal rules of respectable neologising—namely that all the elements of the new word should have their roots in a single language. This was not the first time that Comte had been guilty of introducing a 'barbarous' neologism into the English language. A few years earlier another Comtean term, 'sociology', which similarly combined a Latin stem with a Greek suffix, had made its way into English through the influence of the *Cours de Philosophie Positive*. In 1851 a contributor to *Fraser's Magazine* wrote unhappily about 'The new science of sociology, as it is barbarously termed'.[25] Even a generally sympathetic article in the *Westminster Review* in 1854 regretted the 'barbarous and hybrid designation of *Sociology*'.[26] In a similar vein, a contributor to *Notes and Queries* in 1880 quoted from the French Catholic writer Père Hyacinthe who had written about the adoration of humanity which 'is called to-day, in rather barbarous French, *l'altruisme*'.[27] Even in the 1960s, one commentator on the history of sociology suggested that Comte's works might have had a more lasting impact had they not been written in such 'barbarous French'.[28] Some of Comte's other suggested terminological innovations in the *Politique Positive*, terms such as 'biocracy', 'sociocracy', 'sociolatry', and 'anthropolatry', were equally barbarous but did not have the success enjoyed by 'sociology' and 'altruism'.

If the linguistic construction of 'altruism' was inelegantly hybrid, the social and political system with which it was identified was, to liberal readers, absolutely terrifying. 'Altruism' and living for others were the ideals of an authoritarian, scientific utopia planned by Comte in meticulous detail in which an atheistic priesthood would have total control over science, education, and morality; in which an unelected group of bankers and

---

[24] Anon., 'The Failure of Altruism', *Fraser's Magazine,* 20 (1879), 494–503, at 495. For a further discussion of this article, see Ch. 3, below.

[25] See *OED*; G. Hughes 2000: 51–3.

[26] Anon., 'Comte's Positive Philosophy', *Westminster Review,* 62 (1854), 173–94, at 177. Interestingly, Houghton 1966–89 suggests Richard Congreve as the possible author of this article, which is a review of Harriet Martineau's 1853 condensation of the *Cours de Philosophie Positive*. The article was published shortly before Congreve resigned his Oxford fellowship and announced his conversion to positivism.

[27] This was in response to the query about the origins and meaning of 'altruism' discussed in Ch. 1, above; *Notes and Queries* (3 Apr. 1880), 286; quoting from *Nineteenth Century,* 7 (1880), 265.

[28] Simpson 1969: p. vii.

industrialists would govern all secular affairs (and choose their own successors); in which the middle classes would disappear and the vast majority of
people would be *prolétaires* with no prospect of social mobility; in which
artists as a class would be replaced by the philosophical priesthood, who
would use art as a medium to express facts; in which women would have
supreme authority in the domestic sphere—and even be worshipped—but
would be allowed no active role whatever outside of it; and in which there
were to be no rights for anyone other than the right to do their duty.
Although Comte welcomed the overthrow of the French monarchy by the
democratic revolutions of 1848, he looked towards a future where progress
would be guaranteed through an orderly dictatorship rather than the
'chaos' of democracy; it was for this reason that he had welcomed the acces-
sion of Louis Napoléon at the end of 1851. The mottoes on the title-page
of the first volume of the *Politique Positive* in 1851, capturing the essence of
Comte's political programme, were 'Order and Progress' and 'Live for
Others'.[29]

It was not as a political ideal, however, but as a term of scientific ethics
that 'altruism' would initially be taken up by British readers. Comte's claim,
in the *Politique Positive*, was to have produced the first truly scientific theory of human nature. Whereas the Catholic Church had, according to him,
always taught that human nature was entirely selfish, and that benevolent
affections towards others only existed as a gift of divine grace, modern
biology demonstrated that altruistic propensities were actually innate to
humanity.[30] Comte supported this claim through analyses of animal behaviour and brain science.[31] His claims about animal altruism and egoism were
based on works by much earlier French natural historians including Buffon

---

[29] For an overview of the social and religious tenets of positivism see Comte 1865, which is also
included in vol. i of Comte 1875–7. John Stuart Mill's 1865 book *Auguste Comte and Positivism* is
another very helpful overview; Mill 1963–91: x. 261–368; see also [Leslie Stephen], 'The Comtist
Utopia', *Fraser's Magazine,* 80 (1869), 1–21. Other informative summaries of Comte's social and
religious system and its impact in France, Britain, and beyond are to be found in Wright 1986:
8–39; Cashdollar 1989: 7–12; Brooke and Cantor 1998: 47–57; Pickering 2000. Pickering 1993 is
a detailed intellectual biography of Comte during the first part of his career. Wernick 2001 offers
a polemical account of the failures of Comte's attempt to construct a post-theistic social theory.
[30] Although this was a reasonable summary of one part of Augustinian orthodoxy (as opposed to
the heretical Pelagian view that human nature contained the seeds of its own deification and salvation), it did not do justice to related Christian ideas about divine love and the original goodness of humanity. Jacques Maritain suggests that Comte's view of Catholic doctrine was skewed
by the prevalence of Jansenist rhetoric in the Catholic teachings of his youth; Maritain 1964:
333–4; see also E. Caird 1885: 228–9. On Augustine's and Aquinas's teachings on human nature,
and especially the roles of passions and affections, see Dixon 2003: 26–61.
[31] Comte 1875–7: i. 456–594.

and Georges Leroy.[32] Certain species were marked by particularly pronounced egoism: 'Apart from the periods of sexual desire or maternal activity, the tiger, and even the tigress, and still more the crocodile or boa, are
wholly occupied with themselves.' Other species, including the dog and the
stag, had more developed social and domestic feelings; 'the happiness of living for others is not entirely monopolised by Man'. But it was only in the
human race that the glimmers of animal sympathy were developed into a
larger altruism extending to the whole of humanity.

This transition from the animal mode of life to the human was marked
by the 'development of the internal functions of the brain'.[33] Comte's starting point in discussing the human brain was the work of Franz Joseph Gall
on the structure and function of the different mental 'organs' that made it
up. Gall's system was well known in Britain as the principal source of the
popular science of 'phrenology'.[34] Comte's own cerebral theory similarly
involved enumerating and locating mental organs on the basis of a combination of the basic anatomy of the nervous system, familiarity with human
thought and behaviour, and more or less speculative associated deductions.
The main principle of localization that Comte adopted was that propensities were 'higher in quality and inferior in force as we proceed from behind
forwards'. The necessity of placing the organs of benevolence close to the
intellectual organs further confirmed that the altruistic instincts were
located towards the front, and the egoistic towards the rear of the brain:

> Egoism has no need of intelligence to perceive the object of desire; it has but
> to discover the modes of satisfying it. Altruism on the contrary cannot so
> much as become acquainted, without intellectual effort, with the external
> object towards which it is ever tending. The connection of Intellect with
> Love is more prominent in the Social State, because the collective object of
> sympathy is more difficult of apprehension.[35]

Comte ranked his own discovery of the innateness of the altruistic instincts
alongside the Copernican discovery of the motion of the earth as one of
the two most important findings of modern science.[36] In the *Catéchisme
Positiviste* he went even further: the 'innate existence of the altruistic

[32] The latter's major work was C. G. Leroy 1802, which would later also be cited by Darwin, in
The Descent of Man, as a source of observations of the behaviour of foxes and swallows; C. Darwin
2004: 102, 131.
[33] Comte 1875–7: i. 486–517, quotations at 495, 501.
[34] On phrenology see Cooter 1984; van Wyhe 2004. On Comte's cerebral theory and its influence
on George Eliot, see Wright 1982.
[35] Comte 1875–7: i. 560.
[36] Ibid. iv. 18.

instincts' was 'the chief discovery of modern science'.[37] Thus, the positivist priest explained, science could now improve on the provisional account of human nature offered by St Paul: 'The imaginary conflict between nature and grace' could now be 'replaced by the real opposition between the posterior mass of the brain, the seat of the personal instincts, and its anterior region, where there are distinct organs for the sympathetic impulses and the intellectual faculties.'[38] The 'affective propensities' were ranged in a progressive series which ran from 'pure egoism' to 'pure altruism'. The series started with the nutritive and sexual instincts. Maternal instincts were also included in the 'egoistic' category. In the *Catéchisme*, the priest explained this categorization, which his female interlocutor had found surprising: 'The observation of animals leaves us no doubt . . . for it shows us the maternal relation in animals at too low a point in the scale to have the higher sentiments which are associated with it amongst us.' True altruism, as observed in the instincts of 'attachment', 'veneration', and 'benevolence', was a higher and broader sympathy which went far beyond mere sexual or parental instinct.[39] The highest altruistic instinct—the propensity for universal love—was the feeling that had been 'imperfectly represented by theologians under the name of Christian Charity'.[40] A table illustrating the 'Positive Classification of the Eighteen Internal Functions of the Brain' was appended to both the *Politique Positive* and the *Catéchisme Positiviste* (see Fig. 8).

The fact that the altruistic instincts, in comparison with the egoistic, were 'higher in quality' but 'inferior in force', meant that subordinating egoism to altruism—Comte's 'great problem of human life'—was no easy matter. The regime of religious instruction and social reorganization that Comte hoped to see implemented was designed to achieve this subordination. The task would be made easier by the fact that modifications in the strengths of the various 'affective motors' could be inherited. One of the laws of animal life in Comte's biology was the 'Law of Exercise', according to which the use and disuse of particular organs led to their development or atrophy, respectively. The cerebral organs associated with the affective propensities could, like any other organs, be strengthened by regular exercise. These strengthened and enlarged organs could then be inherited.

---

[37] Comte 1891: 221.
[38] Ibid. 176. For St Paul's account of the internal struggle played out in the individual between the law of the flesh and the law of God, see Romans 7: 14–25.
[39] Ibid. 181–2.
[40] Comte 1875–7: i. 566.

POSITIVE CLASSIFICATION

OF THE EIGHTEEN INTERNAL FUNCTIONS OF THE BRAIN,

OR

SYSTEMATIC VIEW OF THE SOUL.

IMPULSION.
(THE HEART.)

Decrease of energy, increase of dignity, from the back of the head to the front, from the lower part to the higher, from the sides to the middle.

Egoism. | Altruism.

COUNSEL.
(THE INTELLECT.)

Knowledge, or vision, for the sake of prevision, with a view to provision.

EXECUTION.
(THE CHARACTER.)

PRINCIPLE.

INTEREST	Instincts of Preservation	{ of the Individual, or *nutritive Instinct*...... 1 of the race, or ... { *sexual Instinct* ...... 2 { *maternal Instinct* 3
AMBITION	Instincts of Improvement	{ by destruction, or ... *military Instinct* ...... 4 { by construction, or... *industrial Instinct* 5
	Temporal, or Pride, desire of power............ 6	
	Spiritual, or Vanity, desire of approbation 7	
ATTACHMENT 8		
VENERATION 9		
BENEVOLENCE, or Universal Love (sympathy), *humanity* 10		

7 PERSONAL. / 3 SOCIAL. — General, Special.

10 AFFECTIVE MOTORS. Propensities, when active; feelings, when passive.

MEANS.

CONCEPTION
{ Passive, or Contemplation, hence objective materials.
  { Concrete, or relative to Beings, essentially *synthetical*. 11
  { Abstract, or relative to Events, essentially *analytical*. 12
{ Active, or Meditation, hence subjective constructions.
  { Inductive, or by comparison, hence *Generalisation*. 13
  { Deductive, or by co-ordination, hence *Systematisation*. 14

EXPRESSION ...... Mimic, oral, written, hence *Communication* 15

5 INTELLECTUAL FUNCTIONS.

RESULT.

ACTIVITY { Courage 16
{ Prudence 17

FIRMNESS ...... hence *Perseverance* 18

3 PRACTICAL QUALITIES.

ACT FROM AFFECTION, AND THINK IN ORDER TO ACT.
(TO LOVE, TO THINK, TO ACT.)

SUMMARY OF THE CEREBRAL THEORY.

These eighteen organs together form the cerebral apparatus, which, on the one hand, stimulates the life of nutrition, on the other, co-ordinates the life of relation, by connecting its two kinds of external functions. Its speculative region is in direct communication with the nerves of sensation, its active region with the nerves of motion. Its affective region has no direct communication except with the viscera of organic life; it has no immediate correspondence with the external world, its only connection with which is through the other two regions. This part of the brain, the essential centre of the whole of our existence, is in constant activity. It is enabled to be so by the alternate rest of the two symmetrical parts of each of its organs. As for the rest of the brain, its periodical cessation of action is as complete as that of the senses and muscles. Thus, our harmony as living beings depends on the principal region of the brain, the affective: it is from this that the two others derive their impulse, and, in obedience to this impulse, the two others direct the relations of the animal with the external agencies which influence it, whether such relations be active or passive.

Figure 8. Table illustrating Comte's cerebral theory. Of the ten 'affective motors', seven were associated with 'egoism' and three—attachment, veneration, and benevolence—with 'altruism'. Comte 1875–7: i, facing 594.

Comte believed, in other words, in the heritability of acquired characteristics, and recommended the biological teachings of Jean Baptiste Lamarck. Unlike Lamarck, however, he did not believe that species were indefinitely variable; organisms could only evolve within fixed species boundaries.[41] Comte's followers would later consequently also be resistant to the Darwinian theory of evolution.[42]

The positivist hope for the future, then, was that social organization and the structure of the human brain would evolve together until the former was dominated by service to humanity and the latter by the organs of altruism. Through the inheritance of gradually strengthened altruistic propensities, moral and intellectual progress could become ingrained within human nature. Proletarians and capitalists alike would come to see that all their efforts were, and should be, for the good of the *Grand Être*, 'Humanity'. That was the essence of the sociological and biological utopia which the egotistical and humourless Auguste Comte was in the midst of working out, in both old language and new, when Alexander Bain encountered him at 10 Rue Monsieur-le-Prince in the summer of 1851.

142 Strand, City of Westminster

When Bain returned to London after his Parisian summer, he was engaged to give lectures in physical and political geography and moral philosophy at the women's college in Bedford Square.[43] One of the women who attended lectures there was Marian Evans, sometimes accompanied by her employer and landlord, John Chapman.[44] Bain recalled that on his return to London in 1851 he had found 'every place crowded for the great Exhibition'. This included the unusual boarding house run by Chapman and his wife at 142 Strand. When the census enumerators called there in March 1851 they recorded a 'miner and smelter', his wife, and a couple of

---

[41] Comte 1875–7: i. 492–3. Comte recommended Lamarck's *Philosophie Zoologique* amongst the 30 volumes on science in his 'Positivist Library' of 150 books. For an exposition of Comte's three primary biological laws—'Renovation of substance, Destruction of the individual, Conservation of the race'—see Comte 1875–7: i. 474–82. For the 'Positivist Library', see Comte 1875–7: iv. 483–6; Comte 1891: 27–30.

[42] See W. Stanley Jevons, 'Comte's Philosophy', *Nature* (7 Oct. 1875), 491–2; and Patrick Geddes's recollections of positivist distrust of evolutionary theories in his introduction to Liveing 1926: 1–19, at 4–5.

[43] Bain 1904: 228–9. The college had been founded as part of the University of London in 1849.

[44] *ODNB*.

merchants, all visiting from the United States, drawn to London by the Great Exhibition. Elisabeth Tilley, Chapman's mistress, was recorded on the census return as a 'visitor'. If the enumerators had called a week earlier they would also have found both Chapman's wife Susanna and Marian Evans at this address, but an emotional scene had driven Evans temporarily back to Coventry (and Susanna Chapman to stay with family in Truro) a few days earlier.[45] Chapman accompanied Evans to the railway station when she departed. According to the entry in his private journal that day, she had pressed him 'for some intimation of the state of my feelings', to which he had responded 'that I felt great affection for her, but that I loved E. and S. also, though each in a different way'.[46]

142 Strand functioned not only as a somewhat fraught domestic environment and a boarding house, but also as a bookshop and a publisher's office. It was a location for literary dinners attended by some of the leading radical writers and intellectuals of the day, and, most importantly, it was to become the centre of operations for the *Westminster Review*. Chapman was already established as a publisher of progressive works on philosophical and religious subjects when, in October 1851, he took over as proprietor and editor of the radical quarterly.[47] Chapman had previously published Marian Evans's translation of D. F. Strauss's *Das Leben Jesu* in 1846, and from the end of 1851 he employed her as *de facto* editor of the *Westminster*.[48] Despite the backdrop of romantic and emotional unrest, Chapman's and Evans's professional relationship continued fairly smoothly during 1851. Evans set to work drawing up an 'analytic catalogue' of all Chapman's publications. His list for 1851 included the controversial atheistic *Letters on the Laws of Man's Nature and Development* by Harriet Martineau and the mesmerist Henry Atkinson, Herbert Spencer's first book, *Social Statics*, Francis

---

[45] On the American visitors and the census, see Haight 1969: 15–17. The Great Exhibition was officially opened on 1 May 1851, but was open to the public prior to that date. The references for the 1851 Census records for the Chapman household, the Brays (which includes Marian Evans as a visitor), and Susanna Chapman's family in Truro are Public Record Office, HO.101/1511, f. 203, 10–11; HO.107/2068, f. 114, 27; and HO.107/1910, f. 145, 29; all accessed through the website of the UK national archives (see Bibliography for details).

[46] Entry for Monday 24 Mar. 1851, in Haight 1969: 147.

[47] On Chapman's acquisition of the *Westminster*, and the financial and editorial struggles this entailed, see Haight 1969: 28–65. On the broader history of the *Westminster Review*, see Houghton 1966–89: iii. 528–58; Rosenberg 1982.

[48] On Chapman's relationship with Marian Evans in this period, and her associations with Spencer, Lewes, and other members of the Chapman circle, see Haight 1968: 68–147; 1969; Ashton 1991: 115–47; 1996: 77–107. For a recent history of 142 Strand as 'A Radical Address in Victorian London', see Ashton 2006.

Newman's *Lectures on Political Economy,* William Rathbone Greg's sceptical
The Creed of Christendom, and several works by Unitarians, including a commentary on St Paul's epistles to the Corinthians by John Hamilton Thom,
and a sermon entitled 'The God of Revelation His Own Interpreter' by
Harriet Martineau's brother James.

Later the same year, the two Martineaus fell out irrevocably over James's
exceedingly hostile review of Harriet's *Letters*.[49] That review, entitled
'Mesmeric Atheism', appeared in a quarterly devoted to theology and literature, the *Prospective Review,* also published by John Chapman.[50] But
Chapman had his own falling out with James Martineau a few years later.
The *Westminster* had, not for the first time, run into financial difficulties, and
James Martineau hoped to take it over and make it an organ of 'serious and
free theology'. Chapman resisted this proposal, with Harriet Martineau's
financial help. James Martineau recorded in a letter to a friend his disappointment that the *Westminster* had thus been 'delivered into the hands of a
Comtist coterie' with a pronounced 'atheistic tendency'.[51] It was in large
measure thanks to the activities of this 'Comtist coterie' of writers, whose
words were disseminated in books and periodicals published by John
Chapman, that 'altruism' became part of the English language rather than
simply remaining a piece of obscure French scientific jargon. So, while the
French father of *altruisme* was the eccentric and egotistical founder of a new
godless religion, the term's English godfather was a radical and freethinking publisher with a reputation as a womanizer and a financial oppor-
tunist.[52] It was initially through articles in the *Westminster* and through the
English translation of the *Catéchisme,* also published by Chapman, that the
language of altruism was imported from Paris and transmitted to British
readers in the 1850s and 1860s.

It was also through Chapman that Marian Evans got to know two of
the key figures in the transmission of 'altruism' — G. H. Lewes and Herbert
Spencer.[53] After a brief and ultimately unrequited romantic involvement
with Spencer, Marian Evans fell in love with Lewes. The latter was already

[49] On the Martineau and Atkinson *Letters,* and the rift between James and Harriet see Cashdollar
1989: 58–63; C. Roberts 2002: 169–92. On Harriet Martineau's views on religion and positivism
see also Pichanik 1980: 192–203; Hoecker-Drysdale 2001.

[50] [James Martineau], 'Mesmeric Atheism', *Prospective Review,* 7 (1851), 224–62.

[51] James Martineau to Charles Wicksteed, 18 Feb. 1855, quoted in Haight 1969: 78–9. See also
Pichanik 1980: 202–3; Wright 1986: 63. There is also a brief account of this episode in Alexander
Bain's autobiography. He visited Harriet Martineau in the Lake District in 1854 around the time
of this struggle with her brother; Bain 1904: 240–1.

[52] Rosenberg 1982: 169.

[53] See *ODNB* entry for Lewes for a brief account. See also Haight 1969: 68–71.

married and had condoned the adultery of his wife with his friend Thornton Hunt. In the circumstances divorce was not possible. Evans took the decision to live with Lewes nonetheless; the union would last until his death in 1878. During those twenty-five years Marian Evans became 'George Eliot' to some and 'Mrs Lewes' to others. She also came to be perceived as an apostle of the religion of 'altruism'. Although she had more sympathy with the positivist religion than Lewes, and certainly much more than Spencer, it was they rather than she who actually adopted the term in their own writings, as a signal of the scientific nature of their approaches to ethics and society.[54] Aside from one early reference in the pages of the *Westminster* in 1856, and another isolated usage over twenty years later in *Impressions of Theophrastus Such* (1879), George Eliot did not adopt the language of altruism.[55]

It was Lewes who was the first to introduce the Comtean neologism in print. Naturally enough it was in the pages of the *Westminster* that he did so. In an article on the 'Contemporary literature of France' in the April 1852 number—the second produced under the editorial eye of Marian Evans—Lewes had announced Comte's conversion from man of science to moral philosopher and provided a brief account of the first volume of the *Politique Positive*.[56] In the October number he provided a fuller account of some of the teachings of the *Politique Positive*. Comte's social principles, Lewes explained, were all deduced ultimately from biology. This included Comte's observations of how 'the selfish instincts of man lead in their satisfaction to the development of unselfish instincts, how *egotism* is the impulse to *altruism* (to use a felicitous phrase coined by Comte): thus the egoistic instinct of material preservation, which impels to industry, is the foundation of Society, rendering it possible in a higher sense than that of mere aggregation of families'.[57] Lewes had another opportunity to introduce the Comtean distinction between egoism and altruism the following year. *Comte's Philosophy of the Sciences* (1853) was primarily a summary of the *Cours de Philosophie Positive*, but in the later chapters Lewes included some key points of the later works. This included an outline of Comte's analysis of the affective propensities, and his observations about their manifestations

---

[54] On Spencer's life-long attempts to distance himself from Auguste Comte and positivism, despite adopting his terminology, see Ch. 5 below.

[55] Her place in the history of 'altruism' is examined in more detail in Ch. 3, below.

[56] [G. H. Lewes], 'Contemporary Literature of France', *Westminster Review*, 57 (1852), 346–55.

[57] This was the first published use of 'altruism' in English—a year earlier than the earliest quotation given in the *OED*, from Lewes 1853. [G. H. Lewes], 'Contemporary Literature of France', *Westminster Review*, 58 (1852), 614–30, at 617–18.

at different points on the animal scale: 'all the higher animals exhibit
both Personality and Sociality. These may be denominated *Egoism* and
Altruism.'[58] This was the first time the latter term had appeared in a book
in English, a book which was credited by one observer with having
'introduced the name and principles of Comte for the first time to many
readers in this country'.[59]

   Most of the contents of *Comte's Philosophy of the Sciences* had appeared
previously in the *Leader*, a weekly newspaper that Lewes had co-founded
with Thornton Hunt in 1850. Through the pages of the *Leader*, Lewes not
only communicated Comtean philosophy, but also solicited subscriptions
for a fund to support Comte, who, 'in his fifty-fifth year, is thrown upon
the world, with no other resources than such as his friends and admirers can
collect for him!' Lewes invited 'any generous lover of philosophy' to 'forward to me his mite' to add to the subscriptions.[60] The series of articles on
Comte's philosophy ran from April to August 1852. They were often
accompanied by appeals for funds and thanks for contributions received.
Two weeks after the original appeal, Lewes reported that he had received
only three responses but, he trumpeted, 'of the three first respondents, two
were *working-men*—(John Ivory and Charles Clements)—who forwarded
two shillings in postage-stamps'. Subsequent donations ranged from a very
generous £10 from Joseph Livesey of Preston to an offering of two shillings
and sixpence from a young working man calling himself 'Ortis', 'whose letter made my face flush with admiration'.[61] Despite these contributions,
Lewes was disappointed with the total he managed to raise. He wrote to
Comte in August 1852, towards the end of his appeal, that there was 'a
strong prejudice against any subsidy' and that this prejudice was all the
stronger when the intended recipient was a foreigner and an unbeliever
too.[62]

[58] Lewes 1853: 217.
[59] Tulloch 1885: 251–2. For the leading secularist's appreciative review of the book, see G. J.
Holyoake, 'Lewes's *Comte* and Leigh Hunt's *Religion of the Heart*', *The Reasoner and Secular Gazette*,
15 (1853), 273–5. On Holyoake's initial enthusiasm for Comte's philosophy, and on his later
reluctance to endorse the Religion of Humanity, see Wright 1986: 68–9.
[60] G. H. Lewes, 'Comte's Positive Philosophy, Part I: Biographical', *The Leader* (3 Apr. 1852), 327–8.
[61] *The Leader* (17 Apr. 1852), 375; (24 Apr. 1852), 399. The large donation was probably from the
same Joseph Livesey who made his name as founder of the Preston temperance society and pioneer teetotaller, although I have not found any other evidence that he had positivist sympathies;
see *ODNB*; Roberts 2004.
[62] G. H. Lewes to Auguste Comte, 17 Aug. 1852, Maison d'Auguste Comte, Paris; published in
Baker 1995: i. 205–6. The amount Lewes raised was under 400 francs—only a small proportion
of the 5,600 francs which Erskine Perry claimed was raised in subsidies for Comte from all

The other principal popularizer of Comtean positivism in Britain was Harriet Martineau. Her abridged translation of the *Cours*, like Lewes's book on Comte, came out in 1853. Martineau's condensation was published by John Chapman and was strongly recommended in the first of a series of columns on contemporary science written by Thomas Huxley for the *Westminster* between 1854 and 1857.[63] The article praised Martineau for converting the *Cours*, 'without the loss of a sentence that was worth keeping, from six wearisome volumes of indifferent French, into two of very excellent readable English'.[64] As an atheist and positivist, and one known to have a particular interest in morality, Harriet Martineau was someone who might have been expected to embrace the Comtean ideal of 'altruism'. She was certainly associated in the public's eyes with philanthropy: on one occasion a letter reached her addressed simply to 'The Queen of Modern Philanthropists'—the Post Office had written on the envelope 'Try Miss Martineau'.[65] On top of this, Martineau was someone who thought carefully about the need for linguistic change as a prerequisite of religious and intellectual change. In articulating their defence of a morally elevated form of unbelief in their *Letters*, she and Atkinson had thought about whether or not to use traditional terms like 'religion'. Martineau worried that such terms had unwanted theological connotations. Atkinson recognized this but regretted that 'we cannot invent new terms for the sentiments; and by dropping such terms as religion and spirituality, and the like, we shall be equally misinterpreted, in another way, and be called dull, cold, un-impassioned atheists, dry reasoning materialists, and indeed be found wanting in the faculties and feelings more or less common to the human race'.[66]

The way that Comte and some of his British readers solved this problem of seeking to inculcate a certain religious enthusiasm but without using the language of the churches was indeed to 'invent new terms for the sentiments', most notably 'altruism'. Harriet Martineau did not adopt this

---

sources during 1852, which in turn fell short of the 7,000 francs Comte had hoped for; Perry, 'A Morning with Auguste Comte', *Nineteenth Century*, 2 (1877), 621–31, at 629.

[63] It was presumably the fact that Chapman had already commissioned this work from Martineau that prevented him from taking Lewes's book on Comte, for which he would otherwise have been the natural publisher.

[64] [Thomas H. Huxley], 'Contemporary Literature: Science', *Westminster Review*, 61 (1854), 254–70, at 254. Mill had refused Chapman's request to review the work; Wright 1986: 45.

[65] H. Martineau 1877: iii. 62.

[66] Ibid. 301.

language, however. This was most probably because of its association with the religion of humanity. Writing about Comte's later writings for the *Daily News* in 1858, Martineau thought it was a pity 'to bring into fresh notice the melancholy latest works of the great thinker' who, in his 'days of feebleness' had lost sight of his own positive principles. Reading Comte's *Catéchisme Positiviste*, after the *Cours*, was like watching 'a masquerade following a star-gazing night in an observatory'.[67] Consequently she refused to perform the same task of abridgement and translation of the *Catéchisme* or the *Politique* that she had for the *Cours*, despite Comte's requests.[68] Although, as Shelagh Hunter puts it, Martineau's writings offer 'a remarkable glimpse of a struggle to express the new in an inherited vocabulary', she did not in this particular case adopt the new Comtean ethical terminology as part of that struggle. If it is true that Martineau's 'life and work is not understandable if we stray far from the vocabulary in which she addressed her public or came to terms with herself', then it is important to note that she was not what Hunter goes on to suggest she was, namely a proponent of 'Comtean altruism'. Martineau's non-adoption of that terminology revealed her unhappiness with the later direction taken by the Comtean philosophy.[69]

Lewes adopted 'altruistic' as the scientific term for a certain set of instincts, and willingly exercised his own altruistic organs by spreading Comte's scientific ideas and trying to raise money for him.[70] Like Martineau, however, he would not take the extra step of devoting himself to the worship of the *Grand Être*. Lewes may have believed that, as a philosophy, positivism was 'the only true system of thought', as he put it in a letter to Comte.[71] But privately he was embarrassed by many of the detailed proposals of Comte's later works. His friend W. M. W. Call, a poet and clergyman on his way to renouncing his Anglican orders, had been working on a translation of the early parts of the *Politique Positive*, but Lewes wrote to him in 1852 that he did not think it the right time to publish such a work: 'There are so many things in it which lay themselves open

---

[67] [Harriet Martineau], 'Literature', *Daily News* (9 Apr. 1858), 2. On the authorship of this piece see Arbuckle 1983: 165n.

[68] Hoecker-Drysdale 2001: 186.

[69] Hunter 1995: 1, 12.

[70] For Lewes's later discussions of altruistic and egoistic instincts, in his *Problems of Life and Mind*, see Lewes 1874–5: i. 101, 153–4, and esp. 161–2.

[71] G. H. Lewes to Auguste Comte, Oct. 1853, Maison d'Auguste Comte, Paris; published in Baker 1995: i. 229.

to ridicule, & *that* is not desirable.'[72] The reception of Richard Congreve's translation of the *Catéchisme*, published by John Chapman in 1858, would confirm that Lewes's fears were well grounded.

The publication of *The Catechism of Positive Religion* made Comte's own scientific theories about the altruistic sentiments and his proposals for a 'Religion of Humanity' available in English for the first time.[73] This was the only work published in English in the 1850s that contained a sustained discussion of 'altruism'. The 1860s saw the publication of works by Mill and Bridges which included brief analyses of Comtean altruism, which are discussed below. A fuller theoretical analysis of 'altruism' did not come until the 1870s, which saw the appearance of the 2nd edition of Herbert Spencer's *Principles of Psychology* (1870–2), the English translation of the *Positive Polity* (1875–7), and, most importantly of all, Spencer's *Data of Ethics* (1879).[74] Although Richard Congreve and his wife were on friendly terms with Lewes and Marian Evans, and formed part of Chapman's 'Comtist coterie', that did not prevent members of that coterie, including Chapman himself, from drawing the line at the religion of humanity.[75] Chapman wrote to Harriet Martineau of his astonishment that Congreve had spent time and money on this translation of the *Catechism*, which he himself considered a 'melancholy exhibition of egotism, vanity and the marvellous ascendancy of a woman over a great mind'.[76] In his part of a review for the *Westminster*, jointly written with Lewes's friend Call, Chapman continued on a similar theme. He included much detail from the *Catechism* itself about the prescribed public and private forms of devotion to humanity, as well as the many annual positivist festivals, and the nine 'social sacraments'. The form of social and religious 'despotism' envisaged by Comte, Chapman

---

[72] G. H. Lewes to W. M. W. Call, Apr.–Mar. 1852, in Baker 1995: i. 202. On Wathen Mark Wilks Call (1817–90), who renounced his Anglican orders in 1857, the same year as Richard Congreve, see Haight 1954–78: i, p. lviii; Haight 1969: 209n.; Baker 1995: i. 27–9. When Lewes wrote to Comte a few months later that he had a friend who was abridging the sociological volumes, he presumably had Call in mind, rather than Congreve, who is suggested by Baker 1995: i. 206n.

[73] Comte 1858; later edns were published by Trübner, and then by Kegan Paul, Trench, Trübner & Co.

[74] An English translation of Comte's 'General View' of positivism was published in 1865, but the discussion in that work of the need to nurture the social and sympathetic feelings did not make use of the language of altruism; Comte 1865. John Stuart Mill's articles on Comte for the *Westminster Review* in 1865 and John Bridges's response of 1866 contained brief discussions of 'altruism', which are discussed below.

[75] On the support offered by Lewes and Evans to the Congreves, see *ODNB* entry for Congreve.

[76] Quoted in Wright 1986: 64.

concluded, was purportedly 'founded on science and inspired by benevolence' but in reality the whole system was simply the expression of Comte's 'sublime egotism'.[77]

It was at one of John Chapman's regular literary soirées that William Maccall, a Unitarian minister who had recently been ejected by his congregation in Devon for including 'violent political declamation' in his sermons, was encouraged by Thomas Carlyle to 'come out like an athlete' into the worlds of literature and philosophy.[78] Maccall naturally followed the encouraging advice of such an eminent person and amongst the results were a book on *The Elements of Individualism* published by Chapman in 1847 and several exceedingly athletic reviews of works by rationalists and positivists.[79] His review of Marian Evans's translation of Feuerbach was entitled 'Hegelian Atheism'; the Martineau and Atkinson *Letters* he treated as 'Imbecile Atheism'.[80]

Predictably, this Christian individualist was not an admirer of Comte's atheistic altruism. Maccall reviewed both the *Catéchisme* and the *Politique* in the 1850s. Of the former he wrote: 'All M. Comte's books are dull. This is one of the dullest. And yet it is throughout abundantly entertaining.' He likened Comte, in his comic dullness, to a grave goose strutting on the common, and described him as perhaps the most 'unlimited self-idolater' in the history of humanity. Maccall thought it 'monstrous' to try to reconcile science and religion simply by exalting science itself into a new religion which had really resulted from Comte 'falling in love with his neighbour's wife'. In his reviews of both works Maccall particularly complained about Comte's linguistic innovations. Comte's 'ugly and pedantic terminology' made the 'godless ghastliness' of his social gospel even more unbearable. It would not have been necessary to point out the obvious flaws of Comte's works, Maccall wrote, if it were not for the fact that 'M. Comte's wretched jargon had gained a certain currency in England'. It may well have been discussions over the dinner table at 142 Strand that confirmed Maccall's fears of the deleterious impact of Comte's writings on the English

[77] [W. M. W. Call and John Chapman], 'The Religion of Positivism', *Westminster Review,* 69 (1858), 305–50, quotations at 338. This quotation is from the second part of the article, written by Chapman. On the authorship of the article see Houghton 1966–89. It is mistakenly attributed to Harriet Martineau in Arbuckle 1983: 165n.

[78] On Maccall's life and career, see *ODNB*; Maccall's own account of his wife's life and death, Maccall 1880; Espinasse 1893: 247–55, quotation at 250.

[79] Maccall wrote for various publications, including *The Spectator, The Critic, Fraser's Magazine*, and the *Gentleman's Magazine*. Some of his reviews are collected together as Maccall 1873.

[80] Maccall 1873: 98–121.

language. But perhaps he was not listening carefully enough to his dinner companions. His review of the *Politique* informed his readers that Comte had begun to preach 'what he elegantly termed Ultraism, that is to say, the devotion of our energies to the service of others'.[81]

The Mechanics' Institute, Bradford

The obscurity and verbosity of Comte's own writings remained a significant hurdle to his ideas enjoying greater currency. Maccall's shaky grasp of Comte's language in 1858 was not helped by the fact that he had not managed to read the entirety of the *Politique* before reviewing it: 'It is nearly three years since we perused the first page, and we honestly confess that we have not yet arrived at the last.'[82] Even in the 1870s, Mark Pattison diagnosed a similar problem. He wrote that the 'mere bulk of Comte's books is repellent' and that their language 'has been too technical and scholastic'. 'Words ending in "ology" recur too often in their pages', Pattison wrote, and the very terms 'science' and 'philosophy' were enough to deter many readers.[83] However, to assert as Pattison did that positivism had not yet been given an accessible 'superficial presentation' was, in 1876, certainly inaccurate. This was to overlook Harriet Martineau's and Lewes's 1853 books, both of which were generally thought to be very readable. The English versions of the *Catechism of Positive Religion* (1858) and the *General View of Positivism* (1865) were also both concise and quite accessible. In fact, by the 1860s, thanks to the influence of these books, and of the *Westminster Review*, the social and religious aspects of Comtean positivism, including its scientific celebration of the new ideal of 'altruism', were becoming much better known. In 1866, the *Pall Mall Gazette* identified Richard Congreve for its readers as an apostle of a new religious movement committed to 'the direct culture of the altruistic instincts and the subordination to them of the egoistic'.[84] And, according to Leslie Stephen, writing in 1869, Comte had

---

[81] The review of the *Catéchisme* was originally published in 1856, that of the *Politique* in 1858; Maccall 1873: 63–77. 'Ultraism' was a term for extremism or one-sidedness, although not one that was in frequent use.

[82] Maccall 1873: 77.

[83] Mark Pattison, 'The Religion of Positivism', *Contemporary Review*, 27 (1876), 593–614, at 595–6. Pattison himself had read Comte's *Cours* in French in the 1840s; Cashdollar 1989: 52. On Pattison, see H. S. Jones 2007.

[84] *Pall Mall Gazette* (16 July 1866), 4. The whole phrase was placed in quotation marks, indicative of its strangeness.

become such a popular focus for religious and theological debates that 'newspapers are full of allusions to his supposed vagaries, and even at dinner-tables he has become a fashionable subject of conversation'.[85]

'Positivist' was now, according to Stephen, a label which 'many young men are pleased to bear, as indicating that they are up to the very last new thing in religious creeds'.[86] Although he did not himself adopt the label, Stephen was among very many Victorian thinkers, writers, and reformers who made a study of Comte and positivism as part of the process of forging their philosophical and religious identities. Stephen read Comte during the period when, as a young Anglican priest and college fellow in Cambridge, he was gradually deciding that his religious doubts meant he could not continue in his clerical vocation.[87] Others, such as the Congregationalist Henry Reynolds, the Anglicans Brooke Westcott, Frederic Farrar, and Harvey Goodwin, and the Unitarian James Martineau, made serious studies of Comte while retaining their Christian commitments.[88] Eminent philosophical writers also took notice of Comte. One of the very last things that William Whewell wrote, in 1866, was an article on Comte and positivism, responding to a piece by Lewes in the *Fortnightly Review*.[89] The idealist Edward Caird later devoted a whole book to *The Social Philosophy and Religion of Comte* (1885). Others who reflected on Comte's ideas and who feature in the story of the transmission of the language of altruism include novelists (George Eliot, Mrs Humphry Ward, W. H. Mallock, George Gissing, Thomas Hardy), social reformers (Arnold Toynbee, Beatrice Potter, Charles Booth), and scientific writers (Herbert Spencer, James Cotter

[85] [Leslie Stephen], 'The Comtist Utopia', *Fraser's Magazine,* 80 (1869), 1–21, at 1.

[86] Ibid.

[87] *ODNB*; Maitland 1906: 73, 172.

[88] For a comprehensive and extremely illuminating study of the impact of positivism on clergymen and theologians in the Protestant churches of both Britain and America between 1830 and 1890, see Cashdollar 1989. On Reynolds, see Cashdollar 1989 and *ODNB*. Brooke Westcott wrote on 'Aspects of Positivism in Relation to Christianity', *Contemporary Review,* 8 (1868), 371–86. On Farrar see Ch. 3, below. Harvey Goodwin, the bishop of Carlisle, later engaged in debate in print with Frederic Harrison about the value of Comte's doctrine of the three states. See e.g. Harvey Goodwin, 'Comte's Atheism', *Nineteenth Century,* 21 (1887), 873–82. J. Martineau 1885 included a substantial section on Comte.

[89] William Whewell, 'Comte and Positivism', *Macmillan's Magazine,* 13 (1866), 353–62. Whewell wrote that he would not have taken Comte seriously except for the attention paid to him by writers he respected such as Mill and Lewes. The article was a response to G. H. Lewes, 'Auguste Comte', *Fortnightly Review,* 3 (1866), 385–410. This was in turn a review of Mill's *Auguste Comte and Positivism* (1865) and of French works on Comte by Émile Littré and Jean Robinet. Lewes, signing the article as the editor of the *Fortnightly*, urged his readers to learn more about the doctrines of positivism for themselves through their own reading.

Morison, Patrick Geddes).[90] The impact of positivism was also felt in the political arena, especially through the activities of the English positivists Congreve, Bridges, Beesly, and Harrison, who campaigned in favour of trade unions and against British imperialism. Significant figures in later British socialism such as Henry Hyndman, Ernest Belfort Bax, and Sidney Webb had all also studied Comte and positivism.[91]

Although reading and discussing Comte was an activity initially confined to academic circles, and to the pages of the more intellectual periodicals, his ideas were gradually reaching a wider audience. In 1860, Florence Nightingale wrote to Mill about a book she had written on religion. It was aimed, she said, at those artisans and working people who now found the Christian creed unacceptable. She told Mill that, 'many years ago', she had 'a large and very curious acquaintance among the artisans of the North of England and of London' and had discovered that 'they were without any religion whatever—though diligently seeking after one, principally in Comte and his school'.[92] Nightingale must have conceived of the religion of 'Comte and his school' in a rather general sense, since 'many years' before 1860 there was no awareness in Britain of Comte's religious teachings. Shortly after she wrote this, however, more concerted efforts were under way to bring the teachings of Comte to just the sort of audience she had in mind—the working people of the North of England. The Comtist coterie's first emissary to the north was John Henry Bridges.

In 1856, at 23 years of age, Bridges became the second person in England, after his Oxford tutor Richard Congreve, to commit himself completely to Comte's religion of humanity; Bridges's contemporaries at Wadham College, Harrison and Beesly, followed a few years later.[93] John

---

[90] For further details see the sections devoted to these writers below. Spencer denied any significant debt to Comte, but his immersion in the 'Comtist coterie' surrounding Chapman and the *Westminster Review* in the 1850s must have exposed him to regular discussions of Comte's work. On Spencer, see Ch. 5 below.

[91] C. Kent 1978 focuses on politics and on university reform as areas of English life in which Comtist influences were felt, especially through the activities of individuals such as Harrison and John Morley, who wrote the article on Auguste Comte for the 9th edn of the *Encyclopaedia Britannica*; J. Morley 1877. For more on Harrison, see F. Harrison 1911; Vogeler 1984; Royden Harrison 1994. On Bax and Hyndman, see *ODNB*. On Sidney Webb's youthful immersion in both utilitarianism and Comtean positivism, see Bevir 2002.

[92] Nightingale 1994: p. ix. The work, entitled *Suggestions for Thought*, ran to 3 vols and was printed privately by Nightingale in 1860. Mill responded encouragingly but not entirely uncritically; Mill 1963–91: xv. 706–12.

[93] On the life and career of John Bridges, see Liveing 1926; *ODNB*.

Bridges was the son of the Reverend Charles Bridges—an evangelical
Anglican vicar whose commentary on Psalm 119 had gained him some
recognition in religious circles. Having been head boy at Rugby and then
president of the Oxford Union, John Bridges seemed to have all the requi-
site qualities to pursue a career of establishment distinction and Anglican
orthodoxy. His conversion to positivism, however, set him on a different
path, to the anguish and disapproval of his friends and family. For the next
fifty years he devoted himself to the propagation of positivist teachings and
to the embodiment of its motto 'Live for others' through his work as a
physician, an educator, a Poor Law inspector, and an ardent campaigner for
sanitary reforms, social justice, and Irish home rule. He was described as a
'Saint of Rationalism' by L. T. Hobhouse and as 'un saint laïque' by a French
positivist friend.[94] No other individual more consistently embodied the
Comtean ideology of altruism in his personal, professional, and intellectual
life than John Bridges. His very decision to train as a physician was in
conformity with Comte's teaching that those preparing for the positivist
priesthood should first study medicine.

While studying for his medical degree in London in the late 1850s,
Bridges lodged with John Chapman, who had now moved from the Strand
to Albion Street, near Hyde Park. There he had the opportunity to take part
in Chapman's Sunday-night literary soirées, attended by the likes of Mill,
Huxley, Spencer, Eliot and Lewes—the 'lions of literary London'.[95] He
spent a positivist Christmas day with Eliot and Lewes at the Congreves'
home in 1859.[96] By 1860 Bridges's medical training was complete and he
was admitted as a member of the Royal College of Physicians. The same
year, he married his cousin Susan Torlesse. At the wedding, Reverend
Charles Bridges took the opportunity to remind the young couple how
perilously near they were to the road to damnation, on account of their
denial of Christianity. Frederic Harrison gave the best man's speech and
extolled the unbelieving groom's virtuous character.[97] To escape the disap-

---

[94] Liveing 1926: pp. xiii, 234.

[95] The Chapmans moved into 1 Albion Street in Mar. 1858; Haight 1969: 98; the 1861 census
return also confirms the address, although Bridges had moved out by then; Public Record Office,
R.G.9/8, f. 33, 23; accessed through the website of the UK national archives (see Bibliography for
details). Liveing 1926: 61 suggests that when Bridges initially lodged with Chapman, it was at
Spring Gardens. It was at Albion St in 1860 that Frederic Harrison met Herbert Spencer, through
Bridges's membership of the Chapman circle; 'Memoranda as to Herbert Spencer by Frederic
Harrison. Part I. 1860–1870'; a document written by Harrison and held in the Herbert Spencer
papers at the Senate House Library, London; MS.791/355/9.

[96] George Eliot to Sara Hennell, 30 Dec. 1859, in Haight 1954–78: iii. 238.

[97] Liveing 1926: 68.

proval of their evangelical families, the newlyweds decided to emigrate. John Chapman noted in his diary on 10 March 1860: 'J. H. Bridges sailed for Melbourne with his young wife. His friend Harrison tells me that she is 1 or 2 years older than he; plain but possessing a vigorous intellect and excellent heart. Though the daughter of a clergyman and living in a secluded village she has quite freed herself from the popular Christian superstition!'[98] During the three-month voyage on board the *Swiftsure*, Susan Bridges wrote to her sister of her and her husband's happiness in their new altruistic mission in life: 'we both hope to live and work together for others'. Their life in Australia started well. John hoped to build up a successful medical practice. Susan wrote to her sister in September 1860 that she and John were reading Plato's *Republic* together after breakfast each day and, in the evenings, were working through Darwin, 'which is also very interesting; you would be delighted at the wonderful facts he brings forward in natural history'.[99]

A few months later Susan Bridges died from typhoid fever. Her distraught husband brought her body home to England. On the grief-stricken voyage home he occupied himself in his cabin by translating the first volume of Comte's *Politique Positive*. Part of this translation would be published in 1865 as the *General View*. His full translation of the first volume of the *Positive Polity* came out in 1875. Bridges seems to have found some comfort in translating a work which was itself dedicated to the memory of Comte's beloved and departed Clotilde, and which celebrated the centrality of womankind in the hoped-for regeneration of society. We do not know whether Bridges at this time felt any anxieties about his decision to abandon the Christian hope for a future life, along with its associated fears of future punishment—hopes and fears which were still central to the Anglican faith of his father. He wrote to his friend Frederic Harrison in 1861, however, that 'the religion of Humanity stands the test of sorrow'.[100] The following year Harrison would commit himself to the positivist faith.

Back in England, Bridges moved to Bradford where he started to practise as a physician, and to become involved in local educational activities. He became an active member of a radical circle of writers, artists, and thinkers who met in the home of the educationist Fanny Hertz and her husband William, a local mill-owner and yarn merchant.[101] Mrs Hertz was

---

[98] Haight 1969: 221–39.
[99] Liveing 1926: 77, 81.
[100] Ibid. 85.
[101] Ibid. 137.

active in the Mechanics' Institute movement, was instrumental in helping
to found the Bradford Female Educational Institute in 1857, and represented Bradford on the North of England Council for Promoting the
Higher Education of Women. Through her association with Bridges she
became a committed positivist and one of several individuals who collaborated in the English translation of Comte's *Politique Positive*.[102] Bridges
offered courses of lectures both to the Mechanics' Institute and to the
Female Educational Institute. To the latter he lectured on practical subjects
and on one occasion spoke about Florence Nightingale, a fellow enthusiast
for improved sanitation, as an example of the great importance of practical
knowledge.[103] It was in his lectures to the Mechanics' Institute in 1862 that
he introduced the Comtean theory of altruism to some of the working
people of Bradford.

The Bradford Mechanics' Institute had been established in 1832, after
some preliminary resistance from the local churches, as part of a national
movement designed to provide useful secular education for the working
classes through the provision of a library, classes, and public lectures. By
1862 the Bradford institute boasted a library of 8,000 volumes and had
about 1,200 members, most of whom paid an annual subscription of
between eight and twelve shillings. Sixty-five per cent of the membership
was estimated to be 'strictly of the working classes'. The average attendance
at Bridges's lectures was about seventy people. This compared favourably
with the equivalent Anglican institution—the Bradford Church of England
Literary Institute—whose most popular classes (on arithmetic and book-
keeping) attracted an average attendance of only twenty-five.[104] In
February 1862 Bridges wrote to Harrison that he would be lecturing at the
Mechanics Institute the next day on the 'Moral Nature of Animals', which
would be 'preparatory to an explanation of the *Théorie Cérébrale* as relating
to man'. In other words, he would be explaining to his audience the biological and cerebral basis of the Comtean motto 'Live for others'—the theory of 'altruism' contained in the first volume of the *Positive Polity*, which
he had translated two years earlier on his voyage back from Melbourne. 'I
find the whole thing admirable', he told Harrison, 'at all events for
myself.'[105] During his decade in Bradford, Bridges found various ways, in

---

[102] On Hertz, see *ODNB*. The section she translated concerned the contributions of Greek
philosophy to the intellectual, moral, and religious evolution of the west: Comte 1875–7: iii.
211–89.
[103] Liveing 1926: 91.
[104] Godwin 1860; Hastings 1863: pp. lii–lx, at liv; Tylecote 1957: 224–40; Koditschek 1989.
[105] Liveing 1926: 91.

addition to his educational talks, to act out his own commitment to live for others. He tried to use his London contacts to give a voice to the grievances of the textile workers in neighbouring Lancashire during the privations of the cotton famine of 1863. And in 1867 he had an opportunity to express his solidarity with the oppressed Irish by writing to the *Bradford Review* protesting against the arrest, trial, and execution for murder of three Fenian sympathizers in Manchester.[106]

While a few dozen working people in Bradford were introduced to positivist altruism by John Bridges's lectures, those with access to the London press could reach a readership of thousands. And there was no philosophical writer with a greater reputation nor a more influential readership in the 1860s than John Stuart Mill. His contribution to public discussions of Comte's later writings was decisive in giving further authority to the language of altruism as a respectable philosophical idiom but also in establishing a definitive division between the earlier and the later Comte— between the author of the *Cours*, 'the *savant*, historian, and philosopher', and the author of the *Politique* and the *Catéchisme*, 'the High Priest of the Religion of Humanity'.[107] It was further testament to the currency and prominence of Comte and positivism as intellectual subjects in the 1860s that Mill, at the height of his influence and productivity, chose to produce two substantial articles on the thought of Auguste Comte. Mill had been planning the articles since 1863 and they were eventually published in the *Westminster Review* in 1865, the same year that Mill was elected as the radical Liberal MP for Westminster, and that his substantial study of the philosophy of William Hamilton was published. The two articles on Comte were published together as a book at the end of that year.[108]

The very separation by Mill of his reflections on Comte into two articles established the distinction that he, along with many others who admired the *Cours* but were embarrassed by the *Catéchisme* and the *Politique*, wished to make. The first article was a substantial and largely

---

[106] Ibid. 95–103, 128–31.

[107] John Stuart Mill, 'Later Speculations of Auguste Comte', *Westminster Review*, 84 (1865), 1–42, quotation at 2.

[108] The two original articles, both signed 'J.S.M.', were published in Apr. and July 1865: 'The Positive Philosophy of Auguste Comte', *Westminster Review*, 83 (1865), 339–405; 'Later Speculations of Auguste Comte', *Westminster Review*, 84 (1865), 1–42. The two articles were reprinted together by Trübner's as Mill 1865, which went into a 2nd edn in 1866, and 3rd and 4th edns in 1882 and 1891. The 2nd edn is the basis of the version included in the *Collected Works*: Mill 1963–91: x. 261–368. For Mill's earlier letters to Chapman, which reveal the evolution of his plans for the articles on Comte during 1863 and 1864, see Mill 1963–91: xv. 839, 849, 880–1, 884–7, 978.

sympathetic account of 'The Positive Philosophy of Auguste Comte'. The second was a somewhat shorter article and in its very title communicated a certain disdain: 'The Later Speculations of Auguste Comte'. Although Mill was sympathetic to the idea that one could have a religion without God, he was extremely scathing about the details of Comte's religious and social scheme.[109] And as a spokesman of liberal individualism, albeit one with increasing sympathies with certain kinds of collectivism, it was not surprising that Mill found Comte's teachings on altruism excessive and tyrannical. Mill explained that Comte believed that all educational and social arrangements 'should have but one object, namely to make altruism (a word of his own coining) predominate over egoism'. Comte's new golden rule—*Vivre pour autrui*—demanded that we should not love ourselves at all, since loving our neighbour as ourselves was too selfish and calculating a principle. Comte, in other words, Mill wrote was a 'morality-intoxicated man' who made entirely excessive demands for altruism. Mill agreed that there was 'a standard of altruism to which all should be required to come up, and a degree beyond it which is not obligatory, but meritorious'. However, there had to be limits. 'We do not conceive life to be so rich in enjoyments', Mill wrote, 'that it can afford to forego the cultivation of all those which address themselves to what M. Comte terms the egoistic propensities.' These propensities were to be moralized by sharing them with others, rather than by seeking entirely to eliminate them.

Mill traced what was objectionable in Comte's ethics to both philosophical and political causes. The principal philosophical error was the assumption that the criterion or test of virtuous conduct must also be its sole motive. Mill did not dissent from Comte's assumption that what qualified as virtuous conduct was any action which ultimately benefited others. Comte's error was to suppose that such conduct could only be produced by consciously and directly seeking the good of others rather than of oneself. This was not necessarily the case. On the classical utilitarian view, for instance, a society of individuals consciously and directly pursuing their own interests, if properly organized, could still produce the greatest possible general happiness.[110] Another main area of disagreement between Mill and Comte was on the question of individual liberty. In both *On Liberty*

---

[109] On the extent of Mill's own enthusiasm for some kind of religion of humanity, albeit not one resembling Comte's in any of the details, see Hamburger 1999: 108–48; Raeder 2002; Sell 2004: 69–118.

[110] John Stuart Mill, 'Later Speculations of Auguste Comte', *Westminster Review*, 84 (1865), 1–42, quotations at 8, 9, 11; reprinted in Mill 1963–91: x. 328–68, quotations at 335, 336, 339.

(1859) and *Utilitarianism* (1863), Mill had already complained about Comte's illiberal politics. In the former he had described the Comtist utopia as 'a despotism of society over the individual, surpassing anything contemplated in the political ideal of the most rigid disciplinarian among the ancient philosophers'.[111] *Utilitarianism*, as commentators at the time and more recently have noted, was a much less individualistic work. Frederic Harrison felt that Mill had failed to reconcile 'the tone of militant Individualism in the *Liberty* with the tone of enthusiastic Altruism in the *Utilitarianism*'.[112] It was true that Mill wrote in the latter work of that social feeling which, if perfect, would mean that no individual would ever seek any benefit in which the rest of humanity was not included. However, he immediately qualified this statement with a warning that the morals and politics of Comte's *Politique*, while being conducive to the cultivation of just such a feeling of solidarity with humanity, were in danger of making that feeling 'so excessive as to interfere unduly with human freedom and individuality'.[113] In his *Autobiography* Mill would describe the *Politique Positive* as 'the completest system of spiritual and temporal despotism, which ever yet emanated from a human brain, unless possibly that of Ignatius Loyola'.[114]

In Bradford, John Bridges read Mill's second *Westminster* article with dismay. He composed a seventy-page response, published the following year as *The Unity of Comte's Life and Doctrine: A Reply to Strictures on Comte's Later Writings, Addressed to J. S. Mill, Esq., M.P.*[115] The work was composed in the form of a long letter to Mill, which began,

---

[111] Mill 1963–91: xviii. 227.

[112] Frederic Harrison, 'John Stuart Mill', *Nineteenth Century*, 40 (1896), 487–508, at 499–500. Stefan Collini and George W. Carey have both also discussed Mill's approval of the cultivation of altruism and how this related to his commitment to individual liberty; Collini 1991: 67–74; Carey 2002; see also Hamburger 1999. On the intellectual and personal relationship between Mill and Comte, see further Alexander Bain, 'John Stuart Mill', *Mind*, 4 (1879), 520–41; F. Harrison 1918: 203–58; Packe 1954: 273–84; Haac 1995; Raeder 2002: esp. 38–86. For Mill's own account in his *Autobiography* of his relationship with Comte, see Mill 1963–91: i. 173, 217–21, 271–2. Two major political disagreements between Comte and Mill were on the question of the political rights of women, Mill favouring female suffrage and Comte envisaging an exclusively domestic and familial role for women; and on the dictatorial rule of Louis Napoléon after 1851 in France, which Comte admired and Mill despised.

[113] Mill 1963–91: x. 203–59, at 232.

[114] Ibid. i. 221.

[115] The pamphlet was published by Trübner's who had, in 1865, also brought out both Bridges's translation of Comte's *General View* and the book version of Mill's articles on Comte; the pamphlet served as, if nothing else, a small advertisement for both those works.

Sir, Your recent criticism upon Comte will be read by hundreds who are not
likely to test its accuracy by consulting his writings. The legitimate prestige
of your name will induce acquiescence in your judgment with large numbers who have not the power, or who have not the will, to form a judgment
for themselves.[116]

This was true enough and Bridges would undoubtedly have been only too
aware that a pamphlet written by a positivist physician in Bradford was as
unlikely to be consulted by such people as were Comte's own writings. The
essence of Bridges's argument, as his title indicated, was that the *Politique
Positive* represented a continuous development of Comte's thought rather
than a later aberration. Bridges was right that Comte had written about the
need for a spiritual power to facilitate social regeneration from the time of
his earliest political works in the 1820s.[117] However, he was also right to fear
that Mill's attack on the details of Comte's politics and religion, and his separation of these from a positivist approach to the history and philosophy of
the sciences, would prevail amongst British readers.

On the issue of altruism, Bridges argued that Comte had never claimed
the discovery of any new truth in promoting his altruistic ethics. This was
misleading since, as we have seen, Comte claimed the innateness of the
altruistic instincts as a scientific discovery of great novelty and importance,
based on his study of animal life and the human nervous system. And
Bridges himself admitted that Comte had preferred the new motto *Vivre
pour autrui* to the formulae 'Do unto others that which ye would they
should do to you' or 'Love thy neighbour as thyself' because, unlike these,
his maxim 'avoided all mention of self' and was 'not the second of two
commandments: it is the first and there is no other'.[118] Bridges's own formulation of positivist ethics also did little to change the impression formed
by Mill that it was a system of quite extreme individual self-renunciation.
The recognition that life was 'given us not solely or mainly for our own
enjoyment, but mainly, if not solely for the service of others' was, Bridges
wrote, 'the one primary condition of spiritual health'.[119] In his own life he
continued to practise what he preached. A few years after writing his pamphlet on Mill and Comte he was appointed as a medical inspector to the

---

[116] Bridges 1866: 3.
[117] Ibid. 14–15. Through his modern edn of Comte's early political writings, H. S. Jones has provided further support for the idea of an underlying unity and continuity between Comte's earlier and later writings; he suggests that Mill's statement of the gulf between these is overstated;
Comte 1998: esp. pp. ix–xi.
[118] Bridges 1866: 5–6.
[119] Ibid. 30.

Poor Law Board in London. For the next twenty years he devoted himself to improving public health by introducing special hospitals to deal with the threats posed by epidemics of smallpox and of ophthalmia.[120] During this period, Bridges wrote to his second wife: 'Our duty is to annihilate ourselves if need be for the service of Humanity.'[121]

Trinity College, Cambridge

Perhaps there was something in the ethos of self-renunciation and duty inculcated by Thomas Arnold and his successors at Rugby school which made the strict moralism of Comtean positivism attractive to its former pupils. Like Richard Congreve and John Bridges before him, Henry Sidgwick—who arrived at the school in 1852, the year after Bridges left as head boy—would later find himself attracted by the writings of Auguste Comte as he tried to work out alternatives to his waning Christian faith. The son of an Anglican clergyman-headmaster in Yorkshire, Sidgwick remained orthodox throughout his school and undergraduate career, partly through the influence of his cousin Edward White Benson, who was one of the masters at Rugby (and who later became Sidgwick's brother-in-law, and ultimately archbishop of Canterbury). Sidgwick went on to enjoy great academic success at Trinity College, Cambridge, graduating in 1859 with first-class honours in both classics and mathematics, and immediately being elected to a fellowship. In 1869 he would resign that fellowship when he finally felt unable to subscribe to the thirty-nine articles of the Church of England in good conscience. It was at the start of the intervening decade that Sidgwick was most intensely interested in Auguste Comte and positivism. His reading of Comte, and of Mill, along with his historical and

---

[120] It was an outbreak of this eye disease in a private school in Yorkshire, resulting in two boys losing their sight, that had earlier been the basis of the depiction of the dreadful Dotheboys Hall in Dickens's *Nicholas Nickleby* (1838–9).

[121] Liveing 1926: 190–203, quotation at 191. In later contributions to the *Positivist Review* Bridges continued to write on the questions he had grappled with in his encounter with Mill in the 1860s: J. H. Bridges, 'The Correspondence of Mill with Comte', *Positivist Review*, 7 (1899), 89–94; J. H. Bridges, 'Altruism', *Positivist Review*, 7 (1899), 175–9. There is no indication that Mill read Bridges's original pamphlet, although the two did correspond in 1867 on another question about which they both had strong views—the Irish question; Mill 1963–91: xvi. 1328–30; Hamburger 1999: 128.

linguistic studies of the Bible, contributed to his emerging identity as a rational doubter of the teachings of Christianity.[122]

Sidgwick's writings in private notebooks and correspondence between 1860 and 1862 reveal the role that positivism and the language of altruism played in the early, intellectually tumultuous stages of this transitional decade. In early 1860 Sidgwick still identified himself as a Christian. A locked diary that he kept at that time included a prayer—a confession written by Sidgwick before he took communion—which encapsulated the way that he thought about moral duty and Christianity at that time.[123] The young don commenced: 'I confess my errors to Jesus Christ in whom I humbly hope & pray that I believe with a saving faith.' The two principal errors of which Sidgwick convicted himself were 'selfishness' and 'pride of intellect'. He asked God to deliver him from his selfishness and to 'make it my sole aim primarily to do thy will, secondarily to further my own health & self-improvement intellectually, morally & physically; but always relatively if not subordinately to the welfare of others'. This recognition of the combined but distinct demands of God, self, and others was a classic expression of Anglican moralism. William Paley's famous utilitarian definition of Christian virtue had involved the same elements: 'doing good to mankind, in obedience to the will of God, with a view to eternal happiness'.[124] Sidgwick's prayer, in addition to this recognition of legitimate desires for worldly health and eternal happiness, included an expression of a contrasting strain of Christian rhetoric. He asked to be given 'a complete devotion to Jesus Christ & a desire to imitate him in his utter abandonment of self'. Finally, on the subject of his second error of 'pride of intellect', Sidgwick asked God to 'grant me neither to exalt too high nor to despise this gloriously capable part of my nature'. In the coming decades, Sidgwick would

---

[122] The major sources on Sidgwick's life and writings include the very substantial collection of papers and correspondence that comprise the Henry Sidgwick Papers, held in Trinity College Library, Cambridge. The major published sources are the memoir produced by his widow and his brother; Jerome Schneewind's authoritative study of the production and intellectual contexts of Sidgwick's major philosophical work, *The Methods of Ethics*; and Bart Schultz's substantial intellectual biography, which combines biographical, social, cultural, and intellectual perspectives on Sidgwick's career; A. Sidgwick and Sidgwick 1906; Schneewind 1977; Schultz 2004. Other useful secondary studies include Stefan Collini's entry on Sidgwick in the *ODNB*; F. M. Turner 1974: 38–67; Schultz 1992; Singer's introduction to H. Sidgwick 2000; Collini 2001; Ross Harrison 2001.

[123] The diary included entries made by Sidgwick between March and May 1860; it is held in Trinity College Library, Cambridge; Add.ms.d.68. Quoted in Schultz 2004: 40–1. I am grateful to Jonathan Smith, archivist at Trinity College, for confirming the dating of this diary entry.

[124] Paley 1785: bk I, ch. 7.

continue to think and write about the moral demands of self and of others through an application of his 'gloriously capable' intellect.

Looking back on this transitional period of his life, Sidgwick would pick out his commitments to science, reason, and impartiality as the most important factors in changing his outlook. He recalled that in the conversations with Cambridge friends that helped to form his mind in these years the one fixed element, in the midst of much theological disagreement between them about the merits of positivism and the 'Neochristianity' of *Essays and Reviews*, was 'the necessity and duty of examining the evidence for historical Christianity with strict scientific impartiality'. The aim was to 'weigh the *pros* and *cons* on all theological questions as a duly instructed rational being from another planet—or let us say from China—would naturally weigh them'.[125] Early in 1861 Sidgwick wrote to *The Times* (signing himself simply 'A Cambridge Graduate') to complain about the intemperate abuse of the authors of *Essays and Reviews* by conservative churchmen who disapproved of rational, historical, and scientific approaches to scripture and doctrine. The essayists, Sidgwick wrote, should not be condemned but reasoned with. They were not united by any sort of conspiracy against orthodoxy, as their critics alleged, but simply in their 'belief in the advantage of perfectly open discussion and perfectly impartial investigation.'[126] In October of that year, Sidgwick wrote in a private notebook, 'I wish to show forth in my own life the Supremacy of Reason.'[127]

But what did it mean to be supremely rational as a moral agent? Was it rational to prioritize one's duties to God, to others, or to self? What were the methods that Sidgwick's 'duly instructed rational being from another planet' should adopt in order to choose the right conduct in a given situation? These were the questions that would preoccupy Sidgwick both professionally and personally for the rest of his life, and which formed the foundations of his major work, *The Methods of Ethics*, which was first published in 1874, and regularly revised until the posthumous 6th edition of 1901.[128] At the heart of that work was the famous 'dualism of practical

---

[125] Benson 1899: 250; repr. in A. Sidgwick and Sidgwick 1906: 40.

[126] *The Times* (20 Feb. 1861), 12; repr. in A. Sidgwick and Sidgwick 1906: 64–5.

[127] Henry Sidgwick Papers, Trinity College Library, Cambridge; Add.ms.d.70, f.3.

[128] H. Sidgwick 1874. The 7th edn (1907), which was almost identical to the 6th, forms the basis of most modern edns, such as H. Sidgwick 1981. Sidgwick's Cambridge lectures on moral philosophy, as delivered in the 1880s and 1890s, were published posthumously as H. Sidgwick 1902. Other miscellaneous essays, reviews, and lectures on ethical subjects are included in H. Sidgwick 1898, 1904, 2000.

reason', which rested both on the apparent conflict between one's duties to self and to others and also on the related ambiguity of the idea of 'rational' action. Moral actions might be described as 'rational' either because they were self-interested or because they were disinterested. In the first sense, it seemed obvious that it must always be rational for an agent to act in their own interest. But Sidgwick's commitment to impartiality and objectivity also implied that the only truly rational approach was to see moral problems 'from the point of view of the universe' (or of someone from another planet, or from China). Taking this sort of disinterested approach to moral problems would tend towards a utilitarian ethics in which the good of the greatest number must take priority over any one individual's good.

In his mature works Sidgwick expressed this central problem in terms of the equal plausibility of 'rational egoism' on the one hand and 'utilitarianism' or 'universalistic hedonism' on the other as ethical methods; and in terms of the competing claims of 'self-love' and 'benevolence' as moral motives. He only occasionally used the terms 'altruism' or 'altruistic' and then normally within quotation marks and as non-technical terms.[129] In an account of his own intellectual development written towards the end of his life, for instance, Sidgwick wrote that for

> practical men who do not philosophise, the maxim of subordinating self-interest, as commonly conceived, to 'altruistic' impulses and sentiments which they feel to be higher and nobler is, I doubt not, a commendable maxim; but it is surely the business of Ethical Philosophy to find and make explicit the rational ground of such action.[130]

---

[129] Sidgwick used the language of altruism much more freely in his later undergraduate teaching, especially in his lectures on Herbert Spencer's *Data of Ethics* (1879), which are included in H. Sidgwick 1902; he also set his undergraduate students, including G. E. Moore, essays on 'Egoism and Altruism'; see Chs 5 and 8 below, respectively. In a review of J. Martineau 1885, Sidgwick distanced himself from the language of altruism by putting the term in quotation marks and expressed mild disapproval at the amount of Martineau's book taken up with attention to Comte as an ethical theorist; Henry Sidgwick, '*Types of Ethical Theory* by James Martineau', *Mind*, 10 (1885), 426–42, at 433.

[130] This account was appended to the preface to the posthumous 6th edn (1901) of the *Methods*; H. Sidgwick 1981: pp. xvi–xxiii, quotation at xviii. A further example of Sidgwick's use of quotation marks around 'altruistic' can be found in a section of the *Methods* which spells out Sidgwick's critique of Mill's utilitarianism, as developed in the same chapter of *Utilitarianism* that had helped persuade Sidgwick away from Comtism in 1861–2; H. Sidgwick 1874: bk 4, ch. 6, s. 3, pp. 462–6. Collini also notes Sidgwick's caution in using quotation marks around 'altruism'; Collini 1991: 61. By the final edns of the *Methods*, Sidgwick had relegated the critique of Mill just cited to a footnote and removed the quotation marks from 'altruistic', but still retained them in the earlier section noticed by Collini about the 'enlarged "altruism"' to which familial affections might eventually give rise; H. Sidgwick 1981: 439, 499n.

Sidgwick's distancing of himself from the language and ideology of altruism, and his implication that a simple devotion to altruism was appropriate only for 'practical men who do not philosophise', was a rebuke to his former self as well as to his philosophical adversaries. When, as a newly elected fellow of Trinity College, he first encountered the writings of Auguste Comte, Sidgwick had immediately adopted the language of altruism as an expression of his own innermost beliefs. In a 'Bird's eye view of myself' penned in his private notebook on 16 October 1861, Sidgwick wrote of his desire to pursue only those studies that could ultimately result in an increase in the general happiness of humanity. He continued: 'The strongest conviction I have is a belief in what Comte calls *altruisme*: The cardinal doctrine, it seems to me, of Jesus of Nazareth.' Then, as in his prayer the previous year, Sidgwick went on to probe his own motivations and wonder whether his own 'philanthropy' really had its roots in his 'selfishness'. 'Whether a Comtist or not', he concluded, 'I feel as if I never should swerve from my cardinal maxim, wh[ich] is also his: *L'amour pour principe, le progrès pour but.*'[131] It is easy to see how Comte's ethics of altruism would have appealed to Sidgwick, who was looking for a rational and scientific way to think about his duties to others, and who also maintained an affinity to the 'abandonment of self' taught by Jesus of Nazareth. In the following pages of his notebook he wrote that all pleasure ought to contain an altruistic element so that the 'habit of altruism' was not weakened, and wrote of himself as a 'philosophic Altruist'.[132]

Another philosopher, John Venn, when he met Sidgwick in 1862, formed the impression that 'at a still earlier age, he had been so far inclined towards dogma as to have adopted much of the Positive Philosophy' and that as far as he knew Sidgwick was 'the only man in Cambridge' to have studied Comte's writings at first hand at that time.[133] As Venn noted, however, by 1862 Sidgwick's brief positivist phase had passed. Even a month after describing belief in *altruisme* as his own strongest conviction, Sidgwick was having doubts about Comte, as a result of reading John Stuart Mill's warning (in *Utilitarianism*, which was initially published in instalments in *Fraser's Magazine*) about the dangerously anti-individualistic tendencies of

---

[131] The positivist motto means 'Love the principle, progress the goal'. Henry Sidgwick Papers, Trinity College Library, Cambridge; Add.ms.d.70, ff. 1–2. Parts of this note are also quoted in Schneewind 1977: 42; Collini 1991: 86; Schultz 2004: 42.

[132] Henry Sidgwick Papers, Trinity College Library, Cambridge; Add.ms.d.70, ff. 4–5.

[133] In fact Leslie Stephen at Trinity Hall and Thomas Clifford Allbutt at Gonville and Caius College had both also done so; *ODNB*; Maitland 1906: 73, 172. Venn's recollections are in A. Sidgwick and Sidgwick 1906: 134–7, quotation at 136.

the religion of humanity. In a short paper for a philosophical discussion group carried out by correspondence known as the 'Initial Society', Sidgwick wrote that Comte's 'theory of Absorption into Humanity seems to me to correspond to his practical error of subordinating the individual entirely to the species: swallowing up Egotism totally in Altruism—an error which J. S. Mill has lately (*Fraser*) violently repudiated'.[134] In January 1862, he was writing to a friend of his reduced sympathy with Comte's religion of humanity: 'I tried to fancy being a Positivist and adoring Gutenberg, the inventor of printing, but I found the conception impossible.' By March of that year he described himself to his friend Dakyns as 'taking long solitary constitutionals in order to unravel a violent reaction from Comteism which at present holds me'. The next month he explained that one of his main reservations about both Comte and most utilitarians was that they exalted self-sacrifice into 'the supreme Rule of Life' without recognizing the rational demands of self-interest; amongst utilitarians it was only Bain who saw the 'glorious paradox' involved. In May, with his views still in turmoil, Sidgwick wrote to J. J. Cowell that he had now converted back to the Christianity of F. D. Maurice and the 'Broad Church'. But in June he reported to Dakyns that this reconversion had already 'ended in smoke' and had really just been a 'violent reaction' back towards the spiritual after 'soaking myself in much Comte'.[135]

In these intellectually exhausting months following Sidgwick's brief, and largely private, experimentation with the identity of the 'philosophic Altruist' in the winter of 1861–2, it was his reading of Mill and his inability to accept the details of Comte's religion that were the main triggers for his decision not to become a positivist. He also still hungered after some sort of theism, although he found he could swallow Christian theology no more than the religion of humanity. In addition to these factors, there were two fundamental intellectual sticking points arising from Comte's views of knowledge and of ethics. Positivism was an entirely relativistic philosophy. Comte aspired to produce a 'subjective synthesis' of human knowledge. He wrote that the emancipation of philosophy would be achieved only by giving up aspirations to objective knowledge and rec-

[134] Initial Society Papers, in the Henry Sidgwick Papers, Trinity College Library, Cambridge; Add.ms.c.96/4(21). Mill's criticism of Comte, which came at the end of ch. 3 of *Utilitarianism*, was to be found in the Nov. number: *Fraser's Magazine*, 64 (1861), 525–34. On the Initial Society see Schultz 2004: 61–2.
[135] Henry Sidgwick to E. M. Young, 28 Jan. 1862; to H. G. Dakyns, Mar. 1862 and 7 Apr. 1862; to J. J. Cowell, 9 May 1862; and to H. G. Dakyns, 9 June 1862; in A. Sidgwick and Sidgwick 1906: 74–81.

ognizing that 'The only point of view from which the facts of nature can be regarded as a whole, is their relation to Humanity.'[136] Sidgwick still aspired to objectivity, to see things not from the point of view of humanity but from the point of view of the universe. Even more fundamental, though, was Comte's failure to recognize that both egoism and utilitarianism seemed to provide rational bases for ethics. Sidgwick's rejection of positivism, and his distancing of himself from Comtean 'altruism', signified his dissent from the statement put in the mouth of the priest in *The Catechism of Positive Religion* that the positivist motto 'Live for others' had succeeded in 'finally condensing, in one and the same formula, the law of duty and the law of happiness'.[137] Such a motto might serve as a maxim for the practical and the unphilosophical, but not for Henry Sidgwick.

Sidgwick continued to study the Bible as well as becoming increasingly consumed by the construction of his own moral philosophy during the 1860s. The most developed expression of his views on Christianity, which revealed the considerable extent of his own understanding of the latest literary and historical analyses of the gospels, was a long review of *Ecce Homo*, a work depicting the earthly life of Jesus as one of poetic humanism and passionate benevolence.[138] Sidgwick's review admired the author's description of Jesus's teaching as an attempt to inculcate in his disciples a universalised 'enthusiasm of humanity'. As he read through *Ecce Homo*, though, Sidgwick wrote, he felt often that 'if Jesus planted, Jean Jacques and Comte have watered'. If sometimes this Jesus sounded too much like a romantic or a positivist, at other times his teachings seemed 'too nearly akin to Benthamism'. Sidgwick thought that in *Ecce Homo* the egoistic and individualistic elements of Jesus's teachings had been neglected. Jesus had sometimes appealed to self-interest, by telling individuals that their virtuous conduct would have great rewards; and when he told the young man to sell all his goods and give them to the poor this injunction was 'surely given, not primarily for the sake of the poor, but for the sake of the young man himself: it was a test, not of philanthropy, but of faith'.[139] Having criticized

---

[136] Comte 1875–7: i. 477–9. The sentence quoted here was one of many which George Eliot copied into a black leather notebook from the English translation of the *Politique Positive*, which she studied in the 1870s while working on *Daniel Deronda*; George Eliot, Nuneaton Notebook, Warwickshire County Record Office, ff. 25–42, at 27. For more on Eliot and Comtism see Ch. 3 below.

[137] Comte 1891: 215.

[138] The work was written by the historian J. R. Seeley and published anonymously in 1865.

[139] Sidgwick's review initially appeared in the *Westminster Review* in 1866; repr. in H. Sidgwick 1904: 1–39, quotations at 18–20. Thirty years later Oscar Wilde made similar complaints about the attempt to reduce Jesus's teaching to mere philanthropy; see Ch. 8 below.

the Jesus of *Ecce Homo* for being too utilitarian, too positivist, and too philanthropic, Sidgwick wrote to Dakyns at the end of 1866 that he himself had now 'finally parted from Mill and Comte' and had resolved to be an 'eclectic'.[140]

When Sidgwick was invited to join the famous Metaphysical Society in London in 1869, he arrived among the intellectual elite of mid-Victorian Britain as neither a Christian, nor a philosophic altruist, nor even an orthodox utilitarian, but as a professional philosopher and a dispenser of objective truths. In 1873, the year before *The Methods of Ethics* was published, Sidgwick delivered a lucid and polished paper on 'Utilitarianism' to the Metaphysical Society in which, he said, he had been 'careful not to dogmatise upon any point where scientific certainty did not appear to be attainable'. Instead he offered what he hoped was a series of incontrovertible propositions about utilitarianism, which he defined as 'the ethical theory that the externally and objectively right conduct, under any circumstances, is such conduct as tends to produce the greatest possible happiness, to the greatest possible number of all whose interests are affected'. Utilitarianism proper was to be rigorously distinguished from any psychological theory about whether and to what extent human agents were generally motivated by self-interest. Another key distinction was that between the rational proof of utilitarianism (which derived from the universal extension to all individuals of the egoistic belief that one's own happiness was objectively good) and the practical sanctions of utilitarianism (which might or might not be sufficient to persuade the rational egoist to do what was right from an objective point of view). In short, Sidgwick presented himself to the Metaphysical Society in a series of arguments that identified him as an astute and critical commentator within the tradition of English utilitarianism.[141] But, with the Unitarian W. B. Carpenter, the Catholic archbishop of Westminster, Cardinal Manning, and Thomas Huxley, the fiercest scientific antagonist of positivism (he had memorably dismissed it as 'Catholicism *minus* Christianity') all in attendance, the terms 'altruism' and 'altruistic', and their associations with the Comtist coterie, did not pass Henry Sidgwick's lips.[142]

---

[140] A. Sidgwick and Sidgwick 1906: 158. For a condensed summary of Sidgwick's relationship with Comte and positivism in the 1860s and afterwards, see Wright 1986: 146–9.
[141] The paper was delivered on 16 Dec. 1873, and is repr. in H. Sidgwick 2000: 3–9, quotation at 3.
[142] For the attendance at Sidgwick's paper, see A. W. Brown 1947: 326. For Huxley's comments on positivism: Thomas H. Huxley, 'On the Physical Basis of Life', *Fortnightly Review*, 5 (1868), 129–45; repr. in T. H. Huxley 1893: 104–27, quotation at 121–2; also repr. in T. H. Huxley 1893–4: i. 130–65; Thomas H. Huxley, 'The Scientific Aspects of Positivism' in T. H. Huxley 1893: 128–50.

From Philip Terrace, Tottenham to the Grosvenor Hotel

Prior to 1870 there was possibly only one person in Britain, outside of organized positivist circles, who really made the language of altruism his own and started to use it in a sustained and creative way. That individual was the ear surgeon, social reformer, and idiosyncratic philosopher of religion and ethics, James Hinton. Unlike Bridges and Sidgwick who had both come from Anglican families and had been educated at Rugby and then Oxford or Cambridge, James Hinton came from a Nonconformist family and did not enjoy an establishment education. His father John Hinton was a Baptist minister (whom George Eliot had heard preach in her youth), and James himself was a religious young man who was educated at a Nonconformist school before training in medicine at St Bartholomew's hospital in London in the 1840s.[143] What Hinton shared with Bridges and Sidgwick, however, was an intense interest in religious and philosophical questions, an alienation from the Christian orthodoxy of his youth, and an interest in finding alternative ways to think about ethics using scientific and positivist ideas in general, and those of Auguste Comte in particular. Like Bridges, Hinton combined a commitment to altruism with a professional vocation in medicine and a life-long concern about the plight of the poor; and like Sidgwick, he philosophized about the relative moral demands of self and others, and was a founding member of the Metaphysical Society in 1869.

James Hinton's moral philosophy has not generally been remembered. He had neither the political profile, the success as a writer, nor the academic position that allowed others, such as Carlyle, Mill, Ruskin, Eliot, Spencer, Green, or Sidgwick to make an impact. He was primarily a medical practitioner (his patients included G. H. Lewes, whose temporary deafness he cured in 1873); he enjoyed only modest success as a published author.[144] Much the most significant reason for Hinton's failure to enter the canon of Victorian moral thinkers, however, was the sheer obscurity of his writings. He published three books during his lifetime. *Man and his Dwelling Place* (1859) dealt with the relations between science and religion. *Life in Nature* (1861) argued for a distinctive natural philosophy which saw

---

[143] The main sources on Hinton's life are the *ODNB* entry by Neil Weir and Hopkins 1878. See also Perril 1997: 327–31; Koven 2004: 14–18. On Eliot's encounter with John Hinton, and her and Lewes's impressions of him as a philosopher similar to Herbert Spencer, see Eliot's letter to Sara Hennell, 6 Aug. 1860, in Haight 1954–78: iii. 328–30.

[144] On Hinton's treatment of Lewes see George Eliot's letter to Mrs William Cross, 17 Sept. 1873, in Haight 1954–78: v. 436.

life as at once vitalistic and mechanistic. His third book, *The Mystery of Pain* (1866), was a work in which he published some of his speculations on the necessity of pain in moral life, and of its identity with goodness, when properly understood. The large bulk of his writings, however, remained in manuscript form. Between 1870 and 1874 he had these manuscripts privately printed in four substantial volumes.[145] These contained reams of disconnected, stream-of-consciousness, sometimes quite incoherent philosophical speculations about metaphysics, epistemology and ethics. It took the labours of his widow Margaret, his sister-in-law Caroline Haddon, the social purity campaigner Ellice Hopkins, and Hinton's later philosophical admirers, Shadworth Hodgson, Havelock Ellis, and Edith Lees Ellis to collect together and try to form some shape out of this mass of material, and to communicate to a wider audience Hinton's teachings on religion, ethics, and altruism.[146]

Another reason that has been suggested for Hinton's posthumous obscurity was the gradual revelation after his death of the unconventional views he had held about sex and marriage. He considered monogamy a restrictive and selfish institution, and was allegedly an advocate and practitioner of some kind of free love.[147] In his study of the Victorian philanthropic practice of 'slumming', in which bourgeois men and women explored the slums for what he suggests was a mixture of erotic and altruistic reasons, Seth Koven takes James Hinton as his 'philosophical point of departure'. Koven is certainly right to identify Hinton as a philosopher who, as we shall see, espoused his own vision of altruism—a vision which saw moral life as a series of pleasures and pains, and which had both sensual and religious overtones. Koven also speculates about the extent to which the scandal surrounding Hinton's sexual views and practices, and those of his son Howard in the 1880s, posthumously erased the memory of his 'good deeds and philosophy, leaving behind few visible traces of his once formidable influence on contemporaries' understanding of the dynamics of eros and altruism'.[148]

There certainly seems to have been an erotic aspect to Hinton's philanthropy and philosophy, although, perhaps unsurprisingly, it is rarely mentioned in his substantial philosophical writings. One hint at this side of

---

[145] Hinton 1870–4.

[146] Ibid.; Hopkins 1878, 1879, 1881, 1884; Haddon 1886; Ellis 1918. The explanation of Hinton's philosophy that I have found most illuminating is Havelock Ellis, 'Hinton's Later Thought', *Mind*, 9 (1884), 384–405.

[147] See *ODNB*; Havelock Ellis, 'Hinton's Later Thought', *Mind*, 9 (1884), 384–405, at 397.

[148] Koven 2004: 14–18, quotation at 17.

Hinton's enterprise came in an 1870 journal entry, quoted by Koven, in which Hinton wrote that he yearned to live amongst the lowest classes of the poor of Whitechapel 'as a man longs for his wedding-day'.[149] It should be noted, however, that the schemes that Hinton envisaged implementing in his future altruistic life amongst the poor (which he never realized) were conventional paternalistic and philanthropic ones: giving the lower classes access to books, the visual arts, and education, and replacing their gin-shops with establishments providing 'wholesome drinks'.[150] Whatever the exact nature of his views about sex, they did not deter his biographer and disciple Ellice Hopkins from continuing to claim Hinton proudly as the inspiration for her own campaigns for social purity and against the moral and physical contamination of men and women by the institution of prostitution in the 1880s and 1890s.[151] On Hopkins's account at least, Hinton's primary concern about sex was how to prevent it being a source of degradation to women. She recalled how he 'used to wander about Haymarket and Piccadilly at night, and break his heart over the sights he saw and the tales he heard'.[152] A vivid recollection by a friend of Hinton's perhaps best encapsulates this side of his philosophy and his philanthropy. 'Late one evening,' the friend recalled, 'James Hinton took me for a walk in the Strand. He led me into the Alhambra; we were very soon surrounded by women of loose character.' Hinton apparently took no notice of these women but 'began quietly talking about unconscious sacrifice'. Soon the women started to gather around him, as did the policemen who were there to keep order, and 'all were spellbound while he sweetly discoursed on Christ's hatred of sin and pity for the sinner', ending his address by saying that if Christ were on earth he would be there amongst the sinners. Leaving the scene, Hinton 'wiped tears from his eyes'.[153]

This prophet of altruism encountered Comte's new moral language with enthusiasm in the 1850s. He must have first come across 'altruism' either in the original French publications or more likely in Lewes's writings of the early 1850s, since his first uses of the term were in manuscript notes made, according to Hinton's recollections, in 1856. His private manuscripts and letters were peppered with uses of 'altruism' and 'altruistic' and

[149] Hopkins 1878: 290, quoted in Koven 2004: 16. Hinton had spent a short period as a teenager working at a woollen-draper's shop in Whitechapel, and this early contact with the London poor inspired much of his later moral and political thinking; Hopkins 1878: 7–11.
[150] Hopkins 1878: 290.
[151] Hopkins 1909: 4–5. On Hopkins's own religious and moral campaigns, see Morgan 2000.
[152] Hopkins 1909: 5.
[153] Hopkins 1878: 296.

even with his own variants such as 'altruisticness'—a quality he attributed to God.[154] Hinton's interest in positivism and altruism was at its peak at the same time that Bridges was lecturing on altruism in Bradford and Sidgwick was experimenting with the term in his private notebooks. In September 1862 Hinton wrote to a friend, 'My obligations are absolute to the Positive school. I am, indeed, the most advanced Positivist I know.' Although Hinton does not seem ever to have attended any positivist meetings or religious services in London, he was certainly associated with positivism by some, even decades later.[155] A positivist novel, *The New Continent* (1890), written under the pseudonym of 'Mrs Worthey' included a young character called Rose who, in the 1860s, initially inspired by Tennyson and F. D. Maurice, visited hospitals, asylums and the slums of the East End, determined to live a life of some usefulness. Rose was a young woman on her way towards conversion to positivism, and had studied 'all Mr Hinton's books' with great interest. Her companion Ernest agreed with her that 'Hinton's is a grand mind'. Rose replied: 'Yes; sacrifice is his root-idea. Nature's force is grand, wide, deep. We limit that force in our puny personal bodies and become selfish.'[156]

'Sacrifice' and 'service' were terms that featured more in Hinton's published works than 'altruism' and 'altruistic', which were confined to his correspondence and unpublished manuscripts. His adoption of the new terminology occurred during a short period when he had temporarily given up medical practice to devote himself entirely to philosophical writing. This decision had inevitably involved a drastic reduction in his income, and necessitated a move from his comfortable premises in central London to a tiny house in Philip Terrace, Tottenham, where his new neighbours included a commercial traveller and haberdasher, a mariner's wife, a governess, a missionary working for the London Missionary Society, and a family of shoemakers.[157] He tried to reconcile his wife to their new arrangements with moral philosophy. 'You must take into view the want and distress of the other portion of the world', he told her. 'A beautiful

[154] Hinton 1870–4: iii. 467.

[155] His name does not feature in the lists of those who attended services held with Richard Congreve's papers in the British Library, Add.ms.43844; nor does it feature in the list of members of the London Positivist Society held in the London School of Economics library, LPS 1/1.

[156] Worthey 1890: i. 130–8, quotations at 138. The conclusion of the novel was Rose's loss of her Christian faith and her decision to commit herself completely to Comte's Religion of Humanity. 'Mrs Worthey' was the pen-name of Fanny Byse, the wife of a Swiss pastor; Wright 1986: 229.

[157] 1861 census return; Public Record Office, R.G.9/795, f. 11, 16–18; accessed through the website of the UK national archives (see Bibliography for details).

house is not beautiful if other people are starving.' Their domestic staff was reduced to a single servant, and Mrs Hinton was thus often to be found in the kitchen, where her husband would interrupt and, on Ellice Hopkins' account, 'keep up such a distracting blaze of metaphysics and physics, epicycles and parabolas, noumena and phenomena, as threatened to make the light pudding or pastry at dinner-time one of the heaviest problems to solve', causing 'much transcendental confusion' amongst Mrs Hinton's culinary preparations.[158] Among the blaze of distracting jargon in the kitchen at Philip Terrace almost certainly would have been the novel Comtean language of altruism. By way of explanation to a correspondent of this period, Hinton wrote, 'The word "altruistic" I borrow from Comte. Is it not a capital word? I am resolved to naturalise it. We want it. It is the antithesis to "self"; self-being = deadness; altruistic being = life; and so on.'[159] He had come to his view of the centrality of sacrifice and altruism 'from the scientific side' rather than the spiritual, Hinton maintained. Havelock Ellis later wrote that Hinton's greatest distinction was to have been 'the first man of ethical genius who has been deeply and consciously impressed with the methods of science'.[160]

Hinton offered, in his correspondence, a very mundane example of his altruistic philosophy in action—his own decision to get off the omnibus several stops before he was home, in order to allow the driver and conductor to finish work early. As he walked along the road, he reflected, he was 'distinctly glad, not only that the men could go home to their families the sooner, but that it was my walking (and wearing out my shoes) that enabled them'. The true moral 'bigness' of a man's life, he thought, was '*measured by his pains*'.[161] Hinton's 'altruistic' philosophy encompassed much more than an opposition to selfish monogamy and a desire to let bus drivers go home early, however.[162] His extensive private writings, written, as Caroline Haddon recorded, at any moment in the day when he had a thought, wherever he might be, 'in the street, in society, at a concert, in church', suggest the activities of a feverishly eclectic mind. He used 'altruistic' to describe not just philanthropy, nor just the benevolent instincts so named by Comte, but the connectedness and relatedness of all natural phenomena, and the

---

[158] Hopkins 1878: 165–6.
[159] Ibid. 194.
[160] Havelock Ellis, 'Hinton's Later Thought', *Mind*, 9 (1884), 384–405., at 396.
[161] Hopkins 1878: 171–2.
[162] One concise summary of some of Hinton's thinking on altruism, as interpreted by Caroline Haddon is 'Utilitarianism and Altruism: A Discussion', in Haddon 1886: 24–36. See also Hopkins 1878: 258–85; Hinton 1881: 245–88.

possession of 'a consciousness co-extensive with humanity'.[163] He even saw the basic causal relationship in nature as illustrating altruistic self-sacrifice, since an apparently isolated individual cause was destroyed when it merged into its effects.[164] Although he sometimes called himself a positivist, in reality Hinton's philosophy was more Platonist or idealist. He had departed from Christian orthodoxy, but he believed that reality was fundamentally spiritual, and that there was a transcendent life to come after one's earthly existence, in which the connectedness of the illusory worldly 'self' to an even greater divine other might become apparent.

Hinton's influence, like his philosophy, was diffusive and hard to pin down. He clearly passed on his philosophy of altruism to the circle of close associates mentioned above who became exponents of his work. He was also perhaps one of the influences on the artist and critic John T. Nettleship who adopted the language of altruism and egoism in his *Essays on Robert Browning's Poetry* (1868). Nettleship described Browning's Sordello as developing from a 'great egoist' to a 'great altruist', a man who found that sorrow and suffering were the 'portals to altruism'; his altruism consisted in 'taking upon himself the stern practical task of an endeavour to make poor men happy'.[165] Nettleship married Hinton's daughter Ada in 1876, and might also have come into contact with the language of altruism through his brother Edward, who was a member of the London Positivist Society headed by Richard Congreve, and who cooperated with John Bridges's schemes for improved treatment of ophthalmia in the East End in the early 1870s.[166] Nettleship's vision of sorrow and suffering as the 'portals to altruism' had a Hintonian rather than a positivist ring to it, but it is impossible to be sure about the direction of influence. Among theorists and practitioners of social reform, Hinton also had an influence on Jane Hume Clapperton, who cited his work approvingly, Arnold Toynbee, who was the son of Hinton's close friend Joseph Toynbee, and Henrietta Barnett, who attended a school run by Caroline Haddon and her sister and who, with her husband Samuel Barnett founded the famous Toynbee Hall, a

---

[163] Hopkins 1878: 173.

[164] Havelock Ellis, 'Hinton's Later Thought', 389.

[165] Nettleship 1868: 167, 191, 223.

[166] Edward Nettleship, surgeon, is listed as one of the members of the society in the record book for the branch headed by Bridges and Harrison after their separation from Congreve; held at the London School of Economics library, LPS 1/1. On his work with Bridges, see Liveing 1926: 199–201.

university settlement in the East End named in memory of Arnold Toynbee.[167] Hinton's ethics were also well known to Mary Everest Boole, who acted as his secretary for the last two years of his life, and who recalled that in those later years Hinton 'lived to experience bitter self-condemnation for having led young people into the path of *continuous* altruism'.[168]

Undoubtedly the pinnacle of Hinton's recognition as a thinker in his own lifetime came in the invitation to become a founding member of the Metaphysical Society in 1869. Alfred Tennyson, who, along with the editor of the *Contemporary Review*, James Knowles, was one of those involved in the initial conception and construction of the society, had read and admired some of Hinton's writings.[169] He shared with Hinton the view that science and religion could be reconciled through a recognition that the reality underlying all phenomena was ultimately spiritual, and could be described as either God or Nature. Tennyson also agreed with Hinton's idea that some of reality seems dark or dead because of the distorting influence of the self and the individual mind. The vision of nature expressed in the poem which Tennyson composed to be read out on the occasion of the first meeting of the Metaphysical Society would have pleased Hinton. The poem was entitled 'The Higher Pantheism' and included the lines:

> Speak to Him, thou, for He hears, and Spirit with Spirit can meet—
> Closer is He than breathing, and nearer than hands and feet.[170]

A fellow member of the society, the editor of the *Spectator*, R. H. Hutton, later wrote a reminiscence in the form of an imaginary typical meeting. Those attending met at the Grosvenor Hotel, where they dined, before waiters removed the tablecloth and crockery to replace them with sheets of foolscap paper and pens. Hutton recalled that each member of the group had his own 'type of spiritual and moral expression'. 'Then came Mr Hinton, glancing around the room with a modest half-humorous

---

[167] See *ODNB* and Koven 2004: 16–17. On Toynbee Hall and other university settlements of the 1880s and 1890s, see Ch. 6 below.

[168] Boole included this reflection on Hinton's changing attitudes in a short essay on 'Altruism' in 1888 for *Light*, a journal devoted to psychical science, reprinted in Boole 1931: i. 389–90, at 390. Havelock Ellis suggested a similar shift in his later attitudes. The word 'altruism' had characterized his earlier thought, Ellis wrote, and he 'never entirely abandoned the altruistic phraseology' although his emphasis changed from self-sacrifice to pragmatism and empirical study of social and moral 'facts'; Havelock Ellis, 'Hinton's Later Thought', 396–7.

[169] Hopkins 1878: 256. On Hinton's contributions to the Metaphysical Society see A. W. Brown 1947: esp. 123–5 (although I find Brown's view that Hinton would certainly have aired his views on polygamy and free love in this context implausible).

[170] Quoted in A. W. Brown 1947: 42–3.

furtiveness, as he seated himself amongst us'; the suggestion seemed to be
that the eccentric Hinton could sit 'amongst us' but that he was still an out-
sider. 'The wistful and sanguine, I had almost said hectic idealism, of James
Hinton struck me much more than anything he contrived to convey by his
remarks,' Hutton wrote.[171]

The society's discussions were often about epistemology and metaphysics rather than ethics. The nature and justification of belief and the reality of immortality were both central concerns. Ethics was also a frequent
topic of conversation nonetheless. In Hutton's reconstruction of a typical
meeting of the society, he described the Roman Catholic clergyman Father
Dalgairns as discoursing eloquently 'on the noble ethical character of
George Eliot's novels, and the penetrating disbelief in all but human excel-
lence by which they are pervaded'.[172] These meetings of the 1870s provided
a nexus within which 'altruism' could reach a new and exceedingly well
connected group of thinkers and writers. Metaphysical Society meetings
were attended not only by Henry Sidgwick and James Hinton, but also by
others who had written or would later write about 'altruism', namely
Frederic Harrison, James Martineau, and Leslie Stephen. Two others
attending the meetings, Hutton and J. B. Mozley, would play important
roles in transmitting the language of altruism through their resistance both
to the neologism and the ideas with which it was associated.[173] Although
not all the papers, and virtually none of the discussions, have been recorded,
there can be little doubt that Hinton and Harrison, if not Sidgwick,
Martineau, and Stephen, would have introduced the language of altruism
into the proceedings.

The Metaphysical Society had provided the setting for another famous
Victorian neologism, 'agnosticism'. Huxley later recalled that he had felt
like a 'fox without a tail' at a preliminary meeting of the society because,
unlike most of the others present, he did not have his own '-ism'. It was
partly Huxley's desire to dissociate himself from positivism, along with
older 'isms' such as atheism and materialism, that led him to coin the term

---

[171] R. H. Hutton, 'The Metaphysical Society: A Reminiscence', *Nineteenth Century*, 18 (1885),
177–96; quoted in A. W. Brown 1947: 62. Much of Hutton's article is used by Brown in his own
reconstruction of a typical meeting of the society: A. W. Brown 1947: 60–70. Hutton's article is
available online in the 'Victorian Commentary' section of the 'Huxley File' hosted by Clark
University (see Bibliography for details). See also L. Huxley 1903: i. 451–63.
[172] Quoted in A. W. Brown 1947: 61.
[173] On Mozley, see Ch. 3; on Hutton's discussions of 'altruism' in his contributions to the *Spectator*,
see Ch. 4. For a full list of the 62 members of the society who attended its meetings between 1869
and 1880, see A. W. Brown 1947: 307–12.

'agnosticism' to describe his own particular kind of scepticism.[174] And one of the published records of the activities of the Metaphysical Society reveal that 'altruism' existed alongside 'agnosticism' not only in the first fascicle of the *OED* in 1884 but also in the language of the intellectuals who met on Tuesday evenings in the Grosvenor Hotel during the 1870s. The context for the discussion of 'altruism' was a debate about 'The Soul and Future Life' published by James Knowles in his successful new periodical, *The Nineteenth Century*, as the second 'Modern Symposium' in a series of three.[175] Here the leading religious and philosophical minds of the day confronted the question of whether, in the absence of belief in a future life, people could be expected to behave morally. This was to be one of the most persistent questions asked about the new scientific and humanistic commitment to 'altruism': why would anyone who did not believe in God, nor in divine rewards and punishments, live for others rather than for their own pleasure during the short span of earthly life within which they found themselves?

---

[174] See Lightman 1987: 10–13, 188n.; Desmond 1998: 372–5; White 2003: 130–4. For Lightman's more recent reappraisal of the rhetoric and propaganda surrounding the story of Huxley's coining of the term, see Lightman 2002.

[175] Knowles did for the Metaphysical Society, through the *Contemporary Review* and the *Nineteenth Century*, what Chapman had been able to do for his 'Comtist coterie' through the *Westminster Review*, and what Lewes and then John Morley had done for radical thinkers through the *Fortnightly Review* from 1865 onwards. On Knowles as an influential editor, see A. W. Brown 1947: 167–95. On Morley and the *Fortnightly Review*, see Everett 1939; A. W. Brown 1947: 224–30.

Chapter Three

Death and Immortality

For none of us liveth to himself, and no man dieth to himself. For whether we live, we live unto the Lord; and whether we die, we die unto the Lord: whether we live therefore, or die, we are the Lord's. For to this end Christ both died, and rose, and revived, that he might be Lord both of the dead and the living.

St Paul's letter to the Romans, 14: 7–9

'Yet another ism!'

As the *Saturday Review* noted in 1868, 'Christians and Positivists are agreed in acknowledging the higher virtues of self-sacrifice.'[1] They were far from agreed, however, about what language to use to describe those virtues, what reasons one might have for practising them, whether their ultimate basis was physiological or divine, and what future goods they would bring, whether for the individual or for society, whether earthly or heavenly. 'Altruism' in the 1870s was strongly associated with the denial not only of the existence of God but also of the immortality of the soul. It was the watchword of an atheistic and humanistic ethics which claimed that a truly moral person should give up the Christian hope for personal, conscious immortality on the grounds that it was egotistical and selfish. The most celebrated novelist of the day, George Eliot, was perceived by many contemporary critics as a prophet of 'altruism' because of her association with the alternative self-denying positivist ideal of 'subjective immortality'. Christian preachers, meanwhile, commented on, contested, and sometimes collaborated in the spread of the language of 'altruism'. During the three decades after its coining, the religious meaning of 'altruism' evolved from its Comtist origins to become, for some, synonymous with the teachings of Jesus Christ. A sermon on 'Christian Altruism' was even preached in the

[1] *The Saturday Review of Politics, Literature, Science, and Art* (25 Apr. 1868), 541.

presence of Queen Victoria. In all of these developments, to disagree about the meaning of 'altruism' was to disagree about the meaning of life—and about the meaning of death. The responses to death that were experimented with ranged from Christian hope, to stoic resignation, to psychical research, to life insurance.

The arrival of 'altruism' seemed to many to be a linguistic marker of the creeping displacement of Christianity from British moral life. Worries about the secularization of language and belief existed alongside long-established anxieties about the vitality and influence of the churches. The religious census undertaken in Britain on Sunday 30 March 1851 had found, to the consternation of many, that only about half of the population of England and Wales attended church services that Sunday (split equally between Church of England and Nonconformist services, and with generally lower attendances in large cities than in the country). This was interpreted by some as an indication of the prevalence of 'secularism'—a term coined by George Holyoake in 1851 to describe his more moderate form of religious unbelief and its associated campaigns for religious freedom and the separation of church and state. In his report on the religious census, Horace Mann speculated that the millions of working men and women who did not attend church or chapel were 'unconscious secularists'.[2] A study of church attendance in London in 1902–3 found that the proportion attending religious services in the metropolis was now only about one in five.[3] Halfway in time between these two statistical studies, the Anglican clergyman Charles Maurice Davies undertook his own personal, journalistic survey of the religious life of London, which offered a much more colourful, qualitative analysis of phases of spiritual life in the capital.

Davies's accounts of his experiences attending services at a range of Christian, secularist, positivist, freethinking, ethical, and spiritualist institutions were published as newspaper articles in the *Daily Telegraph* and the *Manchester Evening News*, and collected in a series of books from 1873 to 1875, entitled *Orthodox London, Unorthodox London, Heterodox London*, and

---

[2] Royle 1974: 205, 233; see also Secord 2000: 299–335, which approaches the histories of Victorian secularism and respectable unbelief through an examination of both religious and scientific tracts, pamphlets, and books read by working men and women in the 1840s, with a particular focus on *The Vestiges of the Natural History of Creation* (1844) and its identity as a 'dangerous' book.

[3] On the 1851 religious census, see Mann 1854; on the survey undertaken in London for *The Daily News* in 1902–3 see Mudie-Smith 1904: esp. 15–18. These statistics are all open to considerable debate and alternative interpretations. C. G. Brown 2000: 18–30, 145–9 discusses both the 1851 and the 1902–3 statistics, and the reasons for the perpetuation of the 'myth of the unholy city'. See also Gill 2003, and Snell and Ell 2000: esp. 395–420, which tests historical generalizations about urbanization and secularization against a detailed analysis of the 1851 data.

Mystical London.[4] He attended services conducted by Christian denomina-
tions including Unitarians, Presbyterians, Plymouth Brethren, Seventh-Day
Baptists, Roman Catholics, Moravians, and Sandemanians. At the Little
Portland Street Chapel near Oxford Circus, Davies heard James Martineau
preach to his well-to-do Unitarian congregation on the similarity between
the idea of the pre-existence of Christ in the fourth gospel and Plato's
doctrine of *anamnesis* — the soul's memory of itself. Davies noted that
Martineau had recently set up a 'Free Christian Union'. Other founding
members of this short-lived organization included Henry Sidgwick, still
engaged in an attempt to reconcile Christian belief with science and
ethics, John Seeley, author of *Ecce Homo*, and the Oxford moral philosopher
T. H. Green. The organization aimed to unite people in a religious enterprise based on 'filial Piety and brotherly Charity, with or without more
particular agreement in matters of doctrinal theology'.[5]

Moving from the merely 'unorthodox' to the outright 'heterodox',
Davies ventured into the chapels, temples, and halls of secularists, panthe-
ists, atheists, and positivists.[6] Richard Congreve's positivist lecture room in
Chapel Street was adorned with positivist images and mottoes, including
'Live for others', and 'Love for our principle; Order as our basis; Progress
for our object', engraved in bright green letters on a white marble tablet.[7]
There Davies listened to a poorly attended morning lecture by Congreve,
and an evening talk by John Bridges. The latter, which discussed the life and
works of William Shakespeare as part of a series of lectures on the great
men in Comte's calendar of saints, was much better attended. The audience
included many members of trade unions, some '*bona fide* working men' and
'a good many who looked like working women too: many who might have
been decent domestic servants spending their "Sunday out" in that most
unlikely of all places'. Davies recalled that when he had delivered a sermon
on positivism himself a few years earlier, he had 'found the congregation

---

[4] C. M. Davies 1873*b*, 1873*a*, 1874, 1875. Ritchie 1870 was a similar survey produced for the same
religious publisher, Tinsley Brothers, a few years earlier.
[5] Quoted in C. M. Davies 1873*b*: 38. On the Free Christian Union, see J. Martineau 1869; extracts
from which are included in Parsons 1988: iii. 163–9. See also Ritchie 1870: ch. 15. In the Henry
Sidgwick Papers in Trinity College Library, Cambridge, there are papers and correspondence
relating to the founding of this organization and some of its proposed activities and publications;
see Add.ms.c.97/3, Add.ms.c.93/124(3), Add.ms.c.94/18, Add.ms.c.94/117; on Sidgwick's
involvement see also Schultz 2004: 99, 143–4.
[6] On the history of varieties of secularism and free thought in Britain, see W. S. Smith 1967; Royle
1974; S. Budd 1977; Royle 1980; Lightman 1987; Berman 1990.
[7] Wright 1986: 79–86.

greatly interested in the subject'.[8] In 1875, the hero of Davies's novel *Broad Church* was a young clergyman who attended Chapel Street and picked up positivist ideas to work into his latitudinarian sermons.[9]

Davies's survey of 'phases of free thought in the metropolis' in the 1870s revealed that organized positivism and its gospel of altruism jostled for attention alongside a whole range of other movements also seeking moral and political progress independently of the institutions, beliefs, and language of Christianity. Of vegetarianism, Davies wrote that if 'heterodoxy' were taken in its etymological sense of thinking differently from most people then 'there can be no question as to the title of this particular "ism" to stand on my voluminous list of religious and social heresies'.[10] ' "What!" I fancy I hear my readers exclaim, "yet another ism!", Davies wrote apologetically at the start of another of his dispatches from the front of the Victorian struggle against orthodoxy—a report on a lecture on 'humanitarianism'. The unusual teachings of the particular humanitarian lecturer whom Davies heard addressing an almost deserted hall one Sunday morning in Islington included the transmigration of souls and the future universality of the English language.[11]

The majority of the heterodox movements that Davies documented had small memberships and, with some exceptions, tended to attract relatively educated and prosperous individuals who shared with their orthodox neighbours a well developed sense of duty. The working-class masses, whether unconscious secularists or unconscious Christians, were, from the point of view of the orthodox or the heterodox middle classes, in need of material help, cultural education, and religious enlightenment (whatever that might entail). In short, they were potential targets for the activities of the hundreds of philanthropic organizations that were sustained by the donations and the voluntary labour of Christians and secularists alike in Victorian Britain. Charles Dickens's son (also called Charles) produced *A Dictionary of London* in 1879 which listed, amongst many other things, the 'principal Philanthropic Societies, with their objects and terms of subscription'. His list, which excluded those who had not replied to his request for information, included about fifty organizations, ranging from the Aborigines Protection Society, to the Decorative Needlework Society, the Female Mission to the Fallen, the London Anti-Vivisection Society, and

[8] C. M. Davies 1874: ii. 242–63, quotations at 246, 252.
[9] Wright 1986: 229.
[10] C. M. Davies 1874: ii. 282.
[11] Ibid. 55–86, quotation at 55.

the Universal Beneficent Society, whose activities included granting pensions to the aged and infirm, providing homes for destitute children, and 'granting loan without interest to persons of respectability in need of temporary assistance'. The insistence that the recipients of philanthropy should be of good character was, of course, a standard condition. The Mendicity Society, for example, which had branches nationwide, described its dual object tersely as: 'The apprehension of impostors and vagrants, and relief of the deserving poor'.[12]

Institutional, intellectual, and linguistic changes occurred together. To adopt a particular 'ism' could be simultaneously to belong to a sect, to adopt a creed, to take on a moral identity, to strive to change certain aspects of society, and to use special names and categories to communicate one's beliefs, identity, and aspirations. Thus the proliferation of moralism and heterodoxy recorded by Charles Davies and Charles Dickens in their surveys of religious and philanthropic institutions in the 1870s also left its mark on the English language. Alexander Bain's *Companion to the Higher English Grammar* (1874) provides one record of the moral and political language of the 1870s. Bain compared the 'two vocabularies' that comprised modern English, namely the Saxon and the classical. Saxon terms were generally to be preferred on account of being 'more generally understood and more homely in their associations'. The classical vocabulary was more recondite but more elevated in its associations. Bain illustrated the distinction by comparing moral terms from the two stocks of words. Saxon terms for bad qualities were 'evil', 'low', 'selfish', 'worldly', 'one-sided'; those for good qualities included 'great', 'right', 'worthy', 'fair', 'righteous', 'forgiving', 'lovely', 'noble'. Turning to the classical vocabulary, 'bad' words included 'vice', 'improbity', 'degenerate', 'delinquent', 'egotist'; good terms were 'incorruptible', 'meritorious', 'impartial', 'devoted', 'sympathising', '(self)-sacrifice', 'altruism'. In another section, illustrating the construction of words using various suffixes, Bain explained that the Greek suffix '-ism' was 'freely used in new compounds to express state, condition, or action, or a system of principles or doctrines, or adherence to these'. His list of illustrations included many that had resonances with the time and place that he was writing, including 'workingmanism', 'Fenianism', 'Irishism', 'papism', 'secularism', 'pessimism', and 'altruism'.[13]

---

[12] Dickens 1879; consulted through the online *Dictionary of Victorian London* (see Bibliography for details). The Hastings librarian E. H. Marshall, and Henry Sidgwick in Cambridge, both supported the work of their local Mendicity Society; see Ch. 1, above.
[13] Bain 1874: 208–10, 264.

'There is no burning everlasting hell'

Apologists for the Christian establishment in mid-Victorian Britain, seeking to maintain the intellectual plausibility of their faith, as well as the political influence and cultural authority of the church, were confronted with challenges from all sides. They had to justify the hierarchical and monarchical structure of society to republicans, secularists, and socialists; to defend their belief in God and a spiritual world to scientific agnostics and positivists; and to explain to sceptical historians and linguists why the Bible should still be revered as the word of God above any other ancient text. In the midst of the political and intellectual challenges to orthodoxy mounted by the varieties of unbelief, Christians had traditionally been able to take refuge in their moral superiority, if nothing else. The unbeliever's philosophy could be characterized by the biblical phrase 'Let us eat and drink; for to-morrow we die'.[14] The infidel was a decadent, self-indulgent, sensual creature whose casting off of religious belief was undoubtedly motivated by the desire to live a life of indulged appetites and ungoverned passions free from the fear of divine judgement. The invention of 'altruism' was one sign that this superiority of the believer over the unbeliever in the sphere of morals could no longer be taken for granted. Sensual atheists and libertines were being replaced by respectable unbelievers and secular saints. The unbelief of the 1870s, W. H. Mallock complained, was 'associated no longer with any dissolute wit, with any cruel and brilliant cynicism, or with the fascination of lawless love'. On the contrary, it had become 'eminently respectable' and 'somewhat dull'; it was 'the atheism of the vigil, not of the orgy'.[15]

There was an existing tradition of moralistic unbelief. The most widely read anti-Christian work of the first half of the nineteenth century in Britain was Thomas Paine's *Age of Reason* (1794–1807). In his even more widely read radical political work, *The Rights of Man* (1791–2), Paine had announced 'my country is the world, and my religion is to do good'.[16] In *The Age of Reason* he elaborated much further on his religious views. Written in Paris at the height of the Terror, shortly before Paine himself was arrested on suspicion of plotting against Robespierre, *The Age of Reason* combined a full-blooded assault on Christianity and clericalism with a defence of a deistic faith, which he believed necessary for the maintenance

---

[14] 1 Cor. 15: 32; similar phrases occur at Eccles. 8: 15, Isa. 22: 13, and Luke 12: 19–20.
[15] W. H. Mallock, 'Is Life Worth Living?', *Nineteenth Century*, 2 (1877), 251–73, at 255.
[16] Paine 2000: 222.

of true religion and morality: 'I believe in one God, and no more; and I hope for happiness beyond this life. I believe in the equality of man, and I believe that religious duties consist in doing justice, loving mercy, and endeavoring to make our fellow-creatures happy.' All 'national institutions of churches—whether Jewish, Christian, or Turkish' were condemned as 'human inventions set up to terrify and enslave mankind and monopolize power and profit'.[17] A large part of Paine's attack on Christianity consisted in claiming it to be not only morally inferior to his own deism, but an actively immoral religion. Paine's *Age of Reason* set a pattern that was followed by much later nineteenth-century free thought, combining admiration for the moral teachings of Jesus of Nazareth with disdain for the Bible and contempt for 'priestcraft' and the adulterous connections between church and state. The Bible, Paine wrote, was full of 'voluptuous debaucheries' and 'unrelenting vindictiveness'. It was 'a history of wickedness that has served to corrupt and brutalize mankind; and, for my own part, I sincerely detest it, as I detest everything that is cruel'.[18] Jesus Christ, on the other hand, had 'called men to the practice of moral virtues, and the belief of one God'. The great trait in the character of Jesus, Paine thought, was 'philanthropy', and his moral teachings had parallels with those of Confucius, of some Greek philosophers, and of the Quakers.[19]

Despite Paine's vague hope for 'happiness beyond this life', his anti-Christian polemic was perceived as a direct threat to the faith and the morals of the people since it did away with the threat of eternal punishment. The belief in future rewards and punishments had for centuries been seen as one of the cornerstones of Christian morality. Many British children had this belief reinforced by reading the *Divine and Moral Songs for Children* composed by the Congregationalist divine Isaac Watts. These poems, published in their earliest form in 1715, were reproduced in numerous editions throughout the eighteenth and nineteenth centuries (a hundred editions had been produced by 1850), and were widely anthologized and used in schools.[20] The song about heaven and hell offered a clear and simple message:

---

[17] Paine 2000: 267–8.
[18] Ibid. 278.
[19] Ibid. 271, 282; Paine himself came from a Quaker family.
[20] See *ODNB*; Michael 1987: 167–9. On Watts's works of moral philosophy concerning the passions and affections of the soul, see Dixon 2003: 72–81.

There is beyond the sky
　A heaven of joy and love;
And holy children, when they die,
　Go to that world above.

There is a dreadful hell,
　And everlasting pains:
There sinners must with devils dwell
　In darkness, fire, and chains.

Can such a wretch as I
　Escape this cursed end?
And may I hope, whene'er I die,
　I shall to heaven ascend?

Then will I read and pray,
　While I have life and breath,
Lest I should be cut off today,
　And sent t' eternal death.[21]

Ideas such as these were also held to be an important support for British criminal justice. In 1797, when Thomas Williams, a London bookseller, was successfully prosecuted for blasphemy for selling a copy of Paine's *Age of Reason*, the judge passed comment on exactly this question. Justice Ashhurst said that the spread of Paine's anti-Christian works would have the effect of destroying civil obligations, undermining the solemnity of oaths, and depriving the law 'of one of its principal sanctions—the dread of future punishments'.[22] Inspired by Paine, and with increasing confidence and regularity from the 1840s onwards, deists and freethinkers engaged in a concerted effort to undermine this standard view that taking away the belief in rewards and punishments in a future life would lead to moral anarchy.

One of the landmarks in this tradition of religious writing was the publication of the series of letters exchanged by Harriet Martineau and her friend, the mesmerist Henry G. Atkinson. This text used philosophy, phrenology, physiology, mesmerism, and the latest transmutationist natural history to undermine conventional Anglican theology of the kind associated with William Paley. The resulting *Letters on the Laws of Man's Nature and Development* (1851) was a classic and representative example of the attempt to moralize unbelief. Atkinson wrote: 'He who does not suppose a personal God, or look for a future, may, nevertheless, be most unselfish and deeply

---

[21] Watts 1866: 47–8; accessed online through the Christian Classics Ethereal Library (see Bibliography for details). I am grateful to Jane Platt for drawing my attention to this verse.
[22] Nash 1999: 77–8.

religious.' Atkinson elevated the intellectual act of doubt itself, contrasting his heroic truth-seeker with those 'thousands upon thousands who have no clear knowledge on any one question relating to their religion, and yet are most proud in declaring themselves Christian, although it be not certain that they possess any one Christian self-denying virtue'.[23] Harriet Martineau agreed about the moral inferiority of Christianity. 'What an insult it is to our best moral faculties', she wrote, 'to hold over us the promises and threats of heaven and hell, as if there were nothing in us higher than selfish hope and fear!'[24] The *Westminster Review*, shortly before it was taken over by John Chapman and his Comtist coterie, contained a very unsympathetic review of the *Letters*. 'Strange and wonderful is the power of self-delusion!' the reviewer wrote.

> Here we have two clever, well-informed people, persuading themselves that they experience extraordinary raptures mingled with the most exquisite philosophic calm, from believing that unconscious matter is the cause of conscious thought, that the truest human affection is nothing worthier than the love of a spoonful of nitric acid for a copper halfpenny, and that annihilation is the most satisfactory end of human life.

Both the intellect and the heart will recoil from such views, the reviewer concluded, 'with well-founded disgust'.[25]

But other Victorians found that it was the Christian doctrine of eternal damnation rather than materialistic unbelief that filled them with disgust.[26] Harriet Martineau's acquaintance, Charles Darwin, whose own encounters with death had included that of his unbelieving father in 1848, and of his young daughter Annie in 1851, later wrote, in his autobiography, that he considered the doctrine of eternal damnation for unbelievers a 'damnable' one and that he could not see how anyone would wish it to be true.[27] Austin Holyoake, the younger brother of George Holyoake and the author

---

[23] Atkinson and Martineau 1851: 229.

[24] Ibid. 247.

[25] Anon., '*Letters on the Laws of Man's Nature and Development* by Henry George Atkinson and Harriet Martineau', *Westminster Review*, 31 (1851), 83–92.

[26] Major studies of 19th-century attitudes to death, immortality, heaven, and hell are Rowell 1974; Hilton 1988: esp. 270–6; and Wheeler 1990, of which Wheeler 1994 is an abridgement. F. D. Maurice and F. W. Farrar were both influential in transforming mid-Victorian Anglican teaching on the afterlife, partly in response to the critiques of moralistic unbelievers. They taught that warnings about pain and torment in hell were metaphors for alienation from God rather than literal threats of terrifying physical punishments. Two edited collections which reveal how debates about the impact of science on Christian doctrines of immortality and resurrection were carried on in the later 20th century are Penelhum 1973; W. S. Brown *et al.* 1998.

[27] C. Darwin 1958: 87.

of a secularist burial service, had been brought up in a Calvinistic Methodist household, and shared Darwin's disgust. He wrote that the doctrine of an eternal hell seemed to him 'too monstrous for the belief of any humane man or sensitive woman'. He recalled: 'From my earliest childhood I remember being taught to dread the wrath of an avenging God, and to avoid the torments of a brimstone hell. I said prayers twice a day, I went to a Sunday-school where I learnt nothing but religious dogma, and . . . I may sincerely say that up to the age of fourteen I was never free from the haunting fear of the devil.' Holyoake wrote these words on his deathbed many years later. At the same time, he reaffirmed his disbelief in an afterlife and echoed Atkinson and Martineau, saying that he regarded all forms of Christianity 'as founded in selfishness' by offering the reward of eternal bliss in return for professions of faith.[28]

Comte and his followers took the same approach. When Erskine Perry visited Comte in Paris in 1853, Comte explained that he admired the unity of belief and purpose that the Catholic Church had provided in the Middle Ages, but that unfortunately 'the spirit of Christianity is completely egotistical, requiring the sacrifice of everything, even to giving up father and mother, to save a man's own soul, whereas duty, reason, the progress of intellect, incontrovertibly prove that altruism, or the living for others, is the only worthy object of life'.[29] Frederic Harrison (see Fig. 9) delivered his own version of this teaching in a paper to the Metaphysical Society in January 1877 on 'The Soul and Future Life'. He argued that the belief that the 'soul' was an immaterial entity that could survive death went against the teachings of the Bible, as well as against modern science. The term should be used only to refer to those higher 'religious emotions' which man experienced as an organic and bodily being. He regretted the 'suicidal course' taken by Christianity of 'trying to cast out the devil of selfishness by a direct appeal to the personal self' and recommended instead the positivist idea of 'subjective immortality'. For the positivist, the selfish hope for personal immortality was to be replaced as both a consolation and a moral motive by the hope to contribute to the social progress and future happiness of the human race on earth, and to live on in the influence exerted on the higher life of others. 'And the difference between our faith and that of the orthodox is this', Harrison explained to Thomas Huxley, John Tyndall, Cardinal Manning, and others: 'we look to the permanence of the activities which

[28] G. J. Holyoake, 'Thoughts in the Sick Room', written as he approached death from consumption in 1874, quoted in C. M. Davies 1874: ii. 400–3.
[29] Erskine Perry, 'A Morning with Auguste Comte', *Nineteenth Century*, 2 (1877), 621–31, at 628.

Figure 9. Frederic Harrison—'an Apostle of Positivism'—in the *Vanity Fair* 'Men of the Day' series, 25 January 1886.

give others happiness; they look to the permanence of the consciousness which can enjoy happiness. Which is the nobler?'[30]

The title poem in the 1881 collection of the freethinking Mathilde Blind, *The Prophecy of St Oran, and Other Poems*, placed distinctly positivist sentiments on the subject of death and immortality in the mouth of St Oran: 'Poor fools! wild dreamers! No, there is no God / Yon heaven is deaf and dumb to prayer and praise'. Turning to the 'Deluded priests', Oran described their idea of future bliss as 'a sick brain's phantasy'. To his fellow 'sinners' he said:

> To you who hardly dare to live for fright;
> There is no burning everlasting hell
> Where souls shall be tormented day and night:
> The fever ye call life ends with your breath;
> All weary souls set in the night of death.
> Then let your life on earth be life indeed!
> Nor drop the substance, snatching at a shade!
> Ye can have Eden here! ye bear the seed . . .

Blind's St Oran taught, like Frederic Harrison, that thoughts of heaven and hell should be replaced with thoughts of happiness on earth; 'For if within, around, beneath, above / There is a living God, that God is Love.' The poem was described by the *Athenaeum* as a poetic rendition of Harrison's 'dream of universal altruism as the agent which would, one day, turn evil into good, pain into pleasure, death into life', and considered it 'the first attempt to express in poetic form the doctrines of the English Positivists'.[31] Several years earlier, however, someone else had made just such an attempt.

'O may I join the choir invisible'

The first journal article to include 'altruism' in its title, and one of the most energetic and imaginative attacks on the new humanistic ideology it represented, was published in *Fraser's Magazine* in 1879. Its title was 'The Failure of Altruism'. Although the authorship of this article is not certain, it bears strong similarities to a discussion of Comte, altruism, and George

---

[30] Harrison's paper was delivered on 9 Jan. 1877, and was subsequently published in two parts in the *Nineteenth Century*, 1 (1877), 623–36, 832–42, quotations at 838, 840; on the attendance of the paper and its publication by Knowles as the basis of a 'Modern Symposium', see A. W. Brown 1947: 190–1, 332.

[31] Blind 1881: 1–65, quotations at 60–4; *The Athenaeum: Journal of English and Foreign Literature, Science, the Fine Arts, Music and the Drama* (30 July 1881), 136–7.

Eliot in a work of literary criticism and philosophy by the poet Thomas Sinclair published the previous year as *The Mount: Speech from its English Heights* (1878).[32] Some readers of the *Fraser's* article were no doubt surprised to learn of the failure of something of which they had never even heard. However, this exhilarating piece of commentary, in a mere ten pages, forcefully explained the weaknesses of the new 'Positivism of science and Altruism of religion' in the context of the most pressing intellectual and cultural concerns of the day, from Darwinism and positivism, to the relationship between intellect and emotion in Tyndall's famous 'Belfast Address', to Catholic–Protestant relations, and the writings of both George Eliot and Charles Dickens.

The central argument was that the new gospel of altruism and the associated religion of humanity were bound to fail because they appealed to only half of human nature. The Christian commandment to love one's neighbour as oneself implied a dual duty to love oneself as well as others. In a rather stretched application of the story of Icarus, the article continued:

> The altruists, like the cunningest acrobats, now profess to fly the whole human race, on one wing to each individual, in the airy regions of the spiritual life. It is to be feared, perhaps hoped, that the scientific Daedalus will have as little satisfaction out of his youth, Altruism, as the old Greek had of his Icarus, whose waxen back and wings the sun melted inexorably, so that he got down among the dead things.

The article identified George Eliot, a woman 'trained at the scientific school every moment that could be spared', as 'certainly the most popular apostle of the one-winged ideal'. 'The dogma is not hers', the author noted, but was first put forward by 'the too mathematical—in other word, mad—Frenchman, Comte, who struck out the sublime idea that,—blessed be man, man was wholly sufficient unto himself'. But by neglecting self-love, the love of God, and the hope of immortality, the article concluded, Eliot and her gospel of altruism could not hope to inspire virtue and self-sacrifice. Could people, whether philosophers or not, really be persuaded to 'live beautiful lives on the prospect of being fossils, or even spiritual winds of the material future'?

Not much indication was given in 'The Failure of Altruism' of which aspects of Eliot's writings were thought to be representative of Comte's doctrine of altruism, but the article referred to Eliot as the author of *The*

---

[32] Anon., 'The Failure of Altruism', *Fraser's Magazine,* 20 (1879), 494–503; Sinclair 1878.

Mill on the Floss, and also drew a contrast between Comte and Eliot, which made reference to *Daniel Deronda*, published three years earlier:

> Comte himself had decided for woman as the ideal of his religion; the English missionary of most effect, 'George Eliot', chooses man, the pre-Christian Jewish man whose Canaan is entirely of this earth, as the crown of altruistic aspirations. It is a religion of gallantries, of communistic exchanges of the higher affections, sweet to the initiated; but hopelessly obscure and weak in attractive power to all else.[33]

A few years later, in 1884, a tract treating Eliot as a 'Moralist and Thinker' suggested that her novels were underpinned by 'the Positivist conception of Humanity as a collective unity, a *grand être* in which are gathered up the noble deeds, past, present, and to come, to which our race owes its well-being and progress, and in which we find the truest object of our love and reverence'.[34] Another critic, in an article for the *London Quarterly Review* on 'George Eliot and Comtism', had spelt out the apparent congruence between Eliot's novels and the positivist philosophy in a little more detail. The three main features of Eliot's writings picked out as positivist were her characters' general neglect of Christian belief and practice, their over-whelming sense of duty to the human race but not to God, and their lack of any sense of eternity and the immortality of the soul.

The *London Quarterly* reviewer was not alone, however, in finding the clearest expression of Eliot's subscription to the Comtist doctrine of altruism not in her novels but in one particular poem.[35] The poem in question he considered an expression of 'her teaching concentrated and at its highest'. It was described by W. H. Mallock, also in 1877, as the 'whole gospel of atheistic ethics, as it is now preached to us, presented in an impassioned epitome'.[36] One of Eliot's first biographers, the American Unitarian George W. Cooke, described the same poem, in 1883, as having 'made altruism attractive and lovely'.[37] In the same year, Frances Power Cobbe referred to it as an illustration of the 'high altruistic sentiments and hopes of certain

---

[33] Anon., 'Failure of Altruism', quotations at 495, 497, 499, 500.
[34] Anon. 1884b: 7–8. This pamphlet sought to articulate Eliot's 'philosophy of life', often using both Comtean and Spencerian formulations about the conflict between egoistic and altruistic desires and the future hope for a subordination of the former to the latter, or for some kind of identity between the two.
[35] [Frank T. Marzials], 'George Eliot and Comtism', *London Quarterly Review*, 47 (1877), 446–71, at 468.
[36] W. H. Mallock, 'Is Life Worth Living?', *Nineteenth Century*, 2 (1877), 251–73, at 262.
[37] Cooke 1883: 320; see also his comments on Eliot, Comte and altruism at 155–8.

illustrious Agnostics'.[38] The pamphlet on Eliot as 'Moralist and Thinker' published the following year interpreted the poem as teaching that, in 'the highest phases of evolution', which humanity was now entering, 'the altruistic tendencies are dominant' and would drive out the fear of death which was a product of 'unrestrained egoism'.[39] Another critic described the poem as the 'summit of altruism, the classic expression of the sublime morality of a being in renunciation of conscious future existence'.[40] 'Above all,' yet another wrote, this was a work of Eliot's which truly revealed 'the altruism which she believed in and preached' and expressed 'the unselfishness, the real devotion of her nature'.[41] A six-hundred-page survey of *The Systems of Ethics Founded on the Theory of Evolution* (1893), by the American philosophical writer Cora M. Williams, culminated by recommending the unselfish and noble philosophy expressed in the same work by Eliot, whom Williams described as one of 'the great pioneers of Scientific Doubt and pure Humanitarianism'.[42]

The ode in question was composed by Eliot in the summer of 1867 while in Dresden with Lewes. Earlier in the year, this time in Biarritz, Eliot had written to her friend Maria Congreve (the wife of the positivist leader Richard Congreve) that she and Lewes were reading Comte's *Politique Positive* together after breakfast each day—an activity which left her with a 'moral glow' for the rest of the day. A few months later, she and Lewes attended the opening lectures delivered by Congreve to mark the founding of the Positivist Society in London.[43] That summer she composed the poem with these famous opening lines:

> O may I join the choir invisible
> Of those immortal dead who live again
> In minds made better by their presence: live
> In pulses stirr'd to generosity,
> In deeds of daring rectitude, in scorn
> For miserable aims that end with self,
> In thoughts sublime that pierce the night like stars,
> And with their mild persistence urge man's search
> To vaster issues.

[38] Frances Power Cobbe, 'Agnostic Morality', *Contemporary Review* (1883), repr. in *Littell's Living Age,* 158 (1883), 175–82, at 182.
[39] Anon. 1884b: 24.
[40] Gordon 1893: 10.
[41] Crawshaw 1907: 375.
[42] C. M. Williams 1893: 581.
[43] Haight 1954–78: iv. 324, 332–4, 360, 363.

That the piece was of significance to Eliot herself was suggested by her decision to include it as the closing poem in her collection *The Legend of Jubal, and Other Poems* (1874).[44] The central idea was similar to that expressed by the famous closing lines of *Middlemarch* (1871–2), in which the narrator reflected on the impact of Dorothea on the world: 'the effect of her being on those around her was incalculably diffusive: for the growing good of the world is partly dependent on unhistoric acts; and that things are not so ill with you and me as they might have been, is half owing to the number who lived faithfully a hidden life, and rest in unvisited tombs'.[45]

'O may I join the choir invisible' became, as Martha Vogeler has put it, 'a touchstone of humanist piety in the Victorian age'.[46] It was rapidly adopted for use in the positivist liturgy by Richard Congreve, and was quoted approvingly by Frederic Harrison in his paper on 'The Soul and Future Life' delivered to the Metaphysical Society and published in the *Nineteenth Century*.[47] After the positivist schism, which saw Harrison, Bridges, and Beesly separate from Congreve, their former teacher, the new school of positivism at Newton Hall also made use of the ode. A service for the 'Festival of All the Dead' took place on the last day of 1883 in Newton Hall, where positivist mottoes, including 'Live for others', adorned the walls (see Fig. 10). The service included a performance of a setting of Eliot's poem arranged as a cantata by the composer Henry Holmes for the occasion. Harrison told the congregation that Eliot had sympathized with the positivist movement and that this poem 'expressed the inmost belief of her great brain'.[48]

And it was not just positivists who were attracted to this humanistic ode. At the Co-operative Congress in Ipswich in 1889, the Cambridge economist Alfred Marshall ended his address by praising the pioneering co-operators of a previous generation who had, through their selfless labours, given the working classes opportunities for education and improvement. Adapting the closing lines of Eliot's poem, Marshall concluded:

---

[44] On the dating and publication of the poems see Haight 1954–78: vi. 37–9.

[45] Eliot 1871–2: 'Finale'.

[46] Vogeler 1982: 79. Beer 2000: 171–2, notes that Eliot had planned, in the 1850s, to write a book on *The Idea of a Future Life*, exploring the question of immortality. Bevir 2002 discusses the ideological background to Sidney Webb's socialism, including his identification with 'O may I join the choir invisible'; on Beatrice Webb, see Ch. 6, below.

[47] Haight 1954–78: ix. 194; Wright 1986: 84; Frederic Harrison, 'The Soul and Future Life', *Nineteenth Century*, 1 (1877), 623–36, 832–42, at 840. For more on positivist adoption of the poem as a hymn, see Vogeler 1982: 77–8.

[48] *The Times* (1 Jan. 1884), 7.

Figure 10. Newton Hall, the Positivist meeting hall in central London where George Eliot's 'O may I join the choir invisible' was performed as a cantata on 31 December 1883 at the 'Festival of all the Dead'. Reproduced by permission of the Library of the LSE; London Positivist Society Papers 5/4, f. 17.

> And in diffusion ever more intense,
> So shall they join the choir invisible
> Whose music is the gladness of the world.

This peroration was greeted with 'prolonged cheers' from the four hundred or so delegates in the hall.[49] One of those delegates was the secularist George J. Holyoake, at whose memorial service, fifteen years later, a musical setting of the poem would be used as an anthem.[50] Several different musical versions of the work were used as hymns by Unitarians and by London ethical societies in the late nineteenth and early twentieth centuries, perhaps attracted, Vogeler suggests, by the poem's 'earnest, creedless altruism'.[51] The poem was also read at Eliot's own funeral in 1880 and its second and third lines were inscribed on her gravestone at Highgate Cemetery.[52] When John Chapman died in 1894, he was buried in the same cemetery, close to Eliot's grave. The *Westminster Review* wrote of the man who had been its editor for over forty years: 'No more eloquent tribute can be paid to the memory of Dr John Chapman than to think of him as one of the "Choir invisible / Of those immortal dead who live again / In minds made better by their presence".'[53]

But were the critics right to see in this humanistic ode or, indeed, in Eliot's novels, a manifesto for altruism? This question, and the connected one of the exact extent and nature of the influence of Comte on Eliot's works, has been discussed in great detail by Eliot scholars.[54] The additional suggestions that I have to make here arise simply from observations about Eliot's own encounters with the language of altruism, both as an avidly engaged reader of Comte and Lewes, and as a writer who nonetheless almost completely avoided using that language herself. My conclusion will be that, while some of Eliot's readers, whether admirers or critics, saw her as the leading 'apostle of the one-winged ideal' of altruism, as the *Fraser's* article put it, that was not how she saw herself.

---

[49] *The Times* (11 June 1889), 4. The original version of the poem had 'shall *I* join' rather than 'shall *they* join'.

[50] *The Times* (29 Jan. 1906), 4.

[51] Vogeler 1982: 78.

[52] Ibid. 65. The two lines inscribed on Eliot's grave were: 'Of those immortal dead who live again / In minds made better by their presence'.

[53] Quoted in Haight 1969: 118.

[54] The most useful surveys are Vogeler 1980; Wright 1981, 1984, 1986: 173–201. Several specific Eliot characters have been identified by critics as possible positivists. Sally Shuttleworth considers that 'Savonarola preaches the positivist doctrine of altruism outlined by Comte'; Shuttleworth 1984: 101–3, 222n. Wright also suggests that Savonarola paralleled the teachings of the priest in

Eliot first encountered the language of altruism in Lewes's *Westminster Review* article in 1852 and in his *Comte's Philosophy of the Sciences* (1853), the proofs of which she read, and a copy of which Lewes presented to her on its publication.[55] Eliot read and admired the *Catéchisme Positiviste* (1852) in the original French and the passages she marked in her copy included some concerning the positivist cultivation of *altruisme*.[56] During the 1860s, Eliot studied the *Politique Positive*, and came back to it again when working on *Daniel Deronda* in the middle of the 1870s. It was at this time that she copied various passages from the *Politique* into her notebooks, including the table illustrating Comte's cerebral theory (see Fig. 8 above). In fact she copied that table into two different notebooks around this time (see Fig. 11 for one of these copies).[57] In the final years of her life she engaged with theoretical accounts of egoism and altruism again through her editorial work producing the last two volumes of Lewes's *Problems of Life and Mind* (1879), after his death, and in her reading of her friend Herbert Spencer's *Data of Ethics* (1879). Few people can have taken such an interest as George Eliot in both religious and scientific writings about altruism from the 1850s to the 1870s. However, it was not a term that she herself embraced in her own writings, nor one that she used to describe her work or her own moral aspirations in her private correspondence.

As far as I have been able to ascertain, Eliot used the term 'altruism' only twice in her own writings. Each of these occurred during or shortly after a period when Lewes had been working on theories of altruism and egoism. In 1856, a few years after Lewes had introduced the term to the English-speaking world, Eliot included a barbed reference to altruism in an essay for the *Westminster Review*. Her target was Dickens and his unrealistic and sentimentalized accounts of the moral dignity of the working classes. His 'preternaturally virtuous poor children and artisans' and his 'melodramatic boatmen

---

the *Catechism* (Wright 1986: 185) and (ibid. 187) describes Felix Holt's political and moral teachings as 'undiluted Positivism'. Dr Lydgate in *Middlemarch* is another candidate: Wright 1986: 188–9; Haight 1954–78: iv. 171–2n. Deresiewicz 1998 finds points of contrast between Eliot's presentation of Lydgate and the organicism of social thinkers including Comte and Spencer. Beer 2000: 169–95, primarily focuses on the influence on Eliot of Darwinian ideas about descent and time, but also includes reflections on her reading of Comte while working on *Daniel Deronda*.
[55] Haight 1954–78: ii. 162n.; 1968: 135–6; for details of Lewes's uses, see Ch. 2 above.
[56] Haight 1954–78: i, p. xlii; Shuttleworth 1984: 101–3, 222n.
[57] Eliot's notes on the *Politique* from which the image in Fig. 10 is taken, are in the Pforzheimer notebook, MS 707, ff. 73–101, at 87; held in the Carl H Pforzheimer Collection of Shelley and his Circle, New York Public Library. The other notebook into which Eliot copied notes from the *Politique* and a version of this table is George Eliot, Nuneaton Notebook, Warwickshire County Record Office, ff. 25–42, at 34. See also Baker 1976–85; Wright 1986: 192.

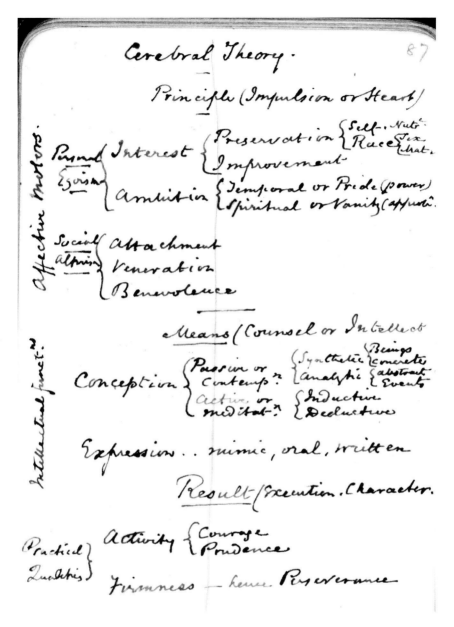

Figure 11. One of two copies made by George Eliot in the 1870s of the table illustrating Comte's cerebral theory, dividing the 'affective motors' into 'personal egoism' and 'social altruism'. Pforzheimer notebook, MS 707, f. 87; held in the Carl H. Pforzheimer Collection of Shelley and his Circle, New York Public Library; reproduced by permission of the Astor, Lenox, and Tilden Foundation.

and courtezans' were in danger, Eliot wrote, of 'encouraging the miserable fallacy that high morality and refined sentiment can grow out of harsh social relations, ignorance, and want; or that the working-classes are in a condition to enter at once into a millennial state of *altruism*, wherein everyone is caring for everyone else, and no one for himself'.[58] The italics might have been intended to convey an emphatic sarcasm, the unfamiliarity of the word, or both. Eliot's only other use of the term came in her last work, *Impressions of Theophrastus Such* (1879), written at the same time that Lewes and she were both working on the final volumes of his *Problems of Life and Mind*. Having recounted a fable about a badger who was stung by bees, and a bear who tried to console him by telling him how sweet the honey of the bees tasted, the narrator continued: 'The badger replied, peevishly, "The stings are in my flesh, and the sweetness is on your muzzle." The bear, it is said, was surprised at the badger's want of altruism.'[59] Again, the tone was playful and in this case perhaps gently mocking of the anthropomorphism of Lewes's and Spencer's discoveries of morality in the animal world, and of their scientific jargon.

A final occasion on which Eliot herself had occasion to use the language of altruism was not in her own work but during the editing and revision of *Problems of Life and Mind* after Lewes's death. One of the sections of Lewes's text which Eliot modified prior to publication was his discussion of the origin of the moral sense. Here she adopted his terminology in discussing the struggle between 'discerned duty, or the altruistic estimate of consequences' and the 'strong promptings of egoistic desire'. In the same section, however, Eliot introduced a warning about 'how short a way the consideration of animal life alone will take us in the appreciation of the moral life of mankind, which is wrought out of innumerable closely interwoven threads of feeling and knowing'.[60] In another section, on 'The Affective States', both Lewes's and Eliot's versions drew a contrast not between egoistic and altruistic instincts, but between egoistic desires and 'sympathy', which, unlike 'altruism', was a key term in Eliot's novels.[61] Eliot here also seems to have altered the emphasis of Lewes's version. Lewes had drawn a distinction between the egoistic desires, which had their roots in the nutritive instincts, and the sympathetic, which arose from the repro-

---

[58] [George Eliot], 'The Natural History of German Life', *Westminster Review*, 66 (1856), 51–79, at 55.

[59] Eliot 1994: ch. 8, p. 69.

[60] Quoted in K. K. Collins 1978: 486.

[61] See Graver 1984: 263–73; C. Jones 2001.

ductive instincts. Eliot revised this section to make it what was, in fact, a more Comtean account, in which both selfish and sympathetic emotions had their original roots in forms of egoism, whether nutritive or reproductive. As Eliot summarized the matter, 'Appetite is the ancestor of tyranny, but it is also the ancestor of love.'[62]

What George Eliot herself believed she had taken most to heart from her reading of Comte was not his celebration of 'altruism' but his recommendation of a combination of resignation and action. Reflecting on life at the start of her thirty-fifth year in 1853, Eliot wrote to her friend Sara Hennell: 'I begin this year more happily than I have done most years of my life. "Notre vraie destinée," says Comte, "se compose de *resignation* et *d'activité*"—and I seem more disposed to both than I have ever been before. Let us hope that we shall both get stronger by the year's activity—calmer by its resignation.' In a letter to the positivist physician Thomas Clifford Allbutt in 1868, Eliot wrote that all the 'devices which men have used under the name of consoling truths, to get rid of this need for *absolute* resignation, are in my deep conviction false and enfeebling'. She went on to note that her current view was that 'a human lot in which there is much direct personal enjoyment must at present be very rare'. Six years later Mary Ponsonby wrote to Eliot, seeking advice on how to keep a sense of moral meaning when one's faith in Christianity, heaven, and hell had gone. The two keynotes of Eliot's response were sympathy and resignation: pity for the suffering of others would remain even if one believed there was nothing beyond this human life; and in the face of the pains and limitations of one's own life, the answer was to be found in 'that stoical resignation which is often a hidden heroism'. These were the bases on which one's own ignorance and selfishness should be resisted.[63]

Why, then, did Eliot not embrace the language of altruism herself? There are several possible answers to this, some of which I have already indicated, such as her desire to distance herself from Lewes's and Spencer's

---

[62] Quoted in K. K. Collins 1978: 491–2; Patrick Geddes, like Lewes and unlike Comte, made a similar suggestion that egoism had its roots in the nutritive instincts, and altruism in the reproductive; see Ch. 7 below.

[63] To Sara Hennell, 25 Nov. 1853; to Clifford Allbutt, 30 Dec. 1868; to Mary Ponsonby, 10 Dec. 1874; Haight 1954–78: ii. 127, iv. 499, vi. 97–100. The section of this letter on stoical resignation and the avoidance of selfishness was headed 'The Need of Altruism' by Eliot's husband John Cross in his edn of her life and letters; Eliot 1885: iii. 248. On Eliot's repeated quotation of the Comtean saying about resignation and action, see Wright 1986: 21, 183.

versions of evolutionary ethics.[64] Another possible answer is suggested by
Carole Jones's distinction between the notion that Eliot promoted sympathy as a moral ideal and the slightly different idea that she was an advocate
of 'altruism'. George W. Cooke had described *Daniel Deronda* in 1883 as a
book that gave the world 'the gospel of altruism, a new preaching of love
to man'.[65] Jones argues, however, that while Eliot condemned selfishness,
she did not necessarily celebrate altruism. For Jones, *Daniel Deronda*, far
from preaching 'the gospel of altruism', constituted 'a damning critique of
altruism' in that Deronda's admirable sympathy was portrayed as developing into a more misguided and extreme selflessness. On this view, it was
Deronda's empathy as opposed to his altruism that was admirable.[66] It
would be consistent with this interpretation to take Eliot's comment that,
despite her admiration for Comte, she found his philosophy 'one-sided' as
an indication that she thought his demands for altruism excessive.[67]

Another interesting study has read Eliot's novels as examples not of the
celebration of 'altruism' but of the playing out and comparison of the consequences of 'lower egoism' and 'higher egoism', analogous with St
Augustine's distinction between different kinds of self-love.[68] 'Higher egoism' pursues self-fulfilment outside the self; for Augustine this higher self-
love was the love of God; for Eliot it was the love of others. Kathleen Blake
similarly suggests that Eliot saw the attempt to connect with others as a way
to fulfil self, not to renounce it.[69] The quest for personal fulfilment through
sympathy, combined with an attitude of 'stoical resignation', captures Eliot's
moral vision better than the idea that she was a prophet of 'altruism'. Eliot

[64] Wright 1986: 191–4 explores possible reflections of Comte's cerebral theory and his related
teachings about egoism and altruism in Eliot's novels. Wright also suggests that the novels can be
understood as 'an attempt to improve her readers by exercising their altruistic instincts' (199). See
also Wright 1981, which looks for signs of Comte's cerebral theory of the egoistic and altruistic
instincts in Eliot's novels. Further relevant critical works which discuss Eliot's representations of
egoism and altruism; the place of the individual in the social organism; and her relationship with
theorists including Comte and Spencer, are Graver 1984; Shuttleworth 1984; Paxton 1991;
Semmel 1994.

[65] Cooke 1883: 284.

[66] See Carole Jones's introduction to Eliot 2003: pp. v–xxxv, quotations at ix, xx; for an extended
analysis of these same questions, see C. Jones 2001.

[67] The comment was in a letter to Sara Hennell, 12 July 1861; Haight 1954–78: iii. 439.

[68] Granlund 1994: 1–28, at 5.

[69] Blake 1976: 297–8. Levine 2002: 171–99 analyses *Daniel Deronda* in a way which is also compatible with this interpretation: 'One may not live adequately with a self-asserting self; but one
cannot live at all without it. *Daniel Deronda* explores the possibility of selflessness derived from
the energies of egoism. Egoistically annihilating egoism, the heroic figure might at last gain access
to a world that is not self, learn from and do justice to that "other" who lies just beyond the walls
of ego' (177).

described 'sympathy' as 'the one poor word which includes all our best insight and our best love'.[70] The stoical character of Eliot's moral philosophy was also indicated by her choice of epigraph for 'O may I join the choir invisible'. The Latin epigraph came from a letter from Cicero to his friend Atticus, in which he reflected on his wish to commemorate the death of his daughter so that she might be remembered by future generations: 'I am more concerned about the long ages, when I shall not be here, than about my short day, which short though it is, seems all too long to me.'[71]

'Eyes turned to that eternal shore'

The many forms of intellectual, religious, and political heterodoxy created in Victorian Britain had a dual relationship with Christianity—one which combined antagonism with mimicry. Unbelievers condemned the selfishness of Christianity at the same time as setting up alternative moralistic religions and sects. Believers proclaimed the moral inferiority of humanistic imitations of Christianity, defended the role of self-love in the moral life, and yet simultaneously went to great lengths to establish that faithful Christians were the least selfish and egotistical of people—that they were every bit as altruistic as the new generation of selfless unbelievers. It suited unbelievers to position themselves as outsiders and pioneers and to define their moral superiority by contrast with the failings of an orthodox establishment. Equally, the intellectual errors, moral pitfalls, and eternal punishments that might be associated with the latest form of unbelief made quite a racy subject for a sermon. Any new movement, consequently, which seemed to pose a threat to Victorian Christianity could rely on the preachers and theologians of the established and dissenting churches for plenty of free publicity. Positivism and altruism were both spread in this way.[72] Leslie Stephen wrote in 1869 that, in recent years, positivism had 'become one of the standard terms of theological denunciation'. Comte had 'been refuted so often by so many ardent young clergymen', Stephen wrote, that it was surprising his doctrines were not now more generally believed.[73]

---

[70] Haight 1954–78: iv. 119; Graver 1984: 263.
[71] Cicero 1961: iii. 35.
[72] On the communication of positivist ideas into British and American culture by the agency of clergymen and theologians, see Cashdollar 1989.
[73] [Leslie Stephen], 'The Comtist Utopia', *Fraser's Magazine,* 80 (1869), 1–21, at 1.

The emergence of a generation of puritanically moralistic unbelievers posed a new challenge for the defenders of the faith. The persistence of apparently irregular marital arrangements even among such morally refined unbelievers as Comte, Mill, and Eliot, as well as the more robust secularist Charles Bradlaugh, however, left some opportunities for more traditional lines of attack. A contributor to *The North American Review* in 1878 alluded to Comte having 'loved adoringly another man's wife'; to Mill associating 'in the tenderest manner with the druggist's wife' (Harriet Taylor's friendship with Mill had started years before the death of her first husband); and to Bradlaugh and his 'lady associate' Annie Besant whose obscene book on birth control had been condemned by the courts (Besant had lost her faith and separated from her clergyman husband a few years earlier; she and Bradlaugh were both convicted of obscene libel in 1877, but the conviction was overturned the following year).[74] The conclusion was that it was no longer possible to boast that the 'freethinkers of this age' were morally superior to 'the infidels of the days of Tom Paine'.[75]

For the most part, however, this sort of gossipy innuendo was not considered a sufficient response to the rapidly spreading belief in the plausibility of basing morality and society on a godless creed. Those wishing to hear a more theological response to atheistic ethics could turn to any number of churchmen who preached and wrote on the subject. For a sense of the role that the clergy of the Church of England played in spreading the language of altruism and shaping its meanings, we can examine three treatments of 'altruism' delivered from pulpits in the universities of Oxford and Cambridge, and in the presence of the Queen at the Private Chapel at Windsor. What did 'altruism' mean in these bastions of established Christianity? These sermons help to illustrate the range of Christian responses, from outright resistance, through partial accommodation, to a more active appropriation.

In his youth Canon James B. Mozley had been a close friend of John Henry Newman. Unlike Newman, Mozley did not convert to Roman Catholicism, but his sympathies remained with the high-church party. Although not considered a very able preacher, Mozley was reckoned one of the most formidable Anglican theologians of the day. His inclusion among the membership of the Metaphysical Society was a recognition of

---

[74] On Bradlaugh and secularism, see Royle 1980.

[75] The article, signed 'An Evolutionist', was a satirical appeal to men of science stressing the urgent need for a new religion fitted to the modern freethinking world; 'An Advertisement for a New Religion', *North American Review,* 127 (1878), 44–61, quotations at 57.

his intellectual credentials. Those attending the third of his University Sermons for 1869–70 in Oxford, on the afternoon of Sunday 20 February 1870, would have been expecting a substantial if not a sparkling discourse. Canon Mozley took as his text Romans 8: 24: 'For we are saved by hope: but hope that is seen is not hope: for what a man seeth, why doth he yet hope for?' The sermon ranged widely in the areas of philosophy of science and religion, with a particular focus on Comte's religion of humanity, his new virtue of altruism, the relationship between morality and religion, and beliefs about the world to come.

'One of the most remarkable combinations which this age has pro- duced', Mozley began, 'is an Atheism which professes a sublime morality. We have been accustomed to connect Atheism with immorality and licen- tiousness; but here the coalition is in theory dissolved.' In practice, however, Mozley was in no doubt that atheism would never be able to deter people from vice in the absence of 'the powerful motives of religious fear and hope'. Belief in a future life was not only useful as a moral deterrent, Mozley went on, but each individual's reflection and conscience in any case revealed it to them as a natural and rational conviction. 'When reason itself has opened a view to immortality,' he said, 'to put up contentedly with annihilation,—what a dreadful stupefaction of the human spirit!' His dis- gust was palpable: 'This horrible materialist indifference to extinction of our being, this taking up with it as the natural end of man, what are we to call it? It is the lapse of human nature. It is a fall. This low apathetic insen- sibility to the continuance of his being, is the recurrence to an animal nature.' And what of the Comtist claim to improve on the morality of Christianity? 'The Gospel says—Love thy neighbour as thyself; the new precept is, Love thy neighbour and not thyself—or Altruism, as it is called.' This precept, and the accompanying idea that Christianity encouraged egotism, was based on the confusion of two different kinds of self-love (the two which Augustine had distinguished). One kind of self-love was the self- ish pursuit of one's own advantage at the expense of others, but the other was the 'pure relation of man to himself'; this desire for his own ultimate good was a natural part of a man's existence and 'no more selfish in him than it is selfish in him to *be* himself'. The desire for immortal happiness for both oneself and others could, in any case, hardly be considered a purely egotistical one.[76]

---

[76] 'Eternal Life' in Mozley 1886: 46–71, quotations at 46, 61, 65.

Some of Mozley's fellow Christians in the Metaphysical Society pro-duced similar arguments in their responses to Harrison's paper on 'The Soul and Future Life' in the 'Modern Symposium' of 1877. R. H. Hutton, who had, the previous year, described Mozley's sermons as the first exam-ple for many years of true 'religious genius' in the English church, insisted that 'selfishness' meant 'the preference for my own happiness at the *expense* of someone else's' but that the desire for an eternity of happiness for one-self and for others did not fit into this category.[77] Canon Alfred Barry, meanwhile, felt the need to come to the defence of Mozley's erstwhile mentor John Henry Newman. Newman had famously stated in his *Apologia Pro Vita Sua* (1864) that at an early period in his religious development he had reached a stage where his distrust of material phenomena had led him to 'rest in the thought of two, and two only absolute and luminously self-evident beings, myself and my Creator'. Even in his maturity, he believed that at the heart of Christianity was the face-to-face relationship between the soul and its Creator, a relationship which he dramatized in one of his mature works, *The Dream of Gerontius* (1865), a poem recounting the jour-ney of a soul towards the judgement seat of God after death.[78] Barry wrote that the 'theory of "Altruism", so eloquently set forth by Mr Harrison and others of his school', by suggesting that such a religious vision as Newman's was 'selfish', simply 'contradicts human nature'. Surely it was not only the 'weakest or ignoblest of human souls' who had at times felt, as Newman did, that the only truly luminous beings were their own self and the 'Supreme Existence'.[79]

So, engagements with 'altruism' led Victorian Christians to defend and reformulate their own beliefs about death, judgement, heaven, and hell. The 1877 'Modern Symposium' included discussions of whether the true Christian future hope was for immaterial spiritual immortality, for physical resurrection, or for both. The biblical teaching and the creeds focused on the physical resurrection, but there was a parallel tradition that represented the world to come as an immaterial one.[80] Different views were presented to the 'Symposium' in response to the arguments put forward by Harrison,

---

[77] R. H. Hutton, 'Mozley's University Sermons' (1876), repr. in Hutton 1894: i. 319–25, at 319–20.
[78] J. H. Newman 1994: 25, 179. *The Dream of Gerontius* was later set to music by Edward Elgar. See Wheeler 1990: 305–39, which describes Newman's poem as, with the exception of Tennyson's *In Memoriam*, 'the best known and most frequently discussed literary work on the subject of death and the future life to be published during the Victorian Age' (305).
[79] 'A Modern Symposium. Subject: "The Soul and Future Life"', *Nineteenth Century*, 2 (1877), 329–54, 497–536; at 331, 505.
[80] On the creeds, see van Inwagen 1995: 478.

Huxley, and W. R. Greg against the plausibility of any kind of Christian hope. Both spiritual and physical conceptions of the world to come were discussed. The view defended by Barry probably best represented Anglican orthodoxy on the subject: between death and the bodily resurrection described by St Paul (in 1 Corinthians 15), the individual would exist, but in an 'intermediate state' characterized by 'suspense and imperfection' until being raised up by the Creator in a new 'glorified body' at the general resurrection.[81]

Another member of the Metaphysical Society for whom the question of survival of death was absolutely central was Henry Sidgwick. The infamously pessimistic conclusion of the 1st edition of Sidgwick's *Methods of Ethics* (1874) was that no solution seemed to be possible to the puzzle of how both egoism and utilitarianism could simultaneously be rational principles of action. Unless there was some greater 'moral order' in the universe, beyond what could be observed in our imperfect actual world, Sidgwick concluded, the 'Cosmos of Duty' would be reduced to a mere chaos. If this were the case, then 'the prolonged effort of the human intellect to frame a perfect ideal of rational conduct is seen to have been foredoomed to inevitable failure'.[82] Sidgwick hoped to avoid this depressing conclusion by using evidence of life after death as the basis for belief in a grander cosmic order.

Mozley, in his 1870 sermon had stated that, despite the reasonableness of the belief in immortality, it could not be proved scientifically. Many travellers had gone to the grave, he said, 'their eyes turned to that eternal shore upon which the voyage of life will land them', but 'none come back to tell us the result of the journey; there is no report, no communication made from the world they have arrived at'.[83] The scientifically minded Sidgwick, however, hoped that just such reports might be received, and in 1882 he became the founding president of the Society for Psychical Research.[84] Around the same time he wrote to Mozley about the moral significance of belief in a future life. He himself had remained publicly silent on theological matters for many years, Sidgwick wrote, since 'I cannot myself discover adequate rational basis for the Christian hope of happy immortality' and 'it seems to me that the general loss of such a hope, from the minds of

---

[81] 'A Modern Symposium', 350, 497, 509, 513–14, 520; Barry's view at 503.
[82] H. Sidgwick 1874: 473.
[83] Mozley 1886: 56.
[84] On Sidgwick's life-long interest in psychical phenomena and his activities in the SPR, see F. M. Turner 1974: 38–67; Schultz 2004: 275–334.

average human beings as now constituted, would be an evil of which I cannot pretend to measure the extent'. Such a general loss of hope would risk bringing about a complete dissolution of the existing social order. Sidgwick held out the hope, however, that in the future human sympathy would have become so strong that thinking about the results of one's actions on others (including those in future generations) would suffice as a motive to benevolence, thus rendering the expectation of 'personal immortality and of God's moral order more realised' less important.[85] In other words, Sidgwick envisaged, in the absence of any conclusive evidence for an objective future life, a future human society of the kind desired by positivism and poetically inaugurated by George Eliot's ode.

'A sweeter or better word than charity?'

After James Murray, the editor of the *New English Dictionary*, had requested illustrative quotations for 'altruism' in *Notes and Queries* in 1882, he was sent examples both from Mozley's 1870 sermon in which he denounced the new gospel of 'Altruism' and from a sermon preached before the University of Cambridge by Frederic Farrar in the same year. Murray included only the latter in the dictionary. Among the reasons for this might have been the feeling that Farrar had made the same point but more forcefully; or that his reference to the language that 'altruism' sought to displace was particularly appropriate for lexicographical purposes; or, most likely of all, that Farrar was a respected philologist (whose expert assistance Murray would acknowledge in the first volume of the dictionary).[86] As an Anglican clergyman and a philologist, Farrar was the perfect person to pass judgement on the Comtean neologism. In the fourth of his Hulsean Lectures at Cambridge in 1870, on 'Christianity and the Individual', Farrar took as his text Acts 17: 28: 'For in him we live, and move, and have our being'. 'Live for others', was indeed a grand motto, Farrar told his Cambridge audience, but he did not see the need for Comte's new terminology. 'Is "altruism" a sweeter or better word than charity?' he asked; 'or has the bare and naked formula "*Vivre pour autrui*" a charm which has been lost from the old commandment, "Thou shalt love thy neighbour as thyself"?' By detaching love

---

[85] A. Sidgwick and Sidgwick 1906: 357–8; Schultz 2004: 248, 269.
[86] Murray 1888: p. xlii.

of neighbour from love of God, Farrar said, the religion of humanity took away the very basis and reality that made such love possible.[87]

Linguistic resistance to 'altruism', as exemplified in Mozley's and Farrar's pronouncements in 1870, became a standard feature of reactions to contemporary atheism in Christian circles. Another Anglican, Charles A. Row, in the Bampton Lectures of 1877, mocked Comtean altruism as an ineffectual 'caricature of Christianity'.[88] In 1890 Row returned to the subject in a popular work defending *Christian Theism*. What he wrote on that occasion encapsulated particularly clearly the standard Anglican response:

> As a substitute for moral obligation as propounded by Christian Theism, modern anti-Christian unbelief has propounded a system of morality designated 'Altruism', which teaches that it is our duty to labour for the good of others, without regard to any other consideration. It therefore dispenses with the being of a God; denies that conscience and a sense of moral obligation are original principles in man; affirms that while each individual man will at death pass into a state of unconsciousness, from which there will be no awakening, yet that it is his duty to labour for the good of future generations, in the elevation of which he will not participate; and that while the combined labours of successive generations, after the lapse (it may be) of millions of years, at last produce an altruistic millennium, in which human nature will be so improved that it will be as natural to seek the good of others as it is in our present low moral condition to seek the good of self.

Row flatly denied that pure disinterestedness was noble for its own sake, disconnected from any duty either to serve God or to elevate one's own self.[89] William Thomson, the archbishop of York, had similarly told the Church Congress in 1880 that lives were shaped to high purpose not 'from a scientific calculation that something called altruism is the best policy, but because of a persuasion that this life is not all, and that it is better to live with a view to connect this life by work and self-denial with the life to come'.[90]

From a Roman Catholic perspective, W. G. Ward regretted that 'love' and 'selfishness' were now called 'altruism' and 'egoism'; and his son Wilfrid, later the biographer of Cardinal Newman, complained of the moral inefficacy of a maternal 'altruism' pursued in the absence of paternal discipline

---

[87] F. W. Farrar 1871: 144–6.
[88] Row 1877: 106.
[89] Row 1890: 202–11, quotation at 202–3.
[90] *The Times* (1 Oct. 1880), 9.

and the fear of future punishments.[91] Dissenting ministers joined in too. The Leeds Congregationalist Eustace Conder, in his Congregational Union Lecture for 1877, unhappily informed his listeners that positivists were now teaching that 'Altruistic brain-instincts, and the organisation of social statics and dynamics, will effect what Christianity has clumsily and vainly attempted by means of love to God, and love to man as the child and image of God'.[92] In Scotland, the Presbyterian theologian Robert Flint, in one of a series of lectures on *Anti-Theistic Theories* (1877), said that positivism may teach universal beneficence, 'under the barbarous name of altruism', but that 'unlike the Gospel, although it enjoins love to one another with the urgency which is due, it unseals no fresh source and brings to light no new motives of love'.[93]

This Christian resistance to 'altruism' would have reached a considerably broader audience than that available to volumes of theological lectures and sermons through its appearance in novels of the period.[94] George Meredith's *One of our Conquerors*, in 1891, included an echo of Mozley's and Farrar's sermons of 1870: ' "And *Altruistic!* another specimen of the modern coinage," a classical Church dignitary, in grammarian disgust, remarked to a lady, as they passed.' Expressing one's ideas using such unpleasant neologisms, the clergyman thought, was equivalent to 'trading with tokens instead of a precious currency'.[95] A few years later the religious novelist Charlotte Yonge, whose works were particularly popular with schoolgirls, produced *The Long Vacation* (1895), which included a discussion between two respectable ladies about the church's lack of progress among the younger generation. The 'younger ones', one of the women thought, 'fancy it is the Church's fault, instead of that of her members' failures, and so they try to walk in the light of the sparks that they have kindled'. Her companion agreed about the new generation's desire for their own ideals: 'Altruism as they call it—love of the neighbour without love of God.' 'But is not each generation a *terra incognita* to the last?' the narrator asked.[96]

---

[91] 'A Modern Symposium', 520; Wilfrid Ward, 'Positivism in Christianity', *Nineteenth Century*, 22 (1887), 403–15, at 413.

[92] Conder 1877: 6.

[93] Flint 1880: 176–210, at 209. Cashdollar 1989: 169 describes these Baird Lectures as the most thorough platform examination of Comtism of the period.

[94] I return to the treatment of altruism and altruists in novels at the end of Ch. 6 below.

[95] Meredith 1891: ii. 144–5.

[96] Yonge 1895: ch. 13, pp. 127–8; accessed online through the Internet Archive Open-Access Text Archive (see Bibliography for details). In an 1888 survey of the reading habits of over a thousand schoolgirls, Yonge was the fourth most popular author, beaten only by Charles Dickens, Walter Scott, and Charles Kingsley; Rose 1995: 196–200.

The language of 'altruism' was again represented as something which placed a division between the older and younger generations in George Gissing's *Our Friend the Charlatan* (1901). The opening chapter introduced a 67-year-old clergyman who 'accepted the theory of organic evolution, reconciling it with a very broad Anglicanism'. As he sat waiting for his breakfast, Reverend Lashmar was reading an article in his weekly newspaper which condemned the 'facile enthusiasm' and 'gross self-interest' of the younger generation, together with their 'tendency to verbose expression'. He started to think that perhaps his own son fitted this description. 'Worst, perhaps, of all these frequent traits', his article continued, 'is the affectation of—to use a silly word—altruism.' The 'most radically selfish of men', the newspaper claimed, could today persuade themselves that their 'prime motive is to "live for others."' This silly, hypocritical altruism, was 'far worse', the vicar read, than 'the unconscious hypocrisy which here and there exists in professors of the old religion; there is something more nauseous about self-deceiving "altruism" than in the attitude of a man who, thoroughly worldly in fact, believes himself a hopeful candidate for personal salvation'.[97] Whether in lectures, sermons, treatises, or novels, it was Christian opponents of 'altruism' as much as anyone who made sure that the term reached the largest possible audience from the 1870s onwards.

'Self less than duty even to the grave!'

There was more to the Christian reaction to 'altruism' than simple opposition, however. Frederic Farrar, whose linguistic resistance in 1870 had set the pattern for later Christian pronouncements, seems himself not to have kept up that attitude of resistance for long. Like Gissing's clergyman in *Our Friend the Charlatan*, Farrar was a broad churchman who was sympathetic to many of the developments of modern science. He was a Fellow of the Royal Society—an honour for which he had been nominated by Charles Darwin in recognition of his services to linguistics and philology. It was also he who helped to make sure, in 1882, that Darwin was honoured with a funeral in Westminster Abbey.[98] On that occasion, Farrar preached a sermon on Darwin's great genius, comparing him to Newton, applauding his broadly religious vision of nature, and cautioning against the setting up of

---

[97] Gissing 1901: 1–6. On the writing and reception of the novel, see Pierre Coustillas's introduction to Gissing 1976: pp. xi–xxv.
[98] On Farrar's career, see *ODNB*; R. Farrar 1904.

theological obstacles to scientific progress.[99] Himself a schoolmaster, he was also an energetic educational reformer, and joined forces with individuals such as Thomas Huxley and Matthew Arnold in pressing for the inclusion of more scientific and practical subjects on the school curriculum. His attitude to positivism was accordingly more accommodating than that of some more conservative churchmen.[100]

Brooke Westcott, a friend of Farrar's who had been unusual amongst Anglican churchmen in taking a serious and sympathetic interest in Comte's work, saw a deep affinity between positivist and Christian teachings. In an 1868 article for the *Contemporary Review* on Comte's religious ideas, Westcott wrote: 'Now these grand and far-reaching ideas of the continuity, the solidarity, the totality of life, which answer equally to the laws of our being and the deepest aspiration of our souls, are not only reconcilable with Christianity, but they are essentially Christian.'[101] Like Westcott, Farrar was critical of his fellow Christians for excluding the worldly too much from their religious vision. In the last of his five Hulsean Lectures in 1870, on 'Christianity and the Race' Farrar echoed the positivist claim that contemporary Christianity was too much focused on 'the doctrine that man's one object in this world is to save his soul'. He even used the quotation from Newman's *Apologia* as evidence of this pernicious Christian tendency to focus only on self and God. As Westcott had already shown, Farrar said, such a Christian tendency would leave the field of social reform open to domination by secularists. Farrar, who was also famous as the author of an extremely popular *Life of Christ* (1874), which went through thirty editions, portrayed Christ in his final Hulsean lecture as a teacher who 'valued charity far above orthodoxy'. His version of Christianity seemed to have been significantly coloured by positivism, especially in his closing summary of the meaning of Christianity as a creed that 'unites us to the Dead—all saints whom we reverence, all souls whom we commemorate; it unites us to the Living, all whom we love and know not, all whom we love and know; it unites us to Posterity, for which, sustained by Faith, inspired by Hope, we labour with patient unselfishness and active love'. Above all, though, Farrar added, presumably to the relief of the more orthodox professors and students of divinity in the audience, 'it unites us to

[99] In F. W. Farrar 1891: 294–310.

[100] Farrar also took a more liberal line than Mozley and others on teachings about death and judgement. On Farrar's rejection of the doctrine of eternal damnation, and his connected attempt to resist teaching universal salvation nonetheless, see Wheeler 1990: 73–7.

[101] Brooke Westcott, 'Aspects of Positivism in Relation to Christianity', *Contemporary Review*, 8 (1868), 371–86, at 383.

the Infinite by making us the children of God and joint-heirs with Christ, if so be that we suffer with Him'.[102]

Farrar's sympathy with a socially oriented version of the gospel, and one that was tinged by positivism, soon seems to have led to a change of heart about 'altruism'. In a sermon to his pupils at Marlborough College in 1873, Farrar described Auguste Comte as 'a good and wise modern philosopher' who had 'summed up the law and duty of life in Altruism— *Vivre pour autrui* —"Live for others"'. In doing so, Farrar said, he had been 'guided by the same conception as that of the sweet and noble Hillel', a great Jewish teacher in the days before Christ.[103] In a footnote to his *Life of Christ* (1874), Farrar further noted the similarities between the moral teachings of Christ, of Hillel, and of Confucius, even suggesting 'altruism' as a synonym for the principal of 'reciprocity' taught by the great Chinese sage.[104] And much later in his career, preaching in Westminster Abbey at a service organized for the members of the Congress of Hygiene and Demography, Farrar said that the foundation and success of that organization, which was devoted to the scientific study and amelioration of insanitary living and working conditions, was a happy proof that 'religious selfishness was being replaced by a more social, a more beneficent, a more nobly altruistic view of life and its duties'.[105] While some continued to accuse positivist altruism of being nothing more than a pale shadow of Christian morality, Farrar seemed instead to be stealing the clothes of the freethinkers and the positivists. In an 1895 article on 'Some Problems of the Age', Farrar argued that neither science nor socialism could truly offer practical or ideological help to the poor, but that Christianity taught that social transformation would be achieved only when all roused themselves to 'genuine Altruism'.[106]

'Altruism' had truly arrived within the pale of Anglican respectability when it was used in 1883 in the title of a tract published on the authority of Queen Victoria herself. The work was a sermon on 'Christian Altruism' preached that year in the chapel at Windsor Castle by the Reverend William Boyd Carpenter. Carpenter was one of Victoria's favourite clergymen. His appointments as royal chaplain and canon of Windsor were followed in 1884 by his elevation to the see of Ripon, where his finely delivered sermons earned him the soubriquet 'the silver-tongued bishop of

---

[102] F. W. Farrar 1871: 169–70, 171, 193; see Romans 8: 17.

[103] F. W. Farrar 1876: 157.

[104] F. W. Farrar 1874: ii. 456n.

[105] *The Times* (17 Aug. 1891), 8.

[106] F. W. Farrar, 'Some Problems of the Age', *North American Review,* 161 (1895), 412–20, at 420.

Ripon'.[107] Carpenter kept a note of every single sermon he preached, from his first, in 1864, on 1 John 1: 7, 'The blood of Jesus Christ his son cleanseth us from all sin', to his last, in 1918, on 1 Peter 2: 16, 'Free—yet servants'. In total he preached over 7,000 sermons.[108] The 2,989th of these represented a significant milestone in the process whereby the heathen term 'altruism' was made safe, converted, and baptized.

Frederic Harrison, in explaining his belief in subjective immortality to his Metaphysical Society colleagues had encapsulated it not only in the words of George Eliot's 'Choir Invisible' but also in a line taken from an American Civil War marching song, which had become famous a decade earlier: 'John Brown's body lies a-mouldering in the grave, but his soul is marching along.'[109] That was also, in a much more literal sense, the message of Carpenter's sermon on 'Christian Altruism' delivered on the morning of 1 April 1883. A few days earlier, at Windsor Castle, Queen Victoria's devoted personal attendant John Brown had died. Carpenter told the grieving Queen, her family and attendants, that human social life was one of 'absolute interdependence', and that the great truth taught by nature was 'the solidarity of all life'.[110] Just as Newton and Galileo had discovered the pre-existing laws of the physical universe, Carpenter said, so St Paul had unveiled the pre-existing moral law that 'No man liveth to himself.'[111] Christ himself had told his disciples that 'The greatest is he that doth serve.'[112] The virtuousness of service was indeed an appropriate theme in the circumstances: 'men may win a glory, than which even those who occupy the higher departments can win no higher, the glory of having done their duty of simple and honest service'. John Brown's 'continuous and unselfish service' had bestowed upon his life a dignity to which all might aspire.[113] So Carpenter's sermon elevated John Brown alongside Christ as an example of true altruism, a living sacrifice labouring and suffering always for others rather than for self. The Queen must have been moved to hear such a eulogy for the man who had devoted himself to her service. Later that year she would erect a statue in Brown's honour at

---

[107] *ODNB*.

[108] The three notebooks containing the list of Carpenter's sermons are in the British Library, Add.Mss.46761–3.

[109] Frederic Harrison, 'The Soul and Future Life', *Nineteenth Century*, 1 (1877), 623–36, 832–42, quotation at 837.

[110] Carpenter 1883: 5.

[111] Rom. 14: 7, quoted in Carpenter 1883: 6.

[112] Luke 22: 26, quoted in Carpenter 1883: 9.

[113] Carpenter 1883: 10–11.

Balmoral, inscribed with lines penned by Tennyson at her request: 'Friend more than servant, loyal, truthful, brave! Self less than duty even to the grave!'[114]

In correspondence exchanged between Carpenter and Queen Victoria around this time, as well as in conversations over dinner at Windsor Castle, the subject of Victoria's anxieties about the nature of heaven came up on many occasions. Her conception of the life to come seems to have been towards the literal end of the spectrum. She wanted to know whether the departed could see the actions of those on earth and, if so, whether they would not feel great 'disdain for our weakness'. Carpenter replied that he was sure the departed would be wise and magnanimous in their judgement. Next Victoria was worried whether those who had gone before would have accumulated so much more knowledge and wisdom than us that, on our arrival in the hereafter, we would seem terribly ignorant to them. Prince Albert, she said, had always been better read than her in any case. Carpenter patiently replied that 'pure, clear, unselfish love would bridge every gap' between the 'newcomer and the old inhabitant of Heaven'. It sounded like a very welcoming and polite English boarding school.

In August 1884, Victoria wrote again to Carpenter of her intense long-ing for reunion with lost loved ones. On this occasion she was worried whether among 'those whom we meet again' there would be some 'who did not know or appreciate each other' and that this might spoil the har-mony of the reunion. Perhaps she was worried whether Prince Albert and John Brown would get along in heaven. The queries to Carpenter contin-ued. In the next letter she wanted to know again 'How will it be? How shall we see them and know them? Clothed or unclothed? Men and women and children, or how? If only we could get some glimpse!' In January 1885, the inquiry continued. Her concern was once more how she would cope with meeting those 'dear ones' who 'knew not each other's great merits'. And, presumably thinking of John Brown, and of Carpenter's sermon, she wrote that those she had lost whom she had been fond of 'were not all highly informed; but it was the worth, the devotion, the self-sacrifice which bound us together'. In an attempt to help Victoria with all these questions, Carpenter sent her Professor Henry Drummond's recent book on *Natural Law in the Spiritual World* (1883) in which the evangelical Drummond sought to establish the harmony and continuity between the worlds revealed by scientific study and by spiritual experience. The Queen

---

[114] Quoted in Dyson and Tennyson 1969: 107.

returned the book to Carpenter with a note saying: 'I think you take me for much more scientific than I am.'[115]

William Boyd Carpenter was attracted to the idea that scientific and spiritual insights could be combined in promoting a morality of self-abnegation. He was, of course, clear that the basis of this morality must remain the love of God. As he put it in 1887: 'The principle of Altruism will, no doubt, win its way in the world . . . But when that vision is realised, it will not be through the unaided sentiments of man—the holy city of universal brotherhood is a city whose builder and maker is God.'[116] This combined strategy of praising 'altruism' and seeking to appropriate it within Christianity was increasingly popular during the 1880s and 1890s as 'altruism' began to appeal within a wider range of religious and ethical movements.[117] The Baptist Timothy Harley delivered a sermon on 'Altruism' in 1890 (the second published tract, after Carpenter's sermon, to have the word in its title) which combined the two Christian strategies of resistance and appropriation somewhat uncomfortably together. On the one hand, Harley reproduced many of the arguments used in the *Fraser's* article on the 'The Failure of Altruism' (1879), some of them almost verbatim. The two main criticisms were that 'altruism' could not motivate humanity since it did not connect people with the infinite, and that the ideal was too much based on science and philosophy, and lacking in emotion.

Having established the defects of 'Comtist Altruism', however, Harley went on to claim, having quoted from Farrar's Hulsean lectures, that altruism was not a new invention but 'a *Christian doctrine*'. This identification was also suggested by the poem composed by Harley as an epigraph for his sermon:

> *To serve not self but others;*
> This was the law of Christ:
> To benefit his brothers
> His life was sacrificed.
> His altruistic action
> Has caused the Christian name
> To fuse in benefaction
> With beatific flame.

---

[115] Carpenter 1911: 279–88.

[116] Carpenter 1889: 219–21.

[117] Another example is to be found in a short work on *Egoism, Altruism, and Christian Eudaimonism* (1890) by Revd Moritz Kaufmann, a Christian socialist and biographer of Charles Kingsley.

The conclusion of the sermon was twofold, both religious and secular. As a religious maxim, Harley recommended that his listeners should imitate Christ, that 'Great Altruist, of whom it is truly written, *Pertransivit benefaciendo*—"He passed through the world doing good."' The surprisingly mundane form that Harley thought this imitation of Christ should take was for all responsible men to guard against the evil effects of their being struck down by disease or by early death by joining a mutual, equitable, or prudential assurance society. To pay the monthly premiums was an act of Christian altruism undertaken out of love for one's dependants. The additional virtues of taking out insurance of this kind were many: 'It necessitates frugality, it systematises thrift, it cultivates independence, it mitigates calamity.'[118] But was taking out life insurance really to imitate Christ? Was this what St Paul had in mind when he announced that death had lost its sting? Harley was, in any case, not alone in connecting 'altruism' with financial prudence; one of the volunteer readers who sent quotation slips to James Murray to illustrate the meanings of 'altruism' in the early 1880s pasted their quotation onto the back of a flyer advertising a meeting of the New Mutual Permanent Benefit Building Society.[119]

What was inevitably forgotten in this process of reconstructing Christianity under the influence of altruistic social and secular movements was the theological rationale articulated by Mozley, Barry, Row, and others for resisting the reduction of Christianity to morality, and the identification of the latter exclusively with self-sacrifice. The author who would ultimately go even further in this direction, and do most to popularize the idea that Christian love and altruism were identical was Henry Drummond, whose first book had been too scientific for the Queen. In 1891 he wrote that 'the new word altruism—the translation of "love thy neighbour as thyself"—is slowly finding its way into current Christian speech'.[120] Drummond's *Ascent of Man* (1894) was the apotheosis not only of the identification of Christian love with 'Altruism', but also of a certain kind of

[118] Harley 1890: 1, 9–10, 20–2; the biblical quotation is from Acts 10: 38.
[119] This is one of the 'superfluous slips' for 'altruism' held in the OUP archive in Oxford. The quotation was taken from *The Reader* (19 May 1866), 494: 'But Mr Mill does more than this. He acknowledges the claim of Positivism to be a religion. He aspires to the direct cultivation of altruism, and the subordination of egoism to it far beyond the point of absolute moral duty.' Overleaf, the flyer read: 'New Mutual Permanent Benefit Building Society. You are hereby requested to attend a Meeting of the Members of the above Society, to be held at the Shaftesbury Hall, 36 Aldersgate Street, on Saturday Evening, 30 June at half-past Eight o'clock, for the purpose of appropriating the sum of £800, and on other business, William Bowman, Secretary.'
[120] Henry Drummond, *The Programme of Christianity*, first published in 1891, and included in Drummond 1903: 69–123, at 77.

progressivist evolutionary vision of nature, of which human motherhood was the crowning glory. The *Ascent of Man* would suggest that the Darwinians were to blame for exaggerating the role of the 'struggle for life' in the history of evolution. There was a second factor which they had overlooked and which Drummond called the 'struggle for the life of others' or 'Altruism'.[121] Drummond acknowledged that Darwin himself had not entirely overlooked this factor in evolution, so how did Darwinism come to be associated with the view that the natural world was an arena of pure competition in which sympathy and cooperation had no place?

---

[121] On Drummond, see Ch. 7 below.

Chapter Four

The Darwinian Conscience

Thus the reproach is removed of laying the foundation of the noblest part of our nature in the base principle of selfishness; unless, indeed, the satisfaction which every animal feels, when it follows its proper instincts, and the dissatisfaction felt when prevented, be called selfish.

Charles Darwin, *The Descent of Man* (1871)[1]

Positivism and Darwinism

Charles Darwin has often been thought of as someone who saw nothing but ruthless conflict in the natural world and who, consequently, could see nothing but individualistic self-assertion in human nature. It has also been supposed that he, like some twentieth-century biologists, agonized over the 'problem of altruism' as he developed the theory of natural selection. In fact, neither of these beliefs is true, as this chapter explains. Darwin sought to overturn the utilitarian assumption that humans were naturally motivated by self-interest rather than by instincts of love and sympathy. And he saw evidence of those parental and social instincts at work throughout the animal world. To those with a vested interest in more recent debates about evolutionary theory, the historical Darwin has sometimes been an embarrassment who needed to be dressed up according to the latest theoretical fashions before he could pass muster in respectable scientific company. Many and various misconceptions about Charles Darwin as a moral theorist have arisen from these attempts to rescue him from himself. The current chapter retells the story of Darwin the moral theorist not through the categories of twentieth-century neo-Darwinism, but rather in Darwin's own words, and in those of his contemporaries.

---

[1] Quotations from *The Descent of Man* are taken from the revised 2nd edn, first published in 1874 and repr. with minor revisions and alterations through the 1870s; C. Darwin 1882: 121.

Many of the moral and philosophical questions that Darwin raised had also been aired in earlier debates about positivism and Christianity. By the time Darwin's theories about human morality came to be debated in the 1870s, 'evolution' and 'Darwinism' had joined 'positivism' and 'altruism' in the philosophical vocabularies of the scientific and the progressive.[2] Although Darwinism and positivism shared certain assumptions about human nature, religion, and morality, those advocating the two doctrines were very clearly, sometimes antagonistically, distinguished from each other during the second half of the nineteenth century. Darwin himself lived in a different social world and hence a different mental world from that inhabited by the 'Comtist coterie' surrounding John Chapman and the *Westminster Review* in the 1850s and 1860s. Their active engagement in the latest political campaigns, philosophical movements, and literary machinations of the metropolis were in sharp contrast with the much more detached life of the naturalist Darwin in his rural home in Kent. His moral vocabulary reflected his way of life. Darwin's own thinking about mental and moral philosophy had largely taken shape during the 1830s, through his reading of works by British moral philosophers of the eighteenth and early nineteenth centuries, such as John Abercrombie and James Mackintosh. It is not surprising therefore that, as we shall see, he did not think about moral questions in terms of 'altruism' and 'egoism', but rather in terms of 'sympathy' and 'selfishness', of 'self-sacrifice' and 'self-preservation', and of the nature and origins of the 'moral sense' or 'conscience'.

Following his return from the *Beagle* voyage, Darwin had set to work collaborating with the leading naturalists of the day studying and classifying the large collections of fossils, plants, and animals he had amassed and sent home during the voyage. He settled in London, where he lived from 1837 until 1842, and rapidly became established in the capital's elite institutions of natural history. In 1837 he was appointed to the council of the Geological Society, and in 1838 became its secretary and also served as vice-president of the Entomological Society. The following year saw the publication of his *Journal of Researches into the Geology and Natural History of the Various Countries Visited by H.M.S. Beagle under the Command of Captain Fitz-Roy, R.N., from 1832–1836*, the success of which started to gain him a modest reputation as an author as well as an expert naturalist.[3] It was

---

[2] 'Evolution' as a general scientific and philosophical term was associated more with Herbert Spencer than with Darwin, who only rarely used the word; see Carneiro 2000.

[3] For authoritative biographical accounts of Darwin's life and scientific career, see Desmond and Moore 1991; Browne 1995, 2002.

during this period that Darwin started to develop his philosophical and scientific theories not only about natural selection and the origin of species but also about the nature and origins of the human mind. Immersing himself in works by natural theologians as well as moral philosophers, he started to develop his own materialistic ideas about instincts, the moral sense, and the emotions, which would form the basis of his major publications on human evolution over thirty years later, namely *The Descent of Man, and Selection in Relation to Sex* (1871) and *The Expression of the Emotions in Man and Animals* (1872).[4]

Although Auguste Comte was not an author who had a very profound impact on Darwin's thinking, he certainly figured amongst the philosophical authors Darwin read in this period of metaphysical speculation in the late 1830s. His 'M' and 'N' notebooks, which dealt with questions concerning mind and morals, contained five explicit allusions to Comte's positive philosophy. Darwin had been introduced to Comte's philosophy through a review of the first two volumes of the *Cours de Philosophie Positive* (1830–42) by David Brewster in the *Edinburgh Review* in 1838. He would also probably have learnt more about Comte's ideas from conversations with his brother Erasmus and other progressive London acquaintances such as Harriet Martineau.[5] Brewster's review warned his readers against Comte's atheism but recommended the law of the three states of development (theological, metaphysical, and positive) as a more reliable account of the history of the sciences than that offered by William Whewell. Darwin seemed particularly sympathetic to the Comtean idea that nature was governed by strict natural laws, which should not be conceived as expressions of a divine will.[6] Twenty years later, however, Darwin would choose natural-theological epigraphs for the *Origin*, including one from Whewell himself, which suggested support for an interpretation of the laws of nature as the means through which God could act in the world. Whatever the extent of his private sympathy with Comte's atheistic metaphysics, Darwin was certainly not influenced by any of his later speculations, including those laying

---

[4] On Darwin's notebooks and early theorizing, see Gruber 1974; Manier 1978; Barrett 1987; R. J. Richards 1987: 83–126; Hodge 2003.

[5] On Darwin's acquaintance with Harriet Martineau and her works, see Desmond and Moore 1991: 153–4, 201, 205–6, 216–17, 244, 270.

[6] Manier 1978: 40–4 discusses the impact of Comtean ideas on Darwin's theorizing and suggests that Darwin's sympathy with Comte's atheistic metaphysics throws doubt on Darwin's own later recollection, in his *Autobiography*, that he remained a theist until after the publication of the *Origin of Species* (1859); see C. Darwin 1958: 85–96. For detailed discussions of Darwin's religious beliefs and his gradual loss of faith, see J. R. Moore 1989b, 1994.

out his cerebral theory of 'altruism' and his plans for the 'Religion of Humanity'. Reading Thomas Huxley's famously antagonistic comments about positivism in 'On the Physical Basis of Life' in 1869 persuaded Darwin not to take his curiosity about the content of Comte's later works any further.[7]

Harriet Martineau's writings had a more direct impact on Darwin's moral thought than anything written by Comte. The first time that Darwin explored the idea of a link between animals' social instincts and the human moral sense in his notebooks came immediately after reading Martineau's relativistic views on human morality in *How to Observe: Morals and Manners* in 1838. Martineau's interest was in how the customs and traditions prevalent during childhood shaped one's moral ideas. However, Martineau agreed with ethical writers such as James Mackintosh that there were some universal moral feelings. Darwin's thought was that these might arise from the fact that human beings were social animals endowed with sexual, parental, and social instincts. Even at this early stage of his theorizing, in mental conversation with Martineau, Mackintosh, and the Christian moral philosopher John Abercrombie, Darwin was trying to work out an understanding of morality which was grounded in innate instincts of 'love' and 'sympathy' and which, consequently, he thought could avoid the accusation, often levelled at utilitarians, including William Paley, that they were trying to explain morality in a way that assumed human nature to be fundamentally selfish.[8]

Darwin's moral language, the product of his reading in the 1830s, had more in common with the sermons of the eighteenth-century Anglican moralist Bishop Butler than with the works of either of the two most famous scientific theorists of 'altruism' of the nineteenth century, Auguste Comte and Herbert Spencer.[9] Darwin's concern to differentiate between the established and stable instincts of love and sympathy on the one hand, and fleeting particular passions and desires on the other; his concern to explain the imperious power of the word 'ought'; and his attempt to offer

---

[7] Browne 2002: 297–8; Thomas H. Huxley, 'On the Physical Basis of Life', *Fortnightly Review*, 5 (1868), 129–45; repr. in T. H. Huxley 1893: 104–27; also repr. in T. H. Huxley 1893–4: i. 130–65.

[8] Manier 1978: 138–46. See also R. J. Richards 1987: 110–56. On Abercrombie, see Dixon 2002; and on Darwin's reading of Abercrombie and Mackintosh while developing his ideas in the 'M' and 'N' notebooks about mind, behaviour, and emotions, see Dixon 2003: 159–65.

[9] I am thinking particularly of Butler's sermons on human nature preached at the Rolls Chapel; Butler 1970. These sermons were often included in 19th-century editions of Butler's *Analogy of Revealed Religion*. Darwin chose a passage from the *Analogy* to include as an epigraph alongside those by Bacon and Whewell in the new edn of the *Origin* in 1860; Browne 2002: 95–6; C. Darwin 2006: p. ii. All three epigraphs made the same point—that God was at work in the fixed and natural as much as in the miraculous and supernatural.

an account of the origins of the 'conscience' or 'moral sense' all revealed that his moral categories were the long-established ones of British moral philosophy.[10] Darwin's explanation of the moral sense, first developed in the 1830s and brought to its most developed form in *The Descent of Man*, represented the recasting of that British philosophical tradition in the light of natural history. The fact that Darwin never employed the language of altruism serves as a useful reminder that the Darwinian account of morality had a distinct pedigree from other influential scientific approaches to ethics in the nineteenth century, such as those of Comte and Spencer. In its basic language, structure, and moral categories, it bore the indelible stamp of its eighteenth-century British origins.

That did not prevent those who were hostile to secular and scientific philosophies from identifying the defenders of the new 'Evolution-theory' with the positivists. Mortimer Collins's satirical verse-drama, *The British Birds: A Communication from the Ghost of Aristophanes* (1872), offers one example of the popular impression that positivists and evolutionists belonged to the same modern philosophical movement, which was responsible both for undermining religious belief and for polluting the English language. The poem included amongst its characters four philosophers. The stage directions explained: 'One slightly resembles a Gorilla, another a Germ, a third a Protoplast, a fourth a Sewing-machine. All four, not to mention several minor philosophers, talk in rigorous defiance of the laws of logic and grammar.' The 'Gorilla' represented Darwin; 'Germ' stood for John Tyndall; 'Protoplast' would probably have been identified by most readers as a reference to Thomas Huxley, whose famous essay 'On the Physical Basis of Life' had introduced the originally German term 'protoplasm' to a broader British readership. When a caricature of Huxley was included in *Vanity Fair's* 'Men of the Day' series in January 1871, the accompanying text identified him as 'the inventor of Protoplasm'.[11] 'Protoplasm' also featured in a large satirical illustrated print depicting the whole range of Victorian religious opinion under the title 'Our National Church'. On that print, produced originally in 1873, the representatives of science (Huxley and Tyndall) were grouped separately but adjacent to the positivists (Frederic Harrison and E. S. Beesly). Tyndall and Huxley held the tail of an ape, which was carrying a banner marked 'Darwinism'. With the ape, the men of science were climbing a hill, at the top of which, from

[10] On the 18th-century British moralism from which these categories derived see Dixon 2003: 81–97.
[11] *Vanity Fair* (28 Jan. 1871), 306.

behind a cloud marked 'Protoplasm', the sun shone out to illuminate a bust of Darwin.[12] The fourth of Collins's philosophers, 'Sewing Machine', stood for the freethinking Unitarian Moncure D. Conway, who was quoted to the effect that man was a machine.

Collins's philosophers represented a mish-mash of scientific and philosophical views, some Darwinian, others positivist, others more generally implying determinism or materialism. 'Protoplast', for instance, although taking his name from the term associated with Huxley, asked the assembled city of birds, 'Will you accept the positivist creed / Which shows that man is true divinity?' The request was greeted by the chorus:

> Life and the universe show spontaneity:
> Down with ridiculous notions of Deity!
> Churches and creeds are all lost in the mists:
> Truth must be sought with the Positivists.

The next intervention by the chorus again revealed that Collins used the term 'positivist' to refer to a fairly broad range of secular and scientific figures:

> Wise are their teachers beyond all comparison,
> Comte, Huxley, Tyndall, Mill, Morley and Harrison:
> Who will adventure to enter the lists
> With such a squadron of Positivists?

Nor did Collins differentiate between positivism and acceptance of the Darwinian teaching of an ape ancestry for humans:

> There was an Ape in the days that were earlier;
> Centuries passed, and his hair became curlier;
> Centuries more gave a thumb to his wrist –
> Then he was Man and a Positivist.

The philosopher 'Gorilla', having made reference to 'my grandfather' (Erasmus Darwin), began his declamation: 'So say I: "Whatsoe'er your brain or shape / I am your father . . . the Ancestral Ape." '[13]

---

[12] Browne 2002: 381. See also White 2003: 132–3, where the later 1882 version is reproduced. 'Protoplasm' was coined by the German naturalist Hugo von Mohl. For Huxley's introduction of the term in his 1869 essay, see T. H. Huxley 1893–4: i. 130–65, at 130. The essay was based on a talk delivered in Edinburgh in Nov. 1868.

[13] M. Collins 1872: 47–9, 53, 76. This poem is also quoted in Wright 1986: 238. Collins is described in the *ODNB* as a journalist with 'strong religious sentiments and an aversion to positivists and freethinkers'.

Collins was not alone in seeing similarities between positivists and Darwinian evolutionists. Positivism, after all, had become established as the leading scientific and developmental philosophy, according to which human individuals, societies, and the sciences themselves, had progressed through the 'three states'. In one of a series of public debates with the leading secularist of the day, Charles Bradlaugh, in June 1875, the Reverend Brewin Grant dismissed 'evolution' and 'selection of the fittest' as 'mystic phrases of juggling positivist philosophy'.[14] The following year, Mark Pattison wrote in the *Contemporary Review* that 'Comte was probably the first writer who endeavoured to grasp the whole evolution of the human race, past, present, and future, as one continuous series.'[15] A French cartoon in 1878 depicted Darwin as a circus monkey leaping through hoops marked '*Credulité*' and '*Superstitions — Erreurs*'. The hoops were being held by the leading French positivist, Émile Littré, also in simian form.[16] In the same year, C. Staniland Wake produced a two-volume study of *The Evolution of Morality* in which 'evolution' stood for the positivist idea of the development of human civilization through fixed stages, rather than for either a Darwinian or a Spencerian theory of biological development. Although there could be some confusion between positivist and Darwinian ideas of progress and evolution in the 1870s, it was not long before Darwinism seemed to many to have displaced positivism as the leading scientific creed. Pattison's judgement, for instance, was that 'even in the thirty years which have elapsed since Comte wrote . . . his crude idea of the three stages has been enveloped in a much more comprehensive conception of the Evolution of the Species'.[17] When Richard Congreve died in 1899, *The Times* noted that it had become common to say that Darwin had made Comte obsolete, 'a saying which has at least the merit of emphasizing the difference between teaching which fully recognizes evolution and that which does not'. *The Times* suggested that the impact of Darwin had been to make Comte's desire to place humanity in 'a position of overwhelming importance' in the scheme of nature seem implausible. As a result, Congreve had spoken and written 'in what is to the majority of scientific workers a dead language, which they do not care to understand'.[18]

---

[14] Quoted in J. Kent 1966: 19.
[15] Mark Pattison, 'The Religion of Positivism', *Contemporary Review*, 27 (1876), 593–614, at 602.
[16] Browne 2002: 379, reproduced opposite 313.
[17] Pattison, 'Religion of Positivism', 613.
[18] *The Times* (10 July 1899), 11.

Although Darwin's natural-historical treatment of human morality owed very little to Comtism in theoretical detail or in language, the questions and assumptions that underlay it were similar. As we have seen in the previous two chapters, positivists and freethinkers were already committed to the idea that men and women should be thought of as purely physical, animal beings, subject to the same laws as the rest of the natural world, and without any supernatural 'soul' which could survive the death of the body. And although Darwin wrote, in his chapter on the moral sense in *The Descent of Man*, that no one had previously, to his knowledge, approached the question of the moral sense 'exclusively from the side of natural history', Comte was a partial exception to this.[19] Like Darwin, he had attempted to provide a naturalistic account of the human mind, and to understand motivation in terms of various basic 'instincts'. Like Darwin, he explicitly contrasted his explanations with theological ideas about human nature.

In addition to these general similarities there were also some more specific parallels. Darwin, like Comte, rejected the view that human beings were driven primarily by selfish motives. The Darwinian theory of human nature, like the Comtist one, saw a struggle between personal instincts and social or sympathetic ones, in which the latter were as natural and innate as the former, but were weaker and needed to be nurtured and strengthened in various ways. Both Darwin and Comte drew attention to natural historians' observations of animal sympathy and cooperation to support their idea that humans were naturally endowed with other-regarding instincts; and both believed that in the future these instincts, through a mixture of social progress and biological inheritance, would become stronger. Finally, they both believed that, although the roots of morality could be perceived in other species, it only reached its full development in humanity. As Darwin put it in *The Descent of Man*, if the anthropomorphous apes were to take 'a dispassionate view' of their own morality, they 'might insist that they were ready to aid their fellow-apes of the same troop in many ways, to risk their lives for them, and to take charge of their orphans; but they would be forced to acknowledge that disinterested love for all living creatures, the most noble attribute of man, was quite beyond their comprehension'.[20]

The rest of this chapter explains Darwin's views on the evolution of the social instincts and the moral sense, and examines some of the ways these

---

[19] On the details of Comte's cerebral theory of the egoistic and altruistic instincts, see Ch. 2 above.
[20] C. Darwin 1882: 126.

views were communicated to Victorian readers. Although the language of altruism always remained foreign to Darwin himself, reviewers, critics, popularizers, and interpreters of his works were soon making connections, positive and negative, between Darwinism and 'altruism'. The science writer Arabella Buckley, through her books for children, her public lectures, and other popular works, such as *Moral Teachings of Science* (1891), spread the idea that the struggle for existence had led to the evolution of noble traits of sympathy, self-sacrifice, and altruism. The literary critic, theological writer, and editor of *The Spectator*, R. H. Hutton, introduced his wary readers to Darwinian ideas about conscience and morality—in both insects and humans—through a series of articles in the 1870s and 1880s, which explored Darwinism in its relations to Christianity. Hutton was not alone in finding the parallels between insect and human societies implied in the writings of both Darwin and his friend John Lubbock particularly suggestive and intriguing. Finally, Darwin's argument that utilitarian morality should be reformed by replacing the 'greatest happiness' principle with the new standard of producing the greatest 'health' or 'welfare' led some to wonder how human reproduction could be managed in a way that would reduce the numbers of physically and mentally unhealthy individuals in society. The positivist James Cotter Morison's proposals for the breeding of a more altruistic society, in *The Service of Man* (1887), represented, for some, the frightening and immoral results of following the dictates of a Darwinian conscience. Of all the threats to established morality posed by Darwinism, its apparent destruction of any objective meaning of 'right' and 'wrong' was the most worrying.

The Charles Darwin problem

How was it possible that Darwin could be simultaneously condemned as a writer who had bestowed scientific legitimacy on rapacious individualism and celebrated as the man who had shown nature to be a teacher of the value of love and cooperation? The problem of interpreting Darwin resembles, at least superficially, the problem of interpreting two other major British moral and social theorists, to both of whom Darwin made reference in *The Descent of Man*: Adam Smith and John Stuart Mill. In the late nineteenth century the German economist August Oncken coined the phrase 'Das Adam Smith Problem' to refer to the apparent tension between the appreciation of sympathy in Smith's *The Theory of Moral Sentiments* (1759) and the more self-interested portrait of human motivation in his *Inquiry into the Nature and Causes of the Wealth of Nations* (1776).[21] We saw in Chapter 2 that some nineteenth-century readers detected a similar problem in John Stuart Mill's works. Frederic Harrison thought that Mill had failed to reconcile the 'militant Individualism' of *On Liberty* (1859) with the 'enthusiastic Altruism' of *Utilitarianism* (1863).[22] There is a comparable tension between *On the Origin of Species* (1859) and *The Descent of Man* (1871). The former has frequently been read as a work that discovered in nature, or read into nature, a world of individualism and ruthless competition. The latter included two substantial chapters emphasizing the importance of mutual help, sympathy, and love in the animal world, and looking forward to a future in which human beings would become endowed with ever stronger social instincts and refined consciences. This apparent inconsistency is the basis of what we could call 'The Charles Darwin Problem'.

There is no doubt that Darwin himself sometimes portrayed natural selection as a ruthless, competitive, individualistic, and amoral process. In a section dealing with insect instincts in the *Origin*, for example, Darwin wrote that, difficult though it may be for us,

> we ought to admire the savage instinctive hatred of the queen-bee, which urges her instantly to destroy the young queens her daughters as soon as born, or to perish herself in the combat; for undoubtedly this is for the good of the community; and maternal love or maternal hatred, though the latter fortunately is most rare, is all the same to the inexorable principle of natural selection.[23]

At the end of the chapter on 'Instinct', Darwin explicitly rejected the idea that each creature had been endowed with its instincts by a wise and benevolent Creator, and proposed instead that such instincts were 'consequences of one general law, leading to the advancement of all organic beings, namely, multiply, vary, let the strongest live and the weakest die'.[24] In the 'Recapitulation and Conclusion' of the *Origin*, Darwin emphasized the individualistic nature of his theory by describing natural selection as a

---

[21] Dickey 1986; Montes 2003.
[22] Frederic Harrison, 'John Stuart Mill', *Nineteenth Century*, 40 (1896), 487–508, at 499–500; for a further discussion, see Ch. 2 above.
[23] Quotations from the *Origin* are taken from the 2006 repr. of the 1959 variorum text collating the successive edns, edited by Morse Peckham. I follow Peckham's system of referencing by giving the chapter number in Roman numerals followed by the sentence number in Arabic numerals; C. Darwin 2006: VI. 241.
[24] Ibid. VII. 288.

process that had achieved its astonishing results by 'the accumulation of innumerable slight variations, each good for the individual possessor'.[25]

From the outset, consequently, one popular reading of the *Origin of Species* was that offered by the *Manchester Guardian*, whose 1860 review of the book was entitled 'National and Individual Rapacity Vindicated by the Laws of Nature'.[26] A couple of years later, Karl Marx would write to Friedrich Engels that Darwin seemed to have discovered in nature a reflection of 'English society with its division of labour, competition, opening up of new markets, "inventions", and the Malthusian "struggle for existence"'.[27] Writing a review of Herbert Spencer's *Principles of Psychology* (1855) along with the *Origin of Species*, R. H. Hutton argued that the Darwinian theory was 'quite incapable of explaining the specifically human phenomenon of the rise of what may be called an anti-Darwinian conscience, which restrains and subordinates the principle of competition, inspiring pity for those poorer types of nature which, on Darwinian principles, simply stand in need of extinction'. Hutton could not see how a system 'sharpened and improved solely by competition' could give rise to creatures who laboured for the good of their weaker brethren. Just as Darwin's theory of natural selection offered 'no explanation of the growth of life out of that which is not living' so it also failed to explain 'the growth of love out of that which is not loving'.[28]

Even after Darwin's works on human evolution had been published and widely discussed in the 1870s, many continued to associate Darwinism exclusively with ruthless competition and with selfish individualism. Such a view was encouraged by the pronouncements of some Darwinians themselves. E. Ray Lankester, in a course of lectures on the theory of natural selection delivered at the London Institution in 1886, laid down the basic Darwinian principle that all physical and mental properties in nature existed for the benefit of their possessor rather than for the amusement or use of humanity, or for the benefit of another species. He used the example of flowers. It had sometimes been supposed, he said, that flowers 'were created for the delectation of man and the decoration of woman, and that they had a special appropriateness as regarded the human race'. The fact was, however, that the colours of the flowers were 'useful to the flowers

---

[25] Ibid. XIV. 7.

[26] Paul 2003: 223–4.

[27] Quoted in Radick 2003: 143. P. Crook 1994: 19–20 provides a useful summary of the various sources and nuances of Darwin's language of 'struggle' and warfare, and its role in the development of his theories from the 1830s onwards.

[28] R. H. Hutton, 'Science and Theism', repr. in Hutton 1888: 39–58, at 55.

themselves' in attracting insects. Lankester interpreted Darwinism as show-ing that just as 'there was no altruism in the flowers' so, more generally, there was no altruism to be found 'anywhere in the whole field of nature'.[29]

Darwin the discoverer of a world of natural strife, selfishness, and 'sur-vival of the fittest', and the legitimator of competition and individualism in human society, however, was never the only Darwin.[30] The Darwin of *The Descent of Man* was quite different.[31] He acknowledged very fully the coop-eration that was evident in the natural order, arguing that it had been to the benefit of the individual, and in the interests of tribes or communities of social animals, to possess the propensity for parental and filial affection, which could develop into social instincts such as sympathy and love. When these instincts were combined, as they were in humans, with the intellec-tual ability to reflect on one's past behaviour, the linguistic ability to com-municate and understand communal approval and disapproval, and the power of hereditary transmission of habits and instincts, Darwin saw every reason to predict an increasingly virtuous future for humanity. Darwin had already implied a belief in some sort of progressivism at the end of the *Origin*, where he had written that 'as natural selection works solely by and for the good of each being, all corporeal and mental endowments will tend to progress towards perfection'.[32] This optimistic tone was intensified and moralized in the *Descent*. 'Looking to future generations,' Darwin predicted, 'there is no cause to fear that the social instincts will grow weaker, and we may expect that virtuous habits will grow stronger, becoming perhaps fixed by inheritance. In this case the struggle between our higher and lower impulses will be less severe, and virtue will be triumphant.'[33] He even went

---

[29] Reported in *The Times* (9 Feb. 1886), 11.

[30] This one-sided representation of Darwin has proved a persistent one. The phrase 'survival of the fittest' was coined by Herbert Spencer in 1864 to express the Darwinian idea of evolution by natural selection; Paul 1988. For various examples of Darwin being characterized as a prophet of selfishness and individualism, from the 1880s onwards, see Percival 1886: 4–5; Clapperton 1904: 125; Grant 2001: 33; A. N. Wilson 2003: 120, 148.

[31] The two key chapters were C. Darwin 1871: i., chs 3 and 5; in 2nd and subsequent edns these became chs 4 and 5. Discussions of Darwin's views on the evolution of morality include R. J. Richards 1987; Cronin 1991: 325–53; P. Crook 1994: 20–8; Cunningham 1996: 43–8; Gayon 1998: 77–83; R. J. Richards 1999, 2003. James Moore and Adrian Desmond's introduction to their new edn of the *Descent* provides a particularly helpful historical and political contextualization of those views; C. Darwin 2004: pp. xi–lviii. Michael Ruse has argued in recent years (1995, 2002) for a Darwinian approach to ethics, in ways that combine a historical approach to Darwin with his own philosophical agenda.

[32] C. Darwin 2006: XIV. 266. This sentence remained unaltered in all edns of the *Origin*.

[33] C. Darwin 1882: 125.

so far as to quote the Bible, telling his readers that the social instincts, with the aid of intellect and habit, 'naturally lead to the golden rule, "As ye would that men should do to you, do ye to them likewise;" and this lies at the foundation of morality'.[34] So elevated was the moral tone of the *Descent* that Darwin wrote to his daughter Henrietta who was reading the manuscript for him in 1870, 'Who would ever have thought that I sh'd turn parson?'[35]

In short, Darwin tried to show in the *Descent* how his competitive mechanism of natural selection could, when acting on tribes rather than individuals, produce love and sympathy rather than selfish individualism. R. H. Hutton had been sceptical, after reading the *Origin*, about the ability of the Darwinian theory to account for the evolution of the conscience. And in 1869, when he read the first paper to be delivered to the Metaphysical Society, he had used the occasion to air his criticisms of Spencer's account of the evolution of the moral sense—an account which, as we shall see below, Darwin later quoted approvingly in the *Descent*.[36] Having read the *Descent*, however, Hutton was at least persuaded that Darwinism need not imply selfishness. He now thought that Darwin's theory had in fact overturned 'the selfish system' of morals. Reviewing Leslie Stephen's *Science of Ethics* (1882) for *The Spectator*, Hutton argued that Darwin had made the selfish system obsolete by contributing to 'the wealth of discoveries recently made in relation to the organic structure and the various origin of the instincts and impulses which beset us'. Hutton approved of the fact that Stephen, like Darwin, recognized the existence of what Bishop Butler had termed the 'disinterestedness' or 'as Mr Leslie Stephen prefers to call it,—not we think, very wisely,—the genuine "altruism," of many of the human sympathies and passions'.[37] Another commentator on *The Science of Ethics* interpreted Stephen as simply following Darwin 'in his insistence upon Altruism as the ground-form of morality, and upon Sympathy as a primary animal instinct'.[38]

---

[34] Ibid. 126. The biblical quotation is from Jesus's sermon on the plain in Luke 6: 31. It is a very slight misquotation—the King James Version included the word 'also' before 'to them'.

[35] Quoted in R. J. Richards 1987: 189.

[36] On Hutton's paper, see A. W. Brown 1947: 43–7, 318.

[37] R. H. Hutton, 'Mr Leslie Stephen's Science of Ethics', originally published in *The Spectator* in 1882, repr. in Hutton 1894: i. 148–63, at 150. For Stephen's analysis of the meaning of 'altruism' and the ethical implications of evolutionary science, see Stephen 1882: 219–63; Collini 1991: 75–9.

[38] James Seth, 'The Evolution of Morality', *Mind,* 14 (1889), 27–49, at 34.

Theoretical problems and moral categories

There were, then, differences of emphasis in Darwin's own writings which, from the outset, gave rise to various misconceptions about his views of human nature and morality. A misconception of more recent origin is the belief that Darwin considered 'altruism', either in neuter insects in particular, or as a more general phenomenon, to be a special problem for his theory.[39] 'Altruism' has, especially since the innovative work of W. D. Hamilton on the theory of 'kin selection' in the 1960s, been recognized as a potential problem for neo-Darwinism.[40] However, Charles Darwin was not a neo-Darwinian. He believed that acquired characteristics (including behavioural habits and social feelings) could be inherited, and he believed that natural selection could preserve well adapted communities or tribes as well as individuals (one form of neo-Darwinian orthodoxy holds that natural selection can operate only at the level of the gene and, indirectly, the individual organism, but not for the good of the group or community).[41] For Darwin, consequently, there was not a special 'problem of altruism'.

There are two distinct but related points to make about this. First, Darwin did not think that cooperative and self-sacrificing actions and feelings were especially difficult to explain on evolutionary principles. Although he thought that no individual could be endowed by natural selection with a trait that existed exclusively to benefit individuals of another species, and that natural selection generally acted for the benefit of each individual, Darwin did not deny the obvious facts of parental care, sympathy, and collaboration amongst social animals, and mutually beneficial cooperation between different species.[42] These were all phenomena

[39] See, for instance, Levine 2002: 281; Schloss 2002: 214; 2004: 10.

[40] Dawkins 1989; Cronin 1991: esp. 253–310; W. D. Hamilton 1996. As Helena Cronin puts it: 'Only once it was solved was the problem clearly seen. Only with gene-centred hindsight were Darwinians able to formulate sharply what really should have been considered altruistic, and why.... For a century, altruistic behaviour was hardly discussed at all; until recently most Darwinians did not even appreciate that altruism posed a problem'; Cronin 1991: 265.

[41] But for a reassertion of the plausibility of group selection as a Darwinian explanation, see Sober and Wilson 1998; D. S. Wilson and Sober 2002.

[42] Darwin's comments, in ch. 6 of the *Origin*, 'Difficulties on Theory', about the impossibility of natural selection producing traits in one species exclusively for the benefit of another species have sometimes been misconstrued as statements about the impossibility of natural selection producing cooperative or self-sacrificing behaviour. The relevant passage is: 'Natural selection cannot possibly produce any modification in any one species exclusively for the good of another species; though throughout nature one species incessantly takes advantage of, and profits by, the structure of another. But natural selection can and does often produce structures for the direct injury of other species, as we see in the fang of the adder, and in the ovipositor of the ichneumon, by which

which he thought he could explain, as we shall see. The second point is that, although Darwin certainly theorized about behaviours and instincts that others, both in the nineteenth century and more recently, would describe as examples of 'altruism', that was not the way that he thought about them himself. The two principal social instincts for Darwin were 'love' and 'sympathy'; associated qualities included 'obedience', 'fidelity', 'courage', 'benevolence', and 'self-command'. Some of Darwin's readers, including E. Ray Lankester and R. H. Hutton, read his works as contributing to debates about 'altruism'. The fact that this was not a term of his own, however, is a helpful reminder that the theoretical problems confronted by Darwin, and the explanatory tools he adopted to deal with them, were different from those of more recent neo-Darwinians for whom 'the problem of altruism' has become such a favourite theoretical topic (as well as from those of Comtists and Spencerians in his own day).

One particular source of misconceptions about Darwin and 'altruism' has been, as Helena Cronin has shown, a misreading of Darwin's discussion of neuter insects in the *Origin*. The problem that Darwin confronted there, one which he wrote he had initially feared was insuperable and might be 'actually fatal to my whole theory', was the fact that in some species of insect there were sterile workers which were very different from their parents, in terms both of their instincts and their anatomy. It was, as Cronin rightly emphasizes, the diversity of structure and behaviour in these neuter insects, who could not pass on their traits themselves, that puzzled Darwin, rather than, as some have claimed, the fact that they laboured altruistically for the good of the community.[43] The 'climax of the difficulty' for Darwin

---

its eggs are deposited in the living bodies of other insects. If it could be proved that any part of the structure of any one species had been formed for the exclusive good of another species, it would annihilate my theory, for such could not have been produced through natural selection. Although many statements may be found in works on natural history to this effect, I cannot find even one which seems to me of any weight. It is admitted that the rattlesnake has a poison-fang for its own defence and for the destruction of its prey; but some authors suppose that at the same time this snake is furnished with a rattle for its own injury, namely, to warn its prey to escape. I would almost as soon believe that the cat curls the end of its tail when preparing to spring, in order to warn the doomed mouse. But I have not space here to enter on this and other such cases. Natural selection will never produce in a being anything injurious to itself, for natural selection acts solely by and for the good of each.' In the 6th edn, Darwin changed the last sentence to 'Natural selection will never produce in a being any structure more injurious than beneficial to that being, for natural selection acts solely by and for the good of each.' C. Darwin 2006: VI. 221–8.

[43] Cronin 1991: 299. For a recent example of the rereading of Darwin's theory of natural selection through the lens of 1970s selfish-gene neo-Darwinism, for which altruism was indeed a central theoretical problem, see Dugatkin 2006: 1–11.

was not anything to do with altruism, but the fact that these sterile females differed in structure and instinct not only from their parents but also from each other, often being divided into several different castes adapted to different kinds of work.[44] How could these strange facts, Darwin asked himself, be accounted for by his theory of natural selection?

'The difficulty, though appearing insuperable,' Darwin argued, 'is lessened, or, as I believe, disappears, when it is remembered that selection may be applied to the family, as well as to the individual, and may thus gain the desired end.' Just as a farmer might select the parents of a desirable ox (which itself would have no offspring) to produce more oxen with the same or similar desired characteristics, so natural selection, Darwin argued, by preserving those communities of ants which produced sterile workers with advantageous modifications, would tend to produce future generations of such workers, despite the fact that the individual workers left no offspring. This reference to natural selection acting on the 'family' has been used by some to cast Darwin as a precursor of modern theorists of 'kin selection'.[45] However, even in this passage he did not discriminate carefully between such terms as 'family', 'tribe', and 'community', explaining that natural selection could preserve modifications that were 'advantageous to the community' as well as those that benefited individuals.[46] The fact that the sterile workers differed not only from their parents but from each other could be accounted for, Darwin thought, by the great variation to which all structures and instincts were susceptible. A very wide spectrum of modifications of a particular trait (whether it was a physical one like jaw size or a behavioural one such as aggression) might become accidentally associated with sterility, and those in the most serviceable part of each spectrum would be preserved by natural selection. Those communities which produced the most well adapted neuters would have had a great benefit in comparison with other communities. Darwin wrote that it was easy to imagine 'how useful their production may have been to a social community of insects, on the same principle that the division of labour is useful to civilised man'.[47]

Darwin's conclusions about the evolution of neuter insects were twofold. First, as we have seen, he argued that this case showed how natural selection could work by preserving those communities that were

---

[44] C. Darwin 2006:VII. 250.
[45] Ibid.VII. 245. See also Dugatkin 2006: 6–8.
[46] C. Darwin 2006: VII. 248. For a more detailed explanation of Darwin's argument here, see R. J. Richards 1987: 142–52; Cronin 1991: 298–308; Gayon 1998: 70–3.
[47] C. Darwin 2006:VII. 270.

favoured in the struggle for existence, not just by selecting successful individuals. Secondly, Darwin emphasized that this was a case that could not be explained 'by the well-known doctrine of Lamarck', according to which instincts and physical structures evolved by the inheritance of modifications made during each individual's lifetime. Since the neuter insects had no off-spring each generation was, on the face of it, a dead-end in terms of Lamarckian inheritance. Darwin believed, then, that his community-selection explanation of the evolution of well adapted neuter insects provided one important example of a case that could not be explained by Lamarckian inheritance of modifications produced by use and disuse: 'For no amount of exercise, or habit, or volition, in the utterly sterile members of a community could possibly have affected the structure or instincts of the fertile members, which alone leave descendants.'[48] That was not to say that Darwin thought such explanations were never appropriate, however—far from it. Throughout the six editions of the *Origin*, Darwin called upon Lamarckian inheritance, or 'use inheritance', alongside his own favoured mechanisms of natural selection and sexual selection to account for various kinds of evolution. His continuing reliance on use inheritance was clearly discernible in the 6th edition of the *Origin* and especially in *The Expression of the Emotions in Man and Animals*, both of which were published in 1872, a year after *The Descent of Man*.[49]

While the central problem that Darwin addressed in connection with neuter insects was not the evolution of 'altruism', but how the traits of individuals that left no progeny could be preserved by natural selection, the problem addressed in the chapters of the *Descent* on the moral sense was different again. This time the problem was how to explain the existence and force of the faculty of conscience. Darwin started by stating his agreement with those who believed that 'of all the differences between man and the lower animals, the moral sense or conscience is by far the most important'. Quoting from moral philosophers including James Mackintosh and Immanuel Kant, Darwin agreed that the imperious sense of duty and obligation felt by man, his willingness to risk his life for the sake of others, and to devote himself unreservedly to what he believed was right, were the highest and noblest of his attributes. Darwin's purpose in addressing the origin and nature of the moral sense was to see what could be added 'from the side of natural history' to this interesting question and also to provide

---

[48] Ibid. VII. 276.
[49] On the *Expression*, see Browne 1985; Montgomery 1985; Fridlund 1992; Campbell 1997; Hartley 2001: ch. 5; Dixon 2003: 159–77; R. J. Richards 2003.

further evidence for the central argument of the first part of the *Descent*, namely that the many physical and mental similarities between man and the lower animals could only be satisfactorily explained with reference to a common ancestry. So, again, Darwin was not trying to solve any 'problem of altruism'. Rather, he was seeking to close the gap between humanity and the rest of the animal world by showing, first, that the moral qualities of sympathy and love were present in lower animals as well as in man and, secondly, that a plausible evolutionary account could be constructed of how those social instincts, in the case of man, could have risen to such a pitch as to produce those intense feelings of moral duty and obligation with which he and his Victorian readers were so familiar.

While some have wrongly suggested that Darwin was, like neo-Darwinians, preoccupied with altruism as a problem for the theory of evolution by natural selection, others have gone so far the other way as to suggest that Darwin had virtually no theory at all about the evolution of what modern scientists describe as 'altruistic' instincts and behaviours—or only a vague and inconsistent one. This is the suggestion in Helena Cronin's book, *The Ant and the Peacock* (1991), for example. Cronin deliberately rewrites the history of biology as a progressive story in which one version of later twentieth-century neo-Darwinism emerged triumphant by solving the problems of altruism and sexual selection. While giving a generally accurate account of Darwin's theorizing, Cronin's own advocacy of a particular kind of neo-Darwinism and her desire to celebrate Darwin's importance in the history of biology come into tension with each other. Cronin mentions only once, very briefly and in passing, that Darwin accepted Lamarckian use inheritance as a 'subsidiary agent in evolution'.[50] She admits that Darwin seemed to offer explanations that involved natural selection acting at the level of the tribe or community. This is certainly true. Both in the *Origin* and the *Descent*, Darwin referred to natural selection preserving traits that benefited the family,[51] the swarm,[52] the community,[53] or the tribe[54] (in competition with other communities or tribes) rather than simply the individual. Alfred Russel Wallace, during the 1860s, had also invoked explanations in terms of the natural selection of tribes (before, to Darwin's dismay, subsequently deciding that man's moral and intellectual

---

[50] Cronin 1991: 36.
[51] C. Darwin 2006: VII. 245.
[52] Ibid. VII. 229.
[53] C. Darwin 1882: 105–6; C. Darwin 2006: VII. 234, 248, 270.
[54] C. Darwin 1882: 128, 130, 132.

faculties could not have been produced by natural selection and were rather evidence of a spiritual force at work in nature).[55] It is therefore misleading to describe, as Cronin does, those twentieth-century biologists who invoked group selection as departing from 'the individual-level orthodoxy of Darwin, Wallace and their contemporaries'.[56]

It is similarly misleading to deny that Darwin ever intentionally adopted an explanation in terms of selection between communities, and to describe Darwin's reference to competition between tribes or groups, rather than between individuals, in the *Descent* as uncharacteristic or unintentional.[57] Cronin prefers to present Darwin as confused and unclear, as a theorist accidentally putting forward non-Darwinian explanations despite himself, than to accept the historically unsurprising truth that the patron saint of modern neo-Darwinism was not himself a neo-Darwinian. Cronin professes to find Darwin's account of the evolution of self-sacrificial behaviour 'puzzling' and claims that it displayed a confusion between the question of how such behaviour could first have become established within a tribe and the secondary question of how, once established, it could have been strengthened by natural selection. Having quoted one key passage from the *Descent*, about the advantages that a tribe with courageous, obedient, and sympathetic members would enjoy over other tribes, Cronin writes of Darwin: 'It is hard to guess what he had in mind here.'[58] As we shall see shortly, Darwin's explanation is fairly complex, but it is not difficult to work out what he had in mind. Guesswork is not required.

Others have used Darwin's own diffidence about the primal origins of the parental and filial affections, which he believed were the original sources of the social instincts, as the basis for a much more general claim that he 'did not offer any explanation' for the evolution of the social instincts; or that he 'did not know how to explain the competitive advantage' such instincts conferred.[59] The key passage comes in the first edition of the *Descent*, where Darwin wrote: 'With respect to the origin of the parental and filial affections, which apparently lie at the basis of the social

[55] Wallace's views prior to his conversion to a spiritualist interpretation were set out in a paper to the Anthropological Society of London in Mar. 1864, 'The Origin of Human Races and the Antiquity of Man Deduced from the Theory of Natural Selection', *Journal of the Anthropological Society of London*, 2 (1864), 158–70. On the development of Wallace's account of human evolution see A. R. Wallace 1891: 186–214; 1912: 445–78; R. J. Richards 1987: 176–84; Cronin 1991: 353–67.
[56] Cronin 1991: 277.
[57] C. Darwin 1882: 132; Cronin 1991: 303, 327–8.
[58] Cronin 1991: 277.
[59] Rachels 1990: 154; Gates 1998: 60.

affections, it is hopeless to speculate; but we may infer that they have been to a large extent gained through natural selection.'[60] This, however, did not mean that he had no account of how the social instincts evolved from such affections. It was, rather, a general statement of the difficulty of explaining the earliest developments of animal mental life. Earlier in the *Descent*, Darwin had similarly written: 'In what manner the mental powers were first developed in the lowest organisms, is as hopeless an enquiry as how life itself first originated. These are problems for the distant future, if they are ever to be solved by man.'[61] But, perhaps unwilling to give the impression that he was unsure of the evolutionary foundations of the social instincts, he changed the passage about the parental and filial affections to read, in the 2nd edition: 'With respect to the origin of the parental and filial affections, which apparently lie at the base of the social instincts, we know not the steps by which they have been gained; but we may infer that it has been to a large extent through natural selection.'[62]

'The noblest part of our nature'

Darwin was neither confused nor unclear nor excessively anxious nor silent about the evolution of the social instincts and the moral sense. In the *Descent*, he drew on the work of many other naturalists who had written about animal cooperation. These included the early nineteenth-century work of the Frenchman Georges Leroy, whose observations Auguste Comte had earlier relied upon in his account of animal cooperation; the German naturalist Alfred Brehm's *Thierleben* (1864–9); Thomas Belt's *The Naturalist in Nicaragua* (1874); as well as the observations of gentleman-naturalists who were part of his own inner circle, including John Lubbock, Joseph Hooker, and Francis Galton. Drawing on these and his own observations, Darwin established the existence of courageous baboons, conscientious dogs, faithful elephants, cooperative pelicans, and many other kinds of loving and sympathetic animals. Darwin explained how, in his view, instincts leading to cooperative and self-sacrificing behaviours could have become established and strengthened among human ancestors, as they had been in the case of these other social animals.

---

[60] C. Darwin 1871: i. 80.
[61] C. Darwin 1882: 66.
[62] Ibid. 105.

There were three stages in Darwin's account: the establishment of social instincts within a group, their strengthening through use inheritance and natural selection, and their development into a moral sense or conscience. The first stage saw parental and filial affections extended to include other members of a social community. There were several ways that Darwin suggested this would have come about. First he thought that natural selection would preserve sympathetic and loving individuals in preference to solitary ones. The latter would have lost out in the struggle for existence in comparison with their more sociable and cooperative competitors. He also offered the standard argument that an individual will soon learn through their own experience that if they do good to one of their fellows they can hope to receive some good in return. Such cooperative habits would then be imitated by others and thus spread through the group. Finally, in communities which had developed a form of language, these sympathetic and loving tendencies would be reinforced by praise and blame. The desire for approval and the avoidance of disapproval were, Darwin thought, powerful motivating factors in any social community. Over many generations these sociable feelings and cooperative habits would become fixed and inherited. In other words, they would become instincts.[63]

Once social instincts had become established within a group Darwin believed that they would be reinforced over time by two principal agencies: use inheritance and natural selection between tribes. At every stage in the process, individuals who developed their social tendencies during their own lifetime could pass on such changes to their offspring. Thus any society which encouraged each generation to be more obedient, courageous, and benevolent than the last, could expect a gradual improvement in the inherited moral standards of its members. This belief in the inheritance of acquired moral improvements was fundamental to a whole range of progressivist visions of society in the nineteenth century, from Comte, to Darwin, to Spencer, and beyond. On the mechanism by which habits which were beneficial to the group might become innate, Darwin approvingly quoted from Herbert Spencer: 'the experiences of utility, organised and consolidated through all past generations of the human race, have been producing corresponding modifications, which, by continued transmission and accumulation, have become in us certain faculties of moral intuition'.[64]

[63] Darwin's protégé, George J. Romanes wrote a helpful explanatory essay on 'The Darwinian Theory of Instinct', published in the *Nineteenth Century* (Sept. 1884) and repr. in Romanes 1897: 25–58.

[64] Quoted in C. Darwin 1882: 123. The source of the quotation was a letter written from Spencer to Mill, which was published as an appendix to Bain 1868, quotation at 722.

In other words, a use-inheritance explanation was superior to the assumption made by associationist philosophers of mind such as Mill and Bain that
the moral sense was acquired afresh by each individual child through their
experiences of pain and pleasure, approval and disapproval in infancy.

The other principal way that Darwin explained the evolutionary
strengthening of social instincts was through natural selection between
tribes. He acknowledged that many noble moral traits might give 'but a
slight or no advantage to each individual man and his children over the
other men of the same tribe'. This had been counteracted, however, by the
fact that a tribe including many members 'possessing in a high degree
the spirit of patriotism, fidelity, obedience, courage, and sympathy', and
who 'were always ready to aid one another, and to sacrifice themselves for
the common good', would generally 'be victorious over most other tribes;
and this would be natural selection'. Natural selection, by thus preserving
the tribes with higher standards of morality, had ensured that, in terms of
morality, 'the number of well-endowed men will thus everywhere tend to
rise and increase'.[65]

Having explained how he believed the social instincts had become
established and strengthened, the final stage—the culmination of the task
Darwin had set himself—was to explain the genesis of the human conscience. At this point Darwin appealed to a distinction between persistent
social instincts and more fleeting, but temporarily more powerful, selfish
instincts that he described as 'desires and passions'.[66] Instincts of self-
preservation, hunger, lust, and the desire for vengeance could all overwhelm
an individual in an instant. The origin of the human conscience lay in the
power of reflection. Looking back on a moment when he had followed his
personal desires rather than his social instincts, a reasoning individual living
in a society that approved of benevolence and sympathy but disapproved of
selfishness, would come to regret having indulged the instinctive desire of
the moment rather than his more persistent and stable social instincts. This
ability to reflect on one's actions, to feel regret, and to resolve to satisfy one's
persistent social instincts rather than one's fleeting personal instincts in
future, through education, religion, and inherited habit, could give rise to
the development of conscience, and thus to the power of 'that short but
imperious word ought, so full of high significance'.[67] This was the complex,
evolved Darwinian conscience, 'originating in the social instincts, largely

---

[65] C. Darwin 1882: 132.
[66] Ibid. 115.
[67] Ibid. 97.

guided by the approbation of our fellow-men, ruled by reason, self-interest, and in later times by deep religious feelings, and confirmed by instruction and habit'.[68]

Far from portraying himself as a prophet of individualism or an apologist for selfishness and competition, Darwin claimed now to have established that humans, as evolved social animals, were by nature loving and sympathetic, courageous and benevolent. He thus believed he had shown that utilitarians and political economists had been wrong to assume that all human behaviour could and should be explained with reference to self-interest. On his new evolutionary account of the origins of morality, Darwin wrote, 'the reproach is removed of laying the foundation of the noblest part of our nature in the base principle of selfishness; unless', he added, 'the satisfaction which every animal feels, when it follows its proper instincts, and the dissatisfaction felt when prevented, be called selfish'.[69] That combination of high Victorian moral rhetoric with the casual identification of virtue with animal instinct encapsulated the essence of Darwin's ethics. He crowned humanity as the noblest and most virtuous of creatures while simultaneously explaining the conscience as nothing more than animal instinct. On the one hand Darwin celebrated heroic human actions, such as those of a man who would unhesitatingly risk his own life to rescue someone else from a fire, as the greatest of human deeds. All were agreed, Darwin wrote, that 'an act cannot be considered as perfect, or as performed in the most noble manner, unless it be done impulsively, without deliberation or effort'. On the other hand, he did not hesitate to state that the man who thus impulsively risked his own life was acting 'in the same manner as does probably a bee or ant, when it blindly follows its instincts'.[70]

Popularizing Darwinian morality: Arabella Buckley

The Darwinian theory of evolution spread rapidly through Victorian culture. Its first public airing had come in a meeting of the Linnean Society in London in 1858, at which Darwin and Alfred Russel Wallace jointly announced their independent arrival at the theory of natural selection. Although the impact was not immediate, within a couple of years the *Origin* had been published, had gone through several editions, had been

[68] Ibid. 132.
[69] Ibid. 121.
[70] Ibid. 120.

reviewed in scientific journals, general periodicals, and newspapers, and had been discussed in public arenas such as the British Association for the Advancement of Science. The BAAS meeting at Oxford in 1860 was the location of the famous debate about Darwinism between Bishop Samuel Wilberforce, Thomas Huxley, Joseph Hooker, and others, which was later dramatized in accounts of a legendary clash between Huxley and Wilberforce, represented as a microcosm of the Victorian battle between science and religion.[71] Darwinism was a gift not only for publicity-hungry men of science and clergymen, but for cartoonists and caricaturists too. From the 1860s onwards, images of human-like apes, ape-like humans, and, especially, ape-like Darwins, became standard visual tropes for illustrators and satirists.[72]

There was an immense range of different media through which a Victorian might learn about Darwinism. Some actively followed expert scientific discussions about the details of Darwin's theories and their implications for natural history, biology, and allied sciences. Such people studied Darwin's published works at first hand, and attended to the debates which took place within learned societies and in the pages of specialist journals. But most came to Darwinism by a less direct route. They might have encountered Darwinism in a sermon, a religious tract, a philosophical work, a textbook, a public lecture, a novel, a cartoon, a poem, a song, a play, a political speech, a pamphlet, a general periodical, or a children's book.[73] Debates about Darwinism in the general culture frequently focused not only on the religious implications of Darwinian evolution, but also on its ethical import.[74] In the rest of this chapter, I trace a few of the ways that Victorian readers came into contact with discussions specifically of the moral meanings of Darwinism. This will include looking at the view of Darwinism on offer in the weekly newspaper edited by R. H. Hutton, *The Spectator*, and in some other general periodicals. One of the most enthusi-

---

[71] Lucas 1979; James 2005.

[72] On visual representations of Darwin, see Browne 1998, 2001. See also J. Smith 2006: 234–44, which examines Darwin in the world of Victorian caricatures as part of a much broader study of Darwin's uses of and contributions to Victorian visual culture.

[73] On the spread of representations of Darwin through popular culture, see Browne 2002: 370–81; on the dissemination of evolutionary debates through the performing arts, see Goodall 2002.

[74] On the reception of the *Descent* in the periodical press, see Ellegård 1990: 293–331. See also Desmond and Moore 1991: 566–86; Browne 2002: 325–69; Moore and Desmond's introd. to C. Darwin 2004: pp. xi–lxvi; and Dawson 2005, which focuses on ways that questions of indecency and sexual immorality were raised by reviewers of the book. On religious and theological aspects of the reception of Darwinism see J. Kent 1966; Chadwick 1966–70: ii. 1–35; J. R. Moore 1979; Livingstone 1987, 1992, 1999; Kohn 1989; Brooke 1991: 275–320; 2003.

astic and successful communicators of Darwinian morality, however, was not a man of science, nor a contributor to the higher journalism of the period, but the popular children's writer Arabella Buckley.

Buckley was the daughter of an Anglican clergyman who, in her mid-twenties, took up the post of personal secretary to the Unitarian geologist Sir Charles Lyell. The latter's gradualist *Principles of Geology* (1830–3) had been, along with Malthus's *Essay on the Principle of Population* (1798) and William Paley's *Natural Theology* (1802), among the leading models of theoretical speculation that influenced Darwin's own thinking about natural history from the 1830s onwards.[75] Through her work as Lyell's secretary between 1864 and 1875, Buckley became well connected with some of the leading figures of British science, including Charles Darwin and Alfred Russel Wallace. From 1876 onwards, Buckley made the transition from secretary to popular author and lecturer on scientific subjects. Her first book was *A Short History of Natural Science and of the Progress of Discovery, from the Time of the Greeks to the Present Day* (1876), intended 'for the use of schools and young persons', but also counting Darwin amongst its readers and admirers.[76] This was followed by several successful books aiming to bring the findings of modern science to life in colourful narratives intended for children.[77] These books included such titles as the particularly popular *The Fairy-Land of Science* (1879) and its sequel *Through Magic Glasses* (1890).[78] It was in three other works, two for children and one for a general readership, that Buckley explained how Darwin had revealed nature to be the most noble and formidable of moral teachers.

The titles of Buckley's two evolutionary books for children indicated clearly enough what she hoped to bring out as the leading ethical qualities of animal life, both of them already familiar to her readers from their experiences at home and at school, namely parental love and competition. The

---

[75] On some of the intellectual sources of Darwin's theories, see Manier 1978; Ospovat 1981; R. J. Richards 1987: 71–156; Hodge 2003. On Lyell's geology, see Secord 1997.

[76] Darwin wrote to Buckley congratulating her on her first book, offering a few criticisms and suggested improvements, and thanking her for doing such justice both to Lyell and to himself: 'You have crowned Wallace and myself with much honour and glory. I heartily congratulate you on having produced so novel and interesting a work.' Darwin to A. B. Buckley, 11 Feb. 1876; Darwin Correspondence, University Library, Cambridge. I am grateful to Paul White for providing me with the text of the correspondence between Darwin and Buckley.

[77] On Buckley's career, see Barbara Gates's entry on her in the *ODNB*, and Gates 1997; 1998: 51–61; 2004; Lightman 2007. A 1922 edn of *The Fairy-Land of Science* was advertised as the 'thirty-eighth thousand'; Buckley 1922.

[78] See Lightman 1997b: esp. 197–9, 205–7. See also the introduction to Fyfe 2003, an anthology of science writing designed for Victorian children, including material by Buckley.

first was called *Life and Her Children: Glimpses of Animal Life from the Amoeba to the Insects* (1880); the sequel was *Winners in Life's Race; or, The Great Backboned Family* (1882). The first began with a question: 'If in a large school every boy had a prize at the end of the half-year, whether he had worked or not, do you think all the boys would work as hard as they do or learn as well?' More generally, without competition could there be any progress in the world at all? The right answer to these questions was clear enough: 'No, it is the struggle for life and the necessity of work which makes people invent and plan, and improve themselves and things around them.' In the natural world, as in the classroom, competition was key: 'Life has to educate all her children, and she does it by giving the prize of success, health, strength, and enjoyment to those who can best fight the battle of existence, and do their work best in the world.'[79] Having surveyed the lives of invertebrates and insects in some detail, including the highly organized and selfless societies of ants, Buckley suggested to her readers that they would still feel that something was wanting from this picture, namely 'mutual sympathy and help between any two beings, independently of mere duty as citizens'. Simultaneously reinforcing the division between humans and lower animals, and setting up the subject matter of her next book, Buckley wrote that 'for the development of fuller sympathy' we must turn to 'that other branch' of life, 'the key-note of whose existence is the relation of parents to children, of family love'. The lesson of the history of the vertebrate animals would be that the struggle for existence, which had taught the ant selfsacrifice, would also teach the higher virtues of love, mutual help, and sympathy. Such qualities, she wrote, 'are among the most powerful weapons, as they are also certainly the most noble incentives, which can be employed in fighting the battle of life'.[80]

Winners in Life's Race; or, The Great Backboned Family (1882) provided the second part of Buckley's version of Darwinian evolution as a morality tale. Delving now into natural theology as well as natural history, she explained how 'that patient lover and searcher after truth, Charles Darwin' had 'opened our eyes gradually to a conception so deep, so true, and so grand, that side by side with it the idea of making an animal from time to time, as a sculptor makes a model of clay, seems too weak and paltry ever to have been attributed to an Almighty Power'. Thanks to 'our great countryman', Darwin, it was now understood that all the wonderful varieties of life had

---

[79] Buckley 1880: 5–6.
[80] Ibid. 300–1.

been produced by 'the working of Nature's laws, which are but the expression to us of the mind of the great Creator'.[81] Among the most wonderful products of those laws were the instincts of the higher animals. Buckley surveyed examples of parental love among fish and sharks, the affection of tame toads and snakes for their owners, the collaborative herding of wolves and jackals, and the posting of sentinels by some species of birds and mammals to warn the group of danger.[82] This last instinct was one of those which Darwin had also particularly commented upon.[83] Buckley's conclusion, like Darwin's, was that all this showed that 'one of the laws of life which is as strong, if not stronger, than the law of force and selfishness, *is that of mutual help and dependence*'. A couple of pages later this italicized lesson was now spelt out in emphatic capitals: 'amidst toil and suffering, struggle and death, the supreme law of life is the law of SELF-DEVOTION AND LOVE'.[84]

Almost a decade later, Buckley produced a short book for a general audience on *Moral Teachings of Science* (1891). This more philosophical and argumentative work started by summarizing the moral and social tenor of the age as one of 'earnest scepticism' in which the 'very fundamental principles of religion and morality are often called in question', and not only by those who 'wish to make an excuse for self-indulgence and vice'. In the face of the failure of doctrinal theology to provide earnest sceptics with a firm foundation for virtuous living, Buckley argued that people should now turn to science instead. Here the moral lessons for adults were the same as those Buckley had drawn for children, namely that the 'high moral instincts and duties which all religions inculcate have their elementary roots deep down in the sub-soil of life'.[85] *Moral Teachings of Science* drew many suggestive parallels between natural and social life. Annual plants were susceptible to being killed by frost or drought, 'as hard times kill the poor and scantily-fed among men'. Parasitic fungi were compared with 'the debased and criminal classes among men'. The fact that parasitic species of plants and animals tended, in general, to be weaker and more stunted than their self-reliant counterparts served as a warning 'of the danger of drifting into helplessness and dependence ourselves, or of driving others into it either by our own greed or injustice, or by the indolence which induces many to

---

[81] Buckley 1882: 345–6.
[82] Ibid. 347–51.
[83] C. Darwin 1882: 100–1, 107.
[84] Ibid. 351, 353. 'Self-devotion' was a common 19th-century term for self-sacrifice or self-denial.
[85] Buckley 1891: 2, 5, 32.

bestow indiscriminate charity rather than take the trouble to help others to help themselves'.[86]

Moral Teachings of Science drew not only on Darwin but on the observations of Kirby and Spence's natural-theological *Introduction to Entomology* (1815–26), Fabre's *Souvenirs Entolomogiques* (1879), and other works by Pierre Huber, Henry McCook, and Auguste Forel. Her interpretation of those colonies of ants in which sterile females watched over eggs and cocoons as if they were their own was that 'self-devotion and self-sacrifice for the good of all have been developed out of the maternal instinct'.[87] On the other hand, she noted that 'we can observe among the insects the evil side of self-interest in the form of selfishness and self-indulgence appearing side by side with self-devotion'. Some bees committed robberies. Ants waged warfare against other nests. Taking an example used by Darwin in the *Origin*, she noted that one species of slave-making ant, *Polyergus rufescens*, had become so dependent on its slaves that it could not even feed itself. This was another instance of 'the lesson of degradation following upon self-indulgence'.[88]

Darwin and Buckley both found in nature not only the evolutionary origins of love and sympathy, but also the values of perseverance and industry celebrated in the works of the great popularizer of self-reliance and cooperation, Samuel Smiles, whose *Self-Help* had been published in 1859, the same year as Darwin's *Origin of Species* (and as John Stuart Mill's *On Liberty*). Smiles visited Darwin at Down House in 1876, taking with him a copy of his latest didactic biography of a self-improving working-class hero. The subject this time was the self-taught Scottish naturalist Thomas Edward. Darwin thanked Smiles for this latest book and assured him he had read all the others too, with 'extreme pleasure'.[89] Arabella Buckley was also a reader of Smiles. She used an anecdote from the life of Thomas Edward to illustrate the sympathy and affection shown by birds. Edward himself had shot a tern, and left it wounded rather than dead. He then watched in admiration as the flock of terns carried the injured bird away from the hunter to safety.[90]

Buckley's moral categories and evolutionary explanations were essentially Darwinian. She celebrated the way that natural selection had preserved

---

[86] Buckley 1891: 38, 41, 58.
[87] Ibid. 64–5.
[88] Ibid. 67–8; C. Darwin 2006: VII. 102–10, 142–3.
[89] Browne 2002: 385.
[90] Buckley 1891: 72–3.

those communities of animals whose members, like the terns hunted by Thomas Edward, displayed 'love', 'sympathy', and 'self-devotion'. Two ways in which she went beyond Darwin were in her emphasis on parenthood and in her theology. Buckley agreed with Darwin that the social instincts were an extension of the parental and filial affections and, like him, she did not offer any account of the primal origins of those affections.[91] In her narrative of the evolution of life, however, she put particular emphasis on the parental feelings in a way that Darwin had not. In describing the higher qualities that were found in the vertebrates as opposed to the insects, for instance, she wrote that 'as each individual life becomes its own centre, creatures live in pairs or family groups, and the father now, for the first time, takes the position of protector and provider'.[92] The contribution of both father and mother to family life was an important sign of moral progress for Buckley. Fatherhood was also a theme that could connect nature, human society, and God. Buckley agreed with her friend Alfred Russel Wallace that psychical research, as well as the higher moral and intellectual qualities of human beings, suggested that the origins of the universe and of human personality were spiritual.[93] She had even acted as a medium at a séance after the death of Wallace's son in 1874.[94] All of these ideas came together in Buckley's celebration of qualities which, by 1891, she had come to call 'altruistic'. The 'care of our "other-selves"', she wrote, 'has, from the very start of life, been educating living beings in the higher altruistic qualities.' Her theological interpretation of this was that the development of the qualities of unselfishness and self-devotion in nature 'have become to us a faint foreshadowing of Infinite Love, Sympathy, and Fatherly Care'.[95]

As Barbara Gates has argued, Arabella Buckley was an important contributor to that alternative Darwinian tradition in which nature was interpreted as a teacher of sympathy and love rather than of individualism and self-assertion. This alternative tradition, like the tradition which emphasized the ruthless and competitive side of natural selection, had its roots in Darwin's own writings. Around the same time that Buckley started to publish her evolutionary popularizations, the French Comtean sociologist

[91] In this I differ from the interpretation of Buckley's theoretical relationship with Darwin proposed by Barbara Gates, who suggests that Buckley's account of the evolutionary origins of sympathy and altruism was innovative and corrective with respect to Darwin; Gates 1997, 1998: 51–61.

[92] Buckley 1891: 69.

[93] On Buckley and Wallace, see Fichman 2004: 83, 181, 302–3.

[94] Browne 2002: 320.

[95] Buckley 1891: 95.

Alfred Espinas, the Russian zoologist Karl Kessler, and the freethinking
German physician Ludwig Büchner were all developing their own versions
of evolutionary theory in which love and mutuality were given prominent
roles. Influential British contributions to ideas about the evolution of altruism in the 1870s and 1880s came from Herbert Spencer and Patrick
Geddes, as we shall see in subsequent chapters.[96] These visions of natural
altruism were developed in religious and political contexts, as well as having a continued existence within natural history and biology. For Buckley,
Darwinian science had been enlisted in defence of a conventional Victorian
morality in which self-reliance, self-help, and competition were encouraged
alongside altruistic qualities of sympathy, love, and parental care. Theistic,
moralistic, and altruistic Darwinism reached its nineteenth-century zenith
in Henry Drummond's lectures on *The Ascent of Man* (1894). Drummond's
vision of the evolution of altruism, which is explored in Chapter 7 below,
had much in common with Buckley's, although in Drummond's version of
the evolutionary epic human motherhood was given an even more prominent place of honour. Cooperation and mutualism amongst animals provided an inspiration to political as well as to religious writers. Socialists and
anarchists, including Peter Kropotkin and Keir Hardie, saw parallels between
their social ideals and mutual aid in nature. There was also a tradition, which
Paul Crook has documented, of 'peace biology', in which both Comte and
Spencer were significant figures, drawing pacifist inferences from coopera-
tionist biology in the late nineteenth and early twentieth centuries. Finally,
ecological theorists also interpreted evolutionary biology in ways that
emphasized how natural selection could preserve altruistic qualities by acting
at the level of the group or community rather than the individual.[97]

---

[96] On Spencer, see Ch. 5 below, on Geddes, Ch. 7.

[97] Alfred Espinas's *Des Sociétés Animales* was published in 1877. Karl Kessler lectured on animal
cooperation at the University of St Petersburg in 1880. Ludwig Büchner's *Liebe und Liebesleben in
der Thierwelt* was published in 1879, and tr. into English by Annie Besant for the Freethought
Publishing Co. the following year. Richard Weikart (2002: 325) describes Büchner as 'one of the
most important popularizers of Darwinian theory in late nineteenth-century Germany'. On
Büchner as a humanist and scientific materialist, see Gregory 1977a, 1977b. Kessler, Büchner, and
their influence on Kropotkin's *Mutual Aid* (1902) are mentioned again in Ch. 7, below. See also
Kelly 1981; Bowler 1983: 54–7; Todes 1989: 104–42; Mitman 1992: 61–71, 78–80; P. Crook 1994;
Clark 1997: 169–72; Peaker 2005. On the adoption of Darwinian ideas by socialists in Britain,
including Alfred Russel Wallace and Peter Kropotkin, see Stack 2003. A wide spectrum of different political groups, including both individualists and socialists, made use of Darwinian theories
in Britain, America, Germany, and elsewhere; see Bannister 1979; Bowler 1988: 152–73; Weikart
1993; Paul 2003. On Hardie, see Bowler 1988: 161. On the development of ecological ideas and
their 19th-century roots, see Allee *et al.* 1949: 13–43, esp. 29–32. Cronin 1991: 274–83 provides a
highly critical account of this kind of 'greater goodism' in the history of biology. Mitman 1992

Insect ethics

Of all the examples of cooperation and selflessness that could be found in nature, none was more striking than that offered by the complex and apparently communistic societies of the social insects. There was a long history of finding moral meanings in insect life.[98] Their highly developed instincts could be interpreted as signs of the power and wisdom of the Creator, as they were in natural theological works such as William Gould's *An Account of English Ants* (1747) and Kirby and Spence's *Introduction to Entomology* (1815–26) — a work which Darwin and Buckley had both studied.[99] Later in the nineteenth century, the beehive particularly appealed to positivists and trade unionists as an orderly and altruistic model for human industry. The positivist E. S. Beesly edited a working-class newspaper called *The Bee-Hive*, to which he and Frederic Harrison both contributed articles advocating a positivist approach to capital and labour.[100] Arabella Buckley also admired the perseverance and obedience of 'the industrious law-abiding bee'.[101] The most widely known lines celebrating insects as moral models in the eighteenth and nineteenth centuries were penned by Isaac Watts in his *Divine and Moral Songs for Children*.[102] These included a tribute to 'the little busy bee', industriously gathering honey and skilfully building her hive:

> In works of labour or of skill
>   I would be busy too:
> For Satan finds some mischief still
>   For idle hands to do.

In another of his verses Watts chose the ant for its exemplary providence in gathering and storing food for winter:

---

gives a fuller and more sympathetic account of ecology and social thought in America in the first half of the 20th century. For a recent brief account of the fortunes of group selection in the history of biology see D. S. Wilson and Sober 2002. Dugatkin 2006 is a concise popular history of the scientific study of 'the origins of goodness' from Charles Darwin to W. D. Hamilton, via W. C. Allee, couched throughout in the language of 'altruism' and 'blood kinship', covering similar material to Todes 1989; Cronin 1991; Mitman 1992.

[98] On the cultural and moral meanings of ants and the history of myrmecology, see Sleigh 2001; 2003: esp. 58–86; 2007; Lustig 2004.

[99] On the natural theology of instincts, and the role it played in shaping Darwin's theories, see R. J. Richards 1987: 127–56.

[100] Liveing 1926: 86; Wright 1986: 104–5, 113. On positivist social policies, see Ch. 2 above.

[101] Buckley 1891: 100. On the cultural history of the bee see Preston 2006.

[102] On the depiction of heaven and hell in Watts's poems, and their multiple 18th- and 19th-century edns, see Ch. 3 above.

But I have less sense than a poor creeping Ant,
If I take not due care for the things I shall want,
   Nor provide against dangers in time;
When death or old age shall once stare in my face,
What a wretch shall I be in the end of my days,
   If I trifle away all their prime![103]

In A. S. Byatt's novella, *Morpho Eugenia* (1992), which explores insect–human parallels in the world of a Victorian upper-class family, the Reverend Harald Alabaster is struck by the moral qualities of ants: 'We have been accustomed to think of *altruism* and *self-sacrifice* as human virtues, essentially human, but this is not apparently so. These little creatures exercise both, in their ways.' He similarly sees in the society of bees 'a primitive form of altruism, self-sacrifice, or loving-kindness'.[104]

Although Darwinism could be used to reinforce this kind of natural-historical moralizing, as it had been by Arabella Buckley, Darwinian accounts of insect life could not be integrated into a cosy and uplifting moral story without some struggle. First, it was quite clear from accounts offered by Darwin and by his neighbour and friend, the politician and naturalist Sir John Lubbock, that the moral qualities of insects were far from universally admirable. Secondly, as Buckley and other commentators noted, although ants and bees displayed self-sacrificial devotion to their communities, there was more to human moral life than mere self-denial. Finally, the Darwinian association of conscience with instinct seemed to leave no room for the spontaneous action of a free will. For these reasons Darwin's comparison between human and insect instincts was just as provocative for Victorian readers as was his more famously troubling suggestion that humans had apes for ancestors. He seemed to be suggesting, as the *Edinburgh Review* put it, that human morality was 'a mere instinct of the same order as that which rules the actions of the worker-bee'.[105]

The most famous of Darwin's own examples of the darker side of insect life was the behaviour of a parasitic wasp—one of Buckley's animal equivalents of 'the debased and criminal classes among men'—the ichneumon, which laid its eggs inside a living caterpillar. On hatching, the wasp larvae

[103] Watts 1866: 65–6, 103–4; accessed online through the Christian Classics Ethereal Library (see Bibliography for details).
[104] Byatt 1992: 85–6. See also Byatt 2000: 91–122; Sturrock 2002.
[105] [W. Boyd Dawkins], 'Charles Darwin, *The Descent of Man and Selection in Relation to Sex*; Alfred R. Wallace, *Contributions to the Theory of Natural Selection*; St George Mivart, *On the Genesis of Species*', *Edinburgh Review*, 134 (1871), 195–235, at 208.

would eat their host alive.[106] As an ardent abolitionist, Darwin also observed with horror that in some species of ant there existed 'so extraordinary and odious an instinct as that of making slaves'.[107] The warlike aggression of ants, sometimes combined with the stealing of the larvae of other species to rear as their own slaves, made these insects ambivalent moral models at best (see Fig. 12). Darwin himself was struck by these facts of insect life. This may have been part of what he had in mind when he wrote to his friend Joseph Hooker in 1856, 'What a book a Devil's Chaplain might write on the clumsy, wasteful, blundering low & horridly cruel works of nature!'[108] The cruelty of some insect behaviours had theological implications for Darwin too. It was his reflection on some of the more unsavoury works of nature in insect instincts that led Darwin, at the end of the chapter on instinct in the *Origin*, to argue against special creation and to offer one of the more brutal formulations of his law of natural selection:

> to my imagination it is far more satisfactory to look at such instincts as the young cuckoo ejecting its foster brothers, — ants making slaves, — the larvae of ichneumonidae feeding within the live bodies of caterpillars, — not as specially endowed or created instincts, but as small consequences of one general law, leading to the advancement of all organic beings, namely, multiply, vary, let the strongest live and the weakest die.[109]

Writing to the American naturalist, Asa Gray, shortly after the publication of the *Origin*, Darwin made the same point: 'I cannot persuade myself that a beneficent and omnipotent God would have designedly created the Ichneumonidae with the express intention of their feeding within the living bodies of Caterpillars.'[110]

In the *Origin*, Darwin had relied largely, although not exclusively, on the observations of other naturalists when it came to describing the behaviour of various species of ants. His principal entomological authorities had included Pierre Huber, August Fabre, and William Tegetmier. In the decades following the *Origin*, the leading exponent of experimental entomology in Britain was Sir John Lubbock. His most popular scientific publication, *Ants, Bees, and Wasps*, was first published in 1882, as volume 40 of the very successful International Scientific Series, and had reached an 18th edition by

---

[106] On Darwin's observation of this wasp, and his reactions to it, see Desmond and Moore 1991: 123, 276, 293, 463, 479.

[107] C. Darwin 2006: VII. 115; in the 6th edn of 1872, this was altered to read simply 'so extraordinary an instinct'.

[108] Darwin to J. D. Hooker, 13 July 1856, quoted in Desmond and Moore 1991: 449.

[109] C. Darwin 2006: VII. 288.

[110] Quoted in Desmond and Moore 1991: 479.

Figure 12. An illustration from the French naturalist Louis Figuier's book on insects showing the 'Return of Ants after a Battle', carrying the young of another species which would subsequently become their slaves. Figuier's *Les Insectes* was first published in 1867; the first English edition was Figuier 1868. Reproduced by permission of the Mary Evans Picture Library.

1929.[111] Lubbock's results were achieved using beehives and pioneering artificial ants' nests. He employed these in a series of experiments during the 1870s, conducted at his home, High Elms, less than a mile away from Down House in Kent, which had been Darwin's home since 1842. Lubbock's new post-Darwinian insights into insect life captured the imagination of Victorian readers such as Richard Holt Hutton, who had grown up with the intelligent and industrious creatures that populated the songs of Isaac Watts.

Hutton, the son of a Unitarian minister, was born in Leeds in 1826. Unlike both Harriet Martineau and Charles Darwin, however, who made the journey from provincial Unitarianism towards some form of scientific unbelief during the middle decades of the nineteenth century, Hutton gradually became more attracted to established Christianity, and, under the influence of F. D. Maurice, joined the Church of England in 1862. Hutton's involvement with *The Spectator* dated from the same period. For about a quarter of a century, starting in 1861, he and Meredith Townsend were joint editor-proprietors of the paper, subtitled *A Weekly Review of Politics, Literature, Theology and Art*. Hutton was extremely productive, contributing hundreds of articles himself, mainly on literary, religious, and philosophical subjects. One friend recalled Hutton as a voracious reader and careful critic who was frequently to be seen 'holding the book or paper' he was currently reviewing 'within an inch or two of his one good eye' (see Fig. 13).[112] Hutton helped to establish a distinctive style of literary criticism characterized by 'careful discriminations, supported by illustrative evidence rather than descriptive adjectives'. Philip Davies describes Hutton as 'one of the age's outstanding critics and reviewers'.[113] As a member of the Metaphysical Society, this philosophical Yorkshireman was at the hub of Victorian intellectual life as well as of the higher journalism. Subjecting scientific books as well as novels, the *Proceedings of the Linnean Society* as well as essays by Matthew Arnold, to critical scrutiny, and publishing his considered responses for an audience of educated readers, he was one of the many conduits through which scientific knowledge was channelled to the Victorian public.[114] Among the employees of the *Spectator* itself Hutton came into

[111] Clark 1997: 158. On the International Scientific Series, which was initiated by Herbert Spencer's friend, the American publisher Edward Youmans, in 1871, see Ch. 5 below; see also Howsam 2000, which explains the genesis and reception of the series and questions the extent to which its new 'editions' of titles generally represented anything more than mere reissues.

[112] The recollection is from A. J. Church's *Men and Memories*, quoted in Thomas 1928: 76.

[113] Davis 2002: 212, 583. On Hutton, see also Thomas 1928: 55–80; G. C. LeRoy 1941; A. W. Brown 1947: 204–7; Woodfield 1986.

[114] On the Metaphysical Society, see Brown 1947, and Chs 2 and 3 above.

Figure 13. The critic at work: R. H. Hutton, editor of *The Spectator*, reading with his one good eye. Reproduced from Thomas 1928, facing 64.

contact with at least one member of that sceptical public whom he hoped to engage. The housekeeper of the *Spectator* office, Mrs Black, had surprised Hutton's co-editor Meredith Townsend by replying, when he asked her about her religion, 'I am a moderate atheist.'[115]

Between 1874 and 1881, Hutton wrote a series of pieces for *The Spectator* inspired by Lubbock's entomological experiments. These had titles such as 'The "Sociology" of Ants', 'Insect Conservatism', and 'Ants as Farmers'.[116] One of the earliest was 'Sir John Lubbock on "The Little Busy Bee"' (1874). Here Hutton described Lubbock's reports on the behaviour of bees and wasps as 'iconoclastic', destroying the picture offered by 'Dr Watts and those other orthodox admirers of the busy bee, who made that insect so obnoxious to our childhood by over-praise and invidious comparisons'. There was a shocking contrast between the picture painted by Lubbock and 'the eulogium uniformly bestowed upon them in moral books for the young'.[117] Although Lubbock did not deny that the bee was industrious, Hutton interpreted his experiments as a clear attack on their intelligence and on their morality. The key experiment here was one in which Lubbock left some honey close to an open door in the back of a beehive. The few bees who found the honey seemed not to have communicated the discovery to their friends in the hive. Hutton compared their behaviour to that of Lord Byron who had on one occasion recorded in his journal that he had not invited a friend to dine with him because 'I had a fine young turbot which I wished to eat myself'. Either the bees were similarly 'governed by the selfish instincts' or else they were lacking the means necessary to gratify their generous instincts by sharing their discovery with other bees. Lubbock had shown, in other words, that either bees lacked the power of communicating ideas, which some had supposed they had, or else that 'they are even more purely devoted to the selfish system, and are less of communists, than men themselves'.[118]

Turning from bees to ants, with their highly organized communities, ruled over by a queen, inhabited by hordes of industrious workers, farming aphids, storing food, making slaves, waging wars, building colonies, and labouring in specialized tasks for the good of the community, the potential comparisons with Victorian society were obvious and plentiful. Hutton

---

[115] Thomas 1928: 78.

[116] These and several others were included in published collections of Hutton's writings. See Hutton 1894: ii.

[117] Ibid. 315–21, at 315–16.

[118] Ibid. at 317–18. For further discussion of the meaning of 'altruism' in the context of discussions of communism and socialism, see Ch. 6, below.

perceived that ants' nests would also be encouraging subjects of study for 'that new school of scientific thought which is endeavouring to show how the principles of morality are a perfectly inevitable outgrowth of the laws which make society coherent and strong'. With this in mind, he turned his critical eye to Lubbock's experiments on ants. Even though Lubbock himself, like Darwin, used an older moral language of 'affection' and 'sympathy' rather than 'altruism', Hutton took the opportunity to insinuate a disapproving reference to the language of altruism into his review. Lubbock had 'carefully studied the domestic and foreign policy of the ant,' Hutton explained, 'with a view to the sentiments, "altruistic" or otherwise, which appear to be indicated, and has come to some very remarkable results indeed'. Lubbock had revealed the foreign policy of the ant to be far from altruistic. As Hutton put it, their foreign policy was 'Chinese (of the old school)'. Lubbock had shown that any foreigner intruding on the territory of an ants' nest would be instantly attacked and killed. This applied not only to ants of other species, but also to ants of the same species but from a different nest.[119]

The experiment of Lubbock's which Hutton found most revealing had first been reported in the *Proceedings of the Linnean Society*, and an account was subsequently also included in Lubbock's *Scientific Lectures* (1879) and in his *Ants, Bees, and Wasps* (1882).[120] The experiment was also discussed in print by the social purity campaigner (and biographer of James Hinton, the early pioneer of 'altruism') Ellice Hopkins, in an 1880 article 'On Ants' for the *Contemporary Review*.[121] The experiment in question was one of a series designed to investigate simultaneously ants' attitudes to friends and to strangers. Lubbock placed several individuals from a nest of *Formica fusca* in a small bottle and covered the end with muslin. The ants could see through the muslin and make contact with each other through it using their antennae, but could not get in or out of the bottle. Lubbock placed nearby a similarly arranged bottle, this time containing ants of the same species but from a different nest. Lubbock was interested to see whether the ants would help their trapped comrades, perhaps by trying to feed them through the muslin, and whether their attitude would be different to the ants from the other nest. The result was the same on all occasions, namely that the trapped

[119] 'The "Sociology" of Ants' (1879) in Hutton 1894: ii. 322–30, at 324–5.

[120] Ibid. ii. 326–8 for Hutton's account of the experiment. See also Lubbock 1890: 106–8.

[121] Ellice Hopkins, 'On Ants', *Contemporary Review* (1880), repr. in *Littell's Living Age,* 146 (1881), 20–30. On James Hinton as a pioneer of 'altruism', see Ch. 2 above. On Hopkins see *ODNB*; Morgan 2000.

comrades were entirely ignored and the trapped strangers were the focus of a great deal of agitated attention culminating in the muslin being eaten through and the foreign ants killed. Lubbock's conclusion was that, in this species at least, 'hatred is a stronger passion than affection'.[122]

Hutton and Hopkins each used their commentary on this experiment as an opportunity to develop their own moral philosophy, and both made similar points. Hutton thought that Lubbock's conclusion that in this case hatred was stronger than affection was too mild. The results pointed rather to the conclusion that in these ants 'fear or hatred' was a very powerful instinct indeed but that there was no sign at all of 'pure affection in the sense of love of fellow-citizens for their own sake—as distinguished from the interest of the nest'. Hutton's point was that hatred of strangers and a blind obedience to the interests of the nest were just the sort of instincts that one would expect to be produced by a process of evolution which preserved the most successful of a series of competing communities, but that acting for the good of the community was only one part of morality. Personal affections were missing from this picture. One could imagine how personal affections between particular individuals could be destructive of the cohesion of an insect community—just as they could be if they existed between soldiers in the different regiments in an army—unless they were regulated by 'that very refined and subtle, and far-reaching principle, of which the human conscience is the highest earthly form'. Social organization could achieve certain cooperative ends, in both insect and human societies, but did not tend towards producing 'that sort of order for which the sense of a moral law, and the existence of a moral government, are the great essentials'.[123]

In another article on John Lubbock's studies of ants, Hutton made an explicit connection between the very limited 'morality' of the ants' nest, and 'the modern sceptic's idea of ethics, which makes ethical progress consist in the gradual, unconscious subordination of the good of the individual to the good of the community'. This modern ethical ideal, Hutton wrote, had been developed to a high state of perfection among the ants, but this had only gone to prove 'that individuality, and the affections which foster individuality, are the most essential conditions' for a society in which individuals can accumulate experience and act voluntarily and intelligently rather than automatically.[124] Ellice Hopkins came to similar conclusions.

---

[122] Lubbock 1890: 108; Hutton 1894: ii. 328.
[123] Hutton 1894: ii. 329–30.
[124] 'Sir John Lubbock on Ants' (1877) in Hutton 1894: ii. 338–9; also ibid. 352.

The way she posed the question incorporated Comtean, Darwinian, and Christian allusions: 'How far does natural selection under socialistic conditions, or the survival of the serviceable to the community, necessitate the gradual evolution of disinterested affection, self-sacrifice, and benevolence, the "*vivre pour autrui*" of Comte and of one greater than Comte?' Hopkins's conclusion, like Hutton's, was that ants represented the kind of social arrangements that would be expected to thrive under natural selection between communities, but that true moral life must involve 'personal affection' between individuals and not 'mere gregariousness'.[125] Arabella Buckley had made exactly the same distinction, between insects, which were endowed with self-sacrificing instincts which they followed mechanically, and the higher vertebrates, which displayed 'individual sympathy' and 'personal affection'. Ants might be devoted to the community but they were not devoted to each other.[126]

Darwin, Lubbock, and Buckley all expressed some sort of disapproval for the more brutal and less sympathetic sides of insect life at the same time as drawing at least tentative parallels with human society. Hutton was right, however, that those who advocated versions of evolutionary progressivism according to which future humans would act spontaneously and unreflectively for the good of others rather than for the good of self were to that extent envisaging a future in which human society increasingly resembled an ants' nest or a beehive. Such an assumption was discernible to some extent in Comtean, Darwinian, and Spencerian visions of human moral progress, and was also one that was made by both Henry Sidgwick and George Eliot.[127] Along with the suggestion that human goodness would in future be simply a matter of the blind following of instinct (if it was not already), these evolutionary speculations also implied that human progress was a matter of the biological inheritance of physical, mental, and moral health as much as it was something to be achieved through culture and education. The common belief in the inheritance of acquired characteristics guaranteed that these two sides of progress were never entirely separate. Darwin's ideas about the ways that this physico-moral progress might be attained took him from the realm of entomology into the new world of eugenics.

---

[125] Hopkins, 'On Ants', *Littell's Living Age,* 146 (1881), 28–9.
[126] Buckley 1880: 300–1; 1891: 67. The eugenicist Caleb Saleeby later similarly complained about the inappropriateness of the social insects as models for human morality; Saleeby 1906*b*: 112. For more on Saleeby, see Ch. 7 below.
[127] See Chs 2 and 3 above, respectively.

Happiness, health, and birth control

Darwin's celebrity status brought him, amongst other things, crank letters from visionaries and social reformers. In 1878, he received one such letter from a Bradford artist and birth-control advocate, George Arthur Gaskell— one of only two letters Darwin ever received making use of the language of altruism.[128] Gaskell thought that humanity could hope for immunity from the more painful parts of the struggle for existence in future through the use of birth control. The modern 'growth of altruism' led Gaskell to believe that a new stage of evolution was now under way—a regime of 'Social Selection' or 'Birth of the Fittest'—in which the healthy would breed and the unfit refrain from reproduction. Gaskell wrote that he had been influenced in his views not only by Darwin's *Descent of Man*, but also by works by W. R. Greg, Francis Galton, and Herbert Spencer.[129]

Darwin agreed with Gaskell about the nature of the Malthusian problem, but did not endorse his neo-Malthusian solution. Darwin had quoted from Greg and Galton in the *Descent* in support of the assertion that 'the very poor and reckless, who are often degraded by vice' tended to marry earlier and to have more children than 'men of a superior class', and that this posed a serious obstacle to the evolution of more civilized society.[130] But, replying to Gaskell in 1878, Darwin wrote that the evil that would follow from checking sympathy and benevolence towards the less vigorous members of society, as Gaskell had suggested in some cases, would be worse than that which would follow from allowing them to survive and procreate. He wished Gaskell well with his further investigations, and recommended an article by Galton 'in which he proposes certificates of health, etc., for marriage, and that the best should be matched'.[131] On the specific question of birth control, Darwin stated his opposition on the grounds that it would lead to profligacy and sexual immorality amongst unmarried

---

[128] I am grateful to Paul White at the Darwin Correspondence Project, Cambridge University Library, for this information. The other was from Anthony Rich to Charles Darwin, 28 Dec. 1879, Darwin Correspondence Project, Cambridge University Library. Rich referred to his preference for a peaceful and 'altruistic' foreign policy rather than an aggressive, acquisitive, and 'egotistic' one. On the connections between altruism and pacifism, see Ch. 5 below.

[129] G. A. Gaskell to Darwin, 13 Nov. 1878; Darwin Correspondence Project, Cambridge University Library. See also F. Darwin and Seward 1903: 49–50; Burkhardt and Smith 1994: 497, nos. 11744, 11745, 11752. On Gaskell, see *ODNB* entry for Jane Hume Clapperton; Soloway 1990. See also Greer 1984: 255–8, where Gaskell is, perhaps mistakenly, given the title of 'Reverend'. Gaskell 1890 was a pamphlet advocating birth control.

[130] C. Darwin 1882: 138.

[131] F. Darwin and Seward 1903: 49–50.

women.[132] Darwin had expressed the same view to Charles Bradlaugh when approached by him for support during his and Annie Besant's obscenity trial for publishing birth-control literature a year earlier: 'I believe that any such practices would in time lead to unsound women & would destroy chastity, on which the family bond depends; & the weakening of this bond would be the greatest of all possible evils to mankind.'[133]

To others, however, birth control seemed both an altruistic and a Darwinian measure. It was altruistic in the sense that it put the interests of humanity, specifically the health and happiness of future generations, ahead of the selfish desire of the profligate and unfit to procreate. It was also altruistic in a more indirect sense, in that it was hoped that it would result in the morally elevated members of society reproducing more prolifically than the base and selfish, tending towards an increase in the moral standards of future generations. As Gaskell put it, in a letter to the *Malthusian* in 1879, the dilemma facing modern society was how to prevent the 'careless, the selfish, and the foolish', in other words 'the worst stock in the species' from propagating their kind.[134] Birth control was Darwinian because using either contraceptive measures or legislation to prevent the mentally and physically unhealthy from reproducing would give the process of natural selection a helping hand. The moral of an 1867 novel entitled *The Lancashire Wedding, or Darwin Moralized* was the foolishness of marrying anyone with a hereditary illness. Emma Darwin read the book herself, but did not think it good enough to read to her husband. She wrote to their daughter Henrietta: 'The moral is that it is not wise to give up a pretty, poor, healthy girl you love and marry a sickly, rich, cross one you don't care for, which does not require a conjuror to tell one.' Emma thought the story would have been more interesting if the moral had been the necessity of 'giving up a pretty, sick girl you love and marrying a healthy one you don't care for'.[135]

Birth control, like refraining from marriage with the sick, was also Darwinian in another sense, namely that it was consistent with Darwin's stated desire to replace the utilitarian ethical goal of achieving the greatest happiness for the greatest number of individuals with the subtly different one of maximizing health or the 'general good'. And it was in these comments that Darwin most clearly set up a moral framework which would

---

[132] Desmond and Moore 1991: 626–8; Browne 2002: 443–4.
[133] Charles Darwin to Charles Bradlaugh, 6 June 1877, quoted in Browne 2002: 443–4.
[134] Soloway 1990: 98.
[135] J. C. Waller 2002: 12; Litchfield 1915: ii. 187.

prove attractive to those, like Gaskell, who were beginning to promote the movement that would come to be known by Galton's term 'eugenics.'

In his 'Concluding Remarks' on morality in the *Descent* Darwin suggested that the standard of morality should be thought of not as conduciveness to the happiness of individual members of a group but as conduciveness to the 'general good'. That term, Darwin argued, should be defined as 'the rearing of the greatest number of individuals in full vigour and health, with all their faculties perfect, under the conditions to which they are subjected'. Darwin cryptically added 'but this definition would perhaps require some limitation on account of political ethics'.[136] Although Darwin added this caveat, and was consistently opposed, as in his reply to Gaskell, to any draconian policies that would reduce benevolence towards those members of society who were less vigorous and healthy than the rest, or whose faculties were less perfect, the suggestion that the proper end of human conduct was physical vigour and health rather than happiness was radical, to say the least.[137] It was not difficult to see how that moral principle, when given the authority of the most celebrated scientific writer of the age, could strike some as necessarily leading to social policies which actively did more to pursue a healthy society, through further restrictions on philanthropy, restrictions on marriage, or birth control.[138] Gaskell's version of 'altruism', which drew just such conclusions, also influenced the social thought of the socialist and eugenic campaigner Jane Hume Clapperton, whose *Scientific Meliorism* (1885) reprinted Gaskell's letters to Darwin, explained how in future the criminal type would be restrained from 'perpetuating his vicious breed', and was described by one reviewer as a 'Bible of Altruism'.[139]

All the worst nightmares of the critics of Darwinian and other scientific approaches to ethics, although not immediately becoming realities, were given full expression in an outlandish utopia entitled *The Service of Man*, written by James Cotter Morison and published in 1887. Morison, a

---

[136] C. Darwin 1882: 121.

[137] Leslie Stephen, in his *Science of Ethics* (1882), similarly sought to reconfigure ethics around the principle that 'social vitality' rather than individual happiness was the goal of human life. For a useful contemporary philosophical discussion of this principle, see James Seth, 'The Evolution of Morality', *Mind*, 14 (1889), 27–49. On Darwin's reformulation of utilitarianism, see R. J. Richards 1987: 219–42; Gayon 1998: 76–9. For Darwin's discussion of his and Mill's views see C. Darwin 1882: 98n.

[138] Paul 1995, 2003.

[139] See *ODNB*; Clapperton 1885: 340–2; Carr 1895: 2, 85–9, 109–14; Greer 1984: 255–8. Gaskell's correspondence with Darwin was again published in a much later book on the subject of heredity; Gaskell 1931.

founding member of Congreve's Positivist Society in 1867, had become convinced of the incoherence of the doctrines of free will and moral responsibility.[140] He argued that Darwinism had shown that there was no divine designer and that all that was left to guide social progress in the absence of theology was a sober appraisal of how to raise the physical and moral health of the nation. A firm believer in the heritable nature of both altruistic tendencies and 'evil passions', Morison argued that moral character was more or less fixed from birth. The only hope, therefore, for those who wished, as he did, to produce a more altruistic society, was to encourage altruists to reproduce and to discourage or prevent those of a selfish and criminal nature from doing so.

Like Darwin, Morison thought of moral virtue in terms of physical vigour and health. Morison's view on criminals was similar to Galton's, in that he held that criminality was a physical condition. Their views differed, however, in one interesting way. Galton had told the anthropological section of the British Association in Plymouth in 1877 that the criminal was an amoral creature who had 'neither the natural regard for others that lies at the base of conscience' nor the ability to pursue rationally 'his own selfish interests'; he could not 'be preserved from criminal misadventure, either by altruistic or by intelligently egoistic sentiments'.[141] As far as Morison was concerned, however, ten years later, the criminal was a 'moral monster . . . born with his evil passions inherited from his progenitors near or remote'.[142] Altruism and egoism, for Morison, as for all orthodox positivists, were correlated with the development of certain brain structures. Those born lacking the appropriate cerebral organisation could not be expected, in Morison's view, to be altruistic. 'If the interest of society requires a due proportion of altruistic sentiment in each of its members,' Morison argued, 'we can only expect them in those individuals who are correspondingly organised.' The conclusion was that altruistic types — 'the good stock' — should be cultivated as actively as possible while the bad stock should be eliminated 'as far as possible'. Morison was vague on how exactly this would be achieved, but he made some suggestive comments. He observed, for instance, that soldiers who deserted in warfare were 'deservedly shot' and that there were some other forms of criminality which were 'worse

[140] Morison separated from Congreve's Positivist Society in 1878 to join Frederic Harrison's Newton Hall positivist group. Morison died in 1888, leaving £500 in his will to support the ongoing activities of the Positivist Society. Papers of the London Positivist Society, London School of Economics Library; LPS 1/1; LPS 5/1/ff.1–2.
[141] *The Times* (18 Aug. 1877), 6.
[142] Morison 1888: 214.

than desertions'.[143] As Hutton explained it to his readers in *The Spectator*, Morison had finally shown that to be a proponent of 'Altruism' was to believe it the height of virtue to 'extirpate a bad moral stock' and to prevent not only the physically sick but the morally inferior from marrying.[144]

It might seem that the extermination of the unfit was an unlikely connotation for 'altruism' to have acquired. However there had been earlier signs of this association. The first such sign had come, in fact, in the very same paragraph in which Auguste Comte first used the term in his *Politique Positive*. Comte believed that certain animals who devoted themselves to the service of humanity through their agricultural or military or domestic labours should be included in the 'Great Being', as honorary members of 'Humanity'. But at the same time as thinking that some animals should be treated like humans, Comte seemed to imply that some humans could be treated like the less serviceable species of animals. Those animals, Comte wrote, who through their great altruism entered into a noble union with humanity, 'should be regarded henceforward as accessory members of the Great Being, a title to which they have a far higher claim than many useless members of the human race who have never been anything but a burden to Humanity'. Comte's attitude to animals was straightforward—only those species that were of real utility to man, materially, physically, intellectually, or morally should be allowed to survive. Similar efforts would also be made to 'restrict the vegetable kingdom to such species as in one way or other are desirable for man's use, or such as serve to nourish the companions of our destiny, the assistants in our work, and the laboratories of our food'.[145] While Comte was happy to propose the extirpation of useless animals and plants, he did not spell out a comparable policy for those 'useless members of the human race' who were less use to humanity than some animals.

The logic seemed clear enough to some, however. Whether in a Comtean or a Darwinian version, any philosophy which identified the good with the health and vigour of the human race seemed unlikely to attribute much value to the unhealthy and the weak. The connection was also made in the trenchant attack on 'altruism' published in *Fraser's Magazine* in 1879 under the title 'The Failure of Altruism'. 'Love of others

---

[143] Ibid. 216, 218.
[144] 'Mr Cotter Morison on "The Service of Man"' (1887) in Hutton 1894: i. 271–80, at 279–80. See also Hutton's 'Ardent Agnosticism' (1888), in Hutton 1894: i. 281–7. For other Christian responses see Wilfrid Ward, 'Positivism in Christianity', *Nineteenth Century*, 22 (1887), 403–14; Row 1890: 207–10.
[145] Comte 1875–7: i. 496–8.

from the basis of exact, secular knowledge', that article warned, would soon become 'love of the best others; and this develops into destruction of the worst others inevitably'. If a religion based on such a view ever acquired popular force, it continued, 'the crowd would soon feel, if they might not be able to see, that, for the real good of others, shooting the weak ones through the head, as on material principles we do to our best loved animals, would be the supreme kindness'. 'Have we not had all this already "wisely" pointed at', the author asked, 'by the positivists, the Darwinians, the Gregs, in their current articles on such questions as population and national advance?'[146]

Reviewers of the *Descent* feared this kind of morality too. The *Edinburgh Review* thought that if the aim of society was to secure the goals of health and vigour aimed at by natural selection then it would be best to adopt 'the Fijian custom of killing the adults at the first approach of old age, or the Esquimaux practice of deserting the aged and the infirm'.[147] In a book published shortly before the *Descent*, St George Mivart—a Roman Catholic naturalist who had fallen out with both Darwin and Huxley— quoted from Darwin's own *Journal of Researches into the Geology and Natural History of the Various Countries Visited by H.M.S. Beagle* in order to make a similar point. Mivart, whose book bore the heavily loaded title *On the Genesis of Species* (1871), asked whether on Darwinian principles it would not be best to do as the Fuegians did, namely to kill and eat the elderly in times of food shortage. The relevant passage from Darwin's *Journal of Researches* had recorded a conversation between a member of the *Beagle's* crew, Mr Low, and a Fuegian boy. Asked by Low why they devoured their old women even before their dogs when short of food in the winter, the boy answered: 'Doggies catch otters, old woman no.'[148]

'A mere inherited prejudice'

It is conventional to assume that the main moral challenges posed by Darwinism to established religious and ethical views were, first, the demon-

---

[146] This article is also discussed in Ch. 3 above. Anon. 'The Failure of Altruism', *Fraser's Magazine*, 20 (1879), 500.

[147] [W. Boyd Dawkins], *Edinburgh Review,* 134 (1871), 220.

[148] Mivart 1871: 206; C. Darwin 1913: 225. Later in 1871, Mivart wrote a very hostile review of the *Descent*: 'Charles Darwin, *The Descent of Man, and Selection in Relation to Sex*', *Quarterly Review,* 47 (1871), 47–90. On Mivart's falling out with Darwin and Huxley in the late 1860s, see Desmond and Moore 1991: 566–86; Browne 2002: 329–31.

stration that human beings were nothing more than animals, and secondly the suggestion that, as products of natural selection, human beings were bound to be selfish, competitive, and ruthless. However, theologians and moral philosophers had always known that man was an animal driven by selfish desires. And, as we have seen in this chapter, it was far from the case that Darwin's own account of human evolution implied that people either were or should be selfish. Arabella Buckley was just one of those who pop-ularized the orthodox Darwinian view that natural selection between com-munities, in tandem with reason, education, and use inheritance, had moulded human beings into naturally loving, cooperative, and sympathetic creatures. The moral questions that more clearly arose from Darwin's account of the social instincts and the human conscience were not whether or not human beings were animals, but whether and in what respect their intelligence and morality was any different from that of lower animals. The question was not whether human beings were necessarily selfish and rapa-cious but what should be done, from a scientific point of view, about those who were. Perhaps the biggest challenges of all came from the casual man-ner in which Darwin proposed that happiness be replaced by health as the proper end of human endeavours, and in which he imagined alternative societies—insect societies in particular—in which an entirely different morality would have been brought about as a result of the different needs of the social community to which it belonged.

There were two points in his writings at which Darwin conducted thought experiments about alternative insect moralities. As we saw above, in the *Origin*, Darwin had written—using that imperious word 'ought'—that we 'ought to admire' the murderous hatred shown by the queen-bee to her daughters, since this was undoubtedly 'for the good of the commu-nity'.[149] He returned to the same case in the *Descent*, suggesting that hatred between near relations amongst bees—the workers who kill their brothers, and the queen who kills her daughters—had evolved because it was 'of service to the community'.[150] This was exactly the same way that the more common feelings of love for near relations had evolved. Darwin did not suggest any difference in principle between the two. And this was consis-tent with Darwin's most general claim in the chapters on morality in the *Descent* that 'any animal whatever, endowed with well-marked social instincts, the parental and filial affections being here included, would inevitably acquire a moral sense or conscience, as soon as its intellectual

---

[149] C. Darwin 2006:VI. 241.
[150] C. Darwin 1882: 106.

powers had become as well, or nearly as well developed, as in man'. Clearly, however, the moral sense would differ depending on the social instincts.

> In the same manner as various animals have some sense of beauty, though they admire widely different objects, so they might have a sense of right and wrong, though led by it to follow widely different lines of conduct. If, for instance, to take an extreme case, men were reared under precisely the same conditions as hive-bees, there can hardly be a doubt that our unmarried females would, like the worker-bees, think it a sacred duty to kill their brothers, and mothers would strive to kill their fertile daughters; and no one would think of interfering.[151]

Since, for Darwin, the 'conscience' was simply the feeling of regret that one had acted on a fleeting impulse rather than a 'stronger or more enduring' instinct, the exact prescriptions of the conscience would depend on the nature of the creature's most enduring instinct. The imperious voice of conscience in a woman raised in similar social conditions to a hive-bee would instruct her to kill her relatives.

While this was all perfectly consistent, some readers undoubtedly found this exceedingly deflated and relativistic sense of conscience hard to square with Darwin's opening assertions in which he stated that, like Mackintosh and Kant, he considered the conscience the most noble and elevated of human faculties. This may well be another case, such as the inclusion of natural-theological epigraphs and biblical language in the *Origin*, where there was some tension between Darwin's private views and those he wished to communicate to his readers.[152] In 1874 Darwin wrote to a liberal American clergyman, Francis Abbot, whose periodical the *Index* he subscribed to for several years, about an article in the *Index* on the moral philosophy that could be derived from *The Descent of Man* and *The Expression of the Emotions in Man and Animals*. Darwin wrote that he could not see how morality could be 'objective and universal'.[153] He wrote, in some parts of the *Descent*, nonetheless, in a way that would have allowed some readers to believe that he measured moral actions and moral instincts according to an absolute standard—a standard according to which Victorian morality was not only more highly evolved and more noble than that of the lower animals and lower races from Darwin's own point of view, but in a final and objective sense.

---

[151] C. Darwin 1882: 98–9.
[152] Brooke 2003: 201.
[153] Browne 2002: 392.

Arabella Buckley undoubtedly believed in an objective and universal morality—one that was guaranteed both by religion and by evolutionary science. She spread the good news that Darwinian science had demonstrated that high moral instincts and duties were 'inherent in the very laws of our being' and 'deep down in the sub-soil of life'.[154] Her didactic moral writings were an attempt to bolster conventional morality with the latest science. But not all read Darwin the same way.

For others it seemed that, according to the Darwinian picture, people were loving and sympathetic towards each other not because they had voluntarily decided to be so, nor because of a fear of future punishment, nor in order to bring about the greatest happiness of the greatest number, nor even out of a calculation about what would be best for the future of the human race, but simply because their ancestors had, for expedient reasons, acted that way. In short, people were good because it used to be useful to their ancestors to be cooperative and now, having inherited ancestral habits, they could not help themselves. If it had been useful to murder their siblings in the past, that would now both seem and be their highest duty. The anti-vivisectionist campaigner and critic of Darwinism, Frances Power Cobbe offered a forceful version of this view.[155] While Buckley thought that Darwinism provided a cure for ethical scepticism by looking at the witness of the natural world, Cobbe thought quite the reverse. Writing on the subject of 'Agnostic Morality' in 1883, Cobbe argued that to adopt a Darwinian account of the nature of conscience was simultaneously to discredit its testimony, since on this account 'our sense of right and wrong is nothing more than the inherited set of our brains in favour of the class of actions which have been found by our ancestors conducive to the welfare of the tribe'. There was no longer any 'eternal' morality on such a theory, and the conscience was no longer a lofty human faculty but a 'mere inherited prejudice'.[156]

To say that conscience was an 'inherited prejudice' was another way of saying, as Buckley had it, that it was 'inherent in the very laws of our being'. And while the latter sounded very elevating it was obvious, of course, that it was not only Buckley's favoured parts of human nature that had their roots in humanity's evolutionary history, but the more violent and troubling

---

[154] Buckley 1891: 6, 32.

[155] On Cobbe's anti-Darwinism in the context of her anti-vivisection campaigns, see Gates 1998: 124–30.

[156] Frances Power Cobbe, 'Agnostic Morality', *Contemporary Review* (1883), repr. in *Littell's Living Age,* 158 (1883), 175–82, at 177.

parts too. That selfishness and criminality appeared to be 'inherent in the very laws of our being', in some cases, was the central contention of Cotter Morison's ethical eugenics. The way that Darwin himself had put it in one of his philosophical notebooks in the late 1830s was equally vivid: 'Our descent, then, is the origin of our evil passions!! The Devil under form of Baboon is our grandfather!'[157] In the *Descent*, Darwin had taken an example from Brehm of a baboon, 'a true hero', who had risked his own life to save a young member of his troop from a pack of dogs; he had also mentioned the same naturalist's observations of baboons acting in concert to turn over large stones to find insects together. But the *Descent* included not only accounts of heroic and cooperative baboons but also of the terrifyingly aggressive baboon that attacked its keeper in the zoo, and of groups of baboons plundering people's gardens in Abyssinia.[158] Humanity's animal ancestry was morally ambivalent.

Finally, the Darwinian picture of human motivation seemed to reviewers to neglect several crucial aspects of established Christian morality, especially an objective sense of right and wrong, an active rational faculty, and a freely acting will. The *Edinburgh Review* was, like Cobbe and others, alarmed at the Darwinian view of the sense of right and wrong, according to which it was the accidental product of natural selection preserving those variations that had served the 'general good' in the past. If this doctrine were generally accepted, the reviewer predicted, 'the constitution of society would be destroyed; for if there be no objective right and wrong, why should we follow one instinct more than the other, excepting so far as it is of direct use to ourselves?'[159] Mivart regretted that the Darwinian view seemed to leave rational judgement out of the picture and instead imagined human motivation as a free play of competing impulses and feelings. It was beside the point, Mivart argued, for Darwin to show that natural selection could preserve 'mutually beneficial acts' or 'altruistic habits', since no amount of such things would account for the 'intellectual perception of "right" and "duty"'.[160] Darwin had made the 'social instinct' synonymous with 'the gregariousness of brutes'; but such gregariousness lacked any moral element 'because the mental powers of brutes are not equal to forming reflective, deliberate, representative judgments'.[161] To bring these vari-

---

[157] Barrett 1987: 549–50.
[158] C. Darwin 1882: 101, 103–4.
[159] [W. Boyd Dawkins], *Edinburgh Review,* 134 (1871), 216.
[160] [St George Mivart], *Quarterly Review,* 47 (1871), 79–80.
[161] Ibid. 87.

ous objections together, one could have said that on the Darwinian view people either could not help acting as they did, since they were following their instincts, like some more complicated bee or ant, or else they were making a decision to act a certain way. In the former case, Cotter Morison seemed to be right, that there was no place left for ideas of free will and responsibility. In the latter case, if people were able to decide which instincts to follow and which to resist, then the observation that all their instincts, whether evil or virtuous, violently aggressive or sympathetic and cooperative, had evolved did not take them much further forward from a moral point of view.

When Charles Darwin died in 1882, Frederic Farrar gave the sermon at his funeral in Westminster Abbey and celebrated him as a great man of science whose discoveries were consistent with an elevated view of the actions of the Creator, even if Darwin himself had not been able to accept entirely orthodox theological views.[162] R. H. Hutton wrote an appreciation of Darwin's life and achievements for *The Spectator*. Like Farrar, he praised Darwin as a great and humble lover of truth and 'a most brilliant, original, and successful student of the secrets of Nature'. Hutton's only regret was that when it came to 'the psychology of human nature' Darwin had not displayed the same 'subtlety and depth' that he had brought to his study of 'the laws of organic change'. Hutton regretted Darwin's misguided attempts to derive 'an "ought" and "a conscience" out of mere victorious sympathy' Darwin had identified conscience as an awareness of a persistent social instinct that had not been satisfied. But that, for Hutton, was 'a mere leap in the dark'. If morality was to be guaranteed by the most 'persistent' instincts, surely there was no more 'persistent' instinct than self-love? The motive which gave birth to obligation, Hutton wrote, must be something other than the persistence of a social instinct.[163] What, then, would Hutton and others like him have thought when they read Darwin's claim to have removed the reproach of laying the foundation of morality in the 'base principle of selfishness; unless, indeed, the satisfaction which every animal feels, which it follows its proper instinct, and the dissatisfaction felt when prevented, be called selfish'?[164] They would have found the statement puzzling. They might not have been inclined to call the satisfaction of an inherited social instinct 'selfish'. But acting to satisfy a persistent social

---

[162] 'Charles Darwin' (1882) in F. W. Farrar 1891: 294–310.
[163] 'Charles Darwin' (1882) in Hutton 1894: ii. 146, 151.
[164] C. Darwin 1882: 121.

instinct—like a more advanced hive-bee prompted by an involuntary 'inherited prejudice'—this was most certainly not what most Victorians had in mind when they thought about the inward promptings of 'that short but imperious word ought, so full of high significance'.[165]

---

[165] C. Darwin 1882: 97.

Chapter Five

Herbert Spencer, the Radical

Altruism is a principle which should govern national conduct, but it is an altruism which naturally and properly begins at home, and rulers who make it begin abroad are guilty of a violation of their trust. Patriotism, therefore, is the first important virtue which finds a place in one system of morality and not in the other.

Lord Lytton, Rectorial Address to the University of Glasgow (1888)[1]

'England's most popular living philosopher'

Herbert Spencer and Charles Darwin were the two names most popularly associated with the new 'evolution-theory' in Victorian Britain. They had other things in common too. Both were products of Dissenting families from the English Midlands. Darwin's upbringing, in Shrewsbury, had been influenced both by his Unitarian mother and his freethinking father. Spencer was from Derby, where Darwin's paternal grandfather Erasmus had practised as a physician. Spencer's mother was a Wesleyan Methodist and his father, a schoolmaster, had drifted from his Methodist beginnings towards a sympathy with Quakerism. Spencer, like Darwin, eventually made the journey from Midlands Dissenting Christianity to religious scepticism and to worldwide fame as a leading proponent of evolution. Spencer's fame was not to be as long-lived as Darwin's, but during their lifetimes both had international reputations, and both were associated with controversial reformulations of moral philosophy on the basis of the latest science.[2]

Despite these similarities, Spencer's and Darwin's social and intellectual lives were very different. Darwin's world was that of a wealthy gentleman living off the profits of large investments in, amongst other things, railway shares. Spencer had started his professional life working as a railway

---

[1] As reported in *The Times* (12 Nov. 1888), 9.
[2] R. J. Richards 2004 compares Darwin and Spencer as evolutionary theorists.

engineer, subsequently turning to political journalism, before finally mak-ing a comfortable living as a writer.[3] Darwin's intellectual world was shaped by the literature of his establishment education at Cambridge in the 1820s and by decades of minute observations of barnacles, beetles, bees, and baboons. Spencer's philosophy bore the marks of the radicalism pursued by his father and uncle in the Derby of the 1830s and 1840s. Born in 1820, Spencer grew up in the context of Midlands Dissenting and working-class rebellion against the established social order, both before and after the Reform Act of 1832. This was the world that would also be the setting for George Eliot's 1866 novel, *Felix Holt, The Radical*.[4] Another major factor determining Spencer's development as an ethicist was his desire to produce a grand overarching theory of the evolution of nature, humanity, and soci-ety. These two evolutionists' ethical theories were correspondingly worked out using different moral languages. It was Spencer, rather than Darwin, who did most 'to put the *word* "evolution" into currency'.[5] He also gener-ally favoured the modern scientific vocabulary of 'biology', 'sociology', and 'ethics' over more traditional categories of 'natural history', 'political econ-omy', and 'moral philosophy'. And while Darwin had written about 'love' and 'sympathy', Spencer was a theorist of 'altruism'. In summary, if Darwin's moral philosophy could be crudely characterized as Bishop Butler (minus God) plus natural history, then Spencer's was Tom Paine plus evolutionary sociology.[6]

---

[3] Desmond and Moore 1991: 396–7.

[4] See J. D.Y. Peel 1971: 33–81, which refers to *Felix Holt, The Radical* at 72–3. Marian Evans, later to become famous as George Eliot, was another product of the world of Midlands dissent, and she and Spencer were extremely close in the 1850s. On the Chapman circle, of which they were both a part, see Ch. 2 above. On the connections between Eliot's works and Spencer's philosophy, see Paxton 1991.

[5] J. D.Y. Peel 2004: 128.

[6] Spencer's own autobiography (1904) and David Duncan's *Life and Letters* (1908) are both rich sources of information on Spencer's life. Francis 2007 is a major new intellectual biography. See also Jose Harris's entry on Spencer in the *ODNB*. The major study of Spencer as a sociological theorist, which also situates his work within the context of the radical politics of his youth, is J. D.Y. Peel 1971. On Spencer as a pioneering sociologist, see also J. H. Turner 1985, 2000. Wiltshire 1978 argues for the primacy of politics rather than evolution as the driving force in Spencer's career and philosophy. M. Taylor 1992 and Gray 1996 also consider Spencer as a political philoso-pher. G. Jones and R. A. Peel 2004 is a useful collection of essays reappraising Spencer's writings, impact, and historical reputation on the centenary of his death (including an earlier version of this chapter). Offer's introduction to Spencer 1994: pp. vii–xxvii, is another useful starting point, as are Taylor's introductions to the separate works reprinted in Spencer 1996. Offer 2000 is an extremely valuable 4–vol. collection of responses to Spencer, including both Victorian and 20th-century critical and interpretative studies of Spencer as a philosopher, evolutionist, ethicist, soci-ologist, and political thinker.

Spencer was by far the most influential theorist of altruism in nineteenth-century Britain. As will become clear in this and subsequent chapters, after the 1870s it was hard to conduct discussions of 'altruism' without the figure of Herbert Spencer being somehow implicated, scientifically, philosophically, or politically. Although Spencer's writings were particularly important, they were not the only route through which 'altruism' became more widely embedded in Victorian culture. Spencer's *Study of Sociology* (1873) and his *Data of Ethics* (1879) took their places on Victorian bookshelves alongside several other widely discussed and even more popular works which between them introduced 'altruism' to large and various readerships through a range of literary genres, including philosophy, fiction, political propaganda, and popular science. One of the best-selling and most controversial novels of the 1880s, Mrs Humphry Ward's *Robert Elsmere* (1888), told the story of a clergyman's transformation from orthodox Anglican to idealistic but heterodox 'altruist'. 'Altruism' was also a key word in the vocabulary of Robert Blatchford, the most widely read British socialist propagandist of the 1890s. Finally, 'altruism' was the central subject of two of the non-fiction best-sellers of the 1890s—works that combined popular science and religion in new ways—Henry Drummond's *Ascent of Man* (1894) and Benjamin Kidd's *Social Evolution* (1894). The uses of the language of altruism in these popular late Victorian works, the new connotations it consequently acquired, and the cultural and political contexts within which its broader significance developed are the central subjects of the next three chapters. The present chapter focuses on Herbert Spencer, examining the places of 'egoism' and 'altruism' in his moral philosophy and in his political opposition to indiscriminate philanthropy and to aggressive imperialism. The next chapter looks especially at practical and theoretical responses to poverty, and how the language of altruism made its way onto the streets and into the settlement houses of the East End of London, as well as into the thoughts of economic and social theorists, and onto the pages of popular novels. Chapter 7 looks at what moral lessons were drawn about motherhood and the future of the race in the 1890s in the light both of Spencerian and neo-Darwinian theories of evolution. The final chapter, 'Egomania', marks the beginnings of the reaction against the Victorian culture of altruism that the writers, readers, and reformers of the 1880s and 1890s had helped to create.

Recent discussions of Herbert Spencer have sometimes asked whether Spencer can be best understood as an advocate of 'Social Darwinism', or perhaps as pioneer of 'evolutionary ethics' and 'evolutionary psychology'.[7] In his own day, however, he was famous primarily simply as a philosopher. The great work on which he was engaged from its first inception in 1857 until the publication of the final volume in 1896 was his multi-volume *Synthetic Philosophy*. This enterprise, financed by sub-scriptions from hundreds of readers, and completed despite regular relapses in Spencer's physical and mental health, was conceived as a reworking of the entirety of philosophy and science from the point of view of evolution. When Spencer appeared in the *Vanity Fair* 'Men of the Day' series in 1879, the caricature was given the one-word caption 'Philosophy' (see Fig. 14). The accompanying text described Spencer as the man who had seen that 'Evolution' might be 'applied to psychologic problems' and had consequently begun 'to publish distressing tomes'. Since no one could understand his philosophy, 'his reputation waxed mightily' and he was now 'the one recognised authority on "Sociology"'. He had also discovered, the *Vanity Fair* pen-portrait noted, that 'the man of science "knows that in its ultimate essence nothing can be known." Yet he goes on writing.'[8]

In the late 1870s, when Spencer was particularly worried about his health, he decided to start work on the *Principles of Ethics* even though the *Principles of Sociology* was not yet completed. He considered the ethics the cornerstone of his system and wanted it produced before he died, even if the rest of the *Synthetic Philosophy* had to be left incomplete. The resulting work was *The Data of Ethics* (1879). Although Darwin had published his natural-historical account of the development of the moral sense several years earlier, and other anthropological and philosophical writers had also approached morality and ethics from the point of view of evolution, Spencer's *Data of Ethics* soon became the definitive statement of the evolu-tionary approach to ethics.[9] Alexander Bain recalled in his autobiography that in 1879 he had 'prepared a notice of Herbert Spencer's *Data of Ethics*; freely commenting on his Evolution point of view, and especially com-mending the two chapters "Egoism *versus* Altruism" and "Altruism *versus* Egoism".' Looking back, Bain interpreted the *Data of Ethics* both as a defin-itive rebuttal of 'popular exaggerations of altruistic duty' and also as the work that marked the arrival of 'the Ethics of Evolution' as a school

---

[7] See Dixon 2004: 85–9; J. D. Y. Peel 2004; R. J. Richards 2004.

[8] On the production of the *Vanity Fair* cartoon, the work of Sir Francis Carruthers Gould, and a facsimile of the original accompanying text, see G. Jones and R. A. Peel 2004: pp. xi–xiii.

[9] Other evolutionary approaches to morality in the 1870s, which displayed the influence of the-orists including Hegel and Comte were Simcox 1877: esp. 209–42; Wake 1878. On Simcox, see *ODNB*; Beer 2001.

Figure 14. The caricature of Herbert Spencer in the *Vanity Fair* 'Men of the Day' series, 26 Apr. 1879, captioned 'Philosophy' and published a few months before his *Data of Ethics*.

occupying 'a place in the standing controversy respecting the true foundation of an ethical system'. In subsequent years, 'Spencer's position was
steadily controverted by Sidgwick in the interest of Utility, while it was
subsequently embraced by Leslie Stephen in his work published two years
later.'[10] *The Times* obituary of Spencer in 1903 considered that, of all his
works, *The Data of Ethics* had occasioned the most 'prolonged and active
controversy', and that its arguments had been 'canvassed by all sections of
the philosophical world'.[11]

For his own part, Leslie Stephen felt the need, in the introduction to
the work Bain was referring to, the *Science of Ethics* (1882), to respond to
the question of whether 'my book has not been made superfluous by the
discussion of the same topic upon the same assumptions by the leading
exponent of the philosophy of evolution in Mr Herbert Spencer's *Data of
Ethics*'.[12] Spencer's international reputation was further enhanced by a successful lecture tour in the United States in 1882.[13] His friend Beatrice
Webb, looking back on the 1880s, thought that the first part of this decade
had marked 'the zenith of his world-fame as England's greatest philosopher'.[14] In her substantial survey of evolutionary approaches to morality ten
years later, C. M. Williams (1893) gave Spencer a central position, and
described him as 'England's most popular living philosopher'.[15] Frederic
Harrison's estimate of Spencer was even more generous. In an article
appraising the posthumous reputation of John Stuart Mill, Harrison wrote
that Mill had been 'neither so original nor so systematic as Bentham or
Spencer', but nevertheless that his name 'must stand as the most important
name in English philosophy between Bentham and Spencer'.[16] The radical
political theorist and campaigner Henry George, who opposed Herbert
Spencer's politics, nonetheless recognized the very high esteem in which he
was held as a philosopher. He wrote in 1892 that Spencer was perceived
within 'a wider circle than any man now living, and perhaps than any man

---

[10] Bain 1904: 341. Stephen's *Science of Ethics* (1882) was in fact published three years later.

[11] *The Times* (9 Dec. 1903), 12.

[12] Stephen 1882: p. viii.

[13] On Spencer's international impact, see J. D. Y. Peel 1971: 1–6; on his particular influence in America, see also J. R. Moore 1985b: 79. American audiences were also being introduced to a very different kind of British philosophical individualism in 1882, by Oscar Wilde, who was touring America and Canada giving lectures on aestheticism as an accompaniment to the touring pro-duction of Gilbert and Sullivan's *Patience*, an opera which satirized the aesthetic movement; *ODNB*.

[14] Webb 1926: 184; also quoted in M. Taylor 1992: 19.

[15] C. M. Williams 1893: 2.

[16] Frederic Harrison, 'John Stuart Mill', *Nineteenth Century*, 235 (1896), 487–508, at 508.

of our century' as a 'profound, original and authoritative thinker'. Some, George believed, even held Spencer to be 'the greatest thinker the world has ever seen'.[17]

Although Spencer was widely eulogized, both before and after his death, as one of the world's great philosophers, that did not necessarily mean that many people actually read his books. It is probably slightly safer to assume a correlation between high sales and large readership in the cases of some literary genres, such as popular novels or weekly newspapers, than it is in the case of others, including works of science and philosophy. Greta Jones suggests that Spencer's name and some general sense of his evolutionary ideas were relatively widely known, but that close reading of his works was confined to a much smaller number of serious students of science and philosophy. Spencer was dismayed when he discovered, for instance, that his good friend Richard Potter (the father of Beatrice Potter, later Beatrice Webb, with whom Spencer also became friends) had never read any of his works.[18]

A similar picture was suggested by some representations of the non-reading of Spencer's works in novels by Mary Elizabeth Braddon and George Gissing. In Braddon's *The Golden Calf* (1883), Brian Walford used his agnosticism as an excuse not to attend church with his wife, despite having only 'dipped into Herbert Spencer'.[19] The deeply religious Nora Beauminster, in *The Rose of Life* (1905), 'loved literature and hated science, had never read a chapter of Darwin or Huxley, knew Herbert Spencer only as a name, and had a shuddering horror of the Immensities and the Unknowable'.[20] Amy Reardon, in Gissing's *New Grub Street* (1891), liked to read 'solid periodicals', and especially 'those articles which dealt with themes of social science' or anything 'that savoured of newness and boldness in philosophic thought'. She preferred to read the kind of literature that 'may be defined as specialism popularised; writing which addresses itself to educated, but not strictly studious, persons'. 'Thus, for instance,' the narrator explained, 'though she could not undertake the volumes of Herbert Spencer, she was intelligently acquainted with the tenor of their contents; and though she had never opened one of Darwin's books, her knowledge of his main theories and illustrations was respectable.' In this way, Amy Reardon was presented as a 'typical woman of the new time, the

---

[17] Quoted in M. Taylor 1992: 19.
[18] G. Jones 2004: 9.
[19] Braddon 1883: ii. 214.
[20] Braddon 1905: ii. 40–1.

woman who has developed concurrently with journalistic enterprise'.[21]
Another type of reader—the working-class autodidact—was represented
by Samuel Barmby in Gissing's *In the Year of the Jubilee* (1894). Barmby had
learnt whatever he knew from 'penny popularities' and as a result his mind
'was packed with the oddest jumble of incongruities; Herbert Spencer jostled with Charles Bradlaugh, Matthew Arnold with Samuel Smiles; in one
breath he lauded George Eliot, in the next was enthusiastic over a novel by
Mrs Henry Wood; from puerile facetiae he passed to speculations on the
origins of being, and with equally light heart'.[22]

On the other hand, there were of course plenty of readers who did
engage with Spencer's writings, and these were also represented in the fiction of the period. Another of Gissing's characters, Lord Dymchurch in *Our
Friend the Charlatan* (1901), sat in the library of his club reading one of
Spencer's best known books, *The Man versus The State* (1884), which Gissing
himself had read a few years earlier. Dymchurch subsequently debated the
book's merits with the idealistic and altruistic Dyce Lashmar.[23] In
Braddon's *The Day Will Come* (1889), Harrington Dalbrook and his intellectual sisters divided their leisure hours between poring over volumes of
Herbert Spencer, and works about Eastern religion, and discussing the latest fashions and the details of each other's love lives.[24] Spencer's books even
appeared in fictional works as accessories to romantic love. A young couple, Gerard and Hester, in another Braddon novel, *Gerard, or, The World, The
Flesh and the Devil* (1891), spent dreamy afternoons together moored in a
punt and reading philosophical works by 'W. K. Clifford and Herbert
Spencer, Comte and Mill—he picking out chapters or essays for her to
read, she accepting meekly whatever he put before her as the best'.[25] In
Chekhov's short story 'The Duel' (1891), Layevsky recalled the beginning
of his affair with a married woman: 'At first there was kissing, and quiet
evenings, and promises, and Spencer, and ideals, and mutual interests . . .
What a sham! Essentially, we were just running away from her husband.' In
the end, Layevsky was disappointed to discover that 'life with a woman
who's read Spencer and gone to the ends of the earth for you is just about
as boring as living with any village girl'.[26] Colonel Colquhoun, in Sarah

[21] Gissing 1985: 397–8.
[22] Gissing 1895: 214 .
[23] Gissing 1901: 43–7. Gissing read *The Man versus The State* in 1896 and sympathized with its
anti-socialist message; see Gissing 1978: 403, 562.
[24] Braddon 1889: i. 26–7, 148.
[25] Braddon 1891: ii. 74.
[26] Chekhov 2001: 253–4; also quoted in J. D.Y. Peel 1971: 3.

Grand's *The Heavenly Twins* (1893), hoped to impress his new wife, the well-read and scientifically minded Evadne, by providing her with good books to read in the marital home. He tried to persuade her that she would prefer Zola and George Sand to Herbert Spencer and Francis Galton, her previous favourites, but bought her all the books she had not already read by those authors nonetheless. This was all part of Colquhoun's unsuccessful attempt to win Evadne round and persuade her to consummate their marriage despite her discovery of his dissolute past. Volumes of the *Synthetic Philosophy* can surely only very rarely, however, have actually been employed as a means of seduction.[27]

Spreading the word

Another of Herbert Spencer's readers was Eliza Lynn Linton. Linton had a controversial and productive literary career as journalist and novelist, gaining particular notoriety for her articles denouncing the advocates of women's rights. In a fictionalized memoir, *The Autobiography of Christopher Kirkland* (1885), in which Linton cast herself as a man, she recalled meeting Herbert Spencer and Marian Evans in John Chapman's house in the 1850s, before Evans had become the 'incomparable George Eliot' and at a time when 'Herbert Spencer's laurel-crown was still growing on the bushes'.[28] Christopher Kirkland also recalled that, in the 1860s he had felt motivated by his desire to alleviate the suffering of humanity. 'What we now call altruism', Kirkland recalled, 'was then as much a fact under another name. And altruism is integral to my nature.'[29] In the final peroration of the book, Kirkland professed a philosophical faith which advocated 'the manly modesty of Agnosticism which knows nothing save the obligation of active well-doing' and 'the practice of altruistic Duty as the absolute law of moral life' instead of superstitious beliefs about 'the heaven that lies Beyond'.[30] The transition from the time when 'altruism' was known 'under another name' to the 1880s when it was a watchword of agnostic moralism was not unrelated to the rise of Herbert Spencer as a famous philosopher. The optimistic and 'altruistic' agnosticism of Christopher Kirkland clearly owed

---

[27] Grand 1992: 175–6; on 'Sarah Grand' (the pen-name of Frances Elizabeth McFall) and *The Heavenly Twins*, see Richardson 2003: 95–131.
[28] Linton 1885: i. 12, iii. 77.
[29] Ibid. ii. 244–5.
[30] Ibid. iii. 320.

much to Spencer's philosophical writings of the 1870s, if not his later works. There would be a connection between Spencer, Linton, and altruism again in 1894 when Spencer called upon Linton to launch an attack on Henry Drummond's misappropriation in his *Ascent of Man* of the account of the evolution of altruism set out in the *Data of Ethics*.[31]

Looking at when and how the language of altruism made its way into some of the established records of national life, the *Annual Register*, the *Oxford English Dictionary*, and *The Times,* also reveals that its association with Spencer was of particular importance. The *Annual Register, or A View of the History, Politics, and Literature of the Year* had been published in London since the mid-eighteenth century. In 1864 its subtitle had changed to *A Review of Public Events at Home and Abroad.* The first time that 'altruism' appeared in its pages was in 1879, in a review of Herbert Spencer's *Data of Ethics.* The term's next appearance in the *Annual Register* came three years later in a discussion of Leslie Stephen's Spencerian *Science of Ethics*, which included a substantial section on 'altruism'.[32] It was also in 1882 that James Murray appealed to readers of *Notes and Queries* for illustrative quotations for 'altruism' and related terms for inclusion in the Philological Society's new dictionary. Of the fifty-two quotations that were sent to him to illustrate these words, seventeen were from works by Herbert Spencer, of which three made it into the first fascicle of the new dictionary, 'A–Ant', in 1884.[33] Some of the earliest references to 'altruism' in *The Times* came in letters written by Spencer and by Frederic Harrison who were conducting a public dispute in 1884 about Spencer's dependence or lack of it on the works of Auguste Comte. Several other early uses in *The Times* occurred in the context of disagreements about British foreign policy, a context into which Spencer himself, as we shall see, had introduced the language of altruism.

Another indication of the connection between 'altruism' and the philosophy of Herbert Spencer is to be found in *Mind*. During the ten years following the founding of *Mind* in 1876, as the first professional philosophical periodical in Britain, thirty-seven articles were published in the journal which referred to 'altruism'. Of these, twenty-four also mentioned Herbert Spencer (in thirteen cases specifically referring to the *Data of Ethics*). Extending the analysis up to 1900 produces a figure of 106 for the

---

[31] See Ch. 7, below.

[32] Stephen 1882: pp. viii, 219–63.

[33] See Ch. 1, above. The definition and quotation slips are held in the OUP archive in Oxford. The copy slips relating to altruism and related words are numbered from 895 to 911. The superfluous slips are not numbered.

number of articles mentioning 'altruism', precisely half of which also mentioned Spencer (in comparison to thirty-five which mentioned Mill, sixteen Comte, and fifteen Darwin).[34] Among these discussions in *Mind* was an article by Bain about the life and philosophy of his friend and mentor, John Stuart Mill. Referring to Mill's later political sympathies with certain forms of 'socialism', Bain wrote that Mill's understanding of the term was very different from that 'of the Socialists commonly so called'. Mill's imagined 'socialism' Bain explained, was to be 'the outcome of a remote future, when human beings shall have made a great stride in moral education or, as Mr Spencer would express it, have evolved a new and advanced phase of altruism'.[35]

In the United States, one of the leading interpreters of Spencer's ideas was the philosopher and religious thinker, John Fiske. Readers of Fiske's *Outlines of Cosmic Philosophy* (1874) were informed, in characteristically Spencerian jargon, that

> it is a corollary from the law of use and disuse, and the kindred biologic laws which sum up the processes of direct and indirect equilibration, that the fundamental characteristic of social progress is *the continuous weakening of selfishness and the continuous strengthening of sympathy.* Or—to use a more convenient and somewhat more accurate expression suggested by Comte— it is a gradual supplanting of *egoism* by *altruism.*[36]

(Spencer himself, as we shall see, also acknowledged the Comtean origins of the language of altruism when he first introduced it into his system.) By 1899, Fiske's view of the term 'altruism', which he employed as part of a Spencerian picture of social evolution, was that it was 'an ugly-sounding word' but that it seemed 'to be the only one available'. The influence of Spencer's philosophy had been such that his categories of thought now were apparently inevitable, even though the title for Fiske's own chapter seemed to suggest two alternatives: 'The Cosmic Roots of Love and Self-Sacrifice'.[37]

A poem entitled 'Altruism. (A Tale)' was published in an American illustrated magazine, *The Century*, in 1885. This satire on the self-interested and self-deceiving 'altruism' of modern philosophers imagined a shipwreck in which two 'scholars', possibly based on Fiske and Spencer, but identified

---

[34] Based on searches of the full text of *Mind*, which is available both through JSTOR and through Oxford Journals Online; see bibliography for details.

[35] Alexander Bain, 'John Stuart Mill', *Mind,* 4 (1879), 520–41, at 540.

[36] Fiske 1874: ii. 201. On Fiske, see Hawkins 1997: 106–8.

[37] Fiske 1899: 105; see also the section on 'Maternity and the Evolution of Altruism', 117–26.

simply as 'Jones, and the yet more famous Brown', were amongst the pas-
sengers on board and were left to fight over the one remaining life-
preserver. Each tried to persuade the other that—for purely altruistic
reasons—their claim to be saved was greater. Jones had a wife and three
children whose happiness depended on his survival. But Brown thought he
had an even stronger altruistic motive, namely his commitment to his
expectant readership, who were eagerly awaiting the third and final volume
of his great 'Cosmogony':

> Oh, were that mighty task complete
> Down to the last corrected sheet,
> Believe me, Jones, to save your life
> To your dear family and wife,
> I'd yield to you, unmurmuring,
> This frail support to which we cling!
> But what are wife and children three
> Compared with a Cosmogony?
> Or what—confess it, dearest Jones—
> Are *many* wives and childrens' moans
> To that loud cry of grief and woe
> With which the learned world shall know
> That it can never hope to see
> The long-expected Volume Three?[38]

The conclusion of the tale saw Jones and Brown both drown, each holding on to the life preserver, convinced of the validity of his altruistic arguments for his own superior claim to it. The connection between Spencer
and 'altruism' was made by philosophers as well as satirists. The philosophical writer George S. Carr wrote of Spencer as 'the very apostle of
Altruism', while a British periodical devoted to the dissemination of the
philosophy of egoism described him, albeit somewhat facetiously, as a
'famous altruist'.[39] An American lecturer even claimed that it was Herbert
Spencer who had invented 'the word "altruism" to take the place of love,
because the old word (sweet word!) was so quivering with life as to be unfit
for the dissecting operations of science'.[40]

'Altruism' started to spread more rapidly in Britain from the later 1870s
partly because it helped people to think and argue, and to position themselves, in relation to two of the most pressing political questions of the time,

---

[38] Robertson Trowbridge, 'Altruism. (A Tale)', *Century Magazine*, 30 (1885), 495.
[39] Carr 1895: 37; *The Eagle and the Serpent* (15 June 1898), 36. For more on Carr, see Ch. 7, and
for more on *The Eagle and the Serpent*, see Ch. 8 below.
[40] Warren 1890: 405.

namely what to do about the empire and what to do about the poor. And it allowed them to do so while using the latest philosophical and scientific vocabulary (whether approvingly or mockingly). While the earlier debates about positivism, science, and Christianity had often focused on the individual and their reasons for acting for the good of others rather than living a life of self-indulgence, these new and wider discussions of 'altruism' marked a shift in perspective from the morality of the individual to the morality of classes and nations. The moral scenarios that were now imagined differed in two ways. Not only did they involve relations between groups or classes rather than between individuals, but those relations were ones of inequality rather than the tacitly assumed equality of some earlier moral philosophizing. Specifically, they concerned the relation of Britain to other nations and races, and the relation of workers to employers, of the poor to the rich. 'Altruism' and 'egoism' thus came to be employed in the context of yet more 'isms' that were being debated at the time, including 'jingoism' and 'imperialism', both of which entered the language in the late 1870s, and 'socialism' and 'individualism', which were terms frequently used to suggest the political polarization experienced by many in the 1880s and 1890s between those who supported and those who resisted increasing state involvement in the provision of education, the regulation of the labour market, and the administering of schemes to improve the health and housing of the poor, and to relieve the financial distress of the unemployed.[41]

One example of how these questions came together in the 1890s can be found in a speech given by Lord Rosebery, Foreign Secretary in Gladstone's final administration at the time, shortly before becoming Prime Minister. Speaking at the opening meeting of the twenty-sixth annual session of the Royal Colonial Institute in 1893, Rosebery was offering a vote of thanks to Lord Onslow for an address on 'State Socialism in New Zealand', which had explored some of the successes and failures of various policies brought in to satisfy the 'labour interest' in New Zealand. In thanking Lord Onslow, Rosebery was led to reflect on the question of whether

---

[41] On 'jingoism' and 'imperialism', see *OED*, which gives 1878 as the earliest use for both terms. The latter was already a term for an imperial form of government but it was only in the 1870s that it took on the more ideological meaning of an expansionist or jingoistic attitude to empire. Political debates about the conduct of the empire are returned to later in this chapter. On 'individualism', see *OED*; M. Taylor 1992: 2–5; Collini 1979: 16. M. Taylor 1992 explores individualism as a political and social theory. For further literary and philosophical connotations of the term, and especially Oscar Wilde's characterisation of Jesus Christ as the greatest of individualists, see Ch. 8 below. On socialism, see Ch. 6.

classes and nations could ever be described as 'selfish'. As Foreign Secretary, he was only too aware that Britain had often been accused of 'selfishness' in her dealings with other nations. Rosebery quoted from 'a very humorous American paper' which had parodied the idea that 'Great Britain is at her old game, pursuing her own selfish aims, while all the other nations of the world are pursuing the aims of others without the slightest regard to the consequences'. Rosebery's audience greeted this with 'laughter and cheers'. Rosebery then compared this charge that nations were motivated by selfishness with the accusations often made that the working classes were driven purely by selfishness in demanding better pay and working conditions. He sometimes asked himself, he said, whether any class existed that was instead 'moved by altruism, by a purely generous regard for the interests of others?' His conclusion was that classes and nations were bound to pursue their own interests and that to expect them to be driven by 'altruism' was unrealistic and unreasonable.[42]

Bentham among the protozoa

Spencer's writings on 'altruism' provide a particularly clear illustration of the connections between the three dimensions of meaning that I distinguished at the outset, namely definition, connotation, and significance. Spencer provided new definitions of 'altruism' and 'altruistic' in theoretical works of psychology, sociology, and ethics in the 1870s. These definitions encouraged the kind of confusion between intentions and actions that has regularly dogged discussions of 'altruism' ever since. In terms of connotations, Spencer suffered particularly from the persistent positivist associations of the language of altruism. Even though his definitions differed from Comte's and the political programme through which he hoped to see altruism of a certain kind increase was almost diametrically opposed to Comte's, the Comtean connotations of the language of altruism led to the mistaken identification of Spencer with the doctrines of positivism, much to his frustration. Finally, the language of 'altruism' and 'egoism' had its greatest significance for Spencer in the contexts of the political debates of the period about governmental policies regarding poverty and empire, to which I have already alluded.

---

[42] *The Times* (15 Nov. 1893), 10.

The three works of Spencer's, all published in the 1870s, which made the most extensive use of the language of altruism were the 2nd edition of *The Principles of Psychology* (1870–2), *The Study of Sociology* (1873), and *The Data of Ethics* (1879). Although these were all scientific and philosophical works, they did not conform to the stricter professional standards of philosophical writing that were established through *Mind* or the writings of someone like Henry Sidgwick. In Spencer's ethical writings, theoretical speculations in biology, psychology, sociology, and philosophy were interspersed with empirical data from the writings of historians, anthropologists, and authors of travellers' tales. And, whatever the ostensible topic, Spencer's self-help sermonizing and political apologetics were never far away. Spencer was a public intellectual who, like Darwin, had no university post. Unlike Darwin, however, Spencer relied on his writing in order to make a living and was more than happy to include controversial and explicitly political argumentation in his published scientific treatises. In his combination of philosophy, science, and political polemic, as well as in his aspiration to produce a systematic philosophy of everything, Spencer had much more in common with Auguste Comte than with Charles Darwin. Comte and Spencer both wrote turgid, multi-volume, jargon-packed philosophical syntheses. Both proposed their own classification of the sciences, both held the sciences of sociology and ethics to be the most important of all, and both were closely associated with 'altruism'.

Spencer's *Principles of Psychology* was first published in 1855 before he had conceived of the ten-volume *Synthetic Philosophy* of which it was to become a part. The conception of the *Synthetic Philosophy* in late 1857, and the publication in 1859 of Darwin's *On the Origin of Species*, both meant that when it came to producing a 2nd edition of the *Principles of Psychology*, a large amount of rewriting and of new material was required. The first volume of the 2nd edition came out in 1870, the second in 1872. It was in the second volume, in a new chapter of 'Corollaries', that Spencer first wrote about the psychology of the 'altruistic' sentiments. Spencer himself explicitly acknowledged the Comtean pedigree of the term 'altruistic' and defended the positivist neologism against its orthodox critics:

> I gladly adopt this word, for which we are indebted to M. Comte. Not long since, some critic, condemning it as new-fangled, asked why we should not be content with such good old-fashioned words as benevolent and beneficent. There is a quite-sufficient reason. Altruism and altruistic, suggesting by their forms as well as their meanings the antitheses of egoism and egoistic, bring quickly and clearly into thought the opposition in a way that benevolence or beneficence and its derivatives do not, because the antitheses are

not directly implied by them. This superior suggestiveness greatly facilitates
the communication of ethical ideas.[43]

This endorsement of the Comtean antithesis between altruism and egoism
as a central tool in the task of communicating ethical ideas scientifically was
a key moment in the history of the transformation of moral philosophy by
the arrival of the language of altruism. It entailed the rejection of the terms
'benevolence' and 'beneficence', which had embodied the distinction
between good intentions and good actions which Spencer's own philosophy blurred. It also seemed to suggest, as Comte's and Lewes's uses of the
terms certainly had, that the distinction between moral badness and moral
goodness could now be mapped onto that between devotion to self and
devotion to others. Of course, Spencer in fact was not such an enthusiast
for altruism as an ethical ideal in the present as were his positivist friends,
but by structuring his ethics around their categories, and in looking forward to a future in which 'altruism' would prevail, he joined them in
enshrining the distinction between self and other at the heart of his ethics.

In contrasting the superior suggestiveness of 'altruism' with inferior
existing terms, Spencer probably had Anglican critics of 'altruism' such as
Frederic Farrar or J. B. Mozley in mind, although neither Farrar or Mozley
compared the term specifically with 'benevolence' or 'beneficence'.[44] Farrar
had asked a Cambridge audience in 1870 'Is "altruism" a sweeter or better
word than charity?'[45] Spencer's answer, in 1872 at least, was 'yes'. In the
Principles of Psychology, the 'altruistic' sentiments comprised one of three
related groups of moral feelings: the 'egoistic', the 'ego-altruistic', and
the 'altruistic'. All of these were classed as sentiments as opposed to appetites
or instincts by virtue of resulting from higher cognitive representations and
re-representations (to use Spencer's terminology) of more basic feelings and
impulses. The egoistic sentiments were those which were related to personal welfare and happiness, such as the remembrance of past pleasures, the
love of acquisition and possession, and the resistance of restraints on
conduct.[46] The ego-altruistic sentiments were those feelings which gave
rise to seemingly altruistic behaviour but which in reality arose from the
recognition of personal benefits which would accrue from such behaviour—benefits such as the approval of others, or rewards in this world or

---

[43] Spencer 1870–2: ii. 607n.
[44] This comparison was made a few years later by the Presbyterian Robert Flint in his Baird
lecture for 1877; Flint 1880: 209.
[45] On Farrar, Mozley, Flint, and other clerical critics of 'altruism', see Ch. 3 above.
[46] Spencer 1870–2: ii. 578–91.

the next. Thus consciousness of right and wrong took its origins in such ego–altruistic feelings, and the standards of right and wrong arising from these feelings would vary widely from place to place depending on 'the theological traditions and social circumstance' that prevailed; in other words, depending on the moral tastes of the local leaders, ancestors, or gods.[47] Finally, the altruistic sentiments, which were increasingly in evidence in 'the philanthropy of modern times', and which would prevail in the perfect social state of the future, were evolved from the ego–altruistic sentiments, and 'not sharply marked off' from them.[48] All altruistic feelings were 'sympathetic excitements of egoistic feelings', whether those feelings were sea-sicknesses, the urge to yawn, or sentiments proper, such as the love of possession, which could be sympathetically felt as the altruistic sentiment of generosity.[49]

Spencer's 1872 treatment of altruism, then, focused on the altruistic feelings and sentiments which would be increasingly felt as the 'predatory' form of social life gave way to the 'industrial'. Now that life was less painful, he thought, the altruistic sentiments, 'which find their satisfaction in conduct that is regardful of others and so conduces to harmonious co-operation', would become ever stronger.[50] In his focus on sentiments (rather than on behaviour); in his view that the roots of these sentiments were to be found both in a mixture of enlightened self-interest with social sympathy and parental instinct; and in his belief that these sentiments would gain in strength as society developed, Spencer echoed the teachings of both Comte and Darwin on the subject.[51] For Comte the great problem of human life had been how to subordinate the egoistic feelings to the altruistic, and it was through studying the laws of life, mind, and society (through the sciences of biology and sociology) that one could come to understand how that subordination might be achieved. Comte had also made use of the distinction between earlier military and later industrial modes of social existence—a distinction that would be of increasing importance to Spencer, as we shall see.[52]

Around the same time, Spencer was persuaded by his friend, the American publisher Edward Youmans, to be one of the first contributors to

---

[47] Ibid. ii. 592–606, at 603.
[48] Ibid. 607–26, at 609, 614.
[49] Ibid. 612–13.
[50] Ibid. 618–19.
[51] Like Darwin, Spencer argued that cooperative behaviour would have evolved, in part, through 'survival of the fittest among tribes'; Spencer 1892–3: i. 314.
[52] Comte 1875–7: i. 456–594.

a new international publishing venture designed to bring the latest scientific knowledge to a popular audience (and to make money and create new readerships for scientific publishers and writers). Youmans, acting as an agent for the American publisher Appleton & Co., enlisted Spencer, along with several other leading men of science, including Bain, Tyndall, Huxley, and Lubbock, to contribute to the new International Scientific Series. The books in this series, in which ninety-six titles were ultimately included, were published by Appleton's in New York and by H. S. King in London, as well as, in some cases, being published in French, Italian, and other European languages too. With an eye to maximizing his readership and his income, Spencer arranged for *The Study of Sociology* to be published in instalments in the *Contemporary Review* in Britain and in Youmans's *Popular Science Monthly* in America prior to its publication as a book in 1873. The series subsequently included John William Draper's *History of the Conflict between Religion and Science* (1875), Thomas Huxley's *The Crayfish: An Introduction to the Study of Zoology* (1880), and John Lubbock's *Ants, Bees, and Wasps* (1882). But the best-seller of the whole list was Spencer's *The Study of Sociology*, which was the fifth title in the series, and sold over 26,000 copies in Britain alone. *The Study of Sociology* was translated into French, Italian, and Swedish, and was the only title in the series also to be translated into Russian.[53]

Although it was through the *Data of Ethics* that Spencer had most impact as a philosophical theorist of 'altruism', it was as a popularizer of social science that his ideas about 'altruism' would have reached a wider readership. The chapter of *The Study of Sociology* in which Spencer had most to say about altruism was entitled 'The Educational Bias'.[54] Here, in describing how he believed religious education could inculcate prejudices that might create biased sociological observers, Spencer developed an account of social evolution in terms of two competing religions—the religion of enmity and the religion of amity. According to Spencer, primitive pagan religions of enmity had encouraged egoism and militarism. A reaction against these religions had given rise to a diametrically opposed religion, the Christian religion of amity, or 'the religion of unqualified altruism', as Spencer also called it, according to which one was to love one's enemies as oneself. To Spencer, both these religions were extreme and one-sided. Each needed to be corrected by the other: 'That altruism is right, but

[53] Howsam 2000: esp. 196–8.
[54] Herbert Spencer, 'The Study of Sociology. VIII—The Educational Bias', *Contemporary Review*, 21 (1873), 315–34; Spencer 1873: 178–203.

that egoism is also right, and that there requires a continual compromise between the two', Spencer wrote, was a position which very few 'consciously formulate and still fewer avow', but it was, he believed, the correct view.[55] So, while 'altruistic' had been used to describe certain sympathetic psychological feelings in 1872, Spencer now used 'altruism' as a term that sometimes signified love for others and sometimes a broader religious ideal. In the *Data of Ethics*, six years later, Spencer's definition of the term would change again, this time to focus on actions rather than on feelings or ideals.

Approximately a quarter of the *Data of Ethics* (1879) was about the relationship between egoism and altruism, in chapters entitled 'Egoism *versus* Altruism', 'Altruism *versus* Egoism', 'Trial and Compromise', and 'Conciliation'. These chapters constituted the most sustained and most influential theoretical discussion of 'altruism' yet to be published.[56] It was this work which first introduced Friedrich Nietzsche to the language of altruism; it confirmed his view that Spencer, like so many other European philosophers, was in the grip of intellectual decadence and a degenerate morality.[57] It was also read and reviewed by many leading members of the emerging profession of philosophy in Britain and America, including Alexander Bain, Henry Sidgwick, and William James. It was also here, in the key chapter on 'Altruism *versus* Egoism', that Spencer developed ideas about 'altruism' being discernible from the very dawn of life, in the lowest and simplest creatures, and especially in the evolution of parental instincts which ultimately evolved into social sympathy. These evolutionary ideas were subsequently enthusiastically taken up by Patrick Geddes, Henry Drummond, and others.[58]

The central note of this work, namely the untenability of either extreme egoism or extreme altruism, was the same one that had been struck in the *Principles of Psychology* and the *Study of Sociology*. 'If the maxim—"Live for self" is wrong,' Spencer wrote, 'so also is the maxim—"Live for others." Hence a compromise is the only possibility.'[59] Spencer also sought to blur the boundary between the two categories of egoism and

---

[55] Spencer 1873: 182–3.

[56] For a thorough and sympathetic reassessment of Spencer's ethics as a valuable and pioneering contribution to the enterprise of evolutionary ethics, see R. J. Richards 1987: 295–330.

[57] On Nietzsche's scathing response to Spencer's 'decadent' moral philosophy, see Ch. 8 below.

[58] Spencer 1879: 201–18. *The Data of Ethics*, *The Principles of Ethics*, and many other of Spencer's works are available online through The Online Library of Liberty (see Bibliography for details). On Geddes and Drummond, see Ch. 7 below.

[59] Spencer 1879: 219.

altruism. He argued that effective altruism could not be undertaken without taking care, egoistically, of one's own mental and bodily well-being and that of one's family; and that altruism, in any case, had many egoistic benefits, such as the pleasure it could bring to the benefactor and the broader rewards of living in a cooperative society. In addition to both Christianity and the positivist 'Religion of Humanity', as examples of ideologies advocating excessive altruism, Spencer, in the *Data of Ethics*, turned to the utilitarianism of Bentham and Mill. Here he developed further the theme of the need for a conciliation between egoism and altruism, and accused the utilitarians of promoting an ideology of 'pure altruism'. Henry Sidgwick thought that Spencer was getting confused between utilitarianism and Comtism. Sidgwick wrote, in *Mind*, that Spencer's apparent antagonism to the utilitarian school depended 'on a mere misunderstanding' and that 'his quarrel is not really with the very sober and guarded "altruism" of Bentham and the Benthamites, but with certain hard sayings of the prophet of the Positivist religion, from whom the term Altruism is taken'.[60] In his undergraduate lectures in Cambridge in the 1880s and 1890s, which were attended by G. E. Moore, amongst others, Sidgwick was even more outspoken in his critique of Spencer on this point: 'the combination of Benthamite Utilitarianism and Comtist Altruism against which Mr Spencer appears to be arguing in chapter xiii is the most grotesque man of straw that a philosopher ever set up in order to knock it down'.[61]

Spencer's attempt in the *Data of Ethics* to redefine 'altruism' as a kind of action rather than a set of instincts, or even as an ethical ideal, also drew comments from reviewers. Spencer had suggested in 1872 that 'altruism' was more suggestive a term than either 'benevolence' or 'beneficence', but he had not acknowledged that in replacing those two words with the solitary term 'altruism' he was tacitly effacing the basic distinction they made, which was evident in their etymologies, between a good will and a good action. In 1879 Spencer for the first time stipulated that 'altruism' was to mean 'all action which, in the normal course of things, benefits others instead of benefiting self'. This was to include all 'acts by which offspring are preserved and the species maintained', in non-human as well as human species, regardless of whether there was any conscious motivation; 'acts of automatic altruism' were to be included along with those motivated by a

[60] Henry Sidgwick, 'Mr Spencer's Ethical System', *Mind*, 5 (1880), 216–26, at 221.
[61] H. Sidgwick 1902: 184–5. Of the 22 lectures included in this posthumous edn produced by E. E. Constance Jones, 10 were about Spencer's ethics, 8 on T. H. Green, and 4 on James Martineau.

desire to help others. At the lowest level, the reproductive cellular fission of the simplest organism, such as an infusorium or a protozoon, was to qualify as an act of 'physical altruism'.[62] Spencer acknowledged that some, who thought altruism meant simply 'conscious sacrifice of self to others among human beings', would find his extension of the definition of altruism so far beyond that meaning, to include the lowest forms of life, to be counterintuitive or absurd. Undeterred, Spencer, in his new scientific and materialistic definition of the term, reduced 'altruism' to those actions which 'involved a loss of bodily substance' (a definition which would later come in for particular mockery from Nietzsche).[63] Spencer presented the evolution of life as a process in which egoism and altruism, defined in his reductive biological senses, were both primordial (although egoism was primary), and both evolved simultaneously, with altruism gradually coming to predominate in more civilized human societies.

This extension of altruism to all acts that benefited others, undertaken by any creature, and which involved the loss of bodily substance, led to certain conceptual difficulties. Those difficulties were caused especially by the fact that Spencer had, both in his earlier writings and in the *Data of Ethics* itself, either tacitly or explicitly used definitions which focused on feelings rather than actions, motivations rather than outcomes. Those other-regarding actions that were motivated by the love of praise or rewards, by the second-rate 'ego-altruistic' sentiments of the *Principles of Psychology*, now seemed to qualify as straightforwardly altruistic, since a benefit to others was now the only requirement for that title. In the *Data of Ethics*, Spencer sometimes stuck with his initial definition in terms of actions, but at other times he applied the adjective 'altruistic' to a sort of motive, a type of character, a sort of sympathetic feeling (as he had in the *Principles of Psychology*), or even to a philosophical doctrine or ideology (as in his allegation that utilitarianism was a form of 'pure altruism'). Reviewers picked up on this from the outset. Writing in the *Princeton Review*, the Princeton President James McCosh alluded to the problem when he wrote: 'I prefer the phrase "love" to altruism, the Comtean one, which the school is seeking to introduce, inasmuch as the former demands an inward affection whereas the latter might be satisfied by an outward act.'[64] Alfred W. Benn, writing the third review of the work to be published in *Mind* (the first two being those by Bain and Sidgwick), identified the problem more directly. He complained

---

[62] Spencer 1879: 201–2.
[63] Ibid. 203.
[64] James McCosh, 'Herbert Spencer's *Data of Ethics*', *Princeton Review*, 4 (1879), 607–36, at 627.

that what Spencer meant by altruism was unclear, and suggested that words ending in 'ism' 'never denote actions but always beliefs or dispositions'. 'Altruism', therefore, should mean not a sort of action but 'the feeling that prompts us to benefit others . . . which is not quite the same thing'. Benn also noted that Spencer introduced further confusion by talking about the pleasurable feelings arising from actions benefiting others as 'altruistic pleasures'. This was misleading since these feelings certainly were not themselves of any benefit to others. Spencer was equivocating, as indeed he had in the *Principles of Psychology*, between 'altruistic' and 'sympathetic'.[65]

It was thanks to Herbert Spencer that, from its earliest uses as a central term in evolutionary ethics, with both biological and moral connotations, the word 'altruism' was beset by definitional problems. James Murray, sorting through the many quotations from Spencer he had been sent to illustrate 'altruism' and related terms, opted to exclude the behavioural meaning of the term and so put aside those slips bearing Spencerian quotations which defined 'altruism' as a kind of action. Although those quotations survived as 'superfluous slips' in the *OED* archives, as well as in their original locations in Spencer's publications of course, these did not contribute to the official definition of 'altruism' given to the public in the first fascicle of the new dictionary in 1884.

Comtean connotations

Back in the 1850s, when Spencer was close friends with Marian Evans and George Henry Lewes and other members of John Chapman's *Westminster Review* circle, he took a trip to Paris. This was in 1856, during a period of recuperation following the nervous breakdown he had suffered after completing the 1st edition of the *Principles of Psychology*. On his way to Paris, Spencer had dropped in on John Chapman's office on the Strand, and Chapman had given him an errand to run. He gave Spencer a 'sum of something under twenty pounds to pay over to Comte' representing the modest royalties due to Comte from the sales of Harriet Martineau's condensation of the *Cours*, published by Chapman in 1853.[66] Spencer, like Bain, who had visited Comte's apartment on Rue Monsieur-le-Prince a few years earlier, did not form a positive impression. To start with, Spencer was unimpressed by Comte's physiognomy: the face was 'unattractive'

[65] Alfred W. Benn, 'Another View of Mr Spencer's Ethics', *Mind*, 5 (1880), 489–512, at 509.
[66] On Martineau and the Chapman circle, see Ch. 2 above.

although, being 'strongly marked', it was at least 'distinguished from the multitudes of meaningless faces one daily sees'. Spencer did not recall a great deal of the conversation that passed between them: 'I remember only that hearing of my nervous disorder, he advised me to marry; saying that the sympathetic companionship of a wife would have a curative influence.' This, Spencer noted, was a point of agreement between Comte and Thomas Huxley who, many years later, also 'suggested that I should try what he facetiously called gynœopathy: admitting however that the remedy had the serious inconvenience that it could not be left off if it proved unsuitable'.[67]

Spencer always insisted that he had taken virtually nothing of any substance from Comte's philosophy, and yet his immersion in the Comtist world of Chapman, Evans, and Lewes in the 1850s clearly had more of an impression on him than he would admit. Spencer's first book had been titled *Social Statics* (1851), which itself was a Comtean phrase. For many years, Spencer denied that he knew the phrase 'social statics' had been used by anyone other than himself when he wrote the book. Eventually, however, in an 1891 footnote to one of his reprinted essays, Spencer admitted that he must have got the idea of dividing social science into 'statics' and 'dynamics' from John Stuart Mill's *Logic* (1843), which, although not naming Comte as the source, had taken the distinction from him.[68] Spencer's adoption of the Comtean neologisms 'altruism' and 'sociology' was similarly a double-edged sword. Using this language helped to mark Spencer's philosophy out as particularly scientific. These were both amongst the newest scientific terms with which to analyse human society. They lent his works an appropriately modern and technical linguistic allure. To write in this way helped Spencer to identify himself as a thinker untainted by the old theological superstitions or metaphysical abstractions. On the other hand, however, it was this adoption of the language of Comte and the positivists, this wearing of their philosophical clothes, which led to the constant perception, by both friends and foes of Comte's philosophy, that Herbert Spencer was himself a follower of Comte.[69] This was an allegation which Spencer resisted vigorously throughout his life, sometimes going to great lengths to prove his lack of dependence on Comte. In 1864, he wrote an appendix to his *Classification of the Sciences*, entitled simply 'Reasons for Dissenting from

[67] Spencer 1904: i. 492–3.
[68] Spencer 1891: 134n.
[69] For a discussion of the recurrent connections made between Spencer and Comte and an analysis of the extent of the dependence, if any, see Eisen 1967.

the Philosophy of M. Comte'. In 1889, Spencer, through Frederic Harrison, paid a researcher a guinea to go to the British Museum to track down some newspaper articles he had written in *The Pilot* in the 1840s, to prove that he had not used the term 'sociology' in them (such a usage would have indicated that, contrary to his constant claims to the contrary, Spencer had indeed read Comte prior to the composition of *Social Statics*).[70] Spencer wrote to Harrison that, despite the toll it was taking on his 'shattered nervous system', he was determined to establish his independence from Comte: 'This thing has been my bane for the last thirty years and more'.[71]

Harrison was only too aware of Spencer's sensitivity on this question, since he had been central to its most public airing a few years earlier. In January 1884, Spencer had published an article on religion in the *Nineteenth Century*, to which Harrison responded in the March issue. Harrison criticized Spencer's description of the unknowable ultimate reality as 'an Infinite and Eternal Energy, from which all things proceed' as an unnecessarily grandiose and theological formulation of what could simply have been designated 'the unknown'.[72] Then in September the two clashed again over claims made by Harrison in an address on 'The Memory of Auguste Comte and his True Work', which was reprinted in *The Times*. Harrison had described Spencer's philosophy as 'nothing but an attempt to play a new tune on Comte's instrument'. This led to an exchange of published letters to the editor from Spencer and Harrison, each penning their claims in the rooms of the gentleman's club to which they both belonged, the Athenaeum. Spencer went over the old ground, already covered in his 1864 pamphlet, and added to this the testimony of a letter from John Stuart Mill supporting his independence from Comte.[73] Central to Harrison's reply was the claim that Spencer, by adopting Comtean terminology, implicitly adopted parts of the doctrine too. It was Harrison's view that 'terms which crystallize entire modes of thought are of crucial import'. The terms he had in mind included sociology, social evolution, social environment and social organism. These were 'terms of art' introduced by Comte as early as 1839, and yet Spencer, he said, 'can hardly write a page without employing them;

---

[70] Correspondence relating to this episode is held in the Frederic Harrison Papers, London School of Economics Library, Harrison 1/43/ff. 19–27. See also Spencer 1904: i. 255–6; Duncan 1908: 287.

[71] Spencer to Frederic Harrison, 5 Apr. 1889; Frederic Harrison Papers, London School of Economics Library, Harrison 1/43/f. 20.

[72] Herbert Spencer, 'Religion: A Retrospect and Prospect', *Nineteenth Century*, 15 (1884), 1–12, at 12; Frederic Harrison, 'The Ghost of Religion', *Nineteenth Century*, 15 (1884), 494–506, at 496.

[73] The text of the letter from Mill is to be found in Mill 1963–91: xiv. 934–5.

and employing also, as I hold, the conception of Comte'. The same was true, Harrison went on, 'of what Mr Spencer writes about "altruism" in ethics, and about an industrial succeeding to a military organization in sociology'. Harrison's conclusion was that Spencer, through his long association and friendship with Lewes and Eliot, had unconsciously appropriated more than he had realized of the positivist philosophy. Spencer's response contained nothing new, and on the question of the term altruism he simply conceded again that the word was indeed Comte's and that it was 'a very useful word'.[74]

Spencer would clearly have been better advised, since he wished to distinguish his own philosophical and political projects very clearly from those of Comte and the positivists, to have steered clear of the language of altruism. Spencer and Comte agreed about many things. They looked forward to a future society where barbarous, militarized forms of society would be replaced by civilized, industrialized ones marked by greater altruism.[75] In this process both expected to see theological dogmas increasingly replaced by scientific facts, and to see God replaced by Humanity as the ultimate focus of men's moral strivings. They both believed in the universal reign of natural law, and interpreted natural laws as empirical generalizations of observed phenomena. For all these similarities between Spencer's and Comte's treatments of altruistic feelings, there were important differences too. While Comte envisaged these sentiments being maximized in an autocratic society in which the autocrat was Auguste Comte, Spencer envisaged them coming about increasingly in a freely cooperating society of individuals, in which the individuals were all Herbert Spencers. For, eventually, on Spencer's model, as the altruistic sentiments, through being associated with the sympathetic pleasures that they produced, became stronger, there would arise individuals so advanced that their altruistic sentiments would 'begin to call into question the authority of the ego-altruistic sentiments'—that is the love of approval and reward which earlier theological systems had played upon. Those men who were prepared to 'brave the frowns of their fellows by pursuing courses at variance with old but injurious customs, and even cause dissent from the current religion', would eventually come to dominate in the ideal future state.[76]

---

[74] 'Mr Herbert Spencer and the Comtists', *The Times* (9 Sept. 1884), 5; (12 Sept. 1884), 8; (15 Sept. 1884), 7.
[75] On Spencer's role in the popularization in America of his secularized 'theodicy' in which the evolution of perfect society in future could justify the natural evils of the present, see J. R. Moore 1985b.
[76] Spencer 1870–2: ii. 622.

Spencer was at least partly right when he protested, for the umpteenth time, in his *Autobiography* (1904), that his adoption of Comtean language did not imply adherence to Comtean philosophy or religion. 'Save in the adoption of his word "altruism," which I have defended,' Spencer wrote, 'and in the adoption of his word "sociology," because there was no other available word (for both which adoptions I have been blamed), the only indebtedness I recognize is the indebtedness of antagonism.'[77] What Spencer's experience proved, however, was that the meanings suggested to readers by key terms were determined not only by the definitions given to them by a particular author, but also by the associations and connotations that were already attached to the word. One of the outcomes of Spencer's own deployment of the language of altruism was that, while not losing its Comtean connotations, it gained new associations with arguments about socialism and imperialism.

'The New Toryism'

Although Spencer and Harrison publicly clashed over the philosophical interpretation of Comtean terminology, there were many other questions on which they found themselves in agreement. In politics they were both Liberals. When a parliamentary seat became vacant in Leicester in 1884, a committee representing the electors of the constituency, which was described in the *Annual Register* as an 'ultra-radical' one, initially approached the secularist George J. Holyoake as a potential candidate.[78] He ruled himself out on the basis of his unwillingness to take the parliamentary oath if elected (this had been a question of much public debate since Bradlaugh's refusal to do so since he was first elected as a radical Liberal MP for Nottingham four years earlier).[79] The Leicester committee charged with the nomination of candidates next turned to Herbert Spencer to ask if his name might be put forward, but he turned them down pleading his fragile health and stating his preference for the role of philosopher over that of

---

[77] Spencer 1904: 445–6. Given the association between 'altruism' and Comte made by Spencer and by his reviewers during the 1870s, I would not go so far as Stefan Collini, who suggests that, by the mid-1870s, the word 'no longer needed to carry its identity papers with it'. The Comtist association lasted, for some, into the 1880s and 1890s. Despite this, Collini is essentially right that the Comtist association faded as the term came into wider use, and that the success of Spencer's work was certainly instrumental in that process. Collini 1991: 61.

[78] *Annual Register* (1884), 166–7.

[79] On the Bradlaugh case, see Arnstein 1965; Royle 1980.

legislator.[80] The Leicester committee's third choice was Frederic Harrison, and he also turned them down. As a positivist he did not wish to align himself with any political party, and even if he did, his views were in some cases radical but in others conservative. He wished to see an end to all hereditary positions in government, and he supported Home Rule in Ireland. On the other hand he had views which he suspected were 'probably out of harmony with Radical majorities'. He was 'opposed to compelling people to become temperate by law, or to force them into State schools'.[81] On these questions of increasing state intervention, and also in his concerns about the increasingly aggressive foreign policy of Gladstone's second administration of 1880–5, Harrison was out of sympathy with the Liberal party but very much in sympathy with Herbert Spencer. On state education, for instance, Spencer had also, in the *Data of* Ethics, expressed his opposition to a system which 'taxes ratepayers that children's minds may be filled with dates, and names, and gossip about kings, and narratives of battles, and other useless information'.[82]

We saw above how Spencer's name was increasingly associated with discussions of 'altruism'. It is notable, however, that different readers understood that association in different ways. Bain recalled Spencer's *Data of Ethics* as a definitive statement of the excesses of altruism and the prior claims of egoism. Others thought of him as a prophet of altruism—partly because of his utopian hope for a future society dominated by spontaneous altruism, and partly, as we shall see, because of his opposition to British military aggression. Spencer's moralizing had strands both of sternness and of kindness which allowed him to be read as an egoist or an altruist. Both of these strands had their roots in his political radicalism. Writing as a radical, Spencer attached the label of 'Toryism' both to authoritarian and interventionist domestic schemes and to militaristic foreign policies. He presented his individualism and his anti-aggression as two different ways to be opposed to Toryism. While some Liberals welcomed proposals for greater state provision of education and poor-relief as evidence of a newly socialistic kind of Liberalism, for Spencer this was better described as 'The New Toryism', which was the title he took for one of his essays in *The Man versus The State*.[83] Spencer was trying to retain the associations of the terms

---

[80] *The Times* (10 Mar. 1884), 7; (15 Mar. 1884), 11. See also Duncan 1908: 240–2.
[81] Letter to the Leicester representation committee as published in *The Times* (19 Mar. 1884), 12.
[82] Spencer 1879: 210–11.
[83] 'New Liberalism' only became current as a political designation in the late 1890s; Himmelfarb 1991: 381.

'Tory' and 'Liberal' with which he had grown up several decades earlier. According to Spencer's definitions, Toryism stood for 'coercion by the State *versus* freedom of the individual', whether that use of state power was for selfish or for unselfish reasons. 'The altruistic Tory', he wrote, 'as well as the egoistic Tory belongs to the genus Tory; though he forms a new species of the genus.' Spencer harked back to 'the days when Liberals were rightly so called'. Liberalism then stood for the freedom of the individual from state interference and also for cooperative 'industrialism' as opposed to Tory 'militancy'.[84]

Spencer himself was aware that his views on the undeserving poor might seem heartless to some. He wrote, in June 1892, in the preface to the first volume of the *Principles of Ethics*, that he was anxious to get to work on the composition of parts 5 and 6, on positive and negative beneficence, which would appear in the second volume, before his strength finally failed him. Without them, he feared, the parts which had been published so far would leave 'a very erroneous impression respecting the general tone of evolutionary ethics'. In its full form, he said, 'the moral system to be set forth unites sternness with kindness; but thus far attention has been drawn almost wholly to the sternness'.[85] The reader of parts 5 and 6, however, when they were published the following year, might well have felt that there was little of this promised kindness on display. Spencer's prioritization of the health of society over the health of the individual, combined with his belief in the inheritance of acquired mental and moral traits, always led to what sounded simply like more sternness. The greatest difficulty, Spencer felt, when it came to relief of the poor (one of the principal kinds of positive beneficence), was how to 'regulate our pecuniary beneficence' so as to 'avoid assisting the incapables and the degraded' in multiplying.[86] And this difficulty seemed to Spencer 'almost insurmountable'. As a result he was as stern as ever. He blamed unconsidered state-funded philanthropy for having brought into existence large numbers who were 'unadapted to social life' and simply 'sources of misery to themselves and others'. The only way that this 'body of relatively worthless people' could be diminished was through the inflicting of pain: 'Cure can come only through affliction.' The affliction he had in mind was the pain that would be endured in the transition from a condition of 'State-beneficence' to one of 'self-help and

---

[84] Spencer 1994: 63–79, at 78–9.
[85] Spencer 1892–3: i, p. vi.
[86] Ibid. ii. 392.

private beneficence'.[87] If there was any solution, Spencer wrote, then that was the only one he could think of. His earlier optimism about the prospects of a more civilized and altruistic society evolving seemed quite shattered. Even his faith in the all-encompassing principle of evolution had been shaken by now. In the preface to the second volume of the work, he wrote words that none of his friends or foes could have expected ever to hear from him: 'The Doctrine of Evolution has not furnished guidance to the extent that I hoped.'[88]

By the time Spencer wrote the final parts of the *Principles of Ethics* in the 1890s, 'altruism' had become associated variously with socialism and Christianity as well as with Comtean positivism. Unsurprisingly, Spencer now greatly reduced his uses of 'altruism' and 'altruistic', which had been central categories in the *Data of Ethics*. Instead he generally preferred the terms 'beneficence' and 'beneficent' (which had been the very terms he had compared unfavourably with 'altruism' and 'altruistic' twenty years earlier in the *Principles of Psychology*). The reason that Spencer gave for his new terminology was that he now thought there was a tendency to overlook important distinctions between different kinds of altruistic conduct.[89] Spencer insisted on one distinction in particular, which he embodied in the titles of parts 5 and 6 of the *Principles of Ethics*: 'Negative Beneficence' and 'Positive Beneficence'. Negative beneficence involved self-restraint in one's dealings with fellow citizens; in short it meant respecting their equal rights to justice in social and economic interactions. Positive beneficence, or generosity, involved, where appropriate, actively promoting the welfare of one's spouse, parents, children, the sick, the poor, and the injured. Although the introduction of this conceptual distinction was, then, the supposed reason for replacing the overly broad 'altruism' with negative and positive 'beneficence', Spencer surely also wished to distance himself from the new sentimental creed of altruism. He was unremittingly critical of the prevalent 'hot-headed philanthropy, impatient of criticism', which ignored the distinction between justice and generosity and which was, 'by helter-skelter legislation destroying normal connexions between conduct and consequence'. The end result of this indiscriminate altruism would be the creation of a state 'having for its motto the words:—It shall be as well for you to be inferior as to be superior.' 'Indiscriminate philanthropy', Spencer feared, was leading to a discouragement of industry amongst the poor and,

---

[87] Ibid. 394.
[88] Ibid., p. v.
[89] Ibid. 268.

through the fostering of the idle and dissolute and their offspring, to a bodily and mental degeneration of the race.[90] His reasons for distancing himself from the language of altruism in the 1890s, like his reasons for adopting it in the 1870s, were strategic and political ones concerning the broader movements with which he wanted to be identified.

'Bibles first, bomb-shells after'

Moving from domestic to international politics, the meanings of 'altruism' were different again. There were two sides to the relationship between altruism and militarism. On the one hand, an ideology of self-sacrifice was clearly a necessary feature of military life, and a prerequisite for a state which sought to recruit volunteers to an army and navy which played major roles in pursuing the political and economic objectives of the government through armed conflict.[91] One of the earliest appearances of the language of altruism in a national newspaper came in a report in the *Pall Mall Gazette* on the military camp at Wimbledon in the summer of 1866. This annual event was organized to allow regiments of volunteers to come together for training and to take part, over a period of three weeks, in such activities as rifle-shooting, boxing, and athletics contests. According to the *Pall Mall Gazette*, however, the most striking aspect of 'volunteer life at Wimbledon' was the church parade on Sundays. All the different regimental camps marched to the central pavilion to take part in a religious service based on Church of England morning prayer, but without the communion service. The *Pall Mall* wondered why 'the *odium theologicum* should still burn so fiercely amongst us' when volunteers of all faiths—Catholics, Presbyterians, Unitarians and 'Churchmen of all shades, from the Ritualist to the Calvinist' could so happily come together in this act of public worship. Amongst the volunteers marching in the parade there was even one 'neophyte of the new sect, church—or what shall we call it—which has Mr Congreve for apostle, abjures Christianity as past work, and believes in "the direct culture of the altruistic instincts and the subordination of them to the egoistic."' The sermon was given by the Harrow schoolmaster Frederic Farrar, acting in his capacity as chaplain of the 18th Middlesex Rifle Volunteer Corps. As we saw in Chapter 3, Farrar would later, after his initial resistance, adopt the language of altruism in

[90] Spencer 1892–3: ii. 270–2.
[91] On the role of militarism in national and religious life, see Wolffe 1994: 213–53; Streets 2004.

his own advocacy of social reform.[92] On this occasion Farrar took as his text 'Quit ye like men; be strong!' and, according to the report, delivered a sermon which was 'a vigorous assault on the doctrines of peace at any price and non-intervention'.[93]

Around the same time, John Stuart Mill, in *Auguste Comte and Positivism* (1865), expressed his admiration for Comte's recognition of the importance of discipline in cultivating a more altruistic society. Agreeing with Comte, Mill wrote that 'Until labourers and employers perform the work of industry in the spirit in which soldiers perform that of an army, industry will never be moralized, and military life will remain, what, in spite of the anti-social character of its direct object, it has hitherto been— the chief school of moral co-operation.'[94] Later, others saw General Gordon's death in the Sudan in the pursuit of Britain's imperial goals as an exemplar of noble moral action. Caroline Haddon, in the context of a discussion of James Hinton's moral philosophy in 1886, and using the term that Hinton himself had pioneered, proposed General Gordon as an archetype of 'altruism'.[95] Arabella Buckley, the popularizer of Darwinian morality, also wrote about General Gordon, along with Buddha, Christ, and Isaac Newton as an example of a higher type of humanity. In her *Moral Teachings of Science* (1891) she wrote of those heroes who 'whether searching after truth like Newton, withstanding wrong and oppressions like Abraham Lincoln, or going to almost certain death like Gordon, in the hope of being of some use to his "poor, ignorant, black children," have all followed the law taught alike by science and religion, that he who devotes his life to duty is fulfilling the truest purpose of existence'.[96]

Herbert Spencer's advocacy of non-aggression sought to undermine these identifications of militarism with admirable social discipline and noble individual altruism by recasting the moral debate in terms of the relationship between nations. Debates about militarism and jingoism were an increasingly prominent feature of national party politics at the time that Spencer was at the height of his fame. Criticisms of the Zulu and Afghan wars conducted under the Tory administration of Lord Beaconsfield (the

---

[92] See Ch. 3 above.

[93] *Pall Mall Gazette* (16 July 1866), 3–4. The event was also reported in *The Times* (11 July 1866), 5; (14 July 1866), 5. On the Volunteer movement, see Wolffe 1994: 229–30.

[94] John Stuart Mill, 'Later Speculations of Auguste Comte', *Westminster Review*, 28 (1865), 1–42, at 14; in Mill 1963–91: x. 328–68, at 341.

[95] 'Utilitarianism and Altruism: A Discussion', in Haddon 1886: 24–36, at 35. Haddon was Hinton's sister-in-law. On Hinton as a pioneer of 'altruism', see Ch. 2 above.

[96] Buckley 1891: 105–6.

title Benjamin Disraeli had taken in 1876) in the late 1870s reached their peak in Gladstone's speeches during his anti-imperialistic Midlothian campaigns of 1879 and 1880, which culminated in a Liberal victory in the 1880 general election.[97] A Liberal campaign meeting held at Exeter Hall in March 1880 heard Beaconsfield's Tory manifesto denounced as 'egotism, Imperialism, and blustering'.[98] It was into this world that the *Data of Ethics* was published, and it was in the context of Liberal anti-imperialist politics that it was both written and read.

Altruism between individuals in Victorian society, Spencer thought, had to be strictly limited. It should be subordinated to rational egoism and should be the result of individual sympathy, moderated by a careful consideration of consequences, rather than being enacted through the indiscriminate and coercive apparatus of the state. This was the only way to avoid multiplying the dependent and degenerate classes still further. Between nations, however, Spencer insisted that altruism needed to be increased dramatically and urgently. One of the themes that came up most consistently in Spencer's writings on beneficence and altruism, from the *Social Statics* of 1851 onwards, was the connection between foreign policy and moral sentiments. The argument was that progress could only be made towards a more freely cooperative and altruistic society internally when external relations were peaceful; when barbarous militancy had evolved into civilized industrialism; when war had been replaced by mutually beneficial trade. Like Comte, Spencer believed that militarism was a feature of primitive theological societies. Once science had replaced theology, militarism should correspondingly be superseded by industry and trade as the leading means of international engagement.[99]

In this, as in his general attitude of hostility towards state intervention, Spencer again revealed his radical roots. The radical republican Thomas Paine, whose *Rights of Man* (1791–2) was one of the most widely read political treatises of the first half of the nineteenth century, had made very similar arguments. These would have been well known in the Dissenting circles

---

[97] Ceadel 2000: 110.

[98] The comment was made by Lord Richard Grosvenor, who was chairing a meeting of the supporters of Sir Arthur Hobhouse and John Morley, the Liberal candidates for the City of Westminster; reported in *The Times* (16 Mar. 1880), 10. Although the Liberals triumphed nationally, neither Hobhouse nor Morley was elected.

[99] On Spencer's place in the history of 'scientific pacificism' and the importance of positivist models of social evolution in the same tradition, see P. Crook 1994: 35–47.

within which Spencer grew up.[100] Paine's critique of the aristocratic form of government was that it was vastly more expensive than government needed to be. A central part of this expense was both incurred and justified by warfare: 'In reviewing the history of the English Government, its wars and its taxes, a bystander, not blinded by prejudice nor warped by interest, would declare that taxes were not raised to carry on wars, but that wars were raised to carry on taxes.'[101] For Paine, a civilized and modern form of government would 'promote a system of peace, as the true means of enriching a nation', through commerce, rather than 'keeping up a system of war' which could be used to raise taxes but was not for the general good.[102]

Spencer, like Paine, had been influenced by a Quaker father, and the Society of Friends had always been active in supporting the peace movement. William George Spencer attended Quaker meetings in Derby, whose calm atmosphere he preferred to the evangelicalism, clericalism, and doctrinal theology on offer at the Methodist chapel where his wife worshipped, and into which their son Herbert had been baptized.[103] Spencer recalled that a compromise had been argued for by his father according to which, 'from about ten years of age to thirteen I habitually on Sunday morning went with him to the Friends' Meeting House and in the evening with my mother to the Methodist Chapel'.[104] Although in later life Spencer certainly did not identify himself as a Christian of any kind, and doubted that his views had been shaped by Quakerism, his passionate hatred of militaristic imperialism almost certainly had its origins in those early contacts with the Society of Friends.[105]

In his writings on altruism in the early 1870s Spencer had already identified the apparent conflict between egoism and altruism with the contrast between the predatory and the industrial regimes, and between the religions of enmity and amity. In the *Data of Ethics*, in 1879, Spencer now used examples of British imperial iniquities in order to persuade readers simultaneously of the connections between international and domestic morality and of the hypocrisy of the current established religion. It was on this

---

[100] On Paine's life and political thought, see Mark Philp's entry in the *ODNB*; Claeys 1989; Keane 1995. On Paine's role in the 'infidel tradition', see Royle 1974, 1976.

[101] *Rights of Man, Part I* (1791); in Paine 2000: 94.

[102] *Rights of Man, Part II* (1792), ch. 3; in Paine 2000: 171.

[103] J. D. Y. Peel, 1971: 7–8; Spencer 1904: i. 44–6, 83–4; Duncan 1908: 5–6.

[104] Spencer 1904: i. 83–4.

[105] On the shaping of Spencer's political and religious outlook by his immersion in radical politics and dissenting religion, and his views on militarism being superseded by industrialism, see J. D. Y. Peel 1971: 56–81, 192–223.

subject of the hypocrisies of the British empire that Spencer was at his most
eloquent. He wrote of the 'unscrupulous greed of conquest cloaked by pre-
tences of spreading the blessings of British rule and British religion' and
explained how this aggressive foreign policy increased government expen-
diture and paralysed international trade. He criticized those of the industrial classes who 'thinking themselves unconcerned in our doings abroad,
are suffering from lack of that wide-reaching altruism which should insist
on just dealings with other peoples, civilized or savage'.[106]

Spencer's most passionate polemic was saved for the bishops (especially
those who had seats in the House of Lords and were thus directly implicated in government policy). Citing as an example the brutal response to
the murder of Bishop John Coleridge Patteson in Melanesia in 1871,
Spencer wrote that the British government had gone even further than the
primitive rule of a life for a life and developed the rule 'For one life many
lives.'[107] Spencer regretted that his new pacific and evolutionary view of
ethics would not appeal to 'those whose reverence for one who told them
to put up the sword is shown by using the sword to spread his doctrine
among the heathens'; nor to the 'ten thousand priests of the religion of
love, who are silent when the nation is moved by the religion of hate'; nor
to the bishops who, 'far from urging the extreme precept of the master they
pretend to follow, to turn the other cheek when one is smitten, vote for
acting on the principle—strike lest ye be struck'. In this moralistic peroration, Spencer drove home his message that those who believed that a
rationalized version of Christian ethical principles could be applied while
rejecting the Christian creed, were altogether morally superior to these
'men who profess Christianity and practise Paganism'.[108]

The weekly journal *The Nation*, published in New York, carried an
unsigned article on Herbert Spencer's *Data of Ethics* in September 1879,
pronouncing it 'the most noteworthy production of its energetic author'.
The author of the review was William James, then an assistant professor of
physiology at Harvard with an interest in evolution, psychology, and philosophy. The article was scathing about Spencer's attempt to apply evolution
to absolutely everything, including moral philosophy, and predicted that
when the intellectual furore surrounding evolution had died down, philosophical discussions about the fundamental reasons for action would continue much as they had before. James somewhat sarcastically went on to

---

[106] Spencer 1879: 218.
[107] Ibid. 240.
[108] Ibid. 257.

describe Spencer's imagined ideal future state, in which all would act out of a spontaneous and unconscious desire to increase the total amount of vitality on the earth, unconscious of their motive, unless 'perchance the theory as well as the practice of evolution shall have become ingrained into the nervous system of us all'.[109] James also expressed scepticism about the possibility of persuading anyone, who happened not to be constituted in a way that was conducive to this altruistic direction of social evolution, to change their behaviour accordingly. Finally, the review pointed out that, whereas in Germany the 'struggle for existence' had been invoked by those defending 'the most cynical assertions of brute egoism', Mr Spencer had used the same scientific theories to argue for 'an almost Quakerish humanitarianism and regard for peace'.[110] 'Frequently in these pages,' James noticed, 'does his indignation at the ruling powers of Britain burst forth, for their policy of conquest over lower races.'[111]

Opposition to expensive, pre-emptive, and hypocritical foreign policy was a cause in support of which the radical Spencer and the positivist Harrison could join forces, despite their philosophical differences. They had both served, along with Mill, Huxley, Darwin, and others on the Jamaica Committee, which had been formed in 1866 with a view to bringing a murder charge against Governor Edward Eyre in connection with his brutal military suppression of an uprising in Morant Bay the previous year.[112] A few months after the publication of Spencer's *Data of Ethics*, Frederic Harrison spoke on the subject of the British empire in his new year's address to the London Positivist Society in 1880. Harrison denounced the government's policies of 'conquest and domination', waging unjust wars against the Zulu and Afghan peoples. 'We who look forward to a purely human religion', Harrison said, 'can hope but little from the Churches in dealing with this Central Asian crime.' He expressed dismay, like Spencer's, at the collusion of the established faiths in the crimes of temporal authorities. Christianity, Harrison said, was complicit in imperialist aggression and commercial exploitation.[113] These sorts of arguments about the empire

---

[109] [William James], 'Herbert Spencer's *Data of Ethics*', *The Nation,* 29 (11 Sept. 1879), 178–9.

[110] James presumably was unaware of Spencer's father's connections with the Quakers.

[111] [William James], 'Herbert Spencer's *Data of Ethics*', 178–9.

[112] On the Eyre case, see Workman 1974; C. Hall 1996, 2002. On Spencer's involvement, see Spencer 1904: ii. 142–3.

[113] Frederic Harrison, 'Empire and Humanity', *Fortnightly Review,* 27 (1880), 288–308, quotations at 292–4. For more on Harrison's attitudes to foreign affairs, see F. Harrison 1908: 1–265; 1911: ii, esp. 118–35.

provided another opportunity for unbelievers to present themselves as morally superior to their selfish and aggressive Christian contemporaries.

Gladstone's victory in the 1880 general election was initially seen as a victory for the opponents of jingoistic imperialism. However, that impression was short-lived, and Spencer himself took the initiative in forming an Anti-Aggression League. The central idea of the league, which was embodied in its name, was to form an association of opinion-formers and politicians who were opposed to pre-emptive, expansionist, aggressive, and interventionist wars, but who did not sign up to the Peace Society's more extreme position of total non-resistance. Spencer and his colleagues in the Anti-Aggression League, which was officially launched in February 1882, agreed that military resistance to any hostilities against British territories and interests was justified, but that military actions such as the second Afghan war of 1879, which had been perceived as pre-emptive, commercially motivated, and expansionist, were not.[114] Harrison, along with other radicals such as John Morley and John Bright MP, about thirty other Liberal MPs, and 'upwards of forty Professors, writers, and politicians' formed the General Council of the League.[115] Another member of that Council was the Reverend W. H. Fremantle, the leading Anglican supporter of the international peace and arbitration movements. Fremantle would, in the 1890s, take up the deanery of Ripon. There, with the bishop, William Boyd Carpenter, who had preached 'Christian Altruism' to Queen Victoria in 1883, Fremantle established a centre for liberal churchmanship, with an emphasis on modern ideas and social reform.[116]

Charles Darwin, in response to a letter from Spencer, expressed his support for the Anti-Aggression League, but declined to join until he had seen how its activities worked in practice; he died a few months later.[117] The intensification of the Egyptian crisis in the summer of 1882 was greeted with outrage on behalf of the League by Frederic Harrison, who wrote a circular suggesting that Gladstone's willingness to authorize British military involvement in Alexandria was motivated only by the desire to protect commercial interests. 'Neither English persons nor English property have

---

[114] Ceadel 2000: 109–20 explains this distinction in terms of the later categories of 'pacifist' (describing a policy of non-resistance) and 'pacificist' (meaning one of non-aggression).

[115] On the Anti-Aggression League, see Spencer 1904: ii. 375–82; Duncan 1908: 220–4; Harrison 1908: 184–94; Ceadel 2000: 116, 119–20; Laity 2001: 96–9; quotation on membership from Harrison 1908: 184.

[116] On Fremantle, see *ODNB*. On Boyd Carpenter, see Ch. 3, above.

[117] Darwin's response to Spencer's invitation was written in Sept. 1881; Burkhardt and Smith 1994: 599. He died in Apr. 1882.

been attacked,' Harrison wrote, 'the English Government has suffered neither injury nor insult; and no treaty has been violated by the Egyptian
nation. Yet we are on the very brink of war, and are dictating a form of
domestic government to a foreign nation.'[118] The protests were not heeded,
despite Spencer meeting with Gladstone in person to press the League's
arguments, and Harrison later considered this yet more proof that 'The
party system, the financial interests, and the thirst of Empire are forces that
do not listen to the voice of reason and of justice.'[119] Morley resigned from
Gladstone's cabinet over the Egyptian war and shortly afterwards Spencer
himself departed for his successful lecture tour of the United States. The
Anti-Aggression League's brief existence came to an end.

The association of anti-aggression with 'altruism' was longer lasting
than the League itself. At a time before the term 'pacificism' existed, some
advocates of a robust and 'forward' foreign policy now saw 'altruism' as their
enemy. The popular novelist 'Ouida' wrote to *The Times* from her home in
Italy during the Egyptian crisis in the summer of 1882. She reported the
opinion of an 'Italian gentleman, for some years resident in Alexandria',
whose property had been destroyed by the British bombardment of the city
following the riots there, which had precipitated British intervention. His
view, despite his own losses, was that 'nothing would serve the interests of
Egypt so well, and nothing so well develop its resources, as an English
Protectorate'. Ouida urged the government to act swiftly and decisively
towards this end, and encouraged all Englishmen openly to avow that they
'are chiefly concerned with the interests and welfare of England'. This
would secure them an international reputation as 'sincere and practical persons'. 'The doctrine of altruism will not apply to politics,' Ouida wrote, 'and
the affectation of it only begets distrust and hypocrisy.'[120]

Lord Lytton, who had been the Viceroy of India during the controversial aggression of the Second Afghan War in 1879, had resigned after
Beaconsfield's defeat by Gladstone in the general election of 1880. He continued to make public pronouncements on foreign affairs however. In 1888,
in his rectorial address to the members of Glasgow University, he took as
his topic the question 'Is morality the same for nations as for individuals?'
The question, as *The Times* noted, 'lies at the root of his own much assailed
Afghan policy'. Lytton suggested several reasons why personal and national

---

[118] The circular was printed in *The Times* (19 June 1882), 8; a slightly different version is included
in F. Harrison 1911: ii. 124–6.
[119] Harrison 1911: ii. 126.
[120] *The Times* (18 Aug. 1882), 5.

morality were not equivalent. One of these was that, while in some cases it might be the height of morality for an individual to sacrifice himself for another, it was surely never appropriate for a nation to extinguish its own existence 'for the sake of other nations or of humanity at large'. The reason for this difference, Lytton suggested, was that an individual had a 'self' but that a nation had no 'self' but was itself an aggregation of individual selves, each of whom had a stronger tie to his fellow countrymen than to the rest of the world. 'Altruism is a principle which should govern national conduct', Lytton thought, but, echoing the famous maxim about charity, he went on 'it is an altruism which naturally and properly begins at home, and rulers who make it begin abroad are guilty of a violation of their trust'. The first and most important virtue was patriotism. This must always take precedence over any doctrine of 'altruism' in international affairs.[121]

In the later years of his life, as Spencer completed his *Synthetic Philosophy* and reflected on the state of modern civilization, he saw a world moving away from rather than towards his radical utopia of sympathetic individualism at home and peaceful cooperation abroad. In 1898, Spencer received a letter from the Unitarian freethinker, peace campaigner, and biographer of Tom Paine, Moncure D. Conway, outlining a proposal for the formation of a body of eminent men, including Spencer, who would be invited to provide arbitration on any international dispute that threatened to escalate into war. The proposed organization would have resembled the Anti-Aggression League, only on an international basis and with greater powers. Spencer's response, however, was indicative of the pessimism that had now overtaken him. He wrote back to Conway that he sympathized with his aims but not with his hopes. The Anti-Aggression League had 'failed utterly', and since that time, he feared, the general appetite for conflict had simply increased. 'Now that the white savages of Europe are overrunning the dark savages everywhere', Spencer wrote, 'it is useless to resist the wave of barbarism. There is a bad time coming, and civilised mankind will (morally) be uncivilised before civilisation can again advance.' He predicted that 'universal aggressiveness and universal culture of blood-thirst will bring back military despotism'. Only 'after many generations' might a partially free form of civilization re-emerge.[122]

The same tone of both personal regret and political despair was captured in the title that Spencer gave to the chapter of his autobiography

---

[121] As reported in *The Times* (12 Nov. 1888), 9.
[122] Conway 1904: ii. 407–8.

about the Anti-Aggression League—'A Grievous Mistake'.[123] The interpretation he gave to the formation of the League was that it had been 'the
greatest disaster of my life—a disaster that resulted from doing more than
I ought to have done'. He had, in his letter to Conway, noted in passing
that the strain caused by the episode had permanently ruined his already
fragile health.[124] In founding the League, giving a public speech, and
actively campaigning, Spencer had contravened a rule he had laid down for
himself that, for the sake of his health, he would never join in public political movements of this kind. Although some support was expressed by
'newspapers representing the dissenters', Spencer noted in his autobiography, he felt that overall the League had made no impact on public opinion.
The movement had failed politically, but Spencer included it in his autobiography 'for the purpose of pointing a moral'. The moral was that sacrifices
made for the good of others were not always compensated by 'the pleasurable feeling caused by the doing of right'. It was not true, in other words,
that virtue was its own reward. 'If I know my own motives', Spencer wrote,
then he had, in founding the Anti-Aggression League, been moved 'exclusively by the desire to further human welfare'. He had spent his own time,
effort, and money. His only reward had been a level of nervous strain that
would ultimately reduce his physical condition to that of 'a confirmed
invalid, leading little more than a vegetative life'.[125] Spencer thus represented his own invalidism as a warning against the contravention of his ethical principle that egoistic self-regard should take priority over altruistic
self-sacrifice, even when pursuing peace and freedom for all humanity.

By the end of his life, Spencer had retreated from both the language and
the optimism of his earlier writings on altruism. He became ever sterner in
the limits he felt must be placed on beneficence towards the morally, mentally, and physically inferior. One of the elements that remained consistent
with his earlier writings, however, was his condemnation of British military
'brigandage' and the hypocrisy of Christian leaders. Both in the *Principles of
Ethics* and in the final volume of the *Principles of Sociology*, which, on its
publication in 1896 marked the completion of the *Synthetic Philosophy*,
Spencer's anti-aggression and his anti-Christianity were still much in evidence. In the final volume of the *Principles of Sociology*, Spencer even managed to find a way of attacking optimism, socialism, British imperialism,

[123] The *Autobiography* was mainly written in the late 1880s, but not published until after Spencer's
death; Spencer 1904: ii, pp. v–vi, 417.
[124] Conway, 1904: ii. 407.
[125] Spencer 1904: ii. 375–82.

Figure 15. A photographic portrait of Spencer at the age of 78, a couple of years after the completion of his *Synthetic Philosophy* in 1896. Frontispiece to Spencer 1904:ii.

militarism, and Christianity all in one breath. His point was that sentimental socialism relied on an unduly optimistic estimate of the current state of
human nature and the altruism of which people were currently capable.
People only needed to look around them, he said, to recognize that they
were living in a world not only populated, but led, by selfish and barbarous
people. He then offered as examples the policy of 'unscrupulous aggran-
dizement' pursued by the British government, the conquests being made
'from base and selfish motives alone', and the violent appropriations that
resulted from quarrels with native peoples. His summary of British imperialism was brutally short: 'First men are sent to teach the heathens
Christianity, and then Christians are sent to mow them down with
machine-guns!' The policy was 'simple and uniform—bibles first, bomb-
shells after'. Spencer went on to cite the terrifying rate of homicides in the
United States, which had risen from twelve per day to thirty per day; and
the corruption that was rife in America both among the police forces and
businessmen.

Now, given all this evidence of the continued selfishness and brutality
of humanity in the 1890s, Spencer asked sarcastically, did the socialists seriously believe they could construct a society 'pervaded by the sentiment of
brotherhood' in which 'regard for others is supreme?'[126] Despite Spencer's
own increasing pessimism, there were plenty in the 1880s and 1890s who
believed that such a society could indeed be constructed.

[126] Spencer 1896: 574–5.

Chapter Six

Poverty and the Ideal Self

So it is always with 'Isms.' They are a battle-cry, a watchword, a catchword: but they are not the name of any definite idea. Their force even depends on a certain necessary vagueness, and their ill-defined forms stand out provocative of curiosity and interest as they loom through the mist. They are none the less real or vital on that account.

William Wallace, 'The Ethics of Socialism' (1898)[1]

Manchester

The first and only person ever to call himself 'Altruism' was the author of a *Gas Consumers' Manual* published under that pen-name in Manchester in 1882 (see Fig. 16). Although he was the only person to adopt the term as a name, this Manchester writer was by no means alone in identifying with 'altruism' as a watchword of political, social, and religious reform in the 1880s and 1890s. To some 'altruism' was virtually synonymous with social-ist collectivism, to others it signified an enthusiasm for humanity pursued outside of traditional Christianity but within existing economic and social structures. The language of altruism was on the lips of reformers and social-ists, and was analysed by them in their notebooks and essays. At the same time it was being deconstructed by philosophers, resisted by individualists, and parodied by novelists. Everyone accused everyone else of being selfish, while disagreeing about whether to be an 'altruist' was to strive for a great social transformation, to legitimate theft from the rich by the poor, to

---

[1] W. Wallace 1898: 400. Lord Milner, in a memoir of his friend Arnold Toynbee, delivered in 1894 on the tenth anniversary of the founding of Toynbee Hall, described 'Socialism' similarly as 'that most vague and misleading of all the catchwords of current controversy'; Toynbee 1908: p. xxvi. In his *Victorian England: Portrait of an Age*, G. M. Young, focusing on the threatening connotations of the term, wrote: 'Any one who set himself to collect all occurrences of the word Socialism in the Victorian age would probably conclude that it might be taken, or made to mean everything which a respectable man saw reason to disapprove of or to fear'; G. M. Young 1960: 169–70. On the many meanings of 'socialism' in the 1880s and 1890s see also Himmelfarb 1991: 309–10.

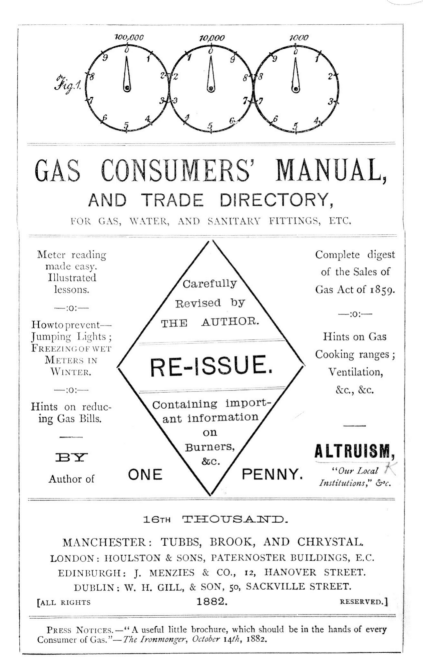

Figure 16. Robert A. S. Melsom's 1882 *Gas Consumers' Manual*, published in Manchester under the pen-name 'Altruism'. Reproduced by permission of the British Library.

endorse an artificial conceptual distinction between the individual and the social organism, or simply to be an impractical, muddle-headed, and super-cilious intellectual idealist. In some cases, the definitions, connotations, and significance of the language of altruism were made quite explicit. In the case of the author of the *Gas Consumers' Manual*, however, we can only approach the meaning he might have found in 'altruism' more indirectly.

After extensive and initially fruitless attempts to discover the identity of 'Altruism', success eventually came when I consulted the records of the Manchester Literary Club, who published an annual 'Manchester Bibliography'. The 1882 bibliography listed the *Gas Consumers' Manual* by 'Altruism' as a work by 'R. A. Melson'. The following year's listing spelled the name 'Melsom' rather than 'Melson'.[2] Further research confirmed that one Robert Melsom was indeed a writer living in Manchester in the early 1880s. Born in Bristol in 1857 or 1858, Robert Melsom was an educated working man with a variety of professional interests. In 1879 Melsom married Agnes Brereton, the daughter of a Wolverhampton boiler-maker. The marriage was registered in Bury, Greater Manchester.[3] Soon afterwards their first child, Florence, was born (possibly named in honour of that eminent and altruistic Victorian, Florence Nightingale). The 1881 census recorded Robert, Agnes, and Florence living at 51 Waterloo Street, in Crumpsall, in the north of Manchester. Robert gave his occupation as 'Herbalist'. Agnes's sister Clara also lived with them, and was apprenticed to a dressmaker. Amongst their neighbours on Waterloo Street were a porter, a warehouseman, a postman, and a printer's clerk. Next door to the Melsoms lived William and Alice Walker, both in their seventies. William was registered as a 'gardener, unemployed', and as being blind.[4] The street

---

[2] 'Altruism' 1882; Melsom 1883. R. A. Melsom's authorship of the 1883 edn of the pamphlet is recorded in Charles William Sutton, 'Manchester Bibliography, 1883', *Papers of the Manchester Literary Club*, 10 (1884), 361–86, at 367; the 1882 pamphlet is listed in Sutton's 'Manchester Bibliography, 1882', *Papers of the Manchester Literary Club*, 9 (1883), 240–63, at 247, where the author's pen-name is given as 'Altruism' and where his name is misspelt as 'Melson'. A copy of the pamphlet bearing Melsom's name as author is held in the Manchester Central Library. I am extremely grateful to George Turnbull, coordinator of Heritage Information, Archives and Local Studies Centre, Manchester Central Library, for supplying me with photocopies of pamphlets by Melsom and of the relevant pages of *Slater's Royal National Commercial Directory of Manchester and Salford* for the years 1881–4. The version of the *Gas Consumers' Manual* giving Melsom as the author is held in the Manchester Central Library under 'Science and Arts Tracts', no. 389/13.

[3] Marriage registered in the third quarter of 1879, in Bury, Greater Manchester, Lancashire, vol. 8c; General Register Office, *England and Wales Civil Registration Indexes*; accessed through the website of the UK national archives (see Bibliography for details).

[4] 1881 census return; Public Record Office, R.G.11/4025, f. 82, 15; accessed through the website of the UK national archives (see Bibliography for details).

directory for Manchester in 1881 and 1882 listed Robert A. S. Melsom as a 'gas inspector' at two different addresses (neither of them Waterloo Street). When Melsom published his *Gas Consumers' Manual* by 'Altruism' in 1882, the Manchester address given at the end of the pamphlet was different again. Neither Melsom's abode nor his profession ever seems to have been entirely fixed.

Melsom produced at least two other works—a pamphlet on the history of marriage customs, illustrated with quotations from Milton and Shakespeare, first published in 1884, and a directory of Cheadle.[5] Melsom's *Courtship and Marriage Customs of Many Nations*, which was advertised by the publisher as '*Amusing! Interesting!! Instructive!!!*' surveyed Chinese, Greek, German, and British marriage traditions, including elopement to Gretna Green, and the history of wedding vows and rings. It also had endorsements and advertisements for the *Gas Consumers' Manual* running along the bottom of each page. Melsom ended the pamphlet by quoting from the eighteenth-century poet and physician, Nathaniel Cotton:

> Though fools spurn Hymen's gentle powers,
> We, who improve his golden hours,
>   By sweet experience know
> That marriage, rightly understood,
> Gives to the tender and the good
>   A paradise below.[6]

But Robert and Agnes's 'paradise below' was soon to end. Later in 1884 Agnes died, at the age of 26, while giving birth to their second daughter, Ruth, who also died.[7] I have not been able to trace any further record of what happened to Robert Melsom and his surviving daughter Florence after that date; it is possible that they also died before the next census in 1891.

What had appealed to Robert Melsom about 'altruism' in 1882? He was in his mid-twenties—a gas inspector, a herbalist, a writer. Perhaps he was a working-class autodidact like Samuel Barmby in Gissing's *In the Year of the Jubilee* (1894), in whose mind 'Herbert Spencer jostled with Charles Bradlaugh, Matthew Arnold with Samuel Smiles'.[8] Or was his

[5] Melsom 1884; the *Cheadle Directory*, possibly the work referred to on the front cover of the *Gas Consumers' Manual* as 'Our Local Institutions', is listed in the 'Manchester Bibliography, 1887', *Papers of the Manchester Literary Club,* 14 (1888), 467–83, at 476.

[6] Melsom 1884: 24.

[7] Both deaths are recorded for the final quarter of 1884, in Manchester, Lancashire, vol. 8d; General Register Office, *England and Wales Civil Registration Indexes*; accessed through the website of the UK national archives (see Bibliography for details).

[8] Gissing 1895: 214; see Ch. 5 above.

identification with 'Altruism', like that of John Bridges and James Hinton,
connected with his work as a practitioner of medicine? There were thousands of unorthodox medical practitioners in Victorian Britain, many of
whom offered traditional and herbal remedies to their patients. A tradition
of working-class herbalism associated with radical politics, primitive
Methodism, and the anti-establishment medical botany of Albert Coffin
had been particularly strong in Lancashire in the 1850s and 1860s.[9] But
perhaps the most likely connotation that Melsom hoped the buyers of his
Gas Consumers' Manual might be attracted to was not a medical one, but the
more general connection between 'altruism' and social conscience. Living
as he did amongst the unemployment, the disease, the unsanitary housing,
and the early death that afflicted the working classes of Manchester,
'altruism' was a word that could imply solidarity and hope. That hope,
specifically, was most often for state legislation that would regulate and
improve the working conditions, wages, housing, and education of the
urban poor. Melsom clearly had at least some taste for politics. He sent
a copy of his *Gas Consumers' Manual* to the Prime Minister, William
Gladstone. The 5th edition of the manual included on its front cover what
was described, entirely inaccurately, as an 'Unsolicited Testimonial' in the
form of a letter from a Downing Street official: 'Mr Gladstone desires me
to thank you for your Gas Consumer's Manual which you have had the
kindness to send him.'[10]

One final possibility is that Robert Melsom was a positivist. The
Manchester publishers of his *Gas Consumers' Manual* were Tubbs, Brook,
& Chrystal. Among their publications in 1884, along with the 7th edition
of Melsom's manual, was a sermon by the Congregationalist minister
Alexander Thomson occasioned by Frederic Harrison's visit to Manchester
to inaugurate a local branch of the Positivist Society. Entitled 'Christianity
and Positivism', the sermon responded to Harrison's allegation that
Christianity was a selfish religion. Thomson denied that Christian men and
women had ever overlooked 'the burdens of poverty and distress among
the lower orders'. He mentioned Temperance Societies, Providence
Societies, and industrial schools as evidence of Christian love for the poor,
but still insisted that 'self-love, self-interest is naturally the predominant
passion in each man's breast' and that it was impossible to persuade a man
to love his neighbour simply 'by plying him with scientific lessons in

---

[9] Berridge 1990: 188–9; *ODNB*.
[10] Melsom 1883.

sociology'.[11] An anonymous rejoinder was published, by 'A Member of the Manchester Positivist Society', and also published by Brook & Chrystal. Its author noted that according to Thomson there seemed to be 'no means of evoking social emotion without recourse to theological artifices', and against this argued for the positivist belief in the naturalness of 'altruism' and in the dependence of the individual on the social organism.[12]

Was it this positivist 'altruism' that particularly appealed to Melsom? Did he even write the response to Thomson? It is impossible to be sure. There is no record of Melsom having attended any positivist meetings in Manchester, and his adoption of 'Altruism' predated the inauguration of organized positivism in the city by a couple of years. At least a few of those amongst whom he lived and worked, however, were attracted to the movement. From 1884, a small group of positivists started to meet in Memorial Hall for Sunday morning meetings and evening lectures on scientific, religious, political, and historical subjects, including physics, metaphysics, chemistry, Auguste Comte, Charles Darwin, Catholicism, Jesus Christ, England's present-day relations with Ireland and Egypt, trade unionism, and co-operation. The occupations of the men and women who attended these meeting, as given on census returns, included railway porter, printer's assistant, book-keeper, confectioner's agent, articled clerk, bank secretary, and a former Unitarian minister, now an insurance company manager.[13] Their president from 1889 was Charles Gaskell Higginson, a former schoolteacher, and a graduate of Owens College, Manchester (Fig. 17 shows the front page of Higginson's first annual circular as president).[14] His father and grandfather had both been Unitarian ministers, the latter having been a tutor to both James Martineau and James B. Mozley (whose 1870 sermon against 'altruism' was discussed in Chapter 3 above). The younger Higginson, however, as readers of a potted biography in the magazine *Manchester Faces and Places* in April 1897 would have learnt, had not been able to accept the tenets of Unitarianism and, having read Comte's *General View of Positivism* in 1881, had resolved to become a positivist, eventually becoming part of the national committee and training as a physician—a

[11] A. Thomson 1884: 12–13, 15.

[12] Anon. 1884a: 13–15.

[13] The last of these was James Odgers; the names of the others whose occupations are given here were John Sanders, William Broyden, Charles Payne, Walter Heywood, and Daniel F. Ramsay; all taken from the 1891 census. Their names are found in the 'Book of Sacraments, Manchester Positivist Society', 1892–9; Manchester Central Library, MS.146.M16.

[14] With a second-class degree in French; *The Times* (12 Dec. 1878), 8.

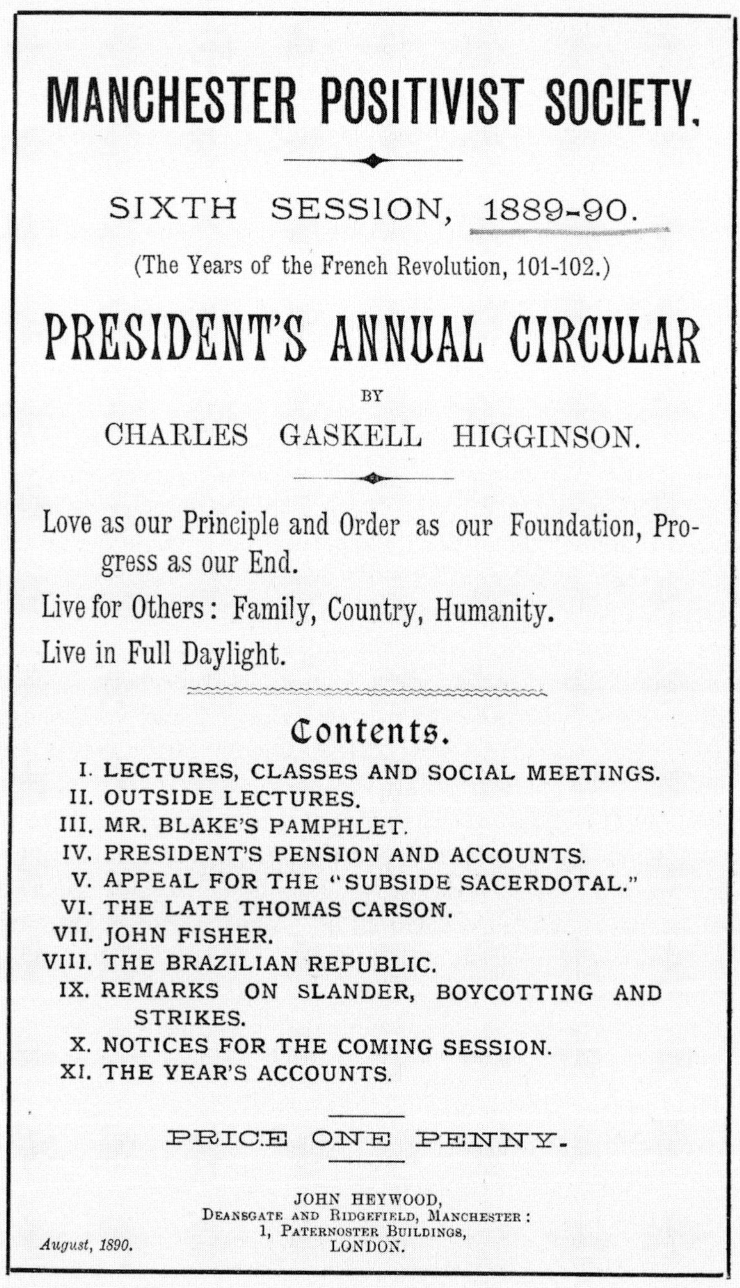

MANCHESTER POSITIVIST SOCIETY.

SIXTH SESSION, 1889-90.

(The Years of the French Revolution, 101-102.)

PRESIDENT'S ANNUAL CIRCULAR

BY

CHARLES GASKELL HIGGINSON.

Love as our Principle and Order as our Foundation, Progress as our End.

Live for Others: Family, Country, Humanity.

Live in Full Daylight.

Contents.

I. LECTURES, CLASSES AND SOCIAL MEETINGS.
II. OUTSIDE LECTURES.
III. MR. BLAKE'S PAMPHLET.
IV. PRESIDENT'S PENSION AND ACCOUNTS.
V. APPEAL FOR THE "SUBSIDE SACERDOTAL."
VI. THE LATE THOMAS CARSON.
VII. JOHN FISHER.
VIII. THE BRAZILIAN REPUBLIC.
IX. REMARKS ON SLANDER, BOYCOTTING AND STRIKES.
X. NOTICES FOR THE COMING SESSION.
XI. THE YEAR'S ACCOUNTS.

PRICE ONE PENNY.

JOHN HEYWOOD,
DEANSGATE AND RIDGEFIELD, MANCHESTER:
1, PATERNOSTER BUILDINGS,
August, 1890.   LONDON.

Figure 17. The annual circular produced by the President of the Manchester Positivist Society for the year 1889–90. Reproduced by permission of La Maison d'Auguste Comte, Paris.

prerequisite of joining the positivist priesthood.[15] In his opening president's letter to the Manchester society, Higginson wrote that theology was no longer either socially or logically useful and that, worst of all, by emphasizing love of God over love of humanity 'it is constantly used hypocritically, in order to turn off the efforts of the people from social reform by offering the illusory bribe of a personal existence after death'. Higginson took particular exception to an article in *The Spectator* which had stated that duty to God was at least as imperative as duty to others, and that 'cases are conceivable in which the highest virtue would be indifferent or even opposed to Altruism'. This last sentence, Higginson thought, should 'open men's eyes to the real position of Theology, and to its power of betraying the Human Cause'.[16]

Higginson's duties as president of the Manchester positivists included 'conferring the due Positivist sacraments at the presentation of children and the burial of the dead'. In this role, which he only performed a handful of times during his ten-year presidency, he offered positivist mourners no 'illusory bribes'. On a February morning in 1895, in Philips Park Cemetery, Manchester, Higginson found himself presiding over the burial of Lilian May Sanders, aged 2 years, daughter of a local printer's assistant, John Sanders, and his wife, Fanny. Higginson wrote in his 'Book of Sacraments' that his duties had involved 'extending sympathy and reminding the mourners of the consolations of the second life'; this second life, of course, being the subjective life that the deceased could live in the lives of others.[17] Three years earlier, Higginson had presided over the burial of the Sanders' infant son, Herbert, also aged 2, and four years later he interred the body of Fanny Sanders, who had died of a gastric ulcer at the age of 44. In his book of sacraments, Higginson wrote, 'The usual address was given by the

---

[15] The papers of the London Positivist Society record that Higginson, like Patrick Geddes, joined the society in 1883; Library of the London School of Economics, LPS 1/1. *The Times* (13 Oct. 1892), 2, noted that Higginson had passed the second examination of the Board of the Royal College of Physicians and Surgeons, in anatomy and physiology, as a student of Owens college, Manchester. 'Mr Charles Gaskell Higginson', *Manchester Faces and Place: An Illustrated Magazine,* 8 (1897), 108–10. On Higginson's grandfather, Edward Higginson (1807–80), see *ODNB*.

[16] Higginson 1889; held in the collection of papers relating to English positivist societies in the Maison d'Auguste Comte, Paris. *The Spectator* (6 July 1889), 20; the article commented on another article by Julia Wedgwood in the *Contemporary Review* entitled 'Male and Female Created He Them', and challenged what it perceived as her tacit assumption that 'virtue and altruism are identical'.

[17] The National Secular Society, founded in 1866, also provided ceremonies for naming, marriage, and burial; see C. M. Davies 1874: ii. 165–87, and see Chs 2 and 3 above.

graveside. Several families were present.'[18] After ten years leading the positivists in Manchester, Higginson later succumbed to what Terence Wright
calls 'the Positivist disease'—depression.[19]

'An awakening of the public conscience'

There was a great moral awakening in later Victorian Britain, of which
the espousal of 'Altruism' amongst the working classes in Manchester
was just one symptom.[20] There were economic, religious, and political
dimensions to this transformation, and it was evident in a wide range of
different activities. The Liberal politician Lord Goschen, addressing the
Edinburgh Philosophical Society in 1883 on the subject of 'Laissez-Faire
and Government Interference', asked what could explain the 'revolution in
public sentiment' that had led to the sudden and, from his point of view,
unwelcome increase in confidence in the right of the state to 'interfere', as
he put it, in such a wide range of activities. The extension of state involvement in 'telegraphy, insurance, annuities, postal orders, and parcels post' was
relatively uncontroversial. But what was 'of far deeper import' was 'its growing interference with the relations between classes, its increased control
over vast categories of transactions between individuals, and the substitu-
tion in many of the dealings of trade and manufacture, of the aggregate
conscience and moral sense of the nation, for the conscience and moral
sense of men as units'. This state interference had an impact on parents,
employers, house-owners, and landowners. Why were the people of Britain
now prepared to tolerate this level of state restriction on their personal and
professional dealings? The leading reason that Goschen thought he could
discern was 'an awakening of the public conscience as to the moral aspects
of many sides of our industrial arrangements'. Specifically, the public had
come to doubt whether those arrangements could produce an improvement in the civilization as well as in the wealth of the nation. Goschen

---

[18] Book of Sacraments, Manchester Positivist Society; Manchester Central Library, MS.146.M16,
f. 7.
[19] Wright 1986: 123.
[20] The late Victorian contexts for discussions of 'altruism' covered in the rest of this chapter,
including philosophical idealism, socialism, philanthropy, the Charity Organisation Society,
university settlements, and social surveying are all covered in illuminating detail in Himmelfarb
1991.

thought that 'facts previously unknown or ignored' had recently 'been revealed in striking colours' in a way that had led the public to demand 'the application of immediate and direct remedies'.[21]

One of the well-known ways that the striking facts of urban poverty had been brought to public attention in 1883 was through a campaign orchestrated by W. T. Stead, the editor of the *Pall Mall Gazette*, and pioneer of what became known as the 'New Journalism'. He publicized a tract by the Congregationalist minister Andrew Mearns entitled *The Bitter Cry of Outcast London: An Inquiry into the Condition of the Abject Poor* (1883). Stead considered the public furore caused by his editorials, highlighting the squalor and immorality in which some of the poorest lived, to have been the 'first great coup' of the *Pall Mall* under his editorship.[22] This was by no means the first time that studies had been published of the lives of the urban poor. One notable precursor was Henry Mayhew's *London Labour and the London Poor* (1851). However, there were many other factors now pushing towards a keener sensitivity to the problem. Economically, the 1880s was a period of recession. Helen Merrell Lynd's study of *England in the Eighteen-Eighties* interprets the period as one in which the ideology and practice of liberal individualism and the unquestioned British dominance of world trade both came to an end. The result was that 'an ideology half a century old yielded to a new phrasing of social problems and an effort to find new paths to their solution'.[23] The 1880s, in short, was a decade in which the economic downturn exacerbated existing privations in the lives of the working classes, and during which a newly sensationalist and moralistic popular press brought those privations to the attention of a curious and conscientious reading public. There was a newly intense concern about a whole range of social problems, especially the housing, health, and morality of the poorest classes. This was the decade that saw the philanthropic pastime of 'slumming' in the East End of London take off.[24] The 'unemployed' as a category were discussed for the first time in the 1880s, as was the problem of 'unemployment', the level of which was estimated to

---

[21] Goschen 1905: 294–325, at 294–5, 297. On Goschen's career as a moderate Liberal and defender of *laissez-faire*, see Spinner 1973. On the shift from old liberalism to New Liberalism and the complaints from old liberals such as Spencer and Goschen about legislation interfering with contracts between labourers and employers, and between landlords and tenants, see M. Taylor 1992: 1–16.

[22] Lynd 1968: 147–8., 333–4. On the context for Mearns's publication see P. d'A. Jones 1968; Stedman Jones 1971.

[23] Lynd 1968: 17–18.

[24] Koven 2004: esp. 6–10.

have risen from about 2 per cent in 1882 to over 10 per cent in 1886.[25] 'Collectivism', a new synonym for 'socialism', also entered the nation's political vocabulary in the 1880s.[26]

According to M. J. D. Roberts, this was also the era in which the state definitively replaced voluntary associations in the public mind as the principal agent of moral reform and philanthropy. From the 1880s onwards, on his account, social and moral campaigners would generally agitate for governmental intervention rather than for action through the voluntary associations that had been a large part of English life from William Wilberforce's anti-slavery campaign to the social purity movement led by figures such as Josephine Butler and Ellice Hopkins, again with the support of Stead and the *Pall Mall Gazette*.[27] These campaigns aimed at legislative outcomes—such as the increase of the age of sexual consent in the 1885 Criminal Law Amendment Act, and the repeal of the Contagious Diseases Acts in 1886. Emphasizing the great availability and credibility of the new campaigning journalism of this era, Jonathan Rose suggests that by the 1880s 'there had been a transference of credulity from the word of God to the word of journalists'.[28] And from 1884 onwards, after the third Reform Act, an even larger number of the working men who read the popular national newspapers could make their political views known through their participation in general elections.[29]

The 1880s was, finally, also a decade in which respectable forms of unbelief advanced ever closer to the heart of national life. It was an 'ethical epoch' in which socialists, secularists, and 'ethicists' (a term coined by Frederic Harrison for members of the freethinking Ethical Societies founded from the 1880s onwards) were challenging the churches' presumed monopoly on the national conscience.[30] In 1880 the secularist leader Charles Bradlaugh was elected as Liberal MP for Northampton. Bradlaugh was not prepared to swear the religious oath required before taking his seat

---

[25] On the emergence of 'unemployment' as a social problem in the 1880s and the middle-class rediscovery of poverty, see Lynd 1968: 55–6; Himmelfarb 1991: esp. 40–53; *OED*.

[26] *OED*; Himmelfarb 1991: 309–10n.

[27] M. J. D. Roberts 2004: 245–89.

[28] Rose 2001: 97.

[29] The effect of the 1884 Reform Act was, roughly, to double the number of voters from about a third of the adult male population to about two-thirds, which in 1885 meant just under six million voters; Pugh 1999: 25–6.

[30] I. D. MacKillop, in his history of the British Ethical Societies, describes 1876–1903 as the 'Ethical Epoch' in which they flourished (1986: 1–40; the reference to Harrison and the coining of 'ethicist', ibid. 1).

in the House of Commons. He asked to affirm instead, as unbelievers were permitted to do in courts of law.[31] This request was refused, however, and it was only after six years of by-elections and legal disputes that Bradlaugh was finally granted the right to take up his seat in 1886.[32] Partly because of the notoriety Bradlaugh succeeded in attaining for himself, the National Secular Society achieved its highest membership level, of over 10,000 people, during the 1880s.[33] In 1883, the famously agnostic Thomas Huxley became the first openly unbelieving president of the Royal Society.[34] The same year saw the publication of *Literature and Dogma,* by his friend the Oxford Professor of Poetry Matthew Arnold, whose preface ended with a striking and simple assertion that 'miracles do not happen'.[35] It was also a landmark year in the history of blasphemy. The secularist George W. Foote was successfully prosecuted for blasphemy in 1883 for the publication of scurrilous cartoons in his *Freethinker* magazine, founded in 1881, such as one depicting Jesus wearing a large canoe on each foot and 'walking' on the water. Although Foote was ultimately found guilty of blasphemy, and sentenced to a year in prison with hard labour, his case gave rise to an historic ruling by Lord Justice Coleridge, who stipulated that if 'the decencies of controversy are observed, even the fundamentals of religion may be attacked without a person being guilty of a blasphemous libel'. As Joss Marsh explains, this overturned a judgement that had stood since 1676, when Chief Justice Hale had stated that 'Christianity is parcel of the laws of England'. Now it was good manners rather than Christian teachings that were protected by the blasphemy laws. As Marsh puts it, blasphemy had now become an offence against literary decency rather than against Christianity. It was on the new grounds of indecency that Foote was imprisoned, despite the overturning of the Hale judgement.[36]

---

[31] There were also Christians who preferred to affirm rather than to swear an oath, in view of Jesus's words in the sermon on the mount: 'But I say unto you, Swear not at all; neither by heaven; for it is God's throne: Nor by the earth; for it is his footstool: neither by Jerusalem; for it is the city of the great King. Neither shalt thou swear by thy head, because thou canst not make one hair white or black. But let your communication be, Yea, yea; Nay, nay: for whatsoever is more than these cometh of evil' (Matt. 5: 34–7; see also James 5: 12).

[32] Bradlaugh's Oaths Act, extending the right to affirm to all MPs, was passed in 1888. See Arnstein 1965; Quinault 1976; Royle 1976.

[33] Royle 1976: 69.

[34] One of his predecessors in the role, his friend Joseph Hooker, was a church-going Anglican but with his own private agnostic doubts; see Jim Endersby's *ODNB* entry on Hooker.

[35] Arnold 1960–77: vi. 146.

[36] Marsh 1998: esp. 197–203, quotation at 200.

'Altruism', you might say, was a word that was in the right place at the right time—in a nation with a newly reawakened awareness of the suffering of the poor, a declining confidence in the beliefs and institutions of traditional Christianity, an urgent desire in some quarters to ensure that moral standards were not a casualty of the decline of orthodoxy, and an increasingly politically engaged population with an appetite for social reform. All these factors were at work in the moral revival discerned by Goschen in his talk to the Edinburgh philosophical society in 1883. He listed among its many characteristics:

> the greater care for the security of the employed, the greater solicitude for the mental and moral welfare of children, the anxiety for sanitary improvements, the desire for better house-accommodation for the poorest classes, the efforts in the cause of temperance, the sympathy for the suffering of dumb animals, and generally the struggles of the philanthropist and the social reformer for the elevation of the masses in comfort and refinement.[37]

Ellice Hopkins, in her book on *The Power of Womanhood* (1899), which urged mothers to raise their sons to be virtuous and chaste, wrote with optimism about the 'new moral forces' that were making themselves felt. She thought she could sense in society the 'deepened sense of moral obligation, the added power of conscience, the altogether new altruistic sense which makes the misery and degradation of others cling to us like a garment we cannot shake off, a sense of others' woes for which we have had to invent a new word'.[38] That word, introduced by Comte and some of his English readers, such as Hopkins's own mentor James Hinton, in the 1850s and 1860s, seemed tailor-made for the activities of the moralists and reformers of late Victorian Britain.

'Altruism' suddenly seemed to be everywhere—in the mouths of anti-vivisectionists, veterinarians, sanitation reformers, and university students, as well as in an ever widening range of published writings, whether by theologians, moral philosophers, social theorists, political idealists, or even authors of children's fiction. Thomas Hardy had originally encountered positivist 'altruism' through works by Mill and Bridges in the 1860s. He was personally acquainted with Frederic Harrison and Edward Beesly, took an interest in the religious aspects of positivism without becoming a positivist himself, and wrote that 'no person of serious thought in these times could

---

[37] Goschen 1905: 324.
[38] Hopkins 1909: 187–8.

be said to stand aloof from Positivist teaching and ideals'.[39] Hardy described the character Lady Constantine in *Two on a Tower* (1882) as being torn between her self-love and a powerful strand of 'altruism'.[40] Later in the 1880s, when Hardy was becoming increasingly interested in Darwinian and Spencerian ideas, he read and admired James Cotter Morison's eugenic and positivist *The Service of Man* (1887), whose approach to altruism was considered in Chapter 4 above.[41] Hardy came to interpret 'altruism' in terms of what Goschen had called 'sympathy for the suffering of dumb animals'. In a letter of 1909 to an American correspondent explaining his opposition to vivisection, Hardy wrote that the 'discovery of the law of evolution, which revealed that all organic creatures are of one family, shifted the centre of altruism from humanity to the whole conscious world collectively'.[42] Some of the critics of Darwinism discussed above, including R. H. Hutton and Frances Power Cobbe, were also opponents of vivisection. Cobbe coined the new term 'zoophily' as the name for her anti-vivisectionist ethics.[43] The Oxford idealist philosopher T. H. Green, who inspired some of the intellectual social reformers discussed later in this chapter, sought to include 'all vertebrate animals' in his extended category of creatures that enjoy some feeling of individuality.[44] Professor John Penberthy, in his address to mark the opening of the 1895–6 academic session, assured the students at the Royal Veterinary College in London of the great usefulness of their chosen profession. Although 'the realization of the teachings of altruism' might be very distant, Penberthy said, veterinary scientists could rest assured that their labours were of the greatest use to society, through their study of the ways that animal diseases could be caught by humans, their ability to improve the health of domestic and military animals, and their contributions to the general understanding of contagious and hereditary diseases, in both humans and lower animals.[45]

[39] Björk 1985: i, pp. xxviii, 67–78, 113–14, 133, 311–12n.; Wright 1986: 202–17. The comment about positivism was in a letter to Lady Grove in 1903; Björk 1985: i. 312n.

[40] T. Hardy 1998: 231, 244.

[41] Björk 1985: i. 189–92, 396–7n.

[42] See Casagrande 1971: 121n. Casagrande gives 1908 as the year for this letter; in fact it was 1909, see F. E. Hardy 1962: 346–7. For more on the influence of religious and evolutionary ideas on Hardy's fiction, see Schweik 1999. For Hardy's later views on religion, Christianity, and altruism, see F. E. Hardy 1962: 332–3. For a detailed study of Hardy's use of language and his interests in dialect and philology, see D. Taylor 1993.

[43] On Cobbe, see Gates 1998: 124–30. On Hutton, see *ODNB*.

[44] Green 2003: ss. 119–20; see also P. Crook 1994: 10.

[45] *The Times* (3 Oct. 1895), 13.

Since the 1880s, university students and others wishing to act on their own altruistic sense, and to encourage its development in others, had been able to do so by volunteering to work at one of the 'settlements' set up in the East End of London, as centres of education and philanthropy, the most famous of which was Toynbee Hall, founded in 1884.[46] An account of the activities of these foundations in 1895 reported that 'The reform of the poor-law is in everybody's mouth, and "altruism" and "collectivism" are the commonplaces of every would-be social reformer.'[47] Mrs H. Percy Boulnois, addressing the Sanitary Institute in Liverpool on the subject of 'The Ethics of Sanitation', maintained that sanitation was necessary for 'the mental, moral, and physical advancement of the race' and argued especially, on sanitary grounds, for the replacement of burial of the dead by cremation, which 'should be encouraged from principles of altruism, the watchword of the day'.[48] The language of altruism even found its way into children's books. *A Girl of To-Day* by Ellinor Davenport Adams was recommended by *The Times* as one of its Christmas books for 1898. The book was not, the reviewer reassured anxious parents, 'the biography of a fast young woman'. Rather it was about a brother and sister who 'arrange with some juvenile friends to form a society of Altruists—the word, by the way must be rather a staggerer for the readers for whom the tale is written'.[49] The Canadian philosopher Eliza Ritchie, writing in the *International Journal of Ethics*, a periodical founded in 1890 and with strong affiliations with the Ethical Societies, gave a long list of the many different embodiments of the new 'conscientiousness-at-large': 'Anarchists, socialists, prohibitionists, female suffragists, Christian scientists, anti-vivisectionists, Christian associations, missionary societies, ethical societies, in addition to the hosts of workers gathered around the different churches.' 'From the nihilist who kills his sovereign to the amiable lady who devotes her spare afternoons to slumming', all were motivated by the beneficence and enthusiasm of the age. In other words, despite the mixed motives that were doubtlessly behind such activities, 'we yet find altruism to be the greatest force in most of the social movements of our day'.[50]

[46] Knapp 1895; Meacham 1987; Himmelfarb 1991: 235–43; Sutherland 1991: 215–29; Koven 2004: 228–81.

[47] Bailward 1895: 167.

[48] As reported in *The Times* (26 Sept. 1894), 8.

[49] *The Times* (3 Dec. 1898), 15.

[50] E. Ritchie, 'Women and the Intellectual Virtues', *International Journal of Ethics,* 12 (1901), 69–80, at 70–1. On the *International Journal of Ethics* as an organ of the ethical movement, see MacKillop 1986: 6.

But of all the moral 'isms' that seemed to be spreading with such vigour in the 1880s and 1890s there was one with which 'altruism' was associated more often than any other—'socialism'. These two watchwords of late Victorian conscientiousness loomed through the moral mists together, their exact form unclear, but their presence unmistakable. 'Socialism' was to some, such as Herbert Spencer, a word that stood for a coming slavery of the individual to the state, for others it represented a happy future of equality and universal brotherhood. While 'socialism' could refer to almost any programme for economic and social change aimed at improving the working and living conditions of the poor, 'altruism' was its comparably vague associate in the moral and religious realms.[51] The two terms were semantically linked by their relationship with 'individualism'. 'Socialism' and 'collectivism' were the antonyms of 'individualism' in political economy and sociology, 'altruism' its opposite in ethics. As a result, 'altruism' and 'socialism' were closely associated in the minds of both their advocates and their critics. In 1894, the Edinburgh Professor of Political Economy, Joseph Shield Nicholson, addressed the British Association for the Advancement of Science in the Sheldonian Theatre in Oxford. The subject of his after-dinner talk was 'Historic Progress and Ideal Socialism'. Nicholson said that the present age was witnessing a 'great wave of altruism' unexampled in modern history, but one that was based on a mistaken conception of human nature, derived from the fashionable doctrines of Karl Marx and his followers. Nicholson, an orthodox follower of Adam Smith, contended that human beings were not so altruistic nor governments so wise as would be necessary if a socialist society were to succeed.[52]

The moral meanings of socialism

Victorian discussions of 'socialism' were highly moralistic. Whether debating the merits of co-operation, trade unionism, state socialism, or revolutionary Marxism, rhetoric about selfishness and altruism was rarely further than a paragraph or two away. References to 'altruism' normally entered into these controversies in one of two ways—either in the context of general questions about human nature, or in relation to the motives of particular social classes or political groupings. Socialists argued that human nature

---

[51] On the many meanings of 'socialism' see n. 1 above.
[52] *The Times* (14 Aug. 1894), 14.

was inherently altruistic; their individualist opponents thought this was unrealistic and idealistic. Socialists accused defenders of the traditional individualism that underlay both classical political economy and the Victorian ideal of self-help of being 'selfish'. Individualists returned the compliment, portraying working-class socialists as motivated by selfish greed expressed in their desire to have a share of the property of others without having to work for it, and a self-interested wish to get their hands on the mechanisms of state legislation. These basic arguments were played out again and again in the 1880s and 1890s. Taking one side or another on these questions of altruism and selfishness was a way to show allegiance with either the socialist or the individualist camp.

As we saw in the previous chapter, Herbert Spencer introduced the language of altruism and egoism into debates about state socialism in his *The Man versus The State* (1884). Spencer's individualistic philosophy, with its warnings both against indiscriminate philanthropy and excessive state intervention, was eagerly adopted by members of the anti-socialist Liberty and Property Defence League, founded by Lord Elcho in 1882.[53] The League took as its slogan 'Individualism *versus* Socialism'.[54] Among the early targets of their disapproval was the enthusiasm being generated by the American Henry George's recently published *Progress and Poverty*, which had proposed a single tax on all land as a radical redistributive measure.[55] The League was unable, however, to halt either the tide of socialism or the 'great wave of altruism'. In 1883 the radical Democratic Federation, under the leadership of H. M. Hyndman, declared itself a 'socialist' organization, and became the Social Democratic Federation; within five years there were more than forty branches nationally. The following year saw the founding of the Fabian Society, and the Socialist League followed in 1885 after a schism in the SDF. Towards the end of the 1880s the enthusiasm for social-ism became associated, by some, with support for the 'new unionism', amongst whose achievements was the attainment of better working condi-tions for the 'match girls' in the Bryant & May factory in 1888, and the securing of an eight-hour working day by the gas workers in 1889. For the thousands who devoted themselves under the banner of socialism to the improvement of the lot of the poor and the campaign against economic inequality, socialist beliefs and causes became central to their identity. Sometimes there was a close identification between socialism and an

[53] E. Bristow 1975; M. Taylor 1992.
[54] Spencer 1994: 79.
[55] Lynd 1968: 141–7.

existing Christian identity; sometimes socialism became a secular religion of its own.[56]

Co-operation, although it was connected with Christian socialism, was something distinct from the newly popular economic socialism of the 1880s. It had existed as an organized movement since the 1840s and was essentially a collaborative form of self-help that need not imply any kind of redistribution of wealth or property. What it shared with socialism in the 1880s, however, was its rhetorical denunciation of the evils of individualism and competition. Preaching the sermon at the annual Co-operative Congress in Plymouth in 1886, the Reverend Canon Percival told delegates that to assent to the modern demand to live a life of competition was nothing less than to give oneself over to 'individual selfishness'. Competition, he went on was the 'form which is assumed in civilised life by that "struggle for existence" which Darwinian investigation has shown to pervade all the lower orders of creation, which ends, as Darwin tells us, in the "survival of the fittest"'.[57] Percival contrasted what he took to be the ethos of the 'Darwinian' world of selfishness and competition with the teachings of Christ and St Paul, which were 'rooted in love and sacrifice'. Like Thomas Hughes, a Christian socialist and supporter of the co-operative movement since the late 1840s, Percival interpreted co-operation as the social application of Christian brotherhood, rather than as a step towards any form of state socialism. 'Wherever you turn', Percival said in 1886, 'men's minds are exercised by thoughts about union, co-operation, Socialism, Democratic change. The ideas represented by such words as these are stirring and fascinating the young.' These new movements would have good results only if it was remembered that they 'must be firmly based on our sense of brotherhood in Christ, of our fellowship in Christ, of our membership in Christ'.[58] Thomas Hughes put the matter even more starkly. For him state socialism was a 'specious' system, which would never be an appropriate one in England. Co-operation was synonymous with Christian socialism which was a religious movement based on sympathy and brotherhood, not a political one advocating state ownership and state action. Hughes saw the question of self-identification presented to modern men and women not as

---

[56] Binyon 1931; P. d'A. Jones 1968; Yeo 1977; Himmelfarb 1991: 307–80; Barrow and Bullock 1996; Bevir 2000; G. Johnson 2000; Haggard 2001.

[57] The phrase 'survival of the fittest' was coined by Herbert Spencer in 1864 to express the Darwinian idea of evolution by natural selection; Paul 1988.

[58] Percival 1886: 4–5, 8. For another Christian socialist perspective on 'altruism', published a few years later, see Kaufmann 1890. On the Christian socialist origins of the Victorian ideal of 'brotherhood' in the context of the university settlement movement, see Koven 2004: 231–6.

a choice between 'Individualism' and 'Socialism' as economic doctrines, but rather between opposed understandings of the religious and moral 'law' of life: 'If "competition" and "self-assertion" be the law, follow that; but if "concert" and "the sacrifice of selfish desires" be the law, then follow that. Believe me there is no halting place between the two—one or the other you may be faithful to, to both ye cannot be faithful. "Ye cannot serve God and Mammon." '[59]

The Spectator shared the anxieties of those like Hughes who did not think Britain was now, or ever would be, ready for a socialist form of government. Articles published in *The Spectator* in the 1880s and 1890s revealed the extent to which 'altruism' had become associated with 'socialism'.[60] An article on 'The Extravagance of Altruism' in 1892 complained about 'the exaggerated altruism of which we hear so much now on all sides' and the consequent neglect of one's own proper interests which was being advocated.[61] By 1897 *The Spectator* perceived the existence of a fanatical new creed of 'universal altruism' which, they warned, would mean in practice 'a universe of spoilt children, a wilderness of men tended, protected, watched over, and cosseted until there is nothing in them but a constant expectation of favour and defence from all above or around them'. The same article ridiculed the idea that Christ 'taught altruism, and altruism as understood by those who have accepted the semi-Socialist or Socialist theory now so prevalent'. This assault on socialistic altruism concluded: '"England," said Nelson, "expects every man to do his duty." "And mine too," whimpers the devotee of altruism, who even when he works faithfully for another expects ten men to work for him. Are all the masculine virtues to disappear in one rush of motherliness?'[62]

This apparently unmanly craze for collectivist altruism reached an even more advanced stage in America. There was an 'Altruist Community' in St Louis, Missouri, whose newspaper, previously *The Communist*, became *The Altruist* in 1885, the motto on its masthead reading: 'Equal Rights, United Labor, and Common Property'. Promoting a mixture of Communism, co-operation, and Christianity, *The Altruist* continued to be published until 1917. Another commune, established in California in the 1890s, was even named 'Altruria'. This colony was meant to be a refuge for those tired by

[59] T. Hughes 1885: 1–3, 8.
[60] 'Prodigality and Altruism', *The Spectator*, 57 (1884), 375–6; 'The Extravagance of Altruism', *The Spectator*, 68 (1892), 671–2; 'The Weak Point in Altruism', *The Spectator*, 79 (1897), 515–16.
[61] 'The Extravagance of Altruism', 671–2.
[62] 'The Weak Point in Altruism', 515–16.

competitive, selfish modern society. The entry requirements were fifty dollars and a moral character. The community met on Sundays for a humanistic religious service involving music and discussion and their ideology was one of brotherhood and mutuality. 'Altruria' was a missionary foundation, committed to founding new settlements on the same model. Like many other utopian schemes, however, this one failed financially.[63]

The leading advocate of socialism-as-altruism in Britain was the journalist Robert Blatchford, the country's most widely read socialist propagandist. He and a group of friends had founded the *Clarion* in 1891 as a weekly socialist newspaper. A series of articles written by Blatchford under the pseudonym 'Nunquam' and published as *Merrie England* in 1893 was an enormous success and introduced hundreds of thousands of people to the principles of socialism. Blatchford himself claimed that *Merrie England* had sold a million copies in Britain alone.[64] The Labour MP Manny Shinwell looked back on his early years and recalled that it was Robert Blatchford's writings more than anything else that 'aroused the sentiments of the working class and social reformers to a height far in excess of anything contributed by Hardie, however well-meaning and sincere the latter was'.[65] One of the ways that Blatchford aroused the sentiments of Shinwell and so many others was through his rhetoric of altruism. Blatchford was one of the leading spokesmen of the late Victorian moral revolution. He was a member of the Humanitarian League, which campaigned on a range of issues, including animal rights, Poor Law reform, and international arbitration. Underpinning all of this was a belief in the natural existence of 'altruism' and its superiority over selfishness.[66] As Stephen Yeo notes of Blatchford, in his study of the religion of socialism in Britain, 'Altruism was one of his favourite words in connection with social-ism.' In the preface to Blatchford's autobiography, his friend Alexander Thompson wrote 'I introduced Blatchford to journalism and he, in his turn—*comme un plaisir en vaut un autre*—introduced me to Socialism, or

---

[63] Microfiche copies of extant numbers of *The Communist* and *The Altruist* are held in Lancaster University Library. On 'Altruria', see Edward B. Payne, 'Altruria', *American Magazine of Civics,* 6 (1895), 168–71; Morrison I. Swift, 'Altruria in California', *Overland Monthly,* 29 (1897), 643–5; see also L. J. Budd 1956 on altruism and collectivism in America.

[64] Rose 2001: 48, 225–6, 279; Alexander M. Thompson, preface to Blatchford 1931: pp. vii–xiv. On Blatchford's career, see *ODNB*; Blatchford 1931; Thompson 1951. On Blatchford's writings and the relationship between socialism and the 'woman question' in the 1890s, see Ledger 1995.

[65] Shinwell 1981: 34.

[66] Weinbren 1994: esp. 90–1.

rather to the system of altruism, rooted in love of this country and its people, which he expounded in *Merrie England*.'[67]

In fact it was not in *Merrie England* but only in his publications in the later 1890s and early 1900s that Blatchford became an enthusiast for 'altruism'. The timing of Blatchford's conversion to 'altruism' in the mid-1890s is consistent with his having been persuaded, possibly by Benjamin Kidd's *Social Evolution* (1894), or Henry Drummond's *Ascent of Man* (1894), or both, of the usefulness of 'altruism' as a term with both scientific and religious rhetorical potential and an appeal to a large audience.[68] It was in an 1898 *Clarion Pamphlet* that Blatchford most clearly echoed the language of Benjamin Kidd. In that pamphlet, entitled 'Altruism: Christ's Glorious Gospel of Love against Man's Dismal Science of Greed', Blatchford wrote: 'Altruism, which is the embodiment of the command "Love thy neighbour as thyself," seems to have originated in the teachings of Christ, but has only attained important development in comparatively modern times.' He went on to describe 'Altruism' as 'the most important consummation in the progress of social evolution' and 'the strongest sentiment of modern times'. The faith he hoped other socialists shared with him, in the importance of spreading universal brotherly love, Blatchford said, was not founded on economic science but must have as its basis 'a religion of passionate love for humanity, a religion of service and sacrifice—a religion of Altruism'. Socialism without passionate altruism would be simply the bare doctrine of collective rather than private ownership. Such a dry creed could never win converts to the cause.[69]

By the time he wrote *God and My Neighbour* (1903), Blatchford's defence of altruism had changed. He had dropped the apparent sympathy with Christianity of his earlier writings and now presented a purely scientific and secular defence of altruism: 'It is not to revelation that we owe the ideal of human brotherhood, but to evolution. It is because altruism is better than selfishness that it has survived.' Recommending Kropotkin's *Mutual Aid*, published the previous year, but also echoing Henry Drummond's version of evolutionary history, Blatchford traced

---

[67] Alexander M. Thompson, preface to Blatchford 1931: pp. vii–xiv, at xii.

[68] On the success of Drummond's and Kidd's books, see Ch. 7 below. Neither book featured amongst the works Blatchford recommended to his readers on the subject, however, in Blatchford 1903: p. xii. As will become clear in the next chapter, neither would have been a respectable book for a socialist to endorse. Instead he recommended Kropotkin's *Mutual Aid* (1902) and Cotter Morison's determinist and eugenic *Service of Man* (1887). Kidd and Blatchford both feature as exponents of 'social-imperial thought' in Semmel 1960.

[69] Blatchford 1898: 3, 6, 8.

human altruism to 'the love of the animal for its mate' and 'the love of the parents for their young'. The next steps were tribal loyalty and national patriotism. These stages of 'altruistic evolution', which could be 'seen among the brutes', only reached their apotheosis in man, who could now 'take the grand step of embracing all humanity as one brotherhood and one nation'.[70] Evolution itself, then, was moving towards the goal of the Clarion movement which was, as Blatchford had articulated it in his earlier pamphlet, 'To make Altruists firstly, and secondly to convert those Altruists into Socialists.'[71]

A living sacrifice: Beatrice Potter

Beatrice Potter was to become a leading figure in a quite different part of the British socialist movement than that represented and led by Blatchford. The rigorously intellectual and scientific Fabian Society, the organization behind the founding of the London School of Economics, had little in common with the more emotional, populist, rural, hearty, even Anglo-Saxon Clarion movement, with its cycling clubs, its hikes, and its socialist sing-alongs. Nonetheless, the transformation of Beatrice Potter, daughter of a wealthy Tory businessman and friend of Herbert Spencer, into Beatrice Webb, one of the intellectual leaders of the British Labour movement, offers an intriguing example of the process Blatchford recommended of conversion to socialism via altruism.[72] Thanks to Beatrice Potter's diaries we can date the key moments of that conversion quite precisely: she became a devotee of 'altruism' in 1884 and of 'socialism' in 1890.

Beatrice Potter was the same age as Robert Melsom. Both were born in Gloucestershire and by the early 1880s both found themselves living amongst the urban poor—Melsom as a gas inspector and herbalist in north Manchester, Webb as a middle-class philanthropic volunteer in London. In

---

[70] Blatchford 1903: 160. On Blatchford's views on science and religion: Bowler 2001: 354–6.

[71] Blatchford 1898: 16.

[72] Potter married Sidney Webb in 1892; together they became the leading lights of the Fabian Society, which in turn was a powerful force in shaping the early Labour Party. For biographical information I have relied on, in addition to Beatrice Potter's diary entries in the 1880s, her later autobiography, *My Apprenticeship* (1926), on Norman Mackenzie's introduction to B. Webb 1979: pp. ix–xlii, and on John Davis's substantial entry on Beatrice and Sidney Webb in *ODNB*. On the roots of Sidney Webb's political thought in 'ethical positivism' and his identification with George Eliot's altruistic 'choir invisible', see Bevir 2002. On the importance of positivism to the Fabian society more generally, and the particular role of the Webbs, see Himmelfarb 1991: 350–80.

their mid-twenties, both found in 'altruism' something that they could identify with. For Melsom, and for those members of the working classes who read socialist literature by Robert Blatchford and the like, 'altruism' might have implied class solidarity, even universal brotherhood, and the hope for legislative action or violent revolution to achieve economic and social equality. For Beatrice Potter and other middle-class intellectuals and affluent philanthropists it meant something else. They encountered poverty not as inhabitants but visitors, not as victims but as observers, theorists, and reformers. For them 'altruism', the devotion to others, was an appropriate term for their concern for the poor, with whom they engaged very much as 'others'. As I noted in the previous chapter, 'altruism' in the 1880s and 1890s was often discussed as a quality of an unequal relationship between classes or nations rather than one between equal individuals. In the case of those who had money, education, and a desire to do something about poverty, 'altruism' stood for what could scarcely fail to be a paternalistic kind of concern of a higher for a lower class. There were still different ways of understanding that concern, however. 'Altruism' could function simply as a new name for the traditional philanthropy that encouraged self-help through donations to the deserving poor or, as in the case of Beatrice Potter, it could signify a vocation realized in deliberate rejection of that old philanthropic model. The aim of this kind of altruist was to fulfil their reformist vocation through self-renunciation and devotion to others. The new altruists immersed themselves in poverty as a lived social reality, a problem to be tackled by the social sciences, and an opportunity for moral self-realisation.

In 1883, while William Boyd Carpenter was preaching to Queen Victoria about the life of John Brown as a model of 'Christian Altruism' and readers of the *Pall Mall Gazette* were learning about the incestuous and insanitary living arrangements of the urban poor, Beatrice Potter was working in Soho as a volunteer for the Charity Organisation Society (see Fig. 18). The COS offered the quintessentially Victorian and individualist form of philanthropy, which was available only to the hard-working and the worthy, rather than the improvident, the lazy, the drunk, or the dissolute, and was administered discriminatingly with a view to encouraging rather than sapping the all-important 'self-reliance' of the labouring classes. This was philanthropy on a Spencerian model. Finding these methods unsatisfactory, Potter turned away from the COS and from Spencer in search of alternatives.[73] During

---

[73] Goodlad 2002 situates the COS philanthropy that Potter rejected within the context of several key intellectual and practical movements, including Fabian socialism, New Liberalism, social surveying, and developments in British sociology in the late 19th and early 20th centuries.

Figure 18. Beatrice Potter in 1883, aged 25. Webb 1926: facing p. 120.

the following years she was a pioneer of alternative ways of studying social problems. To try to reduce the distance between the observer and the poor, she went undercover. In 1883 and again in 1886 she visited the Lancashire town of Bacup as 'Miss Jones', the daughter of a Welsh farmer. She was impressed by the Methodist morality and the successful co-operative stores that she found there, which paid healthy profits to their working-class shareholders. Also in 1886 she had started work as one of a small team of investigators working with the Liverpool businessman Charles Booth on his major study of the living conditions of London's poor. Undertaken originally to test the SDF leader H. M. Hyndman's claim that 25 per cent of Londoners were living in poverty, Booth concluded, in the 1st edition of his multi-volume *Life and Labour of the People in London* (1892–7), that the correct figure could be as high as 30 or 35 per cent.[74]

Charles Booth and Beatrice Potter were both motivated by a mixture of social-scientific, religious, and moral concerns. Booth's cousins Harry and Albert Crompton had introduced him to positivism in Liverpool in the 1860s. Through them he would have learnt about Comtean sociology and the positivist advocacy of 'altruism'. Without becoming an adherent of organized positivism, he remained interested in the positivist combination of social science and humanistic religion throughout his life. Reading J. R. Seeley's *Natural Religion* in 1882, which, like Seeley's earlier work *Ecce Homo* (1865), argued for a human and naturalistic kind of religion, Booth jotted down some of his own thoughts about the basis of religion. Booth thought that there were three groups of ideas on which religions were based: 'Nature and law; Human nature and progress; Ideality and conscience'. Each of these bases led to its own kind of morality: 'Nature and law claiming *obedience* as the one thing needed. Human nature *Altruism*—and Conscience insisting upon *purity*.'[75]

Another Liverpool businessman, John Towne Danson had worked as a journalist and barrister before becoming a marine insurance underwriter in Liverpool (where Booth had made his fortune through the family steamship company). A life-long student of social science and political thought, Danson, like Booth, made notes about the meaning of 'altruism' during the 1880s. In 1884, he wrote in his notebook, 'Is "altruism" anything

---

[74] On Booth and his project, see Himmelfarb 1991: 77–178; see also Booth 1918; Simey and Simey 1960; *ODNB*.

[75] Charles Booth, notes on *Natural Religion* (1882), in the Booth Papers, Senate House Library, London; MS.797/II/26/14. See also an undated essay by Booth on 'Egoism and Altruism', discussing the mixed presence of both these forces in each individual; MS.797/II/16/18.

more than a fine name for our recognition of the corporate liabilities . . . of man?' In an incomplete unpublished essay entitled 'Altruism: What is it?', Danson wrote that it was either a new name for acts of 'benevolence' or it was a word that did not denote anything real at all, since he did not believe there was such a thing as a human motive directed exclusively at the benefit of others. The large collection of notebooks, letters, diaries, papers, and books by himself and others that Danson collected during his lifetime included several pamphlets published by the individualist Liberty and Property Defence League as well as papers produced by the National Association for the Promotion of Social Science. Danson's most successful publication, *The Wealth of Households* (1886), indebted for both its title and its ideology to Adam Smith, defended economic individualism and defined 'socialism' as a system of redistribution of wealth from the rich to the poor which, if voluntary, 'may be termed *Alms*', and if not 'is clearly *Theft*'.[76] An example of the latter appeared in a book published in 1897 entitled *Archie; or, The Confessions of an Old Burglar*. Written by the editor of the *Pall Mall Magazine*, the book claimed to be a reliable record of the recollections of a convict—'Archie'—who had recently been reformed and converted by the Salvation Army. The story entitled 'Altruism' told of Archie's unsuccessful attempts to steal and redistribute the property of an unpopular landowner.[77] 'Altruism', like 'socialism', seemed to some to be synonymous with 'theft'.

In 1884, in the midst of her discovery of her vocation as a social investigator, Beatrice Potter started to take an interest in John Towne Danson's question, 'Altruism: What is it?' Potter's answer was much more enthusiastic than that produced by the sceptical and individualistic Danson. In September 1884 she opened a new notebook for herself, and copied out, as she put it in *My Apprenticeship* (1926), 'in large letters for my own edification', the following passage from Comte's *Catéchisme Positiviste*: 'Our harmony as moral beings is impossible on any other foundation but altruism. Nay more, altruism alone can enable us to live in the highest and truest sense. To live for others is the only means of developing the whole existence of man.' The translation from Comte's French was her

---

[76] John Towne Danson papers, in the Danson Family Archive, National Museums Liverpool, Maritime Archives and Library. 'Notes from Books, 1883–1886', D/D/III/14/1/24; 'Notes and draft essays', D/D/III/14/2/17. The quotations from J.T. Danson 1886 are taken from the galley proofs held in the Danson archive, D/D/III/10/21, paragraph 1140. For a brief summary of Danson's career, see Thomas A. Welton, 'Mr John Towne Danson', *Journal of the Royal Statistical Society*, 61 (1898), 372–4.
[77] C. Morley 1900.

own.[78] Immediately above this she had copied out a passage from Mill's *Utilitarianism*: (1863): 'When people who are tolerably fortunate in their outward lot do not find in life sufficient enjoyment to make it valuable to them, the cause generally is, caring for nobody but themselves.' Potter's desire to live for others rather than herself was articulated in the language of the philosophers of altruism of a previous generation. The location for her enactment of her new-found commitment to altruism was inevitably the East End of London, the place that had inspired James Hinton to a life of 'altruism' decades earlier, and which was the location of the newly opened university settlement named after Hinton's best friend's son, Toynbee Hall.[79]

Potter's thoughts about altruism in the years around 1884 were mixed up with several sources of personal distress. Her mother had died in 1882, and in 1885 her father suffered a stroke which meant that she would spend much of her time as his nurse for the following eight years. But the greatest cause of her unhappiness at this time was her romantic entanglement with the charismatic Liberal politician Joseph Chamberlain. Her infatuation was short-lived but painful. She was at her lowest ebb at the start of 1886 when she drew up an informal will, in which she wrote: 'If Death comes it will be welcome—for life has always been distasteful to me.'[80] A few months later she finally ended her contact with Chamberlain in a letter accusing him of being unnecessarily hurtful towards her. 'Thank God! that when our own happiness is destroyed', she wrote, 'there are still others to live for.'[81] Potter suffered from recurring bouts of depression. During one of these, a few months after she had copied out the quotation from Comte about 'altruism', she wrote in her diary that she felt she was 'stranded in a desolate sort of country—with no hope or faith'. But she immediately chided herself: 'Must pick up and think of others. Altruism is after all the creed of those who are suffering personal misery and yet do not intend to sink into abject wretchedness—it used to be devotion to God, under one

---

[78] The diaries have been edited by Norman and Jeanne Mackenzie and published as B. Webb 1982–5. My references to Potter's diaries for this period are to the typewritten transcript held in the Library of the London School of Economics; Passfield 1/1. Diary, 8 Sept. 1884, Passfield 1/1/1–7, f. 382; also quoted in B. Webb 1926: 149; for Congreve's translation, see Comte 1891: 215.

[79] On the influence of James Hinton on Arnold Toynbee, son of the aurist Joseph Toynbee, see Benjamin Jowett's 'Memoir' of Toynbee in Toynbee 1884: pp. v–xxvii, at vi–vii. On Hinton, see Ch. 2 above.

[80] Diary, 1 Jan. 1886, Passfield 1/1/1–7, f. 482; also quoted in Norman Mackenzie's introd. to B. Webb 1979: pp. ix–xlii, at xxix.

[81] Quoted in Mackenzie's introd. to B. Webb 1979: p. xxxi.

form or another—now this God is dead it must be devotion to other human beings.'[82] On another occasion Potter described her altruistic vocation in terms of the desire to be a 'living sacrifice'. This was an allusion to St Paul's letter to the Romans: 'I beseech you therefore, brethren, by the mercies of God, that ye present your bodies a living sacrifice, holy, acceptable unto God, which is your reasonable service.'[83]

Potter's own interpretation, in *My Apprenticeship*, of her devotion of herself to what St Paul called 'reasonable service' through her work in the East End of London in the 1880s was that she had been seized by the 'time-spirit', which had 'compelled me to concentrate all my free energy in getting the training and the raw material for applied sociology; that is, for research into the constitution and working of social organisation, with a view to bettering the life and labour of the people'. This 'time-spirit' was characterised by two 'idols of the mind', namely belief in the scientific method, and 'the consciousness of a new motive; the transference of the emotion of self-sacrificing service from God to man'.[84] The picture presented in the diary entries Potter made at the time is, unsurprisingly, more complicated than her neat formulation in the 1920s. Romantic disappointment, depression, political theory, and religion were all important parts of Potter's construal of herself as a 'living sacrifice'. In September 1885, for instance, one entry recorded Potter considering whether to write an article in response to the Spencerian Auberon Herbert's claim that 'Individualism' and 'Socialism' were now the only two possible political creeds. At the same time, Potter was thinking about her experiences among the co-operators in Bacup and continuing her work as a rent-collector in Whitechapel. She also continued to suffer from depression: 'Oh! so tired. Struggling through the end of my work with painful effort. The old physical longing for the night that knows no morning.'[85] Later that year she pondered the merits of individualism and socialism again. It seemed to her that the individualists overlooked the 'many complicated forms of altruism which undoubtedly exist and which if a man be totally deficient of them he is regarded as a monstrosity by his fellows'. On the other hand, the socialists seemed quite unrealistic in their expectation that the wealthier classes could be persuaded

---

[82] Diary, 19 Nov. 1884, Passfield 1/1/1–7, f. 398.

[83] Rom. 12: 1. Potter's use of the term was in a diary entry for 28 May 1886, Passfield 1/1/8–12, f. 667.

[84] B. Webb 1926: 129–30.

[85] Diary, 10 Sept. 1885, Passfield 1/1/1–7, f. 428.

it was their moral duty to 'give up their earnings to the poor' and thus to do 'what was positively hurtful to themselves and their offspring'.[86]

Early in 1886, back home caring for her father, Potter returned to the Anglican Church she had attended with him as a child, and took communion. Having declared God to be dead in 1884, she now reflected that she had only 'lost that holy influence as a persistent feeling when first I gave way to that delusion about the Great Man' (her infatuation with Chamberlain). Having prayed to God for guidance prior to writing the letter that cut off her connection with Chamberlain, she now felt comforted. Now she could 'turn with earnestness to my own aims in life—to a loving care of that darling old Father, to a persistent pursuit of truth by the light of the faith that is in me'. It seemed to her that the last two years of obsession with Chamberlain had been an attempt to fulfil her 'lower nature'. Taking the sacrament, that 'great symbol of sacrifice', showed that she was now prepared to make 'the sacrifice of individual life and happiness'.[87] This revived Christian faith remained with her only intermittently, but she did continue to believe in some form of theism. In 1889 she wrote in her diary that she could not join the positivist Religion of Humanity since, although practically 'we are all positivists; we all make the service of man the leading doctrine of our lives', humanity was not a sufficiently inspiring object of worship. In order to serve humanity, she thought, 'we need inspiration from a superhuman force towards which we are perpetually striving'.[88] Potter continued to bring a moral ardour to her work in the East End, driven by these mixed motives of romantic disappointment, a morbid sense of self-renunciation, a religious yearning for some superhuman force, and a gradually increasing sympathy with the doctrines of socialism.

In 1888 Potter undertook another of her incognito experiments—an episode described by John Davis as 'one of the more implausible deceits perpetrated by Victorian social observers'.[89] Masquerading as a jobbing seamstress, Potter took an apartment in the East End, dressed herself in tatty old clothes, and managed to get herself a job finishing trousers in a tailor's workshop on the Mile End Road. Potter had trouble fitting in with the other girls who worked there, one of whom said to her of their colleagues: 'They're an awful bad lot, some o'them. Why bless you; that young woman

---

[86] Diary, Oct. 1885, Passfield 1/1/1–7, f. 450.
[87] Diary, 15 Mar. 1886, Passfield 1/1/8–12, f. 499.
[88] Diary, 15 Mar. 1889, quoted in B. Webb 1926: 149.
[89] ODNB.

just behind us has had three babies by her father; and another here has had one by her brother.' The Jewish woman who ran the shop suspected that Potter was of a higher class than the others who worked there and recommended that she find a respectable man to marry.[90] After this brief experiment, Potter continued her work as a social investigator in the East End, and continued to turn to religion for support: 'Prayer is a constant source of strength. I like to sit in that grand St Paul's, with its still, silent space.' In 1888, Potter started to feel that she could 'realise' the life of the people of the East End in her own mind, their joys and their sorrows, and that through a systematic study of that life she could 'to some extent grasp the forces which are swaying to and fro, raising or depressing this vast herd of human beings'. Facing another bout of 'self-torture' and 'mental misery' a few months later, Potter could find reassurance only in 'Religion—the consciousness of a great Father—the judge of all things—the consciousness of an immortal soul—chastened by suffering, strengthened by repentance.'[91]

The first of the many volumes of Booth's survey of the London poor came out in 1889, including an essay by Potter on her experiences working in the tailor's shop the previous year. At that point Potter was one of the many individuals who comprised the 'great wave of altruism' discerned by contemporary commentators. Her particular combination of depression and disappointment with energetic work in the 'service of man' also had its counterparts in some of the fictional altruists of the 1880s. Eliza Lynn Linton's *Autobiography of Christopher Kirkland* (1885), partly based on her own experiences, included the story of Kirkland's long search for an appropriate wife which ended in his falling in love with a Roman Catholic woman called Cordelia. Kirkland was an ardent rationalist whose only desire was 'to benefit humanity'. This included doing all he could to 'combat everywhere the organized mental tyranny and debasing superstitious ignorance of the Church of Rome—that deadliest enemy to human progress which the modern world possesses'. Naturally this did not make for easy relations with Cordelia. Their religious incompatibility meant that Kirkland, with great regret, had to let his beloved go: 'Life was never the same to me after this. Something had gone from me which could never be replaced. I felt like one who has received some unseen and irreparable hurt which maims, but does not kill. I was not visibly disabled, but living was more difficult.' Kirkland was now resigned to living 'without personal hope

[90] Diary, Apr. 1888, Passfield 1/1/8–12, ff. 918–35, quotation at 923.
[91] Diary, 5 May 1888; 28 Aug. 1888, Passfield 1/1/8–12, ff. 938–9, 960.

or love in my life, and with only work, humanity, and thought to fill up the void'; he recalled how he had buried his sorrow away and

> flung myself more and more into active life. Cordelia was dead to me, but humanity was left alive, and still suffered. There was so much to be done for the world! And after all, what were my individual sorrows compared with those of the race? What we now call altruism was then as much a fact under another name. And altruism is integral to my nature, born as it is of passionate sensation and keen imagination, by which I suffer in my own person and understand that others should feel as I have done.[92]

Another fictional altruist spurred on by romantic disappointment was a creation of George Gissing's. Gissing was of the same generation as Robert Melsom and Beatrice Potter, but unlike them he was no devotee to 'altruism'. His own experiences led him to a more pessimistic philosophy. In the 1870s he had been caught stealing money from fellow students at Owens College, Manchester. (Charles Gaskell Higginson, later the president of the Manchester positivists, was studying French there at the time.) Gissing had been using the stolen money to try to 'save' a girl of the streets called Nell with whom he had fallen in love. He was sentenced, in 1876, to one month's imprisonment with hard labour for the theft. After serving his sentence, and undertaking an unsuccessful trip to America, Gissing settled in London, where he turned to writing fiction. He married Nell, who had moved down to London to join him, in 1879, and in 1880 his first novel, *Workers in the Dawn*, a depiction of lower class London life was published. By Christmas only forty-nine copies had been sold and Gissing had started to sell his clothes to raise money. In July 1880, with sales still almost nil, Gissing sent a copy of *Workers in the Dawn* to Frederic Harrison, asking him if he might read it. Gissing and Harrison became friends and Gissing, briefly, became a positivist. But by 1882 he was composing an essay, 'The Hope of Pessimism', which he never sought to publish for fear of offending Harrison and his other positivist friends. The essay condemned the 'Religion of Humanity' as a form of groundless 'agnostic optimism' which tried, unsuccessfully, to motivate human altruism on philosophical principles alone. In this essay Gissing wrote with contempt and disgust about the egotism and competition of modern society, about the struggle for existence described by modern science, and about the lustful passions that tormented all human beings. He concluded by recommending a

---

[92] Linton 1885: ii. 233, 243–5.

bleak, pessimistic philosophy of pity and sexual abstinence derived from Schopenhauer's philosophy in the place of either Christianity or positivism, either individualism or altruism.[93]

'The Hope of Pessimism' was a dark and heavy-going essay, but in his later published works of fiction Gissing applied his pessimism about contemporary society, human nature, and the creed of altruism with a lighter touch, gently mocking altruists such as Edwin Reardon in *New Grub Street* (1891) and Dyce Lashmar in *Our Friend the Charlatan* (1901). His *The Nether World* (1889) was another portrayal of the life of the working classes, and it included a depiction of the ineffectually philanthropic Miss Lant. A middle-aged woman of 'very plain features', Miss Lant did not resemble Beatrice Potter in all respects. But Gissing proposed her as a type of woman whose early years had been 'joyless' and who 'in the energy which she brought to this self-denying enterprise' displayed 'just a touch of excess, common enough in those who have been defrauded of their natural satisfactions and find a resource in altruism'. Miss Lant was not an orthodox believer—she was 'no pietist, but there is now-a-days coming into existence a class of persons who substitute for the old religious acerbity a narrow and oppressive zeal for good works of purely human sanction, and to this order Miss Lant might be said to belong'.[94]

The events of the early 1890s definitively distinguished Beatrice Potter from the traditional altruistic philanthropy of a spinster like Miss Lant, as she took the step that Blatchford considered the crucial one, from altruist to socialist (as well as the step from Miss Potter to Mrs Webb). Having spent almost a decade reflecting on the shortcomings of the COS methods, and of Herbert Spencer's and Auberon Herbert's philosophy of individualism; experimenting with the alternative theoretical models of the scientific reform of society offered by Auguste Comte and the Fabians respectively; and pioneering new kinds of social work and social surveying among the London poor in collaboration with Charles Booth, in February 1890 Beatrice Potter recorded in her diary, with the momentous fervour of a religious convert, 'at last I am a socialist!'[95] Marrying the Fabian Sidney Webb, who had none of the charm and charisma of Joseph Chamberlain,

---

[93] This essay is included in Gissing 1970: 75–97. On Gissing's relationship with Harrison and positivism, ibid. 11–25; Halperin 1982: 40–1; and letters to his brother Algernon on the subject between 1879 and 1882 in Mattheisen *et al.* 1990–7: i and ii. On *Our Friend the Charlatan*, see also Ch. 3 above.

[94] Gissing 1890: 229.

[95] B. Webb 1982–5: i. 322; *ODNB*. On the religious nature of conversion to socialism in the late 19th century, see Yeo 1977; G. Johnson 2000.

two years later, could be interpreted as Beatrice Potter's final denial of her 'lower nature' and its sacrifice to her intellect and her ideals. During their honeymoon Sidney and Beatrice continued work on their joint project of writing a history of the co-operative movement. In each other they had found 'the other one' to whom they could devote themselves while fulfilling their vocation to secure the good of those other 'others'—the working-class poor. Romantic love and social altruism did not have to be mutually exclusive.[96]

The world of *Robert Elsmere*

Another Victorian marriage that had its origins in a shared commitment to improving the lot of the urban poor was that between Henrietta Rowland and Reverend Samuel Barnett, both stalwarts of the Charity Organisation Society, and later the founders of one of the first university 'settlements', Toynbee Hall in 1884. The Anglican settlement Oxford House, opened in Bethnal Green a few months before the Barnetts' non-denominational Toynbee Hall, and the Women's University Settlement set up in Southwark by Henrietta Barnett in 1887, also served as homes for philanthropic missionaries offering a charitable response to poverty that differed significantly from the belief in state socialism that Beatrice Potter was led towards through her own encounters with the poor.[97] The economic, cultural, and moral development which the educated men and women who volunteered in the settlement houses offered was generally, at least initially, of the more traditional kind favoured by the Charity Organisation Society. One of the tasks identified in 1895 by W. A. Bailward, the honorary secretary of the Bethnal Green COS, and a former member of the Oxford House settlement, was for the 'scattered threads of East End philanthropy', including the work of the settlements and of the COS, to be drawn together into a more systematic and organized whole, rather than working in ignorance of each other's schemes. The current disorganized approach, he thought, increased the danger that excessive alms would be distributed and the dependent and pauperized classes enlarged still further. Bailward's essay on the work of the Oxford House settlement was also the source of the disapproving

---

[96] Beatrice Webb dedicated *My Apprenticeship* 'To The Other One'; B. Webb 1926: p. v.

[97] See Koven 1994, 2004: 228–81. Henrietta Rowland had, as a girl in the 1860s, spent several terms at a Dover boarding school run by the Haddon sisters, the sisters-in-law of James Hinton. On Hinton, see Ch. 2 above.

observation quoted above that 'altruism' and 'collectivism' were 'the commonplaces of every would-be social reformer' in the East End in the 1890s.[98]

The Webbs and the Barnetts, then, in their different beliefs about the best way to deal with urban poverty, illustrated the important fact that a commitment to organized social work amongst the poor did not necessarily lead to a commitment to socialism. (Another nice illustration of the two couples' differing outlooks is that, while the Webbs spent their honeymoon reading about the history of the co-operative movement, the Barnetts had spent theirs reading the Christian socialist F. D. Maurice's lectures on St Paul's Epistles.[99]) Although many went on from their experiences in the university settlements to advocate forms of socialism, the original model was premised on a more conservative ideology.[100] Indeed, amongst conservative thinkers, social work was seen, as Arthur Balfour put it in 1895, as being not only distinct from socialism but 'its most direct opposite and its most effective antidote'.[101] W. A. Bailward, for instance, thought it the responsibility of those who volunteered in settlements and who 'have had greater opportunities of study' to lead the way now that 'the centre of gravity' in politics had shifted, and political power had fallen into 'the hands of those who have not much time to read or think'. Such reading and thinking by university men and women would result, Bailward implied, in a preference not for the creation of 'relief works' for the unemployed, nor for the old-age pensions and free school meals demanded by the proponents of 'altruism' and 'collectivism', but rather in the creation of a democracy whose strength lay in the 'industry and independence of the population'.[102] The conservative politician John Gorst, in his 1894 rectorial address to Glasgow University, similarly envisaged the settlements as providing an opportunity for educated men and women to inform the poor of superior solutions to their problems than those offered by socialist agitators. The poor needed to be saved from falling into the hands of trade unionists and, even worse, of

---

[98] Bailward 1895: 167, 170; see J. Lewis 1996: 159.

[99] Koven 2004: 233.

[100] One example of someone whose philanthropic career started in the settlement movement and who went on to become a supporter of the socialism of the Independent Labour Party was Revd James Adderley, who became the first head of Oxford House, at the age of 24, in 1885. And even Samuel and Henrietta Barnett became more sympathetic to certain forms of socialism as the century progressed, writing a book together entitled *Practicable Socialism* (1888); see *ODNB*; Koven 1994, 2004: 240–1.

[101] Quoted in Himmelfarb 1991: 310.

[102] Bailward 1895: 167–8.

'designing persons, who may for their own selfish ends stir them up by promises of social salvation to revolutionary outbreaks'.[103]

In 1890 another university settlement, University Hall, was opened. Its founder was the great literary celebrity of the moment, Mrs Humphry Ward (see Fig. 19).[104] Her novel, *Robert Elsmere* (1888), which told the story of the transformation of an orthodox Anglican clergyman into a heterodox idealist, and founder of a settlement house resembling Toynbee Hall, home to a 'New Brotherhood' committed to social work amongst the London poor, was the best-selling novel of the 1880s, and possibly of the century.[105] Mary Augusta Ward's grandfather was Thomas Arnold and Matthew Arnold was her uncle. Her creation Robert Elsmere abandoned the muscular Christianity of the former to adopt the naturalistic religious moralism of the latter according to which, in the words which rang in Elsmere's ears at the climax of his religious crisis, '*miracles do not happen!*'[106] Elsmere's religion, like Matthew Arnold's, could be summarized as 'morality touched with emotion' (plus social work). Mary Ward used the fame and influence gained through the success of *Robert Elsmere* to pursue two social causes: opposition to female suffrage and support for the settlement movement. In 1889 she was the driving force behind an 'Appeal Against Female Suffrage', published in *The Nineteenth Century*, and signed by dozens of influential women (including Beatrice Potter, who only later became a supporter of votes for women).[107] The following year, Ward founded University Hall. Finding the ethos of Toynbee Hall too sympathetic to socialism, and that of Oxford House too theologically conservative, Ward's University Hall was based on an idealistic kind of Unitarian theism. In that respect it closely resembled the fictional Elgood Street settlement founded in the East End by Robert Elsmere. University Hall and a related foundation, Marchmont Hall, were later combined by Mrs Ward into the much larger Passmore Edwards Settlement, which was officially opened in 1898.

---

[103] Gorst 1895: 16.

[104] On University Hall and the other institutions, Marchmont Hall and the Passmore Edwards Settlement, which grew out of it, see Sutherland 1991: 215–29.

[105] On *Robert Elsmere* see Peterson 1976; MacKillop 1986: 7–16; Lightman 1990; Sutherland 1991: esp. 106–31; Gouldstone 2005: 64–81; P.Waller 2006: 1030–42. Hapgood 1996 treats *Robert Elsmere* as the first of a group of 'social redemption' novels published between 1888 and 1900; see also Hapgood 1995. For Ward's own recollections of the writing and reception of her most famous novel, see Mrs H.Ward 1918: 162–254. See also Rosemary Ashton's introduction to Mrs H.Ward 1987.

[106] Mrs H.Ward 1888: ch. 26, p. 342.

[107] Mrs Humphry Ward *et al.*, 'An Appeal Against Female Suffrage', *Nineteenth Century*, 25 (1889), 781–8. John Davis's entry on Beatrice and Sidney Webb in *ODNB* notes that Webb recanted her opposition to female suffrage in the early 20th century.

ELLIOTT & FRY

7, GLOUCESTER TERRACE,
ONSLOW GARDENS. S.W.
and at 55, Baker Street. W.

Figure 19. Mary Augusta Ward, known to the reading public as the novelist Mrs Humphry Ward, author of *Robert Elsmere* (1888), the best-selling novel of the 1880s. Date of photograph unknown; © Mary Ward Settlement.

Through the huge impact of *Robert Elsmere*, hundreds of thousands of readers in Britain and America were introduced to the ideals of the settlement movement, the associated idealistic philosophy of T. H. Green, to whom the novel was dedicated, and on whom the character of Mr Grey was based, and also to intellectual debates about the historicity of the scriptures and the plausibility of Christian teachings which had been constant subjects of academic discussion since the 1860s.[108] The novel's hero became one of the most famous 'altruists' of the century. On the strength of word-of-mouth recommendations and requests from the users of circulating libraries, 3,500 thousand copies of the three-volume library edition of the novel were sold within a few months of its publication, establishing Ward as a 'cult author' amongst the reading population of the large cities of Britain.[109] Within two years about 70,000 copies of *Robert Elsmere* had been sold in Britain, along with hundreds of thousands of pirated copies of the novel in the United States (which was not yet bound by an international copyright agreement)—some of which were given away to purchasers of bars of a new brand of 'Balsam Fir Soap'. By 1909, on Ward's own estimate, over a million copies had been sold in English-speaking countries. John Sutherland considers *Robert Elsmere* to have been the 'best-seller of the century'.[110] The book was so widely read that there was apparently even some discussion about whether to include as a question on the census form for 1891, 'What do you think of *Robert Elsmere*?'[111]

Robert Elsmere quickly became the subject of reviews, articles, and sermons all over the country. William Gladstone, who had probably not read the *Gas Consumer's Manual* by 'Altruism' sent to him by Robert Melsom in 1882, when he had been Prime Minister, certainly read *Robert Elsmere* six years later, and even met with Mary Ward on two occasions to discuss with her his reaction to its theology. He wrote in the May number of *The Nineteenth Century* on '*Robert Elsmere* and the Battle of Belief', thus giving the book priceless further publicity. It was also reviewed by Walter

[108] On T. H. Green, idealism, and Victorian social and political thought, see Den Otter 1996; Carter 2003; Leighton 2004. On Green's portrayal as Mr Grey in *Robert Elsmere*, see Leighton 2004: 82–3. On Green's broader intellectual and cultural impact see also Himmelfarb 1991: 247–62. On Christian interpretations of idealist philosophy see especially Sell 1995; Gouldstone 2005. Peterson 1976: 134 notes that after 1888, esp. in America, T. H. Green was often identified as 'the Mr Grey of *Robert Elsmere*'.
[109] Sutherland 1991: 126.
[110] Mrs H. Ward 1918: 252–3; Peterson 1976: 159, 221–2; Sutherland 1991: 128–31, quotation at 108. On Ward's continued success as one of the best-selling novelists of the 1890s and 1900s, see Bassett and Walter 2001: 209.
[111] Lynd 1968: 346.

Pater in the *Guardian* and by R. H. Hutton in the *Spectator*.[112] The leading Wesleyan Methodist, Hugh Price Hughes, himself an admirer of T. H. Green's idealism and a proponent of the 'social gospel', preached on *Robert Elsmere* on two Sunday afternoons in May 1888, welcoming the novel's celebration of the ideal of brotherhood but regretting its hero's abandonment of the living Christ on what Hughes considered the entirely inadequate basis of historical criticism of the documents that recorded his earthly life.[113] While Gladstone, Hutton, Hughes, and others regretted the weakness of the case put for Christianity in *Robert Elsmere*, in Manchester Charles Higginson Gaskell thought the case put against it was also inadequate. Gaskell took the opportunity of his annual newsletter to the Positivist Society a few years later, when the novel was still attracting new readers, to criticize *Robert Elsmere* for the weakness of the arguments it offered against Christianity, specifically its omission of any reference to the problem of evil. To reconcile a supposed divine goodness with 'such varied evils as droughts, floods, earthquakes, cholera, anaemia, neuralgia, early bereavement' was, Higginson wrote, 'of course, impossible', and it was a failure of *Robert Elsmere* that this fact was not faced more squarely.[114] The novel later made a deep and more positive impression on Mrs Ward's nephew, the evolutionary biologist Julian Huxley, who himself recalled it as a factor in converting him to a form of religious humanism.[115]

The particular importance of *Robert Elsmere* in the history of the language of altruism was twofold. Beyond introducing that language to a broader readership than that reached by Comte, Mill, or even Spencer, *Robert Elsmere* communicated to its readers both the ethics of philosophical idealism and also the characteristics of a newly emerging social type, the 'altruist'. Since one of the central claims of idealist ethics was that the dichotomy between 'altruism' and 'egoism' was a false and unhelpful one, the identification of Elsmere as both an idealist and an altruist was

---

[112] W. E. Gladstone, '*Robert Elsmere* and the Battle of Belief', *Nineteenth Century*, 23 (1888), 766–88; Walter Pater, '*Robert Elsmere*' (1888), repr. in Pater 1906: 55–70; R. H. Hutton, 'The Theology of *Robert Elsmere*' (1888), repr. in Hutton 1894: ii. 263–9.

[113] Peterson 1976: 250–1, provides a list of about twenty sermons preached on *Robert Elsmere* in Britain and the USA, of which Hugh Price Hughes's first London sermon was the earliest. H. P. Hughes, '*Robert Elsmere* and Mr Gladstone's Criticism of the Book', a sermon preached on Sunday afternoon, 6 May 1888, in St James's Hall, London; 'The Problem for Unbelief', a sermon preached on Sunday afternoon, 20 May 1888, in St James's Hall, London in H. P. Hughes 1890: 94–105 and 108–17. On Hughes and the social gospel, see King 1984.

[114] Higginson 1892: 4–5; held in the collection of papers relating to English positivist societies in the Maison d'Auguste Comte, Paris.

[115] Peterson 1976: 160.

potentially incoherent. Even the most careful exponents of idealist ethics struggled to articulate entirely consistently the idea that a true system of ethics simultaneously encouraged both self-realization and self-sacrifice, both individual fulfilment and devotion to the common good. It is therefore appropriate that *Robert Elsmere*, which was perceived as a popularization of that ethics, should have embodied these same tensions. Henry Sidgwick, in his undergraduate lectures on Green's posthumously published *Prolegomena to Ethics* (1883), complained of this ambiguity. He noted that Green claimed that no true distinction could be made between the good of the self and the good of others, since all individual lives were so intimately bound up with the social whole. Why, then, Sidgwick asked, did Green celebrate 'self-denial' and 'self-sacrifice' as ideals of the virtuous citizen? If acting for the common good was identical with realizing one's better self, then such actions were not properly acts of self-denial at all, Sidgwick argued.[116] The idealist philosopher would have agreed. 'Self-denial', in this context, they would have explained, was shorthand for the denial of the lower, selfish self in order that the higher, truer, better, best, or 'ideal' self should be realized. Sidgwick was right, however, that these complicated redefinitions of the meanings of self and sacrifice, of altruism and self-realization, were liable to lead to confusion.[117]

Green himself did not express his ethical arguments in terms of 'altruism' and 'egoism' (indeed the only reference to 'Altruism' in the *Prolegomena to Ethics* was when Green used it as a term for Sidgwick's universalistic version of utilitarianism).[118] Other idealist philosophers in the 1880s, however, did see their ethics as involving the problematizing of those terms. The Glasgow-educated philosopher Henry Jones, a lecturer at University College, Aberystwyth, and later Professor of Moral Philosophy at St Andrews and then Glasgow, addressed this question in an 1883 essay on 'The Social Organism'. He took the orthodox idealist line that the individual and society only existed 'in and through each other, and are constituted by their relation.' Consequently, individual aims and interests did not exist independently of social ones, and the welfare of the individual was identical with the good of the community. 'From this point of view', Jones

---

[116] Sidgwick 1902: 67–8; referring to Green 2003: bk 3, chs 4–5.

[117] See David Brink's introd. to Green 2003: pp. xiii–xc, at xxxii, xlviii. On the idealist attempt to transcend the dichotomy between egoism and altruism, see also Brink 1997; Simhony 2001. Granlund 1994 explores related questions about higher and lower forms of egoism through a study of Christian ethics and the novels of George Eliot.

[118] Green 2003: bk 4, ch. 4, s. 366.

argued, with Herbert Spencer's *Data of Ethics* (1879) clearly in his sights, 'it becomes unnecessary to effect a "compromise" or to "conciliate" egoism and altruism—the last effort of inconsistent Hedonism to extend its narrow teachings so as to correspond with the facts of ethical life'. Jones took Rousseau to be the archetypal advocate of individualism and Comte to be the prophet of altruism. The former, he wrote, 'would not wash the feet of his neighbour'. Comte, on the other hand, would 'wash "not his feet only but his hands and his head", and drown himself in addition'.[119] Neither extreme was tenable. But no 'conciliation' was necessary, since in reality there was not a conflict between the welfare of the individual and that of the human race. And moral heroes were those whose '*ideal self* was co-extensive with the larger self of their world'.[120]

The Glasgow idealist Edward Caird made a similar point in his 1885 book on Comte's moral philosophy. A 'deeper analysis' of human motivation would have revealed to Comte that human desires 'in themselves, as mere natural impulses, were neither egoistic nor altruistic' and that 'the *ego* is not absolutely opposed to the *alter ego*, but rather implies it'. The truly 'spiritual or self-conscious being', for Caird, was 'one who can realize his own individual good only as he realizes the good of others' and whose natural desires could be channelled into an 'expression of the better self, which is *ego* and *alter ego* in one'.[121] Idealist philosophers thus endorsed in theory what the settlement movement stood for in practice—an attempt to end the artificial isolation of the individual from the rest of society, of the helping self from the helped others. Settlement houses physically placed educated philanthropists in the midst of the needier parts of the society to which they themselves belonged. Idealist philosophers challenged the distinction between altruism and egoism, between self and others, in order to achieve their own version of that reintegration of individual and society.

Mrs Ward's heretical hero, Robert Elsmere, was an idealist archetype, seeking self-realization through self-denial (to the point of working himself to death, breaking his fragile health with the demands of his East End

---

[119] The quotation is from the story, in St John's gospel, of Jesus washing his disciples' feet at the last supper: 'Peter saith unto him, Thou shalt never wash my feet. Jesus answered him, If I wash thee not, thou hast no part with me. Simon Peter saith unto him, Lord, not my feet only, but also my hands and my head' (John 13: 8–9).

[120] The essay originally appeared in Seth and Haldane 1883, and is repr. in Boucher 1997: 3–29, quotations at 25–7. On Jones's life and career, and his educational experiences, which saw him develop from an ambitious shoemaker's assistant to a professor of philosophy, see *ODNB*; H. Jones 1923; Gardner 2004.

[121] E. Caird 1885: 226–7.

mission). Elsmere's odyssey was one in which the truer self, the best self, the ideal self was gradually realized through a series of painful renunciations. While studying the historical works which would lead to the collapse of his Christian faith, Elsmere reflected that, despite the pain this would cause, 'his mind had grown, had reached to a fuller stature than before, and a man loves, or should love, all that is associated with the maturing of his best self'.[122] On his death bed, pressed by his pious wife to return to orthodox Christianity, Elsmere replied that to do so would be to deny 'my true best self'.[123] Despite this commitment to self-fulfilment, the keynote of Elsmere's new theistic gospel, centred around 'a purely human Christ' and 'a purely human, explicable, yet always wonderful Christianity' without miracles and without revelation, was self-surrender.[124] Elsmere's mentor, the idealist Mr Grey, told him that the true element in all religion could be summarized in the single phrase 'self forsaken, God laid hold of'.[125] Shocked by the cynicism and flippancy of the blasphemous *Freethinker* cartoons for which Foote had been prosecuted in 1883, and which were being sold round the corner from his Elgood Street settlement, Elsmere decided to preach a sermon to the working men of the East End on the kind of humanistic Christianity he now believed in.[126] The faith that Elsmere defended was a belief 'in *God*; and in *Conscience*, which is God's witness in the soul; and in *Experience*, which is at once the record and the instrument of man's education at God's hands'. He saw God primarily in human acts of self-sacrifice. God was revealed he said, 'whenever a man helps his neighbour, or a mother denies herself for her child; whenever a soldier dies without a murmur for his country, or a sailor puts out in the darkness to rescue the perishing; whenever a workman throws mind and conscience into his work, or a statesman labours not for his own gain but for that of the State!'[127]

---

[122] Mrs H. Ward 1888: ch. 19, p. 260.

[123] Ibid., ch. 51, p. 600.

[124] Ibid., ch. 24, p. 321.

[125] Ibid., ch. 19, p. 267.

[126] Ibid., ch. 38, pp. 476–7.

[127] Ibid, ch. 40, p. 494. Among the models for Elsmere's lectures on religious, historical, and scientific subjects to working men in the East End were Thomas Huxley's lectures to working men, which he called 'Lay Sermons'. Mary Ward's sister Julia married the Huxleys' son Leonard in 1885. The following year, during the writing of *Robert Elsmere*, Professor Huxley and his wife dined with Mr and Mrs Humphry Ward at their London home. Elsmere's opening of a scientific Sunday school as part of the activities of his 'New Brotherhood' was described in the novel as 'the direct result of a paragraph in Huxley's Lay Sermons, where the hint of such a school was first thrown out'; Mrs H. Ward 1888: ch. 38, p. 475. See also Sutherland 1991: 114–15.

Elsmere the idealist was thus also Elsmere the altruist. The sinister and cynical intellectual squire Wendover, who was responsible in part for Elsmere's loss of faith, was used by Ward as an egotistical foil for Elsmere's altruism and Mr Grey's idealism.[128] While he was serving as a curate on Wendover's estates, Elsmere's appeals for repairs and sanitation for workers' cottages were met by a resolute refusal to intervene. Wendover was against 'these fine things the altruists talk of' and was opposed to 'all forms of altruistic sentiment'. He taunted Elsmere about his 'altruist emotional temperament'.[129] Ward's contrast between the egotist and the altruist brought out, and contributed to, the new connotations of that language in the later 1880s. Wendover's attack on Elsmere as an altruist had two main elements. It implied that he was someone who allowed emotion and sentiment to predominate over cold reason in social and economic affairs. In objecting to Elsmere's interventionist approach, Wendover also implied that the 'altruists' were those in sympathy with state socialism rather than the doctrines of *laissez-faire*. It is notable, and consistent with the nature of idealist discussions of self-realization and self-denial, and their aversion to 'altruism' as an ideal, that the only uses of the language of altruism in *Robert Elsmere* were hostile uses of the term by Wendover. Similarly, the identification of Elsmere with 'altruism' in reviews of the book tended to be unsympathetic. *The Times*, while admiring some of the book's qualities, thought that 'Elsmere's new religion is either no less untenable than he found Christianity to be, or it is merely altruism, clothed for the sake of old associations with the name of a Deity. In any case, it is just as unlikely as Unitarianism to exercise any great influence over the masses.'[130] The *Catholic World* more simply called Elsmere's religion 'altruistic rubbish'.[131]

Altruists and individualists in late Victorian fiction

Egoism, altruism, and varieties of moral self-discovery or self-deceit were already popular themes in Victorian fiction. George Meredith's *The Egoist* (1879) had portrayed an upper-class individualist, Sir Willoughby Patterne,

---

[128] Mrs H. Ward 1888: ch. 27, p. 353.
[129] Ibid., ch. 18, p. 234; ch. 19, p. 254; ch. 30, p. 382.
[130] *The Times* (7 Apr. 1888), 5.
[131] *Catholic World,* 47 (Sept. 1888), 847–50; quoted in Peterson 1976: 179.

who was ultimately outmanœuvred in his attempts to win the affections of the novel's heroine, Clara Middleton, by the more liberal and sympathetic Vernon Whitford. One of the underlying suggestions of *The Egoist* was the evolutionary idea that assertive individualism was more primitive and uncivilized than were sympathy and cooperation.[132] The book, however, made no use of the language of altruism. By the time 'altruism' and 'altruist' had become ideological catchwords in the 1880s and 1890s, it was the devotees of altruism, more than the increasingly embattled defenders of high-Victorian individualism, who seemed the more appropriate targets of satire. The character of Dyce Lashmar in Gissing's *Our Friend the Charlatan* (1901), in some ways a counterpart of Meredith's egoist, Sir Willoughby, was an advocate of altruism, albeit one whose professed love of others seemed to be only a poorly disguised kind of egoism.[133] In some of Meredith's own works in the 1880s and 1890s, sceptical questions were also posed about 'altruism'. *Diana of the Crossways* (1885) began with an account of Diana Warwick's philosophical views. She thought that the world should guard against sentimental 'feminine' vices of 'hysterical goodness' and 'impatient charity'. In their 'elementary state' she believed that 'the altruistic virtues' were 'distinguishable as the sickness and writhings of our egoism to cast its first slough'.[134] In *One of Our Conquerors* (1891) Meredith included a 'classical Church dignitary' denouncing 'altruistic' as a despicable modern coinage.[135]

The sentimental, idealistic, broadly socialist, frequently self-deceiving and self-serving 'altruist' appeared with increasing regularity as a recognizable social type in the fiction of the 1880s and 1890s. Eliza Lynn Linton's Christopher Kirkland, and Gissing's characters Edwin Reardon, Miss Lant, and Dyce Lashmar have all already been mentioned. A year before *Robert Elsmere* appeared, a short story by William Hardinge, called 'Lucinda's Altruism', was published in *The Hour Glass*, introducing another young altruist. The story was about two unmarried sisters, Lucinda and Nell

---

[132] On Meredith's allusions, in *The Egoist*, to Darwinian theories of the evolution of the social instincts, and of sexual selection, see J. Smith 1995. On Meredith's ideas on the evolution of social sympathy, in comparison with similar themes in works by Eliot, Hardy, and others, see Kucich 2002: 124–31.

[133] On *Our Friend the Charlatan*, see Ch. 3 above. On the similarities between Dyce Lashmar and Sir Willoughby Patterne in *The Egoist* (1879), see Pierre Coustillas's introd. to Gissing 1976: esp. pp. xviii–xx.

[134] Meredith 1909: ch. 1, p. 10.

[135] Meredith 1891: ii. 144. On clerical resistance to 'altruism' in sermons, novels, and elsewhere, see Ch. 3 above.

Somers. The former's altruism consisted largely in taking care of her sister and finding her a good husband. The disciplinarian Lucinda had painted various mottoes and sayings on the walls of the London flat which the sisters shared. Among those was the Comtean phrase '*Le bien d'autrui*'. The story concluded with Lucinda's discovery that her sister had fallen in love with an Italian prince and secretly married him. She wrote to her friend admitting that she should have realized that 'we can't do much in life for each other'. 'Disheartened just now at my own blindness and failure', she wrote that she had gone to tear down one of her mottoes, '"*Le bien d'autrui*." I had aimed at that as long as I can recollect; it meant for me Nell's happiness. But I have just perceived to my surprise and profit what I was a fool not to have perceived before: it's this, "*Autrui*" *is always masculine!*'[136] The moral seemed to be that Lucinda should have worried more about her own marital prospects and less about her sister's—that she should have been seeking out a male other to whom she could devote herself. Other stories similarly poked fun at the sentimental confusions of morally self-aggrandizing altruists, whose compassion for the object of their affections was not clearly distinguished from romantic love. H. V. Brown wrote about 'The Altruist in Corduroy' for the *Gentleman's Magazine* in 1892.[137] And in 1895, the freethinker Walter Gallichan wrote a story about 'An Altruist' for the *Free Review*, in which a young man married a sickly girl out of altruistic pity and then actually fell in love with her before she died.[138]

An Experiment in Altruism (1895), a novel by the American writer Margaret Sherwood, was a much less successful version of *Robert Elsmere*—a tale of faith, doubt, university settlements, and social reform populated by characters referred to as 'The Altruist', 'The Anarchist', 'The Man of the World', 'The Lad', and so on. 'The Altruist' was an inhabitant of a settlement house, clearly based on Toynbee Hall, called 'Barnet House', situated amongst the slums of an unnamed city's East End, where 'the streets were swarming with children, Russian and Jewish children, dirty, ragged, and forlorn'. 'The Altruist', the narrator noted, 'was terribly in earnest. He considered our social system all wrong, and he wrote and lectured and preached about it constantly.' His philosophy was one in which

---

[136] William H. Hardinge, 'Lucinda's Altruism', *The Hour Glass: An Illustrated Monthly Magazine,* 1 (1887), 33–9, at 36, 39. Hardinge is reputed, as an Oxford undergraduate in the 1870s, to have had a romantic relationship with Walter Pater; see Dowling 1994: 100–2, 106–7; *ODNB*.

[137] The story originally appeared in the *Gentleman's Magazine*, and was reprinted in *Littell's Living Age,* 195 (1892), 395–407.

[138] W.M.G. [Walter M. Gallichan], 'An Altruist', *Free Review,* 5 (1895), 91–8.

'positivism, agnosticism, atheism, Schopenhauerism' were all 'recognized and transcended in the creed of the Anglican church'. Another of his fellow residents at Barnet Hall, with a particular interest in 'social investigation', had recently completed a Ph.D. in economics and had just 'become a Socialist', to the pleasure of 'the Altruist'. Beatrice Potter's vocations of social investigation and socialist economics, Robert Elsmere's intellectually renewed Christianity, and the Barnetts' use of art and music as vehicles of cultural philanthropy were all present in *An Experiment in Altruism*. Voice was also given to some of the common critiques of these altruists. According to 'The Doctor', to live in a well-plumbed house in the slums these days was no more of a sacrifice than living anywhere else. The university men who lived in these entirely 'artificial' settlements were, according to him, 'too supercilious' and patronized both humanity and God by presuming to have been the first to discover the 'brotherhood of man'. 'The Altruist', the narrator concluded, did not have all the answers to the problems of human suffering in his convoluted and excessively self-confident social and religious philosophy. She preferred to rest with a simple sense of 'duty to our fellow-man' and resignation in the face of the dual incomprehensibility and inescapability of her faith in God.[139]

In 1897 a comic novel, *An Altruist*, appeared, which spoofed the new generation of idealistic altruists with more open irreverence. The book was by the conservative writer and popular novelist, 'Ouida' (who had written to *The Times* during the Egyptian crisis of 1882 to the effect that 'altruism', contrary to the view of Spencer and his Anti-Aggression League, was not a doctrine applicable to British foreign policy).[140] In the early 1890s, prior to her attack on the 'altruist', she was instrumental in creating and satirizing another modern type—the 'new woman'.[141] The central character of *An Altruist*, the aristocratic Wilfrid Bertram, the younger son of a peer, was described as 'an altruist, a collectivist, a Fourrierist, an Engelist, a Tolstoi-ist'. One listener to Bertram's socialist creed, when asked whether the doctrine

[139] Sherwood 1895: 2–3, 9–10, 39, 42, 82, 214–15. Koven 2004: 257–9, discusses a critique of the artificiality and superficiality of the settlement residents in Margaret Harkness's novel *Out of Work* (1888).

[140] 'Ouida' was the pen-name of Louise de la Ramée; see *ODNB*. On her letter to *The* Times, see Ch. 5 above. On her career as a writer, see Gilbert 1999; Schaffer 2003. The latter compares Ouida with Wilde as popular aesthetic writers; they also shared an affection for individualism and a suspicion of altruism. On Wilde's individualism, see Ch. 8 below. On Ouida's novels as a case-study in the economics of Victorian publishing, see Weedon 2003: 145–56.

[141] On the 'new woman', see Heilmann 1998; Richardson and Willis 2002. On 'Ouida' in particular, see Gilbert 1999. See also Ch. 7, below, which examines how evolutionary theories of altruism were used to reinforce conservative visions of motherhood and femininity.

had been made clear, responded that nothing could be clearer: 'Nobody is to have anything they can call their own, and everybody who likes is to eat in one's plate and bathe in one's bath.' Ouida's crass socialist aristocrat, to prove his political sincerity, proposed marriage to a working-class girl. When asked by him whether he loved her, Bertram replied that he disliked the bestial implications of the word 'love' but that what he felt for her was 'respect, esteem, the sweetness of fulfilled duty, the means of proving to the world the sincerity of my sociology'. The conclusion of *An Altruist* confirmed the shallowness and impracticality of Bertram's creed by having him inherit a large fortune, marry a much better class of girl, and plan a new life in Italy where, a cynical onlooker observed, 'Mosquitoes, malaria, malandrini, and the hourly probability of a shot from behind a hedge, or a dagger-thrust from an irate beggar, will certainly provide you with constant material for the most active altruism.'[142]

An Altruist was a lightweight caricature of the philanthropy and politics of a certain type of educated late Victorian. A somewhat more considered and substantial satire of that same world of sentimental socialism, settlements, and utopian politics was W. H. Mallock's *The Individualist* (1899). Mallock, a prolific writer of political and philosophical journalism as well of works of fiction, was one of the most widely read advocates of anti-socialist individualism in the late nineteenth and early twentieth centuries. His religious and social conservatism included the belief that self-interest was the principal human motive, and that an elite of those with the greatest abilities should take precedence over the voice of the masses in determining the direction of political life.[143] The main focus of Mallock's anti-altruistic satire in *The Individualist* was a character called Mrs Norham—a famous author and social reformer who had founded a settlement house in London called Startfield Hall, as a philanthropic institution 'intended to form in a poor and disreputable district the headquarters of a band of social and intellectual missionaries'. Mrs Norham was 'one of the most famous women in Europe' thanks to the success of 'a novel with a purpose which, despite its length and its solemnity, had achieved an enormous circulation, and had raised her to the ranks of a prophetess'. The religion of which Mrs Norham was the prophetess was a sort of doubting and humanistic Christianity.[144]

---

[142] Ouida 1897: 15, 18, 120, 222–3.
[143] On Mallock as an anti-socialist ideologue, see Freeden 1996: 356–9. See also Ford 1974; Cowling 1985: 297; Barker 1997: 73–6.
[144] Mallock 1899: 20–2.

Although Mallock denied it, there can be little doubt that Mrs Humphry Ward was at least a partial inspiration for the character. The fact that Mrs Norham was also a translator of Comte and had written for the *Daily News* could suggest that Harriet Martineau was also in Mallock's mind.[145] However the references to the serious and very successful novel and to the foundation of a settlement house make the primary identification with Mrs Humphry Ward hard to resist.

Mallock used the contrast between the wealthy, thoughtful, and sincere Tristram Lacy, the hero of *The Individualist*, and the pompous, self-serving, vain, social-climbing Mrs Norham to undermine the fashionable ideal of altruism. Mallock looked at the philanthropy of Mrs Norham in much the same way that squire Wendover had regarded the reformism of Robert Elsmere. Mrs Norham, like Elsmere, founded her schemes on emotion rather than reason. Addressing the opening meeting of Startfield Hall, she told her listeners that 'emotion is our life. We are instinct with all the burning fire of brotherliness, which some of us think is so inadequately expressed in Christianity, and which for us is baptised with a new and a holier name—the holy name of Altruism—Altruism, which is merely social emotion made functional, if I may use the technical terms of the theology of the new religion.' Later Mrs Norham celebrated the superiority of 'this altruistic *Credo* of ours to even the simplest of the *Credos* of Christianity', which were nothing more than a series of 'historical or pseudo-historical assertions' with no scientific or philosophical basis.[146] Amongst Mrs Norham's band of altruists was the working-class alcoholic poet Mr Squelch. Mallock's suggestion in the case of Squelch, who committed suicide when his first published book of poems was savaged by the critics, was that misguided encouragement of those without true ability, undertaken in the name of altruism, could have disastrous consequences.[147] Mrs Norham's entourage of admirers also included two 'solemn and altruistic' positivists, described, in allusion to Frederic Harrison and Richard

---

[145] Yarker 1959: 198–9 suggests Harriet Martineau as one model. Mallock denied the identification of Startfield Hall with the Passmore Edwards Settlement, and of Mrs Norham with Mrs Humphry Ward, who is alluded to without being named, in the preface to *The Individualist* (parts of which had already appeared in instalments in the *Fortnightly Review*); Mallock 1899: pp. v–vii.

[146] Mallock 1899: 37, 272–3.

[147] Ibid. 309–16. It is possible that the character's name was an allusion to the socialist politician and working-class autodidact, Harry Quelch, a leading figure in the Social Democratic Federation.

Congreve, as 'a briefless barrister and a doctor without patients'.[148] Representing Mallock's own preferred disciplinarian and unsentimental moralism were Mrs Tilney and the Tory Prime Minister, Lord Runcorn. Mrs Tilney's philanthropic dealings with the poor were characterized by 'the feelings of the ideal Christian—that is to say, treating them precisely as she would treat herself—she was as severe upon their moral failings as she would have been on her own'. Lord Runcorn expressed to Mrs Norham his hope that the rise of 'altruism' and 'socialism' among the 'propertied and cultured classes' would turn out to be a passing fad, like the fad for medievalism in art, fashion, and architecture. He told the altruistic novelist that he thought they 'need not take either too seriously— the suburban enthusiasm for Humanity, or the suburban enthusiasm for Botticelli'.[149]

The last two decades of the nineteenth century, then, saw 'altruism' become a fashionable political word and the 'altruist' become a recognizable, and easily parodied, social type. This was the time that Beatrice Webb later described as having witnessed 'the transference of the emotion of self-sacrificing service from God to man'.[150] In *Robert Elsmere*, Mrs Humphry Ward pointed to the 'dissociation of the moral judgment from a special series of religious formulae' as 'the crucial, the epoch-making fact of our day' and referred to Elsmere's admiration for 'that potent spirit of social help which in our generation Comtism has done so much to develop, even among those of us who are but moderately influenced by Comte's philosophy, and can make nothing of the religion of Humanity'.[151] But it was not

[148] Mallock had first mocked the 'altruism' of positivists some twenty years earlier in *The New Paul and Virginia, or Positivism on an Island* (1878). One reader sent the following quotation from this earlier novel to James Murray of the *OED* to illustrate an early use of 'altruist': 'It soon, however, occurred to him, that eating and drinking were hardly delights sufficient to justify the highest state of human emotion, and he began to fear he had been feeling sublime prematurely; but in another moment he recollected he was an altruist, and that the secret of their happiness was not that any one of them was happy, but that they each knew the others were.' See Mallock 1878: 62–5, quotation at 63. The quotation slip is one of the unnumbered *OED* 'superfluous slips' for 'altruist' held in the OUP archives in Oxford; on Murray and the *OED*, see Ch. 1 above. On Mallock as a parodist of positivism, see also Wright 1986: 230.

[149] Mallock 1899: 237, 248, 362–3. Mallock also attacked both altruism and socialism in an article about Benjamin Kidd's *Social Evolution* (1894): W. H. Mallock, 'Altruism in Economics', *Forum*, 21 (1896), 690–704. On Kidd, see Ch. 7 below.

[150] B. Webb 1926: 129–30.

[151] Mrs H. Ward 1888: ch. 47, p. 558; ch. 38, p. 470. On the treatment of Comtism and the religion of humanity both in *Robert Elsmere* and also in Ward's later novels, see Wright 1986: 230–2.

as simple as any of these pronouncements suggested. In 1888, Beatrice
Potter sat in St Paul's cathedral, enjoying the vast space, trying to relate her
belief in God the father to the plight of the poor and her own social vocation. At the same time, tens of thousands were reading *Robert Elsmere* and
pondering Elsmere's rallying cry: 'I take my stand on conscience and the
moral life! In them I find my God!'[152] Elsmere's 'New Brotherhood' was
centred on the human Christ but also on a moral God. He looked, in the
social and religious movements of the day, for evidence of God's spirit driving humanity 'towards new ways of worship and new forms of love!'[153] This
was a moment when thousands hoped for moral renewal through religious
reform and thousands more, like W. H. Mallock, looked for the same result
through a return to traditional Christianity and a strengthened social hierarchy. But what they got was not a new religion, nor a reinvigorated
Christian nation, but rather the beginnings of the welfare state. The arrival
of 'altruism' in the hearts and minds of the propertied classes was ultimately
a sign of their conversion to the basic belief in state action rather than
individual action as the best social remedy. In this form, the suburban
enthusiasm for humanity outlasted the suburban enthusiasm for Botticelli.

The ultimate form and function of the Passmore Edwards Settlement
differed markedly both from the Elgood Street premises of the 'New
Brotherhood' in *Robert Elsmere*, and from Ward's original vision for
University Hall in 1890. Those differences signified the passing of the
idealistic and neo-Christian aspirations embodied in Mary Ward's hero-
ically self-sacrificing high-Victorian doubter, and the arrival of a popularly
supported state socialism. When the Passmore Edwards Settlement opened
in 1898 it boasted rooms for a warden and eighteen residents, a library, a
workshop, a gymnasium, numerous classrooms, and a billiard room, all of
which, *The Times* reported, 'are lighted by electric light, and are cheerful
and tastefully decorated'.[154] The settlement offered courses of evening
lectures and pioneering educational opportunities for working-class and
disabled children. It would bring 'good music and rational entertainment
within the reach of the people of this part of London'.[155] But it did not
mark the beginning of a new religion. There was no neo-Christianity, no
preaching of a modern understanding of scripture, no awakening of the
better self through the story of the human Christ. Even the Unitarian

---

[152] Mrs H. Ward 1888: ch. 32, p. 408.
[153] Ibid., ch. 32, p. 411.
[154] *The Times* (11 Feb. 1898), 8.
[155] Ibid.

Christianity that had originally been the faith embodied in University Hall in 1890 now receded into the background. Mr Tatton, the first warden of the Passmore Edwards Settlement, described the institution's ideology in secular terms of 'equality and fraternity'. A settlement where men and women of 'all sorts and conditions' could mix freely together would allow those ideals to be realized 'not only in social, but in educational work as well' (see Fig. 20).[156] The education for disabled children offered at the Passmore Edwards Settlement was, from 1899, formalized as a new school funded by local ratepayers through the London School Board. Agreement to the public funding of this service was secured by, amongst others, the Fabian socialist Graham Wallas.[157]

The vision of Robert Elsmere, the altruist and idealist, had made the transition from fiction to reality. In doing so, however, it had been transformed from a form of neo-Christian philanthropy in to an educational mission partly funded by the state and spreading a secular ideology of equality, fraternity, and social reform. One of the courses of lectures offered at the Passmore Edwards Settlement in 1898–9 on the 'Elements of Ethics' was delivered by a young Cambridge philosopher, G. E. Moore.[158] His secular and aesthetic ethics of emotional self-realization had affinities with Greenian idealism but, along with the incipient state socialism of the 1890s, it belonged to a world quite remote from the religious idealism of *Robert Elsmere* and the original university settlement movement. When Moore, Oscar Wilde, and others reacted against 'altruism' in the 1890s, they did so as an act of rebellion against both the world of *Robert Elsmere* and also the naturalistic evolutionary ethics of Herbert Spencer and his followers. Although by the 1890s Spencer himself was neither advocating 'altruism' nor dominating the philosophical agenda, varieties of post-Spencerian ethical naturalism provided the context in which 'altruism' was to have its final *fin-de-siècle* flourish.

---

[156] Quoted ibid.
[157] Sutherland 1991: 226.
[158] See Ch. 8 below.

A MONDAY EVENING "SOCIAL" IN THE HALL.

CHILDREN'S SATURDAY MORNING PLAY ROOM.

Figure 20. Photographs of some of the early activities at the Passmore Edwards Settlement, which opened in 1898. © Mary Ward Settlement.

Chapter Seven

Motherhood and the Ascent of Man

So it is that the sublime chapter in which the founder of dogmatic Christianity describes that charity which never faileth, that highest expression of the human worship of Love, finds its genesis in the breasts of the mammalian mother.

Caleb Saleeby, 'The Birth of Love' 1904[1]

Three kinds of ethical naturalism

The most influential book by the most influential figure in the international anarchist movement in the early twentieth century was a plea for communism based on observations of ants, bees, crabs, dung beetles, ducks, and donkeys. This was Peter Kropotkin's 1902 book *Mutual Aid: A Factor in Evolution*.[2] Kropotkin was a mathematician and naturalist who had renounced his aristocratic identity as a Russian prince, and been a political prisoner in both Russia and France, before finally settling in Britain. There he made a living by writing about scientific and political subjects. *Mutual Aid* first appeared as a series of eight articles in James Knowles's *Nineteenth Century*. The first two of these articles, both published in 1890, concerned mutual aid amongst animals. The rest were about mutual aid amongst savages, barbarians, medieval peasants, and, finally, modern societies. Having surveyed the various cooperative strategies employed by insects, rodents, ruminants, and monkeys, Kropotkin concluded that, if nature could speak to animals, she would say: 'Don't compete!—competition is always injurious to the species, and you have plenty of resources to avoid it! ...

---

[1] C. W. Saleeby, 'Science: The Birth of Love', *The Academy and Literature*, 66 (26 Mar. 1904), 356–7, at 356.

[2] On Kropotkin, see *ODNB*; P. Crook 1994: 106–12; Peaker 2005. There is not a definitive edn of *Mutual Aid*. References below are to the 1939 Penguin edn with a foreword by the economist and social historian H. L. Beales. I have given chapter numbers as well as page numbers to assist those who have access to a different edn.

Therefore combine—practise mutual aid! That is the surest means of giving to each and to all the greatest safety, the best guarantee of existence and
progress, bodily, intellectual, and moral.'[3] Although acknowledging at the
outset that Darwin himself had recognized the importance of social cooperation in the struggle for existence, Kropotkin frequently sought to draw
a contrast between a broadly 'Darwinist' emphasis on competition between
individuals of the same species and his own focus on intra-species cooperation.[4] He pointed the finger especially at Thomas Huxley as a leading
Darwinist guilty of exaggerating the extent to which the natural world was
an arena of pitiless competition and gladiatorial combat.[5] Kropotkin listed
several significant existing works on the role of cooperation in the animal
world, including a book on the love lives of animals by the German physician and socialist Ludwig Büchner, published in 1879 under the title *Liebe
und Liebesleben in der Thierwelt*. Kropotkin dissented from Büchner's explanation of all animal cooperation in terms of 'love and sympathy', preferring
to refer to cooperation and solidarity, and cited Büchner's book as one of
the works which set the pattern for Henry Drummond's *The Ascent of Man*
(1894).[6] The contribution that Kropotkin himself thought most significant
was a little-known lecture by the Russian zoologist Karl F. Kessler, given at
the University of St Petersburg in 1880. It was this lecture that had first led
Kropotkin to see that there was in nature a law of mutual aid which was
'far more important than the law of mutual contest'.[7]

   Those who sought to take ethical and political morals away from their
reading of the book of nature in this period fell into three broad categories. There were those who, like Kropotkin, thought that nature was essentially cooperative, and that cooperation was thus the policy that humanity
should pursue. There were others who thought that nature was essentially

---

[3] Kropotkin 1939: ch. 2, p. 73.

[4] Ibid.: introd., p. 12, ch. 1, pp. 21–2.

[5] Ibid., ch. 1, p. 23. Kropotkin refers in particular to Thomas Huxley, 'The Struggle for Existence
and its Bearing upon Man', *Nineteenth Century*, 23 (1888), 161–80, repr. as 'The Struggle for
Existence in Human Society', in T. H. Huxley 1893–4: ix. 195–236. On Huxley's portrayal of
nature as an arena of gladiatorial violence, and Kidd's and Drummond's responses, see P. Crook
1994: 54–62. The disagreement between Kropotkin and Huxley is discussed as a pre-experimental
precursor to modern scientific debates about 'altruism' and 'blood kinship' in Dugatkin 2006:
12–36.

[6] See Kropotkin 1939: introd., pp. 14–15, ch. 1, pp. 24–6. Kropotkin gave Büchner's name,
mistakenly, as 'Louis Büchner'.

[7] Kropotkin 1939: introd., p. 14. For more on this alternative tradition of evolutionary thought, to
which Kessler, Büchner, Kropotkin, and Drummond were contributors, see the section on
Arabella Buckley as a popularizer of Darwinism, in Ch. 4 above, esp. n. 97.

competitive and that human progress would only come about by allowing this process of competition to have free play. Thirdly there were those who recognized the presence in nature of both competitive and cooperative traits, and who thought that eugenic policies should be implemented to ensure that, in the case of humanity, the latter came to dominate. As Francis Galton, the father of eugenics, put it, the aim was to work 'both through nature and by nurture' to 'improve the heritable powers of man to their utmost' in pursuit of the 'furtherance of human evolution'.[8] All three groups of ethical naturalists shared some core commitments: they believed that the scientific study of nature was central to a proper understanding of humanity and society; they believed in the possibility and desirability of, as Kropotkin put it, 'progress, bodily, intellectual, and moral'; and finally they thought that ethical and social policies should work with the grain of nature. Although they differed fundamentally over the best way to characterize nature and to achieve progress, they all could have signed up to the general motto, 'Follow nature!' This chapter is about some of the final flourishes of this tradition of Victorian ethical naturalism in the 1890s.

Three different theories of altruism are considered below, each associated with one of the kinds of ethical naturalism just outlined, and each a reinterpretation of, or a response to, the work of Herbert Spencer. Henry Drummond's *Ascent of Man* (1894) was a popularized and Christianized version of Spencerian evolution (a version the agnostic Spencer himself, of course, loathed). The natural-theological vision of the *Ascent of Man* was particularly influenced by a book on the evolution of sex by the biologist Patrick Geddes, who had also been influenced by Spencer. Drummond argued that following nature, following Christ, and following one's own altruistic instincts, all led in the same ethical direction. Benjamin Kidd took opposition to Spencer's belief in the inheritance of acquired characteristics as the starting point of his *Social Evolution* (1894). Kidd defended instead a social application of August Weismann's neo-Darwinian insistence on the primacy of natural selection, arguing that human societies should follow nature by allowing the sort of open competition that alone led to progress.[9] And Caleb Saleeby, in the early twentieth century, presented his eugenic vision of a more truly altruistic future as both a defence of Spencer and an attack on the dangerous views of Nietzscheans and neo-Darwinists. For

[8] Francis Galton, 'The Part of Religion in Human Evolution', *National Review*, 23 (1894), 755–63, at 763.

[9] Darwin himself, like Spencer, and unlike Weismann and other neo-Darwinians, had accepted that acquired characteristics could be inherited. See Ch. 4, above.

him, eugenic policies could be used to work with nature in producing more truly altruistic future generations.

As we shall see below, some clergymen and theologians continued to complain about the scientific language of altruism displacing the language of the New Testament, and to resist this language because of its associations with Herbert Spencer. Discussions of 'altruism' in the 1890s continued to draw, directly or indirectly, sympathetically or critically, on Herbert Spencer's evolutionary philosophy. Spencer himself, however, had his own reasons to distance himself from this terminology, despite having originally done so much to ensure its dissemination.[10] If it was the associations of 'altruism' with positivism and socialism that were originally problematic for Spencer, its connection with the hugely successful popularizations of Kidd and Drummond in the 1890s gave him yet another reason to pause before using the term. Kidd and Drummond, who were not scientific specialists, but a civil servant and a popular theological writer respectively, developed Spencerian and Darwinian biological ideas in highly speculative social and religious directions. As one of the key words of such accounts, it is understandable that 'altruism' might not have appealed to those who hoped to maintain a serious scientific reputation.[11] Huxley (like Darwin before him) never used the term; Spencer belatedly tried to drop it in the 1890s; and Peter Kropotkin preferred to write about 'mutual aid'.[12]

This chapter will provide a different angle on the religious and political meanings of scientific discussions about evolution and ethics in the late nineteenth century, and thus serve to complement existing studies which have focused primarily on canonical figures such as Darwin, Spencer, Huxley, and Kropotkin.[13] As 'altruism' migrated into new territories, the ethical meanings of science as understood by non-specialist writers and their readers continued to evolve. The scientific justification and meaning of altruism mattered in the 1890s and 1900s especially in the context of debates about the differences between the sexes, the importance of

---

[10] See Ch. 5, above.

[11] On Huxley's attempt to hold on to his authority as a 'man of science' to pronounce on political and ethical questions during the 1880s and 1890s, see White 2003: ch. 5.

[12] In all of Huxley's writings I have found no uses of 'altruism', and one use of 'altruistic' in a footnote to his Romanes lecture on 'Evolution and Ethics'. Kropotkin similarly used 'altruistic' once, in a discussion of trade unionism. See T. H. Huxley 1893–4: ix. 111; Kropotkin 1939: ch. 8, p. 213.

[13] Detailed and sophisticated versions of this history are to be found in the work of Robert Richards (1987, 1999, 2003). A rather simpler version of the standard story can be found in Allhoff 2003, which is a recent summary focusing on Darwin, Spencer, Huxley, and G. E. Moore, but not Kropotkin. A recent concise and popular version of this history is Dugatkin 2006.

motherhood and the family, the future of the Anglo-Saxon race, the relative social roles of religion and science, and the prospects for breeding a healthier society through eugenics. While these arguments took scientific research as their starting point, they produced a world of meanings that was growing, irresponsibly some thought, and in ways that were beyond the control of scientific experts, as well as of clergymen and Christian philosophers.

The irresponsible growth of scientific language

'Altruism' was by no means the only controversial scientific neologism of the day. The December 1894 number of the periodical *Science-Gossip* included a protest by its editor, J.T. Carrington, against the adoption of the term 'scientist'. His complaint was reported in several newspapers and, seeking further support for his objection, Carrington wrote to well-known figures in the world of science, seeking an 'authoritative declaration' on the subject.[14] Most condemned the word, some suggesting it was an Americanism. Thomas Huxley compared the term to another American neologism: 'To any one who respects the English language', he wrote, 'I think "Scientist" must be about as pleasing a word as "Electrocution."' Herbert Spencer's friend, the agnostic popular science writer and novelist Grant Allen was also asked his opinion. Allen, like Huxley, compared 'scientist' with other neologisms. He wrote that, personally, he disliked the word 'scientist', but that 'languages grow, and grow irresponsibly' and that if the majority of people adopted a word, little could be done about it. 'We have swallowed "Sociology",' he observed, 'we have swallowed "Altruism" and I don't see why, after camels like those, we need strain at a comparative gnat like "Scientist".'[15]

[14] Those who responded included Lord Kelvin, Lord Rayleigh, Alfred Russel Wallace, Thomas Huxley, and Sir John Lubbock.

[15] All seven of the responses Carrington received are reproduced in Ross 1962: 76–8. I am grateful to Jim Moore for drawing my attention to this article by Ross and to the Allen quotation. The responses were also summarized in *The Times* (29 Dec. 1894), 6. Paul White uses this *Science-Gossip* debate about 'scientist' to introduce his study of Thomas Huxley's creation of the identity of the 'man of science', which differed from both 'natural philosopher' and 'scientist'; see White 2003: 1–5. It is well known that the term 'scientist' was not coined until the 1830s, when it was suggested by William Whewell. It is less well known that the term was still treated with such suspicion sixty years later. In addition to Ross 1962, see also R. Williams 1976: 232–5.

Allen wrote those words at the end of 1894—the year that had seen the publication of Kidd's *Social Evolution* in January, and Drummond's *Ascent of Man* in June. These two books about the scientific and religious meanings of altruism were two of the most popular non-fiction works of the decade. The monthly lists of best-selling books published in *The Bookman* between 1891 and 1906 suggest that Kidd's *Social Evolution* was the best-selling non-fiction work of the entire period. Henry Drummond, who had several best-selling works during the years covered, including *The Ascent of Man*, was the only non-fiction writer amongst the sixteen best-selling authors according to the *Bookman* lists. Drummond was ranked thirteenth, a few places behind Mrs Humphry Ward and Arthur Conan Doyle, but ahead of both Émile Zola and the enduringly popular Walter Scott.[16] It was quite possibly as a result of reading either *Social Evolution* or *The Ascent of Man* that William Kirby, the proprietor and manager of Queen's Gate Mansions in London, got the idea of giving 'Altruistic' as his telegraphic address when advertising sets of well-appointed furnished or unfurnished rooms, benefiting from electric lighting and a hydraulic lift, in *The Times* (see Fig. 21). He had advertised under his own name since 1890 and only from October 1894 started to use the address 'Altruistic', perhaps wishing to establish his credentials as a modern, scientific, and philanthropic landlord, or to suggest a socialistic sympathy with the working classes and the unemployed. The 1881 census had recorded Kirby as an unemployed butler living with his parents in Watford, prior to his later success as the 'Altruistic' manager of Queen's Gate Mansions in Kensington.[17] Other London telegraphic addresses adopted by *Times* advertisers in 1894 included 'Divines' (the Nursing Sisters of St John the Divine), 'Skilful' (Middlesex Hospital Trained Nurses Institute), and 'Bookmen' (Henry Sotheran & Co.,

---

[16] Bassett and Walter 2001: 208–9, 228, 230. Another of Drummond's popular books was *The Programme of Christianity* (1891), in which he wrote: 'But the new word altruism—the translation of "love thy neighbour as thyself"—is slowly finding its way into current Christian speech. The People's Progress, not less than the Pilgrim's Progress, is daily becoming a graver concern to the Church. A popular theology with unselfishness as part at least of its root, a theology which appeals no longer to fear, but to the generous heart in man, has already dawned, and more clearly than ever men are beginning to see what Christ really came into this world to do.' Drummond 1903: 69–123, at 77.

[17] Kirby's first advertisement in *The Times* (1 Apr. 1890), 15; the first using the address 'Altruistic' (8 Oct. 1894), 15. The last of these advertisements was published in *The Times* (22 Sept. 1898), 1. 1881 census return; Public Record Office, R.G.11/1438, f. 75, 1; accessed through the website of the UK national archives (see Bibliography for details). Kirby, born in 1858, was the same age as both Robert Melsom and Beatrice Webb, whose identification with 'altruism' was discussed in Ch. 6 above.

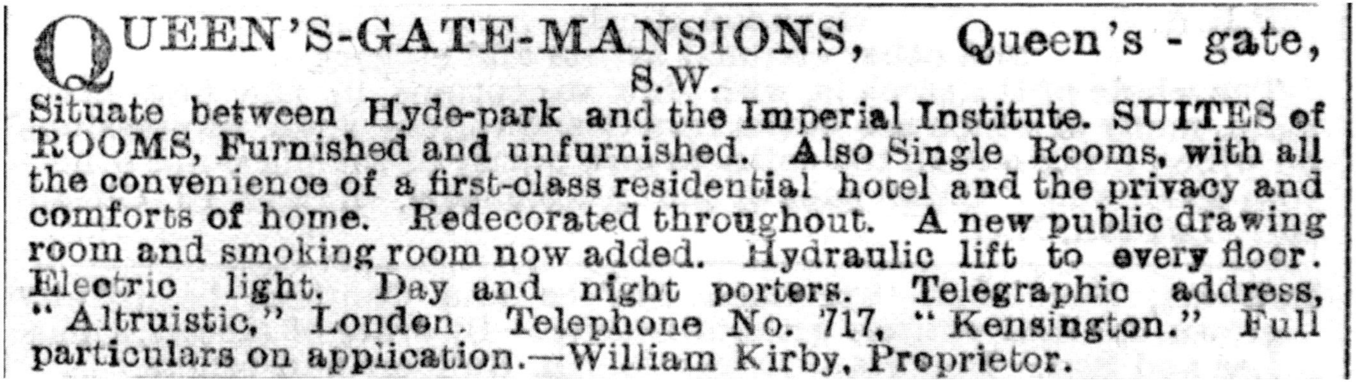

QUEEN'S-GATE-MANSIONS, Queen's - gate, S.W.

Situate between Hyde-park and the Imperial Institute. SUITES of ROOMS, Furnished and unfurnished. Also Single Rooms, with all the convenience of a first-class residential hotel and the privacy and comforts of home. Redecorated throughout. A new public drawing room and smoking room now added. Hydraulic lift to every floor. Electric light. Day and night porters. Telegraphic address, "Altruistic," London. Telephone No. 717, "Kensington." Full particulars on application.—William Kirby, Proprietor.

Figure 21. One of a series of advertisements placed in *The Times* by William Kirby between 1894 and 1898 offering rooms for rent and giving himself the telegraphic address 'Altruistic'. *The Times*, 22 November 1897, 15.

Second-Hand Booksellers).[18] A few years later, W. H. Mallock's novel *The Individualist* (1899) featured a devotee of altruistic socialism who chose 'Revolution' as his telegraphic address.[19]

Writing in 1900, in an article in the American periodical *Catholic World*, James Walsh suggested that the increasing use of biological terminology in everyday speech, itself just one of many indications of the supreme importance of biological science at the close of the nineteenth century, was partly a result of the influence of such widely read 'scientific littérateurs' as Grant Allen himself and Oliver Wendell Holmes. Among the 'technical terms of very special significance' which had 'become current coin of the realm wherever our English tongue is spoken' the article listed 'the struggle for life', 'survival of the fittest', 'natural and sexual selection', 'atavism', 'hereditary transmission', 'environment', 'parallelism', 'adaptation', and 'altruism'.[20] Allen and Walsh were not alone in making a connection between the meaning of 'altruism' and the influence of modern science. In the summer of 1891, the British Association for the Advancement of Science met in Cardiff. The first meeting of 'Section A', the section devoted to the mathematical and physical sciences, took place in the Unitarian Free Christian Church and was addressed by the president of that section, the physicist Oliver Lodge. His speech, taking stock of progress across the sciences, mentioned some of the most exciting recent developments. Lodge said that advances had been made, for instance, in understanding the nature of disease, mental aberrations such as 'duplex personality', and the phenomena associated with hypnotism. 'The phenomenon of crime, the scientific meaning and justification of altruism and other matters relating to life and conduct', Lodge went on, 'are beginning, or perhaps are barely yet beginning, to show a vulnerable front over which the forces of science may pour.'[21] So, what exactly were the 'scientific meaning and justification of altruism' in the 1890s? That depended upon who you asked.

In choosing, in his response to *Science-Gossip*, to compare 'scientist' with two words coined by Auguste Comte, both of which had been popularized in Britain and America by the writings of Herbert Spencer, Grant Allen reinforced linguistic and conceptual connections that had, as we have already seen, been current for some decades. A contributor to *Humanitarian* magazine in 1895 wrote that 'Altruism has hitherto been considered almost

---

[18] *The Times* (4 Jan. 1894), 1; (4 Oct. 1894), 1; (2 Oct. 1894), 1.
[19] Mallock 1899: 339.
[20] James J. Walsh, 'A Half-Century in Biology', *Catholic World*, 70 (1900), 466–79, at 466–7.
[21] Reported in *The Times* (21 Aug. 1891), 6.

entirely from the standpoint of Sociology—undoubtedly its proper sphere.'[22] The article went on, however, to discuss new biological dimensions to the scientific understanding of altruism.[23] The fact that James Walsh, writing five years later, believed that 'altruism' was a term of biological rather than sociological science may be taken as evidence of some of the shifts in scientific associations and connotations that had come about. It would be a mistake, however, to suppose that clear boundaries could be drawn, even in the 1890s, between biological, sociological, and ethical languages. Some complained about biological misappropriations of language that was properly sociological or ethical. But others recognized that the free interplay (or even the identity) between sociological and biological language had long been established, especially through the impact of works by both Comte and Spencer.

One who took this view was the Scottish Congregational minister and theologian Robert Mackintosh, who lectured on sociology to theological students at the Lancashire Independent College in Manchester during the 1890s.[24] In the book based on his lectures, which was published in 1899 under the title *From Comte to Benjamin Kidd: The Appeal to Biology or Evolution for Human Guidance*, Mackintosh wrote that one of the most notable features of 'the science or alleged science of sociology' was its continuing connection with biology. Even in the works of Auguste Comte, he noted, biology had held a very important place and, 'subsequent evolutionary speculation has enlarged its claims to infinity'.[25] Sociology could perhaps be distinguished from the practical world of politics, the older discipline of political economy, and from social philosophy of a more metaphysical kind. However, when it came to writings in the domain of ethics, Mackintosh argued, the distinction between the sciences of sociology and evolutionary biology was very hard to discern, especially since sociologists, including Comte and Spencer, were so keen to draw analogies between the two by treating society as an 'organism'.[26] Comparing Spencer's writings with works on science and ethics by Leslie Stephen and Samuel Alexander published in the 1880s, Mackintosh found it hard to find any real difference between sociological and evolutionary approaches to ethics: 'The brand, no

---

[22] J. Herbert Parsons, 'The Evolution of Altruism', *The Humanitarian: A Monthly Magazine,* 7 (1895), 459–64, at 459.
[23] The works Parsons particularly mentioned were Geddes and Thomson 1889; Drummond 1894.
[24] On Mackintosh, see *ODNB* and Sell 1977.
[25] Mackintosh 1899: 2.
[26] Ibid. 5–6.

doubt is different; the liquor is the same.'[27] (Coming from someone who took immoderate drinking as a prime example of vice, the comparison was certainly not intended to be flattering.[28]) Mackintosh thought that Kidd's *Social Evolution* constituted 'the most extreme form logically possible' of the sociological appeal to biology.[29]

With new scientific connotations to the language of altruism came new reasons for linguistic resistance. Mackintosh observed (not entirely approvingly) in 1899 that 'Innumerable writers, Christian as well as non-Christian, have come to employ the term "Altruism" as a synonym for goodness'.[30] There may have been innumerable writers who employed the term but there were others who, unlike Grant Allen, refused to swallow this Comtean camel.[31] One contributor to the *Agnostic Journal*, the mathematician George Shoobridge Carr, was intrigued by this linguistic resistance amongst the reviewers of Kidd's *Social Evolution*.[32] The two reviewers he drew attention to were the duke of Argyll (who had been among those condemning the neologism 'scientist') and Lord Farrer. Carr quoted Argyll to the effect that 'altruism' was a 'new and very affected name for the old form of things which we used to call charity, benevolence, and love'; while Farrer called altruism an 'odious word'. W. H. Mallock, in his review of Kidd, also preferred to write of the 'Charity' shown by private individuals rather than 'what Mr Kidd calls their "altruism"'.[33] Carr could find no 'objection on philological grounds' made by such writers and concluded instead that 'some hidden reason exists for such a marked antipathy' to the word.[34]

---

[27] Stephen 1882; Alexander 1889; Mackintosh 1899: 6.

[28] Mackintosh 1899: 51.

[29] Kidd 1894; Mackintosh 1899: p. vii. Another writer on this subject, drawing on the work of Sir John Lubbock and George J. Romanes, described the importance of altruism as a natural principle, in insects, birds, primates, and humans as a 'law of social biology'. See T. Gavanescul, 'The Altruistic Impulse in Man and Animals', *International Journal of Ethics,* 5 (1895), 197–205, at 205.

[30] Mackintosh 1899: 45.

[31] Collini 1991: 61, observes that for some writers it had not been necessary to comment upon or justify the use of the language of 'altruism' even in the 1870s, two decades earlier. That was true for a few but many continued to resist the term or place it in disapproving quotation marks in the 1890s.

[32] Carr's 1895 book, *Social Evolution and the Evolution of Socialism: A Critical Essay* was composed of two articles written for the *Agnostic Journal* (on the theme of 'Social Evolution', which reviewed Kidd 1894 and Drummond 1894) and a third, new essay on 'The Evolution of Socialism', which particularly focused on Clapperton 1885. For some brief biographical information on Carr, see Berndt and Rankin 2000: 598–9.

[33] W. H. Mallock, 'Altruism in Economics', *Forum,* 21 (1896), 690–704, at 693. For more on Mallock, see Ch. 6 above.

[34] Carr 1895: 17–18.

The agnostic Carr thought the hidden reason was the term's association with secular systems of ethics, such as Herbert Spencer's. Thus its use was interpreted by 'Christian dogmatists', Carr thought, as a 'red flag of revolt against sacerdotalism'; it was not surprising, then, that 'the innovating word should come under the *odium theologicum*'.[35] Pronouncements by Anglican clergymen continued to provide support for this hypothesis even in the last years of the nineteenth century. Speaking to the Working Men's section of the Church Congress in Nottingham in 1897, the dean of Rochester described secular systems of moral philosophy as repetitions or incomplete extracts from the New Testament. What were Comte's 'Altruism' and Spencer's 'Sacrifice of the individual to the common weal', he asked, but St Paul's 'We that are strong ought to bear the weak', or St John's 'Let us love one another'? And, referring to the well-known story that Queen Victoria had on occasions visited some of her subjects in their homes to read to them from scripture, the dean asked where 'outside the Church of Christ' was 'a communism so comprehensive as that which brought the Queen of England to read the Bible in a cottage home?' *The Times* reported that this speech was greeted with 'Loud cheers' from the audience of working men.[36] At the Church Congress in Bradford the following year, the Reverend Professor Lewis Campbell struck a very similar note, saying that the spirit of Christ was the true source of the selfless devotion of the soldier, the heroism of the common labourer, and the 'so-called "Altruism" of the philanthropist'.[37] And Professor Campbell was not the only person in the 1890s trying to reclaim 'Altruism' for Christianity.

Henry Drummond's *Ascent of Man*

For Henry Drummond, 'Altruism' was spelt with a capital 'A', and was the alpha and omega of evolution. He described it as the 'greatest word of ethics' and used it enthusiastically to describe almost any other-directed behaviour in nature, as well as the sexual, parental, and social instincts that motivated such behaviour, and the divine love that he thought ultimately lay behind and justified both those instincts and the whole process of evolution. Both selfish egoism and altruistic love were

---

[35] Carr 1895: 18.
[36] *The Times* (29 Sept. 1897), 9. On the story of Victoria reading the Bible in cottage homes, see Walsh 1902: 183–4 and 263–4.
[37] Reported in *The Times* (30 Sept. 1898), 4.

great in nature, Drummond wrote, but—echoing St Paul—he concluded that 'the greatest of these is Love'.[38]

With the help of the Romeike and Gurtige Press Cutting and Information Agency, Henry Drummond amassed, during 1894 and 1895, over seventy-five reviews, editorials, letters, sermons, and essays responding to the book in which he developed this account of the meaning and justification of altruism, *The Ascent of Man*.[39] Over the five years following its publication, over 30,000 copies of the book were sold in Britain alone.[40] Newspapers and periodicals in England, Scotland, America and Australia carried responses to the book, written by clergymen, theologians, journalists, and men of science. Inevitably, there was a wide range of opinions about the quality and significance of the work. Some agreed with Robert Mackintosh, who expressed concern to his Manchester theological students that a defender of Christianity was 'casting in his lot so unreservedly with the programme of naturalistic science'.[41] *The Presbyterian Churchman* went further in this direction, telling its readers that 'However beautifully it may be clothed in words', the whole hypothesis of human evolution on which Drummond's book was based, was 'repellent to Christian thought'. Faith in divine revelation, this short review concluded, was inconsistent with belief in the evolutionary origins of human morality: 'One or the other must prevail.'[42] For others, the reverse was the problem: Drummond was not too scientific, but too theological. Writing under the pseudonym Hugh Mortimer Cecil, the president of the Liverpool branch of the National Secular Society, Ernest Newman, complained bitterly of the pseudo-scientific theological distortions perpetrated by Drummond. Newman rejected Drummond's 'bogus analogies between Christianity and evolution' and described his method as 'that of a curate with a fatal felicity in vapid epigram talking to the debating society of a Young Men's Christian Association'.[43] Although there were very various responses to *The Ascent*

---

[38] Drummond 1899: 341. On the earlier history of this alternative, more altruistic, interpretation of Darwinian evolution, see Ch. 4 above. For a sense of Drummond's place in the broader history of Christian interpretations of Darwinism, see J. Kent 1966: 20–8; J. R. Moore 1979: 217–51; 1985a; Livingstone 1999; Bowler 2001: 215–43.

[39] These are held in the National Library of Scotland. NLS/MSS/Acc.5890.14. On the reception of *The Ascent of Man*, see also G. A. Smith 1899: ch. 17.

[40] The 1899 London edn is advertised as 'Thirty-first thousand'.

[41] Mackintosh 1899: 147.

[42] *The Presbyterian Churchman*, undated cutting in NLS/MSS/Acc.5890.14.

[43] Cecil 1897: 105, 175. For more on Ernest Newman see Ch. 8 below. Newman's 1897 pseudonymous book grouped Drummond and Kidd together with Arthur Balfour, author of *The Foundations of Belief* (1895), as an 'Irrationalist Trio'. Others also saw these three, who in various

Figure 22. Portrait of Henry Drummond (1851–1897). Date of photograph unknown; reproduced from frontispiece of G. A. Smith 1899.

of Man, there were three points on which most reviewers of the book agreed: it was not truly a work of science, it certainly was not original, and it drastically overstated the importance of altruism in evolution.

As a young man, Drummond had been swept up in the evangelical mission to Britain of the American preachers Dwight Moody and Ira Sankey in 1874–5, and was subsequently appointed, in 1877, as a lecturer in natural science at the Free Church college in Glasgow. An extremely successful book seeking to demonstrate the compatibility of natural science and Christian faith, *Natural Law in the Spiritual World* (1883), published when Drummond was 31 years old, established his reputation as a powerful and popular writer.[44] By 1885, *Natural Law* had already gone into a 15th British edition and sold 39,000 copies; by 1888 British sales had reached 70,000; and by the end of the century the figure exceeded 120,000.[45] Drummond himself described this early work as the result of the breaking down of a barrier between two different 'compartments of my mind', which related to his activities both as a science lecturer and as a Christian preacher. Gradually, Drummond wrote, 'the wall of partition showed symptoms of giving way', and finally the waters from two separate 'fountains of knowledge', science and religion, met and mingled.[46] The result was a work in which Drummond adopted scientific terms taken from his reading of such authorities as Darwin, Spencer, and E. Ray Lankester, and employed them to explain theological ideas of election and sin. So, for instance, the language of 'natural selection', 'degeneration', and 'reversion to type' was used to explain how a man who ceased to work and strive towards God would risk spiritual decay, death, and damnation. This, Drummond stated, was the spiritual equivalent of the way that a natural organism, in the absence of selective pressure, might revert to a more primitive and degenerate type.[47]

A decade later, when Drummond came to deliver the 1893 Lowell Lectures in Boston, on the theme of 'The Evolution of Man', his vision of the natural world had changed. The Darwinist–Calvinist preoccupation

---

ways reasserted the importance of religion at the end of the 19th century, as forming some sort of triumvirate. Goldwin Smith treated all three together in his 'Guesses at the Riddle of Existence', *North American Review*, 161 (1895), 230–48. Karl Pearson referred to them as a 'delightfully incongruous trinity': quoted in D. P. Crook 1984: 91. Other works treating these three together were Carr 1895; Mackintosh 1899.

[44] This was the book recommended by William Boyd Carpenter to Queen Victoria, who found it too scientific; see Ch. 3 above. On Drummond's life and writings, see *ODNB*; G. A. Smith 1899; Lennox 1901; J. R. Moore 1985a; A. Scott 2004.

[45] Drummond 1885; G. A. Smith 1899: 213.

[46] Drummond 1885: pp. vi–vii.

[47] Ibid.: esp. 95–120, on 'Degeneration'. A. Scott 2004: esp. 440–2.

with the darker sides of natural selection and supernatural election had been replaced by an altogether more optimistic reading of the book of nature. As Drummond's biographer put it, whereas the earlier work had, in its hard distinction between the natural and the gracious, 'excommunicated nature', the Lowell Lectures reclaimed nature as belonging to 'the sphere of the God of Love, and sought to prove the presence of the characteristic forces of Christianity—sympathy and self-sacrifice—upon the lower stages of the evolution of man'.[48] Many of Drummond's former admirers worried that, in moving towards such a naturalistic vindication of Christian teaching, he had abandoned the central Christian message of the power of sin and the necessity of Christ's atoning death. Drummond's uncle, for instance, complained to him in a letter that in 'all your writings and addresses you all but ignore the Atonement'. In his reply, Drummond defended his scientific apologetics on the grounds that other people were publishing plenty of tracts expressly devoted to 'the fundamentals of Christianity' and that he felt called to say in his addresses what *is not being said* otherwise', namely that natural science reinforced the Christian message.[49]

The way that he pursued this mission in *The Ascent of Man* was, as he put it in the preface, to communicate 'in a plain way' some of the latest scientific discoveries about human evolution. Drummond acknowledged that his sweeping narrative was not intended for the scientific expert, nor for the theologian, but for a broader audience who wished to understand the outlines of the theory of evolution.[50] Deliberately mirroring Darwin's *Descent of Man* in his choice of book title, Drummond presented his vision of evolution as an account which would function in two particularly important ways: namely as a corrective to the Darwinian account of human evolution, which, in its most popular forms, omitted one of the most important factors in the history of life; and secondly as a 'connected outline' of the 'great drama' of evolution, drawing together all the most important scientific findings on the subject.[51] As we have seen in Chapter 4, Darwin himself was well aware of the roles of love and sympathy in evolution, and his account of the importance of these instincts had already been

[48] G. A. Smith 1899: 430–1.

[49] This exchange took place in Jan. 1891; G. A. Smith 1899: 410–12.

[50] Quotations are taken from the 1899 edn. Drummond 1899: pp. v–viii.

[51] Drummond 1899: 2. The freethinking poet, and biographer of George Eliot, Mathilde Blind had used the same title, *The Ascent of Man*, for an 1889 collection of poems on evolutionary themes; Blind 1889. On her 1881 'Prophecy of St Oran', see Ch. 3 above.

popularized with some success by Arabella Buckley. Drummond's reassertion of this picture within an evangelical narrative about God's love, however, proved to be more popular still.

Evolutionary philosophy as a whole was guilty, Drummond claimed, of having 'misread Nature herself' by supposing that the sole or even the main actor in the drama of evolution was 'the Struggle for Life'. Drummond continued to echo Kropotkin's *Nineteenth Century* articles when he wrote that, although Darwin was not directly responsible for this misperception, his emphasis on competition had been the start of the error; and that Thomas Huxley's most recent statements, in his 1893 Romanes Lecture on 'Evolution and Ethics', about the conflict between the civilizing human 'ethical process' and the merciless natural 'cosmic process', had greatly exacerbated the mistake.[52] In point of fact, Drummond argued, there was 'a *second* factor which one might venture to call the *Struggle for the Life of Others*, which plays an equally prominent part' in evolution.[53] The 'Struggle for the Life of Others', he explained, was 'the physiological name for the greatest word of ethics—Other-ism, Altruism, Love.'[54] And it was the influence of this second struggle that was at the centre of Drummond's rereading of the book of evolution. Although the first chapter or two of that book might be considered as being about the struggle for life, Drummond argued, taken as a whole the book was not 'a tale of battle' but 'a Love-story'.[55] Even in the early stages of evolution the struggle for the life of others had been important, 'while in the world's later progress—under the name of Altruism—it assumes a sovereignty before which the earlier Struggle sinks into insignificance'.[56] Drummond admitted that both struggles must constantly be kept in view for any truly 'scientific theory of Evolution' to be possible, whether in biology or in sociology.[57] However, he was also clear that, while both factors had shaped evolution in the past, the future would belong increasingly to the struggle for the life of others: 'The path of progress and the path of Altruism are one. Evolution is nothing but the Involution of Love, the revelation of Infinite Spirit, the Eternal Life returning to Itself.'[58] Although many critics considered such romantic

---

[52] On Darwin, see Drummond 1899: 15–16, 279–81; on Huxley, ibid. 26–32.
[53] Ibid. 17.
[54] Ibid. 281.
[55] Ibid. 279.
[56] Ibid. 15–17.
[57] Ibid. 24.
[58] Ibid. 46.

religious rhapsodies unscientific, he himself told his listeners and readers that 'the Evolution of Love is a piece of pure science'.[59]

The distinction between the selfish struggle for life and the altruistic struggle for the life of others was connected in *The Ascent of Man* with three other distinctions: between nutrition and reproduction, between the physiological and the ethical, and between male and female. In making these distinctions, the connections between Drummond's work and what others were writing about science and altruism in the 1880s and 1890s became clear—connections which some unfriendly critics felt Drummond himself had inadequately acknowledged. Drummond did acknowledge that Herbert Spencer, John Fiske, George Romanes, Arabella Buckley, and Peter Kropotkin, amongst others, had already written about the role of altruism in evolution; and he also acknowledged that Patrick Geddes and J. Arthur Thomson's *Evolution of Sex* (1889) had made particularly important advances in the same direction. However, these acknowledgements were somewhat peremptory, covering only a couple of pages.[60] The similarity between Drummond's version of evolution and that developed by Arabella Buckley in *Moral Teachings of Science* (1891), for instance, was more substantial than Drummond's brief acknowledgement suggested. But perhaps the most important of these sources of Drummond's vision of altruism, and one that connected him both with Comtean positivism and Spencerian evolution, was Geddes and Thomson's *The Evolution of Sex*.

'Hunger and love are performing the task'

Patrick Geddes was, despite the best efforts of his mentor Thomas Huxley, steeped both in Spencerian evolutionary biology and in Comtean positivism. Indeed, it was the vehemence of Huxley's attacks on Richard Congreve and the Religion of Humanity that had first aroused Geddes's interest in the latter.[61] Geddes's association with the British positivists started in the 1870s and he officially joined the London Positivist Society

---

[59] On Darwin, see Drummond 1899: 277.

[60] Ibid. 42–4.

[61] I am grateful to Chris Renwick for allowing me to consult his dissertation on the historical and intellectual contexts of Patrick Geddes's career. See Renwick 2005. On Huxley and positivism, see Dixon 2005b: 199–202.

in 1883.[62] Looking back towards the end of his life, by now established as a leading sociologist and town-planner, Geddes acknowledged that his own work had been influenced by positivist teachings, and estimated that Comte's impact on modern thought was more significant than Spencer's. He wrote that Comte's 'truly prophetic' ideas had triumphed, in spite of the failure of organized Positivist Societies, and that as a result 'the man in the street is far more of a positivist than he knows'.[63] Geddes's later recollections of the positivists provide an interesting insight into his biological sensibilities. He recalled that he was very physically impressed by Edward Beesly and Frederic Harrison. The former was 'tall, golden-haired and blue-eyed . . . my ideal Northman'; the latter was broad-chested and energetic, the type of the 'dark Celt'. Congreve and Bridges were his 'ideal Anglo-Saxons'. Geddes also recalled with approval the positivist teaching on the centrality of the family and of the separate spheres of men and women. Remembering these four men and their 'leading ladies', all 'happily, even ideally, mated', Geddes wrote, had helped him in his subsequent reflections on the subject of eugenics.[64]

In 1889, the *Evolution of Sex* (of which Geddes was the senior and principal author) set out Geddes's biological views on the relationship between the sexes in a way that gave an important role to the evolution of altruism. Selfishness and altruism were said each to be associated with the discharging of a basic function of animal life: selfishness with nutrition; altruism with reproduction.[65] Geddes and Thomson illustrated this idea with a diagram of the relationship between 'Nutritive, Self-Maintaining, or Egoistic, and Reproductive, Species-Regarding, or Altruistic Activities' (see Fig. 23).[66] It was this central distinction that Drummond borrowed for his own purposes in *The Ascent of Man*. Geddes and Thomson had traced the influence of the reproductive instincts from multicellular animals in which there was no psychological side to sexual union, through examples of increasingly developed sexual psychologies in dung beetles, parasitic worms, fishes, frogs, and reptiles, and finally to birds and mammals. Among these last two classes of animals, Geddes and Thomson wrote, 'the greater differentiation of the nervous system and the higher pitch of the whole life is associated

---

[62] Records of the London Positivist Society, held in the archives of the London School of Economics. LPS 1/1. Geddes's own recollections are recorded in his 'Introduction' to a memoir of John H. Bridges. See Liveing 1926: 1–19.

[63] Liveing 1926: 9–17.

[64] Ibid. 2–4.

[65] Geddes and Thomson 1889: ch. 19, pp. 264–81. Drummond 1899: 43–4.

[66] Geddes and Thomson 1889: 280.

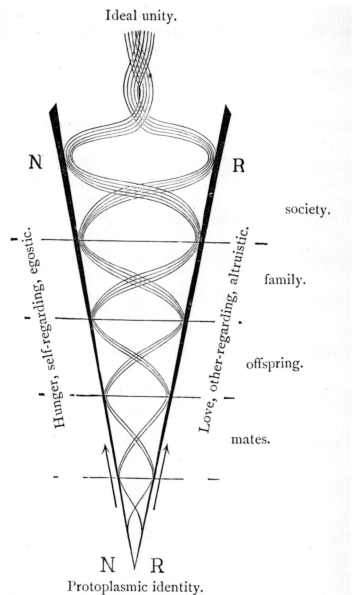

Diagrammatic Representation of the Relations between Nutritive, Self-Maintaining, or Egoistic, and Reproductive, Species-Regarding, or Altruistic Activities.

Figure 23. Diagram representing the evolution of altruistic and egoistic activities in the animal world, from Patrick Geddes and J. Arthur Thomson, *The Evolution of Sex* (1889).

with the development of what pedantry alone can refuse to call love'.
Sceptical readers were referred, for 'an overflowing wealth of instances', to
Ludwig von Büchner's *Liebe und Liebesleben in der Thierwelt* (1879)—the
same book that Kropotkin would cite the following year in his articles on
'mutual aid'.[67] Although Geddes and Thomson, like Kropotkin, disparaged
the idea that the whole of animal life should be read as a 'hymn of love',
they did approve of a maxim due to Schiller, with which they ended their
book: 'While philosophers are disputing about the government of the
world, Hunger and Love are performing the task.'[68] In a later popular work
on evolution for the Home University Library of Modern Knowledge,
Geddes and Thomson described *The Evolution of Sex* as 'essentially an
elaboration of one aspect' of this motto.[69] In the same work, they continued to emphasize the altruistic side of natural history, and recommended Kropotkin's *Mutual Aid* as a 'valuable account of the inadequately
appreciated "other side" of the struggle for existence'.[70]

    Drummond's second important distinction was between physiological
'Other-ism' and the full-fledged psychological and ethical version of that
force, 'Altruism', which was comprised of all the highly developed virtues
connected to sympathy, tenderness, unselfishness, and self-sacrifice.[71]
Drummond thought that, even in the basic activities of 'the humblest
organisms visible by the microscope', one could discern 'the function on
which the stupendous superstructure of Altruism indirectly comes to rest',
namely reproduction by cellular fission. In other words, the basic functions
of nutrition and reproduction were shared by all forms of life and, therefore, 'even in protoplasm is Self-ism and Other-ism'. Herbert Spencer had
been the first to discover altruism, or at least its evolutionary roots, in the
simplest forms of life, and even in single cells. By the 1890s, the idea was
widespread. The novelist Thomas Hardy recorded in his diary in 1893 that,

---

[67] Geddes and Thomson 1889: 266, 282.

[68] Ibid. 314.

[69] Geddes and Thomson 1911: 235.

[70] Ibid. 253. Thomson pursued the same line in his 1915–16 Gifford Lectures (which, in their published form, were dedicated to Geddes), insisting that hunger and love, the egoistic and the altruistic aspects of animal life should both be kept in view: 'The twofold business of living creatures
is caring for self and caring for others.' Thomson reminded his listeners that Darwin had recognized that success in the struggle for life might be best attained by parental devotion and 'self-
subordination'. Thomson went on to list Spencer, Kessler, Geddes, Drummond, and Kropotkin
as those who had done most to correct the idea that the struggle for existence should be
characterized as one of 'internecine competiton'; J. A. Thomson 1920: 289–316, quotations at
314–15.

[71] Drummond 1899: 22, 39.

over dinner at the Conservative Club, the Scottish physician and asylum inspector James Crichton-Browne had told him that the Darwinian view of nature required readjusting to take account of the existence of 'an altruism and coalescence between cells as well as an antagonism'.[72] Similarly, Professor Simon Henry Gage, in his presidential address to the American Microscopic Society in 1895, described how, in an experiment on a salamander, white blood cells had carried carbon out of the creature's tissues, thus saving the animal's life, but in the process sacrificing themselves 'as surely as ever did soldier or philanthropist for the betterment or the preservation of the State'. This *'cellular altruism'*, Gage said, was an example of the exciting new facts of nature that the microscope helped to reveal.[73]

Drummond was not alone, then, in using the language of 'altruism' in a way that blurred the boundary between physiological descriptions of cells and ethical and psychological ideas more applicable to human society. Although he acknowledged that protoplasm could not strictly be described in moral terms, Drummond suggested that in this physiological process of cell-division 'there lies a prophecy, a suggestion of the day of Altruism'.[74] Drummond professed to separate 'Other-ism' from 'Altruism', but also saw a continuity between the two. This tension was evident in a single sentence about the struggle for life and the struggle for the life of others: 'No true moral content can be put into either, yet the one marks the beginning of Egoism, the other of Altruism.'[75] In this respect, Drummond's clearly echoed Herbert Spencer's writings on the subject in *The Data of Ethics* (1879). This similarity provoked a furious review by Spencer's friend, the journalist Eliza Lynn Linton, who was most famous for her assaults on the 'shrieking sisterhood' and the 'wild women', as she characterized campaigners for women's rights, from the 1860s onwards.[76]

Linton launched her assault on Drummond in the pages of the *Fortnightly Review* in September 1894, accusing him simultaneously of 'simple and direct plagiarism' and of reducing Spencer's views to the level of 'unscientific nonsense'. Compare Spencer's *Data of Ethics* with the *Ascent of Man*, Lynn Linton said, and you will see the difference between 'the real scientific thinker' and 'the pseudo-scientist writing clap-trap for an

---

[72] F. E. Hardy 1962: 259.

[73] *Science* (23 Aug. 1895); also reported in *Medical News* (28 Sept. 1895), 355.

[74] Drummond 1899: 282–3.

[75] Ibid. 284–5.

[76] See *ODNB*. On Linton's opposition to the exclusion by Thomas Huxley of women from the Ethnological Society, see E. Richards 1989.

ignorant public'.[77] The article had, in fact, been commissioned by Spencer himself, who had written to Mrs Linton saying that someone should write a reply to Drummond but that he would not like to undertake it himself and that 'looking around for a proxy I thought of you'. Spencer was delighted with the result and applauded her denunciation not only of Drummond, but of 'the public taste which swallows with greediness these semi-scientific sentimentalities'.[78] George Shoobridge Carr, although an agnostic with no sympathy for Drummond's Christian interpretation of Spencerian evolution, objected to Linton's review. Carr argued that Drummond's book included an acknowledgment of Spencer's theories of the evolution of altruism, that it was basically scientifically sound, and that the review's 'furious onslaughts' were more suggestive 'of Mrs Linton's own "Wild Woman" on the war-path than anything else'.[79] Linton might also have paused to reflect that Drummond's account of the evolution of motherhood, whatever its scientific failings, provided useful ideological ammunition for those like herself who wanted to resist the rise of the 'new woman'.

The new woman and the holy family

Drummond's and Kidd's new theories of altruism were both given to the Victorian reading public in 1894—the same year that saw the birth of the 'new woman'.[80] This highly educated, self-confident, cigarette-smoking, trouser-wearing, bicycle-riding, over-sexed, marriage-hating young woman was partly a product of the greater educational and social opportunities opening up to young middle-class women, and partly a stereotype produced by anti-feminist writers such as Eliza Lynn Linton and 'Ouida'.[81] Linton and 'Ouida' were by no means the only writers concerned both with the 'Woman Question' and with debates about altruism. The socialist

[77] Eliza Lynn Linton, 'Professor Henry Drummond's Discovery', *Fortnightly Review,* 56 (1894), 448–57, at 453–4.

[78] Duncan 1908: 363.

[79] See Carr 1895: 38–50, quotation at 47.

[80] The phrase seems to have originated with a pair of articles in the *North American Review*—the first by the feminist writer Frances McFall, who wrote under the pen-name 'Sarah Grand'; and a hostile reply by 'Ouida'. 'Sarah Grand', 'The New Aspect of the Woman Question', *North American Review,* 158 (1894), 270–6. 'Ouida', 'The New Woman', *North American Review,* 158 (1894), 610–19.

[81] On the 'new woman', see Heilmann 1998; Richardson and Willis 2002. On 'Ouida' in particular, see Gilbert 1999. On her satire of the sentimental and socialistic 'altruist' see Ch. 6, above.

and feminist writer Jane Hume Clapperton campaigned both against the arid and repressive convention of marriage and in favour of a eugenic approach to sex and reproduction. She was the author of a didactic novel entitled *Margaret Dunmore, or, A Socialist Home* (1888), and her first book, *Scientific Meliorism and the Evolution of Happiness* (1885) was warmly endorsed by George Shoobridge Carr as the very 'Bible of Altruism'.[82] Grant Allen, who had written about his resigned acceptance of 'scientist', 'sociology', and 'altruism' in 1894, wrote one of the most controversial and popular 'new woman' novels the following year.[83] Mona Caird, a critic of the conventional Victorian marriage and a writer associated with the 'new woman' movement, wrote a reply to Linton's 'Wild Women' articles which was published in the *Nineteenth Century* in 1892.[84] She rejected Linton's project of finding natural and scientific justifications for social arrangements confining men and women to separate spheres, and even quoted Geddes and Thomson in support of the idea that future marriages would see men and women coming together as equals with shared interests.[85] The quotation, however, was selective and creatively interpreted.

In fact, *The Evolution of Sex* supported a very well established and widely held view on the innate differences between the sexes—one which centred on the intellectual superiority of men and the moral superiority of women. A popular book by Sarah Lewis published half a century earlier, *Women's Mission* (1839), for example, had described maternal love as 'the only truly unselfish feeling that exists on this earth', and explained that it was easier for women than for men to practise Christian virtues, since they had fewer worldly interests and were 'by nature and education less selfish'.[86] One study summarizes this mid-Victorian orthodoxy, which many men of science reinforced, in the following terms: 'Women were born to suffer, to nurture and to redeem and were equipped for these tasks with fortitude, altruism and an elevated moral sense.'[87] In an 1887 article on 'Mental

[82] See *ODNB*; Clapperton 1885; Carr 1895: 2, 85–9, 109–14.
[83] Allen 1895 told the story of a young woman, Herminia, who persuaded her lover, Alan, to enter into a state of ecstatically unmarried monogamy. It received a particularly hostile review from the feminist campaigner Millicent Garrett Fawcett: 'The Woman Who Did', *Contemporary Review*, 67 (1895), 625–31.
[84] Mona Caird, 'A Defence of the So-Called "Wild Women"', *Nineteenth Century*, 31 (1892), 811–29; repr. in M. Caird 1897: 159–91. Richardson 2003 is a full and fascinating study of connections between debates about the new woman and scientific views of sex, motherhood and eugenics in the late 19th century; on Caird, see esp. ch. 8.
[85] M. Caird 1897: 188.
[86] Quoted in Perkin 1989: 243. Almost nothing is known about Sarah Lewis; see *ODNB*.
[87] Erskine 1995: 100.

Differences between Men and Women', the Darwinian expert on mental evolution, George J. Romanes had given his support to the same idea: while men had more powerful and original intellects and stronger wills, women were superior in the realms of 'affection, sympathy, devotion, self-denial, modesty; long-suffering, or patience under pain, disappointment, and adversity; reverence, veneration, religious feeling, and general morality'. Romanes described women as confirming more closely than men to the new moral ideals inaugurated by the coming of Christ, and noted that it was women rather than men who were present at the crucifixion. The source of this moral superiority, Romanes wrote, was the evolution of those maternal instincts which accompanied the woman's role as primary protector of her helpless young over a prolonged period of infancy, which was the main 'impetus to the growth in her of all the altruistic feelings most distinctive of woman'.[88]

Although Geddes and Thomson criticized Romanes for falling into a category of writers who, they claimed, wrote about the biological differences between the sexes as if they were merely 'a matter of muscular strength or weight of brain', their own analysis basically reinforced the same picture of intellectual men and altruistic women.[89] As in their consideration of the other-regarding emotions associated with sexual reproduction, so with maternal instincts, Geddes and Thomson traced the development of these propensities through a series of examples taken from different classes of animals. Instances were offered of the maternal care and self-sacrifice observed among crayfish, cuttlefish, bees, spiders, and ants. And, again as with sexual love, Geddes and Thomson saw love for offspring evolving into its fullest forms in the birds and mammals. The female opossum's carrying of her young on her back (see Fig. 24) was used as just one illustration of this more developed parental altruism. On their diagram of egoistic and altruistic activities (see Fig. 23), Geddes and Thomson placed love of offspring higher than love of mates, but lower than that love of family and society at large, which were nearer to the 'ideal unity' in which altruism and egoism finally coalesced.[90]

---

[88] George J. Romanes, 'Mental Differences between Men and Women', *Nineteenth Century,* 21 (1887), 654–72, at 658–9, 663.

[89] Geddes and Thomson 1889: 267. In the same paragraph is Geddes and Thomson's famous statement that 'What was decided among the prehistoric Protozoa cannot be annulled by Act of Parliament.'

[90] Geddes and Thomson 1889: 270–4, 279–81, 312–14. James Crichton-Browne, who discussed altruism with Thomas Hardy in the Conservative Club in 1893, also spoke up in favour of the science of sexual difference. Addressing the Medical Society of London in May 1892, he told his

312   THE EVOLUTION OF SEX.

The corresponding progress in the historic and individual world, from sex and family up to tribe or city, nation and race, and ultimately to the conception of humanity itself, also becomes increasingly apparent. Competition and survival of the fittest are never wholly eliminated, but reappear on each new plane to work out the predominance of the higher, *i.e.*, more integrated and associated type, the phalanx being victorious till in turn it meets the legion. But this service no longer compels us to regard these agencies as the essential mechanism of progress, to the practical exclusion of the associative factor upon which the victory depends, as economist and biologist have too long misled each other into doing. For

An Opossum (*Didelphys dorsigera* carrying its young on its back.—
From Carus Sterne

we see that it is possible to interpret the ideals of ethical progress, through love and sociality, co-operation and sacrifice, not as mere utopias contradicted by experience, but as the highest expressions of the central evolutionary process of the natural world. The ideal of evolution is indeed an Eden; and although competition can never be wholly eliminated, and progress must thus approach without ever completely reaching its ideal, it is much for our pure natural history to recognise that "creation's final law" is not struggle but love. The fuller working out of this thesis, however, would lead us far beyond our present limits, towards a restatement of the

Figure 24. An illustration of the altruistic maternal activities of an opossum, and some of the accompanying text, from Patrick Geddes and J. Arthur Thomson, *The Evolution of Sex* (1889), 312.

Drummond's *Ascent of Man*, by making a distinction between the struggle for life as the domain of the father, and the struggle for the life of others as the world of the altruistic mother, reinforced the Victorian idea that men and women belonged in separate spheres.[91] Drummond again seems to have relied very heavily upon Geddes and Thomson, but to have developed their relatively sober analysis into something more colourful. As Goldwin Smith put it, Drummond's chapters on the evolution of the mother as the crown of creation 'are more than philosophy; they are poetry, soaring almost into rhapsody'.[92] Drummond asked his listeners and readers to run their eye over the scale of animal life from the protozoa, through the invertebrates to the fish, amphibians, reptiles and bird, and 'then—What? The Mammalia, THE MOTHERS. There the series stops. Nature has never made anything since.' Drummond thought it perhaps not even too extreme to wonder whether the 'one motive of organic Nature was to make Mothers'. And the human mother was the most perfect creation of all. The centrality of maternal care and self-sacrifice to the whole process of evolution, Drummond suggested, was the way nature had chosen 'to teach the youth of the world the Fifth Commandment'—that is, to honour their fathers and mothers.[93] Drummond also discussed how nature had brought about 'the evolution of a father', although he thought that it was 'not so beautiful a process as the Evolution of a Mother'; and the defining characteristic of the father was not altruism but 'Righteousness'.[94]

The climax of Drummond's Lowell lectures was a celebration of the new vision of the human family which the study of the natural world suggested. He compared that new picture to a Raphael painting of the 'Holy Family'. Just as Raphael's picture's meaning could not be discerned by analysing the structure of the canvas and the chemical composition of the pigments, nor could the meaning of love be understood by thinking purely in terms of the physical evolution of parental instincts. The picture of the family revealed by a study of evolution was of an institution that had survived through millennia, untarnished by time, and unimprovable by human art or even by religion. This was a spiritual truth which went beyond

---

audience that male and female intellects were not equal, largely as a result of the superior size, density, and blood supply of the male brain (especially the parts concerned with cognition). In 1910, he would join Mrs Humphry Ward in supporting the Anti-Woman Suffrage League. *The Times* (4 May 1892), 10; (21 July 1910), 9.

[91] Drummond 1899: 22–3.

[92] Smith, 'Guesses at the Riddle', 236.

[93] Drummond 1899: 342–3, 355.

[94] Ibid. 376, 403.

natural science and even beyond the old argument from design.[95] The natural evolution of mothers and fathers revealed both that the sacred human family had its roots in biology and that God's love worked through that biology.

In the closing paragraphs of his final lecture, Drummond reminded his audience of 'that Altruism which we found struggling to express itself throughout the whole course of Nature' and asked them simply 'What is it?' He started his answer by quoting from the duke of Argyll's review of Kidd's *Social Evolution*—the same sentence quoted by Carr in his discussion of resistance to scientific language—'Altruism is the new and very affected name for the old familiar things which we used to call Charity, Philanthropy, and Love.' However, while the duke of Argyll's comment signified a simple resistance to the importation of scientific neologisms into moral language, Drummond's strategy was more constructive. Although he sympathized with the idea that, in discovering 'altruism' in nature, scientists had really discovered the very 'roots of Christianity', his own enthusiastic adoption of the language of 'altruism' in the foregoing lectures was part of an attempt to show that Christianity had nothing to fear from the attempt to describe and understand the world in scientific terms. Whether it was called 'Other-ism', 'Altruism', or anything else, Drummond believed that it was only by 'disguising words' that science could deny that this fundamental factor that had been discovered in evolution was identical with Christian love.[96] So, Drummond's ambition was twofold: to re-Christianize the scientific language of 'altruism'; and to maintain and strengthen the associations, which he inherited from Auguste Comte and Patrick Geddes, between the celebration of altruism and the celebration of marriage and motherhood.

In this way Drummond used evolutionary science to reinforce the idea that it was natural for women to subordinate their own needs to those of their husbands and children; to romanticize the institution of Christian marriage; and thus tacitly to resist the rise of feminism and the 'new woman'. At least one woman in Drummond's Boston audience, the American feminist Ellen Batelle Dietrick, understood his argument in this way. Writing for the *Boston Evening Transcript* in April 1893, having heard Drummond lecture, Dietrick contested his use of natural history to support the identification of women with passive self-sacrificing altruism and men with activity and physical courage. Examples could also be found in nature

[95] Ibid. 406–7.
[96] Ibid. 442.

that reversed this picture: female spiders who devoured their male mates, and queen bees who dominated whole droves of males; as well as instances of tender devotion in male parents, such as the selfless feeding of mate and offspring by the male red-beaked hornbill of the tropics. 'Professor Drummond has struck a noble key-note in declaring that the greatest thing in the world is love,' Dietrick concluded, 'but he wanders far from discernment in teaching that it is natural and excellent for the human race to divide itself either in its ideals or in its travel towards those ideals.' [97] Little has been written about Dietrick and her philosophy. She was the secretary of the New England Suffrage Association in 1895; contributed to the individualist-anarchist journal *Liberty*; and has been described as an 'individualist feminist'.[98] In her opposition to the gendered celebration of altruism and in her interest in individualism and anarchism, Dietrick resembled Dora Marsden, the editor of a series of British periodicals between 1911 and 1919, who is considered amongst other post-Victorian egoists in Chapter 8 below.

There were other American feminists who, unlike Dietrick, adopted rather than resisted the scientific idea that women were innately more altruistic than men, and deployed it in their political campaigns. Eliza Burt Gamble's *Evolution of Woman: An Inquiry into the Dogma of Her Inferiority to Men* (1894), published in the same year as Drummond's *Ascent of Man*, appropriated Darwinian ideas to argue that women should now be taking leading social and political roles. The basis of this argument was a speculative evolutionary history in which earlier human societies had been dominated by matriarchal compassion and altruism. The superiority of these female traits, Gamble suggested, which had subsequently been marginalized by the ascendancy of the destructive egoism, competitiveness, and belligerence of men, now needed to be recognized in a feminist renewal of modern society. Charlotte Perkins Gilman pursued Darwinian ideas about evolution and sex differences in support of similar conclusions.[99]

---

[97] Ellen Battelle Dietrick, 'Professor Drummond on Sex', *Boston Evening Transcript* (29 Apr. 1893); cutting in NLS/MSS/Acc.5890.14.

[98] H. K. Johnson 1913: 11 identifies Dietrick as a suffragist. On her individualism and feminism, see McElroy 1996: 176; 2001: 12. Dietrick was also one of the contributors to a sceptical work on the negative portrayals of women in scripture, *The Woman's Bible*, the first part of which was published in 1895 under the editorship of the American suffragist Elizabeth Cady Stanton; Stanton 1971: 542–3.

[99] On Gamble, Perkins, and other feminist writers who engaged with Darwinism in the late 19th century, see Jann 1997; Kohlstedt and Jorgensen 1999; Deutscher 2004; Vandermassen et al. 2005.

Taking a different approach from these American feminists, but one that still accepted the idea of innate female altruism, James Hinton's friend and biographer, the social purity campaigner Ellice Hopkins, welcomed Drummond's vision both of the evolution of parental love and of the special role of women, as mothers, in shaping the morals of the human race. Although Hopkins regretted that Drummond had mixed up his account of the evolution of love with 'a good deal of extraneous sentiment', it was an account which, for her, fulfilled a dual purpose. First, she recommended it to other women as a vehicle for explaining the facts of life to their sons. Hopkins's book, *The Power of Womanhood; or, Mothers and Sons* (1899) was aimed at educated women who wanted to do something to prevent their sons from falling into sexual vice, either at school or in later life. Hopkins thought it was imperative to educate them about sex, but in the right way and at the right time. If a son asked his mother about 'where the little baby brother or sister comes from' at too young an age, Hopkins recommended the following response: 'My child, you have asked me a question about what is very, very sacred. If I were to try to explain it to you, you would not be old enough to understand; for the present you must be content to know that the baby comes from God; how it comes mother will tell you when you grow old enough to understand.' At the stage that the boy was old enough to understand, Hopkins recommended explaining human reproduction as the summit of the natural evolution of sex, and quoted illustrations of plant and animal reproduction taken from Drummond for that purpose.

Secondly, Hopkins used Drummond's account to reinforce the general moral that the 'gradual evolution of the preservative and altruistic elements' showed that the care of the strong for the weak was 'as pervasive an element in Nature as the fierce struggle for existence in which the weak are destroyed by the strong'. Hopkins's advice manual for educated mothers in this way used Drummond's popular science to reinforce her advocacy of moral purity as an 'attitude of soul' that each woman should impart to her sons: 'I do say that early associations are most terribly strong, and if you will secure that those early associations with regard to life and birth shall be bound up with all the sanctities of life—with home, with his mother, with family, with all that is best and highest in life; then his whole attitude in life will be different.'[100] Drummond's *Ascent of Man* was just the book to support the message that the institution of the Victorian family was both

---

[100] Hopkins 1909: 75–87, quotations at 75, 76, 82, 82n., 86–7.

natural and sacred. The idea that altruism was natural, maternal, familial, and was thus associated with 'all that is best and highest in life', was to prove an easy target for those post-Victorian men and women who would seek to construct a more artistic and individualistic philosophy.[101]

Anglo-Saxons and their religion: Benjamin Kidd's *Social Evolution*

One of the dozens of British reviews of Drummond's *Ascent of Man* appeared in a periodical called *The Expositor*, edited by the Free Church minister and journalist, W. Robertson Nicoll.[102] The review rehearsed some of the commonest critical responses to the book: although it dealt with scientific questions, 'its subject is not so much science as the poetry of science . . . the soaring flights of a young and vigorous school of thought'; much of the account offered of human evolution was not original and would be familiar to readers of, for instance, the American Spencerian philosopher John Fiske's book, *The Destiny of Man* (1884); and the sweeping account of the rise of altruism seemed to sacrifice precision and accuracy to the achievement of literary effect; the careful reader would soon notice, for instance, that Drummond had confused and intermingled throughout two different sorts of altruism, namely parental care and social cooperation. The author of this review had more reason than most to view Drummond's book with some suspicion, even rivalry: this was Benjamin Kidd, whose own book had come out a few months earlier and had been explicitly compared with Drummond's by several reviewers.[103]

Among the cuttings carefully collected by Henry Drummond into his scrapbook, several preferred Kidd's analysis of altruism to his own. A generally favourable review of Drummond in *The Methodist Recorder*, for instance, thought that *The Ascent of Man* had appeared at an opportune moment when 'so much interest is being excited by Mr Benjamin Kidd's *Social Evolution*' but that, overall, readers would find that 'Mr Kidd's presentation of Altruism in its relation to the great processes ever going on around us is truer and therefore nearer to the Christian ideal than Mr

---

[101] See Ch. 8 below.
[102] *ODNB.*
[103] This was true of, amongst others, Carr's reviews in the *Agnostic Journal*, repr. in Carr 1895; Smith, 'Guesses at the Riddle', 230–48; Galton, 'Part of Religion'; and Ernest Newman's book comparing Kidd, Drummond, and Arthur Balfour: Cecil 1897; see n. 43 above.

Drummond's', which, the reviewer feared contained 'an undercurrent of fatalism'.[104] *The Methodist Times* praised Drummond's book but thought that it had failed to do justice to the 'selfish factor in human life', which had exercised 'such a tremendous predominance over the altruistic factor that a new intervention of God in the Person of His Son was necessary to restore the balance'. What Drummond's evolutionary story overlooked, according to this review, was the centrality of that 'supernatural factor in religion for which Mr Kidd so brilliantly and so Scripturally contends'.[105] Not all the reviews made disappointing reading for Drummond, however. Writing in the *British Weekly*, Marcus Dods praised *The Ascent of Man* for selecting artistically from the works of scientific specialists such as Haeckel, Darwin, Huxley, and Romanes, and for providing a convincing answer to those, like Huxley and Benjamin Kidd, who believed that the purpose of civilization was to create artificially cooperative systems as a bulwark against the innate selfishness at the heart of nature. Drummond had shown, Dods thought, that 'in nature there is laid a basis for Altruism as deep, firm, and influential as the basis for the struggle for life'.[106] Why did Kidd and others not agree?

The heritability of acquired characteristics was the central plank of Victorian evolutionary moralism. In the 1880s and 1890s, however, it was called into question by the German naturalist August Weismann's famous experiments (including those in which mice with their tails cut off repeatedly produced offspring with full-length tails) and the theoretical framework within which he interpreted them. Weismann himself made claims for the 'all-sufficiency of natural selection' as the mechanism of evolutionary change and denied the heritability of acquired characteristics, believing instead that the immortal 'germ plasm' was passed on unchanged by each organism to its offspring. Such a view of biological evolution, which came to be known as 'neo-Darwinism', 'ultra-Darwinism', or even 'hyper-Darwinism', challenged progressivist visions which depended on the heritability of acquired mental traits.[107] If the results of education and other

---

[104] *Methodist Recorder* (24 May 1894); cutting in NLS/MSS/Acc.5890.14.

[105] *Methodist Times* (24 May 1894), 329; cutting in NLS/MSS/Acc.5890.14.

[106] Marcus Dods, 'The Ascent of Man', *British Weekly* (7 May 1894); cutting in NLS/MSS/Acc.5890.14. See also letter from Dods to Drummond discussing this article, which is in fact a pre-publication preview of the book: NLS/MSS/Acc.5890.2.

[107] On Weismann, see Mackintosh 1899: part IV; Bowler 1983: esp. 40–3; Cronin 1991: 35–47; Gayon 1998: ch. 5. On the roles of Darwinian and non-Darwinian theories of evolution, their religious implications, and their cultural impact in the early 20th century, see Bowler 2001: 122–59. On Kidd's and others' application of the new biology to social evolution, see P. Crook 1994: 70–93.

agents of moral improvement were not passed on from parents to their offspring, then there was no biological reason to believe that each new generation would be more morally elevated than the next.

This question was taken up by the poet and critic Archibald Stodart-Walker in an article for the *Westminster Review* in 1902. Stodart-Walker wrote that biology had revealed no true altruism in nature, if 'altruism' were to be interpreted 'in its most exact meaning', but only forms of cooperative behaviour towards family- and species-members which should really be described as 'protective egoism'. In contrast, he wrote, sociology revealed that society was indeed based upon altruism, which was imposed on individuals against the grain of their natural egoism. Spencer had been wrong, the article argued, to suggest that altruism could be inherited biologically. The 'acquired altruism' of the parent was indeed 'inherited by the offspring' but it was a purely social rather than a biological inheritance. Stodart-Walker cited embryological experiments carried out by the Edinburgh zoologist James Cossar Ewart in support of his own doubts about the heritability of acquired characteristics.[108] The implication was that each generation of human beings was born just as egoistical as the last, regardless of their parentage, and that the 'finely elaborated superstructure of altruistic socialism' could fall to pieces instantaneously as soon as a great disaster threw people back on their natural instincts.[109] The final conclusions were stark, and represented a rejection of the mid-Victorian consensus about evolution and morality: '*Man becomes altruistic as a result of his subjection to a social environment, and as a necessity of self-protection. There is not evolved within himself the altruistic idea.*'[110] Stodart-Walker, then, denied that altruistic instincts were biologically inherited; denied, further, that any acquired characteristics could be inherited; and looked to social evolution alone for a scientific explanation of human altruism. This was exactly the approach that had been popularized by Benjamin Kidd's *Social Evolution* eight years earlier.

Benjamin Kidd came from an Irish Protestant background that would have had theological and cultural similarities with Henry Drummond's Scottish evangelical context. His book, like Drummond's, was seen as an argument for the importance both of altruism and of Christianity. His

---

[108] Archibald Stodart-Walker, 'Is the Altruistic Idea Evolving in Man?', *Westminster Review*, 158 (1902), 375–81.

[109] Ibid. 380. Stodart-Walker referred to a recent storm in Galveston, Texas which, he claimed, had seen people fighting with their friends and family-members in 'scenes of the most frightful description' in their attempts to secure food and water for themselves at all costs.

[110] Ibid. 377.

account of the meaning, origins, and justification of altruism, however, could hardly have been more different from Drummond's hymn to biological love.[111] While Drummond saw the roots of altruism in the feelings associated with both sexual reproduction and parenthood, which evolved throughout the animal kingdom and reached their apotheosis in human motherhood, Kidd denied that altruistic feelings were produced by biological evolution at all. Instead, for him, they were produced by cultural means—specifically, by religion; even more specifically, by the Protestant forms of Christianity that were born in the European Reformation. And whereas Drummond argued that, following the example of nature, following one's own truest instincts, and following the teachings of Christianity all amounted to pursuing some kind of altruism, Kidd distinguished between the natural dictates of reason, which would lead people to behave selfishly, and the countervailing, 'supra-rational' or 'ultra-rational' teachings of religion, which persuaded them to sacrifice their own selfish interests to the greater good of society and the race. Kidd's book was a late Victorian answer to the question that Henry Sidgwick had asked himself from the 1860s onwards: does 'rational' in a moral context mean self-interestedness, disinterestedness, or both?[112] Kidd's answer was that the only rational policy was the pursuit of self-interest, which was why society needed to be persuaded to become less rational.

Central to Kidd's argument was the belief that the progress of the race would only be guaranteed by competition. This was what he believed Darwin and Weismann had shown. Rationally speaking, however, there was no good reason for each individual to submit themselves to a harsh, competitive social environment. Kidd reminded his readers of Mona Caird's observation a couple of years earlier that rational people were beginning to think there was something 'pathetically absurd' in the sacrifices made to their children by 'generation after generation of grown people'.[113] Science taught us, however, that grown people must continue to make such sacrifices if the race was to continue to progress. The only way they could be persuaded to do so, since it was not rational, was by the influence of religion, especially Christian religion, which had provided civilized societies, especially Anglo-Saxon societies, with a great 'fund of altruism'.[114] Kidd

[111] On Kidd's background, life, and career, see *ODNB* and D. P. Crook 1984.

[112] On Sidgwick and *The Methods of Ethics*, see Ch. 2 above.

[113] Mona Caird, 'Defence of "Wild Women"', 824; repr. in M. Caird 1897: 159–91. Kidd quoted this comment twice: Kidd 1894: 210, 294.

[114] This phrase was picked up by several reviewers, and is used, for instance, at Kidd 1894: 165, 181.

believed that it was in those countries most affected by the Protestant Reformation that philanthropic and humanitarian causes had been especially successful, listing campaigns for the abolition of slavery, for women's suffrage, vegetarianism, and the abolition of the Contagious Diseases Acts, amongst many other things, as evidence of this 'great wave of altruistic feeling'.[115] It was the altruism of the Anglo-Saxons as well as their physical vigour and hard work that had secured their place as the most successful and socially efficient of all races.[116] This altruism had inclined the ruling classes to allow freer competition amongst all members of society. This in turn allowed further social progress.

Kidd was very clear, however, unlike others carried along in the 1890s by the 'great wave of altruism', that there was a very great difference between altruism, which encouraged powerful individuals to create a level playing field on which all could compete on equal terms, and socialism, which would redistribute wealth equally in a way that put an end to competition, and thus lead to degeneration. Kidd was not one of those, like Robert Blatchford or Beatrice Webb, who made the transition from proponent of altruism to supporter of socialism. Weismann's form of neo-Darwinism, according to Kidd, endorsed the former but not the latter.[117] Although Kidd and Spencer both rejected socialism, they had different reasons for doing so. Kidd mocked Spencer's 'Utopian dreams' in which the whole race would become more and more altruistic through the inheritance of acquired characteristics. Such views, he wrote, were out of touch with the most 'progressive tendencies of modern biological science'.[118] Although Kidd was an unusual kind of ethical naturalist, in that he did not think that altruistic tendencies were biologically inherited, his belief that

---

[115] Kidd 1894: ch. 10, p. 300.

[116] Race was one of Kidd's primary concerns. Crook has written that Kidd's view of Anglo-Saxon superiority rested 'not upon racist genetics but upon the more flexible concept of "social efficiency"'. D. P. Crook 1984: 4. This is consistent with Kidd's own statement: 'Neither in respect alone of colour, nor of descent, nor even of the possession of high intellectual capacity, can science give us any warrant for speaking of one race as superior to another. The evolution which man is undergoing is, over and above everything else, a social evolution. There is, therefore, but one absolute test of superiority. It is only the race possessing in the highest degree the qualities contributing to social efficiency that can be recognised as having any claim to superiority.' Kidd 1894: ch. 10, pp. 324–5.

[117] Weismann's theory stated that lack of competition would lead to 'panmixia'—that is, the interbreeding of the fit and the unfit alike—and that this would inevitably lead to degeneration. See Gayon 1998: ch. 5.

[118] The key passage comparing Weismann and Spencer is Kidd 1894: ch. 7, pp. 189–92. In 1893 Spencer had published a series of articles in the *Contemporary Review* arguing against Weismann's exclusion of use inheritance.

social policy should be shaped by following the basic principles at work in nature, as revealed by the latest biological science, meant that he was still advocating a naturalistic and scientific kind of ethics. It just happened that it was a kind of naturalistic scientific ethics in which irrational beliefs in supernatural agencies constituted the most important factor in maintaining that state of competition on which the progress of the human race depended.

Benjamin Kidd's counter-intuitive and original argument, appealing to one of the latest developments in evolutionary biology while also arguing for the central role of Protestant Christianity in ensuring progress, succeeded in garnering the attention and admiration of intellectuals and journalists on both sides of the Atlantic, selling between 40,000 and 50,000 copies worldwide in the first fifteen months after publication.[119] W. T. Stead's *Review of Reviews* described *Social Evolution* as 'one of the few philosophic or sociological books of our time which have had the run of a sensational novel'.[120] In its 'Books of the Week' column, *The Times* welcomed Kidd's book as one that 'no serious thinker should neglect and no reader can study without recognizing it as the work of a singularly penetrating and original mind'. Although there was, of course, nothing new about the idea of evolution—'Evolution is the dominant and characteristic category of the age'—Kidd's new, biologically informed approach to society as an organism whose health relied on the altruistic tendencies of the individuals who made it up was, the *Times* reviewer thought, a welcome and original insight.[121] The *Annual Register* for 1894 echoed these praises: Mr Kidd was a 'new and brilliant writer, a deep thinker', whose application of Weismann's biology to social questions was undoubtedly 'the most valuable contribution to the science of sociology' of the year.[122]

In Cambridge, the Knightbridge Professor of Moral Philosophy, Henry Sidgwick (whom Kidd had met the previous year) included a discussion of *Social Evolution* in his undergraduate lectures on 'Ethical Systems' for 1894–5.[123] A couple of years later, at the Lancashire Independent College in Manchester, Robert Mackintosh took *Social Evolution* as the central text

---

[119] This estimate comes from Kidd himself; D. P. Crook 1984: 52.
[120] Kidd himself had written for the *Review of Reviews*, contributing an interview with August Weismann in 1890. See Dawson 2004: 188–91, quotation at 188.
[121] *The Times* (22 Feb. 1894), 8.
[122] 'Retrospect on Literature, Science, and Art in 1894', *Annual Register* (1894), 92.
[123] G. E. Moore undergraduate lecture notes; CUL Add.8875/10/2/1. Kidd had met Sidgwick at a feast at Trinity College, Cambridge, in Dec. 1893; D. P. Crook 1984: 51.

for his senior class in sociology.[124] In January 1895, Kidd was invited, on the strength of his book, to address the Cambridge Ethical Society.[125] The newly formed Socratic Society in Birmingham, whose members included the philosophical idealists Edward Caird and Bernard Bosanquet, also invited Kidd to address them, telling him that, in Birmingham, 'everybody of any note is reading or has read your book'.[126] In America, Theodore Roosevelt described Kidd's work as 'distinctly one of the books of the year' (although he went on to criticize its tendency to dogmatism and superficiality).[127] Two years after its publication, W. H. Mallock wrote that *Social Evolution* was still being widely read in America and was being welcomed as 'an example—some writers have hailed it as being the first example—of true scientific methods applied to social affairs'.[128] *Social Evolution* was one of the most popular books of the altruistic 1890s.

But not everyone was impressed. Substantial and more critical reviews were written by the Scottish idealist philosopher David Ritchie, the 'new liberal' economic and social theorist John Hobson, the agnostic journalist and historian Goldwin Smith, the positivist John Bridges, and the founder of eugenics Francis Galton. They raised questions about Kidd's understanding of history, his definitions of reason and religion, and his interpretations of biology. Kidd's interpretations of history were speculative, to say the least. Among the least plausible were his suggestions that Christianity had always been anti-intellectual, and that the abolition of slavery and parliamentary reform could both be put down solely, or at least primarily, to the altruism of civilized Christian peoples. David Ritchie was scathing about Kidd's attempts to write 'scientific' history. He wondered how the relatively recent rise and growth of slavery in America, for instance, could be explained by Kidd's theory, since that was a country governed by 'his altruistic, humanitarian "Anglo-Saxons"'. He also noted that Kidd never mentioned the encouragement of the slave trade by Britain prior to the campaign for its abolition. It was, in any case, Ritchie argued 'utterly unscientific to trace historical events to isolated single causes'.[129] Goldwin Smith objected

---

[124] Mackintosh 1899: p. viii.
[125] Benjamin Kidd papers; letters from Sheldon Amos dated 23 Jan. and 4 Feb. 1895. CUL Add.8069/A39–40.
[126] Quoted in D. P. Crook 1984: 87.
[127] Theodore Roosevelt, 'Kidd's *Social Evolution*', *North American Review,* 161 (1895), 94–109, at 94. Roosevelt was working in the Washington civil service at this time. In 1901 he would become President of the United States after the assassination of William McKinley.
[128] W. H. Mallock, 'Altruism in Economics', *Forum,* 21 (1896), 690–704, at 690.
[129] D. G. Ritchie, '*Social Evolution* by Benjamin Kidd', *International Journal of Ethics,* 5 (1894), 107–20, at 109–10, 116.

particularly to the idea that the extension of the franchise in Britain in 1832 resulted from the altruism of the upper classes. In fact, Smith wrote, it resulted from 'a conflict between classes and parties carried on in a spirit as far as possible from altruistic and pushed to the very verge of civil war'.[130] John Hobson lectured on *Social Evolution* at the freethinking South Place Ethical Society in north London as well as reviewing it for the *American Journal of Sociology*.[131] He agreed with Ritchie and Smith that the idea that the political reforms brought about through the French Revolution and the English reform movement were the product of a great fund of altruistic feeling amongst the power-holding classes was a 'grotesque contention'.[132]

Kidd's historical incompetence was of less interest to most, however, than his views about rationality, science, and religion. Several reviewers quoted Kidd's own idiosyncratic definition of religion: 'A religion is a form of belief providing an ultra-rational sanction for that large class of conduct in the individual where his interest and the interest of the social organism are antagonistic, and by which the former are rendered subordinate to the latter in the general interests of the evolution which the race is undergoing.' Kidd had also written, while explaining his disapproval of Comte's Religion of Humanity and J. R. Seeley's *Natural Religion*, that a rational religion was a 'scientific impossibility' and an 'inherent contradiction of terms', since the function of religion was, according to his own definition, to provide a motivation for self-sacrifice that reason alone could not provide.[133] These assertions raised all sorts of vexed questions. Critics particularly objected to the identification of religion in general and Christianity in particular with irrationality (or 'supra-rationality', or 'extra-rationality', which both amounted to the same thing). Ritchie noted that Kidd could justifiably apply his analysis to some popular religion but that if he wished to apply it more broadly, 'he will have to exclude every Thomist theologian from the ranks of Christianity'.[134] Although Kidd's definition stipulated that religion was always 'extra-rational', by making no mention of God, it also seemed to allow for the existence of atheistic or secular religions, as Goldwin Smith and Francis Galton both observed.[135]

---

[130] Smith, 'Guesses at the Riddle', 242.
[131] D. P. Crook 1984: 85.
[132] John A. Hobson, 'Mr Kidd's *Social Evolution*', *American Journal of Sociology*, 1 (1895), 299–312, at 305.
[133] Kidd 1894: ch. 5, pp. 100–3.
[134] Ritchie, '*Social Evolution* by Kidd', 113.
[135] Smith, 'Guesses at the Riddle', 240–1. Galton, 'Part of Religion'.

All in all, Christian reviewers, such as those who wrote for *The Methodist Recorder* and *The Methodist Times* and preferred Kidd's views of religion and altruism to Drummond's, should perhaps have read *Social Evolution* more carefully before recommending it to their readers as orthodox and scriptural. Kidd may have placed emphasis on the 'supernatural' factor in religion and on the importance of religion in the evolution of society, but in the end his view of religion was very far from being orthodox. The rhetorical question that John Bridges posed in his review got to the heart of the heterodoxy: 'Is Mr Kidd ready to enter any London pulpit and say "Worship God and do his will: by so doing you and yours will be miserable, but you will promote the ultimate establishment of your race as masters of the world?"'[136]

Another notable feature of Kidd's account was that 'selfish' and 'rational' were treated as synonyms when it came to describing individual human actions. Throughout the book, Kidd assumed that rational behaviour and behaviour that benefited the community or even the whole 'social organism' were always, or virtually always, the products of antagonistic motives. Human motivation was thus reduced to a struggle between individualistic, selfish rationality and religiously inspired counter-rational altruism. Goldwin Smith pointed out that it could be perfectly rational to indulge in self-denial or even self-torture, in cases where the self-torturer believed that his actions were the best way to please the Deity.[137] More fundamentally, other critics noted that an individual's own most cherished interests very frequently extended to include the interests of others. Obvious examples included the identification of one's own interests with those of one's family or nation. It seemed to be stretching the normal meaning of terms too far to suggest that a mother acted irrationally and against her own interests when she made sacrifices for the sake of her children.[138] There were two different strands to this argument—the idealist and the evolutionary. John Hobson praised Kidd for his 'vigorous assertion of the claim of the wider social organism upon the conduct of the several generations' and his recognition that race-preserving instincts were closely analogous to maternal self-sacrifice. But he rejected Kidd's assertion that these altruistic motives were irrational. Hobson denied there was such an antagonism between the individual and the collective, the rational and the irrational. 'The man who reasonably seeks his own interest will (in a socially efficient race)', Hobson

[136] J. H. Bridges, 'The Darwinist Utopia', *Positivist Review*, 2 (1894), 113–18, at 118.
[137] Smith, 'Guesses at the Riddle', 239.
[138] Hobson, 'Mr Kidd's *Social Evolution*', 303.

argued, 'conform to such rules of conduct as make for the welfare of the race, because such conduct will give him most satisfaction.' Putting this in 'the language of a school who mistrust utilitarian language' (in other words the idealist school), Hobson wrote, this amounted to saying that conduct undertaken for the good of the collective 'contributes to the realization of his rational self'.[139] Ritchie agreed. Kidd's claim that the individual's interests were distinct from and antagonistic to those of the whole social organism was untenable: 'Is Mr Kidd's rationalistic individual going to live a hermit's life?'[140]

The second strand of arguments against Kidd's identification of rationality with selfishness drew on the sort of evidence discussed by Spencer, Geddes, Kropotkin, and Drummond of the evolutionary origins of altruistic instincts. The argument here was that instinctively altruistic actions could not properly be described as 'irrational', either because doing so implied a level of cognitive choice which is in fact absent from the motives of such actions, or because actions motivated by innate instincts could not reasonably be described as altruistic. Other animals lived in societies in which individuals acted in the interests of the community. Were they acting irrationally? Or, as Goldwin Smith put the question: 'Is there supernatural or extra-rational sanction in the case of the deer, or the ant, or the bee?' Smith wondered about the true nature of 'this altruism of which we hear so much'. His conclusion was that it was nothing more than man, as a social being, 'gratifying his sympathetic, domestic, or social propensities'; in doing so he was disregarding self no more than when he gratified his desire for food. 'Self is not disregarded because self is sympathetic, domestic, and social.'[141] Galton took the same line. Since altruistic feelings were natural, he argued, they were 'in one sense, selfish'. The love of a cat for her kittens 'is altruistic in its main aspect, though, perhaps, selfish in another; anyhow it cannot be ascribed to the effects of religion'.[142] In rebutting Kidd on this point, reviewers echoed the language popularized by Drummond's *Ascent of Man*. Hobson wrote that the 'struggle for the life of others' was as central a part of the struggle for existence as 'the struggle for one's own life'. The idealist and evolutionary arguments against Kidd emphasized the same single point: 'our own life is organically related to the life of others, the

[139] Ibid. 302–3.
[140] Ritchie, '*Social Evolution* by Kidd', 111.
[141] Smith, 'Guesses at the Riddle', 239–40.
[142] Galton, 'Part of Religion', 756.

family, the generation, the race'.[143] In short, instincts leading to actions for the good of the community were natural (because evolved and shared with other animals) and rational (because the individual shared in the collective's interests) not counter-rational, not dependent entirely on the sanction of religion, and not even necessarily 'altruistic', once a broader sense of self was adopted.

A final, evolutionarily informed criticism of Kidd's vision of social evolution was that, in advocating a kind of altruism according to which individuals in the present consented to live in an uncomfortably harsh and competitive social environment for the sake of the future progress of their race, Kidd was expecting people to go far beyond the limits of that domestic and social sympathy with which they had been endowed by nature. The sympathetic individual certainly identified with offspring, comrades, and compatriots. But there were limits to how far this extended self could be stretched. Goldwin Smith thought that Kidd had gone far beyond these limits: 'Show us the altruist who gives up his dinner to benefit the inhabitants of the planet Mars and we will admit the existence of altruism in the sense in which the term seems to be used by Mr Kidd and some other philosophers today.'[144] Many others had no doubt that altruism directed towards the as-yet-unborn was to be welcomed and encouraged. However, they thought that Kidd's proposed social hyper-Darwinism was not the way to bring this about. Instead of mimicking natural selection by producing large numbers of offspring in a freely competitive environment, Hobson, Ritchie, and Galton all argued that moral progress should be brought about through a process of 'rational artificial selection'—in other words, eugenics.[145] As Hobson put it, every intelligent society 'would consider it a first duty to prohibit unsocial unions' and thus 'to prevent the propagation of physical, mental and moral disease'.[146]

The progress of eugenics

The question of how to breed a more altruistic society had been tacitly raised by earlier scientific moralists, including Comte and Darwin, and had been explored more explicitly by others, including James Cotter Morison

---

[143] Hobson, 'Mr Kidd's *Social Evolution*', 303.
[144] Smith, 'Guesses at the Riddle', 240.
[145] Ritchie, '*Social Evolution* by Kidd', 108.
[146] Hobson, 'Mr Kidd's *Social Evolution*', 309.

and neo–Malthusian advocates of birth control.[147] From the 1890s onwards, scientific controversies surrounding Weismannism and Mendelism, and the rise of organized eugenics movements, gave these debates a new direction and a new institutional platform.[148]

Those who took a eugenic approach to ethics in this period fall into that third category of naturalistic thinkers, mentioned at the start of this chapter, who argued that social and ethical policies should seek to improve humanity by working with the grain of nature. Francis Galton saw the task of eugenics as being to persuade each man to 'co-operate intelligently with what he cannot in the long-run resist'.[149] In his review of Kidd, Galton wrote: 'It has now become a serious necessity to better the breed of the human race. The average citizen is too base for the everyday work of modern civilisation.' Galton agreed with Kidd that religious impulses should be marshalled in support of this much needed racial transformation. However, he disagreed on two other crucial points. He denied that unlimited competition was the key to progress, explaining that 'over-severe competition degrades' both in the natural world and in human society. Fir trees forced by competition to grow unusually tall 'are only just able to hold their own' and 'are stunted specimens of their race'. Similarly, Galton wrote, 'The overworked man or woman is feeble and neurotic.'[150] Instead of free competition, Galton advocated eugenic policies that encouraged those with the highest natural endowments of moral instincts to reproduce. Such policies would make it probable, he hoped, that 'the inefficient multitude of weaklings in brain, character, and physique would be sensibly diminished in thirty years'.[151] Galton also denied that anything supernatural needed to be invoked in the religious realm. He advocated eugenics not only as a scientific discipline and a social programme, but also as a rational religion and a 'national religion' which fulfilled the criteria that Mill had laid down in his posthumously published *Three Essays on Religion* (1874), namely that any religion should direct 'the emotions and desires towards an ideal object,

---

[147] See Ch. 4 above.

[148] For studies of the history of eugenics, see G. Jones 1980, 1986; Kevles 1995; Paul 1995; R. A. Peel 1998; Richardson 2003; J. R. Moore 2004. N. Scott 2002 explores more recent proposals for using eugenic technologies to increase altruism in human societies; this article also brings out the problems that continue to arise from the ambiguity of the word 'altruism'.

[149] Galton, 'Part of Religion', 760.

[150] Ibid. 757.

[151] Ibid. 761.

recognized as rightly paramount over all selfish objects of desire'.[152] That object, for Galton, was the physical, intellectual, and moral perfection of the race.

One arena within which Benjamin Kidd fought out his differences with Francis Galton, and with Galton's protégé Karl Pearson, was the Sociological Society.[153] This society, founded at the London School of Economics in 1903, included amongst its founding members Patrick Geddes, Benjamin Kidd, Francis Galton, John Hobson, and John Bridges. The fact that these figures have all already featured in this chapter as commentators on the social meanings of evolutionary biology during the 1880s and 1890s is indicative of the very porous boundaries that existed between sociology and evolutionary thought in Britain at this time. As Robert Mackintosh put it in a comment quoted above, the brand may have been different, but the liquor was the same. Eugenics was one of the leading topics of debate among the society's members, along with other questions relating to social problems, housing, poverty, and education.[154] From 1907 onwards another London-based forum existed for the discussion and promotion of eugenics, namely the Eugenics Education Society. The society's first president was Francis Galton. On Galton's death in 1911, the presidency passed to Charles Darwin's son, Major Leonard Darwin, who held the post until 1928 and was to remain a central figure in the British eugenics movement until his death in 1943.[155]

Benjamin Kidd was not alone in dissenting from Galtonian orthodoxy within the Sociological Society. The physician, popular science writer, and eugenist Caleb Saleeby was a prominent member of both the Sociological Society and the Eugenics Education Society, and became an increasingly vocal critic of Galton and Pearson from the 1900s onwards.[156] Caleb Saleeby confounds almost every preconceived idea that one might bring to an investigation of Victorian and Edwardian eugenics. Admittedly Saleeby was a dissident within the mainstream movement, but as an articulate and popular spokesman of the broad aims of eugenics, and a passionate writer on the subject of altruism, his writings make a particularly interesting

---

[152] Quoted ibid. 756 (and in modified form again at 763). This definition was first used by Mill in the context of a sympathetic appraisal of the merits of the positivist Religion of Humanity. See Ch. 1, above.

[153] D. P. Crook 1984: 3.

[154] On the new society's membership and concerns, see Branford 1905; Soffer 1982.

[155] *ODNB*.

[156] One of the few secondary sources on Saleeby is G. R. Searle's entry in the *ODNB*. There are also a few references to Saleeby's work on motherhood and eugenics in Richardson 2003.

case study. Saleeby's campaigns, in lectures, essays, and books from the 1900s to the 1920s, had three main elements: an attempt to revive Spencerian evolutionary biology against the increasingly dominant ideas of neo-Darwinism; a defence of a model of individual charity and philanthropy against a cumbersome and coercive form of state socialism; and an attack on the blasphemies of the newly fashionable Nietzschean philosophy. By using Spencerian science in the name of social justice and charity to attack what he saw as the elitist and heartless eugenic policies of the neo-Darwinists and Nietzscheans, Saleeby represents a reversal of one stereo-typed view, according to which eugenics was a product of conservative, *laissez-faire* 'Social Darwinism' which in turn was the product of Spencerian rather than Darwinian thought.

During the 1900s, Saleeby had a 'Science' column in the weekly *Academy and Literature*. In 1904, ten years after the publication of Drummond's and Kidd's books about evolution and altruism, Saleeby took 'The Birth of Love' as the subject for his column. The article was a rehash of Drummond's version of Spencer and Geddes, starting with the appearance of altruism in the first divisions of the living cell, through reproductive and parental instincts, up to the evolution of the mammals, the 'greatest event but one in the history of life', culminating ultimately in 'the great and unique development of altruism in man'. The echo of Drummond was strongest in Saleeby's celebration of the origins of the Christian love celebrated by St Paul. This love, Saleeby wrote, had its source in 'the breasts of the mammalian mother'. It was Spencer, rather than Drummond, however, whom Saleeby named as the source of his view: 'The philosophy of Herbert Spencer has placed maternity and maternal love on an unap-proachable and perdurable pinnacle of glory. In this it resembles Roman Catholicism—which believes that he is burning now.'[157]

The celebration of motherhood certainly did transcend religious dif-ferences. Comte's positivist cult of humanity included a secularized version of the Catholic cult of the Blessed Virgin. Spencer celebrated motherhood as part of his agnostic philosophy of evolution. And Spencerian Christians and religious eugenists in the 1890s and afterwards continued to worship maternity and the family through science. In 1914, Saleeby chose as the frontispiece to his book, *The Progress of Eugenics*, a design for a eugenically inspired stained-glass window by W. J. Ophelia Billinge (see Fig. 25). 'The

[157] C. W. Saleeby, 'Science: The Birth of Love', *Academy and Literature,* 66 (26 Mar. 1904), 356–7. Saleeby developed these views more fully, this time with reference to Geddes and Drummond as well as Spencer, in Saleeby 1906a: 249–90.

Figure 25. 'The Eastward Window' by W. J. Ophelia Billinge, used as the frontispiece to Caleb Saleeby's *The Progress of Eugenics* (1914); reproduced by permission of the Syndics of Cambridge University Library.

Eastward Window' had at its centre a naked (possibly unborn) baby. A young female figure was bent over the child in a devotional attitude while, in a third concentric circle, the father and provider was depicted in medieval dress with a sheaf of wheat. The whole image seemed to celebrate an idealized, rural, medieval, Anglo-Saxonism as well as suggesting an attitude of religious worship towards the unborn. Saleeby's reading of the image was Spencerian and Christian. The infant could be seen both as 'Nature's supreme organ of the Future' and as 'the Christ that is to be'.

Together with its parents, this child represented part of 'the Holy Trinity, Father, Mother and Child'.[158]

Saleeby's devotion to the unborn and to the parents of the future was predicated on his commitment to a Mendelian rather than a statistical approach to understanding heredity, and his continued belief in the heritability of acquired characteristics. In lectures delivered to the Société Francaise d'Eugénique in Paris in January, and the Royal Institution in London in March and April, 1914, which were published later that year as *The Progress of Eugenics*, Saleeby chastized Galton and Pearson for their reliance on statistical methods and their blinkered rejection of Mendelism.[159] Mendel had conclusively shown, Saleeby said, that heredity was not statistical. In other words, offspring did not inherit a merged average of their parents' characteristics, which could be studied by an analysis of averages and probabilities, but instead the 'unit character' of a parent would either be inherited entirely by the child, or not at all. The focus of eugenics, given this discovery, Saleeby insisted had to shift to the particular inheritance of specific individuals. The 'individual youth who wants to know whether he is justified in marrying' needed to know definite facts about his own particular genetic inheritance, not some general statement about averages. Only with this kind of positive information could a future parent who recognized their 'responsibility to the unborn' make an informed decision about whether or not to marry and reproduce.[160]

The real heart of Saleeby's argument, however was his passionate rejection of neo-Darwinism. He reminded his audience that Charles Darwin himself had proposed a 'moderate form' of the theory of natural selection, and had agreed with his 'illustrious predecessor, Lamarck' that physical influences on 'future parents' could affect the character of their offspring. Those eugenists who rejected this view and adopted a strictly neo-Darwinian view of heredity were, in effect, Saleeby said, issuing a 'condemnation of charity and altruism in all their forms'. The view that young people were 'trustees of a certain type of germ plasm *which nothing can alter*', if true, would completely obliterate the eugenic duty to nurture 'future parents', since the physical and moral care of young people would have no impact on their germ plasm and thus no effect on their offspring. In fact, Saleeby concluded, neither the Lamarckian nor the neo-Darwinian view was entirely correct, and it was the duty of eugenists to discover which

[158] Saleeby 1914: 245–7.
[159] Ibid.
[160] Ibid. 4–10, quotation at 9.

changes in the environment could affect an individual's potential as a parent and which could not.[161] He himself was a particular advocate of 'preventive eugenics', which focused on protecting future parents from the influence of 'racial poisons' such as 'intoxication or malnutrition'—the chief causes of degeneracy in offspring.[162]

Like Drummond, Kidd, and their readers in the mid-1890s, Saleeby was still worrying about the meaning of 'altruism' in the 1900s. His most developed statement on the subject came in the context of a series of lectures on 'Individualism and Collectivism' given to the British Constitutional Association during the General Election campaign of 1906 (which resulted in a disastrous defeat for Arthur Balfour's Tories, victory for the Liberals, and an increase in the number of Labour MPs from two to twenty-nine).[163] This was another opportunity for Saleeby to promote his own particular brand of Spencerian social philosophy. He compared the sort of 'ruthless' collectivism that some were advocating to the life lived by social insects, 'where the individual is nought'; and complained that individualism was too frequently confused with egoism or 'the denial of morality'. 'If there is any individualist who denies the duty of altruism,' he told his audience, 'I do not know his name and I am not of his school.' Such a thinker should read Spencer's *Data of Ethics*, Saleeby said, to see how the 'law of love' was grounded in 'cosmic fact'.[164] It was only 'individual altruism'—a direct, sympathetic social bond between giver and receiver—rather than the state-supported, indirect machinery of 'collective altruism'—that was 'really worthy of the name'. Collective altruism was 'a spurious thing to which the name of altruism should properly be denied, love not being a kind of atmosphere or cement but a personal and individual emotion'. All that such

---

[161] Saleeby 1914: 15–17; Richardson 2003: 198–203 compares Saleeby's attitudes to Lamarckism with Mona Caird's. There is a slight ambiguity in Richardson's account, which could lead to the false impression that Saleeby opposed Lamarckism.

[162] Saleeby 1914: 18–21. The previous year, at a breakfast meeting held by the Temperance Society as part of the International Congress of Medicine's meeting in London, Sir Thomas Barlow, the president of the Congress, celebrated the advances being made in the cause of teetotalism in the army and navy. He put this down to 'the growth of an altruistic conscience among the officials of those Services'. *The Times* (9 Aug. 1913), 4.

[163] Twenty-nine was the number of MPs returned who had been officially sponsored by the Labour Representation Committee. Another twenty or thirty members of the new parliament had some kind of Labour affiliation. For an interesting contemporary analysis, see a series of four articles on 'The Labour Members and the Labour Party' published in *The Times* (30 Jan. 1906), 4; (1 Feb. 1906), 13; (10 Feb. 1906), 10; (13 Feb. 1906), 4.

[164] Saleeby 1906b: 112–13. A similar defence of Spencerian, individualistic altruism can be found in J. Herbert Parsons, 'The Evolution of Altruism', *The Humanitarian: A Monthly Magazine,* 7 (1895), 459–64.

a system would achieve, Saleeby thought, was to raise a sense of injury and injustice amongst taxpayers. The effect on the average working man of such a system would be both to empty his pocket and to harden his heart. Finally, Saleeby noted, that it was only individual and not collective altruism that was endorsed by scripture. Jesus had said 'I was an hungred and ye gave me meat: I was thirsty and ye gave me drink . . . I was sick and ye visited me', not 'I was sick, and ye wrote a cheque under compulsion whereby someone else was paid to visit me.'[165]

But were there any individualist philosophers who, although Saleeby did not know their names, really did deny 'the duty of altruism'? There were, and they were even more misguided, in Saleeby's eyes, than neo-Darwinians, anti-Mendelians, or collectivists. They were the advocates of 'the pestilent doctrine of Nietzsche'. Nietzsche—'that brilliant writer but shallow thinker'—wrongly thought that his philosophy was derived from a Darwinian view of nature. He had failed to realize, Saleeby thought, that Spencer had shown that 'from the dawn of life altruism has been no less essential than egoism', and that no human being could ever survive even a single week after their birth without the altruism of others.[166] Only if he was shown a case of a self-sufficient human baby, Saleeby wrote, would he 'be prepared to retract the opinion that Nietzscheanism is the grossest, the most blasphemous, and the most grotesquely imbecile of all lies whatsoever, conceived or conceivable'.[167]

In March 1894, just over a year before his death, Thomas Huxley, now living in Eastbourne on the south coast of England, sat down to reply to a letter from Thomas Common, the country's leading exponent of the gross and blasphemous creed of Nietzscheanism. 'I will look up Nietzsche,' Huxley wrote, 'though I confess that the profit I obtain from German authors on speculative questions is not usually great.' Moving on to reply to a query about evolutionary ethics, Huxley gave a very succinct statement: 'There are two very different questions which people fail to discriminate. One is whether evolution accounts for morality, the other whether the principle of evolution in general can be adopted as an ethical principle.' He told Common that he answered the first question in the affirmative but the second strongly in the negative and that he therefore

---

[165] Saleeby 1906b: 114–21, quotations at 118, 119, 120–1. The biblical quotation is from Matt. 25: 35–6, in the King James Version.
[166] The quotation is from Spencer 1879: 201.
[167] Saleeby 1906a: 285–6.

rejected 'all so-called evolutional ethics'.[168] Common had been thinking about evolution and ethics in 1894 as a result of reading Kidd's *Social Evolution*. Reviewing that work, Common wrote that it was a 'remarkable effort to extend the domain of Darwinian science to social phenomena'; that it was certainly preferable to the popular theological mystifications of Drummond's *Ascent of Man*; and that its success indicated a widespread interest in the subject. However, he added, a much greater 'flood of light' had been shed on this subject by the writings of Nietzsche, who had shown that English and French writers on sociology had mistaken their own decaying and decadent instincts for the highest aspirations of the human character.[169]

Thomas Common, like Thomas Huxley, but for very different reasons, rejected all attempts, such as those made by Drummond, Kidd, and Saleeby, to draw progressivist altruistic morals from evolutionary science. He agreed instead with what Nietzsche had written in *The Twilight of the Idols*, and quoted from his own translation of that work: 'Our Socialists are *décadents*, Mr Herbert Spencer, however, is also a *decadent*—he sees something desirable in the triumph of altruism.'[170] Common and the other early British Nietzscheans were not the only ones starting to rebel against 'altruism' in the closing years of the nineteenth century.

[168] L. Huxley 1903: iii. 302–3.
[169] Thomas Common, 'English Philosophers from Nietzsche's Standpoint I: Mr Benjamin Kidd', *To-Morrow*, 2 (1896), 40–8. Included in box of Benjamin Kidd papers in Cambridge University Library: Add.8069/Misc.1 (Box 6 of 7).
[170] Ibid. 41. Nietzsche's *Götzen-Dämmerung* was first published in 1889. Thomas Common's was the first English translation. See Nietzsche 1896: 201. The quotation is from *Twiliglight of the Idols*, 'Expeditions of an Untimely Man', s. 37; for a translation in a modern edn, see Nietzsche 1990: 103.

Chapter Eight

Egomania

Christ was not merely the supreme individualist, but he was the first individualist in history. People have tried to make him out an ordinary philanthropist, or ranked him as an altruist with the unscientific and sentimental. But he was really neither one nor the other.

Oscar Wilde, *De Profundis* (1905), 176

Post-Victorians

When Friedrich Nietzsche mocked those who saw something desirable in the triumph of altruism, and when Oscar Wilde wrote of his desire to be freed from 'that sordid necessity of living for others', the principal object of their attacks was not, as might be supposed, Christianity.[1] Nietzsche and Wilde were, rather, reacting against the earnestness of George Eliot and the English positivists; the ethical naturalism of Herbert Spencer and his followers; the philanthropy of Mrs Humphry Ward and the university settlements; and the socialism of Robert Blatchford and Beatrice Webb. In short, they were reacting against the Victorian culture of altruism that has been the subject of this book.[2] In doing so, they helped to articulate individualistic, egoistic, and artistic moral visions that appealed to a new generation of post-Victorians.

A commitment to 'altruism' had meant different things to different people. The same was true of opposition to it. Some rejected the language of altruism, as we have seen, because of its associations with atheism, positivism, Spencerian evolution, or socialism. The anti-altruists who form the

---

[1] *Twilight of the Idols*, 'Expeditions of an Untimely Man', s. 37; Nietzsche 1990: 103; Wilde 1999: 1. For the suggestion that Wilde's rejection of living for others was primarily an attack on Christianity, see Murray's explanatory note, ibid. 198.

[2] Of course Nietzsche combined his critique of Victorian moralism with a trenchant attack on Christianity. However, his specific preoccupation with 'altruism' was, as we shall see below, a reaction primarily against Spencerian rather than Christian ethics.

subject of the present chapter, however, were trying to break free from that whole world of characteristically Victorian moral debates. They wanted to create a new moral language and a new kind of ethics. They were not interested in disagreements about whether 'altruism' or 'charity' was a 'sweeter or better word', nor in questions about the exact balance of moral duties one owed to one's family, nation, race, or species. When they thought about altering economic and social arrangements it was with a view to securing a future that was less rather than more altruistic. They did not debate which kinds of conduct were most conducive to the general happiness. Instead, these post-Victorians wanted to talk about friendship, love, art, and the emotions. In their moral lives, they did not seek to follow nature, but to follow their own hearts. By using the term 'post-Victorian', I intend to characterize the writings of these individualists, egoists, and aesthetes as being formed in an antagonistic but intimate relationship with the Victorian moralism that went before.[3]

Earlier Victorian debates were about whether, and to what degree, human beings should primarily love God or love their neighbours. Some loved the poor; others loved their nation; some even loved the whole of humanity, past, present, and future. The resources of Christianity, evolutionary science, and Victorian domestic ideology could all also be marshalled to legitimate and celebrate the reciprocal love between a man and a woman, and between a woman and her children. These were the dominant forms of Victorian love, sanctioned by God and by nature alike. Post-Victorian moral philosophies, in contrast, were produced to legitimate intense Platonic love, homosexual love, love of beauty, and self-love. Aestheticism, decadence, German philosophy, and Hellenism all provided intellectual and artistic resources for the expression of these post-Victorian passions. The valuing of these kinds of love, and their associated ethical doctrines of individualism and egoism, placed discussions of altruism in a new light. Post-Victorian moralists sometimes advocated 'individualism' or 'egoism' in direct opposition to altruism, but sometimes bypassed or rejected the language of 'altruism' and 'egoism' altogether, along with the dichotomies that

---

[3] In other words, I intend 'post-Victorian' to stand in a similar relationship to 'Victorian' as 'post-modern' does to 'modern'—to imply both commonality and antagonism as well as temporal succession. Pedersen and Mandler 1994 is a collection of biographical studies of moralists, intellectuals, and social reformers, including Henrietta Barnett, Leonard Woolf, and J. M. Keynes, which pays attention to questions of continuity and discontinuity between the political and moral outlooks of the Victorian and post-Victorian ages.

it implied. In this they were following philosophical idealists of the 1880s such as T. H. Green, Edward Caird, and Henry Jones.[4]

In his iconoclastic *Principia Ethica*, G. E. Moore provided a bold defence of this new approach. At the outset of that book, Moore signalled that he intended to use the word 'ethics' not, as most Victorian moral philosophers had, to refer to the study of what was 'good or bad in human conduct', but rather to signify 'the general enquiry into what is good'.[5] The celebration of love, beauty, and friendship rather than useful or altruistic conduct was one of the central outcomes of that general enquiry. Published in 1903, this canonical work—which did for Victorian values through analytic philosophy what Lytton Strachey's *Eminent Victorians* (1918) would do through biography—is sometimes treated as if it were both the first and the last word on the pitfalls of ethical naturalism. Moore claimed that Herbert Spencer (and all other major ethical theorists), in identifying the ethical predicate 'good' with non-ethical predicates, such as 'useful' or 'evolved' or 'pleasurable', had committed what Moore called the 'naturalistic fallacy'. The originality and importance of this aspect of Moore's work have sometimes been overstated.[6] *Principia Ethica* features in the current chapter not primarily as the harbinger of the 'naturalistic fallacy' but rather as a retrospective philosophical justification of the cultural and moral movements of the 1890s that formed the context for Moore's young adulthood and Cambridge education.

While it may be true that *Principia Ethica* 'provided the definitive starting-point for twentieth-century ethical theory', the aim of this chapter is rather to consider the prehistory of the work—to read it in the context of the 1890s rather than as a precursor to later twentieth-century philosophy.[7] We can start to get a feel for this prehistory through an

---

[4] See Ch. 6 above.

[5] *Principia Ethica*, ss. 1–2; G. E. Moore 1993: 53–5, quotations at 54.

[6] Hurka 2003 provides a very full analysis of the respects in which Moore's arguments for the indefinable nature of 'good' were similar to ideas found in the published works of Henry Sidgwick and others. A further example not mentioned by Hurka is to be found in Schneewind 1977: 182–3, which gives a summary of an argument used by W. G. Ward, over thirty years before Moore's *Principia Ethica* (1903), and two years before Sidgwick's *Methods of Ethics* (1874), against Mill's attempts to analyse the meaning of 'morally good' in utilitarian terms, focusing on the indefinability and unanalysable nature of the 'good'. The article in question was William George Ward, 'Mr Mill on the Foundations of Morality', *Dublin Review* (1872); repr. in W. G. Ward 1884: i. MacIntyre 1984: 14–20, casts doubt on the philosophical value of Moore's *Principia Ethica* and seeks other explanations for its iconic status.

[7] The quotation about *Principia Ethica* is from Thomas Baldwin's introd. to his revised edn of that work: G. E. Moore 1993: p. xxxvii.

examination of a single key year—1895—before looking at some particular aspects of the individualism, egoism, and aestheticism of Britain in the 1890s in more detail.

1895: New men and degeneration

Two public figures whose careers took particularly dramatic turns during 1895 were Arthur Balfour and Oscar Wilde. January saw the publication of a very well received work of philosophy by Balfour, *The Foundations of Belief*, in which he complained that, according to the creed of evolutionary naturalism, 'the august sentiments which cling to the ideas of duty and sacrifice are nothing better than a device of Nature to trick us into performing altruistic actions'.[8] The philosopher Conwy Lloyd Morgan thought it 'one of the most remarkable books of modern times'. 'Mr Balfour has weighed naturalism in the balance', Morgan announced, 'and found it wanting.'[9] Balfour's proposed alternative to evolutionary naturalism was a kind of theism in which authority and tradition, rather than scientific naturalism, provided a bedrock for morality.[10] On the whole, the British public in 1895 seemed to prefer Balfour's conservative authoritarianism to some of the more radical visions of society on offer. At the general election in the summer, the Liberal government was defeated, and neither the Social Democratic Federation nor the Independent Labour Party won a single seat. The Conservative Party was returned with a huge majority, and the most senior member of Lord Salisbury's government in the House of Commons was Arthur Balfour.[11]

If Balfour stood for authority and tradition, Oscar Wilde represented what was most new and most unsettling in modern culture. At the start of 1895, he was at the height of his fame as a dandy, an aesthete, and the writer of clever and irreverent West End plays. In January *An Ideal Husband* had opened at the Theatre Royal, Haymarket, followed, on St Valentine's day, by the first night of *The Importance of Being Earnest* at the St James's theatre.

---

[8] Balfour 1895: 16.

[9] C. Lloyd Morgan, 'Naturalism', *Monist*, 6 (1895), 76–90, at 76.

[10] On Balfour's philosophical works, see K. Young 1963; Zebel 1973; Jacyna 1980; Root 1980; Lightman 1997a.

[11] The Conservative Party under Salisbury, and then Balfour himself, remained in power for the next ten years. In 1895, Balfour was appointed First Lord of the Treasury. He would become Prime Minister in 1902.

Audiences were delighted by the elegant mockery of their own values of philanthropy, optimism, and earnestness. A few days after the opening of *The Importance of Being Earnest*, the marquess of Queensberry (the father of Wilde's intimate friend Lord Alfred Douglas) left a card for Wilde at the Albermarle Club reading, 'For Oscar Wilde, posing as somdomite'. Despite the poor spelling and syntax, it was clear what was being alleged. Wilde, encouraged by Alfred Douglas, sued Queensberry for libel. Queensberry's lawyers called several young men as witnesses who testified to having had sex with Wilde. The libel action failed and in April Wilde was arrested and charged with gross indecency. By the end of May, Wilde's plays had been closed, his reputation destroyed, and he had started a two-year prison sentence with hard labour. By the end of the year he had, in addition, been declared bankrupt. His home, along with all his books and possessions, were sold to pay Queensberry's legal costs.[12]

The trials of Oscar Wilde represented one dramatic climax of late Victorian debates about the naturalness and morality of different kinds of love. Interrogated in court about the 'Two Loves' referred to in Alfred Douglas's poem of that name, Wilde denied that they could be summarized as 'natural' love on the one had and 'unnatural' love on the other. There was nothing 'unnatural' about 'The love that dare not speak its name', Wilde told the court. It was 'such a great affection of an elder for a younger man as there was between David and Jonathan, such as Plato made the very basis of his philosophy, and such as you find in the sonnets of Michelangelo and Shakespeare'. It was a beautiful and intellectual kind of love.[13] Others in the 1890s named this sort of passion 'Uranian', 'homogenic', or 'inverted'.[14] Havelock Ellis, himself a heterosexual, was at the centre of a group of writers and radicals who were interested in exploring male homosexuality in the 1890s through science, medicine, and philosophy; he was also one of the first serious British commentators on the egoistic philosophy of Friedrich Nietzsche.[15]

Ellis was, in his sexological and philosophical interests, representative of an emerging type that could be called the 'new man'. Alongside that more famous creature of the 1890s, the 'new woman', the new man was searching

[12] *ODNB*; Hyde 1962; Foldy 1997; Raby 1997; Sloan 2003.
[13] Hyde 1962: 200–1.
[14] Weeks 1989, 1990; L. Hall 2000.
[15] *ODNB*; Thatcher 1970: 89–120; Himmelfarb 1995: 189.

for a post-Victorian philosophy of life.[16] He could look for it in cynical and pessimistic novels by George Gissing or Thomas Hardy (whose *Jude the Obscure* came out in 1895) or in the revolutionary revaluations of values performed by Friedrich Nietzsche (whose work was translated into English for the first time in 1895).[17] He could immerse himself in the drama of Richard Wagner's epic operas; quote the clever witticisms of Oscar Wilde; revel in philosophical paradoxes. The new man was unimpressed by traditional morality; rejected the sentimental and earnest philanthropy of his parents; experimented with unconventional sexual relationships. His experiments in modern love could have been with a liberated new woman such as Herminia, the heroine of Grant Allen's 1895 novel, *The Woman Who Did*, who shocked her suitor by proposing an extramarital sexual relationship, or such as her real-life counterpart, the young socialist Edith Lanchester, who was briefly confined to a lunatic asylum by her family in October 1895 when she declared her intention to live with her fellow socialist James Sullivan without marrying him.[18] Alternatively, a new man might have sought his pleasures with another man, moved by the kind of desire made famous by Oscar Wilde.

The new man was also looking for a vision of life and for sources of moral authority that relied upon neither traditional Christianity nor optimistic scientific naturalism. Two young men in their twenties, from quite different backgrounds, were in the midst of just such a quest during 1895. One of them was William Roberts, the son of a Lancashire tailor. He was working as a bank clerk in Liverpool. The other, George Moore (later always known by his initials—G. E.), was from an affluent middle-class family. Having been educated at a London public school, Dulwich College, he was now studying moral philosophy under the supervision of Henry Sidgwick and others at Trinity College, Cambridge. How were these two young men trying to make moral meanings for themselves in 1895?

---

[16] On the 'new woman', see Ch. 7 above. The 'new man', unlike the 'new woman', was not a type recognized and discussed by the late Victorians themselves. The sketch in this paragraph is my own attempt to characterize a certain type of the 1890s. On the ways that 'new men' of the 1880s and 1890s combined asceticism and aestheticism in the activity of 'slumming', see Koven 2004: esp. 273–6. See also Himmelfarb 1995: ch. 7; Tosh 2005.

[17] The earliest published translation of a complete work by Nietzsche was Thomas Common's translation of *The Case of Wagner*, which was published in the *Fortnightly Review* in Sept. 1895; Thatcher 1970: 25. In the following year, the first of a projected 11–vol. edn of Nietzsche's works in English came out, which included this translation and several other works: Nietzsche 1896.

[18] On the Lanchester case see entries for Edith Lanchester and her daughter Elsa Sullivan Lanchester in *ODNB*; *The Times* (28 Oct. 1895), 13 and (30 Oct. 1895), 10; and Hunt 1996: ch. 4.

William Roberts was a young man with an identity problem. He had been born in Everton, Lancashire, in 1868 and brought up in the Anglican faith. Having studied literature, philosophy, and art at University College, Liverpool, his initial plans to join the Indian civil service were frustrated by health problems, and instead he found himself in a clerical job in a local bank. In 1894, at the age of 25, he was elected president of the Liverpool branch of the National Secular Society. It was around this time, having violently rejected the Anglican faith of his childhood, that Roberts began to create an alter ego, 'Ernest Newman'.[19] He started using the name in the early 1890s, and adopted it when writing his first book, *Gluck and the Opera*, which was published in 1895. The name was intended to signify that he wrote as 'a new man in earnest', and he retained the name throughout the rest of his career.[20] Under that name he wrote an appreciative article about Oscar Wilde, which was published in a freethinking monthly, the *Free Review* in June 1895—a time when praise for Wilde was, for obvious reasons, largely absent from the periodical press.[21] The following year Newman wrote about Nietzsche, also for the *Free Review*.[22] It is hard to say exactly what changes of identity accompanied the transition from 'William Roberts' to 'Ernest Newman' since, as his wife later recalled, 'he would not

---

[19] One of the fullest sources on Newman's life is an unpublished work by Henry George Farmer, entitled *Ernest Newman: As I Saw Him.* A bound typescript of this work, dated 1962, is held in the Special Collections of Glasgow University Library (where Farmer held the post of Keeper of Music); MS Farmer 44. The same collection includes an earlier, unbound version of the Farmer typescript, which includes passages that are struck out in pencil and do not appear in the bound typescript; MS Farmer 42. See also the obituary in *The Times* (8 July 1959), 8; *ODNB*; van Thal 1955; E. Newman 1962; V. Newman 1963. On the rise and fall of the secularist movement, which peaked in terms of membership in the mid-1880s, and the National Secular Society, founded in 1866, and dominated by the leadership of Charles Bradlaugh through the 1870s and 1880s, see Royle 1974, 1980.

[20] His earliest writings under the name 'Ernest Newman' were essays for the *National Reformer* and the *Free Review*, written in the late 1880s and early 1890s; see the 2 vols of compilations of Newman's 'Early Press Contributions' in the Glasgow University Library Special Collections, Farmer q493 and Farmer q456. His first book published under that name was the 1895 book on Gluck. See E. Newman 1895; van Thal 1962: p. xii.

[21] Ernest Newman, 'Oscar Wilde: A Literary Appreciation', *Free Review* (1 June 1895), 193–206; reproduced in Beckson 1970: 202–10.

[22] Ernest Newman, 'Friedrich Nietzsche', *Free Review* (1 May 1896), 113–22. Both this article and the article on Wilde were summarized in the *Review of Reviews*. In both cases, Newman's name was given incorrectly—as 'Arthur Newman' on the first occasion and 'Edward Newman' on the second. *Review of Reviews*, 11 (1895), 539; 13 (1896), 421.

discuss his early years with anybody, not even with me'.[23] However, the
basic trajectory is clear.

The Christianity of Newman's childhood was displaced by an aggressive scientific rationalism, inspired by his association with the Liverpool
secularists and his friendship with the freethinker J. M. Robertson in the
early 1890s. As a secularist lecturer, Newman gave public addresses in
Liverpool, Chester, and Manchester between 1894 and 1896 on topics
including 'The Social Philosophy of Ibsen', 'Theism, Atheism, and
Pantheism', 'The Culture of the Emotions', 'Oscar Wilde', 'Life in Ancient
Greece', and 'The Evolution of Humanity'.[24] Newman's secularism also
found its expression in an 1897 book published under yet another name,
Hugh Mortimer Cecil.[25] This book, which was mentioned above among
the many critical responses to Drummond's *Ascent of Man* (1894) and Kidd's
Social Evolution (1894), was entitled *Pseudo-Philosophy at the End of the
Nineteenth Century*, and was dedicated to the memory of Charles Darwin.
In it Newman set out to 'show how three of the modern champions of theology have fared in their attempts to capture the scientific fortress by the
use of pseudo-scientific methods'.[26] For a man seeking to establish his identity as a rationalistic unbeliever, attempts by widely read authors such as
Kidd, Drummond, and Balfour to reconcile religion and morality with science were contemptible. In the persona of Hugh Mortimer Cecil,
Newman ridiculed Kidd's idea that 'altruistic and humanitarian feelings, in
their widest aspect, are purely outgrowths of Christianity'. Even 'the slightest acquaintance with pagan literature' would have revealed to Mr Kidd the

[23] V. Newman 1963: 3. The unpublished book about Ernest Newman by Henry George Farmer,
referenced in n. 20 above, gives more detail on Newman's early life and his career as a rationalist
writer and secularist lecturer. There is correspondence between Farmer and Vera Newman in
1960, partly relating to Newman's early life; Glasgow Special Collections, MS Farmer 47, esp. ff.
58–60, 67.

[24] Lists of Newman's secularist lectures and journal articles are included as appendices to the
unbound version of Farmer's *Ernest Newman: As I Saw Him*, referenced in n. 20 above; Glasgow
University Library Special Collections MS Farmer 43/7.

[25] Cecil 1897. Newman's authorship of this work is asserted in *ODNB* and Cumberland 1919:
146. Glasgow University Library holds a copy of the book into which a letter from the
Superintendent of the British Museum Music Room, dated 6 Apr. 1960, has been pasted. The letter is addressed to H. G. Farmer at Glasgow University Library and confirms that the Museum
now has 'sufficient evidence to introduce Ernest Newman's pseudonymous status into our catalogues, at long last'; Glasgow University Library Special Collections Farmer q218. All this name-
changing has resulted in some understandable confusions. In an anthology of critical responses to
George Meredith, 'Ernest Newman' is described as a pseudonym used by Hugh Mortimer Cecil;
I. Williams 1971: 412.

[26] Cecil 1897: pp. vii–ix.

falsity of that idea, he wrote. Before the Christian era, the Stoics had already recognized that men were made 'to be social and to love one another'.[27] The critique of Drummond focused on the dangers of trying to read ethical 'altruism' into the natural world. 'To credit Nature with intentions in this manner', he argued, 'even when they are good intentions and to call it science, is simply to make a monkey jabber through a human mask and call it acting.'[28]

Having rejected the Christianity of his childhood, the popular scientific 'trash' of Kidd and Drummond, and, ultimately, the activist secularism of Robertson's kind too, where was Ernest Newman now to turn for ethical inspiration?[29] His 1895 article on Wilde provided a clue. He had asked his readers, 'Are we not weary of dull respectability?' He told them that Wilde was right: imaginative hedonism was superior to philistine self-sacrifice as an ethical doctrine; the public should be grateful for the example of a man who 'can love beauty for herself alone'.[30] The fact that Wilde's poems did not lend themselves to quotation in 'the hymn-books of the Independent Labour Party' was a fact very much in their favour. Newman had arrived at an identification with Wildean aestheticism, but through what particular works of art could he live this out?

By his own account, Newman had been drawn towards 'brooding introspection and philosophical melancholy' as a young man. He could be seen with his nose buried in serious philosophical books as he walked the streets of Liverpool, running errands for the bank. 'Street-reading, though, has its perils', Newman recalled. On one occasion he walked into a lamp-post while reading Hegel: 'I had not thought much of the Hegelian philosophy before that, and I thought still less of it after.' It was another brooding German, Richard Wagner, whose works were finally to provide Newman with the inspiration and vision he had been seeking.[31] His first published writing on Wagner was an article on Nietzsche and Wagner for the *Free Review* in 1896.[32] Half a century later, in 1947, the fourth and final volume of his definitive *Life of Richard Wagner* would be published.[33] By that time he had become established as Britain's leading authority on Wagner.

---

[27] Ibid. 71–4.

[28] Ibid. 155.

[29] Newman described Kidd's book as 'trash' in the context of his recollections of his friend J. M. Robertson, included in Robertson 1936: i, pp. xxi–xxvii, at xxvi.

[30] Beckson 1970: 208–10.

[31] E. Newman 1962,:8, 12, 29.

[32] Ernest Newman, 'Friedrich Nietzsche', 113–22.

[33] E. Newman 1933–47.

The formative years of the 1890s were not entirely forgotten, however. During the last Christmas of his long life, in 1958, Ernest Newman spent one evening watching a performance on television of Oscar Wilde's *An Ideal Husband*. He died the following year at the age of 90.[34]

In 1895, as the Wilde scandal unfolded, the conservatives campaigned successfully to get back into government, and Ernest Newman published on Oscar Wilde and hedonism, G. E. Moore was enjoying his first year as a philosophy student in Cambridge.[35] Moore had experienced a brief period of evangelical Christian fervour as a teenager, but he later recalled that 'long before I left school, I was, to use a word then popular, a complete Agnostic'.[36] Like the secularist Ernest Newman, the agnostic George Moore turned to philosophy and the arts in search of alternative sources of meaning. Among the lectures he attended, the ones he found least interesting were those given by Henry Sidgwick on moral philosophy (these included a lengthy critique of Herbert Spencer's treatment of egoism and altruism, and a discussion of *Social Evolution* by Benjamin Kidd, who was himself invited to the Cambridge Ethical Society in early 1895).[37] Moore preferred James Ward's lectures on Lotze and Schopenhauer, and John McTaggart's lectures on Hegel. Again like Ernest Newman, Moore did not retain an interest in Hegel: 'After these two years in which I was obliged to read some Hegel, I never thought it worth while to read him again.'[38]

What Moore did find worthwhile in 1895 was the cultivation of intense Platonic friendships and the enjoyment of music. In the Easter

[34] V. Newman 1963: 263.

[35] Moore went up to Trinity College, Cambridge, in 1892. He was awarded a first in Part I of the Classical Tripos in 1894. From then on he combined his study of classics with work for the Moral Sciences Tripos (within which he concentrated on philosophy). In 1896 he graduated with first-class honours in moral sciences and second-class in classics. The best sources on Moore's life, in addition to the *ODNB*, are G. E. Moore 1968; Levy 1981.

[36] On Moore's period of Christianity, see G. E. Moore 1968: 10–12; Levy 1981: 39–42. Two books of essays written by Moore as a schoolboy for his 'Divinity' lessons between 1889 and 1892 are held in the G. E. Moore papers, CUL Add.8330.5/3/1–2.

[37] G. E. Moore undergraduate lecture notes; CUL Add.8875/10/2/1. For Moore's appraisal for these lectures, see G. E. Moore 1968: 16–17. Kidd had met Sidgwick at a feast at Trinity College, Cambridge, in Dec. 1893; D. P. Crook 1984: 51. For the invitation to the Cambridge Ethical Society, see Benjamin Kidd papers, letters from Sheldon Amos dated 23 Jan. and 4 Feb. 1895; CUL Add.8069/A39–40. On Sidgwick's criticism of Spencer, see Ch. 5 above. The lectures by Sidgwick which Moore attended were later published as H. Sidgwick 1902.

[38] G. E. Moore 1968: 19. Bertrand Russell also rebelled against the Hegelian tendency in Cambridge philosophy around this time. On the dominance of John McTaggart's personality and his neo-Hegelian philosophy in the Cambridge circles in which Russell and Moore both moved in the 1890s, and especially within the 'Apostles', see Russell 1961: 34–5; Levy 1981: 100–9; Griffin 1991: 45–55.

vacation that year, Moore went on a reading party in the Lake District with some fellow Cambridge students, including Ralph Vaughan Williams and George Trevelyan. The comrades kept a log book of the trip which reveals that the group debated theology, literature, and evolution by natural selection, amongst other things.[39] As the 'Wordsworthians of the party', Moore and Trevelyan walked to Grasmere and Rydal.[40] During the summer, Moore spent five weeks at the university of Tübingen. While he was there he attended the Wagner season at the Munich opera, as well as attending lectures on Kant and Plato at the university.[41] In October, Moore was back in Cambridge, planning to read some more Plato himself, practising Schumann sonatas on the piano, and writing to his father that the present he would like to mark his impending twenty-second birthday was the vocal score of Wagner's *Parsifal*.[42]

Towards the end of the year, Moore presented papers to three student societies in Cambridge. He gave a paper on ethics to the Moral Science Club, and one on the relationship between habit and moral character to the 'Apostles'.[43] This last society was a secret intellectual discussion group to which Moore had been elected the previous year. George Trevelyan and Bertrand Russell were also members at the time. The meetings of the 'Apostles', in which philosophical debates were frequently intermingled with far from conventional speculations about sex and homosexuality, was the most important arena within which Moore's personal relationships and his philosophical ethics were to develop side by side, as Paul Levy has shown. In November 1895, Moore gave a paper to the Sunday Essay Society on aesthetics. The central theme of this essay was the meaning of beauty and its relationship with human emotions. Moore's conclusion was that 'a man is essentially more beautiful than a tree, because his nature, as emotion, is higher'; and that the highest forms of human emotion were expressed in works of art.[44] In short, Moore had, like Newman, reached the conclusion by 1895 that it was in art and beauty rather than in Christianity or in science that moral meanings were to be found. As we shall see below, this commitment was also central to Moore's *Principia Ethica*, which was published eight years later.

[39] A photographic copy of the logbook is held in the G. E. Moore papers, CUL Add.8830.6/4.
[40] Levy 1981: 151.
[41] G. E. Moore 1968: 20; Levy 1981: 167.
[42] Levy 1981: 168–9.
[43] Ibid. 169, 173–7.
[44] Ibid. 169–73, quotation at 173.

In taking their inspiration from individualistic and egoistic figures such as Oscar Wilde, Richard Wagner, and Friedrich Nietzsche, the new men of the 1890s were showing clear signs of what the physician and cultural critic Max Nordau had identified as a peculiar psychopathological condition: 'degeneration'. First published in German in 1892, his book *Degeneration* appeared in English in 1895 and was promptly recommended by *The Times*. The book's main message was that 'Degenerates are not always criminals, prostitutes, anarchists, and pronounced lunatics; they are often authors and artists.'[45] The *Review of Reviews* included *Degeneration* in its 'Monthly Parcel of Books' for March, along with Grant Allen's *The Woman Who Did* and Arthur Balfour's *Foundations of Belief*. Nordau's work, the *Review of Reviews* thought, was a 'bad but interesting book', in which the attack on contemporary egoism was 'pressed home unsparingly'.[46] In the following months, the Wilde trials provided a focus for further public debates about aestheticism and decadence as symptoms of a wider degeneration that threatened the health of the social body and the vigour of the British empire.[47] H. G. Wells's scientific romance, *The Time Machine*, which was 'the talk of the town' that summer, centred around the same themes.[48] In this futuristic dystopia, humanity had degenerated into two separate races (descended from the working and upper classes of the nineteenth century): the bestial Morlocks and the effete and ineffectual Eloi.

Nordau divided the degenerates of the 1890s into two basic categories—the mystics and the egomaniacs. Wagner was a mystic, Wilde and Nietzsche were egomaniacs. Nordau quoted from scientific authorities such as the criminologist Cesare Lombroso and the psychologist Paul Sollier to substantiate his claim that one of the leading characteristics of the degenerate was his overweening egoism.[49] The healthy individual, on the other hand, Nordau thought, developed beyond egoism to the stage that had been named 'altruism' by Auguste Comte and Herbert Spencer. In a tacit criticism of Geddes and Thomson's *Evolution of Sex*, Nordau went on to explain that 'altruism' was no mere development of the sexual or reproductive instincts, which treated the other as a satisfaction for

---

[45] *The Times* (8 Mar. 1895), 12; Nordau 1993: p. v. On the history of 'degeneration', see Pick 1989.
[46] *Review of Reviews*, 11 (1895), 291.
[47] Hyde 1962; Foldy 1997; Raby 1997. On the broader cultural milieu of the 1890s see Jackson 1972; Stokes 1989; Beckson 1992; Hill 1997.
[48] The story was serialized in W. E. Henley's *New Review* from January onwards, and appeared as a book in May. See *The Times* (31 May 1895), 8. On the success of the book, see 'Our Monthly Parcel of Books', *Review of Reviews*, 12 (1895), 267–70, at 267.
[49] Nordau 1993: 244.

a pressing physical appetite. Rather, it was a genuine concern for another based on 'sympathy or curiosity'.[50] In summary: 'Not till he attains to altruism is man in a condition to maintain himself in society and in nature.'[51] In a later essay on the 'Philosophy and Morals of War', written for a collection entitled *Briton and Boer: Both Sides of the South African Question*, Nordau warned again that all modern culture was tending to encourage 'ruthless egotism' and the 'delirium of self-love'. Until the individual felt 'his solidarity with the race', society would be dominated by conflicts, wars, and megalomania.[52]

The celebration of art and beauty for their own sakes, the elevation of culture above nature, and the experience of intense aesthetic emotions— all of these things were morally liberating for young men of the 1890s such as Ernest Newman and G. E. Moore. For Max Nordau, however, they were the classic symptoms of degeneration. Oscar Wilde's individualistic aestheticism was nothing more than 'a purely anti-socialistic, ego-maniacal recklessness and hysterical longing to make a sensation'.[53] At the time of his trials, when Oscar Wilde had certainly succeeded in making a sensation, he was denounced in the press for being both artificial and an egotist.[54] In other words, he was the anti-type of those individuals celebrated by Comte, Spencer, Drummond, or Nordau who followed nature and thus became altruists.

Queensberry, Wilde, and Christ

Boxer, jockey, cyclist, poet, secularist, and scourge of the degenerate—the marquess of Queensberry shared Nordau's fears about the health of the modern European races.[55] He had always believed that it was everyone's duty to remain physically vigorous for the future good of the race, and he was an admirer of the evolutionary agnosticism of Herbert Spencer. This philosophy of life was given its idiosyncratic expression in a poem, *The*

---

[50] On Geddes and Thomson and Drummond, see Ch. 7 above. An article by James Bixby, published in the *New World* in Sept. 1895, used both Drummond and Nordau in arguing for the naturalness of altruism, and the altruism of nature. See *Review of Reviews*, 13 (1895), 328.
[51] Nordau 1993: 252–3.
[52] Bryce 1900: 230–51, quotations at 250–1. In this respect, Nordau was in agreement with Spencer's criticism of the lack of altruism between nations; see Ch. 5 above.
[53] Nordau 1993: 319.
[54] See Foldy 1997: 53–4.
[55] On Queensberry's views on decadence, degeneration, health, and sexuality, see Denisoff 1999.

Spirit of the Matterhorn (1881), in which Queensberry communicated his belief that the human soul was the product of the body and that, therefore, there was no personal immortality.[56] Like many positivists and freethinkers before him, he characterized the hope for individual immortality as 'selfish' and contrasted it with his own view, which was that the real happiness that should be hoped for was the happiness of future generations who would inherit 'healthy, evenly-balanced organizations' so long as their parents and grandparents had lived healthy lives, and obeyed 'Nature's laws'.[57]

Queensberry's poem combined positivist ideas about the selfishness of the desire for personal immortality with a Spencerian vision of a future utopia secured by the inheritance of increasingly perfect bodily and moral constitutions. It compared individual souls to drops of water:

> Death sinks all individuality
> In the great essence of an eternal power,
> As rain-drops lose themselves within the sea,
> There find repose: then as those ocean-drops
> Drawn heavenwards to the sky, in mist and spray,
> Each drop becomes a part of millions more,
> Thus ever gaining fresh identity.[58]

Most of the poem was written as a message to humanity spoken by a 'spirit' who had appeared to the author in a dream. The spirit seemed to have been reading works by Herbert Spencer or by neo-Malthusian advocates of birth control:

> Go, tell mankind, see that thy blood be pure,
> And visit not thy sins upon thy race;
> Curse not thy future age with poisoned blood,
> For cursing, it shall curse thee back again.
> And in that distant age, when selfishness,
> The lingering remnant of man's savage state,
> Has been subdued and kept within control
> By true religion of humanity,

---

[56] Queensberry 1881. In a preface to the poem, Queensberry explained that his main reason for publishing it was to provide a response to the peers of Scotland, who at the election in 1880 had deprived him of his seat in the House of Lords on the grounds of his religious infidelity. The preface explained his belief in 'The Inscrutable', which was a god-like if not actually divine power. Queensberry was a committed secularist, serving as president of the British Secularist Union. This organization was a splinter group that broke off from Bradlaugh's National Secular Society in 1877, and was disbanded in 1884. *ODNB*.

[57] Queensberry 1881: 5, 14–17. On earlier arguments about the selfishness of the hope for personal immortality, see Ch. 3 above.

[58] Ibid. 22.

> I can foretell the time when all may claim
> With equal right to reproduce their kind.
> Alas, 'tis not so now; for there are they
> Who, either from hereditary sin,
> Or from the sin they have themselves entailed,
> Possess no right to be progenitors.[59]

The theosophical magazine *Lucifer* reviewed the poem several years later and asserted that its author was clearly 'filled with the spirit of true Theosophy and Altruism', since he accepted that the progress of humanity would only be achieved once man had recognized his 'stern responsibility' both to himself and to the future of the race.[60]

Nordau and Queensberry, then, both saw a strong connection between morality and health, and between immorality and disease. Like other physical diseases, certain kinds of immorality, conceived as forms of insanity such as egomania or monomania, could be passed on through the generations. In a letter to the *Star* on the eve of Wilde's first criminal trial, Queensberry drew an apparently sympathetic conclusion from this view, namely that Wilde, if found guilty, should be treated with all possible consideration, 'as a sexual pervert of an utterly diseased mind, and not as a sane criminal'.[61] In the *Review of Reviews*, W. T. Stead struck a similar note, saying that many people had described Wilde's actions as 'unnatural vices' but that for an 'abnormal person' such as Wilde, they were in fact entirely natural.[62]

On one occasion, at least, Wilde himself adopted the same position, using the language of medical science to argue for the appropriateness of compassion in his case. This was in a petition to the Home Secretary, written in July 1896, after thirteen months of his sentence had been served. Wilde wrote that he was suffering from a form of 'sexual madness' which should be treated by a physician rather than punished by the law. 'In the works of eminent men of science such as Lombroso and Nordau', Wilde noted, 'this is specially insisted on with reference to the intimate

---

[59] Ibid. 25. On Spencerian views about morality and heredity, see Chs 5 and 7 above.
[60] 'The Spirit of the Matterhorn', *Lucifer*, 5 (1889), 352–4, at 352. The review criticized Queensberry for denying personal immortality and describing the soul as the physical product of the body. This review gave rise to a meeting between Queensberry and Mme Blavatsky, and to a published exchange in the *Agnostic Journal* between the two on their differing views about personal immortality. Lord Queensberry's article was published on 27 Sept. 1890, 194–5; Madame Blavatsky's reply on 4 Oct. 1890, 214–15. Both are reproduced on the website of the Blavatsky Study Centre (see Bibliography for details).
[61] Quoted in Foldy 1997: 65.
[62] *Review of Reviews*, 11 (1895), 491–2.

connection between madness and the literary and artistic temperament'. Nordau, in *Degeneration*, had 'devoted an entire chapter to the petitioner as a specially typical example of this fatal flaw', Wilde claimed (with slight exaggeration). 'The petitioner', he went on, had been suffering from 'the most horrible form of erotomania' which had left him 'the most helpless prey of the most revolting passions'. He asked that the rest of his sentence now be remitted so that he could be put under medical care for the treatment of this 'sexual insanity'.[63] This way of writing about himself was adopted, of course, only temporarily and for a very particular purpose.[64] For the most part, Wilde understood himself, his life, and his work not through the criminological and medical categories of Lombroso and Nordau but through philosophical and ethical languages of a quite different character.

Wilde, like Queensberry, had read Herbert Spencer during the 1870s, as the surviving notebooks from his student days reveal.[65] Having read Spencer's *Data of Ethics*, Wilde made a speculative note to himself: 'What is morality but the perfect adjustment of the human organism to the actual conditions of Life, and to the observance of those inexorable Laws to break which is death'.[66] This identification of breaking moral laws with breaking nature's laws was very similar to the Spencerian morality articulated in Queensberry's *Spirit of the Matterhorn*. Wilde's most controversial work, *The Picture of Dorian Gray* (1891), could also be read as asserting the close correlation between immorality and physical degeneration. However, the moral philosophy with which Wilde was most consistently and closely associated was a kind of aesthetic individualism which owed little to his interest in Herbert Spencer.[67] The philosophy that Wilde had come to espouse by the time of the 1895 trials was the product of two decades of life and thought in which Platonic, Aristotelian, and Hegelian philosophical ethics had been read and reinterpreted in the context of one of the most deca-

---

[63] Holland and Hart-Davis 2000: 656. In fact Nordau only devoted a few pages to Wilde as an example of ego-mania: Nordau 1993: 317–20.

[64] Ellis Hanson considers that in his petition Wilde was 'clearly playing an insincere game with language' (Hanson 2003: 106).

[65] P. E. Smith and Helfland 1989: esp. 27–9. On Wilde's use of Spencerian ideas in 'The Soul of Man Under Socialism', see Guy 2003.

[66] P. E. Smith and Helfland 1989: 156.

[67] Wilde gently mocked Herbert Spencer along with 'scientific historians, and the compilers of statistics in general' in his dialogue, 'The Decay of Lying', first published in 1889, and included in *Intentions* in revised form in 1891; Wilde 1909: 27. Wilde's brand of individualism had more in common with that of another aesthetic novelist, 'Ouida', whose anti-altruistic writings were discussed in Ch. 7 above; see Schaffer 2003.

dent, flamboyant, and artistic lives of the age. It was a philosophy that both created and justified his persona, and one which he articulated through the fictional characters he created, in critical essays on the pages of the periodical press, under cross-examination in the Old Bailey, and finally on lined, foolscap sheets of paper in the solitude of a prison cell.[68]

The works in which Wilde developed this philosophy most explicitly were his collection of critical dialogues and essays *Intentions* (1891), his long essay of the same year, 'The Soul of Man Under Socialism', and the spiritual autobiography he wrote while in prison, part of which was posthumously published as *De Profundis* (1905).[69] Wilde's philosophy could be summarized in five words: 'Aesthetics are higher than ethics.' To elaborate slightly, Wilde thought that good conduct and middle-class respectability were easily attained, but that the higher aim of life was to be able to 'discern the beauty of a thing'.[70] Amongst authors writing in English in the nineteenth century whose works most influenced Wilde were the American transcendentalist Ralph Waldo Emerson, and the English critics John Ruskin and Walter Pater.[71] Wilde's own version of aestheticism, if not absolutely original, was nonetheless a coherent philosophy which he used to distance himself from Victorian moralism on the one hand and the more authoritarian kinds of socialism on the other. Wilde developed this philosophy sometimes by explicitly opposing and sometimes by simply neglecting the language of 'altruism'. This new ethics required a new moral lexicon, and 'altruism' functioned, along with other Victorian terms such as 'earnest', as an appropriate target for Wilde's ethical iconoclasm.

During his unsuccessful libel action against Queensberry, Wilde engaged in a celebrated series of exchanges with Edward Carson QC. In their verbal sparring about art, literature, and morality, Carson and Wilde embodied the clash between the languages of Victorian moralism and

---

[68] For a physical description of the manuscript of *De Profundis*, see Wilde 2005: 6.

[69] Wilde 1909, 1999, 2005. 'The Soul of Man Under Socialism' was first published in the *Fortnightly Review* (Feb. 1891). The work published in 1905 as *De Profundis* was an extract from a longer document written by Wilde in the form of a letter to Lord Alfred Douglas towards the end of his two years in prison. The most recent edn, which is the one referred to in this chapter, includes an exhaustive introd. by Ian Small explaining the history of the various versions of the text, as well as extensive explanatory notes.

[70] These sentiments are put in the mouth of the character Gilbert in Wilde's dialogue, 'The Critic as Artist', first published in *Intentions* in 1891. Wilde 1909: 214–15.

[71] On the philosophical influences on Wilde's early thought, see P. E. Smith and Helfland 1989: chs 2–3. Isobel Murray especially emphasizes the influence of Emerson on Wilde in her introd. and explanatory notes to Wilde 1999. For further reflections of Wilde as a writer, philosopher and social critic, see L. Danson 1997*b*, 1997*a*; Gagnier 1997; J. Bristow 2003*b*; Sloan 2003: chs 4–5.

post-Victorian ethics. Carson wanted to talk about conduct and morality, Wilde about literature and aesthetics. Carson asked Wilde's opinion about a scurrilous story entitled 'The Priest and the Acolyte', which had appeared in an issue of an Oxford student magazine called *The Chameleon*, alongside some of Wilde's own aphorisms. The story was about a priest who fell in love with an altar boy and, in a final despairing act, administered poisoned wine to the boy and himself from a chalice, while intoning the words of the sacrament: 'The Blood of our Lord Jesus Christ, which was shed for thee, preserve thy body and soul unto everlasting life.' Carson wanted to know whether Wilde considered the story 'immoral'. Wilde replied: 'It was worse. It was badly written.' Carson persisted. Did Wilde not think it was 'blasphemous'? Wilde's reply this time was that the story 'violated every artistic canon of beauty'. Carson was not satisfied and so asked the question again. This time Wilde answered, 'The story filled me with disgust. The end was wrong.' When pressed twice more, Wilde repeated that the story was 'disgusting', and finally explained, 'I think it is horrible. "Blasphemous" is not a word of mine.'[72]

Edward Carson's cross-examination of Wilde stood for just that world of 'dull respectability' and 'Nonconformist consciences' that someone like Ernest Newman found so unattractive. In his 1895 *Free Review* article celebrating Wilde, Newman described the 'bovine rage' that such dull personalities would fly into when confronted with Wilde's paradoxes. Such philistines would surely be happier reading novels by Mrs Humphry Ward, Newman thought.[73] Wilde himself also enjoyed using the earnestly altruistic *Robert Elsmere* as the moralistic foil to his aestheticism.[74] In his dialogue 'The Decay of Lying', Wilde had placed barbed comments about *Robert Elsmere* into the mouths of both the characters, who described the novel variously as a 'deliberately tedious work'; 'a masterpiece of the "*genre ennuyeux*"'; and as 'Arnold's *Literature and Dogma* with the literature left out'. According to 'a thoughtful young friend' of one of the characters,

[72] Hyde 1962: 106–7. On the *Chameleon* story, which was written by an undergraduate called Jack Bloxam, see Ellmann 1987: 403–4; L. Hamilton 2003: 230, 242–3.

[73] Ernest Newman, 'Oscar Wilde: A Literary Appreciation', reproduced in Beckson 1970: 202–10, quotation at 204.

[74] On Mrs Humphry Ward's popular novel *Robert Elsmere* (1888) and the university settlement movement in the East End with which it and its author became associated, see Ch. 6 above. Maltz 2003 interprets Wilde's critique of 'aesthetic philanthropy' in *The Picture of Dorian Gray* and 'The Soul of Man under Socialism' as a retort to a charitable world with which he had himself been at least indirectly involved in his work as editor of *The Woman's World* from 1887 to 1889. On the aesthetic and ascetic aspects of the university settlements, and their roles as all-male communities, see Koven 2004: 228–81.

Robert Elsmere 'reminded him of the sort of conversation that goes on at a meat tea in the house of a serious Nonconformist family'. After the original publication of this dialogue in the *Nineteenth Century* in January 1889, Wilde replied to a correspondent who had written to congratulate him: 'I have blown my trumpet against the gates of dullness, and I hope some shaft has hit *Robert Elsmere* between the joints of his nineteenth edition.'[75]

The one positive comment that was offered by way of consolation to *Robert Elsmere* in Wilde's dialogue was that 'Green's philosophy very pleasantly sugars the somewhat bitter pill of the author's fiction.'[76] Although Wilde was in sympathy with T. H. Green's doctrine of self-realization, he was, unlike Mrs Ward's earnest doubting cleric, certainly no altruist. That much was clear from the quintessentially Wildean opening line of 'The Soul of Man Under Socialism': 'The chief advantage that would result from the establishment of Socialism is, undoubtedly, the fact that Socialism would relieve us from that sordid necessity of living for others which, in the present condition of things, presses so hardly upon almost everybody.'[77] The majority of people at present, Wilde complained, finding themselves surrounded by poverty and starvation, 'spoil their lives by an unhealthy and exaggerated altruism—are forced, indeed, so to spoil them'. Wilde went on to argue that the redistribution of wealth would have the effect of freeing the wealthy from the sordid duty of philanthropy, and the poor from the cage of poverty. In these new circumstances, everyone, and not just the fortunate few, would be able to 'realise their personality more or less completely'.[78] In short, Wilde's deliberately paradoxical suggestion was that 'Socialism itself will be of value simply because it will lead to Individualism.'[79]

[75] Holland and Hart-Davis 2000: 389.

[76] Wilde 1909: 10, 14.

[77] Ibid. 1. In his discussion of Comte and his British followers, Tony Davies recognizes that the Religion of Humanity was one of Wilde's main targets when he bemoaned the necessity of 'living for others'; T. Davies 1997: 29. Wilde had read and thought about positivism as an undergraduate in the 1870s and had included in his 'Commonplace Book' a paraphrase of Huxley's famous quip that positivism was 'Catholicism minus Christianity'; P. E. Smith and Helfland 1989: 125, 151.

[78] Wilde 1999: 6.

[79] Ibid. 2. For various interpretations of this essay see L. Danson 1997a: ch. 7; Wilde 1999; Guy 2003. Josephine Guy's extremely informative essay considers 'The Soul of Man' as a contribution especially to political debates about the meaning of 'Individualism', and demonstrates similarities between Wilde's views and those put forward by other contributors to the periodical press, including Hugh Price Hughes and Grant Allen. I would dissent from the implication of Guy's essay, however, that recognizing that 'The Soul of Man' was a provocative journalistic contribution to

Wilde's examples of great personalities who had succeeded in realizing themselves included Keats, Flaubert, Byron, Shelley, Browning, Victor Hugo, and Baudelaire. He also included Charles Darwin and Ernst Renan, author of the controversial *Vie de Jésus* (1863).[80] One of the greatest of all those who had taught man to intensify and realise his personality, Wilde wrote, was Christ himself. While the antique world had lived by the motto, 'Know thyself', the message of Christ to man had been simply 'Be thyself'. Wilde's Christ was not opposed to private property and he did not recommend that people live in unwholesome and squalid poverty. What he preached to individuals, rather, was: 'You have a wonderful personality. Develop it. Be yourself. Don't imagine that your perfection lies in accumulating or possessing external things. Your perfection is inside of you. If only you could realise that, you would not want to be rich.' To put it another way, 'he who would lead a Christ-like life is he who is perfectly and absolutely himself'. It did not matter, Wilde argued, whether that person was a poet, a student, a man of science, a shepherd, a fisherman, or a child. Individual self-realization was the duty of all, and this had been the message of Christ.[81]

In prison, Wilde became even more interested in Christ. Attached to the petition he sent to the Home Secretary in the summer of 1896, in which he explained his fear that his 'sexual insanity' would soon take him over completely, Wilde had included a list of books that he hoped might be bought for the prison library and put at his disposal. Reading was one way he thought he might relieve the mental anguish of his solitary confinement. He also requested access to writing materials. The books he asked for included poems by Tennyson, Keats, Chaucer, and Spenser, and prose works by Emerson and Carlyle. At the top of the list, however, were a Greek New Testament, Henry Milman's *History of the Jews*, and Frederic Farrar's *St Paul*. The list also included Renan's *Vie de Jésus* and *Les Apôtres*.[82] His requests for most of these books and for writing materials were successful, with the result that over a third of *De Profundis*, when it was finally published, was taken up by a serious reflection on the life and teachings of Christ.[83]

---

topical debates of the 1880s and 1890s is a reason not to consider it a serious discussion of freedom and authority (Guy 2003: 79–80).

[80] Arata 2003: esp. 261–8, pays attention to the importance of Renan to Wilde.

[81] Wilde 1999: 10, 12.

[82] The list is reproduced in Ellmann 1987: 477–8; Holland and Hart-Davis 2000: 660

[83] The section on Christ is a much smaller proportion of the full text from which *De Profundis* was extracted. See Wilde 2005: 109–25, 173–85.

In *De Profundis*, as in the earlier essay, Wilde depicted Christ as an artist, a poet, and, above all, as 'the most supreme of individualists' and 'the first individualist in history'.[84] While in 'The Soul of Man' Wilde had drawn a contrast between authoritarian socialism and true individualism, in *De Profundis* he emphasized the difference between philanthropy and individualism. Wilde wrote of Christ: 'People have tried to make him out an ordinary philanthropist, or ranked him as an altruist with the unscientific and sentimental. But he was really neither one nor the other.' Unlike the modern philanthropist, Christ had more pity for the wealthy and the hedonistic than he did for the poor. 'And as for altruism', Wilde asked, 'who knew better than he that it is vocation not volition that determines us, and that one cannot gather grapes of thorns or figs from thistles?' Wilde's point here seemed to be that moral character was not something that could be changed by earnest acts of will, but was rather something that had to develop naturally. In any case, Wilde continued, Christ's creed was not that we should 'live for others as a definite self-conscious aim'. One should forgive one's enemies, but for one's own sake, not theirs. And when Christ told the young man to sell all he had and give it to the poor, it was not the state of the poor, but the state of the young man's soul that he was thinking of. This was the same individualistic interpretation that Henry Sidgwick had offered of this particular story in his review of *Ecce Homo*, three decades earlier.[85] Ultimately, on Wilde's reading, Christ did not say to people 'Live for others' but rather showed them that 'there was no difference at all between the lives of others and one's own life'. In this way he connected the history of each individual to the history of the whole of humanity.[86]

The substantial part of Wilde's prison composition that was omitted from the work published as *De Profundis* by Robert Ross in 1905 was a self-justifying autobiography which mercilessly dissected Alfred Douglas's character, explaining the latter's outrageously egotistical and unreasonable behaviour as the result of both his hatred, and his involuntary mimicking, of his father, Lord Queensberry.[87] When Douglas became aware of the

---

[84] For much fuller discussions of the role of Christianity in Wilde's works, see Arata 2003, and the extract from G. Wilson Knight's *The Christian Renaissance* (1962) repr. in Ellmann 1969: 138–49.

[85] See Ch. 2 above.

[86] Wilde 2005: 113–14, 176–7.

[87] Ibid. 37–82 is the bulk of the section about Alfred Douglas, omitted from *De Profundis*. Wilde disapproved of petty selfishness and egotism, while approving of a more broadly egoistic philosophy which celebrated self-development. On this point I disagree with Shewan 1977: p. xii, when he asserts that Wilde used 'egoism' and 'egotism' interchangeably. For further reflections on the difference between 'egoism' and 'egotism', again emphasizing the narrow selfishness of the latter as opposed to the 'self-assertion' of the former, see an article in *The Times* (14 Apr. 1884), 2,

content of this part of the text in 1913, he retaliated with a vicious and often inaccurate book of his own, entitled *Oscar Wilde and Myself* (1914).[88] Douglas later repudiated the book and expressed regret over publishing it, but it is interesting to notice that one of his main accusations against Wilde was that he had failed to understand the importance of altruism. Writing about 'The Soul of Man', Douglas asserted that Wilde would never have written it without the influence of George Bernard Shaw, and that, in any case, its main argument, 'that human beings will never be happy till they have got rid of altruism' was 'the obvious reverse of the truth'. Douglas also discussed the suggestion that Wilde could have saved himself from prison in 1895 if he had been prepared to betray 'a friend' against whom most of the charges of indecency should properly have been brought. Without discussing whether or not he was that 'friend', Douglas dismissed this as an entirely implausible suggestion since Wilde's 'whole principle of life was subversive to any such high altruism; he would not have gone without his dinner to save a friend—much less have faced ruin and imprisonment'. In his life as well as his art, Wilde had been an opponent of altruism, Douglas claimed. The damaging moral of all Wilde's writings was that vice was more interesting than virtue, insincerity better than truth, and that 'cynical carelessness and indifference are more comely than kind feeling and altruism'.[89]

Douglas described *The Picture of Dorian Gray* as a book that Wilde had produced by 'prowling and garbage-hunting among the French decadents' but one which had, by 1914, become 'the gospel and literary stand-by of a world-wide cult of moral and physical leprosy'.[90] In a chapter on 'Literature and Vice' Douglas went on to register his objection to Wilde's belief that 'the sphere of art and the sphere of ethics are absolutely distinct and separate'. Now in his mid-forties, Douglas considered the belief that art was more important than conduct 'a mistake which most of us are prone to make when we are young and dazzled with the beauty and colour of life'.[91] The true character of Wilde's work could be judged by its impact in Europe, Douglas thought. In Russia, for example, Wilde's work was admired by anarchists and revolutionaries 'who, being in a large measure decadents and criminals themselves, had a natural sympathy with the work of a

---

discussing the meaning of the terms in the context of a review of John Stuart Blackie's *The Wisdom of Goethe* (1883).

[88] Douglas 1914. On the circumstances of the composition and publication of the book, see Bendz 1921: 3–29; Holland 1997: 8; J. Bristow 2003a: 8–9.

[89] Douglas 1914: 75, 119, 243–4

[90] Ibid. 278–9.

[91] Ibid. 282, 284.

decadent criminal'.[92] In short, Alfred Douglas, looking for reasons to condemn Wilde in 1914, had reverted to those that had been popularized by
Max Nordau in the 1890s, namely that decadent literature was the product
of egomaniacs, that it was corrosive of public morals, and that it represented
a total failure to recognize the true importance of altruism.[93]

Kein Altruismus!

Friedrich Nietzsche was one of Nordau's prime examples of a degenerate
egomaniac. He was an obvious choice: his whole philosophy revolved
around his contempt for sympathy, pity, and altruism and, since 1889, he had
been entirely debilitated by insanity. Nietzsche himself, however, had also
been warning about degeneration and decadence during the 1870s and
1880s.[94] The view he had arrived at was that degenerates could be identified not by their excessive egoism, as Nordau and others would claim, but
by their altruism.[95] This inversion was not surprising, given Nietzsche's
overall ambition to reverse all conventional moral valuations, whether
Christian or secular. He described Christian morality as a slave-morality—
the product of a revolt of the sickly and weak against their naturally superior masters. This slave-morality was characterized by the celebration of pity
and selflessness. Nietzsche wanted to instigate a counter-revolution against
this slave revolt in morals. He also wanted to invert the modern elevation
of altruism above egoism (partly because he believed that altruism, in any
case, existed only as a distorted kind of unconscious egoism).[96] Indeed the
whole thrust of Nietzsche's philosophy was encapsulated in a violent two-
word exclamation in *The Gay Science*: '*Kein Altruismus!*'—'No altruism!'[97]
His attack on Christianity and his attack on altruism, however, were distinct
if overlapping parts of his moral mission. The former centred on the degenerate nature of pity and the corrupting influence of the church, the latter

[92] Ibid. 300.
[93] For a spirited defence of Wilde's writings against Douglas's charges, see Bendz 1921: 15–19.
Parts of the same essay are also reproduced in Beckson 1970: 366–78.
[94] Nietzsche, unlike Wilde, actually did have a whole chapter of *Degeneration* devoted to him,
namely ch. 5 of bk III, on 'Ego-Mania'; Nordau 1993: 415–72.
[95] For a detailed study of Nietzsche's various uses of the idea of degeneration, see G. Moore 2002:
part II. Nietzsche made the connection between altruism and decadence particularly strongly in
Twilight of the Idols, 'Expeditions of an Untimely Man', ss. 35 and 37; Nietzsche 1990: 98–103.
[96] On altruism as a form of egoism, see *Daybreak*, s. 133, and *Will to Power*, ss. 246, 373; Nietzsche
1997: 83–5; 1968: 141–2, 200–2.
[97] *The Gay Science*, bk III, s. 119; Nietzsche 2001: 116.

on more secular moral errors associated with utilitarianism, Spencerian biology, and socialism.

One of the last works that Nietzsche completed before his final descent into insanity in 1889 was *The Anti-Christ*. This represented the most violent and forceful version of his rejection of Christian morality. Although in some of his writings Nietzsche had made connections between 'altruism' and Christian morality, he did not employ the language of altruism when writing *The Anti-Christ*.[98] In that work, it was the celebration of 'pity' (*Mitleiden*) rather than 'altruism' that Nietzsche especially condemned.[99] Indeed, in *Daybreak*, Nietzsche had written that the central intention of Christianity was to encourage not altruism but extreme self-regard through teaching 'the absolute importance of eternal *personal* salvation'. According to Nietzsche's historical story, this 'strictly egoistic fundamental belief' was gradually displaced by what had been a 'subsidiary belief' in the importance of loving one's neighbour. Finally, those European freethinkers who had liberated themselves entirely from the egoistic dogma of personal salvation, Nietzsche wrote—represented by figures such as Schopenhauer, Comte, and Mill—justified their doctrinal heterodoxy with an increasingly intense commitment to a 'cult of philanthropy'. He later made a similar observation about George Eliot, who had rejected God only to become a 'moral fanatic'.[100] Comte, in particular, with his moral formula *vivre pour autrui* had managed to 'outchristian Christianity'.[101] Nietzsche recognized, then, that it was by the hands of secular and scientific theorists that the modern cult of 'altruism' had been crafted.

As Robin Small has shown, Nietzsche's use of the term *Altruismus* in *Daybreak* (published towards the end of 1880) and subsequent works, was a sign of Herbert Spencer's impact on his moral vocabulary. Earlier debates between Nietzsche and his friend Paul Rée had been about the evolutionary origins not of an 'altruistic' (*altruistisch*) morality but an 'unegoistic' (*unegoistisch*) one. It was only after reading Herbert Spencer's *Data of Ethics* in German translation in 1880 that Nietzsche started to use the language of altruism.[102] Small also suggests that Nietzsche's famous statement that 'there are no moral facts', only moral interpretations, was a tacit

---

[98] The section of Nietzsche's writings that makes the closest connection between Christianity and 'altruism' is *Will to Power*, s. 246; Nietzsche 1968: 141–2.

[99] *The Anti-Christ*, esp. s. 7; Nietzsche 1990: 130–1.

[100] *Twilight of the Idols*, 'Expeditions of an Untimely Man', s. 5; Nietzsche 1990: 80.

[101] *Daybreak*, bk II, s. 132; Nietzsche 1997: 82.

[102] For the material in this and the following paragraphs on the impact of Spencer's writings on Nietzsche, I am dependent on G. Moore 2002: 56–84; Small 2005: 163–77.

allusion to the German title of Spencer's work *Die Thatsachen der Ethik* (The Facts of Ethics).[103] In *The Gay Science* (1882), Nietzsche attacked 'the pedantic Englishman Herbert Spencer' and wondered what made him 'rave' about the future 'reconciliation of "egoism and altruism" about which he spins fables'. Nietzsche found these fables nauseating and wrote that a human race that adopted such a Spencerian perspective 'would strike us as deserving of contempt, of annihilation!'[104]

In 1885 Nietzsche wrote in one of his notebooks: 'Recently Comte's superficial opposition between altruism and egoism—but there is no altruism at all!—was brought out of France into England; and now we see e.g. in Herbert Spencer the attempt to conciliate them again, with a bad willingness to take such a concept so strictly, that in England now even urination is supposed to belong amongst the altruistic activities.'[105] The reference to urination alluded to the stipulation in Spencer and other biological writers that the term 'altruistic' could be applied to any basic physiological activities that involved a loss of substance.[106] 'The false "altruism" of biologists is ridiculous', Nietzsche wrote again in 1887: 'propagation among amoebas seems to be throwing off ballast, a pure advantage. The excretion of useless material.'[107]

In place of the view favoured by both Comte and Spencer, that altruism would gradually come to predominate, Nietzsche suggested that as man evolved he would become increasingly egoistic. He speculated that, unlike other animals, human beings had started their evolution in an unusually altruistic state, which needed to be gradually replaced by a more refined egoism.[108] Two of the main contemporary obstacles to that progression, in Nietzsche's view, were utilitarianism and socialism. Each of these rested on what Nietzsche saw as 'one of the most common lies of the nineteenth century', namely the 'preaching of altruistic morality in the service of individual egoism' (the individual egoism in question being that of the pleasure-seeking utilitarian or the property-grasping socialist).[109] In summary,

---

[103] Small 2005: 168–71.

[104] *The Gay Science*, bk V, s. 373; Nietzsche 2001: 238. Nietzsche had also mocked the Spencerian utopia of universal altruism in *Daybreak*, s. 147; Nietzsche 1997: 93.

[105] This note was made by Nietzsche between May and July 1885. Nietzsche 1974: s. 35[34], 246; 1980: xi. 524, s. 35[34]. Tr. in Small 2005: 174–5. Nietzsche criticized Comte for this elevation of feelings and sensualism above rationality as well as his enthusiasm for altruism. See *Will to Power*, s. 95; Nietzsche 1968: 59.

[106] For examples of these sorts of biological definition of altruism see Chs 5 and 7, above.

[107] This was one of the fragments later published in *The Will to Power*, s. 653; Nietzsche 1968: 345.

[108] *Will to Power*, s. 771; Nietzsche 1968: 404.

[109] *Will to Power*, s. 784; Nietzsche 1968: 412.

Nietzsche believed that, as he put it in one of the first of his works to be translated into English, *The Twilight of the Idols*, 'An "altruistic" morality, a morality under which egoism *languishes*—is under all circumstances a bad sign.'[110] His reasons for believing this were bound up with his rejection of the secular ideologies represented by such insipid and pedantic English philosophers as John Stuart Mill and, especially, Herbert Spencer.[111]

It is easy to imagine how liberating all of this must have seemed to a certain kind of British reader in the 1890s. Writers such as Eliot, Mill, and Spencer had, from the 1850s onwards, created a moral language with which to articulate highly respectable forms of unbelief. Theirs had been an altruistic morality in which each individual was to feel sympathy with everyone else, the greatest good of the collective was to be the criterion of good individual action, and society was evolving towards a state of total altruism. But what if one did not want to follow these respectable unbelievers? What if one found their cult of altruism stifling? Nietzsche's visionary egoism, like Wilde's iconoclastic individualism, provided a new and empowering way of looking at morality at the end of the nineteenth century for those who wanted to reject the respectable unbelief of their parents as well as the Christianity of their grandparents. Although there were certainly important differences between Wilde's aesthetic ideal of self-realization and Nietzsche's much more assertive egoism—and between Wilde's socialist individualism and Nietzsche's aristocratic elitism—Nietzsche and Wilde provided ways of thinking about morality that appealed to the new men and women of the 1890s in similar ways. Both these writers could boast the accolade of having been held up for medico-moral disapproval by the prophet of degeneration, Max Nordau; both were particular admirers of Ralph Waldo Emerson; both expressed themselves in aphorisms and paradoxes that provided a liberating stylistic contrast with the turgid systematizing of thinkers such as Comte, Spencer, or Sidgwick; and both revelled in putting on and taking off philosophical positions like masks.[112] Finally, both set themselves up as opponents of Victorian 'altruism'.

---

[110] *Twilight of the Idols*, 'Expeditions of an Untimely Man', s. 35; Nietzsche 1990: 98.

[111] As Gregory Moore has argued, however, in 'simply substituting egoism for altruism' Nietzsche may have reversed prevailing moral values, but in doing so, especially while maintaining a progressive idea of moral evolution (albeit towards increased egoism rather than increased altruism), he produced a moral philosophy that was not as different from Herbert Spencer's as he might have believed. G. Moore 2002: 83–4. On Nietzsche's critique of altruism in the context of his attacks on Mill and utilitarianism, see Anomaly 2005: esp. 5–7.

[112] Emerson's *Essays* was one of the books Wilde requested when petitioning the Home Secretary in July 1896; Holland and Hart-Davis 2000: 660. On Nietzsche's love of Emerson's *Essays* see Foot 1994: 8. On the use of metaphysical theories as masks see Wilde 1909, 'The Truth of Masks',

The Eagle and the Serpent

New year's day 1914 saw the first appearance of a newly renamed periodical devoted to promoting the philosophies of Nietzsche and Stirner and
the value of art and literature. *The Egoist: An Individualist Review* had been
published from 1911 as *The Freewoman*, then *The New Freewoman*, and continued in existence under its new name until 1919. The changes of title
reflected the intellectual development of the journal's editor Dora Marsden
as she transformed herself from a supporter of democratic suffragism into
an advocate of anarchist individualism and a critic of the culture of altruism. *The Egoist* promoted an assertively individualistic philosophy for both
men and women and also provided an important forum for modernist literary writers, including Ezra Pound and James Joyce, whose *Portrait of the
Artist as a Young Man* was serialized in its pages during 1914 and 1915.[113]
Given the strong Victorian association between altruism, female nature, and
motherhood, a journal that promoted a philosophy of egoism to the modern 'freewoman' was a particularly potent gesture of anti-Victorianism.[114]

Marsden's anarchic modernist gesture had been made possible in part
by the earlier efforts of pioneering British Nietzscheans and egoists.
Amongst those who particularly admired and promoted Nietzsche's philosophy in Britain in the 1890s were the Fabian dramatist George Bernard
Shaw, the 'new woman' novelist George Egerton, and the sexologist
Havelock Ellis, along with many less prominent literary and philosophical
writers such as John Davidson, Thomas Common, and John Basil
Barnhill.[115] It was Barnhill (under the pseudonym of Erwin McCall), with
the assistance of a tireless popularizer of Nietzschean philosophy going by
the name of Malfew Seklew, who was responsible for the founding and

221–63; MacIntyre 1994: 296. Thomas Mann also recognized some interesting similarities
between Wilde and Nietzsche in an essay on Nietzsche's philosophy, an extract from which is
repr. in Ellmann 1969: 169–71.

[113] *The Egoist* (1914–19) can be consulted in the British Library Newspaper Library, Colindale.
On Dora Marsden and her relationships with Ezra Pound, other literary modernists, and the circle of writers connected with the socialist periodical *The New Age*, see Clarke 1992, 1996. The
content of several modernist journals, including *The New Age*, can be accessed and searched online
through The Modernist Journals Project (see Bibliography for details).

[114] On the use of evolutionary science in the 1880s and 1890s to support the distinction between
altruistic women and courageous and intellectual men, see the section on 'The new woman and
the holy family' in Ch. 7 above.

[115] See Thatcher 1970 on the British reception of Nietzsche between 1890 and 1914. 'George
Egerton' was the pen-name of Mary Clairmonte (née Dunne); see *ODNB*; Thatcher 1970: 53,
98–9; Richardson 2003: ch. 7.

editing of a short-lived but flamboyant egoistic periodical called *The Eagle and the Serpent*.[116] The title of the journal referred to the two creatures chosen as companions by Nietzsche's Zarathustra as the proudest and the wisest animals under the sun, respectively. The changing subtitles of the journal during the course of its existence, between 1898 and 1903, indicated the range of aspirations that it hoped to tap into amongst its readers. It started in 1898 as 'A Journal of Egoistic Philosophy and Sociology', changing to 'A Journal of Emersonian Philosophy and Sociology' in July 1900, subsequently to 'A Journal of Wit, Wisdom and Wickedness', and finally to 'A Journal for Free Spirits and for Spirits Struggling to be Free'.[117]

The first number of *The Eagle and the Serpent* came out in February 1898 (see Fig. 26), priced three pence, and announcing on its front page that it was dedicated to 'the Philosophy of Life Enunciated by Nietzsche, Emerson, Stirner, Thoreau and Goethe'. Its motto was: 'A Race of Altruists is Necessarily a Race of Slaves. A Race of Freemen is Necessarily a Race of Egoists.'[118] Turning the page, the reader would have found the 'Creed and Aim' of this new periodical spelt out. This was that the cure for social injustice was not to try to convert 'the exploiters' to altruism—this was a 'maniac's dream'. Rather, the exploited must become 'persistently egoistic'. 'Egoism spells justice and freedom,' the editorial concluded, 'as surely as altruism spells charity and slavery.' Those readers whose interests were more aesthetic than political might have been pleased to read at the end of this creed: 'We stand for the art of life and the life of art'.[119]

The main article of this first number had an uncompromising title: 'Altruism—That is the Enemy'. Readers would have noticed that the arguments against altruism here and in subsequent numbers of the journal had more in common with anarchistic forms of socialism—of the kind developed in Wilde's 'Soul of Man Under Socialism', for instance—than with the more elitist egoism of Nietzsche. The editorial line was that charity and altruism perpetuated social inequalities and that true reform would come about only through self-assertion and self-development, not through more altruism, nor through more democracy:

> Altruism—blessed altruism! Thou art a word to conjure with! Now a lie on the lips of the impostor, and now a *credo* in the mouth of his victim—now an assassin in the hands of the knave, only because thou art a seducer in the

[116] Thatcher 1970: 55–63; McElroy 1981: esp. 25, 30; Bell 2003: 61–2.
[117] McElroy 1981: 37 n. 79.
[118] *The Eagle and the Serpent* (15 Feb. 1898), 1.
[119] Ibid. 3.

THE EAGLE AND THE SERPENT.

A Journal of Egoistic Philosophy and Sociology.

"The proudest animal under the sun and the wisest animal under the sun have set out to reconnoitre."—*Nietzsche*

No. 1.   FEBRUARY 15, 1898.   PRICE THREEPENCE.

THUS SPAKE

NIETZSCHE:

We carry faithfully what we are given, on hard shoulders, over rough mountains! And when perspiring, we are told: "Yea, life is hard to bear!" But man himself only is hard to bear! The reason is that he carrieth too many strange things on his shoulders. Like the camel he kneeleth down and alloweth the heavy load to be put on his back.

EMERSON:

So far as a man thinks, he is free. Nothing is more disgusting than the crowing about liberty by slaves, as most men are, and the flippant mistaking for freedom of some paper preamble like a "Declaration of Independence," or the statute right to vote, by those who have never dared to think or act.

Dedicated to the Philosophy of Life Enunciated by Nietzsche, Emerson, Stirner, Thoreau and Goethe, THE EAGLE AND THE SERPENT Labours for the Recognition of New Ideals in Politics and Sociology, in Ethics and Philosophy, in Literature and Art.

A RACE OF ALTRUISTS IS NECESSARILY A RACE OF SLAVES.
A RACE OF FREEMEN IS NECESSARILY A RACE OF EGOISTS.

"THE GREAT ARE GREAT ONLY BECAUSE WE ARE ON OUR KNEES.   LET US RISE!"

CONTENTS.

*To order of Newsdealers, 3d. or 8 cents. Per Post, 3½d. or 10 cents.
Post free, per year, 1s. 9d. or 60 cents. Issued Bi-monthly.*

The Eagle and the Serpent Office: 185, Fleet Street, London, E.C., England.

Figure 26. The front page of the first number of *The Eagle and the Serpent*, (15 Feb. 1898); reproduced by permission of the British Library.

soul of the believer, always a badge of deception and servitude to the faithful—well may the exploiter say to thee, 'Blessed art thou, holy altruism—
the sole tie which binds our victims to our service.'[120]

This opening salvo concluded by acknowledging that orthodox
Nietzscheans would disagree with the journal's approach to economics,
while expressing the hope that all could agree 'that altruism is a slave-
morality and egoism the only morality possible for those who decline to be
enslaved'.[121]

In subsequent numbers, readers would be treated to serious ideological
debates, such as that between the leading Nietzschean Thomas Common
and the socialist naturalist Alfred Russel Wallace about the relative merits of
aristocracy and equality as principles for social reform. There was also some
more light-hearted material. The third number reproduced a standard reply
the journal had received from Herbert Spencer explaining why his ill-
health and the volume of his correspondence meant he could not reply to
their letter. This was printed as evidence of the egoistic lengths even a
'famous altruist' like Spencer had to go to in order to get anything done.[122]
A couple of short squibs in February 1899 continued the campaign against
altruism. The first was the story of a man 'Prosecuted for Altruism':

> Judge: You are charged with non-support of your wife. Are you guilty?
> Prisoner: My lord, I am guilty of altruism.
> Judge: Guilty of what? (He'd never heard of it before).
> Prisoner: Of altruism: I might have married a rich girl but altruism bade me
> marry a poor girl. By misfortune I have become one of the unemployed.
> Your Honour, an egoist married the rich girl. Please make my sentence a
> heavy one—I deserve all you can give me.
> Judge: But you also stand charged with bigamy.
> Prisoner: That was my second altruistic offence: Do you think my first wife
> was the only woman deserving of my philanthropic devotion?
> Judge: I sentence you to live with two mothers-in-law all your life. (Prisoner
> stabs himself to what is called the heart.)

The second comic tale, entitled 'The Egoist's Temptation', was a reworking
of the story of Christ's temptation in the wilderness. In this story, 'the Devil
of Altruism' beseeched the egoist to convert to altruism—'it's the only
respectable ism now-a-days'. The egoist, of course, was not to be swayed,
replying, 'Get thee behind me, thou Devil of Altruism! Thou never wilt

---

[120] *The Eagle and the Serpent* (15 Feb. 1898), 3.
[121] Ibid. 4–5.
[122] *The Eagle and the Serpent* (15 June 1898), 36.

know the motive of joy in doing helpful things. It is always drudgery with thee and self-sacrifice; something to be entered in the profit and loss column. Let me never hear thy base solicitations again—Scat!'[123]

The secularist Liverpool bank clerk and aspiring writer on philosophy and music, Ernest Newman, also featured in the pages of *The Eagle and the Serpent*, amongst its lively attacks on Christian, utilitarian, and Spencerian ethics. The first number of *The Eagle and the Serpent* had included an attack both on Benjamin Kidd's claims about the importance of altruism in *Social Evolution* and on the inadequate criticism of Kidd on this front by 'Mr Mortimer Cecil' (the pseudonym adopted by Newman for his 1897 book on Kidd, Balfour, and Drummond).[124] Despite this, Newman later replied to a letter from the editor in a supportive way, expressing his hope that 'a paper devoted to Egoism' would succeed.[125] He had expressed sympathy with Nietzsche's philosophy in print on at least two other occasions. He had been at Crystal Palace in 1897 for the first British performance of Richard Strauss's tone poem *Also Sprach Zarathustra*—a work inspired by Nietzsche's book of that name. Newman wrote in defence of Strauss's controversial composition that it was, like Nietzsche's philosophy, a symbol of the destruction 'of all previous values', and that 'no such overwhelming picture of man and the universe has ever before been unfolded to our eyes in music'.[126]

In 1896, Newman had been given the task of reviewing, for the *Free Review*, the first completed volume of a projected eleven-volume collected works of Nietzsche in English.[127] This first translated volume contained *The Case of Wagner, Nietzsche contra Wagner, The Twilight of the Idols*, and *The Anti-Christ*. Newman started by mentioning the work that at that time was the only well-known account of Nietzsche's philosophy in English, namely Nordau's lengthy diatribe against it in *Degeneration*. Although Nordau had succeeded in identifying many weaknesses, Newman thought, he had spoilt his case by 'pushing it to an absurd extreme'. Newman's main complaint was that Nordau was 'too serious, too irritable, too German to write a thoroughly scientific book on modern *decadence*'. 'Who but a German', Newman asked, 'could take Mr Oscar Wilde's delightful paradoxes so seriously' as to deny indignantly that until the impressionists began to paint

---

[123] Ibid.

[124] *The Eagle and the Serpent* (12 Feb. 1899), 100. On Kidd's *Social Evolution*, see Ch. 7, above.

[125] Quoted in Thatcher 1970: 58.

[126] E. Newman 1905: 249–304, at 261, 277; quoted in Thatcher 1970: 32–3.

[127] On these early translations, and the initial problems encountered in completing the project, see Thatcher 1970: 22–7.

London fogs, no such phenomena had existed? Similarly, Nordau's attacks on Nietzsche were evidence of 'how little he knows of literature apart from a few scientific classifications'.[128]

Having established his preference for the playful and paradoxical styles of Wilde and Nietzsche over Nordau's absurd seriousness, Newman turned to his own philosophical reservations about Nietzsche's egoism. These boiled down to a single problem, namely the meaning of the word 'good'. Nietzsche had argued that the slave revolt in morals had seen the word 'good' transferred from noble and assertive traits to weak and sickly ones, such as pity and sympathy. But Newman could not see what, in the light of Nietzsche's revaluation of values, 'good' was now supposed to mean. Nietzsche seemed to argue that a 'good' condition of society was one with good 'physiological conditions', but since different environments favoured different physiological conditions, that answer could give no fixed meaning to 'good'. He also wondered on what basis Nietzsche could defend his view that certain instincts—such as cruel or violent ones—were the most 'healthy': 'And if *our* "instincts" say that cruelty is an abominable instinct, who is to settle between Nietzsche and us?' Similarly, both benevolent and brutal instincts might be considered 'natural' and might be accompanied by 'pleasure'; thus two more of Nietzsche's suggested moral criteria also failed. Newman's conclusion was that the contradictions in Nietzsche's argument were those that would be 'inherent in any theory that begins with the suicidal assumption that certain things are natural and others anti-natural; and the *naïveté* of Nietzsche's assumption that *his* instincts are "natural" because they are *his* instincts, is of a piece with the philosophy he attempts to build upon it'.[129]

---

[128] Ernest Newman, 'Friedrich Nietzsche', 114. For Wilde's original remarks about nature imitating art, and Nordau's rebuttal see: 'The Decay of Lying' in Wilde 1909: esp. 38–41; Nordau 1993: 321–2.

[129] Ernest Newman, 'Friedrich Nietzsche', 121–2. Three years later Newman returned to what he considered to be Nietzsche's confused and contradictory attitudes to altruism in an article entitled 'Nietzsche Once More' published in *The Reformer* (1899), 10–20, where Newman argued that if altruism had evolved to such a high degree in human beings, it could hardly be true, as Nietzsche had claimed, that it was something that was contrary to the law of natural selection. The article is one of many included in the compilation of Newman's 'Early Press Contributions', Glasgow University Library Special Collections, Farmer q493.

Art and emotion in *Principia Ethica*

While Ernest Newman was struggling to understand what 'good' could mean in post-Nietzschean Liverpool, and objecting to any attempt to equate it with 'natural', in Trinity College, Cambridge, another young man was struggling with similar questions about the great German immoralist. That young man was one W. F. Trotter.[130] Trotter had been asked to review the same newly translated volume of Nietzsche for the *International Journal of Ethics*. Like Newman, Trotter was not persuaded of the merit of an ethical outlook which held 'altruism to be immoral' and in which 'physiology is made the criterion of value'.[131] We do not know for certain whether or not W. F. Trotter discussed his thoughts about Nietzsche's ethics with his contemporary as a philosophy student at Trinity, G. E. Moore (although a passing, misspelt reference to Nietzsche in a letter from Moore to a friend in April 1896 is possibly a clue).[132] We do know, however, that during the 1890s, like Newman, Trotter, and others, Moore was puzzling over the meaning of 'good'; its relationship with terms such as 'natural', 'pleasurable', and 'beautiful'; and the merits of altruism and egoism as ethical principles.

As an 18-year-old schoolboy at Dulwich College in 1891 Moore had written an essay on the question 'What is the good of the school mission?'

[130] William Finlayson Trotter and G. E. Moore both achieved first-class honours in Part II of the Moral Sciences Tripos in 1896. Trotter, a Scot, had been awarded a sizarship by Trinity College, Cambridge, in 1891 and admitted to the college in 1892 (*The Times*, 25 Dec. 1891, 8). In the later 1890s he published several short book reviews in *Mind* and the *International Journal of Ethics*, which were signed 'W. F. Trotter, Trinity College, Cambridge'. In 1903 he was awarded a first-class degree in law by the Council of Legal Education in London (*The Times*, 13 Jan. 1903, 9). Around the same time he produced a translation of Pascal's *Pensées*, which became one of the standard translations; Pascal 1904, 1931. He was appointed Professor of Law at Sheffield University in 1909 and King's Counsel in Scotland in 1919, and died in Edinburgh in 1945 (*The Times*, 12 Feb. 1919, 2; 10 June 1936, 18; 10 Feb. 1945, 1). I am grateful to Jonathan Smith at the Trinity College Archives in Cambridge for information about Trotter's career at Trinity; see Trinity College Admissions Book; Venn and Venn 1922–54; Tanner 1984.
[131] W. F. Trotter, 'The Works of Friedrich Nietzsche', *International Journal of Ethics*, 7 (1897), 258–60, at 258.
[132] The volume of Nietzsche, tr. Common, which Newman and Trotter both reviewed was published in Mar. 1896 (*The Times*, 26 Mar. 1896, 8). On 12 Apr. 1896, Moore wrote about his brother breaking off his engagement in a letter to his friend Edward Marsh. This was jokingly described by Moore as evidence of the 'great intellect' of the Moore family, which was 'well-known to be antagonistic to constancy, and Friedrich Nietsche [sic] thinks it much preferable. It is his "master morality", here curiously illustrated in a Christian' (Levy 1981: 187). Nietzsche's views on marriage were also mentioned in Trotter's brief review the following year: Trotter, 'Works of Nietzsche', 259. After graduating in the summer of 1896, Moore worked towards a college fellowship at Trinity which he succeeded in winning in 1898 after an unsuccessful attempt the previous year. G. E. Moore 1968: 20–2; Levy 1981: 168–99.

(The school mission was the college's own version of a university 'settle-ment' house.) Moore started his answer confidently: 'Firstly let it be deter-mined what are the grounds upon which anything may be considered good.' The view he proposed was that the 'ultimate object of each man's endeavour should be to attain for himself the highest possible mental devel-opment', and that the philanthropic and educational activities of the school mission could therefore be justified on the (notably egoistic) grounds that one's own mental development was maximized when one's fellow men's minds were also developed as perfectly as possible.[133] As an undergraduate studying ethics in Cambridge with Henry Sidgwick a few years later, Moore wrote an essay on 'Altruism and egoism, with their relations in the-ory and practice', which discussed the views of Bentham, Comte, Spencer, Green, and Sidgwick himself.[134] As a member of the 'Apostles', Moore had weekly opportunities during term-time to develop his ideas further in the context of intense intellectual discussions with a close group of friends on Saturday evenings. Moore delivered papers with titles such as 'Are we self-ish?' and 'Do we love ourselves best?' in 1898 and 1899.[135] Around the same time, Moore was working on the lectures which formed the original basis for the text of *Principia Ethica*. He delivered these lectures at the Passmore Edwards Settlement, which had grown out of University Hall, founded by Mrs Humphry Ward as an institution inspired by the same principles that had motivated the self-renouncing hero of *Robert Elsmere*.[136] The content of the lectures and the venue in which they were delivered, however, came from different ethical worlds. While Lytton Strachey would later turn his elegantly withering biographer's gaze towards Mrs Ward's grandfather, Thomas Arnold, Moore's *Principia Ethica* represented a rebellion against the neo-Christian philanthropy of Mrs Ward herself.

The brief discussion of altruism and egoism included in the final ver-sion of Moore's *Principia Ethica* in 1903 came in a chapter devoted to crit-icizing the identification of goodness with pleasure in the utilitarian ethics

---

[133] Essay on 'What is the good of the school mission?' dated 22 Nov. 1891, and contained in a book of 'Divinity Essays' held in the G. E. Moore papers, CUL, Add.8330.5/3/1.

[134] CUL, Add.8875.11/2/7.

[135] Apostles papers given by Moore on 26 Feb. 1898 and 4 Feb. 1899; CUL, Add.8875.12/1/16 and 19.

[136] On Mrs Humphry Ward and university settlements, see Ch. 6, above. The lectures that Moore gave at the Passmore Edwards Settlement in 1898–9, under the auspices of the London School of Ethics and Social Philosophy, have been published with an informative introd. by Tom Regan as G. E. Moore 1991.

of both Mill and Sidgwick.[137] Although almost certainly not a reader of *The Eagle and the Serpent*, nor a devotee of Nietzsche, Moore argued in defence of a certain kind of egoism. His discussion of the subject rested on a distinction between egoism as a doctrine of ends and egoism as a doctrine of means.[138] The former was the conviction that the greatest good in life was one's own happiness and all one's actions should be designed to achieve that goal. Moore attributed this position to Hobbes but thought that few still held it. It was only the second kind of egoism that should properly be contrasted with 'altruism', and it was with this form of egoism that Moore had some sympathy. This was egoism as a doctrine of means rather than ends—the belief that the best ethical results (whatever they may be) would generally be achieved if individuals pursued their own happiness directly, rather than if they pursued the happiness of others. Moore rejected egoism as a doctrine of ends but embraced 'this anti-altruistic Egoism, this Egoism as a doctrine of means', and considered that 'Egoism is undoubtedly superior to Altruism as a doctrine of means: in the immense majority of cases the best thing we can do is to aim at securing some good in which we are concerned, since for that very reason we are far more likely to secure it.'[139]

Although Moore argued for egoism over altruism, as a doctrine of means, his very use of that language was confined to a short section of a chapter criticizing Mill and Sidgwick. The language of altruism and egoism was not something that he had made his own. That strange neologism 'altruism'—or *altruisme*—which had, at least initially, been a powerful and inspiring word to Henry Sidgwick as a young man at Trinity in the early 1860s, had become, by the time G. E. Moore arrived at the same Cambridge college thirty years later, a word that smacked both of outdated moral philosophy and of exaggerated Victorian philanthropy.[140] This change in the significance and connotations of the term was a testament to the

---

[137] For detailed interpretations of Moore's arguments in *Principia Ethica*, and the philosophical processes by which he arrived at them, see Baldwin 1990: 66–144; Regan's introd. to G. E. Moore 1991; Baldwin's introd. to G. E. Moore 1993; Cunningham 1996: 31–58; Hutchinson 2001; Hurka 2003, 2005.

[138] *Principia Ethica*, ss. 58–65; G. E. Moore 1993: 147–60.

[139] *Principia Ethica*, ss. 58, 59, 63, 100; G. E. Moore 1993: 148, 216.

[140] On Sidgwick's early reaction to *altruisme*, see Chs 2 and 3, above. Bertrand Russell, in 'My Religious Reminiscences', first published in 1938, reflected on the contrasts between the 1860s and the 1890s. Russell recalled that the young men of Cambridge in the 1890s tended to be agnostic and uninterested in discussions of religion. The 'non-academic heroes' of the 1890s included 'Strindberg, Nietzsche, and (for a time) Oscar Wilde'; whereas in the 1860s the men who commanded respect had been 'Darwin, Huxley, the authors of *Essays and Reviews*, etc.' (Russell 1961: 35).

success that Mill, Spencer, and many others had enjoyed in transforming the moral lexicon of Victorian Britain. The linguistic strategy that Moore pursued in distancing himself from 'altruism' in *Principia Ethica* had two elements. In addition to expressing his preference for egoism over altruism in the earlier sections, when it came to his famous closing chapter on 'The Ideal', he simply used an entirely different moral vocabulary. Key philosophical terms now included 'organic unities' (Moore's term for irreducibly complex states of consciousness) and 'naturalistic fallacy'. 'Personal affections' and 'aesthetic enjoyments'; 'beautiful qualities' and 'appropriate emotion'— these were all phrases to be repeated and savoured.[141] But 'altruism' and 'egoism'? Those were the key words of an earlier generation.

Different readers focused on different parts of Moore's work in their responses.[142] Some philosophical readers found Moore's insistence on the indefinability of 'good' especially frustrating. As one of the leading British idealist philosophers of the period, Bernard Bosanquet, put it, on Moore's terms, argument about goodness simply 'becomes impossible', since whenever any substantive ethical doctrine—such as the Platonic one that the good is that which is desired—might be put forward, 'the naturalistic fallacy is invoked to bar the road by showing that *about good* nothing significant can be said at all'.[143] Another philosophical reviewer thought he detected a certain 'intellectual egotism' in the author of the work, which had prevented 'the sympathetic appreciation of the work of others'.[144]

The Fabian Beatrice Webb who, like Henry Sidgwick, had been inspired by her discovery of Comte and 'altruism' earlier in her life, was baffled by the positive reception *Principia Ethica* had received in Cambridge circles. It seemed to her to be simply a metaphysical justification for doing whatever one pleased. She thought that Moore's book was based on a rejection of both science and religion, and blamed it for encouraging a 'pernicious' Cambridge set which 'makes a sort of ideal of anarchic ways in sexual questions'.[145] The individual Webb believed presided over this unhealthy set, whose intellects and characters were being undermined by Moore's

[141] All of these phrases feature prominently in the famous final chapter of *Principia Ethica*, especially in ss. 113–17; G. E. Moore 1993: 237–44.

[142] On the reception of *Principia Ethica* see Levy 1981: 234–59; Holroyd 1997: 89–92.

[143] Bernard Bosanquet, '*Principia Ethica* by George Edward Moore', *Mind*, 13 (1904), 254–61, at 258, 260. John S. Mackenzie made similar complaints in his review of the work for the *International Journal of Ethics*, 4 (1904), 377–82.

[144] Norman Wilde, '*Principia Ethica* by George Edward Moore', *Journal of Philosophy, Psychology and Scientific Methods*, 2 (1905), 581–3, at 581.

[145] Letter to Lady Courtney, 18 Sept. 1911, quoted in Levy 1981: 4–5.

Principia Ethica, was the writer, lecturer, and former 'Apostle', Goldsworthy Lowes Dickinson.[146] In spite of Webb's identification of Moore and Dickinson with the same degenerate Cambridge set, Dickinson was not a particular admirer of *Principia Ethica*. He had recently finished writing a philosophical dialogue of his own on *The Meaning of Good* (1901) when Moore's book came out.[147] Having read it, Dickinson realized that he had committed 'what Moore called the "naturalistic fallacy"'. This did not trouble him unduly, however, since he was sure, having been involved in philosophical conversations with Moore over several years, that he 'has probably long ago altered his position, on this as on other points'. In his autobiography Dickinson recalled that the phrase 'naturalistic fallacy' had always made him laugh because he thought it suggested 'some kind of unnatural vice'.[148]

It was partly because of its usefulness in defending a sexually unconventional lifestyle of the sort that Webb and Dickinson both alluded to that Lytton Strachey and other members of the Bloomsbury Group welcomed *Principia Ethica* so enthusiastically. Strachey wrote to Moore that the 'Age of Reason' had dawned with the publication of this work and marvelled at the wreckage in which Moore had left all previous ethical theorists, from Aristotle to Christ to Herbert Spencer, Henry Sidgwick, and John McTaggart. To Leonard Woolf, Strachey wrote: 'The last two chapters— glory alleluiah!' According to his biographer, Michael Holroyd, Strachey discovered in *Principia Ethica* a 'moral basis for the love that, since Oscar Wilde's imprisonment, dared not speak its name'. The central message for Strachey was that 'feelings are good', but, he wrote to John Maynard Keynes, it was 'madness' to think that respectable dowagers would be convinced by this celebration of feelings 'when we say in the same breath that the best ones are sodomitical'.[149] Strachey did not broach this particular interpretation of the book with Moore himself.[150]

That readers of *Principia Ethica* were reminded in various ways of Oscar Wilde was not surprising. Wilde's 'The Critic as Artist' had included the assertion that 'To discern the beauty of a thing is the finest point to which we can arrive.'[151] Moore wrote in *Principia Ethica* that the feelings arising from the appreciation of beauty, along with the enjoyment of personal

---

[146] On Dickinson, see *ODNB*; Levy 1981: 97–100.

[147] Dickinson 1901.

[148] Proctor 1973: 164; on Dickinson as an 'Apostle', see also Levy 1981: 97–100. Dickinson, as a homosexual, had some understanding of attitudes to 'unnatural vice'.

[149] Holroyd 1997: 89–92.

[150] Levy 1981: 212–13; Holroyd 1997: 91–2.

[151] Wilde 1909: 215.

affections, constituted '*all* the greatest, and *by far* the greatest, goods we can imagine'.[152] Both Wilde and Moore were making use of the resources of the aesthetic tradition particularly associated with Walter Pater. As an undergraduate at Oxford in the 1870s, Wilde copied down a quotation from an article about Wordsworth in which Pater had written that the end of life was 'not action but contemplation', and that one should aspire to 'witness the spectacle of life with appropriate emotions'.[153] Twenty years later, writing the manuscript that would become *De Profundis*, Wilde mistakenly attributed this same quotation to William Wordsworth himself.[154] In the final chapter of *Principia Ethica*, Moore, who had paid homage to Wordsworth by walking to Grasmere and Rydal during his undergraduate reading party in 1895, repeatedly argued that true appreciation of beauty was marked not only by a cognition of an object's beautiful qualities but by having the 'appropriate emotion' towards those qualities too.[155] For Moore, who enjoyed attending performances of Wagner and playing Schumann sonatas as well as walking in the Lake District, appreciating beauty meant having appropriate emotions in response to 'Art' as well as 'Nature'.[156] While Wilde's motto was 'Aesthetics are higher than ethics', the message of *Principia Ethica* seemed to go even further by suggesting a near-identity between aesthetics and ethics.[157] Moore defined the beautiful as 'that of which the admiring contemplation is good in itself'.[158]

Moore's main achievement in writing *Principia Ethica* was to produce an intellectual rationale for the way of life, and the kinds of love, favoured by a group of educated young men and women in Britain in the late nineteenth and early twentieth centuries. But advocacy of this post-Victorian way of life could not be undertaken in Victorian language. While Max Nordau, Alfred Douglas, and the editors of *The Eagle and the Serpent*, were all still tied to the language of 'egoism' and 'altruism', Moore and his friends were not. Instead of understanding love as something that was given from the 'ego' to a separate 'alter', they understood it as an emotion that brought two people into a unity. In a paper read to the 'Apostles' in 1898, Moore

---

[152] *Principia Ethica*, s. 113; G. E. Moore 1993: 238.
[153] P. E. Smith and Helfland 1989: 141–2, and 194–5, which identifies the source as Walter Pater, 'On Wordsworth', *Fortnightly Review*, 15 (1874), 465.
[154] Wilde 2005: 109, 251.
[155] The first time this point is made is *Principia Ethica*, s. 114; G. E. Moore 1993: 238–9.
[156] *Principia Ethica*, s. 113; G. E. Moore 1993: 238.
[157] On Wilde, see above. The motto is spoken by Gilbert in 'The Critic as Artist'; Wilde 1909: 214–15.
[158] *Principia Ethica*, s. 121; G. E. Moore 1993: 249.

put it this way: 'To be in the right relations with the right persons is all that can here be good; and if you are so, you do not do one thing for self and another for them, but all simply for the sake of the whole that is you and them and what is between you.'[159] The American idealist philosopher, Josiah Royce, like Moore, treated the language of altruism as a relic of Victorian discussions of utilitarianism and evolutionary ethics. For Royce, the terms 'altruistic' and 'egoistic' were inappropriate to discussions of the good life. In 1894, he wrote that two devoted friends, in talking, working, and living together, cooperated in a project that belonged equally to each of them: 'Each friend lives, not "in the other", as other, but in that which is *theirs*.' 'As a fact', Royce concluded, 'no account of the aesthetic element in morality can be complete which fails to take account of the beauty possessed by those forms of conduct which, being moral, are essentially neither egoistic nor altruistic.'[160]

---

[159] From Moore's paper 'Is it Virtuous to Wash?', 26 Feb. 1898. Quoted in Levy 1981: 195–6.
[160] Josiah Royce, '*The Aesthetic Element in Morality, and its Place in a Utilitarian Theory of Morals* by Frank Chapman Sharp', *International Journal of Ethics*, 4 (1894), 395–9, at 397, 399.

Conclusion

On the penultimate day of the nineteenth century, Sunday 30 December 1900, the Reverend Hugh Price Hughes held an afternoon conference for his congregation at the Wesleyan West London Mission at St James's Hall, Piccadilly. The subject of the conference was 'The Altruism of the Nineteenth Century'.[1] Hughes, who had been one of the first to preach on *Robert Elsmere* in 1888, and whose volumes of sermons had titles such as *Social Christianity* (1890) and *Ethical Christianity* (1892), sought to embrace secular philosophy in the service of Christ. He could see in Comtean positivism and in Spencerian evolutionary ethics glimmers of Christian truth and suggestions of a Christian ethics. Himself a devotee of T. H. Green's idealist philosophy as well as a preacher of the social gospel, Hughes's moral teaching captured with absolute clarity the tensions involved in the rhetorical combination of Christianity with the fashionable new ethos of altruism.

In one sermon, on 'The Brotherhood of Mankind', taking as his text Ephesians 4: 25 'We are members of one another', Hughes praised the positivists for emancipating themselves from 'the selfish individualism and parochialism which have so often disfigured conventional Christian thinkers'. He also expressed his admiration for Spencer's discovery in *The Data of Ethics* that egoism and altruism were closely intertwined, and that everyone was therefore 'directly, and even selfishly interested in the true welfare of everyone else'. Hughes went on, in Greenian vein, to emphasize that all social and economic advantages were essentially mutual advantages and that every man 'is consequently a part of my better self, and I am bound by the most sacred obligations to care for his interests precisely as I care for my own'. In other words there was 'no ultimate antagonism between the interest of the Individual and of Society. Legitimate and healthy self-love is in perfect harmony with altruism.' This was orthodox idealist philosophy.

---

[1] Announced in *The Times* (29 Dec. 1900), 6.

By the end of the same sermon, however, this legitimate and healthy self-love seemed to have been set aside, and Christianity to have been reduced to positivist altruism: 'Shall we accept the Pauline, the Christian conception of life, or the Satanic conception of life? Shall we live for self, or shall we live for others—for all?' The love of self which was earlier compatible, even identical, with pursuing the good of others, was now identified with the 'Satanic conception of life', and the only hint that Christian ethics differed from positivism was the two-word afterthought 'for all' tacked on to the end of the Comtean motto 'live for others'. The final moral of this particular sermon, however, was not a recommendation of altruism but a restatement of the Christian-idealist ethos of self-realization through self-denial: 'Happy is the man who understands the characteristic and oft-repeated paradox of Christ, "He that findeth his life shall lose it; and he that loseth his life for my sake shall find it."'[2]

'Paradox' is indeed an appropriate place to end the story of the invention of altruism. The semantic progression that has been revealed by tracing the dissemination of the language of altruism through Victorian culture, like a marker or a dye, culminated in the naturalization of an ethical term fraught with paradox and confusion. Since one of the underlying points of this study has been that, while 'altruism' is a single word, it is one that has historically been used to signify a multiplicity of different concepts, I cannot in this conclusion make any singular statements about 'the' meaning of altruism, either historically or in the present, nor about any absolutely inevitable or inherent semantic difficulties. What I can do, however, is to end by drawing attention to some of the recurring intellectual and political conundrums to which debates about 'altruism' gave rise during the nineteenth century, in the hope that doing so might give present-day users of the language of altruism pause for thought.

Writing about 'earnest', the key word of an earlier Victorian generation, Walter Houghton observes that when a new word 'suddenly comes into fashion to describe a "good" attitude' the historian should be aware that 'the historical context is more useful than the dictionary for understanding its meaning'.[3] In the case of 'altruism', the historical contexts through which that word progressed in the nineteenth century were various. They included not only literary and intellectual contexts such as the writing, reading, and reception of philosophical texts by Comte, Mill, Darwin, Spencer, Green, and Moore, but also such social contexts as James

---

[2] H. P. Hughes 1894: 32–3, 37–8, 41–2. The biblical quotation is from Matt. 10: 39.
[3] Houghton 1957: 218.

Hinton's exploratory tours of London nightlife and John Bridges's talks to the Bradford Mechanics' institute in the 1860s; sermons preached in Oxford, Cambridge, and elsewhere and the deliberations of members of the Metaphysical Society at the Grosvenor Hotel in the 1870s; Beatrice Potter's moments of private reflection in St Paul's Cathedral and Robert Melsom's life in Manchester in the 1880s; Oscar Wilde's prison cell and Ernest Newman's secularist Liverpool in the 1890s; the activities of London's slummers and religious reformers in the East End and Hugh Price Hughes's Wesleyan Mission in the West End.

A word, like a tool, can be used for tasks other than the one for which it was originally designed. Its semantic evolution can see it take on meanings that diverge from, or are even opposed to, its original use and etymology. This happened to a certain extent with 'altruism' as it passed through these various social contexts. It came to stand for actions and ideologies as well as for the set of other-regarding 'affective motors' which Comte had originally used it to denote. Its connotations developed from Comtean to Spencerian, and beyond. In one sense, however, 'altruism' was a word which never broke free from its etymology. Constructed by Comte (or by his teacher Andrieux) from the Italian *altrui* (of or for others), and ultimately from the Latin *alter* (other), 'altruism' was from the outset, and continues to be, a word that draws its primary significance from the distinction between the interests of self and of others. To the extent that this is a problematic distinction, 'altruism' has been a problematic word.

When Lewes introduced the terms 'altruism' and 'altruistic' to readers of his *Comte's Philosophy of the Sciences* in 1853 he did so in terms of this binary opposition: 'Dispositions influenced by the purely egotistic impulses we call popularly "bad", and apply the term "good" to those in which altruism predominates.'[4] One of the earliest definitions of the term, then, not only relied on a stark contrast between self and other, but went further by mapping that distinction onto the moral division between bad and good. Self-ism was bad, other-ism good. Spencer was not so simplistic. Although he also explicitly justified the introduction of 'altruism' on the grounds of its usefulness in denoting a contrast with 'egoism'—something which he thought 'benevolence' or 'beneficence' could not achieve—he did not define the good life as one in which egoism was simply subordinated to altruism, or vice versa. Instead he hoped for a 'conciliation' or 'compromise' between these two powers. It is notable that writers who treated 'altruism'

---

[4] Lewes 1853: 224.

as an established term in the early twentieth century saw it as one half of a well-known dichotomy, rather than as an autonomous term. One author, whom I quoted at the outset, referred in 1910 to 'the two traditional terms, *egoism* and *altruism*, which may be roughly but clearly defined as denoting the self-regarding and the other-regarding impulses, respectively'.[5] The idealist philosopher Bernard Bosanquet wrote in 1919 of the importance of rejecting what he described as 'the popular antithesis of egoism and altruism'.[6] Although the language of altruism had been widely used only since the late 1870s, by the 1910s the contrast between altruism and egoism appeared to be both a traditional and a popular focus for ethical debate.

All the most significant philosophical, religious, and political problems that debates about 'altruism' have involved since its first use have been connected with the problem of explaining and sustaining this distinction between self and other, between ego and alter. It was idealist philosophers inspired by T. H. Green who most clearly identified this as an inherent problem for an ethics of 'altruism' in the nineteenth century. For the idealists, the main point was that each individual was from the outset a social being, whose existence and happiness were inextricably linked with the existence and happiness of many others. It was not out of a love for others directly opposed to a love of self that a mother cared for her children or a social reformer volunteered to work in a settlement house. It was rather that they identified directly with the interests of those they helped, and to that extent, were seeking the fulfilment of their own interests and the cultivation of their own selves in acting as they did. An idealist like Robert Elsmere sought, in undertaking work that some scorned as sentimentally and faddishly 'altruistic', to improve the society of which he himself was a member, and to cultivate his own better self. The ethics of philosophical idealism, as Hugh Price Hughes discovered, resonated more closely with the Christian paradox of self-realization through self-renunciation than it did with the positivist desire to subordinate egoism to altruism.

Coming at the problem from a different angle, those with a Nietzschean suspicion of pity and altruism thought that advocates of these alleged virtues were simply acting as mouthpieces for the selfish desire of the weak and poor for more power and more wealth. From this perspective, the call for 'altruism' reflected not real selflessness but the selfish interests of pleasure-seeking utilitarians and property-hungry socialists. More generally speaking, Victorian commentators of all schools could recognize

---

[5] Sisson 1910: 158.
[6] Bosanquet 1958: p. xv. The quotation is from the preface to the 3rd edn of the work (1919).

that any action undertaken to achieve a desired end, even if that end was the good of others, was undertaken in pursuit of the fulfilment of the agent's own desires and, in that sense, was in their own interest.[7] Agents of altruism could also expect to receive approval, praise, and reward for their selflessness. A secular ideology organized around the social encouragement of altruism, as much as a religion that promised rewards in the hereafter, encountered the problem that there always seemed to be a good self-interested reason to be selfless. A final related paradox was that self-sacrificing acts must be undertaken either spontaneously or after deliberation. While many, including Darwin and Hughes, admired the former more than the latter, it was unusual to express moral approval for involuntary actions.[8] On the other hand, an act of altruism undertaken only after deliberation smacked of a self-interested weighing up of potential consequences.

Victorians certainly worried about these paradoxes of altruism and selfishness, and it would be possible to find evidence to characterize the whole Victorian age as a time either of outstanding benevolence, or alternatively as one of particular selfishness, or perhaps as both. The altruistic interpretation could be substantiated with reference to the money and time devoted by many thousands of Victorians to voluntary philanthropic endeavours, as well as the endless Christian and secular sermonizing recommending such activities, some of which has been explored above.[9] The alternative view—that Victorians were especially selfish—has sometimes been connected with the alleged predominance of a *laissez-faire* economic ethos buttressed by Darwinian science. In his recent portrait of the Victorian age, A. N. Wilson describes Britain in the 1840s as 'a ruthless, grabbing, competitive, male-dominated society, stamping on its victims and discarding its weaker members with all the devastating relentlessness of mutant species in Darwin's vision of Nature itself'. Wilson goes on to describe the condition of the urban poor, the relationship between Britain and her colonies, and the struggle for dominance in Europe as all being 'part of the same selfish Darwinian struggle'. For Wilson, the Darwinian theory was the 'mythopoetic expression' of the capitalist system—a system which itself depended on 'unbridled selfishness'.[10] Another recent writer similarly ponders: 'How different modern life, and not simply biological science, might be, if Darwin

---

[7] See, for instance, Stephen 1882: 219.
[8] C. Darwin 1882: 120. See Ch. 4 above. Hugh Price Hughes used a similar example of spontaneous self-sacrifice as the epitome of moral heroism; H. P. Hughes 1892: 10.
[9] See also Prochaska 1988; Himmelfarb 1991, 1995; Koven 2004.
[10] A. N. Wilson 2003: 120, 148.

had not been consumed by the vision of competition, and had been able to acknowledge the cooperation that is also evident in the natural order.'[11]

As we have seen, these sorts of view seriously misrepresent Darwin's own understanding of the evolution of morality, if not the way that his works have often been read by others. But there is another more fundamental reason to be suspicious of this kind of historical moralizing. Instead of arguing that the Victorians were either particularly selfish or especially altruistic we should recognize instead that it is to them we owe our modern habit of making moral judgements in the rhetorically loaded language of selfishness and altruism. Some Victorian writers themselves recognized that accusations of selfishness against others could easily descend into mere name-calling. An 1869 article in the *Westminster Review* took the ethical writer William Lecky to task for dividing the rival theories of morals into two schools, the first of which was known as 'the stoical, the intuitive, the independent or the sentimental', and the second of which was called 'the epicurean, the inductive, the utilitarian, or the selfish.' The reviewer thought that Lecky was guilty of using what Bentham had termed 'question-begging appellatives', and added the following commentary:

> It is to beg the question at once to describe your opponent's theory as 'self-ish.' Students of morals know that such language means no more than that you dislike the theory in question; but the public at large believe that you start with a moral superiority over your adversaries: the superiority, however, consists in this, that you deliberately use language which cannot mislead the wise, and cannot instruct the foolish, which we venture to think is a superiority the reverse of moral.[12]

Writing in 1882, Leslie Stephen made the similar point that by 'fixing upon an antagonist the imputation of egoism you give him a bad name, and have an easy opportunity for a rhetoric which reflects credit upon the assailant'. This had become common, Stephen wrote, even though only 'a cynic or a satirist here and there' actually maintained 'the thesis of universal selfishness'.[13]

To praise the Victorians for their altruism or to denounce them for their selfishness is to mimic their own moral rhetoric, and to see things their way, rather than to offer a plausible historical characterization of their age. The story of the invention of altruism reveals that ethical judgements had not always been made this way. Moral thought did not have to be organized

---

[11] Grant 2001: 33.
[12] Anon., 'The Natural History of Morals', *Westminster Review*, 36 (1869), 494–531, at 497–8; repr. in Pyle 1998: ii. 351–86.
[13] Stephen 1882: 219.

around the dichotomy between self and other, and had not always been so. Some Victorian moralists preferred to continue thinking about ethical life in terms not of a contrast between altruism and selfishness, but of the love of an individual for God, self, and others, or perhaps as a struggle between a virtuous rational will and troublesome passions and appetites. Others distinguished between a good will and good actions, something that proponents of 'altruism' struggled to do, by using the terms 'benevolence' and 'beneficence'. Others still rejected the distinction between egoism and altruism on idealist or socialist grounds, or because they preferred to trace all human action back to a single motive—whether love or self-interest—rather than to two antagonistic sets of instincts.

The invention of altruism drew attention not only to the paradoxes inherent in the ethical celebration of social selflessness, but also to the problems involved in trying to produce a naturalistic and scientific ethics. Spencer justified his adoption of the term on the grounds that it provided a much needed antonym for 'egoism', but he surely also preferred its modern scientific register to the old-fashioned and religious sound of words such as 'charity', 'philanthropy', and 'beneficence'. Spencer took what had been a term of Comtean cerebral science and gave it a new, extended, and evolutionary set of meanings. In doing so he was contributing to the established tradition, to which Comte and Darwin were also contributors, of connecting ethics with the study of the natural world. Spencer's *Data of Ethics* (1879) and Drummond's *Ascent of Man* (1894) both demonstrated especially clearly the difficulties that arose from juxtaposing ethical propositions with scientific descriptions of non-ethical natural phenomena. What was supposed to be the relationship between these two kinds of discourse? On the one hand, the whole interest of these works lay in their attempt to find the roots of human morality in its evolutionary history, as reconstructed through observations of lower forms of life. On the other hand, it had to be admitted that certainly cellular fission in protozoa, and possibly also the instinctive self-sacrificing, parental, or cooperative behaviours of ants, birds, or monkeys, were quite different in character from the kind of 'altruism' celebrated in human moral life. If mere 'loss of bodily substance' in a protozoon was to qualify, as Spencer had suggested it should, as a rudimentary act of 'physical altruism' then, as Nietzsche put it, even urination could be considered an altruistic activity.[14]

---

[14] Spencer 1879: 201–3; Nietzsche 1974: s. 35[34], 246; 1980: xi. 524, s. 35[34]. Tr. in Small 2005: 174–5. See also Chs 5 and 8 above.

Part of the appeal of the language of altruism had been that it seemed able to contribute to a scientific ethics constructed independently of Christianity and metaphysics, and one which connected humanity with the rest of nature. But by stretching the meaning of 'altruism' to include not only human motives but also physical actions in the natural world that appeared to be entirely automatic and involuntary, Spencer and others who attempted to create a natural history for human morality made the term seem less and less relevant to the very ethical endeavour which had made the scientific project interesting in the first place. The same problem can be discerned in more recent attempts to make use of scientific studies of altruism to contribute to philosophical or theological discussions of ethics. Modern scientific studies generally use the term 'altruism' to refer to any behaviour or trait which increases the reproductive fitness of the recipient while reducing the reproductive fitness of the actor (where 'reproductive fitness' is a measure of an individual's success in leaving offspring in the next generation). On this biological definition, the deaths of slime mould cells when they are turned into a stalk for the dispersal of spores; the release of digestive enzymes by individual microbes which break down food for the benefit of genetically related cells; the donation of regurgitated blood among vampire bats; and the human menopause are all described as 'altruistic'.[15] These seem no more relevant to human moral life than did Spencer's and Drummond's cellular fission or Lubbock's self-sacrificing ants. It is not difficult to understand why some suggest making a firm distinction between an everyday moral sense of 'altruism' and a technical neo-Darwinian sense of the term.[16] To avoid confusion, perhaps we should go one step further and simply drop the terms 'altruism' and 'altruistic' from philosophical, ethical, and theological discussions altogether. They would then be retained simply as technical theoretical terms in the natural and social sciences, where they are still widely used (with attendant mathematical formulae defining their meaning and explaining the existence of the phenomena they denote).

In the nineteenth century, critics of Darwin and Spencer, and of later exponents of ethical naturalism such as Drummond and Kidd, had already noted that there was a gap between the cooperation and self-sacrifice

---

[15] These examples are taken from Foster forthcoming. See also Okasha 2005; Foster *et al.* 2007. Cronin 1991: 265 refers to an example given by Richard Dawkins in *The Selfish Gene* (1976) which explains how a gene for bad teeth could, in certain circumstances, be described as a gene for altruism.

[16] See e.g. Dawkins 1989: 4; Sober and Wilson 1998: 6–8; Sober 2002; Dawkins 2006: 214–22.

discerned in the natural world on the one hand and what they considered to be distinctively human moral life on the other. Conscious, reflective, and affectionate relationships between particular individuals were at the heart of many Victorian visions of morality, but were not to be found in the division of cells or in the social instincts of insects. R. H. Hutton, Ellice Hopkins, and Frances Power Cobbe were amongst the critics of Darwin who held that there was much more to 'that short but imperious word ought' than either the 'mere gregariousness' or the 'inherited prejudice', to which they believed Darwin had reduced it. The Darwinian Arabella Buckley could also see that there was more to the good life than mere insect-like self-sacrifice.[17] If animal behaviour were to be taken either as evidence of the roots of human morality or as some kind of template for human goodness, it was not clear that 'altruism' was the best term to describe what was being invoked as either origin or model. This single term could obscure distinctions between different instincts and behaviours. Darwin wrote about 'love', 'sympathy', and 'conscience' rather than 'altruism'. Benjamin Kidd pointed out that Drummond's use of 'altruism' confused together two quite different things—parental care and social cooperation. And Kropotkin's idea of 'mutual aid' was a reciprocal rather than a simply altruistic ideal.

Even with a richer sense of the different sorts of love and cooperation observable in the animal world, the point remained that there was more to the well-lived individual life than devotion to the family and society. In addition to this qualitative gap between the instincts of animals and human moral experience there was, of course, an argumentative gap between the observation that certain animals (including humans) had a natural tendency to feel, think, and act a particular way and the judgement that they ought to follow rather than resist that particular tendency. Arabella Buckley tacitly acknowledged this argumentative gap by treating natural history as a source of moral parables rather than of logical inferences about ethics. She knew that insects, for example, could be selfish and aggressive as well as cooperative and industrious, and so drew morals from nature only tentatively. Some natural urges should be followed, but others overcome. We were born with the tendency to be violent as well as loving. Although Darwin was certain that human love and sympathy were natural products of evolution, and that they would continue to become stronger in future, he equally recognized that each individual inherited ancestral impulses to

---

[17] See Ch. 4 above.

violence and destruction. As he had put it in one of his early notebooks: 'Our descent, then, is the origin of our evil passions!! The Devil under form of Baboon is our grandfather!'[18] Humanity's natural inheritance was morally mixed. As George Eliot had put it, 'Appetite is the ancestor of tyranny, but it is also the ancestor of love.'[19]

So it was abundantly clear to critics of scientific ethics that even the most persuasive account of the evolutionary history of human morality was ethically incomplete. It could not, in itself, say anything about the desirability or moral worth of particular individual or social ways of life, nor about the merit of following or resisting particular instincts. G. E. Moore put this well-known problem in a slightly different way when he included Spencer's evolutionary ethics (along with almost every other existing ethical philosophy) in the category of those systems which fell foul of his 'naturalistic fallacy'. According to Moore's mystical approach to ethics, any definition at all of the ethical term 'good' in terms of non-ethical categories such as 'pleasurable', 'useful', 'for the greater good', or 'in accordance with nature' was guilty of committing the naturalistic fallacy. As indicated above, Moore's *Principia Ethica* (1903) should be read primarily as a justification of *fin-de-siècle* aesthetic individualism, rather than as a particularly significant contribution to well-established debates about the problem of how to draw morals from the natural world.[20] Moore aside, it remains the case that the scientific question about innate human instincts and the ethical question about how we should live are quite separate. Richard Dawkins made this separation clear in *The Selfish Gene* (1976). Having warned that those who wished to create a cooperative and unselfish society could expect 'little help from biological nature', Dawkins issued his defiant moralistic rallying cry: 'Let us try to *teach* generosity and altruism, because we are born selfish.'[21] Someone with a different moral philosophy and a different interpretation of evolutionary science might prefer to say: 'Let us try to *teach* self-realization and individualism, because we are born altruistic.'

---

[18] Barrett 1987: 549–50.

[19] Quoted in K. K. Collins 1978: 491–2; see Ch. 3 above.

[20] See Ch. 8 above.

[21] Dawkins 1989: 3. Later in the same book Dawkins elaborated on the same manifesto: 'We have the power to defy the selfish genes of our birth and, if necessary, the selfish memes of our indoctrination. We can even discuss ways of deliberately cultivating and nurturing pure, disinterested altruism—something that has no place in nature, something that has never existed before in the whole history of the world. We are built as gene machines and cultured as meme machines, but we have the power to turn against our creators. We, alone on earth, can rebel against the tyranny of the selfish replicators' (200–1).

One of the most interesting features of the arrival and survival of 'altruism' in the moral lexicon, as Hugh Price Hughes's sermons brought out very clearly, was the role that the term's users supposed it to play in relation to Christianity. The key question here, both for Victorian moralists and for those of us seeking a historical perspective on moral philosophy, is whether 'altruism' represented an ideal that was consistent, or even identical, with Christian ethics, or whether it was, on the contrary, one that was in some respects anti-Christian. Comte had, of course, introduced the term as part of an avowedly godless philosophy, and had asserted that his discovery of the innateness of altruism overturned the Christian notion that all human beings were innately selfish and sinful. English positivists who championed Comte's ethics further argued that to replace the Christian hope for a personal afterlife with a belief in personal annihilation and a 'subjective immortality' in the memories of others was to replace an essentially selfish creed with a superior altruistic one. In the place of the self-centred Christian quest for salvation the positivists proposed the self-effacing pursuit of social progress in the name of their *Grand Être*, humanity.

We have also seen that there was a strong body of mid-Victorian Christian opinion according to which 'altruism' was indeed the watchword of an atheistic ethics which either contradicted or at best caricatured Christian teaching by eliminating from the ethical picture the legitimate love both of God and of self. Henry Sidgwick and Oscar Wilde both made the point that the gospel story of Christ's injunction to the young man to sell all he had and give the proceeds to the poor was advice offered for the good of the young man rather than for the good of the poor. Christianity, in the eyes of Victorian idealists and individualists, was a creed of self-realization as much as of self-renunciation. Christ was not a mere philanthropist. The author of the *Fraser's Magazine* article on 'The Failure of Altruism' in 1879 denounced the ideal of 'altruism' as a secular caricature of Christianity, a 'one-winged ideal' which unrealistically denied the power of human self-interest and unreasonably advocated its total elimination. 'Altruism' was, in the eyes of the duke of Argyll in the 1890s, a 'new and very affected name for the old form of things which we used to call charity, benevolence, and love'.[22] For many critics as well as advocates, then, 'altruism' stood for an ideology which opposed Christian ideas about human nature and ethics. Linguistic resistance was closely correlated with ideological resistance, from Canon Mozley's Oxford sermons in the 1870s to W. H. Mallock's and Ouida's novels in the 1890s.

---

[22] Quoted in Carr 1895: 17–18.

In 1870, Mozley had drawn a contrast between the gospel injunction, 'Love thy neighbour as thyself' and the new precept of 'Altruism'—'Love thy neighbour and not thyself.'[23] For others, however, this distinction was soon left behind. In the rush to keep up with the prevailing secular rhetoric of selflessness, and the desire not to be outdone in their denunciation of egotism and selfishness, Christian apologists, including Farrar and Drummond, came to adopt 'altruism' as a synonym for Christian love. Drummond had written in 1891 that 'the new word altruism—the translation of "love thy neighbour as thyself"—is slowly finding its way into current Christian speech'.[24] In 1894, John Gorst MP, in his address to the students of Glasgow University, identified 'the life of devotion to the good of the human race at large' with 'the religion of Jesus Christ'.[25] Robert Blatchford considered that 'Altruism, which is the embodiment of the command "Love thy neighbour as thyself," seems to have originated in the teachings of Christ, but has only attained important development in comparatively modern times.'[26] And in 1899 Robert Mackintosh told his Manchester students (not entirely approvingly) that 'Innumerable writers, Christian as well as non-Christian, have come to employ the term "Altruism" as a synonym for goodness'.[27] Some theologians had even come to interpret Christ's death on the cross as an act of 'altruism'. In his Wilde Lectures for 1911–12, the Oxford philosopher of religion Clement Webb considered modern interpretations of the atonement according to which Christ's death was not a propitiatory sacrifice but was instead a noble example of giving one's life for the sake of others—an action comparable to that of a man on a sinking vessel who puts others rather than himself into the life-boats. To accept this interpretation, Webb noted with some concern, would be to see Christ's death as nothing more than 'a great example of what Comte and Herbert Spencer call "altruism"'.[28]

By the time that 'altruism' had become a standard ethical term in the early twentieth century, its anti-Christian pedigree had been largely forgotten. A word which had only a few decades earlier stood for the atheistic denial of Christianity, and for a set of other-regarding instincts which science had discovered to be innate, had come to stand, for some, for the

[23] 'Eternal Life', in Mozley 1886: 46–71, at 65.
[24] Henry Drummond, *The Programme of Christianity* (1891), included in Drummond 1903: 69–123, at 77.
[25] Gorst 1895: 9–10.
[26] Blatchford 1898: 3.
[27] Mackintosh 1899: 45.
[28] C. Webb 1915: 121–2, quotation at 121. This passage is also quoted in Hilton 1988: 296n.

epitome of Christian morality and, furthermore, for a kind of moral motivation which science could not hope to explain. Alfred Russel Wallace, for
instance, had written to Herbert Spencer about the latter's recently published *Data of Ethics* in 1879, that although he found much to admire in that
book, he doubted that evolution alone could 'account for the development
of the advanced and enthusiastic *altruism* that not only exists now, but apparently has always existed among men'. Wallace thought that this altruism
demanded a supernatural explanation.[29] When Nietzsche described the
positivist celebration of altruism as an ethics which had managed to 'outchristian Christianity' he was only partly right. It had its origins in one part
of Christianity, but combined an extreme caricature of that part with an
outright rejection of many associated teachings. What was surprising was
how quickly this secular caricature became, for many, indistinguishable from
the real thing. After 1900 it was only rarely that the anti-Christian roots of
'altruism' were remembered. The Catholic moral philosopher Jacques
Maritain, writing in the 1960s, provided a rare echo of Victorian criticisms
when he described Comtean 'altruism' as an atheistic and sentimental ideal
which enslaved rather than liberated by denying the importance of self-love,
and thus also of individual rights and social justice.[30]

To the extent that 'altruism' today still seems to signify an admirable
kind of motivation, behaviour, or ethical ideal—in some cases to the extent
of producing the peculiarly modern belief that the very best actions are
those with no discernible benefit to oneself—we can say that we are still
living with the legacy of the inventors of altruism. Even the possibility of
formulating and assenting to such views in the twenty-first century is testimony to those innovators' success in overcoming the linguistic and ideological resistance they encountered from nineteenth-century Christians,
individualists, and idealists. Underlying the problems already surveyed—of
clearly distinguishing between the interests of self and others, of moving
from naturalistic descriptions to ethical prescriptions, and of seeking to
eliminate self-love from ethics—was the fundamental issue of whether and
to what extent 'altruism' represented a desirable ethical or political ideal at
all. There were plenty of Victorian writers who doubted it. Indeed, aside

---

[29] A. R. Wallace to Herbert Spencer, 2 July 1879, quoted in Duncan 1908: 199. An interesting
modern equivalent of this denial that altruism can be explained purely scientifically can be found
in a recent book by Francis Collins, who was previously the director of the Human Genome
Project. He wrote to explain how he combined his scientific beliefs with his Christian faith. See
F. S. Collins 2006: 24–31, which treats 'altruism' both as synonymous with Christian *agape* and as
inexplicable on a purely naturalistic basis.
[30] Maritain 1964: 327–50.

from the two writers who stand at the beginning and the end of the process which saw the meaning of 'altruism' change from atheistic devotion to humanity to the epitome of Christian love, namely Auguste Comte and Henry Drummond, there were very few straightforward advocates of altruism as an ethical ideal. Those who have sometimes been thought of as exponents of Victorian 'altruism', such as George Eliot and T. H. Green, seem on closer examination to have been committed to subtly different ethical philosophies in which self-realization, social solidarity, and sympathy, rather than simple self-sacrifice, were the key notes. Herbert Spencer argued (before being overcome by pessimism later in his life) for a 'compromise' and 'conciliation' between egoism and altruism in the short term, which might in the longer term evolve into a utopian identity between the two.

While early resistance to ideals of 'altruism' had frequently come from Christian quarters, the later Victorian period saw the emergence of a new political sense to the term and at the same time a range of more secular reasons for resistance, from Wildean individualism and Nietzschean egoism to feminism and anarchism. The pivotal decade here was the 1880s. This was a time that saw public life in Britain transformed by an increase in political participation, by the new social acceptability of religious unbelief, and by the birth of a popular socialist faith in state agency. This was the decade that Beatrice Webb retrospectively described as the time that saw the arrival of 'the consciousness of a new motive; the transference of the emotion of self-sacrificing service from God to man'.[31] The name of that new motive was 'altruism'. Although, as we have seen, the process was much more complex than such a neat summary suggests, the language of altruism seems to have come into its own and, for a short time, encapsulated the aspirations of a new generation of idealistic socialists at exactly the time that Webb was forging her own political identity in the 1880s and 1890s. The 1895 General Election was a disaster for the British socialists, but in 1906 they saw their representation increase from two to twenty-nine MPs. That success was a sign that those like Caleb Saleeby who celebrated 'altruism' as the motive of unmediated individual acts of generosity from the giver to the receiver were losing the argument with those who, like Robert Blatchford and Beatrice Webb, thought that the aims of true altruism could only be achieved through the machinery of the state. In 1906 Saleeby memorably parodied supporters of socialism by suggesting that they would rephrase Jesus's saying 'I was sick and ye

---

[31] Webb 1926: 129–30.

visited me' as 'I was sick, and ye wrote a cheque under compulsion whereby someone else was paid to visit me.'[32]

The twentieth century saw large-scale experiments in state socialism flourishing to different extents in different countries. Those regimes that most resembled Auguste Comte's altruistic utopia were those at the totalitarian end of the spectrum. It is therefore not altogether surprising to note that Beatrice Webb's enthusiasm for Comtean 'altruism' in the 1880s had evolved by the 1930s into her identification with the collectivist creed of the Communist Party in Soviet Russia.[33] To others, the emergence of such a regime might have seemed a vindication of the warnings of those Victorians who had suggested that a society based on an ideology of pure altruism—perhaps modelled on the regimented self-sacrifice of the ants' nest—would be one in which the individual would count for nothing. Whether being used to honour soldiers who have given their lives in pursuit of their government's objectives, or to celebrate motherhood, or to encourage behaviour undertaken in the interests of other nations or of future human generations, the rhetoric of altruism, and the associated disavowal of selfishness, remain potent political weapons.

We now live with the intellectual as well as the social and political structures that were the outcomes of our Victorian predecessors' engagements with these philosophical, religious, and political questions. We experience and make sense of ourselves and our society, in part, through the categories we inherited from them. By using their words we see things their way. Uncovering the historical processes that produced our moral language is therefore part of an attempt to understand ourselves. Those who resisted 'altruism' as a psychological category and as an ethical ideal lost the Victorian argument. To remember their reasons for resistance is to remind ourselves that the distinction between altruism and egoism was neither a traditional nor an inevitable part of the study of ethics. It was a Victorian invention.

---

[32] Saleeby 1906b: 114–21, at 120–1. The biblical quotation is from Matt. 25: 35–6.
[33] *ODNB*.

Bibliography

Websites

I have divided the online resources used in researching this book into two categories—those that include at least some publicly available texts at the time of writing, and those that I have accessed through an institutional or individual subscription. Only for those in the former category have I included a web address as well as a title.

Publicly available

A2A—Access to Archives, UK
    http://www.a2a.org.uk/
American Council of Learned Societies History E-Book Project
    http://www.historyebook.org/
Bartleby.com Online Books
    http://www.bartleby.com/
Blavatsky Study Center
    http://www.blavatskyarchives.com/
CELT—The Online Resource for Irish History, Literature and Politics
    http://celt.ucc.ie/
Christian Classics Ethereal Library
    http://www.ccel.org/
The Complete Works of Charles Darwin Online
    http://darwin-online.org.uk/
Dictionary of Victorian London
    http://www.victorianlondon.org/
ECO—Early Canadiana Online
    http://www.canadiana.org/
Electronic Text Center at University of Virginia Library
    http://etext.lib.virginia.edu/
Fair Use Repository
    http://fair-use.org/
Gallica—La Bibliothèque Numérique de la Bibliothèque Nationale de France
    http://gallica.bnf.fr/
Google Book Search
    http://books.google.co.uk/
The Huxley File—The Life and Writings of Thomas Henry Huxley
    http://alepho.clarku.edu/huxley/
Internet Archive: Open-Access Text Archive
    http://www.archive.org/details/texts

The Making of America
  Cornell collection: http://cdl.library.cornell.edu/moa/
  Michigan collection: http://www.hti.umich.edu/m/moagrp/
The Modernist Journals Project at Brown University
  http://www.modjourn.org/
The National Archives of the United Kingdom
  http://www.nationalarchives.gov.uk/
The Online Books Page at the University of Pennsylvania
  http://onlinebooks.library.upenn.edu/
The Online Library of Liberty
  http://oll.libertyfund.org/
Project Gutenberg
  http://www.gutenberg.org/

Available through subscription

Ancestry.co.uk
Annual Register Online
JSTOR—The Scholarly Journal Archive
Nineteenth-Century Fiction
Oxford Dictionary of National Biography
Oxford English Dictionary
Oxford Journals Digital Archive
Poole's Plus
ProQuest: American Periodical Series 1740–1900; American Historical
  Newspapers; House of Commons Parliamentary Papers 1801–1900
The Times Digital Archive 1785–1985

References

Periodical and newspaper articles published before 1914, along with all archival
material, are cited fully in the notes and are not included in this list of references.

Alexander, Samuel (1889). *Moral Order and Progress: An Analysis of Ethical Conceptions.*
  London: Trübner.
Allee, W. C., *et al.* (1949). *Principles of Animal Ecology.* Philadelphia and London: W. B. Saunders.
Allen, Grant (1895). *The Woman Who Did.* London: John Lane.
Allhoff, Fritz (2003). 'Evolutionary Ethics from Darwin to Moore', *History and Philosophy of
  the Life Sciences,* 25: 51–79.
'Altruism' (1882). *Gas Consumers' Manual and Trade Directory.* Manchester: Tubbs, Brook, &
  Chrystal.
Anomaly, Jonny (2005). 'Nietzsche's Critique of Utilitarianism', *Journal of Nietzsche Studies,*
  29: 1–15.
Anon. (1884*a*). *Positivism and Christianity: A Rejoinder.* Manchester: Brook & Chrystal.
—— (1884*b*). *George Eliot: Moralist and Thinker.* The Round Table Series, 2; Edinburgh:
  William Brown.
Arata, Stephen (2003). 'Oscar Wilde and Jesus Christ', in J. Bristow (ed.), *Wilde Writings:
  Contextual Conditions,* pp. 254–72. Toronto and Buffalo, NY: University of Toronto

Press in association with the UCLA Center for Seventeenth- and Eighteenth-Century Studies and the William Andrews Clark Memorial Library.

Arbuckle, Elisabeth Sanders (ed.) (1983). *Harriet Martineau's Letters to Fanny Wedgwood*. Stanford, CA: Stanford University Press.

Arnold, Matthew (1960–77). *The Complete Prose Works of Matthew Arnold*, 11 vols, ed. R. H. Super. Ann Arbor: University of Michigan Press.

Arnstein, Walter L. (1965). *The Bradlaugh Case: A Study in Late Victorian Opinion and Politics*. Oxford: Clarendon Press.

Ashton, Rosemary (1991). *G. H. Lewes: A Life*. Oxford: Clarendon Press.

—— (1996). *George Eliot: A Life*. London: Allen Lane.

—— (2006). *142 Strand: A Radical Address in Victorian London*. London: Chatto & Windus.

Atkinson, Henry G., and Harriet Martineau (1851). *Letters on the Laws of Man's Nature and Development*. London: John Chapman.

Bailward, W. A. (1895). 'The Oxford House and the Organization of Charity', in J. M. Knapp (ed.), *The Universities and the Social Problem: An Account of the University Settlements in East London*, pp. 149–70. London: Rivington, Percival, & Co.

Bain, Alexander (1868). *Mental and Moral Science: A Compendium of Psychology and Ethics*. London: Longmans, Green, & Co.

—— (1874). *A Companion to the Higher English Grammar*. London: Longmans, Green, & Co.

—— (1904). *Autobiography*. London, Longmans, Green & Co.

Baker, William (ed.) (1976–85). *Some George Eliot Notebooks: An Edition of the Carl H. Pforzheimer Library's George Eliot Holograph Notebooks, MSS 707, 708, 709, 710, 711*, 4 vols. Salzburg: Institut für Englische Sprache und Literatur.

—— (ed.) (1995). *The Letters of George Henry Lewes*, 2 vols. Victoria: University of Victoria.

Baldwin, Thomas (1990). *G. E. Moore*. London and New York: Routledge.

Balfour, Arthur James (1895). *The Foundations of Belief: Being Notes Introductory to the Study of Theology*. London: Longmans, Green, & Co.

Bannister, Robert C. (1979). *Social Darwinism: Science and Myth in Anglo-American Social Thought*. Philadelphia: Temple University Press.

Barfield, Owen (1954). *History in English Words*, new edn. London: Faber & Faber (1st edn 1926).

Barker, Rodney (1997). *Political Ideas in Modern Britain: In and After the Twentieth Century*, 2nd edn. London: Routledge (1st edn 1978).

Barrett, Paul H. *et al.* (eds) (1987). *Charles Darwin's Notebooks, 1836–1844: Geology, Transmutation of Species, Metaphysical Enquiries*. Cambridge: Cambridge University Press.

Barrow, Logie, and Ian Bullock (1996). *Democratic Ideas and the British Labour Movement, 1880–1914*. Cambridge: Cambridge University Press.

Bassett, Troy J., and Christina M. Walter (2001). 'Booksellers and Bestsellers: British Book Sales as Documented by *The Bookman*, 1891–1906', *Book History*, 4: 205–36.

Beckson, Karl (ed.) (1970). *Oscar Wilde: The Critical Heritage*. London: Routledge & Kegan Paul.

—— (1992). *London in the 1890s: A Cultural History*. New York and London: W. W. Norton & Co.

Beer, Gillian (2000). *Darwin's Plots: Evolutionary Narrative in Darwin, George Eliot and Nineteenth-Century Fiction*, 2nd edn. Cambridge: Cambridge University Press (1st edn 1983).

Beer, Gillian (2001). 'Knowing a Life: Edith Simcox—*Sat est vixisse?*', in S. Anger (ed.), *Knowing the Past: Victorian Literature and Culture*, pp. 252–66. Ithaca, NY, and London: Cornell University Press.

Bell, Michael (2003). 'Nietzscheanism: "The Superman and the All-Too-Human"', in D. Bradsaw (ed.), *A Concise Companion to Modernism*. Malden, MA, and Oxford: Blackwell, pp. 56–74.

Bendz, Ernst (1921). *Oscar Wilde: A Retrospect.* Vienna: Alfred Hölder.

Bennett, Tony, *et al.* (eds) (2005). *New Keywords: A Revised Vocabulary of Culture and Society.* Oxford: Blackwell.

Benson, Arthur Christopher (1899). *The Life of Edward White Benson, Sometime Archbishop of Canterbury,* 2 vols. London: Macmillan & Co.

Berman, David (1990). *A History of Atheism in Britain: From Hobbes to Russell.* London: Routledge.

Berndt, Cruce C., and Robert A. Rankin (2000). 'The Books Studied by Ramanujan in India', *American Mathematical Monthly,* 107: 595–601.

Berridge, Virginia (1990). 'Health and Medicine', in F. M. L. Thompson (ed.), *The Cambridge Social History of Britain, 1750–1950,* pp. 171–242. Cambridge: Cambridge University Press.

Bevir, Mark (2000). 'Republicanism, Socialism, and Democracy in Britain: The Origins of the Radical Left', *Journal of Social History,* 34: 351–68.

—— (2001). 'Taking Holism Seriously: A Reply to Critics', *Philosophical Books,* 42: 187–95.

—— (2002). 'Sidney Webb: Utilitarianism, Positivism, and Social Democracy', *Journal of Modern History,* 74: 217–52.

Binyon, Gilbert C. (1931). *The Christian Socialist Movement in England: An Introduction to the Study of its History.* London: SPCK.

Björk, Lennart A. (ed.) (1985). *The Literary Notebooks of Thomas Hardy,* 2 vols. London and Basingstoke: Macmillan.

Blake, Kathleen (1976). '*Middlemarch* and the Woman Question', *Nineteenth-Century Fiction,* 31: 285–312.

Blatchford, Robert (1898). *Altruism: Christ's Glorious Gospel of Love Against Man's Dismal Science of Greed.* Clarion Pamphlet, 22; London: Clarion Press.

—— (1903). *God and my Neighbour.* London: Clarion Press.

—— (1931). *My Eighty Years.* London: Cassell.

Blind, Mathilde (1881). *The Prophecy of St Oran, and Other Poems.* London: Newman & Co.

—— (1889). *The Ascent of Man.* London: Chatto & Windus.

Boole, Mary Everest (1931). *Collected Works,* 4 vols, ed. E. M. Cobham with a preface by Ethel S. Dummer. London: C. W. Daniel Co.

Booth, Mary (1918). *Charles Booth: A Memoir.* London: Macmillan.

Bosanquet, Bernard (1958). *The Philosophical Theory of the State,* 4th edn. London: Macmillan (1st edn 1899).

Boucher, David (ed.) (1997). *The British Idealists.* Cambridge: Cambridge University Press.

Bowler, Peter J. (1983). *The Eclipse of Darwinism: Anti-Darwinian Evolution Theories in the Decades around 1900.* Baltimore and London: Johns Hopkins University Press.

—— (1988). *The Non-Darwinian Revolution: Reinterpreting a Historical Myth.* Baltimore: Johns Hopkins University Press.

—— (2001). *Reconciling Science and Religion: The Debate in Early Twentieth-Century Britain.* Chicago: University of Chicago Press.

Braddon, M. E. (1883). *The Golden Calf,* 2 vols. Leipzig: Bernhard Tauchnitz.

—— (1889). *The Day Will Come,* 2 vols. Leipzig: Bernhard Tauchnitz.

—— (1891). *Gerard, or, The World, the Flesh, and the Devil,* 2 vols. Leipzig: Bernhard Tauchnitz.

—— (1905). *The Rose of Life,* 2 vols. Leipzig: Bernhard Tauchnitz.

Branford, V. V. (1905). 'Sociology in Some of its Educational Aspects', *American Journal of Sociology,* 11: 85–9.

Bridges, J. H. (1866). *The Unity of Comte's Life and Doctrine: A Reply to Strictures on Comte's Later Writings, Addressed to J. S. Mill, Esq., M.P.* London: N. Trübner & Co.

Brink, David O. (1997). 'Self-Love and Altruism', *Social Philosophy and Policy,* 14: 122–57.

Bristow, E. (1975). 'The Liberty and Property Defence League and Individualism', *Historical Journal,* 18: 761–89.

Bristow, Joseph (2003a). 'Introduction', in J. Bristow (ed.), *Wilde Writings: Contextual Conditions,* pp. 3–38. Toronto and Buffalo, NY: University of Toronto Press in association with the UCLA Center for Seventeenth- and Eighteenth-Century Studies and the William Andrews Clark Memorial Library.

—— (2003b). *Wilde Writings: Contextual Conditions.* Toronto and Buffalo, NY: University of Toronto Press in association with the UCLA Center for Seventeenth- and Eighteenth-Century Studies and the William Andrews Clark Memorial Library.

Brooke, John Hedley (1991). *Science and Religion: Some Historical Perspectives.* Cambridge: Cambridge University Press.

—— (2003). 'Darwin and Victorian Christianity', in J. Hodge and G. Radick (eds), *The Cambridge Companion to Darwin,* pp. 192–213. Cambridge: Cambridge University Press.

—— and Geoffrey Cantor (1998). *Reconstructing Nature: The Engagement of Science and Religion.* Edinburgh: T. & T. Clark.

Brown, Alan W. (1947). *The Metaphysical Society: Victorian Minds in Crisis 1869–1880.* New York: Columbia University Press.

Brown, Callum G. (2000). *The Death of Christian Britain: Understanding Secularisation 1800–2000.* London and New York: Routledge.

Brown, Warren S., et al. (eds) (1998). *Whatever Happened to the Soul? Scientific and Theological Portraits of Human Nature.* Minneapolis: Fortress Press.

Browne, Janet (1985). 'Darwin and the Expression of Emotions', in D. Kohn (ed.), *The Darwinian Heritage,* pp. 307–26. Princeton: Princeton University Press.

—— (1995). *Charles Darwin: Voyaging.* London: Jonathan Cape.

—— (1998). 'I Could Have Retched All Night: Charles Darwin and his Body', in C. Lawrence and S. Shapin (eds), *Science Incarnate: Historical Embodiments of Natural Knowledge,* pp. 240–87. Chicago and London: University of Chicago Press.

—— (2001). 'Darwin in Caricature: A Study in the Popularisation and Dissemination of Evolution', *Proceedings of the American Philosophical Society,* 145: 496–509.

—— (2002). *Charles Darwin: The Power of Place.* London: Jonathan Cape.

Bryce, James et al. (1900). *Briton and Boer: Both Sides of the South African Question.* New York and London: Harpers & Brothers.

Büchner, Ludwig (1880). *Mind in Animals,* tr. A. Besant. London: Freethought Publishing Co.

Buckley, Arabella B. (1880). *Life and her Children: Glimpses of Animal Life, from the Amoeba to the Insects.* London: Edward Stanford.

—— (1882). *Winners in Life's Race; or, The Great Backboned Family.* London: Edward Stanford.

—— (1891). *Moral Teachings of Science.* London: Edward Stanford.

—— (1922). *The Fairy-Land of Science.* London: Macmillan.

Budd, Louis J. (1956). 'Altruism Arrives in America', *American Quarterly,* 8(1): 40–52.

Budd, Susan (1977). *Varieties of Unbelief: Atheists and Agnostics in English Society, 1850–1960*. London: Heinemann.

Burkhardt, Frederick, and Sydney Smith (eds) (1994). *A Calendar of the Correspondence of Charles Darwin, 1821–1882, with Supplement*. Cambridge and New York: Cambridge University Press.

Butler, Joseph (1970). *Fifteen Sermons Preached at the Rolls Chapel, and A Dissertation on the Nature of Virtue,* ed. with an introduction and additional notes by T. A. Roberts. London: SPCK (1st edn 1726).

Byatt, A. S. (1992). *Angels and Insects*. London: Chatto & Windus.

—— (2000). *On Histories and Stories: Selected Essays*. London: Chatto & Windus.

Caird, Edward (1885). *The Social Philosophy and Religion of Comte*. Glasgow: James Maclehose & Sons.

Caird, Mona (1897). *The Morality of Marriage, and Other Essays on the Status and Destiny of Woman*. London: George Redway.

Campbell, S. (1997). 'Emotion as an Explanatory Principle in Early Evolutionary Theory', *Studies in History and Philosophy of Science,* 28: 453–73.

Carey, George W. (2002). 'The Authoritarian Secularism of John Stuart Mill', *Humanitas,* 15: 107–19.

Carneiro, Robert L. (2000). 'Structure, Function and Equilibrium in the Evolutionism of Herbert Spencer', in J. Offer (ed.), *Herbert Spencer: Critical Assessments,* 4 vols, ii. 441–59. London and New York: Routledge (1st published in 1973).

Carpenter, William Boyd (1883). *Christian Altruism: A Sermon Preached in the Private Chapel, Windsor Castle, Sunday 1 April, 1883.* Printed by the Queen's Command.

—— (1889). *The Permanent Elements of Religion: The Bampton Lectures of 1887*. London: Macmillan.

—— (1911). *Some Pages of My Life*. London: Williams & Norgate.

Carr, George Shoobridge (1895). *Social Evolution and the Evolution of Socialism: A Critical Essay*. London: W. Stewart & Co.

Carter, Matt (2003). *T. H. Green and the Development of Ethical Socialism*. Exeter: Imprint Academic.

Casagrande, Peter J. (1971). 'The Shifted "Centre of Altruism" in the Woodlanders: Thomas Hardy's Third "Return of a Native"', *ELH: A Journal of English Literary History,* 38: 104–25.

Cashdollar, Charles D. (1989). *The Transformation of Theology, 1830–1890: Positivism and Protestant Thought in Britain and America*. Princeton: Princeton University Press.

Ceadel, Martin (2000). *Semi-Detached Idealists: The British Peace Movement and International Relations, 1854–1945*. Oxford: Oxford University Press.

Cecil, Hugh Mortimer (1897). *Pseudo-Philosophy at the End of the Nineteenth Century,* i. *An Irrationalist Trio: Kidd-Drummond-Balfour.* London: The University Press.

Chadwick, Owen (1966–70). *The Victorian Church,* 2 vols. London: Adam & Charles Black.

Chambers, Robert (1994). *Vestiges of the Natural History of Creation, and Other Evolutionary Writings,* ed. with a new introd. by James A. Secord. Chicago and London: University of Chicago Press (anonymous 1st edn 1844).

Chekhov, Anton (2001). *The Steppe and Other Stories*. Penguin Classics edn, tr. with notes by Ronald Wilks, and an introd. by Donald Rayfield. London: Penguin.

Cheung, Tobias (2006). 'From the Organism of a Body to the Body of an Organism: Occurrence and Meaning of the Word "Organism" from the Seventeenth to the Nineteenth Centuries', *British Journal for the History of Science,* 39: 319–39.

Cicero (1961). *Letters to Atticus,* 3 vols, tr. E. O. Winstedt. London: Heinemann.

Claeys, Gregory (1989). *Thomas Paine: Social and Political Thought.* Boston: Unwin Hyman.

Clapperton, Jane Hume (1885). *Scientific Meliorism and the Evolution of Happiness.* London: Kegan Paul, Trench & Co.

—— (1904). *A Vision of the Future, Based on the Application of Ethical Principles.* London: Swan Sonnenschein & Co.

Clark, J. F. M. (1997). '"The Ants were Duly Visited": Making Sense of John Lubbock, Scientific Naturalism, and the Senses of Social Insects', *British Journal for the History of Science,* 30: 151–76.

Clarke, Bruce (1992). 'Dora Marsden and Ezra Pound: "The New Freewoman" and "The Serious Artist"', *Contemporary Literature,* 33: 91–112.

—— (1996). *Dora Marsden and Early Modernism: Gender, Individualism, Science.* Ann Arbor: University of Michigan Press.

Clifford, David (2003). *Reform, the Novel and the Origins of Neo-Lamarckism.* Aldershot: Ashgate.

Collini, Stefan (1979). *Liberalism and Sociology: L. T. Hobhouse and Political Argument in England, 1880–1914.* Cambridge: Cambridge University Press.

—— (1991). *Public Moralists: Political Thought and Intellectual Life in Britain 1850–1930.* Oxford: Clarendon Press.

—— (2001). 'My Roles and their Duties: Sidgwick as Philosopher, Professor and Public Moralist', in R. Harrison (ed.), *Henry Sidgwick,* pp. 9–49. Oxford and New York: Oxford University Press for the British Academy.

—— (2006). *Absent Minds: Intellectuals in Britain.* Oxford: Oxford University Press.

Collins, Francis S. (2006). *The Language of God: A Scientist Presents Evidence for Belief.* New York: Free Press.

Collins, K. K. (1978). 'G. H. Lewes Revised: George Eliot and the Moral Sense', *Victorian Studies,* 21: 463–92.

Collins, Mortimer (1872). *The British Birds: A Communication from the Ghost of Aristophanes.* London: The Publishing Co.

Comte, Auguste (1858). *The Catechism of Positive Religion,* tr. R. Congreve. London: John Chapman.

—— (1865). *A General View of Positivism,* tr. J. H. Bridges. London: Trübner & Co.

—— (1875–7). *System of Positive Polity, or Treatise on Sociology, Instituting the Religion of Humanity,* 4 vols, tr. E. S. Beesly *et al.* London: Longmans, Green & Co. (1st published in French 1851–4).

—— (1891). *The Catechism of Positive Religion,* tr. R. Congreve, 3rd edn. London: Kegan Paul, Trench, Trübner & Co. (1st published in French 1852; in English tr. 1858).

—— (1998). *Early Political Writings,* ed., tr., and with an introd. by H. S. Jones. Cambridge: Cambridge University Press.

Conder, Eustace R. (1877). *The Basis of Faith: A Critical Survey of the Grounds of Christian Theism.* London: Hodder & Stoughton.

Conway, Mocure D. (1904). *Autobiography: Memories and Experiences,* 2 vols. London: Cassell & Co.

Cooke, George Willis (1883). *George Eliot: A Critical Study of her Life, Writings, and Philosophy.* Boston: Houghton Mifflin.

Cooter, Roger (1984). *The Cultural Meaning of Popular Science: Phrenology and the Organization of Consent in Nineteenth-Century Britain.* Cambridge: Cambridge University Press.

Cowling, Maurice (1985). *Religion and Public Doctrine in Modern England*, ii. *Assaults*. Cambridge: Cambridge University Press.

Crawshaw, William H. (1907). *The Making of English Literature*. Boston: D. C. Heath.

Cronin, Helena (1991). *The Ant and the Peacock: Altruism and Sexual Selection from Darwin to Today*. Cambridge: Cambridge University Press.

Crook, D. P. (1984). *Benjamin Kidd: Portrait of a Social Darwinist*. Cambridge: Cambridge University Press.

Crook, Paul (1994). *Darwinism, War and History: The Debate over the Biology of War from the 'Origin of Species' to the First World War*. Cambridge: Cambridge University Press.

Cumberland, Gerald (1919). *Set Down in Malice: A Book of Reminiscences*. London: Grant Richards.

Cunningham, Suzanne (1996). *Philosophy and the Darwinian Legacy*. Rochester, NY: University of Rochester Press.

Danson, John Towne (1886). *The Wealth of Households*. Oxford: Clarendon Press.

Danson, Lawrence (1997a). *Wilde's Intentions: The Artist in his Criticism*. Oxford: Clarendon Press.

—— (1997b). 'Wilde as Critic and Theorist', in P. Raby (ed.), *The Cambridge Companion to Oscar Wilde*, pp. 80–95. Cambridge: Cambridge University Press.

Darwin, Charles (1871). *The Descent of Man, and Selection in Relation to Sex,* 2 vols. London: Murray.

—— (1882). *The Descent of Man, and Selection in Relation to Sex,* 2nd edn, revised and augmented. London: John Murray.

—— (1913). *Journal of Researches into the Natural History and Geology of the Countries Visited During the Voyage Round the World of H.M.S. Beagle,* 11th edn. London: John Murray (1st edn 1839).

—— (1958). *The Autobiography of Charles Darwin*, ed. Nora Barlow. London: Collins.

—— (2004). *The Descent of Man, and Selection in Relation to Sex,* Penguin Classics edn, with an introd. by James Moore and Adrian Desmond. London: Penguin (1st edn 1871).

—— (2006). *The Origin of Species: A Variorum Text*, ed. Morse Peckham (paperback reprint of original 1959 edn). Philadelphia: University of Pennsylvania Press.

Darwin, Francis, and A. C. Seward (eds) (1903). *More Letters of Charles Darwin: A Record of his Work in a Series of Hitherto Unpublished Letters,* 2 vols. London: John Murray.

Davies, Charles Maurice (1873a). *Orthodox London: or, Phases of Religious Life in the Church of England*. London: Tinsley Brothers.

—— (1873b). *Unorthodox London: or, Phases of Religious Life in the Metropolis*. London: Tinsley Brothers.

—— (1874). *Heterodox London: or, Phases of Free Thought in the Metropolis,* 2 vols. London: Tinsley Brothers.

—— (1875). *Mystic London: or, Phases of Occult Life in the Metropolis*. London: Tinsley Brothers.

Davies, Tony (1997). *Humanism*. London: Routledge.

Davis, Philip (2002). *The Victorians: The Oxford English Literary History*, viii. *1830–1880*. Oxford: Oxford University Press.

Dawkins, Richard (1989). *The Selfish Gene,* new edn. Oxford: Oxford University Press (1st edn 1976).

—— (2006). *The God Delusion*. London: Bantam Press.

Dawson, Gowan (2004). 'The *Review of Reviews* and the New Journalism in Late-Victorian Britain', in G. Cantor *et al.* (eds), *Science in the Nineteenth-Century Periodical: Reading the Magazine of Nature*, pp. 172–98. Cambridge: Cambridge University Press.

—— (2005). 'Aestheticism, Immorality and the Reception of Darwinism in Victorian Britain', in A. Zwierlein (ed.), *Unmapped Countries: Biological Visions in Nineteenth Century Literature and Culture*, pp. 43–54. London: Anthem Press.

Den Otter, Sandra M. (1996). *British Idealism and Social Explanation: A Study in Late Victorian Thought*. Oxford: Clarendon Press.

Denisoff, Dennis (1999). 'Posing a Threat: Queensberry, Wilde, and the Portrayal of Decadence', in L. Constable, D. Denisoff, and M. Potolsky (eds), *Perennial Decay: On the Aesthetics and Politics of Decadence*, pp. 83–100. Philadelphia: University of Pennsylvania Press.

Deresiewicz, William (1998). 'Heroism and Organicism in the Case of Lydgate', *Studies in English Literature,* 38: 723–40.

Deroisin, Hippolyte Philémon (1909). *Notes sur Auguste Comte par un de ses Disciples*. Paris: Georges Crès.

Desmond, Adrian (1989). *The Politics of Evolution: Morphology, Medicine, and Reform in Radical London*. Chicago: University of Chicago Press.

—— (1998). *Huxley: From Devil's Disciple to Evolution's High Priest*. London: Penguin.

—— and James R. Moore (1991). *Darwin*. London: Penguin.

Deutscher, Penelope (2004). 'The Descent of Man and the Evolution of Woman: Antoinette Blackwell, Charlotte Perkins Gilman and Eliza Gamble', *Hypatia: A Journal of Feminist Philosophy,* 19: 35–55.

Dickens, Charles (1879). *Dickens's Dictionary of London, 1879: An Unconventional Handbook*. London: Charles Dickens.

Dickey, Laurence (1986). 'Historicizing the "Adam Smith Problem": Conceptual, Historiographical, and Textual Issues', *Journal of Modern History,* 58: 579–609.

Dickinson, Goldsworthy Lowes (1901). *The Meaning of Good: A Dialogue*. Glasgow: J. Maclehose.

Dixon, Thomas (2002). 'John Abercrombie', in W. J. Mander and A. P. F. Sell (eds), *Dictionary of Nineteenth-Century British Philosophers,* 2 vols. Bristol: Thoemmes Press.

—— (2003). *From Passions to Emotions: The Creation of a Secular Psychological Category*. Cambridge: Cambridge University Press.

—— (2004). 'Herbert Spencer and Altruism: The Sternness and Kindness of a Victorian Moralist', in G. Jones and R. A. Peel (eds), *Herbert Spencer: The Intellectual Legacy*, pp. 85–124. London: Galton Institute.

—— (2005a). 'Altruism', in M. C. Horowitz (ed.), *New Dictionary of the History of Ideas,* 6 vols, i. 49–53. New York: Scribner's.

—— (2005b). 'The Invention of Altruism: Auguste Comte's *Positive Polity* and Respectable Unbelief in Victorian Britain', in D. Knight and M. Eddy (eds), *Science and Beliefs: From Natural Philosophy to Natural Science*, pp. 195–211. Aldershot: Ashgate.

—— (2006). 'Patients and Passions: Languages of Medicine and Emotion, 1789–1850', in F. Bound Alberti (ed.), *Medicine, Emotion and Disease, 1700–1950*, pp. 22–52. Basingstoke: Palgrave Macmillan.

Douglas, Lord Alfred (1914). *Oscar Wilde and Myself*. London: John Long.

Dowling, Linda (1994). *Hellenism and Homosexuality in Victorian Oxford*. Ithaca, NY: Cornell University Press.

Drummond, Henry (1885). *Natural Law in the Spiritual World*, 15th edn. London: Hodder & Stoughton (1st edn 1883).

—— (1894). *The Lowell Lectures on the Ascent of Man*. London: Hodder & Stoughton.

—— (1899). *The Lowell Lectures on the Ascent of Man*. London: Hodder & Stoughton (1st edn 1894).

—— (1903). *The Greatest Thing in the World and Other Addresses*. London: Hodder & Stoughton (1st edn 1894).

Dugatkin, Lee Alan (2006). *The Altruism Equation: Seven Scientists Search for the Origins of Goodness*. Princeton: Princeton University Press.

Duncan, David (1908). *The Life and Letters of Herbert Spencer*. London: Methuen.

Dunn, John (2005). *Setting the People Free: The Story of Democracy*. London: Atlantic.

Dyson, Hope, and Charles Tennyson (eds) (1969). *Dear and Honoured Lady: The Correspondence between Queen Victoria and Alfred Tennyson*. London: Macmillan.

Eisen, Sydney (1967). 'Herbert Spencer and the Spectre of Comte', *Journal of British Studies*, 7: 48–67.

Eliot, George (1871–2). *Middlemarch: A Study of Provincial Life*, 4 vols. Edinburgh: Blackwood.

—— (1885). *George Eliot's Life as Related in her Letters and Journals*, 3 vols, arranged and ed. by her husband, J. W. Cross. Edinburgh: Blackwood.

—— (1994). *Impressions of Theophrastus Such*, ed. with an introd. and notes by Nancy Henry. London: William Pickering (1st edn 1879).

—— (2003). *Daniel Deronda*, Wordsworth Classics edn, with an introd. and notes by Carole Jones. Ware: Wordsworth (1st edn 1876).

Ellegård, Alvar (1990). *Darwin and the General Reader: The Reception of Darwin's Theory of Evolution in the British Periodical Press, 1859–1872*, with a new foreword by David L. Hull. Chicago: University of Chicago Press (1st edn 1958).

Ellis, Mrs Havelock (1918). *James Hinton: A Sketch*. London: Stanley Paul.

Ellmann, Richard (ed.) (1969). *Oscar Wilde: A Collection of Critical Essays*. Englewood Cliffs, NJ: Prentice-Hall.

—— Richard (1987). *Oscar Wilde*. London: Hamish Hamilton.

Erskine, Fiona (1995). '*The Origin of Species* and the Science of Female Inferiority', in D. Amigoni and J. Wallace (eds), *Charles Darwin's The Origin of Species: New Interdisciplinary Essays*, pp. 95–121. Manchester: Manchester University Press.

Espinasse, Francis (1893). *Literary Recollections and Sketches*. London: Hodder & Stoughton.

Everett, Edwin M. (1939). *The Party of Humanity: The Fortnightly Review and its Contributors, 1865–1874*. Chapel Hill, NC: University of North Carolina Press.

Farrar, Frederic W. (1871). *The Witness of Christ to History, Being the Hulsean Lectures for the Year 1870*. London and New York: Macmillan.

—— (1874). *The Life of Christ*, 2 vols. London: Cassell, Petter, & Galpin.

—— (1876). '*In the Days of thy Youth*': *Sermons Preached in Marlborough College*, 2nd edn. London: Macmillan (1st edn 1876).

—— (1891). *Social and Present-Day Questions*. London: Hodder & Stoughton.

Farrar, Reginald (1904). *The Life of Frederic William Farrar, Sometime Dean of Canterbury*. London: James Nisbet & Co.

Fichman, Martin (2004). *An Elusive Victorian: The Evolution of Alfred Russel Wallace*. Chicago and London: University of Chicago Press.

Figuier, Louis (1868). *The Insect World: Being a Popular Account of the Orders of Insects, together with a Description of the Habits and Economy of some of the most Interesting Species*. London: Chapman & Hall (1st published in French 1867).

Fiske, John (1874). *Outlines of Cosmic Philosophy, Based on the Doctrine of Evolution, with Criticisms on the Positive Philosophy,* 2 vols. London: Macmillan & Co.

—— (1899). *Through Nature to God.* London: Macmillan & Co.

Flint, Robert (1880). *Anti-Theistic Theories. Being the Baird Lecture for 1877,* 2nd edn. Edinburgh: Blackwood & Sons (1st edn 1879).

Foldy, Michael (1997). *The Trials of Oscar Wilde: Deviance, Morality, and Late-Victorian Society.* New Haven and London: Yale University Press.

Foot, Philippa (1994). 'Nietzsche's Immoralism', in R. Schacht (ed.), *Nietzsche, Genealogy, Morality: Essays on Nietzsche's On the Genealogy of Morals,* pp. 3–14. Berkeley and Los Angeles, CA, and London: University of California Press.

Ford, D. J. (1974). 'W. H. Mallock and Socialism in England, 1880–1918', in K. D. Brown (ed.), *Essays in Anti-Labour History: Responses to the Rise of Labour in Britain,* pp. 317–42. London: Macmillan.

Foster, Kevin R. (forthcoming). 'Behavioral Ecology: Altruism', in S. E. Jørgensen (ed.), *Encyclopedia of Ecology,* 8 vols. Amsterdam: Elsevier.

—— et al. (2007). 'What can Microbial Genetics Teach Sociobiology?', *Trends in Genetics,* 23: 74–80.

Francis, Mark (2007). *Herbert Spencer and the Invention of Modern Life.* Chesham: Acumen.

Freeden, Michael (1996). *Ideologies and Political Theory: A Conceptual Approach.* Oxford: Clarendon Press.

Fridlund, Alan (1992). 'Darwin's Anti-Darwinism in the *Expression of the Emotions in Man and Animals*', in K. T. Strongman (ed.), *International Review of Studies on Emotion,* 2 vols, ii. 117–37. Chichester: Wiley.

Fyfe, Aileen (ed.) (2003). *Science for Children,* 7 vols. Bristol: Thoemmes.

Gagnier, Regenia (1997). 'Wilde and the Victorians', in P. Raby (ed.), *The Cambridge Companion to Oscar Wilde,* pp. 18–33. Cambridge: Cambridge University Press.

Gardner, Philip (2004). 'Literacy, Learning, and Education', in C. Williams (ed.), *A Companion to Nineteenth-Century Britain,* pp. 353–68. Oxford: Blackwell.

Gaskell, George Arthur (1890). *Social Control of the Birth-Rate and Endowment of Mothers.* London: Freethought Publishing.

—— (1931). *A New Theory of Heredity.* London: The C. W. Daniel Co.

Gates, Barbara T. (1997). 'Revisioning Darwinism with Sympathy: Arabella Buckley', in B. T. Gates and A. B. Shteir (eds), *Natural Eloquence: Women Reinscribe Science,* pp. 164–76. Madison: University of Wisconsin Press.

—— (1998). *Kindred Nature: Victorian and Edwardian Women Embrace the Living World.* Chicago and London: University of Chicago Press.

—— (2004). 'Arabella Buckley', in B. Lightman (ed.), *The Dictionary of Nineteenth-Century British Scientists,* 4 vols, i. 337–9. Bristol: Thoemmes Continuum.

Gayon, Jean (1998). *Darwinism's Struggle for Survival: Heredity and the Hypothesis of Natural Selection,* tr. M. Cobb. Cambridge: Cambridge University Press.

Geddes, Patrick, and J. Arthur Thomson (1889). *The Evolution of Sex.* London: Walter Scott.

—— and —— (1911). *Evolution.* London: Williams & Norgate.

Gilbert, Pamela (1999). 'Ouida and the Other New Woman', in N. D. Thompson (ed.), *Victorian Women Writers and the Woman Question,* pp. 170–88. Cambridge: Cambridge University Press.

Gill, Robin (2003). *The 'Empty' Church Revisited,* new edn. Aldershot: Ashgate (1st published 1993 as *The Myth of the Empty Church*).

Gissing, George (1890). *The Nether World: A Novel,* new edn. London: Smith, Elder (1st edn 1889).

Gissing, George (1895). *In the Year of the Jubilee,* new edn. London: Lawrence & Bullen (1st edn 1894).

—— (1901). *Our Friend the Charlatan.* London: Chapman & Hall.

—— (1970). *Essays and Fiction,* ed. with an introd. by Pierre Coustillas. Baltimore and London: Johns Hopkins Press.

—— (1976). *Our Friend the Charlatan,* ed. with a new introd. and notes by Pierre Coustillas. Hassocks: Harvester Press (1st edn 1901).

—— (1978). *London and the Life of Literature in Late Victorian England: The Diary of George Gissing, Novelist,* ed. Pierre Coustillas. Hassocks: Harvester Press.

—— (1985). *New Grub Street,* ed. with an introd. by Bernard Bergonzi. Harmondsworth: Penguin (1st edn 1891).

Godwin, John V. (1860). 'The Bradford Mechanics' Institute', in G. W. Hastings (ed.), *Transactions of the National Association for the Promotion of Social Science, 1859,* pp. 340–5. London: John W. Parker & Son.

Goodall, Jane R. (2002). *Performance and Evolution in the Age of Darwin: Out of the Natural Order.* London: Routledge.

Goodlad, Lauren M. E. (2002). 'Character and Pastorship in Two British "Sociological" Traditions: Organized Charity, Fabian Socialism, and the Invention of New Liberalism', in A. Anderson and J. Valente (eds), *Disciplinarity at the Fin de Siècle,* pp. 235–60. Princeton: Princeton University Press.

Gordon, George A. (1893). *The Witness to Immortality in Literature, Philosophy and Life.* Boston: Houghton, Mifflin, & Co.

Gorst, John (1895). 'Introduction: "Settlements" in England and America', in J. M. Knapp (ed.), *The Universities and the Social Problem: An Account of the University Settlements in East London,* pp. 1–29. London: Rivington, Percival, & Co.

Goschen, Viscount (1905). *Essays and Addresses on Economic Questions (1865–1893) with Introductory Notes (1905).* London: Edward Arnold.

Gouhier, Henri (1933). *La Jeunesse D'Auguste Comte et la Formation du Positivisme,* 3 vols. Paris: Librairie Philosophique J. Vrin.

Gouldstone, Timothy Maxwell (2005). *The Rise and Decline of Anglican Idealism in the Nineteenth Century.* Basingstoke: Palgrave Macmillan.

Grand, Sarah (1992). *The Heavenly Twins,* with an introd. by Carol A. Senf. Ann Arbor: University of Michigan Press (1st edn 1893).

Granlund, Helena (1994). *The Paradox of Self-Love: Christian Elements in George Eliot's Treatment of Egoism.* Stockholm: Almqvist & Wiksell International.

Grant, Colin (2001). *Altruism and Christian Ethics.* Cambridge: Cambridge University Press.

Graver, Suzanne (1984). *George Eliot and Community: A Study in Social Theory and Fictional Form.* Berkeley, CA: University of California Press.

Gray, Tim S. (1996). *The Political Philosophy of Herbert Spencer: Individualism and Organicism.* Aldershot: Avebury.

Green, Thomas Hill (2003). *Prolegomena to Ethics,* ed. with an introd. by David O. Brink. Oxford: Oxford University Press (1st edn 1883).

Greer, Germaine (1984). *Sex and Destiny: The Politics of Human Fertility.* London: Secker & Warburg.

Gregory, Frederick (1977a). *Scientific Materialism in Nineteenth-Century Germany.* Dordrecht and Boston: D. Reidel.

—— (1977*b*). 'Scientific versus Dialectical Materialism: A Clash of Ideologies in Nineteenth-Century German Radicalism', *Isis,* 68: 206–23.

Griffin, Nicholas (1991). *Russell's Idealist Apprenticeship.* Oxford: Clarendon Press.

Gruber, Howard E. (1974). *Darwin on Man: A Psychological Study of Scientific Creativity. Together with Darwin's Early and Unpublished Notebooks,* transcribed and annotated by Paul H. Barrett. London: Wildwood House.

Guy, Josephine (2003). '"The Soul of Man Under Socialism": A (Con)Textual History', in J. Bristow (ed.), *Wilde Writings: Contextual Conditions,* pp. 59–85. Toronto and Buffalo, NY: University of Toronto Press in association with the UCLA Center for Seventeenth- and Eighteenth-Century Studies and the William Andrews Clark Memorial Library.

Haac, Oscar (ed.) (1995). *The Correspondence of John Stuart Mill and Auguste Comte.* New Brunswick, NJ: Transaction.

Haddon, Caroline (1886). *The Larger Life: Studies in Hinton's Ethics.* London, Kegan Paul, Trench & Co.

Haggard, Robert F. (2001). *The Persistence of Victorian Liberalism: The Politics of Social Reform in Britain, 1870–1900.* Westport, CT, and London: Greenwood Press.

Haight, Gordon S. (1968). *George Eliot: A Biography.* Oxford: Clarendon Press.

—— (1969). *George Eliot and John Chapman, with Chapman's Diaries,* 2nd edn. Hamden, CT: Archon Books (1st edn 1940).

—— (ed.) (1954–78). *The George Eliot Letters,* 9 vols. New Haven, CT: Yale University Press.

Hall, Catherine (1996). 'Imperial Man: Edward Eyre in Australia and the West Indies, 1833–66', in B. Schwarz (ed.), *The Expansion of England: Race, Ethnicity, and Cultural History,* pp. 130–70. London and New York: Routledge.

—— (2002). *Civilising Subjects: Metropole and Colony in the English Imagination, 1830–1867.* Cambridge: Polity.

Hall, Lesley (2000). *Sex, Gender, and Social Change in Britain since 1880.* Basingstoke: Macmillan.

Halperin, John (1982). *Gissing: A Life in Books.* Oxford: Oxford University Press.

Hamburger, Joseph (1999). *John Stuart Mill on Liberty and Control.* Princeton: Princeton University Press.

Hamilton, Lisa (2003). 'Oscar Wilde, New Women, and the Rhetoric of Effeminacy', in J. Bristow (ed.), *Wilde Writings: Contextual Conditions,* pp. 230–53. Toronto and Buffalo, NY: University of Toronto Press in association with the UCLA Center for Seventeenth- and Eighteenth-Century Studies and the William Andrews Clark Memorial Library.

Hamilton, W. D. (1996). *Narrow Roads of Gene Land: The Collected Papers of W. D. Hamilton,* i. *Evolution of Social Behaviour.* Oxford: W. H. Freeman.

Hanson, Ellis (2003). 'Wilde's Exquisite Pain', in J. Bristow (ed.), *Wilde Writings: Contextual Conditions,* pp. 101–23. Toronto and Buffalo, NY: University of Toronto Press in association with the UCLA Center for Seventeenth- and Eighteenth-Century Studies and the William Andrews Clark Memorial Library.

Hapgood, Lynne (1995). 'Urban Utopias: Socialism, Religion, and the City, 1880 to 1900', in S. Ledger and S. McCracken (eds), *Cultural Politics ad the Fin de Siècle,* pp. 184–201. Cambridge: Cambridge University Press.

—— (1996). '"The Reconceiving of Christianity": Secularisation, Realism, and the Religious Novel, 1888–1900', *Literature and Theology,* 10: 329–50.

Hardy, Florence Emily (1962). *The Life of Thomas Hardy, 1840–1928.* London: Macmillan.

Hardy, Thomas (1998). *Two on a Tower*, ed. with an introd. by Suleiman M. Ahmad. Oxford: Oxford University Press (1st edn 1882).

Harley, T. (1890). *Altruism*. London: Alexander & Shepheard.

Harrison, Frederic (1908). *National and Social Problems*. London: Macmillan & Co.

—— (1911). *Autobiographic Memoirs*, 2 vols. London: Macmillan & Co.

—— (1918). *On Society*. London: Macmillan & Co.

Harrison, Ross (2001). 'The Sanctions of Utilitarianism', in R. Harrison (ed.), *Henry Sidgwick*, pp. 93–116. Oxford and New York: Oxford University Press for the British Academy.

Harrison, Royden (1994). *Before the Socialists: Studies in Labour and Politics 1861–1881*. Aldershot: Gregg Revivals (1st edn 1965).

Hartley, Lucy (2001). *Physiognomy and the Meaning of Expression*. Cambridge: Cambridge University Press.

Hastings, George W. (ed.) (1863). *Transactions of the National Association for the Promotion of Social Science. London Meeting, 1862*. London: John W. Parker, Son, & Bourne.

Hawkins, Mike (1997). *Social Darwinism in European and American Thought, 1860–1945: Nature as Model and Nature as Threat*. Cambridge: Cambridge University Press.

Heilmann, Ann (1998). 'Introduction', in *The Late-Victorian Marriage Question: A Collection of Key New Woman Texts*, 5 vols, i, pp. ix–xxxi. London: Routledge-Thoemmes.

Helmstadter, Richard J., and Bernard Lightman (eds) (1990). *Victorian Faith in Crisis: Essays on Continuity and Change in Nineteenth-Century Religious Belief*. London: Macmillan.

Higginson, Charles Gaskell (1889). *Manchester Positivist Society, Fifth Session, 1888–89. President's Annual Circular*. Manchester and London: John Heywood.

—— (1892). *Manchester Positivist Society, Eighth Session, 1891–92. President's Annual Circular*. Manchester and London: John Heywood.

Hill, Tracey (ed.) (1997). *Decadence and Danger: Writing, History, and the Fin de Siècle*. Bath: Sulis.

Hilton, Boyd (1988). *The Age of Atonement: The Influence of Evangelicalism on Social and Economic Thought, 1795–1865*. Oxford: Clarendon Press.

—— (2000). 'The Politics of Anatomy and an Anatomy of Politics c. 1825–1850', in S. Collini, R. Whatmore, and B. Young (eds), *History, Religion, and Culture: British Intellectual History 1750–1950*, pp. 179–97. Cambridge: Cambridge University Press.

Himmelfarb, Gertrude (1991). *Poverty and Compassion: The Moral Imagination of the Late Victorians*. New York: Knopf.

—— (1995). *The De-Moralization of Society: From Victorian Virtues to Modern Values*. London: Institute of Economic Affairs Health and Welfare Unit.

Hinton, James (1870–4). *Selections from Manuscripts*, 4 vols. London: Printed for the Author by Theo Johnson.

—— (1879). *Chapters on the Art of Thinking and Other Essays*, ed. C. H. Hinton, with an introd. by Shadworth Hodgson. London:, Kegan Paul & Co.

—— (1881). *Philosophy and Religion: Selections from the Manuscripts of the Late James Hinton*, ed. Caroline Haddon. London: Kegan Paul, Trench & Co.

—— (1884). *The Law-Breaker and the Coming of the Law*, ed. Margaret Hinton. London: Kegan Paul, Trench & Co.

Hobsbawm, Eric (1973). *The Age of Revolution: Europe 1789–1848*. London: Cardinal (1st edn 1962).

Hodge, Jonathan (2003). 'The Notebook Programmes and Projects of Darwin's London Years', in J. Hodge and G. Radick (eds), *The Cambridge Companion to Darwin*, pp. 40–68. Cambridge: Cambridge University Press.

Hoecker-Drysdale, Susan (2001). 'Harriet Martineau and the Positivism of Auguste Comte', in M. R. Hill and S. Hoecker-Drysdale (eds), *Harriet Martineau: Theoretical and Methodological Perspectives*, pp. 169–89. New York and London: Routledge.

Holland, Merlin (1997). 'Biography and the Art of Lying', in P. Raby (ed.), *The Cambridge Companion to Oscar Wilde*, pp. 3–17. Cambridge: Cambridge University Press.

—— and Rupert Hart-Davis (eds) (2000). *The Complete Letters of Oscar Wilde*. London: Fourth Estate.

Holroyd, Michael (1997). *Lytton Strachey: The New Biography*. London: Chatto & Windus.

Hopkins, Ellice (ed.) (1878). *Life and Letters of James Hinton*. London: Kegan Paul & Co.

—— (1909). *The Power of Womanhood; or, Mothers and Sons. A Book for Parents and Those in Loco Parentis,* 16th edn. London: Wells Gardner, Darton & Co. (1st edn 1899).

Houghton, Walter E. (1957). *The Victorian Frame of Mind, 1830–1870*. New Haven and London: Yale University Press.

—— (ed.) (1966–89). *The Wellesley Index to Victorian Periodicals, 1824–1900,* 5 vols. Toronto: University of Toronto Press.

Howsam, Leslie (2000). 'An Experiment with Science for the Nineteenth-Century Book Trade: The International Scientific Series', *British Journal for the History of Science,* 33: 187–207.

Hughes, Geoffrey (1988). *Words in Time: A Social History of the English Vocabulary*. Oxford: Basil Blackwell.

—— (2000). *A History of English Words*. Oxford: Blackwell.

Hughes, Hugh Price (1890). *Social Christianity: Sermons Delivered in St James's Hall, London,* 3rd edn. London: Hodder & Stoughton (1st edn 1889).

—— (1892). *Ethical Christianity: A Series of Sermons*. London: Sampson Low, Marston & Co.

—— (1894). *Essential Christianity: A Series of Explanatory Sermons*. London: Ibister & Co.

Hughes, Thomas (1885). *Address by His Honour Thomas Hughes QC, on the Occasion of the Presentation of a Testimonial in Recognition of his Services to the Cause of Co-Operation, December 6th 1884*. Manchester: Co-Operative Printing Society.

Hunt, Karen (1996). *Equivocal Feminists: The Social Democratic Federation and the Woman Question 1884–1911*. Cambridge and New York: Cambridge University Press.

Hunter, Shelagh (1995). *Harriet Martineau: The Poetics of Moralism*. Aldershot: Scolar Press.

Hurka, Thomas (2003). 'Moore in the Middle', *Ethics,* 113: 599–628.

—— (2005). 'Moore's Moral Philosophy', in E. N. Zalta (ed.), *The Stanford Encyclopedia of Philosophy* (spring 2005 edn): [http://plato.stanford.edu/archives/spr2005/entries/moore-moral/]

Hutchinson, Brian (2001). *G. E. Moore's Ethical Theory: Resistance and Reconciliation*. Cambridge and New York: Cambridge University Press.

Hutton, Richard Holt (1888). *Theological Essays*. London: Macmillan & Co.

—— (1894). *Criticisms on Contemporary Thought and Thinkers: Selected from The Spectator,* 2 vols. London: Macmillan & Co.

Huxley, Leonard (1903). *Life and Letters of Thomas Henry Huxley,* 3 vols, 2nd edn. London: Macmillan (1st edn 1900).

Huxley, Thomas H. (1893). *Lay Sermons, Addresses and Reviews,* 3rd edn. London: Macmillan (1st edn 1870).

—— (1893–4). *Collected Essays,* 9 vols. London: Macmillan.

Hyde, H. Montgomery (1962). *The Trials of Oscar Wilde.* New York: Dover.

Jackson, Holbrook (1972). *The Eighteen Nineties: A Review of Art and Ideas at the Close of the Nineteenth Century.* St Clair Shores, MI: Scholarly Press (1st edn 1922).

Jacyna, L. S. (1980). 'Science and Social Order in the Thought of A. J. Balfour', *Isis,* 71: 11–34.

James, Frank (2005). 'An "Open Clash between Science and the Church"? Wilberforce, Huxley and Hooker on Darwin at the British Association, Oxford, 1860', in D. Knight and M. Eddy (eds), *Science and Beliefs: From Natural Philosophy to Natural Science, 1700–1900,* pp. 171–93. Aldershot: Ashgate.

Jann, Rosemary (1997). 'Revising the Descent of Woman: Eliza Burt Gamble', in B. T. Gates and A. B. Shteir (eds), *Natural Eloquence: Women Reinscribe Science,* pp. 147–63. Madison: University of Wisconsin Press.

Jardine, Nick (2000). 'Uses and Abuses of Anachronism in the History of the Sciences', *History of Science,* 38: 251–70.

Johnson, Graham (2000). 'British Social Democracy and Religion, 1881–1911', *Journal of Ecclesiastical History,* 51: 91–115.

Johnson, Helen K. (1913). *Woman and the Republic: A Survey of the Woman-Suffrage Movement in the United States,* new edn. New York: Guidon Club (1st edn 1897).

Jones, Carole (2001). 'George Eliot's Sympathy and Duty: The Nature and Function of Sympathy and Duty in George Eliot's Fiction in Relation to Nineteenth-Century Theories of Egoism, Altruism and Gender and Twentieth-Century Feminist Object-Relations Theory', Ph.D. dissertation, University of Hull.

Jones, Greta (1980). *Social Darwinism and English Thought: The Interaction between Biological and Social Theory.* Brighton: Harvester.

—— (1986). *Social Hygiene in Twentieth-Century Britain.* London: Croom Helm.

—— (2004). 'Spencer and his Circle', in G. Jones and R. A. Peel (eds), *Herbert Spencer: The Intellectual Legacy,* pp. 1–16. London, Galton Institute.

—— and Robert A. Peel (eds) (2004). *Herbert Spencer: The Intellectual Legacy.* London: Galton Institute.

Jones, H. Stuart (2007). *Intellect and Character in Victorian England: Mark Pattison and the Invention of the Don.* Cambridge: Cambridge University Press.

Jones, Henry (1923). *Old Memories: Autobiography,* ed. Thomas Jones. London: Hodder & Stoughton.

Jones, Peter d'Alroy (1968). *The Christian Socialist Revival, 1877–1914: Religion, Class, and Social Conscience in Late-Victorian England.* Princeton: Princeton University Press.

Kaufmann, Moritz (1890). *Egoism, Altruism, and Christian Eudaimonism.* London: Religious Tract Society.

Keane, John (1995). *Tom Paine: A Political Life.* London: Bloomsbury.

Kelly, Alfred (1981). *The Descent of Darwin: The Popularization of Darwinism in Germany, 1860–1914.* Chapel Hill, NC: University of North Carolina Press.

Kenny, Neil (2004). *The Uses of Curiosity in Early Modern France and Germany.* Oxford: Oxford University Press.

Kent, Christopher (1978). *Brains and Numbers: Elitism, Comtism, and Democracy in Mid-Victorian England.* Toronto: University of Toronto Press.

Kent, John (1966). *From Darwin to Blatchford: The Role of Darwinism in Christian Apologetic, 1875–1910,* The Friends of Dr Williams's Library, twentieth annual lecture. London: Dr Williams's Trust.

Kevles, Daniel (1995). *In the Name of Eugenics: Genetics and the Uses of Human Heredity,* new edn. Cambridge, MA: Harvard University Press (1st edn 1985).

Kidd, Benjamin (1894). *Social Evolution.* London: Macmillan & Co.

King, William McGuire (1984). 'Hugh Price Hughes and the British "Social Gospel"', *Journal of Religious History,* 13: 66–82.

Knapp, John M. (ed.) (1895). *The Universities and the Social Problem: An Account of the University Settlements in East London.* London: Rivington, Percival, & Co.

Koditschek, Theodore (1989). 'The Dynamics of Class Formation in Nineteenth-Century Bradford', in A. L. Beier, D. Cannadine and J. M. Rosenheim (eds), *The First Modern Society: Essays in English History in Honour of Lawrence Stone,* pp. 511–48. Cambridge: Cambridge University Press.

Kohlstedt, Sally Gregory, and Mark Jorgensen (1999). '"The Irrepressible Woman Question": Women's Responses to Darwinian Evolutionary Ideology', in R. L. Numbers and J. Stenhouse (eds), *Disseminating Darwinism: The Role of Place, Race, Religion, and Gender,* pp. 267–93. Cambridge: Cambridge University Press.

Kohn, David (1989). 'Darwin's Ambiguity: The Secularization of Biological Meaning', *British Journal for the History of Science,* 22: 215–39.

Koselleck, Reinhart (1985). *Futures Past: On the Semantics of Historical Time,* tr. K. Tribe. Cambridge, MA: MIT Press.

—— (2002). *The Practice of Conceptual History: Timing History, Spacing Concepts,* tr. T. S. Presner *et al.* Stanford, CA: Stanford University Press.

Koven, Seth (1994). 'Henrietta Barnett (1851–1936): The (Auto)biography of a Late Victorian Marriage', in S. Pedersen and P. Mandler (eds), *After the Victorians: Private Conscience and Public Duty in Modern Britain. Essays in Memory of John Clive,* pp. 31–53. London and New York: Routledge.

—— (2004). *Slumming: Social and Sexual Politics in Victorian London.* Princeton and Oxford: Princeton University Press.

Kropotkin, Petr (1939). *Mutual Aid: A Factor of Evolution.* Harmondsworth: Penguin.

Kucich, John (2002). 'Scientific Ascendancy', in P. Brantlinger and W. B. Thesing (eds), *A Companion to the Victorian Novel,* pp. 119–36. Oxford: Blackwell.

Laity, Paul (2001). *The British Peace Movement, 1870–1914.* Oxford: Clarendon Press.

Ledger, Sally (1995). 'The New Woman and the Crisis of Victorianism', in S. Ledger and S. McCracken (eds), *Cultural Politics at the Fin de Siècle,* pp. 22–44. Cambridge: Cambridge University Press.

Le Goff, Jacques (1984). *The Birth of Purgatory,* tr. A Goldhammer. London: Scolar Press (1st published in French 1981).

Leighton, Denys (2004). *The Greenian Moment: T. H. Green, Religion and Political Argument in Victorian Britain.* Exeter: Imprint Academic.

Lennox, Cuthbert (1901). *Henry Drummond: A Biographical Sketch.* London: Andrew Melrose.

Leroy, Charles Georges (1802). *Lettres Philosophiques sur l'Intelligence et la Perfectibilité des Animaux.* Paris: Valade.

LeRoy, G. C. (1941). 'Richard Holt Hutton', *Publications of the Modern Language Association of America,* 56: 809–40.

Leroy, Maxime (1946–1954). *Histoire des Idées Sociales en France,* 3 vols. Paris: Gallimard.

Levine, George (2002). *Dying to Know: Scientific Epistemology and Narrative in Victorian England*. Chicago and London: University of Chicago Press.

Levy, Paul (1981). *Moore: G. E. Moore and the Cambridge Apostles*. Oxford: Oxford University Press.

Lewes, George Henry (1853). *Comte's Philosophy of the Sciences: Being an Exposition of the Principles of the Cours de Philosophie Positive of Auguste Comte*. London: Bohn.

—— (1874–5). *Problems of Life and Mind. First Series: The Foundations of a Creed*. 2 vols. Boston: James R. Osgood & Co.

Lewis, C. S. (1967). *Studies in Words*, 2nd edn. Cambridge: Cambridge University Press (1st edn 1960).

Lewis, Jane (1996). 'The Boundary between Voluntary and Statutory Social Service in the Late Nineteenth and Early Twentieth Centuries', *Historical Journal*, 39: 155–77.

Lightman, Bernard (1987). *The Origins of Agnosticism: Victorian Unbelief and the Limits of Knowledge*. Baltimore and London: Johns Hopkins University Press.

—— (1990). '*Robert Elsmere* and the Agnostic Crises of Faith', in R. J. Helmstadter and B. Lightman (eds), *Victorian Faith in Crisis: Essays on Continuity and Change in Nineteenth-Century Religious Belief*, pp. 283–311. London: Macmillan.

—— (1997a). '"Fighting even with Death": Balfour, Scientific Naturalism, and Thomas Henry Huxley's Final Battle', in A. P. Barr (ed.), *Thomas Henry Huxley's Place in Science and Letters: Centenary Essays*, pp. 323–50. Athens, GA, and London: University of Georgia Press.

—— (1997b). '"Voices of Nature": Popularizers of Victorian Science', in B. Lightman (ed.), *Victorian Science in Context*, pp. 187–211. Chicago and London: University of Chicago Press.

—— (2002). 'Huxley and Scientific Agnosticism: The Strange Case of a Failed Rhetorical Strategy', *British Journal for the History of Science*, 35: 271–90.

—— (2007). *Victorian Popularizers of Science: Designing Nature for New Audiences*. Chicago and London: University of Chicago Press.

Linton, Eliza Lynn (1885). *The Autobiography of Christopher Kirkland*, 3 vols. London: R. Bentley.

Litchfield, Henrietta (ed.) (1915). *Emma Darwin: A Century of Family Letters, 1792–1896*, 2 vols. London: John Murray.

Littré, Émile (1863). *Dictionnaire de la Langue Française*. Paris: Hachette.

Liveing, Susan (1926). *A Nineteenth-Century Teacher: John Henry Bridges. With a Preface by Professor L. T. Hobhouse and an Introduction by Professor Patrick Geddes*. London: Kegan Paul, Trench, Trübner & Co.

Livingstone, David N. (1987). *Darwin's Forgotten Defenders: The Encounter between Evangelical Theology and Evolutionary Thought*. Grand Rapids, MI: Eerdmans.

—— (1992). 'Darwinism and Calvinism: the Belfast-Princeton Connection', *Isis*, 83: 408–28.

—— (1994). 'Science and Religion: Foreword to the Historical Geography of an Encounter', *Journal of Historical Geography*, 20: 367–83.

—— (1999). 'Situating Evangelical Responses to Evolution', in D. N. Livingstone, D. G. Hart and M. A. Noll (eds), *Evangelicals and Science in Historical Perspective*, pp. 193–219. New York and Oxford, Oxford University Press.

—— (2003). *Putting Science in its Place: Geographies of Scientific Knowledge*. Chicago and London: University of Chicago Press.

Lubbock, John (1890). *Scientific Lectures*, 2nd edn. London: Macmillan & Co. (1st edn 1879).

Lucas, J. R. (1979). 'Wilberforce and Huxley: A Legendary Encounter', *Historical Journal*, 22: 313–30.

Lustig, Abigail (2004). 'Ants and the Nature of Nature in Auguste Forel, Erich Wasmann, and William Morton Wheeler', in L. Daston and F. Vidal (eds), *The Moral Authority of Nature*, pp. 282–307. Chicago: University of Chicago Press.

Lynd, Helen Merrell (1968). *England in the Eighteen-Eighties: Toward a Social Basis for Freedom*. London: Frank Cass & Co. (1st edn 1945).

Maccall, William (1873). *The Newest Materialism: Sundry Papers on the Books of Mill, Comte, Bain, Spencer, Atkinson and Feuerbach*. London: Farrah.

—— (1880). *Via Crucis: A Record of a Divine Life and Picture of a Divine Death*. London: George Standring.

McElroy, Wendy (1981). 'Benjamin Tucker, Individualism, and *Liberty*: Not the Daughter but the Mother of Order', *Literature of Liberty*, 4: 7–39.

—— (1996). *Sexual Correctness: The Gender-Feminist Attack on Women*. London: McFarland.

—— (2001). *Individualist Feminism of the Nineteenth Century*. London: McFarland.

McGee, John Edwin (1931). *A Crusade for Humanity: The History of Organized Positivism in England*. London: Watts & Co.

MacIntyre, Alasdair (1984). *After Virtue: A Study in Moral Theory*, 2nd edn. Notre Dame, IN, University of Notre Dame Press (1st edn 1981).

—— (1994). 'Genealogies and Subversions', in R. Schacht (ed.), *Nietzsche, Genealogy, Morality: Essays on Nietzsche's On the Genealogy of Morals*, pp. 284–305. Berkeley and Los Angeles, CA, and London: University of California Press.

MacKillop, I. D. (1986). *The British Ethical Societies*. Cambridge: Cambridge University Press.

Mackintosh, Robert (1899). *From Comte to Benjamin Kidd: The Appeal to Biology or Evolution for Human Guidance*. London and New York: Macmillan.

McKusick, James C. (1992). '"Living Words": Samuel Taylor Coleridge and the Genesis of the *OED*', *Modern Philology*, 90: 1–45.

Maitland, Frederic W. (1906). *The Life and Letters of Leslie Stephen*. London: Duckworth & Co.

Mallock, W. H. (1878). *The New Paul and Virginia, or Positivism on an Island*. London: Chatto & Windus.

—— (1899). *The Individualist*. London: Chapman & Hall.

Maltz, Diana (2003). 'Wilde's *The Woman's World* and the Culture of Aesthetic Philanthropy', in J. Bristow (ed.), *Wilde Writings: Contextual Conditions*, pp. 185–211. Toronto and Buffalo, NY: University of Toronto Press in association with the UCLA Center for Seventeenth- and Eighteenth-Century Studies and the William Andrews Clark Memorial Library.

Manier, Edward (1978). *The Young Darwin and his Cultural Circle: A Study of the Influences which Helped Shape the Language and Logic of the First Drafts of the Theory of Natural Selection*. Dordrecht: Reidel.

Mann, Horace (1854). *Census of Great Britain, 1851: Religious Worship in England and Wales*. London: George Routledge & Co.

Maritain, Jacques (1964). *Moral Philosophy: An Historical and Critical Survey of the Great Systems*. London: Geoffrey Bles.

Marsh, Joss (1998). *Word Crimes: Blasphemy, Culture, and Literature in Nineteenth-Century England*. Chicago and London: University of Chicago Press.

Martineau, Harriet (1877). *Autobiography, With Memorials by Maria Weston Chapman*, 3 vols. London: Smith, Elder, & Co.

Martineau, James (1869). *The New Affinities of Faith: A Plea for Free Christian Union*. London: Williams & Norgate.

—— (1885). *Types of Ethical Theory*. 2 vols. Oxford: Clarendon Press.

Matoré, Georges (1953). *La Méthode en Lexicologie: Domaine Français*. Paris: Didier.

Mattheisen, Paul F., *et al.* (eds) (1990–7). *The Collected Letters of George Gissing*, 10 vols. Athens, OH: Ohio University Press.

Meacham, Standish (1987). *Toynbee Hall and Social Reform 1880–1914: The Search for Community*. New Haven: Yale University Press.

Melsom, R. A. (1883). *Gas Consumer's Manual*, 5th edn. Manchester: Tubbs, Brook & Chrystal (1st published 1882 under the pseudonym 'Altruism': see above).

—— (1884). *Courtship and Marriage Customs of Many Nations, With Quotations from Shakespeare and Milton*. London and Manchester: John Heywood.

Meredith, George (1891). *One of our Conquerors*, 3 vols. London: Chapman & Hall.

—— (1909). *Diana of the Crossways*. London: Archibald Constable & Co. (1st edn 1885).

Merton, Robert K., and Elinor Barber (2004). *The Travels and Adventures of Serendipity: A Study in Historical Semantics and the Sociology of Science*. Princeton: Princeton University Press.

Michael, Ian (1987). *The Teaching of English: From the Sixteenth Century to 1870*. Cambridge: Cambridge University Press.

Mill, John Stuart (1865). *Auguste Comte and Positivism*. London: Trübner.

—— (1963–91). *The Collected Works of John Stuart Mill*, 33 vols, ed. John M. Robson *et al.* Toronto: University of Toronto Press.

Mitman, Gregg (1992). *The State of Nature: Ecology, Community, and American Social Thought, 1900–1950*. Chicago and London: University of Chicago Press.

Mivart, St George (1871). *On the Genesis of Species*. New York, D. Appleton & Co.

Montes, Leonidas (2003). 'Das *Adam Smith Problem*: Its Origins, the Stages of the Current Debate, and One Implication for our Understanding of Sympathy', *Journal of the History of Economic Thought*, 25: 63–90.

Montgomery, William (1985). 'Charles Darwin's Thought on Expressive Mechanisms in Evolution', in G. Zivin (ed.), *The Development of Expressive Behavior*, pp. 27–50. Orlando, FL, Academic Press.

Moore, G. E. (1968). 'An Autobiography', in P. A. Schilpp (ed.), *The Philosophy of G. E. Moore*, 3rd edn, pp. 1–39. La Salle, IL, Open Court (1st edn 1942).

—— (1991). *The Elements of Ethics*, ed. and with an introd. by Tom Regan. Philadelphia: Temple University Press.

—— (1993). *Principia Ethica*, rev. edn, ed. and with an introd. by Thomas Baldwin. Cambridge: Cambridge University Press (1st edn 1903).

Moore, Gregory (2002). *Nietzsche, Biology, and Metaphor*. Cambridge: Cambridge University Press.

Moore, James R. (1979). *The Post-Darwinian Controversies: A Study of the Protestant Struggle to Come to Terms with Darwin in Great Britain and America, 1870–1900*. Cambridge: Cambridge University Press.

—— (1985a). 'Evangelicals and Evolution: Henry Drummond, Herbert Spencer, and the Naturalization of the Spiritual World', *Scottish Journal of Theology*, 38: 383–417.

—— (1985b). 'Herbert Spencer's Henchmen: The Evolution of Protestant Liberals in Late Nineteenth-Century America', in J. R. Durant (ed.), *Darwinism and Divinity: Essays on Evolution and Religious Belief*, pp. 76–100. Oxford, Blackwell.

—— (ed.) (1989a). *History, Humanity and Evolution: Essays for John C. Greene*. Cambridge: Cambridge University Press.

—— (1989b). 'Of Love and Death: Why Darwin "Gave up Christianity" ', in J. R. Moore (ed.), *History, Humanity and Evolution: Essays for John C. Greene*, pp. 195–229. Cambridge: Cambridge University Press.

—— (1994). *The Darwin Legend*. London: Hodder & Stoughton.

—— (2004). 'The Fortunes of Eugenics', in D. Brunton (ed.), *Medicine Transformed: Health, Disease, and Society in Europe, 1800–1930*, pp. 266–97. Manchester: Manchester University Press in association with the Open University.

Morgan, Sue (2000). 'Faith, Sex and Purity: The Religio-Feminist Theory of Ellice Hopkins', *Women's History Review*, 9: 13–34.

Morison, James Cotter (1888). *The Service of Man: An Essay Towards the Religion of the Future* 3rd edn. London: Kegan Paul, Trench & Co. (1st edn 1887).

Morley, Charles (1900). *Archie; or, The Confessions of an Old Burglar*. London: G. Newnes (1st edn 1897).

Morley, John (1877). 'Comte', in T. S. Baynes and W. R. Smith (eds), *Encyclopaedia Britannica*, 24 vols, 9th edn, vi. 229–38. Edinburgh: Adam & Charles Black.

Mozley, J. B. (1886). *Sermons Preached Before the University of Oxford and on Various Occasions*, 6th edn. London: Rivingtons (1st edn 1876).

Mudie-Smith, Richard (ed.) (1904). *The Religious Life of London*. London: Hodder & Stoughton.

Murray, James A. H. (1888). *A New English Dictionary on Historical Principles: Founded Mainly on the Materials Collected by the Philological Society*, i. *A and B*. Oxford: Clarendon Press.

Nash, David (1999). *Blasphemy in Modern Britain, 1789 to the Present*. Aldershot: Ashgate.

Nettleship, John T. (1868). *Essays on Robert Browning's Poetry*. London: Macmillan.

Newman, Ernest (1895). *Gluck and the Opera: A Study in Musical History*. London: Bertram Dobell.

—— (1905). *Musical Studies*. London and New York: John Lane.

—— (1933–47). *The Life of Richard Wagner*, 4 vols. London: Cassell.

—— (1962). 'Confessions of a Musical Critic', in H. van Thal (ed.), *Testament of Music: Essays and Papers by Ernest Newman*, pp. 1–41. London: Putnam.

Newman, John Henry (1994). *Apologia Pro Vita Sua*, Penguin Classics edn, ed. Ian Ker. London: Penguin (1st edn 1864).

Newman, Vera (1963). *Ernest Newman: A Memoir*. London: Putnam.

Nietzsche, Friedrich (1896). *The Case of Wagner; Nietzsche contra Wagner; The Twilight of the Idols; The Anti-Christ*, tr. T. Common, ed. Alexander Tille. London: H. Henry.

—— (1968). *The Will to Power*, tr. W. Kaufmann and R. J. Hollingdale, ed. with a commentary by Walter Kaufmann. London: Weidenfeld & Nicolson. (1st German edn 1901).

—— (1974). *Nietzsche Werke: Kritische Gesamtausgabe*, vii/3. *Nachgelassene Fragmente: Herbst 1884 bis Herbst 1885*, ed. Giorgio Colli and Mazzino Montinari. Berlin and New York: de Gruyter.

—— (1980). *Kritische Studienausgabe: Sämtliche Werke*, 15 vols, ed. Giorgio Colli and Mazzino Montinari. Berlin: de Gruyter.

Nietzsche, Friedrich (1990). *Twilight of the Idols, and the Anti-Christ*, tr. R. J. Hollingdale, Penguin classics edn. London: Penguin. (1st German edn 1888).

—— (1997). *Daybreak: Thoughts on the Prejudices of Morality*, tr. R. J. Hollingdale, ed. Maudemarie Clark and Brian Leiter. Cambridge: Cambridge University Press (1st German edn 1881).

—— (2001). *The Gay Science: With a Prelude in German Rhymes and an Appendix of Songs*, tr. J. Nauckhoff and A. D. Caro, ed. Bernard Williams. Cambridge: Cambridge University Press. (1st German edn 1882).

Nightingale, Florence (1994). *Suggestions for Thought: Selections and Commentaries,* ed. Michael D. Calabria and Janet A. Macrae. Philadelphia: University of Pennsylvania Press.

Nordau, Max (1993). *Degeneration,* tr. from the 2nd edn of the German work, with an introd. by George L. Mosse. Lincoln, NE: University of Nebraska Press (1st English-language edn 1895).

Numbers, Ronald L., and John Stenhouse (eds) (1999). *Disseminating Darwinism: The Role of Place, Race, Religion, and Gender.* Cambridge: Cambridge University Press.

Offer, John (ed.) (2000). *Herbert Spencer: Critical Assessments,* 4 vols. London and New York: Routledge.

—— (2006). *An Intellectual History of British Social Policy: Idealism versus Non-Idealism.* Bristol: Policy.

Okasha, Samir (2005). 'Biological Altruism', in E. N. Zalta (ed.), *The Stanford Encyclopedia of Philosophy* (summer 2005 edn): [http://plato.stanford.edu/archives/sum2005/entries/altruism-biological/]

Ospovat, Dov (1981). *The Development of Darwin's Theory: Natural History, Natural Theology, and Natural Selection, 1838–1859.* Cambridge: Cambridge University Press.

'Ouida' (1897). *An Altruist,* 2nd edn. London: T. Fisher Unwin (1st edn 1897).

Packe, Michael St J. (1954). *The Life of John Stuart Mill.* London: Secker & Warburg.

Paine, Thomas (2000). *Political Writings,* ed. with an introd. by Bruce Kuklick. Cambridge: Cambridge University Press.

Paley, William (1785). *The Principles of Moral and Political Philosophy.* London: R. Faulder.

Parsons, Gerald (ed.) (1988). *Religion in Victorian Britain,* 4 vols. Manchester: Manchester University Press in association with the Open University.

Pascal, Blaise (1904). *The Thoughts of Blaise Pascal,* tr. W. F. Trotter, Temple Classics edn. London: Dent.

—— (1931). *Pascal's Pensées,* tr. W. F. Trotter, Everyman edn with an introd. by T. S. Eliot. London: Dent.

Pater, Walter (1906). *Essays from 'The Guardian'.* London and New York: Macmillan.

Paul, Diane B. (1988). 'The Selection of the "Survival of the Fittest"', *Journal of the History of Biology,* 21: 411–24.

—— (1995). *Controlling Human Heredity: 1865 to the Present.* Atlantic Highlands, NJ: Humanities Press.

—— (2003). 'Darwin, Social Darwinism, and Eugenics', in J. Hodge and G. Radick (eds), *The Cambridge Companion to Darwin*, pp. 214–39. Cambridge: Cambridge University Press.

Paxton, Nancy (1991). *George Eliot and Herbert Spencer: Feminism, Evolutionism, and the Reconstruction of Gender.* Princeton: Princeton University Press.

Peaker, Carol (2005). 'Mutual Aid, a Factor of Peter Kropotkin's Literary Criticism', in A. Zwierlein (ed.), *Unmapped Countries: Biological Visions in Nineteenth Century Literature and Culture*, pp. 83–93. London: Anthem Press.

Pearson, Heath (2004). 'Economics and Altruism at the *Fin de Siècle*', in M. J. Daunton and F. Trentmann (eds), *Worlds of Political Economy: Knowledge and Power in the Nineteenth and Twentieth Centuries*, pp. 24–46. Basingstoke: Palgrave Macmillan.

Pedersen, Susan, and Peter Mandler (eds) (1994). *After the Victorians: Private Conscience and Public Duty in Modern Britain. Essays in Memory of John Clive*. London and New York: Routledge.

Peel, J. D. Y. (1971). *Herbert Spencer: The Evolution of a Sociologist*. London: Heinemann.

—— (2004). 'Spencer in History: The Second Century', in G. Jones and R. A. Peel (eds), *Herbert Spencer: The Intellectual Legacy*, pp. 125–49. London: Galton Institute.

Peel, Robert A. (ed.) (1998). *Essays in the History of Eugenics*. London: Galton Institute.

Penelhum, Terence (ed.) (1973). *Immortality*. Belmont, CA: Wadsworth.

Percival, Revd Canon (1886). *A Sermon Preached in St Andrew's Parish Church, Plymouth on Whit-Sunday Afternoon, June 13th 1886*. Manchester: Central Co-operative Board.

Perkin, Joan (1989). *Women and Marriage in Nineteenth-Century England*. London: Routledge.

Perril, Simon (1997). 'A Cartography of Absence: The Work of Iain Sinclair', *Comparative Criticism: An Annual Journal*, 19: 309–40.

Peterson, William S. (1976). *Victorian Heretic: Mrs Humphry Ward's Robert Elsmere*. Leicester: Leicester University Press.

Pichanik, Valerie Kossew (1980). *Harriet Martineau: The Woman and her Work, 1802–76*. Ann Arbor: University of Michigan Press.

Pick, Daniel (1989). *Faces of Degeneration: Aspects of a European Disorder, c. 1848–1918*. Cambridge: Cambridge University Press.

Pickering, Mary (1993). *Auguste Comte: An Intellectual Biography*, i. Cambridge: Cambridge University Press.

—— (2000). 'Auguste Comte', in G. Ritzer (ed.), *The Blackwell Companion to Major Social Theorists*, pp. 25–52. Malden, MA, and Oxford: Blackwell.

Post, Stephen G., *et al.* (eds) (2002). *Altruism and Altruistic Love: Science, Philosophy and Religion in Dialogue*. Oxford and New York: Oxford University Press.

Preston, Claire (2006). *Bee*. London: Reaktion Books.

Prochaska, Frank K. (1988). *The Voluntary Impulse: Philanthropy in Modern Britain*. London: Faber.

Proctor, Dennis (ed.) (1973). *The Autobiography of G. Lowes Dickinson and Other Unpublished Writings*. London: Duckworth.

Pugh, Martin (1999). *State and Society: A Social and Political History of Britain, 1870–1997*, 2nd edn. London: Arnold (1st edn 1993).

Pyle, Andrew (ed.) (1998). *Utilitarianism: Key Nineteenth-Century Journal Sources*, 4 vols. London: Routledge.

Queensberry, Lord (1881). *The Spirit of the Matterhorn*. London: W. Mitchell.

Quinault, R. E. (1976). 'The Fourth Party and the Conservative Opposition to Bradlaugh, 1880–1888', *English Historical Review*, 91: 315–40.

Raby, Peter (ed.) (1997). *The Cambridge Companion to Oscar Wilde*. Cambridge: Cambridge University Press.

Rachels, James (1990). *Created from Animals: The Moral Implications of Darwinism*. Oxford: Oxford University Press.

Radick, Gregory (2003). 'Is the Theory of Natural Selection Independent of its History?', in J. Hodge and G. Radick (eds), *The Cambridge Companion to Darwin*, pp. 143–67. Cambridge: Cambridge University Press.

Raeder, Linda C. (2002). *John Stuart Mill and the Religion of Humanity*. Columbia, MO, and London: University of Missouri Press.

Renwick, Chris (2005). 'Sex and the City: The Evolution of Patrick Geddes, 1874–1889', M.Phil. dissertation, History and Philosophy of Science, University of Leeds.

Richards, Evelleen (1989). 'Huxley and Woman's Place in Science: The "Woman Question" and the Control of Victorian Anthropology', in J. R. Moore (ed.), *History, Humanity and Evolution: Essays for John C. Greene*, pp. 253–84. Cambridge: Cambridge University Press.

Richards, Robert J. (1987). *Darwin and the Emergence of Evolutionary Theories of Mind and Behavior*. Chicago: University of Chicago Press.

—— (1999). 'Darwin's Romantic Biology: The Foundation of his Evolutionary Ethics', in J. Maienschein and M. Ruse (eds), *Biology and the Foundation of Ethics*, pp. 113–53. Cambridge: Cambridge University Press.

—— (2003). 'Darwin on Mind, Morals and Emotions', in J. Hodge and G. Radick (eds), *The Cambridge Companion to Darwin*, pp. 92–115. Cambridge: Cambridge University Press.

—— (2004). 'The Relation of Spencer's Evolutionary Theory to Darwin's', in G. Jones and R. A. Peel (eds), *Herbert Spencer: The Intellectual Legacy*, pp. 17–36. London: Galton Institute.

Richardson, Angelique (2003). *Love and Eugenics in the Late Nineteenth Century*. Oxford: Oxford University Press.

—— and Chris Willis (eds) (2002). *The New Woman in Fiction and in Fact: Fin-de-Siècle Feminisms*. Basingstoke: Palgrave.

Richter, Melvin (1995). *The History of Political and Social Concepts: A Critical Introduction*. New York: Oxford University Press.

Ritchie, J. Ewing (1870). *The Religious Life of London*. London: Tinsley Brothers.

Roberts, Caroline (2002). *The Woman and the Hour: Harriet Martineau and Victorian Ideologies*. Toronto: University of Toronto Press.

Roberts, M. J. D. (2004). *Making English Morals: Voluntary Association and Moral Reform in England, 1787–1886*. Cambridge: Cambridge University Press.

Robertson, J. M. (1936). *A History of Freethought Ancient and Modern to the Period of the French Revolution*, 2 vols, 4th edn. London: Watts & Co. (1st published in 1899 as *A Short History of Freethought: Ancient and Modern*).

Romanes, George J. (1897). *Essays,* ed. C. Lloyd Morgan. London, New York, and Bombay: Longmans, Green & Co.

Root, John David (1980). 'The Philosophical and Religious Thought of Arthur James Balfour (1848–1930)', *Journal of British Studies,* 19: 120–41.

Rose, Jonathan (1995). 'How Historians Study Reader Response: or, What Did Jo Think of *Bleak House*?', in J. O. Jordan and R. L. Patten (eds), *Literature in the Marketplace: Nineteenth-Century British Publishing and Reading Practices*, pp. 195–212. Cambridge: Cambridge University Press.

—— (2001). *The Intellectual Life of the British Working Classes*. New Haven and London: Yale University Press.

Rosenberg, Sheila (1982). 'The Financing of Radical Opinion: John Chapman and the *Westminster Review*', in J. Shattock and M. Wolff (eds), *The Victorian Press: Samplings and Soundings*, pp. 167–92. Leicester: Leicester University Press.

Ross, Sydney (1962). 'Scientist: The Story of a Word', *Annals of Science,* 18(2): 65–85.

Row, C. A. (1877). *Christian Evidences Viewed in Relation to Modern Thought*. London: Norgate.

—— (1890). *Christian Theism: A Brief and Popular Survey of the Evidence upon which it*

Rests: and the Objections Urged against it Considered and Refuted. London: Hodder & Stoughton.

Rowell, Geoffrey (1974). *Hell and the Victorians: A Study of the Nineteenth-Century Theological Controversies Concerning Eternal Punishment and the Future Life*. Oxford: Clarendon Press.

Royle, Edward (1974). *Victorian Infidels: The Origins of the British Secularist Movement, 1791–1866*. Manchester: Manchester University Press.

—— (1980). *Radicals Secularists and Republicans: Popular Freethought in Britain 1866–1915*. Manchester: Manchester University Press.

—— (ed.) (1976). *The Infidel Tradition: From Paine to Bradlaugh*. London: Macmillan.

Ruse, Michael (1995). *Evolutionary Naturalism: Selected Essays*. London and New York: Routledge.

—— (2002). 'A Darwinian Naturalist's Perspective on Altruism', in S. G. Post *et al.* (eds), *Altruism and Altruistic Love: Science, Philosophy, and Religion in Dialogue*, pp. 151–67. Oxford: Oxford University Press.

Russell, Bertrand (1961). 'My Religious Reminiscences', in R. E. Egner and L. E. Denonn (eds), *The Basic Writings of Bertrand Russell 1903–1959*, pp. 31–6. London: George Allen & Unwin.

Rylance, Rick (2000). *Victorian Psychology and British Culture 1850–1880*. New York and Oxford: Oxford University Press.

Saleeby, Caleb W. (1906a). *Evolution the Master-Key: A Discussion of the Principles of Evolution as Illustrated in Atoms, Stars, Organic Species, Mind, Society, and Morals*. London and New York: Harper & Brothers.

—— (1906b). *Individualism and Collectivism: Four Lectures*. London: Williams & Norgate.

—— (1914). *The Progress of Eugenics*. London: Cassell.

Schaffer, Talia (2003). 'The Origins of the Aesthetic Novel: Ouida, Wilde, and the Popular Romance', in J. Bristow (ed.), *Wilde Writings: Contextual Conditions*, pp. 212–29. Toronto and Buffalo, NY: University of Toronto Press in association with the UCLA Center for Seventeenth- and Eighteenth-Century Studies and the William Andrews Clark Memorial Library.

Schloss, Jeffrey P. (2002). 'Emerging Accounts of Altruism: "Love Creation's Final Law"?' in S. G. Post *et al.* (eds), *Altruism and Altruistic Love: Science, Philosophy, and Religion in Dialogue*, pp. 212–42. Oxford, Oxford University Press.

—— (2004). 'Introduction: Evolutionary Ethics and Christian Morality: Surveying the Issues', in P. Clayton and J. P. Schloss (eds), *Evolution and Ethics: Human Morality in Biological and Religious Perspective*, pp. 1–26. Grand Rapids, MI: Wm.B. Eerdmans.

Schneewind, J. B. (1977). *Sidgwick's Ethics and Victorian Moral Philosophy*. Oxford: Clarendon Press.

Schultz, Bart (ed.) (1992). *Essays on Henry Sidgwick*. Cambridge: Cambridge University Press.

—— (2004). *Henry Sidgwick: Eye of the Universe. An Intellectual Biography*. Cambridge: Cambridge University Press.

Schweik, Robert (1999). 'The Influence of Science, Religion, and Philosophy on Hardy's Writings', in D. Kramer (ed.), *The Cambridge Companion to Thomas Hardy*, pp. 54–72. Cambridge: Cambridge University Press.

Scott, Anne (2004). '"Visible Incarnations of the Unseen": Henry Drummond and the Practice of Typological Exegesis', *British Journal for the History of Science*, 37: 435–54.

Scott, Niall (2002). 'Eugenics Perpetuated by Altruism', *Science as Culture*, 11: 505–21.

Searle, G. R. (1998). *Morality and the Market in Victorian Britain*. Oxford: Clarendon Press.

Secord, James A. (1997). 'Introduction', in J. A. Secord (ed.), *Charles Lyell's Principles of Geology*, pp. ix–xliii. London: Penguin.

Secord, James A. (2000). *Victorian Sensation: The Extraordinary Publication, Reception, and Secret Authorship of Vestiges of the Natural History of Creation*. Chicago and London: University of Chicago Press.

Sell, Alan P. F. (1977). *Robert Mackintosh: Theologian of Integrity*. Berne: P. Lang.

—— (1995). *Philosophical Idealism and Christian Belief*. Cardiff: University of Wales Press.

—— (2004). *Mill on God: The Pervasiveness and Elusiveness of Mill's Religious Thought*. Aldershot: Ashgate.

Semmel, Bernard (1960). *Imperialism and Social Reform: English Social-Imperial Thought, 1895–1914*. London: George Allen & Unwin.

—— (1994). *George Eliot and the Politics of National Inheritance*. New York and Oxford: Oxford University Press.

Seth, Andrew, and R. B. Haldane (eds) (1883). *Essays in Philosophical Criticism*. London: Longmans, Green, & Co.

Sherwood, Margaret (1895). *An Experiment in Altruism*. New York and London: Macmillan & Co.

Shewan, Rodney (1977). *Oscar Wilde: Art and Egotism*. London: Macmillan.

Shinwell, Manny (1981). *Lead with the Left: My First Ninety-Six Years*. London: Cassell.

Shuttleworth, Sally (1984). *George Eliot and Nineteenth-Century Science: The Make-Believe of a Beginning*. Cambridge: Cambridge University Press.

Sidgwick, Arthur, and Eleanor Mildred Sidgwick (1906). *Henry Sidgwick: A Memoir*. London: Macmillan & Co.

Sidgwick, Henry (1874). *The Methods of Ethics*. London: Macmillan.

—— (1898). *Practical Ethics: A Collection of Addresses and Essays*. London: Swan Sonnenschein.

—— (1902). *Lectures on the Ethics of T. H. Green, Mr Herbert Spencer, and J. Martineau*. London: Macmillan & Co.

—— (1904). *Miscellaneous Essays and Addresses*. London: Macmillan & Co.

—— (1981). *The Methods of Ethics,* 7th edn. Indianapolis: Hackett.

—— (2000). *Essays on Ethics and Method,* ed. with an introd. by Marcus G. Singer. Oxford: Clarendon Press.

Simcox, Edith (1877). *Natural Law: An Essay in Ethics*. London: Trübner & Co.

Simey, T. S., and M. B. Simey (1960). *Charles Booth, Social Scientist*. London: Oxford University Press.

Simhony, Avital (2001). 'T. H. Green's Complex Common Good: Between Liberalism and Communitarianism', in A. Simhony and D. Weinstein (eds), *The New Liberalism: Reconciling Liberty and Community*, pp. 69–91. Cambridge: Cambridge University Press.

Simpson, George (1969). *Auguste Comte: Sire of Sociology*. New York: Thomas Y. Cromwell.

Sinclair, Thomas (1878). *The Mount: Speech from its English Heights*. London: Trübner & Co.

Sisson, Edward O. (1910). 'Egoism, Altruism, Catholism: A Note on Ethical Terminology', *Journal of Philosophy, Psychology and Scientific Methods*, 7: 158–61.

Skinner, Quentin (2002). *Visions of Politics*, i. *Regarding Method*. Cambridge: Cambridge University Press.

Sleigh, Charlotte (2001). 'Empire of the Ants: H. G. Wells and Tropical Entomology', *Science as Culture,* 10: 33–71.

—— (2003). *Ant*. London: Reaktion Books.

—— (2007). *Six Legs Better: A Cultural History of Myrmecology*. Baltimore and London: Johns Hopkins University Press.

Sloan, John (2003). *Oscar Wilde*. Oxford: Oxford University Press.

Small, Robin (2005). *Nietzsche and Rée: A Star Friendship*. Oxford: Clarendon Press.

Smith, George Adam (1899). *The Life of Henry Drummond*. London: Hodder & Stoughton.

Smith, Jonathan (1995). ' "The Cock of Lordly Plume": Sexual Selection and *The Egoist*', *Nineteenth-Century Literature*, 50: 51–77.

—— (2006). *Charles Darwin and Victorian Visual Culture*. Cambridge: Cambridge University Press.

Smith, Philip E., and Michael S. Helfland (eds) (1989). *Oscar Wilde's Oxford Notebooks: A Portrait of Mind in the Making*. New York and Oxford: Oxford University Press.

Smith, Roger (1992). *Inhibition: History and Meaning in the Sciences of Mind and Brain*. London: Free Association Books.

Smith, Warren S. (1967). *The London Heretics, 1870–1914*. London: Constable.

Snell, K. D. M., and Paul S. Ell (2000). *Rival Jerusalems: The Geography of Victorian Religion*. Cambridge: Cambridge University Press.

Sober, Elliott (2002). 'The ABCs of Altruism', in S. G. Post *et al.* (eds), *Altruism and Altruistic Love: Science, Philosophy and Religion in Dialogue*, pp. 17–28. Oxford and New York: Oxford University Press.

—— and David Sloan Wilson (1998). *Unto Others: The Evolution and Psychology of Unselfish Behavior*. Cambridge, MA, and London: Harvard University Press.

Soffer, Reba N. (1982). 'Why do Disciplines Fail? The Strange Case of British Sociology', *English Historical Review*, 97: 767–802.

Soloway, Richard A. (1990). *Demography and Degeneration: Eugenics and the Declining Birthrate in Twentieth-Century Britain*. Chapel Hill, NC, and London: University of North Carolina Press.

Spencer, Herbert (1870–2). *The Principles of Psychology*, 2 vols, 2nd edn. London: Williams & Norgate (1st edn 1855).

—— (1873). *The Study of Sociology*. London: H. S. King.

—— (1879). *The Data of Ethics*. London: Williams & Norgate.

—— (1891). 'Reasons for Dissenting from the Philosophy of M. Comte', in *Essays: Scientific, Political, and Speculative*, 3 vols, ii. 118–44. London: Williams & Norgate (1st published Apr. 1864).

—— (1892–3). *The Principles of Ethics*, 2 vols. London: Williams & Norgate.

—— (1896). *The Principles of Sociology*, 3 vols. London: Williams & Norgate.

—— (1904). *An Autobiography*, 2 vols. London: Williams & Norgate.

—— (1994). *Political Writings*, ed. John Offer. Cambridge: Cambridge University Press.

—— Herbert (1996). *Collected Writings*, 12 vols, ed. and introd. by Michael W. Taylor. London: Routledge/Thoemmes Press.

Spinner, Thomas J. (1973). *George Joachim Goschen: The Transformation of a Victorian Liberal*. London: Cambridge University Press.

Stack, David (2003). *The First Darwinian Left: Socialism and Darwinism, 1859–1914*. Cheltenham: New Clarion.

Stanton, Elizabeth Cody (1971). *Eighty Years and More: Reminiscences 1815–1897*. New York: Schocken Books (1st edn 1898).

Stedman Jones, Gareth (1971). *Outcast London: A Study in the Relationship between Classes in Victorian Society*. Oxford: Clarendon Press.

Stephen, Leslie (1882). *The Science of Ethics*. London: Smith, Elder, & Co.

Stokes, John (1989). *In the Nineties*. New York: Harvester Wheatsheaf.

Streets, Heather (2004). *Martial Races: The Military, Race and Masculinity in British Imperial Culture, 1857–1914*. Manchester and New York: Manchester University Press.

Sturrock, June (2002). 'Angels, Insects, and Analogy: A. S. Byatt's "Morpho Eugenia"', *Connotations*, 12: 93–104.

Sutcliffe, Peter (1978). *The Oxford University Press: An Informal History*. Oxford: Oxford University Press.

Sutherland, John (1991). *Mrs Humphry Ward: Eminent Victorian, Pre-Eminent Edwardian*. Oxford and New York: Oxford University Press.

Tanner, J. R. (ed.) (1984). *The Historical Register of the University of Cambridge: Being a Supplement to the Calendar with a Record of University Offices Honours and Distinctions to the Year 1910*. Cambridge: Cambridge University Press (1st edn 1917).

Taylor, Dennis (1993). *Hardy's Literary Language and Victorian Philology*. Oxford: Clarendon Press.

Taylor, Michael (1992). *Men versus the State: Herbert Spencer and Late Victorian Individualism*. Oxford and New York: Oxford University Press.

Thatcher, David S. (1970). *Nietzsche in England 1890–1914: The Growth of a Reputation*. Toronto: University of Toronto Press.

Thomas, William Beach (1928). *The Story of The Spectator, 1828–1928*. London: Methuen & Co.

Thompson, Laurence (1951). *Robert Blatchford: Portrait of an Englishman*. London: Gollancz.

Thomson, Alexander (1884). *Christianity and Positivism: A Sermon*. Manchester: Brook & Chrystal.

Thomson, J. Arthur (1920). *The System of Animate Nature: The Gifford Lectures Delivered in the University of St Andrews in the Years 1915 and 1916*. London: Williams & Norgate.

Todes, Daniel P. (1989). *Darwin without Malthus: The Struggle for Existence in Russian Evolutionary Thought*. Oxford: Oxford University Press.

Tosh, John (2005). *Manliness and Masculinities in Nineteenth-Century Britain: Essays on Gender, Family, and Empire*. Harlow: Pearson.

Toynbee, Arnold (1884). *Lectures on the Industrial Revolution in England; Popular Addresses, Notes, and Other Fragments*, with a short memoir by Benjamin Jowett. London: Rivingtons.

—— (1908). *Lectures on the Industrial Revolution of the Eighteenth Century in England, Popular Addresses, Notes, and Other Fragments*, new edn with a reminiscence by Lord Milner. London: Longmans, Green, & Co.

Trench, Richard Chenevix (n.d.). *On the Study of Words; and English Past and Present*, Everyman's Library. London: J. M. Dent & Sons (1st edn 1851).

Tucker, Susie I. (1972). *Enthusiasm: A Study in Semantic Change*. Cambridge: Cambridge University Press.

Tulloch, John (1885). *Movements of Religious Thought in Britain during the Nineteenth Century*. London: Longmans, Green, & Co.

Turner, Frank M. (1974). *Between Science and Religion: The Reaction to Scientific Naturalism in Late Victorian England*. New Haven and London: Yale University Press.

—— (1993). *Contesting Cultural Authority: Essays in Victorian Intellectual Life.* Cambridge: Cambridge University Press.

Turner, Jonathan H. (1985). *Herbert Spencer: A Renewed Appreciation.* London: Sage.

—— (2000). 'Herbert Spencer', in G. Ritzer (ed.), *The Blackwell Companion to Major Social Theorists*, pp. 81–104. Malden, MA, and Oxford, Blackwell.

Tylecote, Mabel (1957). *The Mechanics' Institutes of Lancashire and Yorkshire before 1851.* Manchester: Manchester University Press.

Vandermassen, Griet *et al.* (2005). 'Close Encounters with a New Species: Darwin's Clash with the Feminists at the End of the Nineteenth Century', in A. Zwierlein (ed.), *Unmapped Countries: Biological Visions in Nineteenth Century Literature and Culture*, pp. 71–81. London: Anthem Press.

van Inwagen, Peter (1995). 'Dualism and Materialism: Athens and Jerusalem?', *Faith and Philosophy*, 12: 475–88.

van Thal, Herbert (ed.) (1955). *Fanfare for Ernest Newman.* London: Arthur Barker.

van Thal, Herbert (ed.) (1962). *Testament of Music: Essays and Papers by Ernest Newman.* London: Putnam.

van Wyhe, John (2004). *Phrenology and the Origins of Victorian Scientific Naturalism.* Aldershot: Ashgate.

Venn, John, and J. A. Venn (1922–54). *Alumni Cantabrigienses: A Biographical List of All Known Students, Graduates and Holders of Office at the University of Cambridge: From the Earliest Times to 1900,* 10 vols. Cambridge: Cambridge University Press.

Vogeler, Martha S. (1980). 'George Eliot and the Positivists', *Nineteenth-Century Fiction,* 35: 406–31.

—— (1982). 'The Choir Invisible: The Poetics of Humanist Piety', in G. S. Haight and R. T. VanArsdel (eds), *George Eliot: A Centenary Tribute*, pp. 64–81. London and Basingstoke: Macmillan.

—— (1984). *Frederic Harrison: The Vocations of a Postivist.* Oxford: Clarendon Press.

Wake, C. Staniland (1878). *The Evolution of Morality, Being a History of the Development of Moral Culture,* 2 vols. London: Trübner & Co.

Wallace, Alfred Russel (1891). *Natural Selection and Tropical Nature: Essays on Descriptive and Theoretical Biology,* new edn. London: Macmillan & Co. (1st published separately as *Contributions to the Theory of Natural Selection* (1870) and *Tropical Nature and Other Essays* (1878)).

—— (1912). *Darwinism: An Exposition of the Theory of Natural Selection, with Some of its Applications,* 3rd edn. London: Macmillan & Co. (1st edn 1889).

Wallace, William (1898). *Lectures and Essays on Natural Theology and Ethics,* ed., with a biographical introd. by Edward Caird. Oxford: Clarendon Press.

Waller, John C. (2002). '"The Illusion of an Explanation": The Concept of Hereditary Disease, 1770–1870', *Journal of the History of Medicine and Allied Sciences,* 57: 410–48.

Waller, Philip (2006). *Writers, Readers, and Reputations: Literary Life in Britain, 1870–1918.* Oxford: Oxford University Press.

Walsh, Walter (1902). *The Religious Life and Influence of Queen Victoria.* London: Swan Sonnenschein & Co.

Ward, Mrs Humphry (1888). *Robert Elsmere,* new edn. London: Smith, Elder & Co. (1st edn 1888).

—— (1918). *A Writer's Recollections.* London: W. Collins Sons & Co.

Ward, Mrs Humphry (1987). *Robert Elsmere*, World's Classics edn, ed. with an introd. by Rosemary Ashton. Oxford: Oxford University Press (1st edn 1888).

Ward, William G. (1884). *Essays on the Philosophy of Theism*, 2 vols, ed. with an introd. by Wilfrid Ward. London: Kegan Paul, Trench, & Co.

Warren, O. H. (1890). 'Woman in the Social Structure', in B. F. Austin (ed.), *Woman: Her Character, Culture and Calling*, pp. 393–409. Bradford, Ontario: The Book and Bible House.

Watts, Isaac (1866). *Divine and Moral Songs for Children*. New York: Hurd & Houghton (1st published as *Divine Songs* in 1715).

Webb, Beatrice (1926). *My Apprenticeship*. London: Longmans, Green & Co.

—— (1979). *My Apprenticeship*, with an introd. by Norman Mackenzie. Cambridge: Cambridge University Press.

—— (1982–5). *The Diary of Beatrice Webb*, 4 vols, ed. Norman and Jeanne Mackenzie. London: Virago in association with the London School of Economics and Political Science.

Webb, Clement C. J. (1915). *Studies in the History of Natural Theology*. Oxford: Clarendon Press.

Weedon, Alexis (2003). *Victorian Publishing: The Economics of Book Production for a Mass Market, 1836–1916*. Aldershot: Ashgate.

Weeks, Jeffrey (1989). *Sex, Politics, and Society: The Regulation of Sexuality since 1800*, 2nd edn. London: Longman (1st edn 1981).

—— (1990). *Coming out: Homosexual Politics in Britain from the Nineteenth Century to the Present*, rev. edn. London: Quartet (1st edn 1977).

Weikart, Richard (1993). 'The Origins of Social Darwinism in Germany, 1859–1895', *Journal of the History of Ideas*, 54: 469–88.

—— (2002). 'Darwinism and Death: Devaluing Human Life in Germany 1859–1920', *Journal of the History of Ideas*, 63: 323–44.

Weinbren, Dan (1994). 'Against *All* Cruelty: The Humanitarian League, 1891–1919', *History Workshop Journal*, 38: 86–105.

Weiner, Martin J. (1990). *Reconstructing the Criminal: Culture, Law and Policy in England, 1830–1914*. Cambridge: Cambridge University Press.

Wernick, Andrew (2001). *Auguste Comte and the Religion of Humanity: The Post-Theistic Program of French Social Theory*. Cambridge: Cambridge University Press.

Wheeler, Michael (1990). *Death and the Future Life in Victorian Literature and Theology*. Cambridge: Cambridge University Press.

—— (1994). *Heaven, Hell, and the Victorians*. Cambridge: Cambridge University Press.

White, Paul (2003). *Thomas Huxley: Making the 'Man of Science'*. Cambridge: Cambridge University Press.

Wilde, Oscar (1909). *Intentions*, 4th edn. London: Methuen (1st edn 1891).

—— (1999). *The Soul of Man and Prison Writings*, ed. with an introd. and notes by Isobel Murray. Oxford: Oxford University Press.

—— (2005). *The Complete Works of Oscar Wilde*, ii. *De Profundis: 'Epistola in Carcere et Vinculis'*, ed. with an introd. and notes by Ian Small. Oxford: Oxford University Press.

Williams, C. M. (1893). *A Review of the Systems of Ethics Founded on the Theory of Evolution*. London: Macmillan & Co.

Williams, Ioan (ed.) (1971). *George Meredith: The Critical Heritage*. London: Routledge & Kegan Paul.

Williams, Raymond (1976). *Keywords: A Vocabulary of Culture and Society*. London: Croom Helm.

Wilson, A. N. (2003). *The Victorians*. London: Arrow Books.

Wilson, David Sloan, and Elliott Sober (2002). 'The Fall and Rise and Fall and Rise and Fall and Rise of Altruism in Biology', in S. G. Post *et al.* (eds), *Altruism and Altruistic Love: Science, Philosophy and Religion in Dialogue*, pp. 182–91. Oxford and New York: Oxford University Press.

Wiltshire, David (1978). *The Social and Political Thought of Herbert Spencer*. Oxford: Oxford University Press.

Winchester, Simon (2003). *The Meaning of Everything: The Story of the Oxford English Dictionary*. Oxford: Oxford University Press.

Wolffe, John (1994). *God and Greater Britain: Religion and National Life in Britain and Ireland 1843–1945*. London and New York: Routledge.

Woodfield, Malcolm (1986). *R. H. Hutton: Critic and Theologian: The Writings of R. H. Hutton on Newman, Arnold, Tennyson, Wordsworth and George Eliot*. Oxford: Clarendon Press.

Wootton, David (2005). 'Oxbridge Model', *Times Literary Supplement* (23 Sept.): 7–10.

Workman, Gillian (1974). 'Thomas Carlyle and the Governor Eyre Controversy', *Victorian Studies*, 18: 77–102.

Worthey, Mrs (1890). *The New Continent*, 2 vols. London and New York: Macmillan & Co.

Wright, Terence R. (1981). 'George Eliot and Positivism: A Reassessment', *Modern Language Review*, 76: 257–72.

—— (1982). 'From Bumps to Morals: The Phrenological Background to George Eliot's Moral Framework', *Review of English Studies*, 33: 35–46.

—— (1984). '*Middlemarch* as a Religious Novel, or Life without God', in D. Jasper (ed.), *Images of Belief in Literature*, pp. 138–52. New York: St Martin's Press.

—— (1986). *The Religion of Humanity: The Impact of Comtean Positivism on Victorian Britain*. Cambridge: Cambridge University Press.

Yarker, P. M. (1959). 'W. H. Mallock's Other Novels', *Nineteenth-Century Fiction*, 14: 189–205.

Yeo, Stephen (1977). 'A New Life: The Religion of Socialism in Britain, 1883–1896', *History Workshop Journal*, 4: 5–56.

Yonge, Charlotte M. (1895). *The Long Vacation*. London: Macmillan.

Young, G. M. (1960). *Victorian England: Portrait of an Age*, 2nd edn. London: Oxford University Press (1st edn 1936).

Young, Kenneth (1963). *Arthur James Balfour: The Happy Life of the Politician, Prime Minister, Statesman, and Philosopher, 1848–1930*. London: G. Bell & Sons.

Zebel, Sydney H. (1973). *Balfour: A Political Biography*. Cambridge: Cambridge University Press.

Index